Sense to Soul How To Have A Personal Relationship With God Through Mystical Interpretation of Scripture

Kelly Logan

Published by Better By Intent Publishing, 2024.

While every precaution has been taken in the preparation of this book, the publisher assumes no responsibility for errors or omissions, or for damages resulting from the use of the information contained herein.

SENSE TO SOUL HOW TO HAVE A PERSONAL RELATIONSHIP WITH GOD THROUGH MYSTICAL INTERPRETATION OF SCRIPTURE

First edition. March 24, 2024.

Copyright © 2024 Kelly Logan.

ISBN: 978-1971255019

Written by Kelly Logan.

Table of Contents

Sense to Soul 1

Questions and Answers 13

Stepping onto the path 55

Old Testament vs. New Testament 61

Eden and the fall from grace 79

What is God? 83

Truth and the principles of Truth 107

Metaphysics, Mysticism and Manifesting 147

Consciousness and prayer 167

What is prayer/meditation/silent inner listening? 219

What is sin, error and duality? 257

What is grace and demonstration? 287

Healing and Treatment 305

Dying daily 339

What is supply? 355

The Branch connected to the Tree of Life 363

Human man juxtaposed to Spiritual man 365

Mystical Terminology 421

Sense to Soul

The life you are experiencing is not the Truth of who you are.

You are living a life you didn't actually chose, it is a life lived of the atmosphere of man born of centuries of erroneous thoughts that has become the external soup, the atmosphere of man of conflicting fears, desires, wants and hates that come at you like whispers on the breeze for you to accept or swat away as mere annoyances. But you didn't realize you could chose to accept or chose to deny what comes into your experience did you?

The atmosphere of this world was born in the first man who thought himself **separate and apart** from God which according to the Bible was Adam and Eve newly out of the garden of Eden. **This study teaches you Truth and the principles of that Truth by which to live a different version of life right where you are.** This study you are embarking on is that of getting back into oneness with God to have a personal relationship with God which is the way it was in the beginning and the only way to live above the chaos of man to live under grace.

This is the study of how to live a true Christ expression, living by the **Truth** of God and not the *beliefs* of man about God man has been fed for thousands and thousands of years. God is not what you think and when you know God aright you will see you have been kept in the dark. The Truth you will learn will take the God of man away and for some this is not something they willingly relinquish but it must happen because you cannot keep your *perceptions* of a God prayed to outside of man and rise to the **Truth** of God through conscious oneness with God.

You have to know your choices to chose one to live by completely ignoring the one you give up. It is a process of emptying the cup and filling the cup back up, you, with fresh clean water, Truth.

Why should you know God? To know what it feels like. How does God feel? You have to experience it for yourself to know and in that moment of basking in God ask yourself if you have ever felt this way in any part of your human experience out in the world. Has this feeling ever graced you before from gift, surprise, anything man has provided for you? No. And it can't because this amazing feeling is **of** God, specific to God, it is what man calls "heaven on earth" and is not of the world of man to be found.

Another book of God? Aren't there already enough books about God?

Yes, there are many books about what man *thinks* of God but there are only a handful of books that **reveal the Truth of God,** that teach you how to have an actual experience of God to know what and where God is to have a personal relationship with God.

What is taught as orthodox Christianity is not the Truth of God. I am not telling you this for you to believe me nor is this a segway into a new iteration of pseudo Christianity. I am telling you this so you can chose to **free** yourself of false beliefs that have been the cause of all the chaos, pain and fear you have suffered in this life to live the life of the risen Christ in a personal relationship with God as it was in the beginning.

A **personal** relationship with God is only possible when you know **what** and **where** God is and who you are in relationship to God.

Therefore the God man has prayed to outside of themselves for thousands of years is **not** the God of creation that when known through **inner** awareness can and does change the entire experience of your life.

The God man prays to outside of himself does not exist and that is why prayer as has been prayed up until now has been completely useless and why so many people believe there is no God or God has left.

Have you ever wondered why there are thousands of different sects, divisions, and iterations of "Truth" based on a singular Godhead? Why are there so many interpretations of God and why, if it doesn't fit one's own interpretation of Truth it can't be Truth? What makes one person's *beliefs* Truth and another's not Truth? Nothing because man does not have access to Truth because all man knows of God is supposition until they have what is called the mystical experience which reveals the what and where of God in awareness.

Regardless of name of church or doctrine **current** theology says Christianity is a *belief* in a singular source of expression that **created** this universe in its **image** and **likeness** and that it is of higher knowing than man therefore is **not** of the **conscious** knowing of human man thus is outside of man to be prayed *to*.

You have been told God is the face value of the *words* written *about* God, that if you know the *words* by heart, can pull them out of a hat like bunnies at a party you *know* God. You have been told *words* of God are the **Truth** of how God wants you to act and react, what is just according to God is just according to you.

God is not in words, ritual or ceremony, not in buildings, person or idol. God is within each and every person as the Christ **consciousness** that was awakened, illumined **in** Jesus and is that which allows you to receive Truth, God knowing, within your own being thereby having a **personal relationship** with Source, the I of you when you learn how to release the *i,* personality, ego of individual man who *thinks* he is separated from God and in lack and fear for his mortal life.

You cannot be separated from God but you can be **unaware** of the presence of God. You are of the nature and eternality of God when you **know,** by way of what is called the **mystical experience,** to be the prodigal son returned home to once again be in the flow, in the harmony and wholeness of Life in conscious oneness with God instead of the chaos of duality man experiences.

Therefore human man no longer ignorant of Truth, living the principles of Truth **returns to** spiritual man in **expression** living under grace.

Psalm 91:1 He that dwelleth in the secret place of the most High shall abide under the shadow of the Almighty.

From just the tiny bit of Truth that has been revealed to you can you discern what is meant by the words? **He that dwelleth in the secret place of the most High.** Where is something secret from the world? **Within** your own being. Where is God found? **Within** your own being when you know what God is and who you are.

The God you have been given to pray to out there somewhere does not exist. There is no God outside of you if you understand you are **of** the creative intelligence of the universe as is everything else seen and unseen. So if you are **of** God, **of** the universal Law that is creative consciousness in expression, how could the God you are **of** be outside of you? Doesn't it stand to reason that which you are **of** would be **of** you?

Therefore the meaning of Psalm 91:1 is that you can know Truth, capital T, God, if you can learn to get quiet within your own being, get behind the thinking mind into the silence where you wait for God to say hello. You are **expectant** of meeting the Father face to face which results in an experience, a feeling, sensation, vision, that which comes **unbidden,** not of your thinking mind but from that which you are aware of as a presence **within** you that you had never been aware of.

This, in an over simplified example, is how you begin your eternal journey with the God of creation at the helm, shouldering all the weight with you gaining all the reward just for depending on and **responding** to the soft small voice of love, of peace, of harmony and Truth within instead of *reacting* to the duality of man's emotions and environment.

The Old Testament is of human law, Lord, God outside of man and is essentially the laws still in effect today, those of morality and personal compliance or resistance to human laws of acceptable conduct.

The New Testament reveals the way man can free himself from living under law, Lord, man, to rise above the chaos of man to live Truth, is, in conscious oneness with God thereby living under grace, harmonious expression and experience, the promised life of heaven on earth, living in the garden of Eden supplied, maintained and sustained by your Source and that is why spiritual man has **no personal desires or need of anything from man, from the world because all comes from within to the without as is the way of spiritual union with the Source of all that is.**

So if union, communion, oneness with God is the revelation of the New Testament, of God governed spiritual living, of True Christianity, why are we still living by the *laws* of the Old Testament, the Ten Commandments given to Moses to help gentrify, educate and moralize the slaves he became leader of?

Why have the religions of the world not revealed the Truth of God which is how to free yourself from most, 80-90% of the duality of man, the chaos of man to rise above, grow in conscious understanding of God, Self and live that bountiful life? Because when you know Truth you know who you are and when you know who you are you are **free,** have no fear of anything man can do to you or threaten you with. Why? **Because man who is free cannot be controlled** by outside forces and as we all know, control is the only language human man understands.

The orthodox view of the New Testament is that **Jesus was the only Christ** and that we are doomed to hell until he decides to come back and save us. Do we even listen to the words spoken by someone of supposed higher knowing of God than ourselves?

So much of what is given as Truth is nothing more than gibberish when you stop and really listen. Why? Because those with their mouths open have not had the **mystical** experience, do not know where God is and do not know who they are therefore cannot say anything of value you can hang your hat on because Truth cannot come from man unless that man knows God, knows the Truth of error, and expresses the singular nature of God which is harmony, is, good.

All over the world you see these hopeful reminders "Jesus is coming!" "Put your faith in Jesus!" "The second coming of Jesus is near!" "Jesus Lives!" All false but more to the point: Why would you worship a mere man who lived 2000 years ago when what was being brought into conscious understanding in the New Testament is that the **Christ, the seed, essence of God expressing through and as Jesus is what gave him the designation of Jesus *the* Christ.** The Christ is inherent in **all** and it is because of Jesus's illumined consciousness, his **awareness** of the Christ within, that allowed miracles to be performed **through** him **not** by him.

It was Jesus **knowing God aright** that allowed God to come forth to aid, comfort, enlighten and heal not only himself but all seeking Truth.

You do not see God, God is the word man uses for the personal of the impersonal of the invisible universal Law of creation that is the all of all there is. However what you do see are the manifestations, visible forms **of** that Law in action, being, expressing itself in forms necessary for other expressions to benefit by in a closed system of Life, singular source expressing, being, doing what is normal and natural for it to do.

What is Law?

Laws are invisible, unchangeable and eternal expressions governed by principles/rules/boundaries which dictate the way the Law operates, comes into visible form. Mathematics is, music is, gravity is, electricity is, magnetism is, thermodynamics is. You cannot see them but **by their expression in the visible they are known to exist in the invisible as a reality; from the invisible into visible expression is the order of all things.**

You don't need to know how it works, why it works or how to make it work correctly. You just know that it **is** and if you plug something into a socket that has electricity going to it you will get the desired result-light, music, heat, etc. You are **of** these invisible laws, able to partake of their expression and benefit by them when you stay within the boundaries, know the principles of, the do and don't, of the law in expression meaning you know what you can and cannot do within each law that brings about the results desired ie harmony. It is when you lose respect for the law, lose self respect for the return of the law upon you that *you* incur the error of your *thinking* because the law didn't change just to mess with you, you tried to change the immutable universal law of creation silly wabbit.

The goal of any spiritual practice is to have a personal relationship with the singular source of creation to bring you back into the flow of creation that moves you through this life so you experience it as you were meant to and that is accomplished through **silent, sacred, secret communion/prayer/inner listening** wherein you receive Truth, hear the voice of God within your own being which is the personal relationship that returns you to the Father's house to live connected, joined, communed as one for **your** benefit.

There is no other way to receive grace, live under grace or express grace than through knowing God aright and that knowing is what allows you to live the first chapter of Genesis, in conscious oneness with God, heaven on earth in the garden of Eden maintained, sustained and supported eternally.

Learning about God is like learning a different language by which to interpret the world and it takes dedication, practice and living what you learn so you can more fully partake of the harmony you are learning to express. You can only experience what you are aware of and right now all you are aware of as a way of existence is human duality, chaos, opposites, labels and judgements. You have no awareness of the presence within your own being that is peace, harmony, abundance, supply, and joy unto you therefore you cannot experience it or express it.

When learning a new language you study the words and their meaning, repeat them, memorize them but they are only words until you **experience** them in action. However you must be willing to let go of what you *think* you already know and allow yourself to absorb the teachings being given or you won't ever be able to live/experience the language as your expression ie book learning vs fluency. It will always feel like sophomore Spanish where you struggled to make sense of the words because you only used them on paper, you never **became** them, they never came **through** you as your expression. Why? Because you didn't open yourself to it, didn't practice it, implement it or live it on any level higher than that of the *thinking* mind, the academics, the rote mechanics of it.

The desire to learn is a desire to increase your conscious understanding of something because you desire to express/do/be what is being taught. The Bible is no different in that to understand it you must know the language in which it was written-**mystical.** The Bible was written by **mystics,** those who lived in conscious union with God therefore the Bible can only be understood by one in conscious union with God.

The True God you are able to have a relationship with is of one nature of expression, **is,** which is what man terms good, peace, harmony, love. God is kind, funny, gentle, great company and is your rock, your shoulder, your resting place and your comfort. But what you will also come to understand is though you have a **personal** relationship with this transcendental consciousness, spirit, essence, God, Father etc, because it is known to you, the **impersonal** of the **personal** is **Law** unchangeable, immutable, unstoppable, maintenance, support and sustainment of Self. The universal Law of creation becomes personal when you are aware of it and only when it is personal can it be expressed as your nature.

If you are still reading this you desire to know the principles of Truth which will allow you to have a personal relationship with God. Truth is going to reveal that a lot of what you thought were Truths are merely beliefs based on the **original sin**-man thinking he is separate and apart from God. However if you are ready to know Truth you will eagerly let go of what you think you know in favor of finally knowing what will **actually allow you to experience God and live under grace.**

Everything written here came through me by way of my conscious union with God. They are not my words, my conjecture or my random thoughts. This is God through me for you. What was given to me for my enlightenment was also given to those reaching out for God and that is why you are here.

From this point forward you will learn how to live true Christianity, in oneness with God through the Christ consciousness or transcendental consciousness inherent in all man as your birthright just as of now unknown to you.

There are only a few things needed for you to have a relationship with God and they are:

1. a desire to know God
2. you are done with this world, the good and the bad, the confusion, the pain, the lack and the struggle, the highs and the lows
3. are willing to empty yourself of all preconceived ideas of God and make space for Truth.

This book reveals the Truth of God and the how-to, ie the rules, boundaries or principles of living a true spiritual life that if **practiced and lived** will give you the means by which to have a personal relationship with God where you are supplied, maintained and sustained by Self and no longer dependent on man and the world for supply, companionship, understanding, direction or purpose.

There is no right or wrong way to work through this book as each person is searching for something first that must be answered. The most important thing for you to remember is you cannot mix God and man. You cannot add God to human living to have better humanhood, more *material* wealth, better health, more toys, more indulgences. If you try you will fail. If you try to use God for personal gain you will fail. If you do not put into practice what you want to become your expression you will fail. If you talk about this practice to others before you are of sufficient knowing you will fail.

The only way you will succeed on the spiritual path is if you want God over all earthly, material things. You have to want God to receive God because only in your desire for that which is not of this world will you receive the allness of what is not available to you in this world. "This world" is what Jesus called the world of man ie duality, opposites, the way man has been living for thousands and thousands of years as opposed to God's kingdom, conscious oneness with God, singular expression/nature of is, perfect harmony.

The Truths being revealed are going to hit up against every conventional thought of being you have ever had whether it be of creation or evolution, earth science or medical science, birth, death or heredity because all *knowledge of man is belief,* is of the mind thus are illusion not reality. The reason is, and it will become Truth to you as you progress with your studies, nothing of man's thinking mind, nothing of how you perceive this world through the *senses* is the actual reality/Truth of what you experience.

This book is going to peel the onion, remove the layers of erroneous belief by presenting Truth, God. The thing you have to understand about Truth is that it is an experience, it is felt, you **feel** the Truth of what is being given, it resonates not with your mind but with your being, your soul, your conscious knowing of who you are. Truth isn't felt like a reaction to outer stimulus/emotional response but of the within as the nature it is which is harmony, peace, good. Truth drops you, stuns you, mouth open, holy crap! "That makes so much sense! Thank you Father, I see another one of my false beliefs being dissolved!"

This is the only way to uncover and reveal your Truth buried under all the humanhood controlling your every move. Yes, controlling you. You think you are free as a human and that God is the constraint, control, removal of the fun button of life. What about the horror button? That sucker gets pushed a hell of a lot more than the fun or good button doesn't it?

Don't you feel like Pavlov's dog, salivating for a vacation, salivating for a pay check, salivating for a house? Praying to win something, anything to not have to work to have? Trying to make a go of this life on your own always worrying "is this going to work? Am I doing the right thing? Is this going to be ok? What can I do to move things along?"

When you know God those questions don't arise because you are free. Free of the consequences of *your* choices and decisions because they are no longer *yours* to make because you have given all choice to God for harmony and grace to be your experience. What consequences can come when the cause and effect are harmonious? None. Like begets like, harmony can only come from a source of harmony and God is the only source of harmony there is to be found in this experience called life.

God is not religion:

God is not a religious belief, God is not religion, God is the unseen, singular presence of creation harmonious and good. God is nothing you can define for yourself because you would be trying to define that which man doesn't truly know because man has not been face to face with the Father within. Therefore anything you think you know about God is solely conjecture based on ignorance of Truth.

Spiritual man who has the companionship of the Father 24/7 knows God and nothing man says about God is true because you cannot know God until you have an experience of God and when that happens, when you find the Father within, you are no longer man, cannot unfeel what you have felt and now know yourself to be spirit.

You can reject it, a lot of people do and they are miserable because the human side of them, their upbringing, their parents' demoralizing chatter, their schooling, religious learnings etc, will not let the God of them be heard. This dichotomy of mind is that which literally makes people insane. They are trying to negate their Truth and in that loss of hope hate life, hate themselves, hate the fact that they cannot go to God and cry like the child they are and get the comfort that is their birth right.

Insanity is doing the same thing over and over expecting different results. That is humanity in one sentence. Break free of the insanity and for goodness sake do something different, take a leap of faith, take a different way home, shop at a different store, buy a different coffee concoction. Come on! Live a little! Shake that little sugar shack! Enjoy life, take a break, feel the sun on your face even if it is through high rise glass.

Let the possibilities of your life become realities. I'm not just talking about God I'm talking about living. Let yourself live but to live you must change and to change you must be open, release old concepts (die daily) and see the world in a different way (one expression not two) and soon you will be living a completely different life but you have to **allow** yourself to do so. Forgive yourself, forgive the world, forgive 70x7 and just keep **open,** keep **silent,** keep sacred the experiences you have in this new consciousness of good and let the living begin.

Do you see what it takes to find the Father within is nothing weird? It is just foreign as it has never been available to you to learn but it is nothing more than learning how to become a good Hebrew by following the Ten Commandments ie the laws of man and then nudging you over the finish line into spiritual awareness where you live by the Truth of God which is harmony unto your expression and experiences.

It is a natural progression for man of slavery to become man of spirit. It is no different than the evolutionary chart of man as that from ape-ish to "modern" man and all the iterations in between. The evolution expressing isn't of the form it is of the **consciousness of the form** expressing as the change in appearance. It is the progression from one state of consciousness/being/expressing to another until the final state of consciousness is reached-Christ consciousness.

Who is this study for?

The audience for this book is the "dying of thirst" seeker of Truth. If you are ready this book will keep your interest to the point of obsession because you want the Truth it reveals, you want to know God more than anything in the world. Not the God of the world of man but the true God of creation. It will take time and it absolutely requires practice but if you feel what is being given you can receive of what is being given.

The Truth of God could be revealed on one sheet of paper but reading Truth has nothing to do with **living the experience** of what the words reveal within your own being. The necessity for this book is to explain to you what those words mean in application to have oneness with God, conscious knowing of Truth. If you do not have an understanding of what is being revealed you cannot emulate by practical application that which brings about the mystical experience nor be of the understanding of the mystical experience to partake of what is being offered-conscious oneness with God living harmony and peace eternal and infinite as known child of God.

There are a thousand and one ways to express the same thing because of the different levels of consciousness of the student and that is why sometimes you need to hear the same thing twenty different ways before understanding dawns in consciousness as the ah ha moment you experience within your own being, a feeling that comes unbidden, not of you but **for** you, love, peace, joy, relief.

Who you are matters not. What you know to this point of life is irrelevant. If you desire to know and are willing to be other than you are, completely different than who you are, this book is for you. This is a study, a journey, a livingness and as such will evolve, change and deepen in understanding as you practice what you are learning. The understanding of God is available to all but it is a progression, an opening, a deepening of conscious knowing that must be taken in steps otherwise it is like having a bag of Legos with no picture to show you how they go together to produce what is wanting to be experienced.

At this moment you are being given an opportunity to transcend the finite human experience of duality and chaos, of identifying as flesh and blood that is born and dies to that of spiritual man, son, child, individual expression of God supported, maintained and supplied living eternal harmony and wholeness.

Questions and Answers

Basic questions and answers about God and spiritual living

To begin your journey I am going to ease you onto the path with the questions I had and the answers received that helped pave my way forward and I believe them to be fairly universal in nature. The answers may not make sense in the moment but they will; spiritual knowing is cumulative as is any other learning. You have to get a certain amount of book learning in that doesn't necessarily make cohesive sense before it can coalesce, come into understanding before you begin to express what you have been studying and practicing. This is the meaning of signs following, seed time and harvest.

This is a livingness, a way of being. This isn't something you read, put down and hope it does something for you. It won't. It can't. Everything in your life is dependent on your degree of participation as to what degree of satisfaction you get out of it. If you want to know God because you **need** to know God you will put in the effort but if you want God because you want a better house or a better bank account you are wasting your time.

I only say this to make sure you have no misunderstanding what this book is about-true **Christ** living **not** better *human* living but what you will soon understand is human living was an un-fulfilling illusion, a knock off life, pseudo reality and that living out from God instead of your individual consciousness of separation from God is where all you could ever want to experience is found.

There is no right or wrong way to work through this book as each person is searching for something that must be answered first. The most important thing for you to remember is you **cannot** add God to human man. You **cannot** add the principles of spiritual living to human living to have better humanhood-more material wealth, better health, more joy, more indulgences **because those are merely opposites of what you are currently experiencing** which you will come to understand to be *duality* which is the hallmark of what is termed *human* man.

God is not better than what you have God is that which you have never experienced so have no comparison as human man. God **is** perfection of living, **is** harmony, **is** peace, **is** abundance unto your experience. If you try to add God to your human life you will fail. If you try to alter the words given as universal Truth for personal gain you will fail. If you do not put into practice that which is to be your expression you will fail.

The only way you will succeed on the spiritual path is if you want God over all earthly, material things. You have to want God to receive God because only in your desire for that which is not of this world will you receive the allness of what is not **of** this world.

"This world" is what Jesus called the world of human man ie duality, opposites, the way man has been living for thousands and thousands of years believing they are separate and apart from God instead of living **as** spiritual man **of** God's kingdom, in conscious oneness **with** God of singular expression/nature of **is,** perfect harmony.

Why God?

Why go through all the hassle of unlearning all you know just to learn something that *could* change your life? Because it is how you become **fulfilled,** something the world of man cannot offer nor provide. If it had you wouldn't still be seeking. What you are seeking is wholeness, completeness, no place within that feels inharmonious, in lack or fear. You seek to find that resting place so often talked about and wonder if they have good pillows. You want answers dang it and when you get them you can make up your own mind on how you want to express to the world-as human man or spiritual man now knowing there is a definite difference.

A lot of this may not make sense in the moment but it will, think *out of the blue aha moment that gives you goosebumps.* Everything I have written came straight from God, its Word, its Truth to me through the study of mystical writings like those of Joel S Goldsmith so God could more fully express in this world. I did not think this up; how could *i*? There is absolutely no way *i* could put together the words to make it make sense, it takes the Author, God, **I**, dictating to get it right. This book is not about me or any other mystic past, **it is about the mystic in the making learning to live the Word of God reading this.**

There will be many terms that have mystical meaning different than human meaning and I encourage you to look them up in the mystical terminology chapter as you go if in the context it is used it does not make sense. The reason is the words used in mystical writing are of those who lived the consciousness of God, who saw past the visible to the consciousness **of** the words and not the literal meaning of the words, and wrote from that higher or illumined perspective. This is why the Bible doesn't make sense at this time, you do not have the conscious understanding to read it aright. But you will!

God is freedom

Moses put a **veil** on Truth and gave us Lord God, God of human laws and punishment.

Jesus **unveiled** Truth by revealing to all who could understand the meaning of the words **I am I am.**

Jesus was crucified for this because it teaches a slave how to be free, sinless within his own being and rise above the conscious knowing of human man which threatens the powerful man who only knows freedom through force. How do you control one you are no longer able to control through fear and lack? Hunger and cold? How do you use the fear of death against one who knows they are deathless? What power is left to human man when all their power is shown to be an illusion?

Governments and churches do not want you to know Truth **because man who knows he is free cannot be corrupted** so it has been their goal to keep **man in the dark as to the way to man's salvation.**

Why is spiritual man **incorruptible?** Mainly and most importantly a free man of God knows there can be no true death and there is no thing of the world that can be used as a bargaining chip, cause or reason to do something against their nature because spiritual man does not live in the world of birth and death but in the world of eternal harmony in this expression or the next, visible or invisible form makes no difference, spirit cannot die therefore you are eternal and as such incorruptible, pure as snow, child of God, joint heir to the kingdom.

The reason for needing God:

If you are not allowed to bring out your individuality, if you are held down, forbidden or restricted in the development of yourself, who you know yourself to be or want to be, if your access to Truth by which to grow in conscious understanding is not available to you, if you are not being allowed to be who you are and who you want to be separate and apart from others through different avenues of personal education beyond the education offered by government you are being controlled.

The reason man is still living the Ten Commandments of the Old Testament instead of under grace of the New Testament is because the New Testament teaches **individuality.** The Old Testament teaches mass compliance and reward. Therefore under rules that govern masses individuality is stifled, restricted, basically forbidden in a society united by group think instead of a society united by individual thinkers that raise the consciousness of the society to higher and higher plains of consciousness.

If man were of a higher level of consciousness governance over man would not be necessary thus the reason those in positions of power fight so hard to keep Truth hidden-they would lose *their* way to avail *their* need for a sense of power-but at the same time power wouldn't be a sought after expression if man knew they didn't need power or any other human emotion or expression to feel fulfilled because spiritual man is Self complete.

Why do you need religion?

You need religion for fulfillment, to be whole, complete and know you exist because you are witness to it. As *human* man you are barren and empty of **Truth,** spiritual Life, of knowledge of Source and are living as a branch of a tree that is cut off and withers therefore the spiritual Life is the way by which to get back into oneness with the Tree of Life, God.

Religion is your relationship with God by which to experience wholeness of being.

It is only by an actual experience of God that you put yourself back in the Father's house, consciousness of Truth, one with Source eternally fulfilled. Now you can say through religion, your relationship with God, "I and my Father are one, all that the Father has is thine, his grace is upon me, his spirit is upon me," for its Life has become your Life as you truly have no Life separate and apart from God.

The **erroneous belief** that has caused spiritual man to suffer as human man is because he *thinks* he is separate and apart from God.

When you become at one with God you are **of** the Life of God, the wholeness and allness that is God. You are back in the consciousness of oneness and not separateness. **You need a relationship with the Father to bring you back to the Father's house and that is done by having conscious awareness of the Father within** which is where you experience the kingdom of heaven supplied, maintained and sustained eternally by the allness you are **of.**

Religious Belief is not Religious Truth

Believing something does not make it Truth therefore can do nothing for you because *belief* is *personal* and **Truth** is **universal.** This error has been perpetuated by churches because they impress upon man the *belief* that if you attend church, support it, get baptized and observe the holy days you will attain your freedom through those *acts.*

No religious *activity* has ever *freed* its people.

As a matter of fact *religion* has bound them more tightly, enslaved them into error, ingrained it and used it as control instead of freedom. Man must live by the Word of God, consciousness of God through consciously knowing God. Freedom can only come from God and that can only take place as an **activity** within your own consciousness and that activity of consciousness is **awareness** of the presence of God within and has absolutely nothing to do with orthodox religion as it has been practiced for thousands of years.

What do you gain knowing God aright?

Have you ever thought of what you would **gain knowing God aright?** The entire world wide religious community is based on the idea that God/Diety has what you need and that you should want what this is but have you been told what **benefit** God brings during this life? What is the **why** you should be knowing God aright?

Not knowing the true God has been the way of man for 2000 years and has in its absence **removed from memory the reasons to know the God of Self, true Christianity or Christ living.** As most understand it orthodox religion is trying to save you from the devil, the evils of this world by praying to a God outside of you (first untruth) to protect you from something called the Devil, or that which is evil of person, place or thing (second untruth).

So what are you going to gain by knowing the true God? First is gratitude, that sigh of relief, like you are holding that thing that has centered you since childhood, it was lost and now it is found and you hold it close and relax, feel the world right itself and you can stop the monkey mind and just grin a bit because you are at peace. That is the feeling of God on the field, in your awareness, sitting with you just relaxing and enjoying each other's company.

You **feel** God in your midst, you **feel** God as the peace, the joy, the beauty that just cannot be held back and it floods you with tears, damn I'm crying right now, and you just feel it, you **feel** the Truth of your being giving you itself, its allness, its wholeness. You **feel** peace, harmony, safety, security and so many other humanly labeled feelings as to never feel the need to look outside yourself ever again for receipt of those feelings. They are yours whenever you want, they are your experiences, you felt them, responded to them because they happened to you, you had face time with the Father. Because you experienced these things you can bring them back time and time again.

This is not living in the past wishing for that feeling to come back from some outside source, you are remembering an event that happened **within you** and you feel the same way you did the first time you had that particular experience. You not only brought God on the field very smoothly and without effort but brought God to bear for yourself and those around you, a breath of fresh air, woosah to those receptive of grace, harmony in their midst.

You have to stop *reading* the Bible

You have to stop hanging on every word in the Bible as Truth, gospel, the Bible says it so it must be Truth. Stop memorizing words as if theorem to be repeated at lectures. The Bible is God consciousness in written form, the source of the Truth of God by which to live a spiritual life. It is an experience for you to have, not read about. The Bible was never meant to be read and memorized, parroted and used for personal reasons. It is **the story of you** and who you can be **when** you know how to read it to get the **consciousness** of it as it was intended.

God is **I** and you are **I** when you **know** yourself to be **I**, of the consciousness of God and not *i* separate from God with the consciousness of individual man, by way of a **mystical** experience called meeting the Father face to face within your own being. The rest of the words are a story, an allegorical story about human man's life, how you as human man separated from God suffer that separation.

The Bible is allegorical of the life you are experiencing and are going to experience. You were in the kingdom, you are now living a life seemingly separated from God but have been given the tools to rise once again into the consciousness of the Father from whence you came if you chose to.

The Bible could be completely blank but for these words:

I am I am, I am of the I of all that is

The Father and I are one

All that I have is thine

Yours is the kingdom of heaven who dwell in the place of the most high

I will never leave you nor forsake you

Your grace is my sufficiency in all ways

You can live your entire life on just one single Truth of God because if you take that one Truth into the silence God will reveal the allness of life, the purpose of life, the riches and the richness of life waiting for you to experience.

99% of the Bible doesn't matter. It is just fattening of the story of you to give you time to open to the revealing of God's name in the New Testament-I am that I am.

The words are not important. What is important is you understand the experiences of the people in the bible because they **are allegoric to your experience of separation from God at this moment.** The Bible is **your** story of life, of good and evil. Cain and Abel are the evil of man and the harmony of spiritual man, pain of separation then union through repentance and surrender of personal will. Human man Cain vs. Spiritual man Abel are examples of how they expressed to the world, their lack or abundance, their jealousy or their peace, their consciousness of man or consciousness of God in expression.

The majority of the Bible is fluff, filler, to get you to see yourself in the stories, the stories of man separated from God, you. What is important is the taking in of the Word of God, the red letter words spoken by Jesus the Christ who knew God to be within and not outside of himself and others.

When you get the correct persepective of the contents of the Bible and the correct perspective of I when reading the New Testament you will have all you will ever need to know because you are learning Truth of who you are as child of God and not the erroneous beliefs of man who knows not who he is.

The reason I want this to be clear is I see so many videos made by people who love God and want to share God on facebook and Tik Tok but they are focusing on the wrong things. There are those that have you hang on the exact words of a passage without knowing it is the deeper meaning that is meant to be known. Another was horrified there were passages that had been omitted from some Bibles because to most people of faith it is the words that count, following them to the letter, thou shall not, etc. They read the words and humanly interpret them through the laws of man thinking I is them personally not I God.

Right there shows the first and most significant error of orthodox religion: you have never been given the opportunity to know the name of God by which to know your association to God. This has forced man to seek outside for God, the mythical being with powers to make or break your life to be feared and worshiped at the same time. Utter nonsense as you will soon see.

What is God?

When people think of God, even mystics to some extent because God is a personal relationship, they associate God with something they already know, another expression but bigger in stature, that God must think like a human to keep the wheels from falling off this bus but **God isn't a man, God isn't any kind of being, God itself is the all of being.** The Alpha and the Omega, the consciousness that **is** eternity unto itself for consciousness **is** self perpetuating; God, universal Law of creative expression, is renewing itself perpetually.

Perpetuating: illimitable, unlimited, numberless, overlong, perpetual, unbroken, undivided, undying, uninterrupted, unsurpassable, that which has the power to continue indefinitely.

Every single one of those words from wordhippo.com and yourdictionary.com is Truth unto God. God is. **Is** is the definition of self perpetuating expression, being, aliveness. That which **is** will always be unto eternity.

Where is God?

God isn't of this world so if you start a conversation with it while you are taking a shower, sitting on the toilet, driving, walking the dog or making dinner, know that there is no wrong time to communicate with God. It knows **nothing** of the human world because the human world is not **of** its consciousness of harmony. God doesn't see you from outside, God only knows you, the **consciousness** from which you express.

For the consciousness of God to work in your life you must have **conscious** recognition of its presence **within** you. This presence makes itself known when your human thinking mind is quiet.

It is the answer to a question you couldn't grasp on your own, the inspiration for a new thing, a song, a painting, a skill. It is the feeling of love and harmony where before you felt fear. It is the gentle feeling of peace that descends upon you in times of chaos, the feeling of grace in your midst that lets you know everything will work out.

All have experienced God's presence but most dismissed it, ignored it, or re-labeled it as something else because the reality just didn't fit in with your finite understanding that only that which is seen and sensed is real. This is the tragedy I hope to help you avert. If people knew God, not the God of man thought of today from all false avenues, you would never question this voice inside as being anything other than the Truth of your being desiring to express as harmony and peace. God is the artist and you are the art. The artist is greater than the art but the art has all the quality, quantity and expression of the artist.

Who am I?

Your birth wasn't creation, your birth was the **expression** of your eternal consciousness in form that was created in the beginning before time was. You are not *created* of the physical union of your human parents, "parents" are the vehicle by which eternal souls come back into expression time and time again to continue growing and evolving in consciousness.

You are an individualized expression of God in form but because you are born into an atmosphere of duality you have to learn how not to be human and that is by knowing Truth to live that Truth in expression.

What does it mean to be spiritual man?

Spiritual man through conscious knowing of Source allows Source, God, to **manifest** through them as the added and needed things. These things are not *matter/material* but **God** in form and with this clarification you can understand Joel S Goldsmith's revelation:

"My conscious oneness with God constitutes my oneness with all spiritual being and idea."

The only thing spiritual man can manifest is God because God is as all. This is why you do not manifest, bring forth into expression cars, persons, relationships, cash money as those who try to manifest using *mind* over *matter* do. Why? Because there is nothing separate and apart from God. There is no such thing as matter ie metal, paper, flesh and blood, trees, germs. Those are *names* given to things seen as separate and apart from God thus the perceived finite nature of worldly resources.

You bring forth God in awareness, **know God is,** and that knowing is the key to your eternal supply. This is why spiritual man will never be seen begging bread ie in lack of any kind. You receive from that which you are **of** to become more and more of that which you are becoming-harmony, harmonious, spiritual perfection-and this is accomplished by knowing Truth, dying daily, practicing the presence of God within and bringing God into awareness for healing, comfort and companionship.

What do I have to do to get ready to know God?

People say "I need to stop smoking, drinking, fornicating, I need to be a better person before God would want to help me." Stop it! There is nothing you can do humanly to get ready for God except say you are ready for God! If you say it and mean it the path you have entered on is one of dying daily to the erroneous beliefs you have been living under and filling back up with the principles of Truth which are the "how and why" of having a relationship with God.

It is in this way you are being **purified,** transformed, **not of your own doing** but the doing of God that you are **allowing** to be the change of your consciousness. To try to be and do different than you are through human means, self hypnosis, denials or affirmations, psychologists, pills, I can't and I won't's is merely a contest of wills, yours over yours which you wish to change. You are literally fighting yourself, the proverbial two wolves duking it out for supremacy with your sanity stuck in the middle with no neutral ground to be found.

The transformation done by God is much easier and everlasting to boot because it doesn't change your bad into good or your lack into riches, **it reveals the Truth of you.** When you know your Truth and can look at who you thought you were you can see the error of your previous understanding. What happens when you recognize an error? You correct it and move on. You let go of a belief when faced with Truth because you can see the unreality of what you formerly believed.

Do you hold onto both the belief and the Truth? No, you hold onto Truth and let the belief go. Do you wear shoes that are too small? No, they served their purpose, fit when they fit, but now they don't, are of no use so you let them go, they serve no purpose but to clutter up your closet. No matter how precious they were to you, what memories they hold, they serve no further purpose.

Spiritual life is about purging, letting go, dying daily. It is the letting go of that which no longer serves your higher understanding of life in this moment. There is never any shame or remorse in realizing the things you held onto were erroneous. We all have done it and will do it even as we rise; it is the **realization** of the errors held as Truth that allows God to bring more Truth to you to reveal more error to be recognized and released.

Purification is not about changing something into something else, it is revealing the Truth to let go of the error/erroneous belief.

Why am I here on earth now?

The experiences you have encountered as man separated from God have been the **ongoing presentation of the opportunity** to grown in conscious knowing to find that which has been missing.

The purpose of all your lifetimes has been to continually evolve in consciousness from one of low moral standing to one who knows they are the child of God. The Truth of existence is circular not linear ie doesn't end rather you go around and around hopefully rising higher and higher in conscious understanding with each successive iteration/rebirth. What is the purpose of evolving? To live a more evolved ie peaceful and easy existence because you know things you didn't which have allowed you to grow, thrive, burst forth renewed. What you haven't understood is the real reason for evolving your consciousness is to rise above human consciousness of good and bad, chaos, to live harmony knowing God.

This lifetime is but a speck of your existence within a continuous existence that merely marks a certain state of conscious development or enlightenment. Each moment in this existence is now because each moment is the continuation of the one before it and in this way each moment is an opportunity to rise in conscious understanding which is the definition of spiritual living.

What is human man?

Human man is the only expression in the universe that is not under the governance of God, under grace, nor can ever be. Why? Because *human* man does not know God through experience. They may *believe* in God but also *believe* God is separate and apart from them out there somewhere. To know God aright you must have an awareness of the presence of God **within your own being.**

When this happens it is called the **mystical** experience of meeting the Father face to face and it is this experience that allows you to have a true **relationship** with God, God in action, alive and being. God is at this point a reality to you, you now **know** God because you have **met** God face to face, you have experienced a presence within your own being not you but **of** you, **with** you, **available** to you right where you are.

This presence is within each man and is the embodiment of peace, it is joy, it is release and relief, it is wholeness, completeness, it is divine love unlike anything you have ever experienced and it is yours as long as you desire to have it above everything in and of the world of man ie duality and material things.

So if this presence is within all man, why aren't all man expressing it? Because to be active in your life you must have an **awareness** that it exists and cultivate a **relationship** with this presence.

Human man cannot have this relationship with an inner God because human man thinks God to be outside of himself to be prayed to, begged, threatened and manipulated for personal gain. **Human man prays out to a God that does not exist** thinking it does exist and this is why so many prayers miss the mark, fall short, are in the dead letter file. How can a prayer be answered if you are praying to a humanly conceived God instead of the true God?

Man is the only creation that has the ability to think thereby created a false reality based on a *sense* of separation from God which is the atmosphere of man, duality, opposites ie lack *and* wealth, health *and* disease, happiness *and* sadness, good *and* bad, free *or* limited.

Man *reacts* to the opposites that present in the world around him while the whole of the universe **rests**, is in perfect harmony under the governance of that which it is **of**, Life expressing, universal consciousness, invisible substance in form, God.

Human man is the only expression that *reacts* to their surroundings because of perceived powers *outside* of their control *believed* to be able to affect their circumstances positively or negatively, ie good and bad things can happen which is the reason for man's duality: the need to meet the ever changing expressions of the world around them. They must chose carefully the persona they employ to make sure they come out on top. Man *reacts* to protect themselves from the literal game of chance man calls living.

Spiritual creation, the entirety of all that is, animals, vegetables and mineral, **respond** to the governance of the Life **of** them, a closed system eternal in nature simply because of its singularity of expression, Self, what we call God.

The universe is under the harmonious governance of itself and is being what is normal and natural for it to be. The forms that seem innate ie dirt, rock, water etc, are as enlivened as you are, alive with the Life that is their source. All is and is is God being God, expressing its nature of harmony as both cause and effect.

To be a part of the natural flow of Life, to be in the harmony of universal intelligence you have to **stop creating chaos** and the only way to stop creating chaos is to stop judging, labeling, qualifying, comparing and disparaging. You have to stop using *opposites* as qualifiers. You have to become an observer of life, not a reactor, not a helper, not a judge, not a jury.

You cannot know God aright if you judge God's creations as less than yourself. Matthew 25:40 "The King will reply, 'truly I tell you, whatsoever you did for one of the least of these my brothers and sisters of mine, you did for Me.'"

Until you can see the Christ in **all** man no matter how man is presenting whether thief, murderer, addict, drop out, cheater, in lack or illness, you can never know God. Why? Because until you can see the Truth of **all** man and not just the Truth of yourself you are still judging. If you weren't judging you would instantly see we are all peas of the same pod, we are at our base the individual expressions of the one consciousness of which all of what is visible and invisible is of-creative intelligence, spirit, God.

All that is needed to regain the harmony that was is to know the source of harmony that is. **Harmony is of God. That is the secret to spiritual living.** If God is omnipotent, omniscient and omnipresent then how can there be other than all power, all knowing all the time? There can't but no one ever stopped to question the source of that which is said to be the opposite of God which God must be a power over to prove its existence.

Spiritual living is living within the consciousness, atmosphere of God-good, harmony, peace, supply and prosperity. This is why you must be connected to Source and the only way is though conscious knowing otherwise you are a branch that has been cut off from the Tree, withers and dies. You have no life force in your body beyond the ability of your cells through nourishment, activity, materia medica and sleep to provide the environment that allows the body to be "alive." Everlasting life is only available when you are aware of your Source.

You are never asked to believe a single thing you read, you are to prove it to yourself by following the steps to God realization where at that point you chose to continue to learn this path or return to the path of man.

What is consciousness?

Consciousness is who you think yourself to be and it becomes the outward expression of you in visible form. Emerson said "who you are shrieks so loudly I cannot hear what you are saying." In other words there is no need to voice your convictions because you cannot hide them, they become your nature, how you express to the world, **who you are** by your beliefs and actions of right and wrong according to you *personally.*

Consciousness is the link that allows human man to know God. If you have the consciousness of human man you do not have the consciousness of God therefore you do not know God. But if you have the consciousness of God then you know God aright and can **chose** to no longer live as *human* man.

The missing link to God man has searched for outside of himself through ritual and sacrifice is **within** each individual as your **consciousness** of being as either the I of God or the i of man you currently think yourself to be. To "know thyself" doesn't mean humanly ie good/bad rather it means to know what **nature** you are expressing to the world-human man living *duality* or spiritual man living **is.**

The kingdom of God **is** already within you but overlayed with centuries of *materialistic* thinking and living which has brought about a sense of separation from God. Not **a** separation, a *sense* of separation.

Once you can see you are not separated from God because you now know where God is you are at a crossroad. You now know the Truth of Life, where it is, what it is and how to have it but **it is up to you** to chose-stay in man's world of chaos and shifting sand or run as fast as your feet can take you to God.

What is the Truth of you?

Your relationship with God is the proverbial universe whispering your Truth of being, your true nature and birthright. It is the universe breathing into you the secrets of its perfection and you are **of** that spiritual perfection. When you put a shell to your ear you hear the ocean living in your consiousness and all that it contains just in that single expression. Sit with your eyes closed and let that which is Life itself speak to you, let it touch you, let yourself become aware of it. This is the creative energy, the consciousness of the universe, of all that is of it.

God is not something you read, God is an experience and to experience God you must let down your guard. Think of that monster ride that scares the rubber right off your shoes; you want to ride it so badly and you know it will be worth it but you just cannot get over the hump. You are afraid you are going to lose bodily fluid from some opening or another or that you are going to scream like the hyenas of the African plains. Doesn't matter the reason, you are torn, stuck, on the fence.

I think we actually fear finding God because of all the human things we have done out of ignorance which have caused us pain, grief, sorrow, guilt, and so many other human emotions. Who wants to expose their dirty laundry, the whole basketful to *that guy*. If this is where you find yourself at I am going to let you in on what should not be a secret:

God knows **nothing** of your human life. Nothing. Nada. You know what you did and you know that the consequences of your actions are upon you in some way but that is **not** God bringing punishment down on you that was ignorance or willful disobedience, same potato. This is what man calls sin and man associates the sin with the person doing the act but that is not true. Sins are not of you but on you and the moment you meet the God within "though your sins are like scarlet, they shall be as white as snow." Isaiah 1:18

How? Nothing changes the Truth of you because **nothing** can change the I of you. Sins are like mud on your shoes, face, clothing, a little grit around the mouth. Maybe a little egg here and there and definitely some cow pie material to boot. But it matters not. You are not i, personality, ego, thief, murderer, wife beater, cheater, you are not Malia, Geronimo, Khan. You are not a "you" as if spoken from the outside, separate, you are **of** I. It is received within, felt, then known in consciousness: "I am. I exist. I know myself to be." You are not just a you, a generic "hey you!" You are I. I am.

To live the spiritual life you have to know the **name** of God: I. God's true name is I. Now, when you speak of yourself what do you say? You say I. I is Truth. I is God. One consciousness of all, the Elohim.

I am I am. I am of I am. Pause for a moment please, just rest for a couple of seconds. I want you to let that just float around within you. Don't think about what the words mean, just feel how the words express their meaning **to** you within your secret place where you meet God. Do you feel the Truth of those words awakening something within you? A stirring, a shiver, a quickening, a slowing, a realization beginning to take shape just out of reach of full conscious knowing?

This feeling is confirmation that you are connected, though may not understand at this moment, to God, that you **are of** universal creative intelligence in visible form **of** invisible substance of all that is. You are not flesh and blood; that belief is the cause and effect of all error in this world of human man because this belief is what perpetuates the idea of birth and death ie separation from God thus separate from Life, all that is.

All is God. You are **of** God, invisible/etherial spirit in form. You are one with the Father for the Father is Source, cause of your being, effect of your experience as your supply, your fount, your wholeness in this experiential world. God is and there is no other.

God is the Creator, you are the creation. God is the pod and you are the pea and I am the pea and all are the peas. We are all peas of the same pod. This entire universe is the pod, a closed system fed eternally of itself perpetually maintaining its nature of harmony, peace, order and perfection. All of this universal expression **is** God, creation. All that is seen and unseen **is** the expression of a singular universal creative consciousness and it **is** the Life, Law, Source and nature of what man calls God and there **is** no other.

Human man, or man is **not** of the singular consciousness of harmony rather is of the consciousness of good *and* bad ie duality therefore man is an aberration of Truth. Man is spiritual man who has forgotten their true nature of being-harmonious. Human is the name given to spiritual man who is ignorant of their Truth that God is always being God therefore all their needs are met in God so there is no lack, no illness, no discord and no death ie no inharmony. Human man dissapears the moment he knows his Truth to be spiritual man.

There are only two steps to living the spiritual life:

1. finding God within and
2. living your life according to the God within.

You are the traveler and God is the guide in this relationship where wholeness of being is found. You pay attention to the signs the guide points out as possible complications to your smooth sailing. You defer to the wisdom of your guide because your guide knows more than you do that is why he is the guide and you are the traveler.

But after you have been with your guide for a while you begin to feel that you are no longer a mere traveler but of use to the guide with other travelers. Soon you are allowed to lead your own group on the well worn path because you know it like the back of your hand. Your guide taught you well and now you teach others the way to safely get to their destination.

Just like the guide is not responsible for the choices of the travelers neither is God going to tell you not to do something. You have free will at all times to do your will and you are free at all times to let God do the heavy lifting while you defer to what is revealed within the silence. God is a choice, your choice; just remember all choices have consequences born of their source/nature- belief or Truth, duality or harmony.

What do I have to give up to live in God consciousness?

Man fears what they have to give up to live a spiritual existence but have you considered what you will **gain?** Without going into all the details here know this: knowing God by experience is the key to all you wanted humanly **but it is given, received, not gotten by your hand.** When you express from the consciousness of harmony and peace these expressions return in proportion to your devotion to the path, to God, the principles, the practice and the healing of self and others.

You control the amount of grace, God in activity in your life. You are not mindlessly following rules, you are **learning** Truth by which to live, **actual principles of Truth** by which to build a life on, a life on solid rock not shifting sand. You do not **act** good to appease God to get something rather you know when you are with God you receive all the good there is because you are one with good, God. You are being supported, supplied and maintained by the source of your being just as everything else in this universe under its governance is supported, maintained and supplied eternally and this consciousness is the **singularity of all expression and it is Good.**

How does God benefit you?

God is individual consciousness, your consciousness of being once you get past the thinking mind into the quiet beyond, beyond your education and life experiences to where you find the infinite invisible as so many great inventors and wordsmiths of the past have. Edison would hold his hand behind his ear when he needed answers to problems that arose either for himself or other inventor; it was his way of getting still, stopping his own mind to wait for the intuition, the **knowing** to come forth from the within.

You may already do this to some degree in some fashion. If during a struggle of mind you stop and say "it will come to me, it always does," this is the exact same thing I am talking about. It is a letting go of personal struggling, a letting go of what you *think* you know to let fresh life be blown in amongst the cobwebs of confusion and break them apart to give room for new concepts and ideas to flow forth from the within. It is giving up the dependence on the world to supply the answer and asking God to provide it for you, your dependence now firmly on the Father for all things.

All those who bring forth something new in the outer world that came from the within of their own being have tapped into God consciousness without knowing the name of the source but they have learned to depend on that deeper sense because it is always exactly what was needed. Man calls it intuition and those who rely upon it continue to be encouraged because what they receive is always the best and only solution/answer and usually so far out of the normal train of human thought, duality, to be a head scratcher "why didn't I think of that?" Kind of moment.

Why? Because man cannot *think* of an harmonious solution because harmony is an **expression** of **being** not a *choice* to be made. The choice is already made because of the consciousness you consciously chose to express from/as.

All original work comes from going beyond that which is already known and this is only accomplished by going within and letting it be **given** through you either as heightened consciousness, intuition, or oneness with God. **Everything new comes from the invisible.**

Why is secret, silent and sacred of the utmost importance?

Think of man and their judgements and beliefs. Anyone who is not of the mass mind is ridiculed, cast down and cast out from society and **until** you have imbibed enough Truth to know who you are and why you are, **you cannot share with others.** Why? Because man will tear at you until you think you were wrong to believe in God the way you do, the only way, the truthful way. Man will bring you back down to earth because man destroys that which it doesn't understand and in this case that will be you. Keep this inside until you can stand on it in the middle of the valley of death, in the middle of chaos, in the center of the storm and know you will be safe even if this body is lifeless because you are not the body, you are eternal spirit in form.

At the point you are strong, when you know Truth and are past the confusion of this new way of living, then and only then can you share because your expression of Truth speaks louder than the words uttered and it is your expression that keeps the wolves from attacking for they feel your Truth and walk away. Your strength is in your knowing Truth and man knows no Truth but will try their hardest to take yours from you if you are not at the point where the weapons of man cannot hurt you/have no effect on you because you now know by way of **experienced** Truth the powerlessness of man's weapons.

How do you behave when you are on the spiritual path? I mean seriously, we are talking about having a personal relationship with God here!

I know right?! Is it formal or casual? Pot luck or catered? Shoes on or off? Visitor or ohana/family?

God is my best friend, solid, dependable, reliable, constant. I never get tired of his company, his sense of humor, the fuzzy, warm feeling that envelops me out of no where making me smile or cry like a dang fool in the middle of Walmart. I never feel alone and in all honesty don't feel fear anymore just harmony, peace, the ebb and flow of being because I am not thinking of the world, I understand the world now and am not concerned with the world. Why? Because no amount of thinking or worrying or orthodox prayer or even physical doing will change the world. The only thing that will change the world is when more people are **of** the consciousness **of** peace and harmony and **not** of the consciousness of i, me, my, the personal of the impersonal chaos of the world.

Do you see the difference between the thinking mind and the receiving mind? That what you are doing within defines your nature, your expression as human man or spiritual man? Are you thinking and chewing or just chillin' up in there, maybe smiling, maybe just humming? Are you mentally out in the world of man taking on the fear and pain or listening within so you don't miss a Truth bomb that just lights your being, makes you swoon with delight at what you just learned, received, were given?

Your relationship with God is secret, silent and sacred and the **quality** of this relationship is dependent on your devotion to that principle and the other few that will be presented. You cannot mix and match, take what you want of God and sprinkle it over your humanity to make it look pretty. It is still lipstick on a pig, costume, cover, paint, illusion.

God is Law and if you don't abide by the principles of the Law, live the Truths that **are** harmony unto your being, you don't get the desired result but not because these principles don't work.

They do, impeccably, perfectly and eternally. It is merely showing you **you cannot have the good of God without being under the gentle governance of the good you desire.** Not to over simplify but rules are rules and all actions have consequences. Cause and effect of God consciousness is always good because God is harmony in expression and like begets like.

The cause and effect of human consciousness is of duality therefore all outcomes are going to be of duality, good and bad, horrible or great. Duality creates the proverbial crap shoot with every choice you make from the perspective of i and not the perspective of I because of the Law of like begets like. You reap what you sow, get what you give, tit for tat.

The spiritual path is nothing more than learning from the errors that present, learning from the pain you don't want to feel again and asking God within to tell you exactly what you need to go forward more enlightened for the experience. "What is my take away Father?" And wait to be floored because Truth is a bomb, it shatters belief and puts you on solid ground.

This letting go of erroneous beliefs is called **dying daily** and it is what man calls peeling the onion, letting go of belief to get to the Truth of you-spirit in form, eternal. When all the erroneous human beliefs held as Truth are gone because you can see why they were not the Truth you thought they were you can easily let them go and live Truth that has been revealed that never changes, never fails and never ends. The spiritual path is nothing more and nothing less that learning to be one with the Law of universal creation instead of being the log jam in the river trying to make a go of life by yourself.

So how do you act with God? Devoted to, thankful for, joyous. You love God with all your heart, all your soul and that is what is returned to you pressed down and flowing over as visible abundance, peace and harmony. You receive what you give of the way you feel within, God expressing, and this is what brings grace to bear in your life and among man where there was no grace before.

What is Truth, capital T? And why is it different than truth, little t?

Truth is God, truth is man's personal *belief* based on other's beliefs or general consensus.

There is no Truth among man who doesn't know where and what God is because Truth, capital T, is synonymous with God as are Word, Water, Law, Substance, Spirit. They all denote that which is God in expression therefore when you see capitalized nouns by themselves they always and only refer to God and only one of spiritual understanding, one in conscious oneness with God knows the subtle yet profound difference this makes in understanding the Bible.

Truth is what you know by revelation, that which comes from within unbidden, not of you but **for** you for peace, for healing, for release and relief of pain, sorrow or fear. What God reveals is Truth that is, always is, will never change or let you down, forget about you or take back what has been given. **Truth, capital T, God,** releases you from *belief* in a power outside of you as *illusion* when known aright.

Why is the Bible so confusing?

Two reasons. Firstly the Bible is not meant to be read but interpreted, **not** by man outside of you **but by the God within each man** and this is only possible to one who has had the mystical experience of meeting the Father face to face ie knows the source of Truth.

Second, you have to know the name of God and **your** true name before you will be able to experience the Bible because how do you understand a story if you are not aware of who the main character is to understand what is happening and why? Perspective is paramount to understanding the Bible.

Man thinks the Bible is written about a God outside of them when it is actually the story of **you, the I of you, the awakened Christ consciousness of you.** In the first chapter of Genesis all are of God consciousness in the garden of Eden supplied and maintained **then** as spiritual man separate and apart from God in the second chapter of Genesis which is the Old Testament completely devoid of God, governed completely by *Lord* God of Mosaic law which is nothing more than cause and effect or karma.

The New Testament reveals how to have conscious oneness with God to be under God governance, grace, and not under Mosaic law. Unfortunately the reason for the coming of Jesus was not understood as the savior of man but was seen by the Romans as one who had come to set up a new *physical* kingdom of men **and** the Orthodox Jews felt he was not *their* Messiah because he didn't fit the warrior they envisioned to smite their enemy **therefore didn't believe him to be the Christ promised and Jesus the Christ was crucified.** Human greed, human power and judgement over Truth.

The reason the interpretation got so messed up and is still messed up is because man with their thinking, fearing, desiring minds are unable to understand the **expression** of Jesus the Christ was not the expression of his *human thinking mind* but the expression of his **union with God.** Most man of that time *reacted* to his *human* coming, ie could only experience *visible* events in which they *perceived* Jesus to be a threat to the current establishment of church and state and could not understand Jesus was the **expression of peace** sent to save mankind from living in chaos/duality.

Jesus the man was crucified by human man out of fear of *their* loss of power and their *judgement* of him not being the risen Christ. They thought Jesus must be a usurper of power not the returning Messiah. Why? Because the God of the Old Testament was that of law, of wrath, of punishment, big and powerful, therefore they expected a giant, a fighter, a champion for *their* cause to smite *their* enemies, to do *their* bidding, to part the seas for *them*.

Jesus the man did not fit the bill of what they imagined *their* God should *look* or *act* like. Jesus preached peace when *they* wanted a warrior and that is why they felt Jesus could not possibly be the Messiah *they* were waiting for.

Isaiah and Saul of Tarsus returning to the consciousness of God to become Paul are two examples of how Christ consciousness will completely change your entire existence when the weight of the world becomes too much and one cries out in earnest for that which is peace unto your being. It will be received each time you ask for it but understand **each time you ask for peace it is because you forgot where peace was** and went on walk about back to the consciousness of duality where chaos invaded, ie you reacted to the words, emotions and events of *man* and why you must again ask for peace, God, to be in your midst, consciousness.

Do I stop going to my current church services?

Man goes to church to be filled up, to be kept on track, to have something to think about during the week that might make them a better person or to feel cleansed of sins. You cannot begin to learn how to be a true Christian until you start **wanting** to be a true Christian. If you go to church once a week or on holidays you are paying lip service, want something for nothing ie only willing to expend a few hours a month or year. You can continue on that path until the dogs come home and never know what spiritual life is all about. You can devote hours a day to reading the Bible and memorizing verses to bring up at parties and discussions but until you take the time to stop, get quiet and **listen for God within** that is all you will be doing-waiting.

The actual meaning of the word **learn** doesn't mean to pump in, it means to allow what is within to flow out to bring Truth to individual consciousness, that is what you are learning, what comes from within you that is new and not a rehashing of man's words from human mouth to human ears. I am not saying don't go to church, it serves a purpose **just don't put your faith in what**

is being taught. Take yourself there with God awareness and see if the people, the sermon, the preacher don't start to change their ways.

Churches and religious gatherings are not to go to learn from **but to release Truth to** not by words but through conscious oneness with all who are there, seeing others as the Christ and see if the atmosphere doesn't begin to change to more reflect the peace **your** knowing Truth bringing when you bring God into their midst.

What do you have to do?

To succeed in this you have to stop being afraid of everything you think is out of your control because you only believe you have control, you do not so stop thinking you do. It is only when you give up trying to control the uncontrollable-all other individual consciousness or the world at large-that your life begins to take on the expression it is supposed to because only when you stop fighting, using your thinking mind to scheme and plan and figure stuff out are you then able to hear what is being given within that you respond to to reap all the good you had nothing to do with the creation of.

God created all in the beginning and as your conscious understanding of Truth deepens the expressions created in the beginning specifically for you start to express in your life as harmony, peace, rest, relief and then out in the world as your perfect expression of Self, God in form, the added and needed things of a tangible, abundant experience.

You have to be willing **to defer** to an experienced guide on this journey because right now you are running amok somewhere ill prepared and will continue to suffer the consequences of human living/duality. Stop trying to figure life out on your own, you cannot because it has never been your life to figure out. You as human man do not exist, what you believe yourself to be is not real rather an illusion caused by ignorance of Truth.

The spiritual life only requires one thing of you-letting go of your ego, what you think you know, your puff, your protection from supposed outside forces and just melt into a puddle and say "yes please Father! I'll take my place in the driver's seat following only the map you put in front of me. I now know my side jaunts on roads not on the map are full of things I don't want to experience."

God, universal Law of creative expression, is a numbers game. For some of you this is going to be a relief because it is just that simple to live under grace in conscious oneness with God. You get out of spiritual living what you put into **living** the principles that make up the foundation of knowing God aright.

This isn't some book of magic spells, the anti christ to deceive you, mental manipulation or hypnosis, self or otherwise, that casts the universe under your spell so you can act out your fantasy of being God. Muaaahahhh! (Subtext: power tripping hysteria.)

It is quite the opposite actually. It is you who has finally realized you need to be where God is to receive that which is of God and that is within in a secret, silent, sacred relationship not spoken of to the world through the lips but revealed by your expression in the world.

Why are you free when you know God aright?

When you know God aright you are free from the duality of man, the pain of man, the living as man separate from Source. You are free because you know who you are and you are free because you do not need to think or do to create your life rather you rest and let God give you the map, supply travel tunes, navigation and gas money to this new consciousness called heaven on earth.

You are free from the fear of death and free from having to suffer your ignorance of Truth-karma or negative consequences of your actions-ever again because if you are **of** the consciousness **of** God you are **of** the consciousness **of** peace and forgive 70x7 so what could you ever do that would bring negative consequences to bear? Nothing. This is how being **of** the consciousness of Good/God keeps you free from the duality of man. **It isn't a power of God that protects you it is you knowing the boundaries/principles that keep you within God consciousness, the how to and why for of Truth that keeps you right where you want to be.** Remember it is always your choice how you chose to live, by God's gentle governance that is more like a daily adventure or by your knowledge, degrees, personal power, mental power, mental control of self and others.

You are always under the Law of like begets like regardless of which nature you are expressing from. What you sow you reap. What you give you get. There is no escape, no amount of repentance and no amount of money that can change Law into something other than what it is being which in this example is like begetting like. You don't get roses from apple trees and you don't get dogs from donkeys. If you are mean chances are someone is going to be mean back and you have surely recognized when you are nice first others are nice back.

You cannot change an immutable principle of universal creation through mere belief which is no more successful than you trying to have God's allness in your experience while holding onto the judgements and false beliefs of man separated from the source of all that would bring peace to bear.

So if you take the time to separate Truth from fiction and begin to live the Truth you are realizing to be Truth you will live Truth free from judgement and enslavement to self or any one or anything of the world of man. You are free of all human constraints of sin and death to live eternal harmony.

This is the freedom you experience when you **know** God and is the freedom not afforded in the human experience.

What is a metaphor for how God is harmony unto you?

God can be thought of as the conductor of an orchestra. The orchestra is the entirety of the universe, each musician, form, integral in their individual expression of the music, life. Each musician knows their part, their purpose, their function within the whole doing only and exactly what the conductor desires for perfect harmony of all. One musician comes in as another dies off in silence but the note is never gone it just recedes until it is played again.

The perfect harmony of the orchestra is possible because there is only **one** consciousness of the orchestra and it is that of the conductor, the one who directs, maintains and sustains the harmony of the expression because all is under his higher knowing.

Now if one of the musicians starts playing their own song creating chaos within the eternal harmony the conductor doesn't notice that one musician get up and leave. The harmony of the orchestra is **not** dependent on the number of musicians, there is harmony because of the **conductor** not the musicians therefore to have the harmony they know the conductor brings forth in them they will seek to be with the conductor because of the beauty of their expression under his tutelage.

Therefore those who play their own song are no longer heard within the orchestra but they always have a place to come back to when they finally decide to play the music of the conductor and not of their own desire.

Right now as human man you are off on a solo tour but at some time you will yearn for what was, the harmony of your fellow musicians, your brothers and sisters but until you are done playing solo you will not experience the harmony the conductor brings to your music.

You are missing that which the conductor has which is a harmonizing influence that brings individuals together in an expression of the highest order and when you are with the conductor the world falls away, your music is perfect, the presentation, the execution all beyond words and not because of you **but because of the conductor as your consciousness producing/revealing the harmony of itself through you as you.**

How do you have a personal relationship with the God within?

First you have to be done with this world of man, of duality, confusion and pain, ready to wash your hands of the whole basket of crazy, metaphorically not physically, and be open and desirous of knowing that which is not found among man, in or of the knowledge of man.

Second you are willing to devote yourself to learning and practicing the principles of Truth that you have never been given the opportunity to know which is the **only** means by which you develop the connection and subsequent relationship with God.

Knowing God aright is as simple, and as difficult, as sitting in the silence of your own being desirous to know Truth, not what man knows but what God knows and in this way and this way only will you know what it means to experience God and live in the kingdom of heaven.

The majority of spiritual living has been revealed in just these few pages however reading Truth is **not** knowing Truth and is not living Truth.

Spiritual living is a life of expressing the nature of your being, your Source of being, God, spiritual perfection, good, harmony. You know God because you have met God face to face so to speak, are aware of a presence within the silence that is not you but with/of you thus you express the nature of God which is harmony and not the duality of human man. That is what takes the time, the learning **to be** not the *reading* of.

How to know who is being spoken of, God or man?

Capital **I** is **God** and little *i*, personality, ego is *human* man. Spiritual man **is** an expression **of** God while human man only knows how to express what is of themselves.

As *man* you are individual, separate, alone, i, me, my and as such are always going to be in opposition to every other individual i on the planet because there is more than one nature being expressed, more than one expression of being which is the definition of duality.

As **spirit** you are an individual expression **of** the **one** consciousness of creation thus you listen to, do the will of the **one** consciousness and not that of your own will/thinking mind/desires. The difference is subtle but written of in the Bible as one of the names of God-**Elohim,** One of many, many of One.

Now that you are getting your mystical sight can you see how this was plain as day once you knew from what consciousness you were to experience the Bible? That you are **of** the One, are one of the many of the One.

What is meant by "this world is an illusion"?

This is one of the higher conscious understandings that may not make as much sense as some of the other revealed Truth given so far. Don't try to make sense of it, God will bring it to you in perfect timing for your complete understanding because that is how this spiritual path works, all Truth is revealed **within** not *outside* of you from *man* and the world.

We have all heard "this world is an illusion", "the fabric of this world is illusion", "nothing is real" which leads you to think Matrix movie scenario. Nope. It has nothing to do with the **forms** of this world being an *illusion* or your experiences being an illusion **it has to do with what man believes is the makeup of all that is.** Man calls everything seen *matter or material* form.

Man calls all that is *matter or material* in nature when Truth reveals **all is God.** Therefore **spirit** is the substance of all that is therefore what man calls *matter* is truly **spirit in form, God expressing.**

All is God, there is no such thing as *matter or material*-that is the *illusion*.

God **is** as all, the visible and invisible therefore all of what is **is** spiritual consciousness expressing in forms necessary for the conscious advancement of humanity as a whole from immoral man slave to their desires to moral man trying to be and do good to spiritual man who is walking the path back to wholeness.

What is God Power/Spiritual Power?

It is nothing the world can conceive of as power for it is not the power of physical strength or mental ability, in fact it isn't a power that can be used by man.

The power of God is **knowing** Truth and that Truth keeps you from making the errors of man, from believing what presents as duality is reality and reacting.

The power of God is knowing the Truth of one Presence, one Expression, on Law, one Life and one Source of all and it is of you and you are **of** it.

Knowing the principles/rules of Truth and **abiding** in and by those principles **is** what makes you free from duality/consequences to live under grace.

Knowing Truth **protects** you by revealing your place as a willing helper of God as God governs your life with the harmony of a Zen master, nary a ripple on the water.

Through these teachings you will find an inner peace and quiet in which you can actually realize what is behind the words "*i* of my own self can do nothing" so you trust and let the Law of Truth work behind the visible/let God do what God does in its own time, own harmony, own process, own will.

What is manifesting?

Human man thinks they can create matter in form out of thin air just by thinking thoughts. Man believes he can manifest, bring forth into visible expression material good through the application of their mind, that their thinking mind has been endowed with special abilities and is somehow capable of creating.

Truth reveals there is only one thing to manifest and that is God in awareness. Because this is **not** a *matter/material* world there is no matter/material to create from. All **is** spirit in form created in the beginning thus all **is** God **as** individual expressions for the function it provides within this closed system called Life. Therefore the only thing that can be manifested is God in your awareness which is the activity of God of your experience.

Anything man "manifests" is nothing more than manipulation of circumstances and people to get what they want, nothing was created it was only *taken* or *gotten* because they were the stronger will power, stronger force, meaner or more convincing which are all characteristics of one of *dual* expression and not one of **harmonious** expression.

What is duality?

God **is** and the expression of God **is** because the nature of God **is.** Is is the unqualified, no label, no judgement, no personal descriptor of what is that **man adds their interpretation to.** Bailey **is** a dog, **is** vs Bailey is a *bad* dog or Bailey is a *mean* dog or a *good* dog or an *old* dog or a *sick* dog none of which are the Truth of Bailey.

Therefore when you qualify anything you are lying, coloring, embellishing, adding to what **is** already spiritual perfection out of ignorance and will suffer the consequences of your personal judgements and actions.

When you qualify according to personal perspective you are adding human traits to God's perfect creation. You, little i, cannot add anything to creation! What you *think* you add to understand the world around you is exactly what keeps you mired in the world you don't understand.

Duality is anything other than the consciousness of God expressing as **is.**

Duality in spiritual study most simply put is:

- Individual perspective, point of view, expression of emotions ie yelling, fear, anger, sadness, lack; that which has an opposite ie good or bad, any label, qualifier or designation other than is.

- The duality of consciousness', that of God of perfect harmony and that of man of chaos and lack.

- The duality of your own thinking mind, i should, i shouldn't, i want, i need

Man thinks from the standpoint of this or that, right or wrong, kill or be killed, take or be taken. If in your mind there is a choice to be made determined by *you* you are expressing duality. This *or* that, this *and* that. You *or* the other person. However, if in the same situation you see **is,** not a choice of how to accept it, ie by label or judgement, you are expressing oneness, singularity of expression, grace.

Singularity of expression: expressing the consciousness of God, Source.

- God expressing itself as all that is is singularity

- You expressing God/harmony is singularity

- The true atmosphere of the universe is IS, being, harmonious, eternal expression of Self, which is singularity of expression

Therefore **knowing** God aright is the reason for **your** singularity of expression, your harmony and peace, because knowing God reveals the Truth **of** your singularity of expression **as** your true nature of being.

Duality of expression:

- The atmosphere of the world, the way the world works with its good and bad, highs and lows, haves and have nots is duality predicated on the belief of being separate and apart from God, good, allness.

- Man expressing *himself* because what else is man who only knows of man to express as? Man doesn't express duality by choice but because it is the literal atmosphere you live in, it is the atmosphere you were born into, believe in and live by as your operating system and have never been given an other option of how to live.

- Duality is always personal i, me, mine not yours and it is this way for every individual.

The human mind is a dual mind, of both good and evil thoughts and deeds but only because the world around you has the same mind resulting in the literal atmosphere being of this dual expression. Spiritual man only has the consciousness of God, of harmony, of good thoughts and deeds thus sees the world as God does-all is and it is good.

It is this way that you see everything with the single I.

Morally flexible

Why is man of earth human man and not spiritual man?

There are two basic reasons:

1. Human man does not know God therefore has no relationship with God thus knows no

Truth of God
2. Human man is morally flexible which is the meaning of duality.

"Duality" isn't used often in human language and if it is it refers to that outside of man, never of man himself. Duality is choice which is the definition of morally flexible, able to be/do whatever expression/deed/action is needed at the moment to satisfy *self*.

To say man is of duality is to say man is morally flexible in that depending on the wind, the mood, the need and experience desired man will bend their morals, find a reason why they should be the one to get what they desire over another regardless of what that entails if the personal desire is strong enough to engage their moral flexibility.

This moral flexibility is what allows man to think their actions are justified no matter the outcome, it was their right as a human to defend/protect/keep what is theirs whether it be wife, money, job, sanity or life.

Spiritual man has no morality because spiritual man does not live out from human consciousness of choice, moral flexibility. Morality you will come to understand is a quality of human man who doesn't know God therefore doesn't know grace, the singular expression of God, the allness of God in action. Why does spiritual man have no need of morality/moral code? Because spiritual man lives above the law of good or else and lives by Love, good for all no matter the circumstances. How is this possible without one becoming a door mat of life? By living the Truth of God and not the beliefs of human man who knows no Truth of God.

Duality is two-ness, more than one expression of the being you are. As human man you think you are separate and alone from all others and because of this separation human man created two-ness, personal choice-this or that, good for one screw the rest, more for me less for you to protect self from harm/death because man has no idea of their infinite supply/abundance.

Duality is **personal choice to be and do as you chose depending on circumstances.** Man will bend their moral code of living ie do that which normally wouldn't even cross their mind to be or do but because man of earth *thinks* for himself and only himself and all others do the same there is a constant exchange, malleability, flexibility, latitude, wiggle room, of each person's code of ethics thus being of duality ie two minds, good and bad, this or that, me or them.

Duality is personal choice and is the operating system of human man but you will come to find that duality is not of one who has risen back to the consciousness of Truth. Why? Because when you **chose** to live out from the consciousness of Truth, God, you have **chosen** to live by the singular expression of the consciousness you are of which is the consciousness of is. Is **is,** ie cannot be good or bad, this or that but is and this is how spiritual man can be of one expression and not become a door mat of the world by not reacting, holding their own, being strong, protective.

The singular expression of is isn't a neutral place between good and bad it is divine Love, compassion, benevolence, it is not reacting to stimuli presenting because where God is there is peace. The is of God is a feeling of peace, of no thing of the world ie no jealousy, pain, anger, fear, want or need. When you are not dependent on man or the world for what you need you are harmonious because there is no chaos of your wants and needs hitting up against another's wants and needs.

The is of God is a resting place to all who can feel it, become aware of it and it is this feeling of rest, of relief and release that is the is of God, the perfection of God, the love of God and the desire of God for all to experience.

Why is it said God punishes you?

God knows nothing about you as a human, you are not **of** its consciousness of being therefore you are not known to God because you are not aware of God and not able to partake of the allness God is. The pain or punishment you think you are feeling is merely **the sin punishing the sin, actions have real world consequences that are *your* return for your actions.**

All that you do in this world that brings consequences to bear are the consequences **you willingly chose** when you chose to use your thinking mind to figure life out. You *reacted,* shit hit the fan, someone got hurt and you are going to jail. You are not being punished by God, you are feeling the return of your own actions upon you because you *reacted*.

This is the key! Tell me, if you don't react to your child having a melt down, if you don't react to the driver that cut you off, if you don't react to the person who was nasty on the phone, **if you don't react you cannot feed into the chaos being expressed** and therefore **are not of it** therefore not embroiled in what always becomes a mess you have to extricate yourself from. Why? Because you didn't *react,* didn't express from your *human* nature of *duality* rather remained in harmony knowing what was encountered was duality, no Truth within to release, no God of peace to express as their being.

The ego of some of you will say "but they started it! It was their fault!" Yes, when you were four and another kid pushed you and took your toy. So what! Seriously! Just stop interjecting yourself into the errors of the world around you, just for one day, then two days and then a week and see if your insides, your being, your demeanor and your patience are not different, better, if your relationships at work and at home are not better in some way and that life seems smoother, **less emotionally charged,** less snap and bitter, less of the perceived injustices, slights and *imagined* offenses you used to chew and stew on for hours, days, years even.

How does God do what you say God does?

Remember God is Universal Law of creative expression, impersonal, **not** person, not a thinking devising mind but creation doing and being what is normal and natural for it to do. God does what God does because God is merely the human term for Universal Law of creative expression, that which is the entirety, warp and woof, of all existence.

Law **is** and **is** means unchangeable, immutable, eternal in nature. You are **of** the Law when you are **of** the one consciousness that **is** the Law, God.

How do you understand the Bible?

The Bible is not for you to understand through the human mind rather are to allow the words read to **speak** back to you from their Source, God consciousness that is the consciousness of those who wrote the books of the Bible.

The Bible was written by those who had direct union with the Father therefore the words, just like every other thing that presents to spiritual man, is experienced without judgement so that God can speak back to you what you are to know about what you experienced and not what *seemed* to be the experience or the meaning of the words read.

What does it mean "you express as the nature of God when you are in oneness with God?"

As Mike, Paul or Rose you are your personality and as such your emotions, your likes and dislikes, what triggers you, what calms you and what sends you over the edge seeing red come what may dictate how you react which is your expression to the world.

When you are of the consciousness of God, of peace, know the Truth of error that nothing of the perceived forces of the world can do anything to you that is your expression because that is the Truth you embody.

Why has this not been known before?

Truth has been known since before time was but after man walked out of Eden, conscious awareness of God as source of all, God was **separated** from **spiritual** man's conscious knowing and *human* man has been left to suffer their *belief* in separation from God ever since.

Thankfully there have been those notable few down through the ages who had conscious union with God and gave to the world what came into their conscious knowing by way of this relationship. The problem was though they knew they were in oneness with God they had no understanding of **how** they came into that awareness meaning they had no understanding **the act of turning in to hear was what created the mystical experience,** brought God into individual awareness by which to have a personal relationship with and no longer pray outside to a God that doesn't exist ie false theology.

Because these mystics didn't know the **how** of how they had a relationship with God within they could not impart the how for another to emulate and validate as words of Truth.

Jacob Boehme 1575-1624 was a German cobbler who wrote many **mystical** books about God knowing he was in **conscious oneness** with God and was harassed during and after life for revealing **Truth** that went against *orthodox beliefs* of the time.

In The Signature of all things pg. 5 of 293, Boehme said **"the purpose of the mystic is the mightiest and the most solemn that can ever be, for the central aim of all mysticism is to soar out of separate personality up to the very consciousness of God."**

How to have a personal relationship with God by knowing what and where God is has been known since the beginning of time through those few higher of conscious knowing for some reason or another. The Order of the Essenes, a mystic jewish sect of which Jesus was a member, knew this Truth. The reason Jesus is said to have left, or been asked to leave the Essenes was because he wanted to share this Truth with mankind but the church felt knowing the name of God would lead man to conclude *they* were God because the majority of people barely understood the concept of personal responsibility and morality let alone comprehend the difference between *i* personality and **I** which is **felt** as a presence that reminds you where Truth is.

Jesus knew **how** to have a relationship with the Father within-inner listening and deferment of personal will to do the will of the Father which is to heal the sick, feed the hungry, clothe the poor and raise the dead. Jesus walked on his own sharing Truth all the while **being** the expression of this Truth.

Unfortunately man of low conscious awareness paid attention to the *words* and not the **source** of the words, God expressing **through** Jesus thereby missing the Truth being imparted **by** the **expressed nature** of Jesus the **Christ** and that is why there were so few true followers of Christ Jesus and why there were so many more who denounced him, feared him and crucified him.

But recognize too that most of those who did understand the message fell away after his crucifixion because their teacher, their *messenger,* their *visible* connection to God was no longer available to them. That was and is the hiccup. Man is so conditioned to look outside of himself for that which to hold onto that **when the visible is gone so is their religion.** When Jesus was crucified he was no longer of the *visible* world and only those who were **mystics,** knew God to be within, those who lived in the kingdom not of this world (of duality), were left to carry Truth out into the world.

Do not depend on the words of any man, not even a mystic. All should be taken within that needs further explanation and God will bring it forth in its own time, usually when there is a real world example to punctuate what is being given and then the **spiritual healing** is done and you are returned to harmony, oneness.

What is death?

That depends on who is answering, human man or spiritual man. To human man death is what man experiences at the end of this life. Done. Kaput. End of story.

Spiritual man knows their Truth to be consciousness that expresses as form which is your visible body but you are not the body, you are not in or of the body, this body is an **expression** of the **consciousness** you are **of** expressing as you, the individual expression of God known to the world as Jeremy, Pat or Brian. Therefore that which human man calls death spiritual man knows to be a transition from one state of expression, visible human form, to whatever comes next on your spiritual path as you grow higher and higher in conscious knowing.

Understand man who has no desire to find their Truth will come back time and time as human man until somewhere along the line consciousness is awakened and the journey to Truth begins. This journey reveals higher states of consciousness freeing you from the loop of ignorance called human man. You are getting your wings, your illumination, which spirals you higher and higher in conscious understanding until your return home is complete and there is no humanhood left on your spiritual perfect self all the while reaping the bounty, the peace and ease this life of oneness provides.

Honestly, it just keeps getting better and better unless you muck it up going back to doing your own thinking out of fear that this isn't real and one morning you are going to wake up proverbially screwed six ways from Sunday. You can think that, react to it, fall for it, play into it and walk away from the best thing you will ever know or you can stay, go within and scream at the top of your silent voice "I need you Father!" and the Father will come. It will always come.

Do you understand the import of that Truth? You are communicating with the Truth **of** you, the future you, the higher conscious you. You are communicating with the universe **of** which you are and are returning to. Think of walking a path dropping everything from your being to end up naked then gone not as disappeared but back to consciousness, invisible, incorporeal, eternal Truth of being.

Where is your God in all this evil and pain? Why does your God not help with the suffering of this world as it is said to?

Ah, the money question. Yes. Where is God in all this evil? In all this pain and suffering if God is omnipotent, omniscient and omnipresent?

First and most importantly God is an **individual** experience, not a blanket over all because it is dependent on the state of consciousness of the individual whether they are ready to accept the teachings of living the spiritual life and second, to be under grace you must know what grace is and grace is God in action, what is termed miracles to man, those things that just come into being without your effort/hands.

Where is God? God is **only** where God is **known in consciousness** and that awareness is your protection from living duality/chaos.

God is omnipresent, God is everywhere God is known in consciousness. The omnipresence of God means God is always with you **when you are expressing from the consciousness of God.**

If you don't **know** God by way of an actual experience of the presence within, have not had the mystical experience, you live duality and suffer the consequences of your actions.

Therefore God is always present where there is an awareness of God within individual man. When the presence of God is known within a person that becomes their atmosphere, their aura, the way they express, the way you **feel** them in your midst. It is their kindness, peace, their smile that sees past last year's clothes, lack of resources or pain expressed as anger to the Truth of you and when someone sees you, sees you for who you don't know yourself to be, that is what begins to free you from the weight of the world.

Why? Because you feel something within you don't feel from others and that feeling is harmony, kindness, benevolence, a place to rest because you feel the peace you are being given and not the want or desire of another individual in opposition to you.

This is the expression of the nature of God and if you are of the consciousness of God this is your nature expressing as one risen Christ seeing the un-illumined Christ of another because all are equal in the eyes of God for all are **of** God you just aren't aware of your perfection yet.

Understanding Sin

Sin is not what you have done out in the world the **original sin,** the only sin is the **belief you are separated from God** and as such pray to a God outside of you. You suffer solely because you *believe* something that isn't true and when you stop living beliefs and start living Truth right then your world begins to right itself to north, God, home.

The original sin that has caused spiritual man to suffer as human man is the *belief* that they are separate and apart from God, allness and wholeness of being, that which satisfies the soul. This *belief* has caused all the suffering, all the horrors and all the injustices of the world. If not for that first thought *outside* of the consciousness of God, ie an individual expression of God had a *personal i, me, my, mine* thought, a question maybe asked out loud for an answer *from another* form instead of asking God within like always and forever previous.

The original sin translates into the *belief* you are mere flesh and blood, is born and dies and is separate from the source of allness believed to be a God somewhere outside of you. Therefore whatever acts of omission or commission you do aren't your fault personally, it is the fault of the **atmosphere** of the world, the *hypnotism* of man that has said from time immemorial you can do whatever you want if you are willing to suffer the **consequences** of your actions.

However though you erred in ignorance of Truth you cannot be ignorant of the **consequences** of your actions because they are the atmosphere of your human experience, good and bad. Consequences, karma, cause and effect are **opportunities** man does not take to rise in conscious understanding of their actions and the relationship between actions, consequences, personal accountability and quality of life.

The cause of all suffering, damage to the world, cruelty to animals and disregard for life is because man *thinks* he is alone and must get, do and be all he can at any cost their morality deems acceptable. Man judges and compares self by appearances as to strength, wealth, health and happiness of others and *reacts* to that *illusion* of *appearance* solely determined by their *perception* of what is being presented and not what is **actually** being presented. Subtle difference but huge in effect.

What you perceive by your senses is **not** real and not to be trusted because all that you think, witness and hear is not the Truth of what is actually happening rather your personal interpretation filtered through your history-your fears, your joys and your perspective of right and wrong in that moment. **All that you take in by your senses is not the Truth of what is going on** because Truth is **received** from within your own being and it brings peace, harmony, understanding which is the proof that what is sensed outside of you is no thing that can change your expression of harmony.

What is illusion, what human man calls reality known through the senses?

Illusion is all that is interpreted by the senses of the body as being real and present and causes one to react because **all** illusion is charged with emotional history, both good and bad. When you understand this you must realize when you *react* to that which is only in your head you have given your mind permission to control and direct your behavior **not** to improve your life but to protect your *life,* protect the *form* you think is flesh and blood which is the hallmark of human man-kill or be killed because your life is always more important than anyone else's.

Man's thinking mind has put him at a crossroads that is always this *or* that: work or family, time or money, me or them, selfish or unselfish and this constant tug of will and want is the running in place that gets you no where but exhausts you just the same. The thinking mind creates the illusion you accept as reality and react to *as* reality but since your reality isn't real nothing you do changes your life permanently into the good you are trying to *get.*

Who you *think* yourself to be determines your expression, your actions. Whether you react or remain unaffected, get angry or remain unaffected is predicated on your consciousness of being-human man with personal history, personal desires and a personal level of morality by which to judge everyone else or spirit man with no history to color reality and no judgement because Truth is known.

Can you see how chaos is inevitable when each expresses from i, personality, ego? This is the mystical meaning of "too many cooks in the kitchen" ie separate, different, conflicting, no harmony, no peace and no perfect outcome if there is a "fly in the ointment."

Why do people say God takes his children home when there is a death?

Ezekiel 18:32. "For I take no pleasure in the death of one who dies," says the Lord God: wherefore turn yourself/repent and live.

God doesn't "take you home" when you die and you don't go to hell, you just come back again and again until you begin to awaken to the consciousness that allows you to step away from man and hug yourself close to God because you are now able to understand on a conscious level, not an academic level or level of the finite human mind, what God is and is not.

Once you know God aright you cannot die because you know yourself to be spirit and nothing but nothing can take you from your Truth because your Truth can never leave you, never forsake you for you **are** Truth when you are **of** the consciousness of Truth.

What is sin?

Sin is impersonal error that man has attached to a person, place or thing. The sin isn't **of** the person, place or thing, it is a label you have *attached* to a person, place or thing and what you think about something can in no way change what that something is in reality. What you *think* with your mind is an *illusion* not real because what you think has been *qualified* according to you, what is good and what is bad to you.

Sin is merely ignorance of Truth which makes you err; you screw up when you don't know the rules of the game and the rule of this game called spiritual living is **there is only one presence and it is good/harmonious so all else must be an illusion, outward expression of continued ignorance of Truth.**

What is error/illusion/duality? Anything that has an opposite meaning a dog cannot be both a *good* dog and a *bad* dog; it **is** a dog that is being *labeled*, judged, qualified according to *individual* perspective. The same vacation cannot be qualified truthfully as a great vacation or a bad vacation because it is *subject* to individual perspective as to what good or bad encompasses and not **objective** to what **is,** God in expression therefore it was a vacation with human emotions and actions laced in.

What is Duality/error?

Duality=individual i, me, mine

Duality=matter/material perception of reality

Duality=appearances perceived by senses, man's thinking mind that can think good and bad.

Duality is the atmosphere of man.

Just as a fish doesn't know it exists in a wet environment man doesn't know he exists in an atmosphere of good and bad and that atmosphere of good and bad is your operating system, monkey see monkey do, or don't depending on their moral code of ethics/rules of man/religion.

Duality is not reality because **God is as all** and God does not know anything other than itself-all seen and unseen creation that is harmonious in expression.

Human man **is** duality. He expresses it and experiences it but as you can see it all stems from a *belief* you are separated from God, oneness, wholeness and completeness, that which supports, maintains and sustains itself, you.

When error hits up against Truth it dies no different than when you answer a question truthfully. Where else can the conversation go? It is and nothing can change is. Truth lays the ax at the root of duality and drops it clean. What power can a judgement have against Truth? How do you judge someone who is pure of judgement? Tells the Truth?

Truth is and Truth is the mike drop, end of anything unlike itself.

What is the anti christ?

The anti christ is **not** a person it is the carnal/mortal/human/material thinking mind; the anti/*unlike* of God and which, if it is believed to be a power, will destroy you. The anti-christ in all its forms stems from human fear and one who fears is not of the consciousness of peace, not in oneness with the source of harmony therefore is *unlike* God; not against God merely unlike God thus not real.

Anti christ to spiritual man is that which is *unlike* Self and since God is all there is there is **no** thing that is unlike Self. Therefore there is no anti-christ coming as an individual/power against God; all man living as *human* man and not as their true nature of **spiritual** man **are** the *anti-christ* because they have no awareness of the Christ within thus they are anti, unlike, Christ/God **in expression.**

The universal belief in two powers is the impersonal source of all that is judged good and bad and evil in the world.

This belief is ingrained in your psyche from before you were born, it is your conditioning, your programming, your family histories and those of every single person who ever walked this earth around and through the environment in which you were born. The consciousness of man's belief in duality has become the atmosphere of the world to the point no one understands the atmosphere of man **is not Truth, not the reality you are to be experiencing** but a subliminal soup of error, the fearful consciousness of human man who thinks himself separated from God.

It is for this reason instead of seeing the world as it **is** your mind interprets what you are seeing through your history and that becomes your ingrained *reaction* to life, not your response but those of others *held by you,* their fears, loves, hates, desires and biases. There is probably nothing of your own choices/thoughts within you because you have not made any of your own, you have taken the world's views and beliefs at face value never questioning why or how or to what end.

These generational fears exist in the atmosphere of the child before conception and onward being the food, the life breath of the child until the child decides to think with their own mind which many parents rebel against because it usually goes against their way of seeing the world thus wrong on every level. This dissent among family members is why so many seeking God stop seeking, because it is seen as weird, wrong, not our way, fairy tale, never worked for me, can't hack the real world so you live in an invisible world etc. All are fears and biases based on duality which is ignorance of Truth.

Everything you have learned was condition based, punishment and reward, be this way or else, do this or else, this or that, duality, and the way you respond to the world is in ways that your mind feels will protect you from harm, lack, illness, loneliness but it does the opposite. Duality can only beget duality thus your thoughts predicate the outcome and in the human world the result is always duality so you are rolling the dice every time you make a decision because you are making a decision between opposites which allows for both to be the result of your experience.

In the human way of expressing you make choices based on *personal* desires and the desired outcome. In the spiritual way of expressing you rest in the words God speaks within for the harmonious and always perfect solution.

What is Spiritual power?

Spiritual power is the realization of **your** name and nature: **I am** the individual expression of the one God that is the creator of all that is seen and unseen.

What is a spiritual healing?

Spiritual healing means healing *human* man of his *belief* in being *separate* and apart from **God.** It is the term used when Truth has been revealed that dissolves illusion so you are once more in harmony, back where harmony is, in conscious oneness with God.

A large portion of your study will be on healing. Not the physical or mental healing of the human body or mind but the healing of **spiritual separateness.** Man separated from God in conscious knowing must be healed, must have revealed in consciousness the **error** of the *belief* of separation. When that illusion is dispelled because you have had the mystical experience of meeting the Father face to face within your own being you are no longer of the *belief* of being separate and apart from God because you have **experienced** oneness **with** God.

Spiritual healing is the revelation of Truth which brings peace into your midst; when God is present, within your conscious knowing everything else falls away as the illusion it is and you rest. Why? because no matter what presents to you in the world God is with you always as your way shower and rear guard, your Truth and your Life eternal, your best friend and your greatest love.

Stepping onto the path

I hope you are no longer afraid of God because you now know the Truth of God and that God is your biggest supporter and best friend that is eternally dependable, reliable and perfect. I hope you no longer feel God is a being that judges and withholds but universal Law of creative expression that is the ebb and flow of Life, what man calls nature that is harmonious and eternal in expression. That the reason human man is not experiencing the harmony of creation in expression is because man thinks he is separate from creation thus living chaos, that which is unlike the harmony of God.

You have been shown how sin is of the atmosphere of man and sin is not of person, place or thing. That the Truth of you no matter your human expression or label given or received is spiritual perfection just as of yet not in awareness to be known as Truth to you.

There are rules to spiritual living by which you stay within the consciousness of harmony, in conscious oneness with God, harmony in expression. God cannot therefore does not punish you; the sin punishes the sin meaning you are aware of the consequences of your actions and if you chose to do the action you chose to accept the consequences ie punishment, incarceration, death or anything in between which is a result of your *reaction* to the world around you instead of letting God bring Truth to your consciousness.

You have been given a glimpse into what is Truth and what is illusion enough to see the difference thereby knowing Truth is God and illusion is what man calls life. A mystic is one who has met the Father within, knows God exists, God is and God is within individual man when the presence is known and felt. **God is an experience** not words and the only way to understand what the words of the Bible mean is to allow God to bring the understanding to you from within, Truth bomb, mike drop. Peace out.

You have never been alone and in fact you come with your own built in best friend that won't tell you what to do, will always be there when you come back on bended knee, scratched and bruised from another go around with duality. God doesn't judge you, will forgive you 70x7 but at some point you will have to decide which side of the fence you want to be on permanently because the more times you leave God to go play with rocks and hand grenades the longer it takes you to recover from the karma you incur, longer to bring back the peace you had already found.

As you can see spiritual life isn't difficult rather different. It is **responding** instead of *reacting* and the difference depends on who you know yourself to be. The reason man *reacts* is because they have no understanding of peace. If they did they would cling to it but man doesn't know the **source** of peace and harmony as that of God therefore man doesn't experience God, good, grace, love, peace, benevolence etc, within to be able to express them because they are **of** God and not available to *man*.

The expression of God is peace, harmony and love and you have to allow it to flow **from** the source **within** you out into the world for all to feel.

The only reason for knowing God is to find your peace but in doing so afford peace to be available to those in the world seeking as you were. We of the Christ become the light unto the world, the lamp uncovered, the beacon of hope, not in words, **never** in words, but in expression. Have you ever been around someone you just wanted to stay near not because of how they looked or what they did but because of **who** they were, the way they felt-safe, inviting, long lost friend feeling of comfort, openness, free to be yourself around. They had something you wanted and hoped to glean some understanding of what it was by proximity.

That which is in your proximity is by default in your conscious awareness therefore you can emulate, take on the mannerisms, nature of expression of that which you are in proximity to, family for example. This is the meaning of "birds of a feather flock together," ie they think and act alike, sometimes as one as in military or orthodox religious training and also the reason addicts are reminded that the people they used to hang with were of the "flock," the consciousness, they no longer want to be their consciousness thus must separate themselves from the forms expressing that consciousness ie enablers and other addicts.

Therefore if God is an experience you must learn how to have that experience and that is accomplished by knowing Truth about God and then how to let that Truth be the guidance and governance of your experience.

Your state of consciousness, who you think you are, is broadcast to the world louder than if you were to say it yourself. You cannot hide who you are from the world, if one is in conscious union with God, no matter the form/costume presented, one with God can always see the God, the Truth of being, though dormant, unrecognized or unaware of, of the person before them. There is nothing more beautiful to a person than to be seen as their reality of being-the child of God, and not how they present to the world because of circumstances.

Being one with God and recognizing brotherhood in all awakens the spirit in those who become aware of your nature, harmony. This is why it is so vitally important that you not bottle up God within but allow it to flow.

I say all the time when I am out and about, "flow Father, flow" and smile because I know what I have found that gives peace and meaning to my life is available to all in proportion to their awareness of it, walking in it and **living from it.** You live outwardly from oneness with God and it is this awareness of the God within that allows you to be an instrument of God, let loose God through and as all your actions.

All you as Mike or Stephan do is let God go first in all ways to express as I the Father instead of i the personality of duality. First thoughts, first words, first actions. In this way you will never err, never misstep on your path. You of yourself do nothing, it is the God within who doeth the work so put yourself in the driver's seat and just relax, God's navigating.

God is a much better navigator-misses all the pot holes, knows different more scenic routes, has a clean windshield, unlimited fuel and drives at a pace that allows you to enjoy the scenery.

You give up nothing but the weight, duality and confusion of the world and gain a kingdom of supply, peace and ease. It sounds like a no brainer but for most it sounds to good to be true-what is the catch?

The catch is it is **your** choice, always and only your choice and I can understand if you don't have enough information yet to make a choice but I couldn't be more excited for you because before you didn't realize you had an option in how to live your life and now you do and you are willing to find out more instead of rejecting it right out of hand. That is you letting down the wall between you and the unknown. You may not have conscious awareness of God but you are allowing yourself to entertain that which you have been told about God or learned in church etc, may not be the Truth you thought it was.

You are in the process of peeling back your long held beliefs to reveal that underneath all the humanity that confuses and suffocates you is the light unto your being, that which you were missing-**your connection, conscious awareness of being the child of God** you are, joint heir to the kingdom of God, the walking, talking individuated expression of God perfect in every way.

You don't learn God, God reveals itself to you at the level of your desire to know God. All of God consciousness is within you but just as a kindergartner has all the potential of a college professor there are continuous levels of raised conscious awareness, the knowing of things that happen in a progressive manner. The more you desire to know God the more you desire to rest in it instead of the world the faster it may seem that God consciousness is revealed to you.

Think of your consciousness of God at the moment as a mountain top covered by clouds. The more you immerse yourself in God the more the mountaintop is revealed. Soon not only will the clouds have dissipated but you find you have risen to the top of the mountain, God, and no longer look up or at God but are **with** God, seeing what it sees from the vantage point of raised consciousness.

There is a progression of understanding/enlightenment that comes with the order of the following sections but within each section the order is less defined as it all relates to the same subject but from different angles and avenues of awareness ie we have all been in discussions where in the end you realized you were saying essentially the same thing but the words and the way they were used or the way it was explained just didn't click and that has to do with individual consciousness.

Therefore redundancy serves a purpose, not for mere memorization of the words to be thrown down as river cards but to enrich your conscious understanding, give you a more well rounded, more broadly understood picture of what God is, what sin is, what Truth is and how to journey back to the Father's house.

Sense to Soul contains the principles of spiritual living and with study and practice you can free yourself of the limitations of this world if you live the principles of Truth and practice the presence of God.

You cannot fail to find God if you seek in earnest for God hears every call for grace and fulfills the Law unto itself-harmony in your midst, eternal supply and support at your back.

Do not say after one month this isn't working. It isn't that **it** isn't working it is that *you* aren't working it, you aren't studying and practicing and giving up duality. You want to, you say you do, you try but give up saying it isn't working.

The degree you allow God to have governance over your life is the degree of expression of God **as** your life. If you are not expressing the nature of God more and more and human traits less and less you are not walking the talk you are *reading* words *hoping* they do something *for* you.

God is always known by its nature which is harmony. If you are not getting more and more harmonious you are lying to yourself about the work you are actually doing to know God. **Knowing God is up to you and you alone, no one can do it for you** so if you aren't seeing results you aren't doing the work. Plain and simple. God is and when you know this for yourself and stop screwing around with duality it is then that you reap the benefits of knowing God aright.

Old Testament vs. New Testament

Getting started

To begin your study you need to understand why man is in the predicament he is in and that is through understanding the difference between the Old Testament and the New Testament. This distinction allows you to see the life you are living as that of the Old Testament and how you could be living as that of spiritual man of the New Testament which is the life all are going to rise to experience when they awaken to Truth.

In ordering the chapters of this book it was impossible to put them in an order of importance or an A to B to C type of progression because all of the subjects work in concert so if something is mentioned you do not have understanding of take a peek in the terminology chapter to get the spiritual meaning as it is intended because the word used as man uses it will give you an incorrect understanding.

Old Testament vs New Testament

There is an error in orthodox religion and the opposite/correction of this error is found in all metaphysical religions.

In *orthodox* religions Jesus is set apart as *the* Christ consciousness in the sense of his being *separate and apart* from any other individual/man, as if he of his born humanhood was it, the Christ, that Jesus was the *only* man to ever to have conscious union with God. False. All have the spirit of God within them **but until it is known** it is no different than a million dollars in a bank account you have no idea is yours. It does you no good if you have no conscious awareness of it. For something to have an effect on your life you must be aware of it, know it, experience it thus are conscious of it.

Jesus was not the only Christ. Jesus the man had an awareness of the Christ consciousness **within** which was what **made** him Jesus **the** Christ just as Gautama became Gautama **the** Buddha when he too knew Truth within. Human man thinks a man, Jesus, to be the salvation of human man because man's concepts of Truth can go no higher than that which is available to the mind of man. But before Jesus was the Christ by awareness of his Christ, he was no different than you are now, human, not spiritual man under the knowing or protection of God.

The ignorance of Truth is why religious organizations say Jesus, *the man,* is your salvation. *Come to Jesus and you are saved!* and this error is perpetuated on posters, bumper stickers, church reader boards, by clergy and congregations that parrot the lie that your salvation comes through Jesus *the man* because the Bible gives the example of Jesus as being the one **at that time** with a true knowing, connection to God though the Bible also states how Peter knew God because he knew the Truth of Jesus: "who do you say that I am?" "You are the Christ." Only one of Christ consciousness knows the Truth that all human man is spiritual man unaware/ignorant of their true nature.

The way Christianity is taught today you are told to put your faith in Jesus: know Jesus, love Jesus and pray to Jesus. *Jesus* not God. Like God is secondary or not even on the playbill. Such ignorance!

Jesus **is** the example of what it looks like to have a personal relationship with God for you to do likewise. Jesus **became** the Christ though inner knowing of God and that is what Jesus was bringing to the consciousness of man-that **if you dwell in the place of the most high** you will walk beside the Father, know the Father and live as the Father intended.

We are all Masters ordained to heal the sick and feed the hungry **when** we know the God within. Not just Jesus but **any** man can do/be what Jesus showed us was possible **when you know the Father within.** But understand Jesus was just a man like you and me until the Christ entered in, until the teachings, the preparation for the experience was complete and he was ready to meet God within and share Truth with the world. Your correct knowing of God, of Truth, **is** your relationship, your oneness with God and it is **direct, personal, private, secret, sacred and silent.**

Jesus was a man just like you. The only difference between Jesus the Christ and most other men of that time was Jesus had **awakened** to the Christ within through his study as an Essene.

Jesus came to reveal that all men could have personal contact with the Father and he was the example of what inner knowing would do for self and the world when this inner knowing is contacted and allowed to act on your behalf. What does hinder you? Rise, pick up your bed and walk.

The difference between the Old Testament and the New Testament:

-**Old Testament-**God outside of you to be prayed to with moral/mortal law of reward and punishment not spiritual/God. Be good or else. The "or else" is the other shoe dropping, the as yet unknown, the bad, the evil, the unwanted happenings that man believes are powers of the universe set against them, the **I just can't catch a break** sentiments.

-**New Testament-**the revealing of the Christ within and the name of God, I am. Jesus the Christ was the way shower, the example of what **all** man could become when they know Truth and by this knowing the disciples were ordained to heal the sick, feed the hungry and raise the dead. The knowing of the Truth Jesus brought to man as the Christ, the living God, was to reveal God is closer than breathing, nearer than hands and feet when you know what and where God is.

The Hebrews do not acknowledge the Messiah has come, the Christ. The Christians acknowledge that the Christ came for 3 years then went away and are waiting for the second coming therefore both the Hebrews and the Christians are without a Christ, one waiting, the other waiting for the return of the Christ but **both acknowledging the absence of Christ here and now** in this very temple where it has been presented to you over and and over again **the Christ dwelleth in you.** God did not send you to earth without an indewelling Christ otherwise it would be equivalent to turning you loose on earth with no conscious awareness of being.

Man has abandoned the Christ within but only out of ignorance but God has never abandoned you and since nothing can happen to you except through your own consciousness you cannot benefit by the presence of the Christ except by the acknowledgment that **Christ dwelleth in you.**

Whatever is to take place in your life must take place though the activity of your consciousness.

You must know Truth, the Christ, dwelleth in you and that the function of the Christ in you is still, as it was for Jesus the Christ, to heal the sick, raise the dead, feed the hungry and forgive the sinner. Acknowledge Christ dwelleth in you. You can do all things through this indwelling Christ, there is no power outside of you to act upon you because the only Truth of Life is within yourself and it is the harmony unto your being when it is known.

Do not misunderstand there are lots of power in the world to act on *human* man, on those who have not acknowledged Christ dwelleth in them. The moment you have accepted the indwelling Christ the Christ liveth your life and you are no longer man of earth who lives and dies but eternal, immortal being that no power lest given by God can have any effect on you.

You now find that you are not living your own life exclusively but that you have a partner, an invisible, senior partner of power, not the power of man but the still small voice of Truth that says "I've got this, I'm here" that allows you to rest, not be taken in by the appearance/error and continue on your way.

This is the mistake the Hebrews made. Because they lived under the *law* and not **grace** they expected a warrior, a king, someone of earthly power to *vanquish their enemy and set them free* so when they were given Jesus the Christ, of no law of punishment rather grace, love, kindness and Truth but no sword, no visible, physical, *measurable power* by which to *overcome* the armies of nations it is easy to see why they couldn't accept Jesus the Christ as the Messiah-**he wasn't their idea of the power necessary for a God in their image to have.**

They wanted their God to wield a sword but Jesus the Christ brought Truth that the sword cannot be picked up, that it was their dependence on God that dispelled the enemy as the arm of flesh, nothingness in the presence of the Truth of God.

Old Testament-Hebrew dispensation of God is an eye for an eye

New Testament-Christian dispensation of God is forgive your enemy 70x7

What is the difference between old and new that produced the change in the dispensation of God? Knowing the Truth of God which Jesus the Christ, the Master in oneness with God, brought to mankind-**all are the Christ** just not risen into awareness as their Truth of being at the moment to be witnessed.

The entire message of Jesus the Christ was to reveal to man that the kingdom of God is not in holy mountains or holy temples, not in holy books or holy people, that the kingdom of God is not lo here nor lo there but is **within** you.

Then you must accept as a major premise if we are to die to our humanhood, if we are to be reborn of the spirit, you must accept that whatever change is to take place in you is not going to take place because you go to some holy place or find some holy man or holy book. The change is going to take place only if you allow that holy place, or holy book or holy man **to reveal to you first that the kingdom of God is within you and the spirit of God is within you.**

You the human are the tomb the Christ rises from through **awareness of Truth** and you are risen, reborn anew. The old, the outer man of earth must die for God to express as your Truth-child of God, risen Christ, one with the Father knowing Truth by way of an actual experience of the presence within.

This is knowing God aright and this is the salvation that takes you out of death into eternal life as you were meant to experience, to live under grace, in conscious oneness with Source, Creator, God.

The Sermon on the Mount

The Sermon on the Mount, the Beatitudes, Matthew 5:3-12 reveals that there are two ways of life:

The way the world is living now, the old Hebraic way and the new dispensation which Jesus the Christ gave, that of living by a divine grace/harmonious influence, living according to a Law of love, loving your neighbor who is your friend but also loving the friend who is at the moment a perceived enemy. You cannot entertain any idea of an enemy because all are your brother and the only difference between me and you is **our level of conscious understanding of God.** Man who murders is still the same pure child of God because the sins of man cannot change the purity of God. Sins are dirt, they wash off and do not in any way change or compromise the skin below.

Sin is an error of universal belief not individual action. If there weren't the universal belief in two powers the error would never have been committed because the atmosphere would be that of harmony, of God. When you are of God consciousness the cause and the effect are the same- good, harmonious. This is what makes God dependable, reliable, repeatable, trustable. God is Law, not super human something or other. God is universal Law of creative expression expressing, is-ing, be-ing.

When we come to the New Testament Jesus gives man two rules to live by, two commandments which when seen with no judgment, ego or pride, make absolute sense and instantly reveal why we have failed as humans; **we were never meant to succeed as humans because we are not human.** "Human" is a construct in the mind of man who does not know his nature as infinite spirit rather thinks himself finite, killable, as something that lives and dies. Within that construct no wonder man fights for survival!

The two commandments given are:

1. You will have no power beside me. Deuteronomy 6:4-5. Hear O Israel, the Lord is **Our God,** the Lord alone. You shall love the lord **your God** with all your heart, with all your soul and with all your might.
2. Love thy neighbor as thyself. Leviticus 19:18. You shall not take vengeance or bear grudge against any of your people, but shall love your neighbor as yourself. All man are one with God so to harm your neighbor/enemy is to say you would harm yourself and the God of the other person.

Love thy neighbor means to never take an attitude of condemnation/judgement toward another because of outward appearances or perceived intelligence, ignorance, success or lack. That is merely the awareness of the consciousness they have within externalized. We have all worn different costumes-child, teenager, young adult, adult, elderly etc, and we have also worn the costumes of free, bond, slave, happy, sad, fearful, rich, poor, sick, well and in the presence of spiritual man the costume drops so that all that is seen is the brother of my brother, gosh it is so good to see you!

This is the attitude of kinship, of kindness, of **I want nothing from you so what can I help you with?** This is harmony between man, it is the ultimate of utopia, the individual recognition of the God within freeing each man to be supply unto themselves knowingly and that being their way of life.

Do, be, and receive living your life of God's expression and just rest and soak it all up, you are only in this form for a blink so feel the sun, hear the birds, see the children grow, keep your peace wrapped around you like your favorite blanket with the silky edge and breathe deeply of the air provided to sustain this form, feel the chest rise then slowly fall, feel the glory in the ability to breath and know beyond doubt you are home.

The mission of the Master wasn't merely to multiply loaves and fishes nor was it to transform physical bodies from sickness to health nor to raise them from the dead. **The mission of the Master was to take you into a new dimension of life in which you find the reality of your being which is spirit in nature through realization of the Christ within that is the transcendental consciousness that is your connection to all that is.**

Einstein used to tell his students that it was a mistake to think that vegetable and mineral life is different than man and animal, that even a stone has a soul and it does; soul is the very essence and substance of stone, rocks, sand, soil, earth, just as much as that soul, spirit or God is the nature of your true identity.

This spiritual universe becomes apparent to you through the instrument of the mind and it becomes apparent to you in proportion to the purity of your mind. **Not human purity but purity in the sense of freedom from superstition, ignorance and the adulterations of religious beliefs.**

There is one element that entered the mind almost from the beginning that has wrecked man's perception of Truth and it is the basic error that constitutes humanhood. It has been sought for a long time and only recently discovered why it is and what it is that causes man to have a world of sin, disease, lack and limitation. What is it that makes human beings go from the cradle to the grave with little pleasure and a lot of trouble?

When we lived in Eden, in the consciousness of harmony and perfection as pure offspring of God we were as angels and we were perfect. **But into that Eden crept a sin and the sin was the acceptance of a suggestion from outside of Eve; she accepted the *words* of the serpent over the inner knowing given her of God not to eat the fruit. Eve made a *choice* of her own. The choice she made was to know knowledge, that of man unlike God.**

That was the sin, the sin wasn't the quince or the eating of it but the *personal choice* Eve made which began the separation from God in conscious knowing to know that which wasn't of God. Poof. Out of the kingdom of heaven, consciousness of harmonious expression, because she was no longer **of** the consciousness of **harmonious** expression but of *human* man, that which is not of God.

When man began to **eat or imbibe or live by the expression/suggestion of the world around/outside of him he found himself beholden to the belief in good and evil, the laws of man thus took upon himself the mask of duality,** multiple expressions of self, impulses according to personal desire which allowed for expression of either good or evil, and no longer could it be said they were too pure to behold inequity. Why? because they were of the consciousness of man of *earth* where there is a *belief* of power in and of persons, conditions and things.

In that day symbolically it is said that Adam hid because he was naked and God asked him "**who told you** you were naked?" There in you have the whole essence of human life.

Who told you something is good or something is bad?

Who told you there was anything wrong in this entire world?

Not God. God never said there was anything wrong with a naked body, that there was anything wrong on the face of **God's** earth. Peter had to learn this same lesson in a different way. Because of his Judaic background he couldn't eat pork because it was vile but through a dream learned **thou must call nothing on this earth vile that God has made.** Even though Peter had been three years with the Master, even though he had learned all that he had and become so close to the Master he was still a Hebrew, he was still in slavery to religious *beliefs and doctrines* and had never been able to enter Christianity until that very moment in which he perceived that pork wasn't vile **because if God made it it is good and in that moment Peter became a true Christian.**

So it is with us, you don't become a Christian because you accept the teachings of Jesus Christ, you don't become a Christian because you join a Christian church, you become a Christian **in proportion to your acceptance of the revelation that came through Christ Jesus' lips in the Sermon on the Mount.**

That teaching reveals that even Pilate has no power since God is the only power. That teaching reveals that disease of any kind isn't a power since you can put your finger on it or walk through it without "getting it." That teaching reveals there is neither Jew nor Greek, that ye are one in spiritual divine sonship.

Have you stopped praying overly much for your own family and friends and learned to spend more time in praying for the enemy? That is what constitutes being a Christian. It profits you nothing according to God to pray for your friends; you must pray for your enemies and forgive 70x7 which is a principle of Truth.

Understand when you bring grace to bear, forgive time and time again man's indiscretions you are **not** absolving them of their punishment, you are **not** saying what they did was ok, you are **not** trying to white wash the hurt or damage they did. They will have to do what the laws of man require to pay for their crimes. You forgive all error because **all error is ignorance of their true nature** of spirit and illusion with no objectivity. Each time you forgive you release a weight one carries thinking the sin is within them, is **of** them. Forgiving them allows them to be taken into heaven that night, that second, to know their Truth and be "born" again but there will still be things to be taken care of in the world of man.

If you ask for forgiveness, you will get it that moment because forgiveness is a dispensation of God not man. What seems to slip the mind of the one sinning is *to stop and sin no more lest a worse fate befall you.* Know this, you are never cheating God of your life, you are cheating yourself of a life with God every time you use your will, your power for personal gain or personal pleasure.

Each time you ask for forgiveness you are forgiven but it is up to you to take the next step that determines your life-sin or find what lifted your burdens for a moment. They didn't lift themselves or you would be in heaven right now. Something other than you, something other than the world has to offer touched you and you felt it. You felt space to breath, a brighter day, a smile for no reason.

Ask why! What was that? What just touched me? And be curious, expectant, alive and **interactive** because you are going to get conversation, believe me, God is a chatty one when it knows it has a captive audience!

God will wait an eternity for you to come home. Can you wait that long to go home?

―――――――

Under Moses the Israelites experienced a greater area of land, more fertile land on which to live, a greater freedom of physical movement, a freer sense of religious worship and a more abundant supply. All of this represents a greater degree of *human* good. So far though there is no spiritual development-even their religious worship was human form and ceremony.

There was also a constant fluctuation between good and evil, plenty and lack, freedom and slavery, human good and human ill in their experience-further proof that their demonstration was wholly on the human plain and subject to duality.

As you look back upon your own experiences in metaphysics or other mind healing modalities you will find that you also were only experiencing, even in healings, a greater degree of *human* good. You had not made the transition to spiritual understanding which destroys the fluctuating/pendulum swing of good and bad in your life.

No doubt many inharmonious physical and financial conditions will disappear to give place for physical conditions of harmony and increase, this was Moses promise being fulfilled with human good. During this period of human improvement you, just as the Hebrews of old, are under the law. Ten Commandments, church laws, rules and regulations, all of which are necessary progressive steps as Moses led the animal man up to the good human.

Moses is the first Promise in your consciousness of a better life-learn to go along to get along and prosper along the way the best you can while maintaining your health and possessions through your human means of an eye for an eye.

When Christ dawns in your consciousness you are under grace. You are no longer righteous/good/behaving because a law decrees it, you are not good because there is a regulation requiring it, you are not healthy because of some thinking a certain way nor wealthy through affirmations and denials.

As you advance from Moses and improved humanhood into Christ or spiritual consciousness you touch the spiritual sense of health, wealth, harmony and peace.

In the Old Testament it is good and evil with good being invoked to overcome evil. In the New Testament there is only the divine Presence of God, one source of good; one presence of grace, one expression, one impulse and the **power of God** which is the protection afforded you when you know the Truth I am I am, the Father and I are one.

Moses and the 10 commandments

When Moses received the 10 Commandments from God it was at the time of out and out slavery/subjugation of man under the whim of Pharaoh, King, or priest which basically meant man was nothing more than a servant bound to the powerful and left to subsist on whatever was left.

When God revealed to Moses the 10 Commandments it was a baby step in the introduction of moral behavior to the world. Man cannot go from man of earth to spirit of God without steps and stages so first was introduced rules of conduct to be considered a good person thereby securing the favor of God, *Lord* God, the punisher, the gift giver, the one to try to find favor with by being good.

This was and still is the intermediary stage of humanhood and it became necessary to have such a code of acceptable conduct to try to ensure the safety, prosperity, livelihood and equality of men released from slavery running wild in their new found freedom in ways that endangered not only themselves but the lives and livelihood of others thus the need for a *justice system based on karma, an eye for an eye, punishment for sins.*

The 10 commandments are nothing more than suggestions, parameters or guidelines for the man beast to become less beast thereby being a better human who doesn't rock the boat but if provoked will sink someone else's boat to ensure their survival. So much for the 10 commandments. Nothing based in human thinking will ever raise man above human thinking and that is the whole problem of the life man is living. **Nothing you can think, say or do will take you any further than being a good human being which means you also have the potential to be a bad human if threatened.**

These steps and stages are those of an awakening consciousness, greater and greater depths of understanding of yourself and the world around you because one cannot fly if they think themselves grounded.

The only way to rise above the duality of man is to rise above the limited thinking of man and go straight to the creator of you for answers. I always get a kick out of the commercials for insurance-you could ask your dentist about insurance but … he's a dentist and not an insurance broker so the information you get is going to be dual in nature, filled with errors, judgements and omissions because you are not going to the one who can answer your question at the level of Truth.

Moses represents that type of leadership which orders man by laws and rules to lower the chaos of man, the brutality with judgements and punishments.

Christ consciousness is the next step which frees you from the mindset of the 10 Commandments to the reality of being which has nothing to do with who or what you *thought* you were, human man separated from God, and nothing resembling the world viewed through human eyes.

The Christ consciousness makes you free from the desire for that which does not belong to you, makes you free from erroneous traits of character, from limitation of any sort.

It is wonderful to realize that the man who is set free in Christ, who is free of all human entanglements, was at best only a short time before a *good human!* It is merely a transition from one sense or state of consciousness/realization/understanding to another. All the experiences under Moses and Christ will be those of you and me; you won't be crucified but you will die and you will rise from the tomb of humanhood when your conviction is of sufficient degree.

Old Testament

The Old Testament was written from the standpoint of *morality*. The people of that time were newly freed from slavery and had no education of any kind in either manners or morals. They had been told who they were and how to be all their lives and then found themselves free to do as they pleased with no master to beat them and you had people doing and being all they felt they wanted to be without restriction.

The law as it was given by Moses was for *moral* reasons, to give people rules of acceptable expression as well as the subsequent punishment for errant behavior. The Ten Commandments came about to give these newly freed people a sense of their own autonomy through governing self ie live within these rules and you are golden. Break them and you get punished.

Morality, rule following, is only a step on the way to spiritual consciousness and a person may achieve the absolute life of obedience to the Ten Commandments and still be a million miles away from the God life, the spiritual way of life **because the spiritual way of life is above the pairs of opposites** and this is where you have to pay particular attention because in your metaphysical experience you have probably devoted yourself to *overcoming* error, making something the opposite of what you have you don't want.

The laws of man mirrored what the slave owners did, punish behavior. Laws of man are a *moral* code, how to live together without bloodshed because of the uneducated state of the minds of these people. To ask them to accept more than that at their level of consciousness is no different than asking mortal man to accept the reality of God because *you* have had the experience of God.

This is why we don't share this work with anyone not on the same path, on the same level of consciousness because it won't make sense to them and will label you as that person who "talks about God as if they know God!" Which to human man is not only impossible but utterly blasphemous, unfathomable, ridiculous and grounds for public flogging.

Save yourself the heartache, remember silent, secret and sacred, not from the lips but from the consciousness of God for the harmony of God to touch all man to bring peace on earth. Always remember true peace can only come **without** might, **without** personal sense and **without** struggle to **individual** man in consciousness.

New Testament

Peter to Jesus-"thou art the Christ."

Jesus to Peter-"flesh and blood," your eyes and ears, intelligence, "hath not told you this, the Father within **revealed it to you.**"

The Christ of Peter which had been raised up knew the Truth of Jesus because he knew the Truth of himself. Peter was able to say "**I know** who thou art" because he had been raised up to the **same** conscious understanding as Jesus-God **is** within all man to be known and lived in expression as given through the **example of** Jesus **as** the Christ in **expression.**

Hebrews do not recognize the spirit of God within themselves. Man of today does not recognize the spirit of God within themselves either therefore **99.5% of man on earth do not know God is within them** and are living the same experience of being separated from God in conscious knowing as man who lived 2000 years ago. Yet 2000 years ago man was given an **option**-to live as *human* man or to live as the **risen Christ.**

That same option is being presented to you here and now along with how that can be individually accomplished if that is your desire.

In the beginning

In the beginning God constituted our being and was all there was to experience which was peace, harmony and perfection. We were all angels, the image and likeness of God and knew it, lived it and expressed it as the harmony of being known to man as the Garden of Eden, heaven on earth, the consciousness of harmonious living/expressing.

Before we were prodigals and came down (in consciousness) to that famous banquet with the swine/unbelievers/human man we were children of God and the Father consciousness. We were both God the Father and God the son and that was our consciousness before the *material* world was, the world that Jesus overcame/rose above through the knowing of Truth that I and the Father are one. "I have overcome the world" he said **but before there was a world there was I.**

To over come the world means nothing more nor less than knowing this world of sense is not reality and to live from the sense of oneness, consciousness with God to experience the Truth that God gave in the beginning-I am, I am the only, everything and in me there is no inharmony only the perfection of **is.**

The Old Testament is devoted to warfare against evil forces-religious wars-utilizing the power of *good* to destroy the evil/enemy; the enemy being one who thinks/believes/lives differently than the ruling class therefore *they* needed to be educated and brought under submission/same way of thinking or at least not outwardly expressing a different opinion.

The Old Testament ascribed all evil done not to the person, which is correct, a person is never their actions, but to an entity separate and apart from man, a force, some unexplainable thing out of a person's control that over takes them, *makes* them do things. The Old Testament doesn't remove personal accountability **it doesn't even acknowledge it.** All acts were accepted as those of *an other* power working through/against man *making* him the pawn of the evil power thereby subverting personal accountability-"I didn't do it, it wasn't me, it was a power, entity that took me over and *made* me do X."

There is no *other* power. There is only man *thinking* there is and this is why you cannot condemn those who are still ignorant of Truth-you were as well not long ago. Each person has the individual choice to drop their ignorance but until the world loses its hold on them, until the desires and pleasures of the world have become bland, beige, milk toast, will he seek greener pastures to lie down in.

All men will rise but until then those who have risen are the light emanating, illuminating the path for others. It is only by releasing grace, knowing the Truth of error and healing ourselves when error presents do we facilitate **another's** journey to spiritual awareness, help to break the mesmerism of duality by being the expression of what it looks like in evidence to be one with God.

You the human are not resurrected but the I AM of you is the resurrection, the power of resurrection, the I am **is** the Presence of resurrection. You are risen, returned when you **know** I am that I am.

Let the world see by your fruitage that you have discovered the pearl of great price.

Your consciousness is the temple of God because God abides there. Your body is not something separate and apart from your consciousness, your body is spirit/consciousness in form and this is how God expresses **as** you because God is you and I am is its name.

In the New Testament the Master gave as one of his reasons for being on earth the forgiveness of sinners. You are forgiven the *mental* burden of your past when you consciously realize the presence of God within because that realization is the Truth that allows you to see the error of the beliefs you were living under and can now move forward in this expression knowing who you are.

This in no way means the human consequences of your actions are gone-judgment and punishment according to the laws of man-because your error was done in the consciousness of *human* man and will be met out by human laws.

It is important to understand that **the consciousness in which an act is committed determines the karma returned** therefore that which was done as human man, even if you are spirit man now by experience, will present as negative karma to contend with. However after you have been walking the path for a while incurring only good karma/grace that is what you find as your experience more and more.

When you are one with God your capacity to sin, to desire of yourself, to want that of the world doesn't exist. Your oneness with God, your desire to stay in the kingdom wipes out your capacity to sin and the will to sin. It becomes an "unwelcome feeling, ickiness" which is now easily recognized and Truth uttered within the silence dissolves the illusion and places you right back in Truth-the Father and I are one.

This isn't a one and done never going to sin again kinda thing. Even as you gain the awareness of God you will still make mistakes but don't fret! Go within and give forgiveness, ask forgiveness and you are back in the kingdom of peace just remember to sin no more lest a worse fate befall you.

The Old Testament was acquisition, getting something from someone subject to resentments, fears, envies and jealousies. The Old Testament is always concerning itself with self, i, and not I, Self, God, except the few Hebrew leaders that had spiritual vision but couldn't impart it to the masses. Why not? Because if you say to the masses to stop desiring something they take it as not having to have desire, ambition, drive, focus, that they can just be lazy. **Man who is not ready for the step above human living will take spiritual Truth and twist it to fit their desires so they can sit back and do nothing.**

It is not that way at all. You are merely relinquishing *personal* desire in the realization of fullfilment, God's allness and wholeness. You are relinquishing, deferring the direction of your life to God, to Self, omnipresence, omnipotence, and omniscience.

All of us have lived as human beings of the Old Testament under mosaic law, the law given by Moses, the law of cause and effect, karma, you reap what you sow. In spiritual treatments healers understand those who come to us for healing are not truly under the law of cause and effect but *think* they are therefore respond as if they are. The role of a healer is to realize for themselves, **not** the one suffering the error, that they are indeed **not** under the law by bringing Truth to bear/God on the field and then let God reveal what Truth it wants you to feel/know.

A way of doing this is:

I realize Father there is no law of man in activity, there is only the divine Law of grace in which your children do not live by bread alone (the things of man) but by every word that proceedeth out of the mouth of God.

In this way you are holding another in spiritual freedom, you are using your higher consciousness to bring God to earth, to your patient, so God may, through you as an instrument of grace, of harmony, be released to touch others desiring Truth, peace be with you. Within this atmosphere of God as consciousness no one in the world is under the law anymore if they desire grace, higher, better, not of this world. Right this instant God is bringing Truth to man who is ready and you are passing from cause and effect into the New Testament where you live by grace, not by personal effort, not by struggling, not by strife; lay down the sword of man, the ego of man and become joint heirs with God to all the heavenly riches.

You are that spiritual man when you desire wholeheartedly the spirit of God dwell in you.

As spiritual man you do not live under the law of cause and effect, you live under grace and your home is in heaven, heaven being the state of consciousness that is completely with God, oneness, and not the consciousness of man/duality. **Heaven is a state of being, expressing** in which all that is needed, wanted and desired comes to you solely by your devotion, love and sharing of the God that you have found to be the reason for your existence and that existence is supported, maintained and supplied by that which you are devoted to, God.

God is all, God is your all and that is why it is said you will never see a spiritual man begging bread. Why? Because spiritual man knows where his supply lies and that it is infinite thus there is no lack of any kind in his experience.

Christ consciousness is the fulfillment of Life because it is the avenue of awareness to the Father within.

The Master said "ye shall know the Truth and the Truth shall make you free" but only to the degree that you accept the guidance of God will you receive God's grace.

What is the Truth that will make you free?

I and the Father are one.

I am the way. Not anything of the world, not conditions, fears or circumstances. I. I Am the way, consciousness is your resting place always.

I am come that you may have Life and that you might have it more abundantly.

I will never leave thee nor forsake thee

I am with you always, even unto the end of the world

Moses put a **veil** on Truth and gave us Lord God, God of *human* laws and punishment.

Jesus **unveiled** Truth by revealing **I am that I am,** I am of the consciousness of I am therefore I express as I am-peace, benevolence, love, harmony and healing to all man.

Jesus was crucified for this because it teaches a slave how to be free, sinless within his own being and rise above the conscious knowing of human man which threatens the powerful man who only knows control through force. How do you control one you are no longer able to control through fear and lack? Hunger and cold? How do you use the fear of death against one who knows they are deathless? What power is left to human man when all their power is shown to be an illusion?

Governments and churches do not want you to know Truth **because man who knows he is free cannot be corrupted** so it has been their goal to keep **man in the dark as to the way to man's salvation.**

Why is spiritual man incorruptible? Mainly and most importantly a free man of God knows there can be no true death and there is no thing of the world that can be used as a bargaining chip, a cause or reason to do something against their nature because spiritual man does not live in the world of birth and death but in the world of eternal harmony in this expression or the next, visible or invisible form makes no difference, spirit cannot die therefore you are eternal and as such incorruptible, pure as snow, child of God, joint heir to the kingdom.

Eden and the fall from grace

It is at this moment you can change your life and the lives of others not by physical or material means but by silent contemplation of Truth heard from within and being that Truth in expression to bless and awaken those ready to experience the world as it was mean to be experienced in the 1st chapter of Genesis.

Human man does not live the 1st chapter of Genesis, living in the kingdom. Man lives the 2nd chapter of Genesis where man has eaten of the fruit of good and evil, of the *knowledge* of man. The first fruits/taste of human knowledge was brought into awareness by Eve *choosing* to do that which was not given by God to do-**she made a choice outside of the consciousness of God.**

You have to understand the meaning of the word knowledge before this makes any sense. Knowledge is of man's *thinking* mind not Truth given from God. Knowledge comes from *outside* of man rather than being revealed within. Knowledge has nothing to do with God and cannot be lived in conjunction with God for knowledge is of man's finite cumulative understanding of the world around them **and this knowledge can be used for good or evil.** Knowledge is subject to duality because its source is of duality-man.

But knowledge is good right?

Knowledge is what man has surmised about the universe not knowing the **Truth** of the universe. Knowledge is that which man puts into his mind to make sense of this world but Truth functioning as consciousness negates the need for thinking, learning, stuffing in of information because there is nothing man needs to know that God cannot **give** him by going into the silence and listening for the soft, small voice to impart all that is necessary to know: **I am, I will never leave you nor forsake you and the reason I am presenting to you is for your benefit so you may have life and have it more abundantly.**

In the beginning God was all the knowing spiritual man needed, it was God that provided all for his children. So what was it of the tree of Knowledge that caused so much pain? *Knowledge* is of man, **Truth** is of God. Man and God are separate therefore if you live by knowledge, man's finite knowing, you are of the consciousness of good and evil and are **not** of the consciousness of harmony thus are **not** of the nature of God, good, harmony, is.

Man is not known to God because man is an aberration of spiritual man because it lives by its own thinking and not by God's be-ing. Being out of the kingdom merely means being out of the consciousness in which all is already created ready for expression. If you are not **of** the consciousness which provides all that is good you are not able to receive **of** that which is good.

That is all that the fall from grace means: **you are no longer of the consciousness of God by which to receive the things of God.** You have to be in it to win it! Remember that!

First chapter of Genesis: Creation

-Life lived by conscious awareness of God

-Life lived by the Word/consciousness of God, the atmosphere of harmonious eternal expression.

-Singular expression/nature of harmony

Second Chapter of Genesis: construction/destruction

-Life lived in the mind of man who thinks himself separated from God

-Life lived by the word of man/thinking mind of *individual* man in the atmosphere of duality caused by a *sense* of separation from source.

Adam and Eve in their original estate were **being** and they loved it. They were just being and they had all that they needed by grace; why not, they were constituted of God and in oneness/conscious awareness of God at all times, God **was** their being, God **was** their life, God was all they knew and that is why they were pure, why they were desire-less and knew no other, no different. Without desire all they had to do was do that which was given within to do and the rest of the time enjoy life.

Regardless of actual circumstances there was a point in harmonious living that was the advent of inharmonious living-man thinking for himself thus fearing all others. This is how spiritual man found himself out of heaven, out of the allness of God living as man of earth of good and evil thinking and return.

Human man is a house divided against itself and is no longer of harmony but of duality because they believe they are separated from their source of harmony-God.

The understanding of how to get back into oneness with the Father should be clear now-duality is caused by a belief in separation from God so prove to yourself through inner listening this is not Truth by hearing the Father's voice say hello.

In the garden of Eden all communed together, all received Life ie all that is necessary for abundant living from God not from each other. All received supply from God, they knew no other existence. They didn't take thought for their lives, what they would eat, drink, wear, live. They took no thought for their lives by physical or mental labor because by virtue of the relationship they had with God all was provided.

Know ye not are the sons of God? Joint heirs to the kingdom? All that I have, all that **is** is within you but you have to **know the source of the allness before you can partake of it.**

In Eden, the consciousness of God in spiritual man on earth, each person was only dependent on the Father, the creative principle within their own being. In that relationship they didn't mentally think, figure out, devise or plan but merely lived out from their relationship with God, walking the walk, talking the talk and that was their expression.

From here on out you are hereby released from thinking meaning by giving yourself **back** to God what you now experience is what flows from the kingdom, the allness that is good; you are no longer the navigator of the bus, you are the driver going according to the GPS-**God positioning system**-within your being. God navigates you here and there, to meet, to do, to see, day in and day out creating the atmosphere where God is known and seen visibly to you.

How? God is as all therefore the consciousness of all is of one, God, therefore the communication, the impulse to do and be comes from within, from consciousness, your conscious at one-ment with God and not a human response to stimulus which is the consciousness of man/duality.

That still small voice is waiting for you to open the door wide and see the glory and splendor that is your birth right but only you can choose to lay down your sword and joyously give God back the job of living your life as it was in the beginning in the 1st chapter of Genesis.

All men of earth are living in the 2nd chapter of Genesis after the fall of man which was when the belief in two powers began and has been the atmosphere of duality all man are *born into* thus keeping him from knowing the true atmosphere of God, one Presence, one Law, one Life eternally expressing.

It is believed the 10 commandments are spiritual commandments, having to do with spiritual or religious life. This is not true. The 10 commandments, with the exception of the first, constitutes a code of *human conduct*.

The remaining nine commandments constitute law and so now as with Moses and the Hebrews in that intermediary stage of humanhood, it becomes necessary to have such a code of laws, *human* laws in order to teach men how to be just ordinary good humans. At no time does Jesus talk about human good. You are told rather "my kingdom is not of this world." You are lifted into a spiritual atmosphere in which there is not even a thought or a temptation of being humanly bad. This is why you are told **the law was given by Moses, but grace and Truth came by Jesus.**

What is God?

I want you to take a moment and think of all the things you know about God, whether you believe them or not, just bring up all the things of/about God that you know. Got them? Now toss them out the window because they are all wrong. Every single one of them. Why? Because anything you have heard from the lips of man is false because **it came from the mouth of man and not the consciousness of God.**

God is life, God is love, God is good, God is vengeful, God is jealous, gives or withholds, favors or ignores. All incorrect. Go through every synonym you have ever heard in the Bible or metaphysics or mystical writings until you don't have one *word* left in your *mind,* not a single *concept* by which to *define* God. Then you will find yourself face to face with God, **but not as long as you have a *concept* of God.**

Why? Because you would be depending on a *concept, on a word*. In fact as long as you are depending *on* God to do something for you, you will fail. Why? Because you don't depend *on* God, you rest **in** God and there is a difference. Dependent on implies needing something from outside of you, **resting in** means absolute knowing **I is God and there is no other besides that.**

Therefore if you would like to depend on something depend on Truth: I AM the Truth, the Way, the Life, the Bread, the Meat, the Wine and the Water and I is the God of you therefore everything unto your existence, your eternal life is found within your **relationship** with God.

There is no passage or message you can rely on to do something for you because they are **not** meant to be mantras for "protection" but are meant to **reveal** the Truth of God for you to know, live by, express as.

Relying on a passage or message is acceptable for the **new student** to help bring them back into the consciousness of God, of the atmosphere of peace, Truth and love. It isn't to be relied on as a mindless offhanded platitude.

There is only one Truth to depend on and that is **I am the Truth, I am the Way, I am Life eternal.** When you are in communion there is a movement from the I that flows through you as action, as being, as life. So you could say with Paul "Christ liveth my life, he performeth that which is given me to do," that which is appointed for you because it is the **I** performing as you, as me, as each and every individual who attains Christ consciousness.

Original:

That which is therefore there is no other. Original is. It is the only because it is the original. Anything other than what **is** is not of the original because that which **is** is not divisible, changeable or dependent on anything else and is infinite in nature.

That which **is** cannot be altered nor can it ever stop being.

That which **is** is eternal because that which came into being out of itself is only and always itself: harmonious, pure, and singular of source.

Anything that isn't original isn't real, isn't of the Substance, Life and Law of the original. This is what is meant when it is read "if it wasn't made by God it wasn't made." That which isn't **of** God isn't real because all there **is** is God in expression and it is this expression, all that **is** that man misunderstands:

Man believes all visible forms of this world are independent, separate from each other as matter/material and are defined by their base chemical makeup for classification and codifying. That this world and all that is in it is separate and apart from God, original source, because man sees this world as *material* and have been told God is **spiritual.**

This is why it is said, and is absolute Truth, "this world is an illusion," ie **man's finite understanding of the world and all that is viewed as *matter/material* separate and apart from God is the *illusion,* unreality.**

God:

God is an experience. To know God is to experience God within your own being.

God is not a religious anything, God is a personal relationship you willingly enter into.

God is the unseen singular presence and expression of eternal harmonious creation.

God is nothing you can define beyond saying it is intelligent, directive harmony of all that is created and you are an individual identity of this intelligent, directive harmony **when** you are of its consciousness by having an awareness of it within by way of an actual experience of its presence.

Personal/human expression of emotions vs. God expressing as allness through you:

All was created in the beginning and is good and if it isn't good it wasn't created. Only God created and it can only create itself, good/harmony. Man in his belief of separation from God is no longer under grace and brings the opposite to bear in his life thus creating inharmony, chaos-physical death as a result of the ignorance of God within.

The Creator, God, is the only expression of all creation. You are of God therefore God/good/grace flows through you. It is God flowing through you, the **embodiment** of all that is harmonious/spiritual. Your feelings, your emotions of love and peace, joy and companionship are **not** yours, they are of God and if you have an awareness of God then you have all that is of God flowing in and through you as you.

This is the hang up a lot of people have-they think they *personally* are able to give or withhold love. You cannot. You either radiate what is **of** your consciousness or you don't. You can only show forth God, good, in proportion to your openness, your understanding, your awareness, your devotion to God which in turn is seen outwardly as harmony and visible supply.

A child may think when they get older that their parent withheld love from them. That is incorrect. The parent cannot withhold love **however** their lack of God consciousness, lack of awareness of Truth looks to the world as if the parent had no love to give. Why? Because God is the only source of harmony of all its expressions. When you are in a relationship with the God within, desire its presence, this relationship of oneness is the alchemy that allows all that is of God to flow through you out to the world perceived as love being given **of** the one God is flowing through.

Therefore the flow of God **through and out** from a person is the only way they are able to express anything good/harmonious to the world. Otherwise it is all personal ego expressing in a way to elicit some personally directed response for their selfish purposes.

God is unable to be selfish. All God **is** is for all God **is.** Human man in his finite existence struggles for survival because he thinks he can die and must protect at all cost that which he has struggled to acquire. Those who have returned to the spiritual path know all they have is God in form and theirs as long as they have need of it because no man can take what is given of God.

The reign of God on earth is NOT over

The consensus of man who looks out at the world and judges by appearances is that God is gone; what other explanation could there be for the state of this world and the people in it?

The reign of God on earth cannot be over because God is all that is. What is Truth is that **the knowing of Truth, the knowing of God in consciousness is no longer the reigning/overarching consciousness of man of earth** which would express as peace among man.

Remember God, Law of like begets like, is a numbers game. The more who are of God consciousness the more that conciousness of peace, harmony and prosperity becomes the expression of the people, the city, the country, the world.

God isn't gone however the **knowing of how to be in oneness** with God that expresses as peace on earth and goodwill toward man is not in evidence as the consciousness in expression/reign rather that which is perceived as the opposite/unlike of God.

When you understand Truth of God and not the lies of orthodox religion you too will be able to say with confidence, as the Father sits within smiling, "**God is not gone, God lives and God lives in each and every one of us when there is awareness of God within.**"

You may call It God, Divine Love, Universal Life, the Great Architect of the universe or the Spirit of creation. Regardless of what name or term you use God is Truth. God is and God is as all.

As you acknowledge there is this infinite Source of good you go on to the next step and realize that in the degree that the infinite good comes into your consciousness do you **bring forth** the beauty and bounty of that consciousness.

This is a transcendental teaching and it is the opposite or reversal of the ordinary human sense of existence. In man's world man goes out and *gets* supply-works, plans, schemes, steals, lies, cheats- in some way gets what they want.

This transcendental teaching reverses that thinking of man and reveals the secret of supply as the Spirit of God **in you and out from you to the degree of your knowing of God/Truth.**

God is consciousness and God is individual consciousness.

God is the **consciousness** of individual you and me, **not** a consciousness out in space, **not** a consciousness in heaven or on a cross but a consciousness that **is** functioning your life and mine.

God is as all that is visible and invisible

All form is God expressing. There is nothing separate and apart from God because God is the universal Law of creative expression governing itself in a closed system of perfect harmony.

Central Intelligence

God is the central intelligence of the universe, God **is** the universe. God is the only actor and you, spirit in form in conscious union with God are an individual expression of that central intelligence. You do not possess the intelligence of the creator of the universe but you have **access** to it. What is this intelligence? In human terms there is no comparison. The word intelligence to man is so finite and minuscule to use it to try to define that which is the substance and form of your being would be impossible.

Let us just say this about the creative intelligence of the universe: this we call creative intelligence is the creative intelligence of you and me. It is of itself we are formed. We are literally the dust and the air, all is of the same substance, creative intelligence, in forms necessary for the human form to unfold as the risen Christ.

Man is the image and likeness of God, consciousness. Man can know beyond himself but no other living creature can. Man is the only one, when in spiritual oneness with this creative intelligence, that can be assisted to grow beyond the confines and limitations of man's knowing. It is only this knowing beyond what is currently known that propels humanity into the next generation with more conscious understanding of the world around them than the previous. This is evolution and it is God governed by those who knowingly or unknowingly contact the spirit within and bring forth new invention, understanding, bettering the world for man to continue to grow in conscious understanding but most of all freeing man to begin the journey back to the central intelligence which you are of and stop living this life of duality, this life separated from the Father, the comforter.

Life never began and will never end, it is cyclical. For thousands of years you have been on your way to this exact moment. Everything that has ever been of the consciousness that you are, not known to you though some do know their past iterations, every thought, error, pain, pleasure, choice, leap of faith, every literal breath has been to get you to this moment. Why? Because the moment you meet God and understand the upside down nature of man's world and see the practicality and literal common sense of God's world you are beginning the much shorter leg of this visible journey because you are now the prodigal son returned home. You know your Truth and you are willing to learn how to live this path, practice the presence of God to bring the allness of God to bear in your life and in the world for all man for no man is your enemy when you know the nature of all called man.

Why do we exist? God just said for its pleasure. Expression is its pleasure because it is its nature. It does what it does and because it is Law there is no limit to what you receive because as ye sow so shall ye reap. Tit for tat, degree for degree. The entire purpose of getting to this point of conscious understanding is to gain the conscious understanding of **how to go home,** to know and live heaven on earth, sharing God's grace and have a damn good life until you transition out of this form.

The central intelligence monicker makes me think of a cell. A cell **is,** exists only because it is ordered by an invisible intelligence that is the life of that cell, the intelligence necessary for it to divide, serve its purpose of being.

The reason for disease among human man is the actual God of you is not what is living the form because you are unaware of your nature as spirit. Therefore the cells are living themselves by the innate *physical* nature of their *material* expression rather than spiritual expression of wholeness. Therefore when a few go rouge, get drunk and multiply they start popping out funky cells and then you have cells creating erroneous copies of themselves. In human man each cell has its own intelligence and though they work in concert they are free to be as individual cells.

When man knows his connection to God and is in oneness with this consciousness this immediately brings you into eternity because you are **of** the consciousness of that which is eternal therefore you are as well. In this light your body is not made up of individual organs and tissues and billions of cells but **one** substance in the forms necessary to perform the functions of this body **when** spiritually connected to God.

A child born into the world of duality is being brought into an atmosphere of chance, unrealities and illusions thus will suffer the consequences of the duality inherent in the world. This is why "bad things happen to good people." First, there are no truly good humans because they are of both good and evil thinking and doing and second, this world is a crap shoot held together by a shoestring strung between two red hot pokers. No one said this life was going to be easy and they weren't kidding!

A child born into this world from parents on the spiritual path will be born as spiritual child already of the knowing of Truth, it will have its Christ consciousness already open and ready for more Truth in the atmosphere of their home. This child will seem to thrive, be beyond understanding in personality and ability and will be the light unto the next generation which is the only way to perpetuate the knowing of God by bringing as much grace as possible to bear in the world **therefore for the next generation to be more spiritually governed those of this generation must have their awakening to Truth.**

God is impersonal Law

God is not nor has ever been a *man;* God has **always** been incorporeal creative intelligence doing what it does-express **itself.** God is the God of all man. Israelite, Hebrew or Jew, Buddhist, Catholic, Christian or Muslim it is the same God because there **is** only one God.

Regardless of what individual man thinks himself or another to be all are and can only be individual expressions of the one God made manifest in visible form.

God is the God of the just and the unjust. God is no respecter of persons, God is the God of the saint and the sinner. This destroys fear and allows you to relax and rest in the assurance "My peace is at hand, My grace is at hand." It doesn't have to be earned or deserved or paid for, it is without money and without price, neither life nor death can separate you from God.

Purity cannot give it to you and sin cannot take it away from you.

Because the only thing that makes God available is **awareness** and you can have that awareness in the deepest sin and become pure whereas the human who perceives *themselves* good, righteous, upstanding, of great *human* purity has no awareness of God thus has **no** God.

Ye shall know the Truth and the Truth shall make you free. Truth itself doesn't make you free, **living** Truth in expression frees you from the duality of man to live under grace with God.

The greatest healing influence in the world is: Be still and know I Am. Nearer than hands and feet. I. I in the midst of thee am God.

Protective *power* of God:

God is not "protection or power" in the sense of man. God's protection for/of us doesn't go and subdue those we encounter on our path rather brings harmony to them in whatever way is needed so those we encounter have been touched by God, given some relief, brought peace to mind, brought money for a lunch they wouldn't have had and are not *hangry* when they are in your midst.

Know this Truth: God goes before you to make the crooked places straight when grace is your expression.

God will never tell you to do or be anything that is not harmonious so if you think you "hear" God telling you to do things of man, of duality **know you are not hearing Truth.**

Whether by ignorance or choice if you try to stand on false words know they are the shifting sand of error/illusion because you are building them on the *word of man, the thinking mind of duality.*

God can never be anything other than its nature-good, harmony, love and to twist God for personal gain ie anything that sounds like "God told me, God said I was the one, God said" you do not know God thus are expressing duality. Why? Because no one expression of Self is above, greater than or put in a position of power by God. You may be used as an instrument of God to bring harmony to a situation by being put in a position of power but it isn't the power you seek rather the position to do **God's work.**

By your name are ye known so make sure when you say your name you know of whom you speak, God or man.

Everything is of God in its unqualified state. The atomic, hydrogen and nuclear power revealed to man is of God, of the Law of God and **only becomes of duality when man misuses the things of God for personal gain/use/desire.**

God is as all form

There is no matter/material substance or form.

To mortal man the natural makeup (base chemical makeup) of man, animal, mineral or plant is not spirit in form, God, rather a limited concept of life called matter/material. This is why any attempt to heal, change or correct the *physical/material* universe is evidence that you have not develop sufficient spiritual consciousness to understand that **there is no changing of the human scene through spiritual knowing** rather a growing into a conscious reality above human duality where you live with a conscious connection to the one power of creation which is the Truth of you.

Christ consciousness recognizes all life to be of God. But realize what appears as material to the human senses is not reality but merely the illusion or false sense of what it is ie it isn't wood, it is God in form man calls wood. This is also a duality not always recognized. Man thinks of God *and*. Always God *and* you, God *and* the world when the reality is God **is** as all that is. Spiritual consciousness discerns the life which is real-that all is of God and not matter/material in nature.

There is no matter or material in all of the universe because the creator of all that is termed physical, that which is experienced by the five senses, is spiritual consciousness manifest in form. Therefore you cannot think from that level of sense perception but must remember to disregard appearances, turn from the picture before your eyes and become aware of the eternal Truth which is that **spirit** is the substance of all that is visible and invisible.

All that is of the world as form is of the same source no matter the outward expression or form. It may look like gold, steel, a dog, a lustrous diamond or a dead tree but the Truth is all is of God substance in the form expressed/seen and all is enlivened, lived by Source.

There is no separating God from form because God is the source of all form.

There is no God on earth and there is no God among men **except in proportion as God is realized/known by individual man.** That is why you can have sin, disease, death, lack, limitation, all of man's inhumanity to man inspite of God because there is no God in the world that does not individually have awareness of God within.

God is only where God is realized/known in the consciousness of individual man

This doesn't take away from omnipresence, no not at all! Omnipresence is **within you.** One with God is a majority, the allness of God is available to all at all times for God is the omnipotence, omnipresence and omniscience of all that is when you know that it is.

God is not the cause of your suffering, you are the cause of your suffering by believing you are something you are not and by living that belief suffer the consequences of that belief.

God is the cause and effect of your salvation, not your suffering, you suffer because you express as i and not I. **Hell** is a state of consciousness you inhabit, it isn't a physical place. **Heaven** is a state of consciousness you inhabit, it isn't a physical place. Both are experienced within your own being depending on the consciousness from which you express-Truth or duality, God or human man.

The human consensus of God is that it is restrictive, that you have to suffer for your sins, that you cannot do, be or have certain things because they go against God or, and this is the **biggest misconception** of all, that you will have to give up your freedom to make your own choices thereby becoming robotic, un alive of yourself being puppeted by an unseen force.

Patently false. God has been falsely used as a weapon to keep people in check. Don't do this or that or you will be punished by God. It is a good idea not to do certain things because of their **inherent consequences** visited upon you. The thief goes to jail not because of the person who caught them but because they broke the law. The man caught in adultery blames another for their own actions but all actions are of personal thought and have consequences good or bad or somewhere between the two.

People think God is to be feared, that God punishes and rewards, gives and withholds. Human living/duality does that, not God. God wants to give you Life and give it more abundantly than what you are experiencing as a human.

In the Old Testament Moses gave us the laws, the 10 Commandments. Basic *be good human rules.* But the New Testament of Jesus reveals the true nature of man as that of the transcendental consciousness/Christ consciousness which acknowledges the ability to have a personal relationship with God through communion, prayer, inner listening.

Jesus the *man* didn't heal, he didn't multiply loaves and fishes; Jesus was an **instrument of God.** God expressed itself as and through Jesus **the** Christ to bring grace to the world, to show the love of God, the supply of God, the health of God, the allness of what it means to live in God's grace. God's grace is God's allness **in action** expressing in form as that which you need.

Seek ye the kingdom of heaven and all things will be added. The Kingdom is the Christ **consciousness** where you go for the Truth about life and it is always answered at the level of consciousness you need at the moment and those answers will essentially be the **red letter words in the New Testament** because those words are the Truth of God through/from/by way of the Master and are the Truth that guide, protect and provide for the grace of God to flow through you and from you to bless, be a benediction to the world. Some of these are:

I and the Father are one

I will never leave you nor forsake you

I have been with you since before time

I am all supply unto your eternal existence

Your grace is my supply in all ways for all that is needed

They are Truth that bring comfort and understanding, joy and peace. Peace is the dwelling place of the most high. The Prince of peace is within you, the Comforter is within you. All supply is within you. It isn't a matter of faith or belief, it is a matter of **fact** and of Truth but until you get quiet inside and **invite** God to express in your life it will remain on the sidelines, **never** judging your life merely waiting for you to run off the field to greet it like the prodigal son returning to his Father's house where there will be a feast set and rejoicing.

It is the consciousness of the Christ within that allows your life to take on the fullness you were meant to experience. Despite appearances, illusion, error I will not fear/react. I will let it play out without judgement. It just **is.** That which **is** is of God and that which is experienced from the world outside of you is the *illusion* or error that can be judged good, bad or otherwise and are nothing more than personal biases and judgements that govern your life.

What are forms of judgement? Oh, they can be really sneaky and so ingrained in you as to be your only language of life. Anything that you say, think or feel that is anything other that **is** is a *judgement:*

Good dog/bad dog

Fat/thin/ugly/pretty

Old/young/deformed/happy/sad

Privileged/lacking

Skin color/ethnicity/background/education/birth status

Maybe there is a car that to another would be seen as broken and get all worked up about it. If you see a broken car as is, God is free to **bring** to you the solution because you are not all twisted up wondering how *you* are going to fix it. You aren't. **God is.** It may be the money you already received as a blessing which now is available to use to fix your car. No emotion, you have already what you need as it was already given. Or it could be that this car will be replaced with one better, maybe a relative passes and you get one of their vehicles or your perfect car comes available at a price that definitely lets you know God brought it to you.

Everything **is** when you are in the atmosphere/consciousness of **is,** God consciousness, for in the atmosphere of God is the answer to every question because under grace the questions have already been answered before the creation of their need. Why? Because when you have conscious oneness with Source, you have access to Source, you are in the atmosphere of grace, you are **of** God and all that is **of** God. You exist as spirit in form in an atmosphere of grace, like an aura of God in, through and radiating from you to a world atmosphere of duality, pain, suffering and mediocrity. You in your Christhood bring light to the darkness, relief from suffering, peace that passeth understanding just by being of the consciousness of God sharing secretly, silently and sacredly.

Man has confused the word *control* with **governance.** You control your fate, human man or spiritual man, finite or eternal. You are only under the governance of God when you **allow** it to be so. When you are under the governance of God willingly, desirously, then you are of the allness of God which is omniscience, omnipresence and omnipotence.

Omniscience, all knowing, doesn't mean knowing like man knows by thinking; omniscience is the automatic, normal and natural expression of a closed system of singular source eternally bringing forth itself in form as constant renewal of Self, this universe, you, all that is. God doesn't think, God **is** because God is not a being God is **Law** of creation personified within each of us as your guide, your teacher and your resting place.

Your body in man's view is as close to a closed system as you can get biologically because all living things needs things from the outside to survive but the system called body, if it were self sustaining, would be akin to the point I am trying to make to God, the universe, being a closed system.

Your body functions in and of itself so it seems, the systems that make up the body work together without thought, independent of *your* thinking. The body is **being,** the body is **living** itself. When we talk about God **being** this is what is meant. What **it is** perpetuates what it is through self creation and expression therefore if you have the consciousness of God that is what perpetuates and if you have the consciousness of man that is what perpetuates.

There is no such thing as God doing something *for* you or for me. God fulfills itself and the most wonderful things are added unto you. As soon as you inject "i" or "me" or "mine", "my child or my neighbor", you lose God. You need to willingly deny yourself, not deny that there is a you, rather denying your own perspective which is myopic and let God have at it!

Power of God:

The power of God is not a power as man understands power to be-force, of one over another, one killing or subduing, bringing under control person, condition or situation.

The power of God is you knowing the only true expression of being is harmonious and if you are in oneness with God that is also the expression (for the most part, we aren't perfect for a loonnnngg time) of you and back to you as bread on the water, grace returned for grace released. Remember, God is **Law** not a super being therefore is *impersonal* and your return of grace is also impersonal as a measure, degree to which you shared grace. You get back what you give. Technically you get more so if you keep that in mind it does help to keep you in the safety zone of God consciousness.

Yes there are times things aren't completely harmonious but that is a human perception because you may be holding onto a judgement causing you to feel this way ie you had a determination/ desire in mind for yourself. Harmony is a state of being and it is a choice. I can let people get to me if I have not had a moment with Father to get into his sunny vibe first thing in the morning but because I don't want to experience inharmony **I make sure I am the harmony wherever I go so I am never out of harmony unless I drop it.**

Does **harmony** for all always satisfy those new to the spiritual path, those used to *winning or getting?* Not always because the personal sense of i is still very strong and fights against both parties involved getting harmony which doesn't always mean getting what you wanted for yourself. Ahh, there it is. *You didn't get.* You tried to use God to get what you wanted and just found out you can't have your way and God's harmony. It is one or the other because the two cannot ever exist in the same atmosphere/situation. Why? Because one is of God and one is of man; one is real and one is illusion.

The illusion of man is that you can get something by your own power but *you* have no power; all power is of God and it is harmonious. Harmony is a state of being you **choose** to express as. As the expression of harmony you cannot express inharmony/duality at the same time because it is not of your consciousness and in this way **the consciousness of God is your protection from living in error, duality and death.**

Knowing Truth is what protects you from living a false life and dying. Truth is what allows you to rest knowing whatever you may go through on this path will be harmonious unto you because it is God walking with you making the crooked places straight.

You can feel when you are with God because God is a place of harmony, is, and it is a choice you must make consciously, willingly and honestly for fruit to be borne of the relationship out in the visible world and within your own being. **To know God to be the source of your harmony protects you from falling for the duality of man perceived as reality.**

Living the principles of Truth/God is what keeps you from erring, **has** the potential to keep you from making mistakes **if you lean on it in all ways.** Why does this keep you safe/out of duality? Because you only encounter error/duality when you are *thinking* and not **leaning** on God in all ways.

God is not a physical power to be called upon to destroy the enemy outside of you, God is the gentle presence of Truth that destroys the enemy within you-the belief in a power apart from the allness of God.

What is the enemy within you? The belief that you are mortal man that is born and dies separated from a God outside of you.

Knowing the Truth of who you are destroys the illusion of who you thought you were and in that moment the power of the presence of God has been revealed-the presence that reveals Truth of error as illusion which allows you to rest in God's Truth.

God is both your morality and your spiritual development

God is first higher morality through metaphysical Truth then spiritually through mystical Truth/mysticism.

When this Truth came to me it brought forth the understanding of the evolution of my spiritual history/path which may help you see more clearly how far you have come and why there are no mistakes in life, only lessons by which to grow in conscious understanding toward an unknown but nevertheless compelling and necessary goal-knowing Truth, God in awareness.

The first time I heard God speak I was in my early twenties. I was experiencing some really negative consequences of my actions and I distinctly heard God speak. "This is your warning. This is a turning point. Stop now or be responsible for what comes of your actions. This is bad; do you want worse?"

Holy shit! I thought, that was definite and absolutely for me, it was spoken **to** me and I remember choosing right there a different path. "You got it Father, freaking done being that way! Full stop."

It took time to change my consciousness of being from that of who I was to who I wanted to be by thinking and doing differently to get different results but each time I passed through an experience unscathed I would mentally pat myself on my back, phew! "Dodged that bullet! Thank you Father!"

I didn't know it but by silently thanking God for keeping me safe I was praying aright and I realize now it was God in my midst cheering me on in the only way I could at that time consciously accept God-as that part of me that was trying to help me out when I was having trouble.

This I called Soul, the smarter me because it was unfathomable that I could be talking to God, I wasn't that special. I knew there was a part of me that wasn't me because I felt **it** within me. **It** would knock in my heart/chest like "hey! Haven't we had this discussion before? Didn't you learn the last time? Aren't you still licking your wounds?"

I soon realized if I did what Soul was asking me to do I felt peaceful, light, not in trouble, not having to lie, and more importantly not having to confess to errors made from lack of impulse control of my mouth or body. This place within was nice as it kept me from myself.

The first thing I did was stop lying. Lying had been my entire life. I don't know why but it was always my go to. When I gave up lying I gave up a lot of erroneous behaviors because, well, if I was giving up lying and confessing wasn't an option I couldn't do X. I soon realized when you don't do X it can't come back to haunt you and life gets infinitely easier.

Soul and I began having regular conversations and it was nice, an inner light came on and I felt cheerier when *she* was with me. I started a life coaching service based on what I called myself, a **Soul communication facilitator,** I helped people communicate with this inner place of morality, good, that helped keep them on an harmonious path.

It didn't catch on because it was flawed-it was not of God but still of man, of morality, of not doing bad to get good. It was a start, it was what people could understand **but** because what I was trying to share **wasn't** coming from the consciousness of God but my human, thinking mind I was still in the realm of duality having no effect, being of no actual benefit to man because I

1. Didn't know God was within
2. Didn't know the Truth of error
3. Hadn't had the mystical experience

All that I had to offer was of duality, good and bad not God and grace.

It had to fail as it did because it was not Truth. It was what leads up to Truth, knowing God aright, is a step to Truth and thank God it failed because it kept me searching.

Why tell you my story? So you know that as your story unfolds you see that where you are is always and only the place you are supposed to be. Anything of the "I wish, if I could go back I would already be past this point or better off, if I hadn't made all those stupid mistakes" you would not be exactly where you are supposed to be this moment. Nothing of this life is an accident or mere human coincidence when you want other than human living. Even in the slightest amount of being open as you saw I was as I progressed, you get results, you feel the results and you experience the results. This is right thinking, metaphysics/metaphysical Truth, and it leads up to a better *human* life which prepares you for the **mystical experience of knowing God aright** and living under grace, the allness of God in activity as your eternal experience.

The mistake of man is that it isn't a better human life you are seeking but **spiritual Truth which is the Life eternal your soul yearns for you to return to.** That feeling in the chest, pit of the stomach, throat are all God trying to get your attention. "Hey!! In here!! Listen to me!! I want to help you! Just stop for one freaking second and let me take over! Let me get you out of this jam, just move over and let me out."

What comes out isn't ninja skills suddenly downloaded matrix style rather peace in your awareness that is **harmony for all** not *victory for you*. This is the sticking point for man who only thinks of i, me, mine and is what keeps the wheels of anger and hate rolling along-someone is always the victor and someone is always the victim, human powers of duality that cause internal and external chaos man calls life and living.

The life of human man is pure chance controlled only by your moral compass by which to navigate to procure, produce or experience the life you *think* you *want*. The life of spiritual man is spiritually governed which means it is neither good nor bad but the all of God, harmony in expression.

When you feel something stir, tingle, knock, squeeze, stop, take a second to **seek** to know **why** it has come at that particular point and you will soon realize it is your safely net unrolling beneath your feet, it is what you are to do to land safely and softly from this precarious place of duality you find yourself balanced. You do nothing but move over and let God go first and if you do this, concede and defer to all that comes of this silent, sacred, secret relationship you will be in the land of milk and honey, peace and prosperity without ever having to pick up a sword against another brother.

The key to eternal harmony is knowing **why** you never need to aught against another: you are already whole and complete, lacking nothing therefore in need of nothing you just don't know it yet. God's Truth reveals I am that I am, the Father and I are one, all that the Father has is thine, I am joint heir to the kingdom, child of God of the allness, fullness, quality and quantity that is God in expression-all that is. You are Child of the Most High with all the quality and quantity of God available to you when you live in the atmosphere, consciousness of that which you know yourself to be.

When you know **why** there is no need of *personal* want and desire you receive all that you could desire but more importantly you are giving man of earth the means by which to open their consciousness to God just as those before me of raised consciousness opened the way for their imprisoned splendor to escape so that my hungry soul could be fed. Curiosity gave way to a **need** to find the source of happiness, the **purpose** of being, experiencing more than the living, working, birthing and dying of man. Life as man lives made no sense to me and that frustration is what led to change.

I'll tell you right now change is painful but the pain is temporary as you learn this new way of being but the pain of apathy, of not doing anything to change the pain you feel will stay with you until the day you **chose** to awaken to, become aware of Truth, God within asking to be known to take you from this life of confusion and pain to that of peace and understanding.

God can only be found in the present moment. There is no past and there is no future in God's world, only this moment. What you call the future is merely **another now** when it is present. There is only now, **this** moment and if you live in the past or in the future you are missing the opportunity to change the now you are to experience as a future now. Your life is only different in the "future" if you make changes **now** that are reflected in you in a future now.

God is the absence of fear. If you have fear you are an atheist because fear is a human reaction to that which has perceived power over or against you. If you have fear of any kind you cannot be in conscious oneness with God because God is the harmony, supply, peace and good of your experience so how in that atmosphere of spiritual perfection could you have fear of lack, illness, separateness?

The only power is spiritual power and that power is **not** power per se but **protection** through **knowing** Truth: God is omnipotent, omnipresent and omniscient **where it is known.**

If something is the **only** presence, the **only** power and the **only** consciousness of harmonious expression called the universe, there **cannot** be what man calls good *and* bad/evil thus the *belief* in a power *opposite* good/God is not a **Truth** but an *unreality* thus rendering all that is *labeled* or *judged* bad/evil as *illusory*, a false belief in power in *opposition* to the only power there **is.** Sounds kind of obvious when you say it out loud doesn't it?

Life is your sail to the wind being moved along not of your own power or direction but **along for the ride,** to do as given but mostly to be. This is the **gift** of the spirit-not doing of yourself for yourself but being an instrument through which God functions your life.

Being is how you as spiritual man do the work of God and reap the good of God. Just by **being** an expression of Truth you are knowing Truth within. Your only job is to be the poster child for knowing God aright by **being** an expression of what can be for others if they are interested in knowing what **it** is. That is the key. Catching the scent and following the trail.

Your senses are the outer activities of consciousness, ie you become conscious of the world by being aware of it through the senses of the body. That is their **only** purpose, to bring **awareness** to you, not for you to *interpret and react* to what is *perceived* to be there. Spiritual man listens for God to reveal Truth of what the senses have revealed and not what you humanly *think* is happening through your finite sense of right and wrong.

By waiting for God to give you Truth you are not embroiling yourself in error by reacting to something *believed* to be real.

The **only** way by which grace reaches the mortal man starving for spiritual understanding is by way of those already of the awareness of oneness within and are living with God at the helm thereby placing themselves in the constant influx and outflow of God's grace, an atmosphere of ease rather than being a conduit for man's chaos.

This atmosphere **is** the power of the presence/knowing of God. It is the power of knowing your true identity as child of God and in that relationship now understand that all supply comes from God within and not from man or the world outside of you.

So the love that you feel in a room is merely **your** inner atmosphere/consciousness of being expressed outwardly. You are filled and flowing over with God and this is the **feeling** of the presence of God among man. This is the way all are supposed to feel if all had the consciousness of the kingdom within.

You become a channel, river, vessel, a place through which and by which the allness of God, grace, can come to earth to heal those that seek. **There will be a second coming of the Christ and it is when individual man awakens to Truth** because the Christ comes pre packaged inside each and every one of us just awaiting recognition from you to become active in your life as it is supposed to.

The only God that exists already exists within you and praying isn't talking it is actually an act of **listening** for God's voice, its presence to be felt within. So along with most people praying to a God that doesn't exist outside of them and praying to God by begging, pleading, beseeching you see how 99.99% of prayers are prayed incorrectly which has led to this sorry state of affairs where only a few people know, understand and live in a way that brings heaven on earth, a return to Eden.

I want this for you because I have it. Others have it and it is beautiful. **God doesn't change you, God reveals you in all your amazing perfection** envisioned as you from before the earth was. I want you to feel peace, not the peace of man but something completely outside of your understanding. This feeling can be foreign and in a way frightening because you may feel by letting yourself feel, really feel something good, it will someday leave you so better not to even go there. I humbly ask you to stop resisting. Please. Just stop and be.

God clearly states "I will never leave you nor forsake you, You are my child in whom I am well pleased." If you open yourself to anything in this life let it be the soft, small voice of the Father. You are **of** God, you are the individualized expression **of** God. It can no more leave you than it could punish you. You are of it, creation, you **are** the creation forever connected as one. If you trust only one thing in your life let it be the voice within that is only that of peace and harmony to all.

God by its very nature of being is good-harmony, peace, joy, all the plus side emotions ticked. Therefore all of the holy wars, all of the things done in the name of God, anything invoking the name of God as the reason for the carnage was purely the selfishness of man to have power and wealth over others intoxicated by *their* desires and willfulness to have, be or do. It makes no matter the reason given, the source of the *reasoning* was *man* with no relationship **with** God to know the **Truth** of God to share the **love** of God.

Are you beginning to see that maybe you have not known the real God, the God that in all ways sustains, maintains and supplies itself as you, the individualized identity of God? When you live with it and it lives with you, you are one. You are an expression of the consciousness man calls God. You are the child of the most high, you are joint heir to the kingdom of God.

Understanding omnipresence

How to understand omnipresence when so few feel God's presence or understand the implications of it.

Envision the sun shining on a scene in your mind, some place where there are at least a couple of people walking around. Now watch as a cloud goes between you and the sun. That cloud is like an umbrella keeping the sun from you, shadowing you, cutting you off from the sun that is all around you but at the moment, though sun shine is omnipresent where you are there is a cloud, a cover, something keeping the sun from reaching you.

God is omnipresent but unless you know God, are aware of God, know where God is and who you are in relationship to God you are cut off from God. There is a cloud, a barrier, between you and God and God knows nothing of the barrier. Does the sun know a cloud is shielding its rays from hitting the ground? No! The sun does what the sun does because it can do no different.

God is the same. God is not a thing, a person or anything you can name or identify, label or think. God is a name designating that which created this world that is unexplainable and unknowable to *man*.

The barrier, that which is keeping God from being active in your life **is your name,** what you identify yourself as, your nature of being. 99.99% of people will identify as human, flesh and blood Roger, Doug or Pat. If you have a name God knows nothing about you because you are man, disconnected, unaware of God, you are under a cloud stuck in the shadows while at the same time another stands under the full glory and warmth of the sun soaking it in, basking in it, reveling in it.

Man's barrier, cloud or umbrella is his identity-i, me, mine, Erik, the man with an ego/personality separate and apart from every other person on earth. Human man is an island alone and adrift always protecting its own at all cost.

You come out from under duality, that which is "blocking" the sun, by breaking down the illusion of darkness by dying daily to error by knowing Truth until the cloud is no more, cannot keep the glory of the sun from you so you run free in the warmth, free in the arms of God, free knowing **your name as I am, Child of God.**

When you know who you are you know your name and by your name shall ye be known.

The clouds are only there because *you* are holding them there through ignorance of the sun on the other side. Let them disburse, let them become the nothingness they truly are, blow them to the four corners and watch the earth melt, error dissolve.

God is omnipresent and God is the same for all, but no one has God until they **experience** God. Attaining the experience of God is the attainment of all the added things with no asking, no begging and no directing. Through prayer/inner listening/meditation, knowing Truth and expectant listening you have the ability to come into the presence of God and in this presence you are once again whole and complete with all things **added** unto you.

Omnipotent:

Since God is omnipotent, the only power/presence where it is known, there is no outer/other presence, so **evil is not a power** in the presence of one knowing God aright. Sin, disease, lack, limitation, etc, are **not** powers in the presence of God/one of God consciousness or knowing. Why? You are **not affected** by the duality of man when you know Truth because you live above, out of, away from, separate from the errors of man who believes in two powers which is the **only** error of man keeping him from the allness of God.

Let us say you know how to drive a car correctly, aright. You are safe in your understanding, knowing of how a car works, how to control it properly and the functions and limitations of the car, what makes it go and what makes it stop. This knowing of **how** to drive a car correctly is your **protection** from errors or accidents that could have occurred if you had been driving without knowing how to drive.

You **knowing** the Truth of God is your **protection** from the accidents, errors and words of man who doesn't know the Truth of God, ie doesn't know how to really live this life, are driving without knowing how to drive, are just winging it with every other person on the road and you can see the ensuing chaos as most are expressing it.

How to have the awareness of God within

There is only one thing you need and that is the awareness of the presence of God within. Dandy. Sweet! How the heck do you do that?

Having an awareness of the presence of God begins with you wanting to know God. You want to know God therefore you study and practice what is between these pages, 365 Days of Truth volume 1-3, Joel S Goldsmith's treasure trove of works, 18th century poetry like Browning, Blake, Emerson, Whitman and philosophers like Jacob Boehme, Marcus Aurelius, Lao Tzu and Plotinus. Truth, God, is the foundation of their work, is the all of their work just unrecognized by most because of the mystical nature of the consciousness behind the words.

You can no more separate yourself from God than you could separate gold from a ring. Gold is the substance of the ring, it is not gold *and* a ring it is a gold ring. So it is with you. You cannot be separated from God. Why? Because there is **no** we, me or i. There is **no** such thing in all the world as you or me because God being infinite **God is all there is.** God **is** you, your being, your life, mind, soul just as much as "gold" is the substance of the ring and then knowing gold **is** God you can understand all is God, **all that is visible and invisible is God expressing as all that is.**

Truth and the principles of Truth

———

Truth is not available to *man* but that doesn't mean Truth isn't available. Truth is only for those who know where Truth is and how it presents.

Please make sure when you are reading things such as the above that says "Truth is not available to *man*" you are understanding the term *man* to mean "a person who does **not** know God" therefore is **not** spiritual man. When man, human, carnal or mortal are used alone or in any combination to denote a person/presence they are strictly talking about *human* man not **spiritual** man.

You must make sure you make this **distinction** clear in your understanding otherwise when the above is read without that understanding it says **you have no chance in hell of knowing Truth** because up until this point had thought yourself to be man, human man, mortal man, carnal man or material man. But that is absolutely **not** what it says. It says *man* cannot, but you who are on the spiritual path, **spiritual man,** know Truth because you are in a relationship **with** Truth/God.

This distinction **must** be understood. **Only the designation of spiritual man** denotes man in oneness with God, of the consciousness, the nature of God which is harmony.

Spiritual man is always called spiritual man because it is **spiritual** man who has returned to the consciousness of Christ living, living the life of God governance. When the awareness of God has come and you are **one,** you are **spiritual** man because you know God aright, by actual **experience.**

Man does not know God nor can ever know God, Truth or know heaven on earth.

Spiritual man lives heaven on earth beause heaven isn't a *place* it is a **state of being** born of knowing the Truth of your being, the Truth of your existence and a great desire to go back to the way life was before man messed it up with its belief in a presence/reality apart from the allness of God.

This is why man, human man, mortal man, carnal man or material man can never experience heaven because **heaven is a state of consciousness born of knowing God by way of an actual experience of God within.** This is the singular step that reveals man of earth as child of God. Right now you know the world and nothing of the true God but once you have the experience of God within you know God and are shown how man is living an illusion of life, a version of life, a perception of life that is not the reality of the life God created his expressions to experience.

Man has appropriated a belief in two powers to the status of Truth and because not more than a handful of people in the world chose to know the **difference** between belief and Truth, belief is used almost synonymously with Truth which it definitely is not nor can be. One is false and one is real. One cannot become the other and one is not a version of the other. They are separate because one does not exist except in the mind of man who believes himself mortal, lives and dies.

This is why Truth cannot be known by *man*. Man cannot know Truth because Truth is God and God is within man but man is unaware of this presence, this eternal supply and support.

Truth is the result of an awareness that knows **God is** because you just had a conversation with or felt its presence within your own being.

Man has no desire to know God for any of a million reasons thus man cannot know Truth, cannot experience heaven on earth and thinks death is when the physical body gives out.

Read carefully so as not to bring misunderstanding and confusion to yourself. This teaching teaches you to understand the world from a different level of understanding/consciousness and that consciousness is harmony, is. To understand the words of Truth written like the Bible and other mystical writings you must read them from the consciousness they were written from which is that of one in conscious union with God.

When you read spiritual Truth without spiritual Truth as your operating system it makes no sense because you don't understand the language. Of course you don't, it wasn't written by a *human* man, the guy next door of your level of understanding; it was written by one in conscious oneness with God, spiritual man, therefore the perspective of the words, the consciousness that **is** the words, though not stated, is not that of man but of spiritual man knowing only God, good, harmony and love.

This is why when you read "though a thousand will fall at your side and ten thousand at your right hand, nigh will come near your door" you think God is a physical force that will kill to protect you or gives you the right to kill but what it **means** is when God is your consciousness nothing, or very little, of the world comes into your experience, your house, your consciousness, to make life hard regardless of what is happening around you. **Living** the Truth of God is your **protection** from those things of the world knocking on your door, into your life, into your experiences.

Spiritual Truth is very specific and the use of words, or lack there of is **intentional** because it denotes a difference you are to pay attention to. One misunderstood word can change the entire understanding of a Truth, the meaning of what you are reading therefore you must be careful not to overlay human thinking that you "already know this stuff" and gloss over it. This is not conjecture and it is not of the human mind, it is Truth given straight from God within to bring harmony to you, to show you what God **is** and not what man *believes* God is.

I guarantee you have never been given the opportunity to understand Truth because Truth is the consciousness of mystics, those who have an awareness of God, a presence within their own being no matter the name given. It is the conscious oneness of mystics, Jesus the Christ, Gautama the Buddha, Lao Tzu, Peter, Paul, Isaiah, and others who shared the Truth of God, the God within to dispel the errors of the Old Testament of a God separate and apart from man awaiting the coming or second coming of the Christ.

To know God aright is life eternal because by knowing God aright you know yourself aright and know yourself to be infinite eternal being.

God is not in the whirlwind, the chaos of man; God is in the calm within your own being where peace reigns.

In an absolute sense God is omnipresence **but** God is **only** omnipresent **as** the consciousness **of** individual man, not a consciousness/omnipresence *outside* of you meaning the expression, harmonious presence of God is not outside of you, present everywhere like the atmosphere because the atmosphere of man is duality.

Therefore God must be **known** to be within you for the presence of God to express as you, your atmosphere of harmony omnipresent, the only presence/expression where you are.

All holy books are mystical writings and contain mystical Truth but it takes one of a mystical nature to understand the meaning **of** the Truth being revealed and not the face value of the words. Man has taken the literal definition of *words* within holy books and used them as weapons ie an eye for an eye, vengeance, retaliation, rights, personal power instead of universal harmony as intended.

The Truth within holy books can only be understood by those who have God awareness, ie God consciousness. Man has the consciousness of man, duality and judgement therefore when words are read they are experienced within according to *personal* history.

Spiritual man has the consciousness of God therefore has no personal history because spiritual man now knows all those beliefs, errors, omissions and commissions were based on a belief in two powers thus have no power to force opinion to try to negate Truth. Truth is. Take it or leave it, it doesn't change and it doesn't go anywhere just because you don't believe it. Truth is Law, Law is eternal and God is Law unto eternity-harmonious expression seen and unseen.

Truth experienced is the result of oneness with God. Truth is God revealing itself to you through awareness-communion, prayer, meditation. Truth is God revealing itself to you so you can grow in conscious understanding of the God you are returning to the nature of.

Mystics from every part of the world from the beginning of time have been saying the same thing over and over in different ways but all revealing Truth: **there is only one God and that God is within each individual and that all of life as man understands it and lives it is not the reality of the life God created for his expressions.**

Up until now becoming a mystic was an accident born of desire for union with the Father but when this union was created it was created **without** true understanding of what it was they had **done** that produced the results thus could not repeat it or teach it to proliferate the Truth of God more consistently and consciously.

Ahhhh. That's it. **Consciousness.** Knowing God **is** by being **aware** of God **within** you. You open to God through **conscious awareness** of its presence and have a **relationship** with this presence by being **of** the consciousness of this presence.

Three main Truths make up the foundation for spiritual awareness:

1. The Truth of God
2. The Truth of you
3. The Truth of error

Knowing the answers to these three questions leads you to an actual experience which reveals **where** God is, the nature of God and how to be where God is so you can live in this God governed, God supplied, maintained and supported experience of peace and harmony or continue to live the experiences of human duality.

When you search, search in earnest for that which is **new and unknown** to you for only those things bring an opening for more to be known. If you are looking for that which *validates* the views you already have you will never move past where you are because you are not asking for change, you are asking *conformity* to your will and not God's and that is what got man into this predicament in the first place-man's will over the will of the Father for you as his perfect expression.

Truth is an experience of the reality of God within.

To know God you must become aware of the Truth of God:

1. there is only **one God,** one nature of expression of being and it is harmonious
2. **love your neighbor as yourself** which is to know the Truth of all man-spirit in form, brethren
3. **forgive 70x7,** ie hold no one including yourself in judgment, bondage or condemnation for you were ignorant once and will be ignorant again even on this path as it is a learning journey and God brings peace to bear each and every time you ask forgiveness for your ignorance but you must **grow** from your mistakes otherwise you are not growing in consciousness just going around and around the circle track missing the exit.

All are created equal when you know who did the creating and it is by this knowing that **all are of God** you begin to understand by knowing Truth you give others the opportunity to know Truth because more Truth is being shared in the consciousness of man of earth because spiritual man is doing what spiritual man does-share the love of God through grace by expressing the nature of your being-harmony, peace, good will toward man.

The understanding of **consciousness as the link between God and man** was brought forth into awareness through the mystical work of Joel S Goldsmith who was a teacher, philosopher and healer of the early/mid 20th century whose work spanned more than 40 years and brought forth 47 books on God and mysticism. I highly encourage you to read his work as it was the teaching that allowed God to come forth in expression to begin my never ending journey.

This mystical Truth brought forth into expression was **that which mystics all through the ages had not been able to express**-the **how** of how to have a personal relationship with God.

These four foundational principles of Truth make up the entirety of True Christianity, Christ living when **lived as your expression of being.**

1. **Communion** meditation, silent inner listening for the voice of God. Listening is the true activity of prayer and it is only through inner listening that you can have the mystical experience and live under grace.
2. **God is your individual consciousness** when God is known aright. God is found in the silence behind the thinking mind. The thinking mind knows no Truth of God and demonstration/expression of God **by way of conscious oneness/union** is the Truth of being-I am that I am, the Father and I are one.
3. **The Truth of God**-all is God in form therefore there is no matter/material substance separate and apart from the allness of God therefore there is no matter/material reality to be experienced as this is a spiritual universe in form and function.
4. **The Truth of error**-error is no thing, illusion. Error is merely what you judge it to be according to personal history. What man calls error, the devil, bad or good is a thought of the mind not objective/visible therefore has no power to take you from the harmony of God.

Freedom is not won or gained, it is realized.

You can never be persecuted for your religion if your religion is but the outward expression of your inner knowing and living of Truth. Words and actions are persecutable, grace through silence is not. You cannot be persecuted for being a person who sees no evil and expresses no evil.

Evil is nothing more than a personal perception of right and wrong according to you. Therefore one who doesn't express evil or see evil is one who sees and expresses is, good, peace and harmony. One who is not engaging in the errors of man cannot be persecuted for the errors of man thus lives above the consciousness of man which is the protection afforded you when you know God, is, good, peace and harmony.

You must know Truth before you can demonstrate Truth.

Healing work is accomplished by realizing the Truth of error, of duality as no thing and until you understand what that means and is your expression you are not knowing Truth to be able to demonstrate Truth, God in action, grace in your midst.

Every time you accept an evil/error as Truth you are trying to divide God. It isn't possible to divide God against itself, it isn't possible for infinite intelligence to act destructively against itself, all of creation. God is perfection itself, all that is **is** good and anything not made by God wasn't made **therefore only appears to you out of this mesmeric/hypnotic sense and your realization of this Truth is the healing influence,** is the very presence and power that nullifies error; nothing else can.

"You shall know the Truth and the Truth will make you free." That is the way the Master did his healing work. He never healed a crippled or blind man he merely asked "what does hinder you? open your eyes/pick up your bed and walk."

Jesus never healed a condition he healed the belief that one could have a condition, that you of your spiritual perfection could be other than spiritual perfect in expression.

No amount of Truth can benefit you no matter how profound it is.

You are benefitted **only by your living of Truth.** Truth in and of itself will not make you free. "Ye shall know the Truth" and it is **knowing** this Truth, **living** this Truth and **being** this Truth that frees you from the duality of man and the illusions of man as finite being separate and apart from God. It is only when you know the Truth of God do you know the Truth of yourself and all man and in that knowing are able to rise back to the kingdom, the consciousness of harmony, at one with your creative source, what man calls God or infinite being.

Righteousness

Your righteousness must exceed the righteousness of the scribes and the Pharisees, both obedient to Hebrew law but of no knowledge of spiritual law. Your righteousness must exceed that of one who is a 10 commandment *law* follower. How? By knowing God aright which allows you to live above the laws of man to live by grace, the allness of God expressing as one who neither wants or needs, judges or defiles, is of no human expression by which to bring chaos into expression.

Your righteousness has to be beyond the rules, laws and emotions of man. Your righteousness has to go beyond being angry with your brother/mankind, beyond retaliation, revenge, anger, desire, pain or lack. Your righteousness has to be that of **understanding the ignorance of man** and in that knowing do not pin a sin to a person thereby freeing them from that burden.

Understand righteous means **knowing God aright.** Some people understand the word incorrectly which brings to mind a particular personality no one cares to associate with. There is no correlation between *human* righteousness which is ego and hubris and **spiritual** righteousness which is **no** ego, **no** hubris, **nothing** of your human self. Righteous merely means to know God aright/correctly/in its Truth and silently make the correction that brings Truth to bear: God is and God is harmony, all else is of the duality of man and since duality is nothing more than the thinking mind thinking good and bad the effect, what you are momentarily experiencing is nothing more than the *expression* of good and bad *thoughts* thus no thing real ie *subjective* not **objective.**

If you resist not evil by knowing the Truth of error as merely *expressions* of *personal* perspective, a spiritual presence comes into your awareness. All through the sermon on the mount you are given the Law about which it says **as ye sow so shall ye reap.** If you sow to the human law of doing to others as they do to you or defending yourself with human weapons you are told definitely **if you live by the sword you will die by the sword** and yet people believe they are praying to God when they are living in violation of the Christ rules of life. **You cannot pray to God and violate God in the same breath.**

While you are living by the standards of the scribes and Pharisees, which is the same standard held today for the Jews, Protestants, Catholics, Christians, human man in general, you are under the *law* of man and as long as you are living by the laws of man you suffer the laws of man and will die according to the *beliefs* of man. In proportion as you gave to man you get from man and there is no God in the picture; God cannot save you, there is no way because you have never known God therefore have left God out of your life and are not in the realm where God operates.

God doesn't operate in the world of *human* man. God is not operating when you are violating the commandments, not the Ten Commandments of Mosaic law but the two commandments of Jesus the Christ. You can obey nine of the 10 Commandments to the nth degree and still never come under grace because

1. grace is a state of consciousness only attained when you know the Truth of duality as illusion and know God through actual experience.
2. There is no God in the laws of man, no grace just cause and effect/punishment and reward but never grace because grace is God in action, the living Christ and man knows no God by which to receive grace.

There is only one error man is making that is keeping him from God and that is the ignorance of Truth of your nature which is what is being presented to you here in this writing. If you read this and other works of Truth you will lose your ignorance, you will lose the God outside of you and you will lose your life, the life of duality, chaos and fear to live eternity within the allness of that which you are.

The first few steps on your path every day are inscribed with these reminders: I am that I am, I and the Father are one, grace is the substance of my life, your grace is my sufficiency, or a few of your own choosing. They remind you, as if you could ever forget, of your Truth so duality has no chance of rattling your cage, cannot have entrance into your expression.

Truth

The Truth of God found in the red letter words of the Bible are for one purpose and one purpose only-**to know the Truth about your existence**-which is that of individual expression of the one expression called God or universal creative consciousness. The New Testament is all about **you,** how you were meant to live and how to once again have that life but you must open your conscious awareness to Truth and let it work in and on you.

God determines your course by revealing error on your path for you to release so you can continue to flow freely. Think of Truth like water than over time erodes all that hinders it until it has determined its course.

God allowed to flow by way of constant communion/communication is the water that erodes the mountain of errors, the water that makes clear and defined its path/course, that which shows you the fallacy of duality so you **willingly** desire to live under one expression, God, harmonious, joyous, peace and abundance knowing that even if this body is lifeless you still exist.

When Truth dispels long held beliefs there can be an uncomfortable emptiness within. Like hunger without the pain, that hollowness of feeling. This is **normal;** you have to drop the old leaves, go within/pull back the sap/hold and wait for life/God to bring new growth, new fruit in due time.

The life of human man is that of constant motion ie thinking, planning, devising, inventing, working, supplying; it is all on you to use your MBA or School of Hard Knocks degree, your finite supply of energy and finances to make something of yourself in this life and live as long as you can as well as you can no matter how that is accomplished. But even with all you invest in time and money there is no guarantee of success, only luck, chance, the alignment of the stars with fingers crossed.

The life of the spiritual man is based on trust because you know God is and have begun to bear the fruits of your relationship as a better mood, an easier smile, a lighter load on your back and a feeling that tells you you are on the right track by the ease that has been more in your awareness.

As spiritual man your morning begins with a meet and greet, touching base. "Good morning Father! So excited to see what you have in store for us today! Thank you for always being my rock, I love you!"

You go about your day doing what you are prompted to do ie work, laundry, make a phone call, clean the closet. Life is normal but for **one** thing-you are **listening** and **being** not thinking and reacting other than that life is normal.

We all know in general what we have to do each day but be open to the flow of grace taking you in a different direction, in other words don't get so tied to your habits and patterns that an adventure with God is pushed aside because you have things to do. God won't give you the impulse to go do something else instead of picking up your kids or to abandon responsibility or family in any way. The impulses of God are subtle and you have to learn to relax and feel what you are doing is a bit of a game, a segway with a purpose like this:

Grace is God in action therefore the impulses to be and do throughout the day are God guiding and directing your life harmoniously through your conscious oneness **with** God. An example would be you get an impulse to get a bottle of water from the fridge and on your short jaunt down the hallway a fleeting thought is brought into awareness and when you get to the kitchen a song is playing on the radio that makes the fleeting thought come into full awareness, becomes flesh- what is revealed within is what God has given you to do or know to facilitate its life of harmony as your life of harmony.

Protection:

The protection of God is the living of your life within the oneness, the singular expression of peace, chill, harmony thereby protecting yourself from the duality of man which leaves your life to chance, like a pendulum swinging back and forth between good and bad. Oneness with God stops the pendulum swing and rises you above the need to express as good or bad. Your protection, God's protection, is this atmosphere, consciousness, place of harmony, balance, neither good nor bad but perfect, God's perfect which becomes your expression to the world.

The purpose of the Teacher and the responsibility of the Student

A righteous teacher does not want to hold their students in bondage to being students forever, they want to see them go out and be likewise.

The whole purpose of this book is to be your teacher but I can bring nothing to you if you are not open but if you are open you will learn from one who has seen the face of the Father within, has had the mystical experience and lives oneness, allness, in the consciousness of God with the express purpose of being a light by which to bring others into the glory of God. I wish to teach you so you can fly on your own to teach others.

There are rules to living the spiritual life called principles of Truth. They are simplistic in nature and few but simplicity doesn't imply easy. They must be studied, practiced, lived as your expression and **bear fruit** in your experience before they can be shared with those who ask to know what you have and with **no** others. **This work is secret, sacred and silent** and the quality of your life, your return for living secretly, sacredly and silently in God consciousness is the degree of harmony you experience.

If however you decide to mix and match, some from Truth and some from man by which to continue your living, you will find worse fates befalling you because you are not living spiritually, you are trying to *add* **God** to your *human* experience to have more and better *material* things and it won't work because God is not of the world of matter/material.

I am the way. I am that I am. God known in your awareness is the way by which you enjoy harmonious living/heaven on earth in visible form now.

Sword of the Spirit:

The Master said "I am come not to bring peace but a sword."

Man's purpose in life and the Christ purpose in life are two completely different things. Man is set on *getting* security, economic/material good, physical good, peace, physical health, visible abundance etc. by any means they can employ.

Man seeks that which they feel will bring joy, happiness, peace and security. Always is the drive to *acquire* some form of material good that is to *bring* you your peace, harmony, wholeness, completeness. Man depends on bombs for peace, domination for peace but also on money and physical health for peace but all have witnessed the failure of any of these to give man peace, security or happiness.

The sword of God is Truth to help you cut away the kudzu that has taken over your mind, all minds of man, to reveal the true landscape God created in the beginning so you can once again flourish in this earthly garden.

The sword the Master brought-Truth in awareness-is to help you break your reliance, your faith in and on material means, on your having to *get* or *take* to receive. Truth known in consciousness allows you to break free of all *hope* and *reliance* on *external powers* whether those be of a God outside of you, idols, rituals, ceremony, medicine, metaphysical/occult "powers", your mental or physical strength, money in the bank or four leaf clovers.

No matter where you have put your dependence Truth must come to your consciousness and sever from you all such hopes, faiths and confidences until you understand why man shall not live by bread alone, not by *material* means, not by force, not by power; not by anything in the realm of effect/duality/human man but by every Word out of the mouth of God.

The Truth and principles of true Christ living are not of any of the religions being practiced today because spiritual Truth is based on two principles no one else has chosen to recognize that are clear as day and found in the Bible:

1. God is within you, I am that I am
2. Error is merely illusion, nothingness thus no power. What does hinder you? pick up your bed and walk.

Your awareness of God's presence within you confirms that there is only one expression of good and that expression just announced its residency within you. You are admitting freely, joyously, "here in the midst of me is Life, Truth and Grace. All is of the Father and it is of me when I dwell in the place of the most high-the consciousness of being, God." I of my own self can do nothing, it is the Father within, he doeth the works appointed me to do."

All error is personal, of only you, subjective, of the mind and not objective, of the visible world. What man labels and judges as good and bad **does not** give the object the ability to express as good or bad because judgement is not real but of the thinking mind.

All **is** therefore that which is viewed/judged as other than is, harmonious, is nothing more than a *personal perception of your thinking mind,* illusion, maya, "this world," arm of flesh, no thing, an echo of a past consciousness that is no more.

Definition of Laws: Spiritual and Human

The Universal Law of Creative Expression is **the Law unto God** which is the only Law because it is the Law of Life expressing. God **is** Law unto Life, eternal harmony. God is spirit, consciousness, therefore the universe is spiritual Law **being** the expression of all that is. God is what man calls nature-life, evolution and creation-but all **is** God in form not *matter/material* in form as man calls all that is. All that God is **is** the directive, creative intelligence that **is** Law unto the whole of existence, it **is** the Divine Idea expressing.

laws of nature are *man's* scientific interpretation of the world around them as *matter/material.*

Universal law-those laws that are most universally accepted rules of governing *human* conduct.

Cosmic law-Cause and effect, karma, *man's* laws. As ye sow so shall ye reap. The entire teaching of the Master, the New Testament, was to teach you/show you what cosmic law was and then how to **surmount it**/get out of the duality of man and back under grace.

Natural law is a legal philosophy that deals with questions of how *human* man aught to behave and treat each other.

Only the **Universal Law of Creative expression** is Truth, God, the only reality. All other *laws* are nothing more than man's *thinking* mind trying to *understand* the world around them.

The only law there can be is the Universal Law of Creative expression, universal consciousness of being expressing as is normal and natural for it to do and there can be no other Law because God is the one source of infinite being therefore God's Law is the only expression in activity therefore there cannot be any other expression.

The *human* laws of material/matter, ie man's *laws* of weather, age, infection and contagion, sin and disease only operate on the physical and mental levels of human life and the moment you come to the spiritual level in which you recognize God as infinite being you nulify the belief there are laws of matter or laws of mind.

The reason you can be sure laws of matter and laws of mind are not spiritual Law is because:

All material and mental laws can be used for good or evil.

Therefore they cannot be of God because that which is of God can be neither good nor evil it can only be what it **is**-harmonious. There is no such thing as a degree of good, there is no such thing as evil in the Law of God **therefore wherever you find the pairs of opposites, the good *and* the evil, you are dealing with either *matter or mind* which is always *man* and not God.**

The very moment you rise above using these powers to justify your life, fuel your actions and existence as little i, personality, and rise to that which is above personal survival, i, me, mine, to resting and receiving you are in the atmosphere of God where you know you cannot die, you need do nothing to support your life because your life isn't yours to support and if you have given up using good and bad you are being supported by God. Therefore by becoming one in consciousness **with** it you are **of** it and no longer *separated* from Truth, good, harmonious expression and no longer suffering what human man experiences.

Why did Jesus come more than 2000 years ago? Why didn't man of that time just look to the Hebrew Rabbis for this information of God and individual Christ consciousness? What did Jesus have that the Rabbis didn't?

Jesus had a Truth that the Rabbis were unable to give because they didn't know it or in the case of the Essenes, didn't want to share it with common man for they felt it was too powerful and would be misinterpreted thus misused.

What was this Truth Jesus knew? The world as human man experiences it is not the Truth of the experience rather is an illusion/perception of reality filtered over personal history thus causing an illusion of mind to be experienced as if it were real and tangible in the outer world and not just in your imagination.

What man experiences is an illusion, adulteration, embellishment of what **is** and not the reality/Truth of the experience.

How do you not let illusion/error get to you? **by recognizing it as the illusion it is** and that **recognition** is what brings peace to your being in some way that reveals the nothingness of the perceived error. How? If peace descends how can what you were feeling/experiencing be real? What is real is only what comes from within you and you just experienced peace expressing within you releasing you from the expression of error presenting.

The only reason for learning what God is and how to have it active in your life is not to improve your human life but to attain God realization and when that is attained you **automatically** become the child of God, child of the one spiritual household. Not yet under grace but back where grace can be found.

It is the **experience of God** that sets the stage for your freedom from the duality of man, the death of man, the hardship and the confusion of man and places you in the kingdom where there is harmony with God as supplier, provider, protector and comforter unto eternity.

To love your neighbor as yourself is to acknowledge God as the very being of all that appears regardless of the mesmeric appearances that confront you as reality; it is the knowing that the Father is within regardless of appearances.

Matthew 25:40 "And the King shall answer and say unto them, Verily I say unto you, In as much as ye have done it unto one of the least of these my brethren, ye have done it unto me."

Appearances mean nothing, all are the children of God. Period.

The sins of the father:

In old Hebraic time there were many poor widows who had to sell their sons into slavery to pay debts due to poverty. In this way a child was the proof of the errors of his family-they had to sell their children to cover debts or to make ends meet. The child's life was the product of **the sins of the father,** the *human* father or mother or previous. The child always knew they were the price that was paid to cover another's mistakes. They suffered the sins of their father as a mental burden that marked their life with hardship, shame, pain and suffering because it became their identity, their burden to bear.

As you now know there is nothing that can keep you from God. No thing and nothing if you want God, desire to know God and to live God. No condition, circumstance, person or sin can keep you from God. It is impossible because there is only one Father who art in heaven therefore the sins of the human father/parent are the same *illusion* you bear as the guilt, pain or lack you have accepted as your label.

"Thou your sins may be scarlet, ye are as white as snow." Horse's mouth and all, might want to believe it and not the preacher that has no idea of the love of God while they spew the fear of God.

Never trust anyone but God for God is the only Truth. There is nothing of you other than God, no thing and nothing. We all sin, we all do things we wish we hadn't and we all suffer the sin. We all cause others pain and we cause ourselves pain but only because **that is the nature of the *human* world** and up until now did not know there was another way, an **option** to living this experience of duality.

Your Father has not been present to sit with you and have conversations, a back and forth dialog of "how can I help you son?" when you ask to learn what is expected of you and what the result for you is when you are of God governance.

God is always dependable and reliable and I know not one of us can say we have ever encountered likewise in man. Your Father can be your guide this minute to the unfolding Truth of this life if you want, it is always and only up to you how illumined you become, what you express as your progress in fruitage, outward abundance and healing ability but there are rules, boundaries.

Good old boundaries. Just knowing what you can and cannot do to get into and remain in the kingdom with God. No rituals, rights, gutting or pouring of icky stuff. No starving, carving or crying. Just stay within the lines and all is good. Yes, it is truly that simple, hard at times but absolutely simple in application.

There are rules to the kingdom and I'm not talking about wearing shoes in the house. Through study and application of Truth, reading metaphysical Truth, meditation, practicing the presence, healing and forgiving 70x7 you are living God, the nature of God-harmony in expression-and your peace, your joy, your ease of being attests to the degree of God governance in your life. These are the **rules/principles** of Truth, of living in the kingdom. This is the Truth that must express as you to the world if God is governing your life. That's it.

Every time you have an experience that absolutely proves the non power of something the world has given power to you are not only lessening the universal belief in duality but you are also making it possible for someone else to pick up what you have loosed in consciousness-grace, God in action where God was not previously available/known.

What this means is if I receive peace within myself others of God consciousness will feel peace as it was given through **universal** consciousness and is received in consciousness. This is how one may rise all. If you desire that which is not of this world you will receive that which is not of this world and it is that which is felt within as peace, joy, relief. What you received within didn't come from the world, the world produced the reaction you sought refuge from. So if peace and joy are your experience now it must be of God because there is no other option possible.

The mystical knowing of Truth develops the healing consciousness or the Christ consciousness that is your personal relationship with God.

Spiritual teaching comes out of an **attained consciousness** not out of *intellectual knowledge*. Anyone with a quick mind can read books and *memorize* principles but there is no **benefit** in reading or memorizing, only in awareness and practicing the presence.

Spiritual Truth deals with what is termed the **power** of God. The power of God is the **benefit** to you byway of your awareness of the presence of God within your own being, that is the power afforded you, the protection of knowing God aright and knowing how that presence benefits you and keeps you from falling back into duality.

Spiritual man does not use physical, mental or material power to *get* from the world what they want rather **rests in the awareness** of all that is and **receives** of all that it is. The power of God is knowing the Truth of God and expresses as the ease of living unto your experience, it is the gentle voice from within that keeps you from erring, it is that which furnishes your life merely by being where it is-in the silence behind the thinking mind.

Children:

Children need to be directed, not disciplined. There can be discipline in direction but it is not the discipline of force, anger or irritation. It is the discipline of Truth, knowing Truth and living

Truth. Children are animals and must be directed or they become the lower consicousness of the next generation instead of the higher. We are not to teach children like they are taught in school where things are shoved in and learned by rote rather by example, understanding and quiet time. Children today are kept so busy trying to *make* adults that succeed in life by having numerous skills and talents along with intelligence and standing **but this only perpetuates the belief in duality, that you of yourself must do something.** You cannot *make* a child into your image and likeness rather are to allow their true image and likeness to emerge as that of child of God.

Nothing of the outer world matters to a child and it should definitely not matter to you. What is important is bringing up the next generation in an understanding that is different than the world around them and to do that you must employ different ways of getting through to the soul of the child, the consciousness and not just punishing according to outward expression.

Parents do not know, or lose sight of, the reality of their children as God's children when they are the screaming foul monkey demons of horror movies. But if parents know how to correct along spiritual lines there should be no reason for the rebellion in them that makes them problem children later.

Man looks at children as extensions of themselves and this is the problem with human parenting. Your children are of God, are of the consciousness they were when they left their last iteration. **Your children are complete strangers to you because their consciousness was already formed before inception** and why you cannot make children into your image and likeness through fear, control, manipulation and punishment. They are not your children they are God's trying to find their way home as are all that are born and die as human man.

When a parent raises children from this perspective of God realization most of what you are doing as a parent happens in the silence of your being which becomes the atmosphere of your home which becomes the atmosphere from which the child expresses as a more calm, observant child that **gives** to the world instead of *demanding from* the world.

Your children, though not your children, for a time or for life are a reflection of the atmosphere outside of them until something tells them the true reality is the atmosphere within the silence, invisible, sacred and secret. Then and only then does consciousness begin to change to that which is Truth, that which it has been seeking thousands and thousands of years and it is in this way the old man of *earth* dies and you are reborn as the new man of **spiritual** understanding.

Discipline is not punishment and the child can feel this. Punishment is for who you *believe* they are by their actions, discipline is behavior correction through knowing the Truth that they are not bad or sinful but pure and **discipline is to reveal the purity without demoralizing, malpracticing or damaging the child's sense of self which you are revealing as God.** God could no more punish you than it could stop being itself. Therefore you in the consciousness of God cannot punish because it is not of your nature. You heal, you correct and you pray and that brings more and more grace to bear in your children. Even the hardest nut to crack will open at the softest whisper of that which feels to be missing.

The conduct of all those around you is dependent on your consciousness because your consciousness brings the Law of your consciousness to bear. Therefore the consciousness of a human teacher becomes the consciousness of the child **if** the child has not already started to be filled with a consciousness higher than that of the teachers out in the world.

If children are not rightly directed at home through the spiritual consciousness of the parents the child will be educated by the masses, by those of duality and will need to wander this earth as you did before finding Truth. The children of each successive generation are begging, pleading, screaming at the top of their lungs to be given something different than what has gone before so they don't have to suffer and their children's children no longer have to suffer. The only way this world can change is with you knowing and living your Truth to impart it to your children so that as they continue to transition into different phases of this eternal experience they are doing it as raised consciousness instead of human consciousness of duality.

Source of all form:

The source of all form is invisible, incorporeal, eternal creative consciousness expressing. When you place a seed in the ground there is that which is invisible but it acts upon the seed and soil and later appears as blossoms, flower and fruit. The visible is the result of an invisible action in agriculture/horticulture man calls nature but by whatever name you call it it is God, infinite creative consciousness expressing as all form.

There is a Law operating, the Law of like begetting like and that Law is invisible but the result of the Law in action becomes visible and then becomes tangible as flowers, fruit, seed. There is within all this invisible Law in operation and you experience this Law as supply that comes to you without *human* means when you are of the Law that is the supply unto you-God in awareness.

Prayer is an action, a doing, a being, a listening, a living and an expression of the consciousness you share with God.

There is no prayer/praying being done where there is no resultant change of consciousness. There may be some kind of an attempt at prayer, a mix of begging and listening which cancels out the listening part, there may be some false concept of prayer but true prayer, living out from God's consciousness, must result in a change of your conscious expression. If you don't feel different, don't see and experience the world differently you are praying amiss because if you were praying aright you would be expressing the consciousness of God, the nature of God which is good/harmonious.

The practice of the principles of spiritual living absolutely has to bring change to your life because your consciousness is that which you express outwardly as who you are therefore consciousness is always expressed as your being, it can be no other way.

Even if the prayers were carried out in an orthodox way, out instead of in, as long as the **intent** of the prayers was for **Truth** and not *things* they would most definitely lead to a change of consciousness which would in its turn lead to a changed life.

If you do not feel to be a different person, one with more understanding of the world around you by way of more understanding of the world within you need to go back to foundational Truth and see where you are erring. It is just a side jaunt, no biggy, just get your compass out and find your way back to your path.

Never give/share that which you have not attained the consciousness of. If you learn of a principle that seems reasonable to you, practice it until your life shows it forth-visible fruitage. Then when someone is led to you you can share it because it will then multiply itself.

The more you express **as** the Truth you are learning to be the more it will express through you but if you try to give Truth to another through *words* before you have experienced the fruit/validation **of** that Truth it cannot bear fruit for yourself or the one you are trying to *give* it to because you are giving *words* which have no power to change/help a person.

Spiritual Truth will **always be devoid** of human nature/desire because spiritual Truth has nothing to do with man, only God; this is why man cannot understand God because God doesn't give you *things* when you pray, it gives you **itself** ie peace, harmony, rest.

You cannot reach the realm of God except through silence. Eventually you must come to the conclusion that no activity of your mind/thinking will get you into the kingdom of God. Then you will be consciously conscious and the first thing you will become consciously conscious of is God, even if it is just a glimmer to instill in you a deep longing to know it more.

When you no longer are dependent on corporeal effect, matter/material, when you no longer feel that person or thing is the essential of your life but that your demonstration is to be God then it is that God appears as your shade during the day and your torch at night, food, clothing, raiment, companionship, housing but they aren't *things* ie it isn't *a* cloud, *a* torch, *a* person, *clothing* or *housing,* it is God itself **expressing as** these forms, these added and needed things for your experience.

This Truth is the heart and soul of Christ living.

You do not need a sun, you do not need a moon, you do not need clothing, housing or companionship, an earth to stand upon or air to breathe. You need nothing of this world of material sense/matter to support, supply, maintain or enhance your life, all you need is the **realization** of God as all that is and by that knowing are the prodigal son returned home once again able to partake of all that is.

The same expression that causes the sun to rise and set, the earth to turn, the waves to ebb and flow, the expression that is the fish in the sea and the birds in the air, the expression that is maintaining and sustaining the universe in its perfect rhythm is the **same** expression operating in your consciousness.

There is no expression of the nature of God in the things of man-contagion, infection, time, lack, pain, fear, the calendar, the bank account, illness, hate, ill will, spells, hexes or wishes. There is no expression of God, grace, in the human world because the human world is of duality, good and bad, this and that.

You must give up control of your life and to do that you have to stop being a sponge and let your inner Self, the true Self, through consciousness of that inner Self as the true nature of being, direct your life. **God in consciousness is an activity, it is a living presence thus has to be consciously known.** You cannot just say "God will take care of it, I trust God" and blithely turn from the problem. There is no such God. God does not fix, overcome or annihilate anything for you or for anyone else.

God is and must be an **activity** of Truth in your consciousness and that activity of Truth has to be **built**. To build up the activity of Truth is the same way you would build your understanding of a new hobby, profession or skill. You don't just instantly know it all rather it is a going within and giving yourself treatments of Truth pertaining to the illusion presenting. Constantly, **consciously bringing Truth back into awareness in the midst of error is your freedom and liberty** from the illusion of human man's beliefs and fears-nothingness, illusion, universal mesmerism.

Your responsibility is to "awaken thou that sleepest!" And "Christ will give thee light" but you must wake up to the fact that what you experience **is your own consciousness objectified, made form/consequence in your experience.** In oneness your cause and effect is God therefore both are harmonious thus you **are** harmonious but in the world of man cause and effect are of *duality* so you never know what you are going to get in return pressed down and flowing over; it could be good, it could be bad but that is the luck of the draw, chance, statical nature of human/mortal man and not the safety and security of God by being of the consciousness of is, always is, perfect is.

Acknowledge Christ dwelleth in you. You can do all things through this indwelling Christ. There aren't any powers/expressions of man to act upon **spiritual man** but there are all kinds of *perceived* power/expression out in the world to act on *human man,* on those who have not acknowledged God within as the only power/expression.

Your **acceptance** of the indwelling Christ is what allows God to live your life. You then find it to be a presence, grace, that goes before you to make the crooked places straight, bless those around you and stays to bless those after you have taken your leave. You find that you are not just living for yourself, your purposes but that you have an invisible presence, senior partner of universal intelligence unavailable to human man.

This presence within is power unto you but not the physical/mental power of man that goes out to destroy their enemies with a sword, personal might, or the power of a general or a king but the power of Truth, the Christ within you, the still, small voice, the singular consciousness of the universe and this singularity is the reason, the cause and effect of the harmony and peace to all that are accepting and desirous of this consciousness of perfect peace.

The power of God is not a power like what power means to man. The power of God lies in its hierarchy so to speak. In the beginning God. God is and is good. All that God created is good and all that isn't wasn't. What? God could not create anything unlike itself, how could it? Like produces like, like attracts like.

In this hierarchy God is above man in all ways because God is the creator and we are the creation. We have the characteristics of our creator however we will never be the creator, that is not our place. Our place is to be the expressions of the One expression, the Elohim, One of many, many of One. One nature of good, of love out into the world so that others may open to the awareness that you are living somehow differently than they are as a mortal man.

You have a peace, a softness, a gentleness, an atmosphere that is foreign to the senses of the natural man but at the same time there is something within them highly desirable of that which you possess/express.

If you have it then why, they might think, have they never found it? Because the kingdom of God is not of the world of man and man has no concept of anything other than what is of this *visible* world. As spiritual man you live in the world of human duality but do not **partake of,** react to, the atmosphere of duality. You live spiritually, in the atmosphere of grace, is, amongst the natural/human man looking exactly like the natural man in form but expressing out from an entirely different conscious understanding of the world around them-spirit in form, God as all and not matter/material separate and apart from God in form and expression.

To rise in consciousness you must be a blessing to the world that comes into your consciousness.

Consciousness is the link between man and God.

If you live out from the consciousness of man you do not have the consciousness of God therefore you do not know the true God. But if you live out from the consciousness of God then you know God aright and no longer live as man.

The Word, Word of God means the consciousness of God. Consciousness of the presence of God within you is your link to God, is the means of contact whereby spiritual Truth works in and through you opening pathways, channels by which you become more and more aware of the kingdom of God already within you.

The missing link to God man has searched for outside of himself through ritual and sacrifice is within each individual as the consciousness of being I. To know thyself means to know what nature you express to the world as-man or spirit.

The kingdom of God is already within you but overlayed with centuries of materialistic thinking and living which has brought about a sense of separation from God. Not **a** separation rather a *sense* of separation.

Developing the connection between you and God is as simple, and as difficult, as sitting in the silence of your own being desirous to know Truth, not what man knows but what God knows. Ask and and it shall be given but again the warning: be careful what you wish for for wishes are of man, Truth is of God.

There are 2 Truths of God that are the basis of spiritual living, 2 things you most likely have never thought of. They are plain as day when you finally understand what is needed to understand the Bible.

1. God is only where there is conscious awareness of its presence. It is everywhere, omnipresent, but until the sleeper awakes-you-and you are aware of its presence **within your own being,** it can be of no benefit to you.
2. There are no powers of good and evil, there is only the belief in a power separate and apart from God because human man himself is separated from God and suffers that sin as duality, the consequences of the good and evil expressed as the life of human man of the world rather than living under grace in the kingdom of heaven in conscious oneness with God.

Man fights against powers that don't exist and that is the exact reason and understanding for "put up thy sword, resist not evil" because evil is no thing, nothing, unreal, illusion, maya, "this world" as Jesus called the world of man.

Are you beginning to see why there is only harmony and peace in the expression of spiritual man? Because spiritual man knows Truth: that all of what man experiences as reality, as error, sin, pain, lack, illness, fear etc, is the *effect of a belief* of being alone, unsupported, unknown, adrift with no freaking idea what it is supposed to be doing to become what it is supposed to become because it is no longer connected to source to know Truth so it fakes it til it makes it which is never.

Spiritual Truth reveals:

1. The nature of God-good/harmonious/**is**
2. The nature of prayer-meditation/communion/**inner listening**
3. The nature of man-**duality.** Ability to express more than one nature, ie emotion, attitude, good or bad thus subject to good and bad in their experience.
4. The nature of error-**illusion**, duality, opposites, carnal/mortal mind, universal hypnotism.

All error, individual or collective, of person or thing, is actually **no thing** meaning error/evil/bad/power has no objectivity ie has no source, no form, and no Law to support it because it is based on personal history and biases, *thoughts of the thinking mind,* and are nothing more than conjecture, illusion, rose colored glasses.

God is Truth, God is Law, Substance and Expression of all form.

You can only get from God what God **is.** You don't receive *material* things from God rather grace, God in action, appearing **as** the visible supply of man without any labor from you. The more you dwell with the Father in consciousness the less of the world you are entertaining and peace is a result of the time spent with the Father. When I first started my journey I thought to myself "this is going to be exhausting!" **But I was so wrong!**

To spend time with Father, to be in the consciousness of God merely means to **not** be in the consciousness of *man* therefore if your mind is still, nothing to chew on, worry about, fear or desire you are in God consciousness because your human mind is quiet, **waiting, expectant.** If you see everyone and everything around you as yourself, spirit in form, you are in God consciousness. If you encounter error and know error is the result of the thinking mind of man expressing their thoughts you are in God consciousness. If you ask God's grace to flow wherever you go, on errands, at work, at the drive through, at your favorite lunch stop you are in God consciousness. If you do these or things akin to these you are in God consciousness.

Being in God consciousness doesn't mean being in the meditative state for hours on end nor does it mean remembering scripture, reciting scripture or anything. Honestly there is so very little you have to do. In fact there is nothing for you to do but rest. Rest in the Truth of what you are to know of God, rest in the realization of the impartations you have or will be given, rest in the Truth that you are of God and by grace, the activity of God unto you, you have Life. Go to work, love your family, do your favorite things, explore, enjoy all that you would as human man and just be in the moment, present, open, receptive, observing, seeing, being and listening for that still small voice that is the light unto the path your feet shall take that carries you home completely free of humanity.

Truth: There is no selfishness in God therefore there can be no selfishness in you.

When you pray you pray for all to come under the governance of God you do not pray for one over another deeming one more deserving than another. Anything and everything that you do in the spiritual life is **only** for the glory of God because the only thing you can manifest and show forth is your oneness with God in demonstration.

You cannot use God for personal power, personal wants and desires. You are God's willing, desirous servant, you are under its will, its dominion, its governance and it is this deferment of personal will that allows you to live by grace. The minute you believe that the good of God you receive is yours, *of you,* because of how good *you* are you will lose your demonstration ie you will lose the grace of God and once more be living the duality of man.

God is for all and can only bless you if you are a benediction to others. If you believe you can pick and chose who gets God's abundance, grace, supply *you* will lose your demonstration of God because God is harmony for all not just those you deem deserving or worthy.

It is no different than an addict thinking they can cheat and not suffer. You cannot cheat God and you cannot hide from God. Nothing you do is in secret if God is your consciousness-what is done in secret will be shouted from the roof tops. This means nothing is ever a secret, it will appear outwardly as either God's grace or the error of man in your experience.

You can only walk one road if you want to get anywhere. This is the road. It is straight and narrow and few be that enter. My prayer for all is that there comes a time when the knowing of God becomes the desire for your life and in that desire return home as the prodigal son, back to the Father's house for all eternity, to rest in the arms of the Father now knowing what you desire isn't a *thing* but an **experience**.

Worldwide warfare against individuality, individual identity is against your relationship with God.

All of that which sets men in herds or unites them for a common *good* **is a denial of the spirit of individuality, is the denial of freedom to individual man.**

Governments want you to believe freedom comes *from* the government you are under, mass freedom *under* a ruler but there is only **one** freedom and it is **individual** not blanket. Freedom is dependent on **your** understanding of what freedom really is and it isn't what man thinks or experiences therefore man cannot live freely under rules that pretend to give man freedom.

The freedom man experiences is merely the neutral ground within boundaries/laws set by man for moral and ethical averaging of expression ie not good or bad but towing the party line, mass compliance which is the definition of mindlessness, a puppet of another, of being controlled, handled, no free will. And here you have stayed away from God because you didn't want to be controlled by an unseen force **and yet you live exactly how you don't want to live without even realizing it.**

Truth is a bomb and it explodes your reality, dissolves it into the nothingness it is to reveal true freedom is found only when you find God within which frees you from the false freedom of human living.

The God you know is the God you get.

If you know Truth you get the God within. If you know duality you continue to pray to a God that doesn't nor can ever exist and that is why all but a few prayers of *man* are ever answered.

Spiritual power is the realization of **your** name and nature: **I am** the individual expression of the one God within me that is the creator of all that is seen and unseen.

You must leave your nets-your dependence on the world for supply.

You must leave your mother and your father-universal mesmerism you have imbibed as reality.

You must put all your trust in God because that is the only Truth in which to put any trust.

Divine Love:

To be forgiven you must forgive yourself and others, you cannot go to God for freedom when you hold others in bondage and in this way only can you obtain forgiveness of your own errors.

What is divine love if not forgiveness? Isn't forgiving another and knowing you are forgiven the greatest feeling in the world? The greatest release and relief to your being? Does it not give one a second breath, a second look, a second chance? Is that not what God is? 70x7 you will be forgiven. Why? Because no matter what you do as a human nothing can keep you from God if you desire God over man.

The only thing that will keep you from God is the bondage you place on yourself and others and this bondage/inprisonment is enslavement to a pain, an injustice, a hurt, a transgression, lack, fear, disease, omission or commission. You must forgive as you would be forgiven for **only in forgiveness is there total and complete freedom of being** and that is what God is when it is known in awareness.

God is a willing choice.

It is a yielding of personal desires, a yielding of the personal self to be **receptive of spiritual guidance**. It is not an outlining and a determining of what *you* want or how you are to attain it, it is a complete yielding of oneself so that you may be the instrument through which a divine intelligence can operate bringing abundance and harmony into your expression.

There is no can't in this work, there is only that which you haven't attained the understanding of. To say you can't implies you are leaning on your own knowledge and not living by the consciousness of God otherwise it would be obvious you can have all that is of the Father because you are **of** the Father.

It isn't what goes into the mouth that defiles you/makes you impure/sinful it is what your consciousness of being reveals outwardly-you either bear witness as man of duality or man of spirit by how you express.

God doesn't care if you smoke or what you smoke, drink, eat rich foods or snack on crickets as long as your *dependence* is not on the things of the world but on God for all need. The more of God consciousness you imbibe, live in and express the less vices, proclivities, habits or substances attract you, demand your attention and soon they may not even be a part of you.

The point is this: God asks you give up **nothing** of your human ways except the belief in duality. All the rest comes in due time.

Do not think you must be pure before you present to God, God is the purity you already are, God just helps you uncover it and live it to its fullest.

Does that mean you will never partake of the things of the world? Of course not! A drink, a smoke, decadent foods may be part of how you enjoy life but **only** if you are not desirous, dependent or give it powers of good or bad or experience karma as a result.

Moderation in all, attachment to none.

God doesn't make you give stuff up, you desire less because God fills the emptiness that those things once **tried** to fill. I smoke and will continue to until God releases it from my consciousness which will allow the habit to just fade away with no fight, no resistance, no thought like every other erroneous expression that has left my awareness. Do I worry about my health? No, because rightly understood I have no health, no body of my own. I have the countenance of God dependent only on my living Truth in expression and in this consciousness of being I am not flesh and blood I am spirit in form as are you.

Understand: it isn't what goes in the body it is what comes *from* the mouth, that which you express *as* determines whether you should worry about *your* body or not.

If this doesn't instantly make clear sense sit with it and ask God to clarify because it is a **healing** principle being expressed and giving it to God to give back to you is the way you grow in conscious understanding of this new way of life. **Ask God. Always and only.** Don't worry if after a minute or so in the silence you have no feeling or awareness, go about your business. Come back later and ask again and just relax. It will come in perfect timing to illustrate and demonstrate it to you because what I find is when something catches my attention in the outer world, something odd or curious, that is when I get the aha moment. It is like what is being given as Truth within is exemplified by a snap shot of something in your awareness to drive the point home.

I was standing in Walmart waiting to get a prescription when an older lady locked eyes on me from 20 feet away, made a bee line for me and started to tell me the most incredible story of how her sister who is a well known heart surgeon gave her, the woman telling me this story, almost $70,000 for her birthday, this day. The joy I felt for this woman and the joy coming off of her still overwhelms me as I write this. She was behind in her bills, had a negative balance and then showed me, on the broken phone screen because she dropped it when she saw her new balance, the before and the after. She was just bursting with gratitude.

Did I know her? No. But I knew I was supposed to witness her. I finished my shopping and got back in the car and that is when God spoke. "That is what you are bringing to your community. Could you imagine more of you?" I freaking lost it, big ugly happy tears, cathartic and messy and so amazing! To know that my oneness with God had blessed someone so greatly was beyond imagination!

This is what I mean when I say what you get from God, the gift that **is** the Father, **must** be **experienced** to be understood. When you are happier seeing someone else happy than if you had been the one receiving you know Truth, abundance and the infinite nature there of.

The feeling of God becomes the one addiction you can have, the singular desire you as spiritual man are allowed to embrace and in doing so bless yourself beyond measure and bring grace to bear where you are, the town you live in, the streets you drive. No it is not a physical thing per se but when you are driving around talk to God, "hey Father, let's spread some love!" And you are connected with Source and sharing grace wherever you go and out into universal consciousness.

Just think of all those looking for what you have found able to receive it because you know it and are sharing it! This is how the light of Truth spreads dispelling darkness, duality from the minds of man so they too may know perfect peace.

God cannot operate when the mind is active thus God cannot be found in the mind.

Man is praying with their mind using *words* and *thoughts* instead of **listening** within their being to **receive** Truth.

Every person who finds God within makes it more attainable for others to find God. You are a source, an outlet for grace to flow from to awaken others. Your purpose and your job as willing instrument of God in a nut shell is to:

1. Find God, good/harmony
2. Want God, good/harmony
3. Learn God through prayer and practice
4. Share God/good/harmony
5. Reap God, good/harmony
6. Live eternally with God, good/harmony

The seeker and the sought are one (in the same).

The principle of healing works without you taking thought, without you making statements, without you doing mental work-affirmations/denials-and without you begging or pleading or beseeching God. It operates completely without what the metaphysical world calls treatment ie knowing Truth.

The healing principle is a state of peace you achieve through the realization of the presence of God.

This is the spiritual form of prayer-just the abiding in the silence, experiencing peace because you are of that peace, God consciousness.

Once you have been on this path for a while you are more often than not in the consciousness of God, just chilling inside, not thinking of the things of the world, not stressing or worrying or rushing, but just being in the silence knowing God is right there.

In this consciousness of oneness you heal automatically. You don't have to do anything to bring God on the field because God is always on the field when you are **of** its consciousness. You don't need a click, you don't need a feeling or experience as your relationship with the Father deepens because those things show you God is, but you already know God is and are just hanging in the silence with your best friend.

Truth is given only to those who seek it and those who seek Truth never fail to find it.

The spirit draws everything necessary for your unfoldment to you.

God is the one/single/only source and expression of all that is therefore the Law of God is the only Law in activity therefore there cannot be any *other* **Law.** Understand **Law** is **God** and *law* is *man's* rules and regulations.

The *material* laws or *laws* of matter ie laws of *man*-of weather, age, infection and contagion, sin, lack and disease-only operate on the *physical* and *mental* levels of life but the moment you come to the **spiritual** level in which you recognize God as infinite being you nulify the *belief* there are *laws* of matter or laws of mind. The reason you can be certain *laws* of *matter* and *laws* of *mind* are not the **Law** of **God** is:

All material and mental laws can be expressed as/used for good or evil.

There is no duality in God, God **is.** There is no such thing as a degree of good, there is no such thing as evil in the **Life** or **Law** of God therefore wherever you find the pairs of opposites, the good and the evil, the would do, should do, the better for me worse for you scenarios, you are thinking, using the mind, which is always *man* and not **God.**

If you take the time to think of a solution you are of duality because you are thinking to make a choice, this or that, me or them, good or bad, moral or immoral, win or lose, better or worse. However if you observe what is presenting and let God speak within you as to what is really being witnessed you are living in conscious union with God **because you are letting God tell you, you aren't reacting to what** *you* **think is going on.**

The very moment you rise above using thoughts and beliefs to justify your life, fuel your actions and existence as little i, personality and begin to rest and receive you are of the atmosphere of God where you know you cannot die, you do not *get* by your own hand or mind that which is needed to support your life rather you are supported by God, that which you are **of** therefore by becoming one in consciousness with it you are **of** it and no longer separated from Truth, good, harmonious expression.

Understand you job is to give of grace at every opportunity so that God can be present with those in need open to the understanding behind what is going on through intuition, knowing, God within. It is not your job to do for another in any physical or material/financial way unless it is given from within to do. You as child of God heal but are in no way responsible for anything other than your own expression by which you help those who desire to rise above duality, humanhood. You give all man the opportunity to live harmoniously knowing Truth by you living Truth in expression and healing error.

Revelations/mystical Truth are not just pretty sayings, they are Law in every case. Violation brings consequences upon you. You are never punished **for** your sins but *by* the sins you commit by choosing man's chaos over God's harmony.

Revelations are given and passed on to enlighten others, not made up by me or other mystics. They are received, that is how Truth comes into outward expression, and it is the Truth of God from God to bring peace to the heart of man, rest to the weary and salvation if the opportunity is taken to know what changed and where it came from-within.

Truth is not a discussion.

There is nothing to discuss about Truth because I have no opinion of it, it **is** to me and nothing I can say will make it so to you, only you can facilitate that through your own desire to know more.

Truth does not lend itself to discussion because Truth **is.** There are many spiritual Truths but not one single one of them lends itself to discussion. We give of the Truth we have to share but there is nothing to discuss, no what if or why for's. What is **is.** 2x2 is 4. **Is.** What is there to discuss about **is?** Is talking about is going to change is into something else? No. Spiritual principles are Law, never change, never stop being.

Man's laws are *words,* ever changing/personal, *subjective* not **objective** therefore not **Law** unto the universe as man would think them to be rather judgment, duality, cause and effect with no God involved merely human morality and conduct.

Truths are always revealed within you in a way you understand.

You do not receive Truth from a person, a book or a lecture. What comes to you by way of another is **their** revealed Truth they are sharing for you to **contemplate in the silence.** That which you don't understand is easily taken into the kingdom, the inner sanctuary of your being where you ask for understanding, explanation, an example and let God unfold the answer to you. In this way what was taken in as another's Truth has become your revealed Truth because God spoke Truth to you. Now it is yours, it was revealed to you and now can be shared because you have experienced it, it is real to you, it is your Truth forever and always to lean on.

Mortal man only knows what is sensed outside of him but spiritual man knows the unseen, the within therefore each looks at the same thing from a different perspective, **a different state of conscious understanding.**

Understanding consciousness can be confusing because man has never been taught of consciousness because consciousness involves listening not talking so in essence it is a new concept, you are becoming aware of a part of you you did not know as a part of your being because consciousness to man merely means being awake, conscious **not** expression of being.

Spiritual man is **aware** of being **of** all that is and expresses from this consciousness of wholeness which is the expression of harmony, peace and love because what other than contentment can wholeness and allness of being express as?

Face value for a spiritual man is always experienced through the consciousness of harmony thereby knowing any error/discord/sin/inharmony in their experience is not of their making, is not personal, of them rather it is the atmosphere of human man who wants and needs thereby expressing to the world in a way they feel will return what it is they want, need or deserve.

Human man isn't reacting to you personally; what you are witness to/experiencing is not *because* of you **rather it is human man expressing his helplessness to resolve the errors of his life** and is letting the poison created by those unresolved errors infect those they encounter. Man is only reacting to the circumstances they set in motion by their own choices instead of listening for God to be released once and for all from the burdens of self to live free in God, Self.

When you understand error in all its forms to be nothing more than *personal* fear or desire expressing, both of which are creations of the *mind* and have no objectivity or Law to support them, you are then able to start dying daily/healing the errors you encounter thereby lessening the chaos of your own experience.

What this means is every time something bad is sensed, seen or heard you do not react according to human standards of contempt, ridicule, grandeur, sympathy, empathy, pity etc, rather you keep your lips zipped and await the Truth you know will come and the error will soon be dispelled from your awareness because your focus is in with God and not out with man and appearances.

When you experience error do not let it affect your inner peace because that allows the *false* expressions, illusions to alter your state of being when you are working daily to see past false illusions to **is.** This takes practice and nothing is going to happen to you when you mess up except possibly some duality meaning if you react humanly *then* remember Truth you will need to apologize for judging, apologize for not remembering Truth before adding your two cents.

I just went through this with my son; I let him have five cents of my mind. My mind not God's. And I had egg on my face and dirt on my knees; I judged and reacted and then had to make amends. If I had rested and just let God do its harmony ... hind sight. That is all there is to this life, learning not to make personal comments/judging rather rest in the Truth you know of God and the *feeling* of inharmony will leave because Truth, peace, God **is** felt within you.

If you do mess up go within and talk to God and get the peace you should have reached for before running the mouth. We all mess up on this path no matter how far along the key is getting right with Self as soon as you can which is usually right when you press the send button! Oh crap, that was human lol.

It is a new way of thinking and you have to remind yourself each time error presents until it becomes your nature which is why you practice. You are not pretending poverty, illness, greed, power etc, do not exist, they do exist and have real consequences for those who *believe* there is power in and can suffer from the perceived good and bad forces in the world outside of their control.

It is the consciousness of God that allows you to navigate this life smoothly and abundantly. If you know you are the child of God then you know you lack nothing and are protected from the fear of lack in any form because your consciousness is not of man but God. Therefore when you experience or are witness to the errors of man's *thinking* you do not get down in the dumps with them rather lift them by healing the situation by bringing God into awareness, grace in your midst.

The reason you know error is not real is because God has imparted Truth to you that clearly defines God's world from man's world and in the knowing of this Truth you can see, though it does take time to accept Truth that is taking away your deep beliefs, **that the errors man encounters are completely of his own making by the way his mind judges and reacts to outer stimuli.**

Man's mind labels everything by putting it into categories according to good and bad, safe or unsafe. But what you put into one category I might put into another so how can something be both good and bad at the same time? It cannot. At its base or core everything **is.**

Let's use alcohol for an example. For some it's evil, horrible because they or another they know have had circumstances in their lives stemming from alcohol that have been unsavory but for others alcohol is just something to have occasionally and is enjoyable. So you can see the alcohol itself has no qualities of good or bad. It just is therefore how it is viewed is the *judgment* which is the *error* of man giving *power* to that which has no power, no Law. If it did then it would be bad for all or good for all because Law is all or nothing, always, unchangeable, is.

Once man judges something one way or the other it is being viewed in the context of good or bad. Your neighbor is just your neighbor. Man may qualify them as a difficult neighbor or a good neighbor. But a difficult neighbor can become a good neighbor and a good neighbor can become a difficult neighbor.

However if you **know** the Truth of your neighbor regardless of their outward appearance or action then no neighbor and no thing can ever be viewed as other than is or harmonious because you are looking at it from its creative base of God, Truth-all is God in substance and form.

Ceremony and rituals of modern religion veil the Truth.

The Truth lies **hidden** in the ceremony and ritual awaiting your discovery by seeing through the *appearance* of what is being done, the ritual, to the **Truth** behind/of the ritual.

Orthodox religions have watered down Truth by covering it up with actions/ceremonies that entice human man into coming to see a show not receive Truth. Man must be entertained, enticed to do something therefore the songs, the performances, the lights, the largest of churches is nothing more than to get people to come to fill their coffers with money instead of coming to know God aright. The reason? Not more than a handful throughout the world know Truth therefore the rest proselytize *beliefs* as Truth trying to find God in the ceremonies of man.

This isn't to say don't go to church. Go to church, enjoy the atmosphere and the people therein but do not partake of the *duality* preached rather go as a beacon of Truth silent, secret and sacred to bring grace to bear where grace should already be and in this way you are healing those who have congregated for the purpose of receiving Truth whether that is their known intention or their soul seeking.

Now:

To live oneness in the atmosphere of God you must live in the present moment. The past doesn't exist and the future is merely a now moment a little beyond this moment but all time is NOW.

There is no mark of time in the kingdom of heaven, in God's awareness for there is only the now. Whatever life you are living **now** is the only now you have any control over. Time is a human construct and has nothing to do with God. God is now. So if the only time is now what you are conscious of now-consciously being/living/understanding-is what you will be conscious of being/living/understanding when tomorrow is now.

Therefore if you want a different tomorrow than you are living today you must change your **now** to change your tomorrow. Everything is now so if you begin to walk the spiritual path now then two weeks from now you will embody more of God consciousness/awareness which will present itself to you as a higher awareness now.

The understanding that needs to be clear is you cannot hope for a better tomorrow because there is only now. So if you want a better tomorrow you have to chose to be different *now*.

All the "I'll be nicer *next* time", or "I'll do the right thing *next* time" or "I'll be more loving/kind/considerate *tomorrow*" creates exactly what tomorrow will hold-all the lack of yesterday because you cannot change the future, you can only change the now. The now becomes the now *later* so who you are now is who you are tomorrow unless your today is other than it was yesterday.

Yes this sounds like the old joke "whose on first" but this is key to successful spiritual living so if you don't get it just come back to it every now and again and at some point it will click and you will follow the understanding easily because you are at the higher consciousness needed to understand it, you just weren't ready for it until you were ie you were not expected to understand it at your previous level of conscious knowing of Truth.

This is all of spiritual life. If it doesn't stick don't worry about it just circle back, give it a little try on again and go about your business. It will come, it has to come because your ascension back to the full consciousness of God is Law unto your being.

Man *believes* in God with their *mind,* what they *think* God is, but you can only **know** the Truth of God through an absence of thought because God is not found in the thinking mind but in the silence behind the thinking mind where Truth is given to you from the source of Truth, God, consciousness.

You can however think Truth to get your mind off of an error that has captured your attention enough to treat yourself for it by getting silent and waiting for God to come onto the field to prove that what is of the world is illusion and all that is real is within you revealed by its presence.

The activity of Truth in your consciousness is the light which dispels the darkness of human sense. It is not what you *think* is Truth but what Truth **declares** to you from within, not what you *tell* God but what God **reveals** to you.

This is the power of silence.

In quietness and confidence, in stillness and silence Love reveals its comforting presence and assures you that **underneath all are the everlasting arms** upholding and supporting you, even in trail and tribulation for at any point of sin or sorrow you can turn within and find that which will bring harmony.

Silence is the creative principle of existence.

In the silence the Christ of your being speaks to the Christ of another since the Christ of your being is the Christ of another's being for all are of one Source. In the silence you become receptive to the inner voice, the voice of Self and as Truth expresses itself in your listening ear you become aware of the healing influence with signs following. You can never be God but because God is inseparable from your very being you are **of** the nature and expression of God therefore the qualities and quantities of God as well.

The healing principle, what brings healing, is a state of peace you achieve through the realization of the Presence.

This is the spiritual form of prayer-just the realization of the Presence, just the feeling of a state of peace because that is the Truth of you.

You remain in communion, silent receptivity, until a sense of peace steals over you, a sense of peace which comes from but one recognition:

I am with you. I will never leave you nor forsake you. I, in the midst of you, am mighty. My presence will go before you to make the crooked places straight. I will go before you to prepare a place for you. There are many mansions in my kingdom (level of conscious knowing), My peace I give unto you not as the world giveth but a peace transcending man's comprehension, a peace that comes when the Christ is enthroned in your consciousness as the source of your health and supply.

No other peace can be lasting except the peace that comes when the Christ is enthroned as the only presence, being, expression, power back of individual experience.

You can only heal on the level of your consciousness and that is why all healing modalities based in thought/on mind/man are doomed to fail in the long run because only the consciousness of God as your consciousness begets healing because the definition of spiritual healing is **God in awareness.**

Only that which is not **of** the problem can solve/heal the problem ie **you cannot solve a problem on the level of the problem** therefore you cannot solve human problems with human solutions because all humans have an agenda, a desire loaded in their favor therefore there will never be harmony, just a winner and a loser.

Therefore to have a true healing, to receive harmony and peace, it must be spiritually based, of consciousness and result in harmony for all involved thus solving the problem by realizing the nothingness/the non power of error and grace comes on the scene.

When you leave this visible experience the only thing that goes with you is you, your consciousness, who you know yourself to be. What you attain in consciousness in this life is the **foundation** of your next experience. You are storing up spiritual treasure, God knowing, not trying to build up *material* wealth which is not of God. You are establishing an understanding that **the spiritual principles which you learn, the Truth of God, is your protection, your companionship, your profession, your security, your supply, your peace, harmony and love.**

When the principles of Truth are lived as your expression they reveal freedom and liberty to you and to every individual who awakens to them.

Spiritual principles, when applied to self ie treatment and practicing the presence, bring into expression new forms of music, art, literature, inventions and scientific discovery for the benefit and enjoyment of all mankind which results in abundance, joy, prosperity and ease of life.

The major reason for living a spiritually focused, spiritually led life is to bring forth greater beauty, greater harmony than this world has ever known and bring it through from every direction.

Son, all I have is thine, not money but Life, wisdom, love, peace and dominion over the world of man, duality. In Thy presence the earth melteth-duality is revealed in its nothingness and the grace of God is brought to bear bringing with it the only Truth you ever need to know: God is and God is within you.

This returns you to the kingdom, to the knowing of God, the flow of universal spiritual perfection and the allness of heaven on earth. This is your Truth and the sooner you feel it within your being the sooner you begin to experience peace and prosperity man of earth is still searching for outside of himself.

Metaphysics, Mysticism and Manifesting

Like most I couldn't understand the Bible because I didn't have the understanding of God within, oneness, **I**, Self and *i,* self, personality, i, me, mine. Once I had my mystical experience, became aware of God within, the Bible began to pour its meaning out to me on a level never experienced as God brought the words alive in inner communion.

The Bible reveals the story of man as man of duality of the Old Testament to the story of man as risen spirit **in the example of** Jesus the Christ, the risen son of God in **expression** to show all that they too can awaken their individual Christ and be **like** Jesus the Christ ie ordained to heal the sick, feed the hungry and raise the dead.

It is context you are missing-you have to know **who is speaking or is referenced when I is spoken about** in both the Old and New Testaments, who God is to you and where God is before the Bible makes sense because without knowing who you are the Bible seems to be talking about a God outside of you. Until you know who you are in relationship to the Father that which is being read reveals nothing of your Truth of being rather is a confusing collection of long ago stories that seemingly have no connection to present life.

The human experience of life, the expressions and emotions of duality are the same as they were 5000 years past and will be hence unless God becomes known to you, then to others and then to the world. Individual awareness is the only way to attain universal awareness and universal awareness is when all children have risen back to the kingdom knowing conscious oneness with God living their Truth-spirit in form, deathless, ageless, timeless.

There have been mystics all down the ages but it is only now that an important understanding has been revealed. Mystics of the past found the God within by trial and error, tapped into God and knew it but didn't know **how** they did what they did to have the experience again and again **by which to have a relationship,** have direct communication with God and as such couldn't teach it because they didn't know what part of their spiritual practice produced the realization of the Truth within.

That which has been the missing piece to understanding God and living a spiritual life receiving the abundance set forth for God's children is:

1. Conscious awareness of the presence within as that of God and in this knowing of God as Self the union is formed 1+1=1, wholeness, Self completeness, oneness, union with Source, your true nature and expression.
2. By this conscious understanding of oneness you live in the kingdom/consciousness of God here on earth, living among mortal man calling no attention to oneself but silently, secretly and sacredly correcting error and releasing God's healing grace to the world.
3. In this inner contact all reality of being is received and the Truth of error, all error is revealed to be caused by the *universal belief in separation from God*
4. **Only as you become consciously aware of the presence of God does the presence of God function within you.**
5. It is only your acceptance of God, your conscious realization of God through an actual experience of God that allows God to function in **your** life, be **your** life, do **your** life with you just doing what you are needed to do through impartation and the rest of the time enjoy your family, your work and your relationship with God.

This is mysticism and the way of the mystic, you when you are in conscious oneness with God living revealed Truth.

Living in a mystical/spiritual world:

Mysticism is the belief you can know God through an actual experience of meeting the Father face to face within your own being and a mystic is one who lives the outward expression of their inner union with God continually fed/illumined by prayer ie inner listening/communion. Mystical knowledge, illumination, Truth, is attainable through **immediate intuition** or insight and in this way **differs** from ordinary *sense* perception ie the *thinking* mind thinking.

The difference is simple when understood: **that which is of God drops in, swoops in, comes unbidden, mike drop.** My work here is done for the moment, signed, God. It is these moments of aha! The feeling of peace that takes away your worry, it is the response/words that were not of you and were perfect. God is that which is not you but **of** you, gives **of** itself to help you make sense of this world, to make life easier, to know how to have life eternal and have a freaking blast along the way!

The mystical message of the ages, independent of race, color, creed or religion, is the same-**you can and you are supposed to have a personal relationship with God, creation, creator of your**

expression. The language or mode of approach may be different but the message and goal-the attainment of conscious union with God-never changes.

No one can become a seeker of God in his humanhood but when God touches a person to some measure of awakening that person is led to find some kind of spiritual teaching which leads unerringly to that one goal. Nothing can equal the fascination and adventure of the mystical life, it is a life of discoveries which forever lay ahead of you, never behind. You may have had an experience yesterday that lifted you up to the top of the mountains but you cannot live on yesterday's manna, money, occurrences, emotions etc. No matter how great or soul stirring it may have been, it is only a **preparation** for the greater ones that lie ahead.

Metaphysics:

A branch of philosophy defined as the study/theorization of things that are theorized, hypothesized but unable to be proven scientifically ie that which is not seen but is felt to exist.

Even if man were able to prove the unseen *scientifically* it would only be proven to the *intellectual* capacity of the smartest *man* in the field thus still not at all about the unseen rather what is *thought* about the unseen. The things of **God** are nonsense to man and always will be as man cannot understand that which is spiritual, of a completely different state of conscious understanding, invisible to the senses but real to those who have experienced this higher state of consciousness man calls God within their own being.

Metaphysics is supported by *logical argument* and this is why metaphysics cannot reveal the Truth of the unseen/the mystical because they are trying to use *human logic* to unlock the **Truth** of spirituality/the unseen. Apples and oranges. Man will never understand the unseen because logic is of the human mind and Truth is of God.

To understand the unseen you must use a different toolbox from which to work and this is the difference between man and spiritual man. Man works from the toolbox of many tools from good to bad, spiritual man only has one thing in his toolbox-God/good/harmony.

To understand the unseen you have to **be** the Unseen.

To be the Unseen is to not see the world around you as your senses impart it to you. To be the Unseen is to close your eyes and rest in that place you sense, can feel like an openness, spaciousness behind closed eyes. This place within is the unseen of you isn't it? You sense this place/space within your head/mind/behind the eye area of your being and when you close your eyes you are teleported there, to that place.

In this place is quietness and peace. Nothing can enter this sacred place completely separate from man's world, it is unseen and no man of earth knows where you go when you close your eyes. Human man sees the chaos he has created behind closed lids because he brings what he experiences in life within. Man's mind is thinking, visioning, working, cranking, rarely quiet.

The unseen is not in the thinking mind but behind it, where human thought drops off and there is stillness, an emptiness. Not stillness of thought through trying but stillness/lack of the outer world of you. The world is still doing what it is doing around you but within you have a place, a refuge of stillness, a sacred place all to yourself to enjoy the company of your new best friend. It is a place you can visit only when you are focused on being there. Where? In the quiet place within to be with God.

This runs in the background of you, like your chaotic mind used to run in the background. But now it is quiet because you are with God in consciousness instead of with man jumbling up your mind. It is merely a spin of the dial to a different station to listen to. The station of man that is like nails on a chalk board or God within where thoughts come in and thoughts go out but they are not yours or of the world outside but a secret conversation that is your meat, your wine and your water, the sustenance, food that satisfies and you begin to live in that happy place like a person with a new puppy, go ahead, try to take me out of this happy place, I dare you kind of happy place.

Why? Man cannot find peace because man can't be quiet in the mind for more than a few seconds before it begins to feel *empty and uncomfortable* and they once again begin thinking, chewing, stewing and planning.

Silent, sacred and secret is a principle of mystical living and to live with God you have to learn to abide where God is, in the silence of the sacred secret place within that is the Truth of you, in the place behind the thinking mind where Truth drops in from God and not thought by you.

This is the easiest way to understand God's impartations-they come to you from within you, the proverbial mike drop. Boom. There ya go. And you melt because the peace, Truth, allness wrapped up in that single communication has removed duality from you and are now knowing Truth instead of unreality.

To live the mystical life you must take away the mystery connected with the word mysticism.

The problem isn't with the word rather its humanly defined meaning. For years only one of the major dictionaries carried the true definition of mysticism.

The real meaning of mysticism can be found in Webster dictionary. **Mysticism is any teaching that teaches direct or the ability to have direct communion with God.** The ability to pray to God and to receive answer. The ability to have direct contact with God and this does include Christianity because Christianity as understood from the Truth revealed in the New Testament is by definition mysticism-to pray and get answers, communion, to be in direct contact with God.

91st Psalm: He that dwelleth in the secret place of the most High shall abide under the shadow of the Almighty. He with the consciousness of the most High receives of all that is of the Almighty. You commune within yourself at the center of your being at the seat of creation to learn how to be in this place aright, knowing the rules, the whys and wherefores.

To live the mystical life it becomes necessary to understand the part you play in the experience. The Master Christ Jesus taught throughout his whole ministry how to prepare for the experience of meeting the Father within. He taught the need for **prayer** (inner communion with God, listening attitude, not talking or thinking), meditation, going off to commune inwardly.

He taught you cannot add to a vessel already full, that you must purify the temple of your being in order to make room for God to enter. **Purity is not the purity of man but the purity of God.** To be pure in God's knowing is to forgive as you would be forgiven, be benevolent, charitable, be comfort, etc. share food and clothing, serve even the least of these my brethren. Heal the sick, feed the hungry, release/heal error and you **must** free all those you have held in bondage and help to free those holding themselves in bondage.

Your first responsibility of living the mystical life is the **preparation.** When you think back on the woman asking to be healed note how she looked up at the Master. This is preparation, **expecting** something of the Christ therefore her consciousness was prepared for the Christ to enter, purify and release her from the bondage of the world ie **release her from the belief of being separated from God** and in this emptiness of being was made whole once again, perfect in every way no longer of the expression of the *belief* she bore the burden of that caused her to seek God through the worldly expression of God-Jesus the Christ.

Therefore the Master standing there endowed with spiritual expression could do nothing for her until she looked up and virtually created a vacuum within herself in declaring her helplessness/

hopelessness of the situation, that of herself she could do nothing more to remedy her situation but in the **recognition** of the spiritual nature of **his** mission came to him **empty of self** and in that very instant was **prepared** to receive that which she desired-to be made whole, complete and perfect by knowing Truth and through expectancy of the spirit being upon her received the spirit upon her.

The thief on the cross prepared himself by his very recognition of the Christ beside him, by the very recognition that the Christ had power to stave off death and take him into heaven that night. This was acknowledgment, recognition, preparedness/readiness for different than death. Yes! I want that! I give you myself if that is my reward!

As you study scripture of all known mystics there is always preparation before the experience. The life of Gautama that became the Buddha prepared mostly in the wrong direction but sitting under the bohdi tree resting in silence in an attitude of expectancy all night was preparing himself, readying his consciousness for the revelation that came and has become the Buddhist religion of millions.

Read the experiences of the scripture and you will always find a period of **preparation** and that period enables you to receive/accept the spirit which brings with it purification, forgiveness and healing.

The key to this entire spiritual life is this:

God is your individual consciousness and that is why the place whereon thou standeth is holy ground. God is your very consciousness therefore God at all times is closer to you than breathing, nearer than hands and feet.

All that you have to do to receive God is to close your eyes and right there within your consciousness is the kingdom of God because your individual consciousness **is** the access to the whole of infinity. All of it, immortality, eternality, infinite good, abundance etc, is available to you in the very space you occupy.

Your access to infinity is through your own consciousness.

Even the woman taken in adultery did not have to go outside herself to recognize and acknowledge the Christ. For the thief there were no years of punishment or repentance. "No, I will take you to heaven this night" was the Master's benediction as it will be for you.

Intellectual knowledge of God vs. knowing God:

Metaphysical vs. Mystical

You do not memorize spiritual words, you do not remember them to bring up for general conversation rather you take them within and let God bring forth the Truth unto **your** being. You do not live on *words,* someone else's Truth, you live on the **awareness** of Truth from within.

Trying to understand spirit through the intellect makes it an absolute impossibility to arrive at a satisfactory understanding because the subject deals with contradictions in scripture and no one who has tried to figure it out with the mind, with reason, with intellect has come to any satisfactory conclusion.

The secret of life lies in right identification as **Self** not *self.* Knowing your true identity changes intellectual *knowledge,* philosophy, to absolute **Truth** and reality byway of an actual experience of your name and nature revealed within your own being as I am.

The search for the holy grail has been the search for God and it has been a failure until that person came **home** in consciousness and there Truth was revealed: **I am that I am.**

The purpose of metaphysical treatment understood is the development of spiritual consciousness or the conscious awareness of the presence of God within.

A mystic is one who has a personal relationship by way of an actual experience of the presence of God within their own consciousness and now lives in oneness with this presence man calls God.

Mystical teachings reveal man's true nature of being as spirit. That which brings conscious awareness of God where it can be active in your life and the life of others is what is called treatments/revealing Truth/healing.

The **secret** of healing is not in the mysticism but in the **metaphysical Truth,** the written Truth already out in the world. Metaphysical Truth is the written Truth of God which when taken into the silence will lead to the **mystical experience** in which one finds complete spiritual freedom.

Mystics like Jesus who knew this principle could say to Pilate "Thou couldest have no power over me lest it were give to thee of God." **What you just read is a metaphysical Truth,** it is Truth **received** by Jesus from God stating the Truth of God.

You have to understand what God is to have union with God. You know what God is byway of metaphysical Truth which **allows** you to have the **mystical** experience in which you meet the Father face to face which begins the **personal relationship** you are supposed to have with the Father within.

Metaphysics is the study of the unseen but it is still in the realm of man because the mind is being used. **Mysticism** is the conscious knowing of God by way of an actual experience of God within your own being and has nothing to do with the mind of man or man at all.

Knowing Truth is what allows for the mystical experience that rises man from that of mortal man to that of spiritual man not by degree but out of one into another, completely separate states of conscious knowing. *Man* only knows man, the things of man and a **mystic** is one who **knows** God by way of an **actual experience of God** and this Truth, God is and God is within every man, reveals the nothingness of man's duality, of the belief in good and bad caused by *believing* you are separated from God.

Metaphysical Truth is the *written* Truth of God, is what has been given to mystics from God for you to take into the silence to get understanding straight from God. It is this act of **listening** that allows you to **receive** Truth from within that bears witness to the metaphysical Truth you read.

This is mysticism. It is the taking in of Truth to receive Truth unto you that you can stand on because it was **given** to you not *read* by you. If you know Truth you can bring Truth to bear. If you don't know Truth you cannot bring Truth to bear. You can know the words but the words do nothing if they aren't preparation for the experience of God in awareness to reveal Truth, God is and God is within you.

Spouting words does not bring God to bear; listening for God in the silence and abiding by what is given is what allows God to function in your life.

Ordination:

Man's ordination of clergy and other holy people is **not** the ordination of God but of man. Man determines when other man have reached a sufficient understanding of man's *interpretation* of God to spread the fallacy to others. The ordination of man means nothing because you cannot be ordained by God for that which you have no understanding of because that understanding **only comes from an actual experience of the Father within.**

This and only this is true spiritual ordination, the mystical experience, it is the passing from man to spirit in conscious understanding of Self and that is what ordains you, gives you the **permission** to be a servant of God knowing Truth and releasing it to free all of humanity from its universal hypnotism in the belief there are two powers in this world that must be mitigated, avoided or controlled in a way that makes you feel you are in control of your life.

All religions of today are nothing more than spouting what is *thought* of God with no **knowing** of God therefore religion practiced in this way is nothing more than philosophy, *what is thought about God*, not Truth, **knowing God through an actual experience of God in awareness.**

What is *thought* of God, what is theorized and hypothesized of all that is unseen and unknown is called *metaphysics* which is a branch of *philosophy* because it is the *supposition* of what is unknown.

That which spiritual man uses to learn about God is called *metaphysical* **Truth,** the Truth of mystics given to the world so others can take that Truth into silent contemplation to receive Truth straight from the source of Truth. **When you receive an answer from within you have had the mystical experience** and what has been given is now Truth unto you because **Truth spoke it to you.** This is the difference between *metaphysical* and **mystical** but to have the mystical you must study the metaphysical to prime your consciousness so to speak. It is the segway from human man of thinking to the listening man of God.

Metaphysics is the general term for the *academic* study of what is unknown/unseen/invisible and not to be confused with Metaphysical **Truth** which is written **Truth** ie the red letter words of the Bible, mystical poetry etc, that makes no sense to the *human* mind because what is given is of the **consciousness of God** not the *thinking mind of man*.

It is only when you desires to rise above the consciousness of human man that you will rise in conscious knowing to find God and become a mystic, one who has seen the face of the Father. **This is the purpose of Truth,** to rouse you from the confines of your finite human life to live the infinity of Life already within yourself.

Mysticism:

All mystical teachings at their base are revealed Truth through **conscious union with God,** ie realized oneness. It is an actual experience of God's presence within as the Truth unto your being that makes you a mystic but **being a mystic does not mean you are a healer or under grace; it is a designation of conscious understanding and nothing more.**

To be more than an empty designation you must be active, **doing** what a mystic does-heal error and bringing grace to bear where there was none. Therefore a healing mystic is one **living** true Christianity because they are **knowing** Truth and knowing the Truth of error and doing what they are ordained to do as mystics-heal the sick, feed the hungry and raise the dead as Jesus the Christ was ordained to do.

Mysticism:

Mysticism acknowledges that everything in the visible realm comes forth from the invisible. Everything that is visible is an expression **of** the invisible and that is why there is no *matter/material* world of things separate and apart from God when you understand **God is as all.**

I am that I am: what it means:

Every person must come to the place of "I am that I am." This **is** the definition of the word **mystic,** one in conscious union with God, realized oneness with God and the actual experience of God-conscious awareness of its presence within you, felt, communed with and rested upon for the things of God-its wisdom, peace, patience, benevolence, supply, understanding.

Mysticism is the **practical application** of this union to bring about a life lived with God as God's expression to the world. Every mystic that walks the spiritual path knows and reveals through silent meditation, prayer and treatment that I am that I am. I am **of** God in form, maintained and sustained **by** God, eternal Self perpetuation of harmonious expression.

Mystic-one who has oneness with God

There is only one **mystical** teaching-mysticism-and it is based on you having conscious union with God, realized oneness, have had the actual experience of the presence of God.

Metaphysical Truth is *written* Truth which will lead to mysticism, the mystical experience, the awareness of the presence of God within which reveals man's true nature as spirit.

In this oneness with spirit you are called a mystic, one who has conscious knowing of the unseen, invisible Truth of all existence.

Metaphysics is a major branch of philosophy and it concerns the nature of and relationship between the visible and the invisible. The *metaphysical idea* is that reality exists independently of one's (thinking) mind yet can be known. This is true because you do not know Truth, reality with your *mind* but through your **consciousness.**

The only reality is that of God and to be of this reality, the real of Life, you must be aware of God's presence expressing itself through you as you and see the world through the only Law of expression there is-the spiritual law of **is** that has no opposite therefore has no competition, is, only.

Metaphysical-Greek-meta ta physika, "after the things of nature" referring to an idea, doctrine, or posited reality outside of human *sense* perception. In modern philosophical terminology metaphysics refers to the study of what cannot be reached through objective studies of material reality ie *it is a study of what isn't visible by way of the thinking mind that cannot **know** the invisible* and why to man it is *philosophy* and not **Truth.** Man is trying to understand the unseen using the wrong tool-the mind, instead of the correct tool-inner listening through conscious awareness.

Mystic

One who has had the **experience** of God within by which to develop a personal relationship with God, the unseen and only source of creation and expression of all that is.

Metaphysics is the *study* of the unseen which to us on the spiritual path is the study of God. Metaphysics is of man's intellect and is the *study and supposition* of the unseen whereas the next step is **mysticism** which is the **experience** of the unseen, having had an experience of God within as a manifest reality. Remember words only take on importance as they become imbued in your consciousness and their meaning becomes Truth to you.

The purpose of **treatment** metaphysically understood, is the development of spiritual consciousness or the conscious awareness of that which is invisible. This is done byway of resting with Truths like the red letter words of the Bible, Truth all, in silence and **await** Truth from God as to the Truth you took into meditation or contemplation before silent anticipation of a response.

Taking a Truth into meditation before silence helps you get more grounded in the consciousness of God because you are resting on the things of God and not of man and the world. Bringing in Truth is priming the pump for good results because it releases you from man and puts you squarely within yourself where the real party happens.

You cannot read the Bible with your mind because it wasn't written by a mind or through a mind. The entire message of the New Testament is a transcendental message that came through transcendental consciousness. It was imparted to Matthew, Mark, Luke, John, Paul, James, Simon Peter and Jude among others for them to write down and because it came **from** the source of consciousness it **is** revealed Truth from the source of Truth.

This is why most people do not understand the Bible. They are trying to read that which is in a different language, the language of soul, of God, of a consciousness of harmony that is unknown to man therefore they *read* the words, try to string together a human interpretation of spiritual Truth and that is how you come up with the ideology, theology and false beliefs.

The writings of the books of the Bible were not brought into existence by mere mortal men rather individuals who were of a higher understanding by way of communion with the higher consciousness they found within.

The Bible wasn't meant to be confusing, it wasn't meant to hide the Truth it just came through in a different form of expression than the *mortal* mind could grasp and that is because **it was never meant to be read and taken at face value,** it was meant to be taken in to allow God to bring forth the understanding behind the words written.

The Bible is not veiled when read by one with the higher conscious awareness of which it was written. You have to have the consciousness of God, are a mystic, know God by actual experience, know who the I of the New Testament is and who you are in relationship to I before written words transform into poetry for the soul, the allness of existence tucked right within you.

Mystics are not the cause/source/creator of manifestations because *you* cannot demonstrate/bring into form of your own accord. **All demonstrations of supply are God's grace returning to you** so you may glorify, give praise and thanks to God for its care of those who have conscious awareness of it.

There is only one demonstration to make as a mystic-to demonstrate God's existence, to know God as source and form of all that is good.

What are the things of God? Love, grace, benevolence, peace, harmony, joy, supply, support, abundance, ease, ie the good stuff.

You have to die out of *metaphysics* to be born into the realization of your true nature/identity by letting **Truth you know become Truth you experience.**

To do this you must understand the *mind* of man is an instrument, it is **not** God; God doesn't think, God **is** being itself. God cannot stop anything or start anything, there is no beginning and no end of Self. God is being and God is being the same now as it was a 40 billion years ago, ten thousand years ago, yesterday, seven billion years from now for **God changeth not.**

God doesn't *do,* God **is** and **is being** as it has always been because God is Law, unchangeable, immutable and eternal. God doesn't think any more than the principles of mathematics thinks, or the principles of gravity thinks or the principles of chemistry thinks. **The Principle of all certainly does not think.** It is never *thought* 2x2=4 because there never could have been a time when 2x2 was anything other than 4 because it **is** 4. It never *thought* H20 into water because H2O has never been other than what it **is** as an expression of God.

Man thinks man is evolving, getting smarter in and of themselves but it has been those few men and women of every era, continent, race, religion and standing who have been more open to the unseen and have brought forth that which was previously unknowable to benefit mankind.

Man thinks invisible means empty. **Invisible or unseen merely means without form for light to refract off of.** Electricity is and it is unseen. The internet is and it is unseen, the Law of creation and expression are unseen but real none the less as you can attest to existing in a world governed by invisible laws of creation and expression.

All that is given from within is for you and those accepting of spiritual revelation. No matter what you think personally about nuclear power, space exploration, medicine etc. that which comes into expression that was not in the world before came through contact with Source initially for the **benefit** of all man, as solutions to world problems of energy, medicine, protection, food production, navigation, transportation, for the good of life as we know it.

It is human man in his selfishness who uses that which was given for the good of all for personal reasons and there in is the perfect example of how man takes that which at its base **is, God,** perfect and good, and through personal desire of all manner weaponize the good for themselves or a select few for personal gain. Do you see how personal desire turns that which is pure and freely given by God to those who love their Father, brothers and sisters into chaos for themselves and sometimes the world?

It is always wondered why some succeed in causing others a lot of pain but never seem to suffer. Man rails at the injustice of God to let the evil roam free. Who is evil? What is evil? Who judges it to be so? You? Me? No. That is what has gotten us into this predicament-giving a toss about what the world is doing and not minding your own store as the rats and spiders take over. **Not one thing in this world is going to change until each individual man realizes the only thing they need be doing is learning how to have a personal relationship with God** and all the rest falls into place. Not over night mind you but much quicker than it took you to get to this point of surrender meaning this relationship, this life with God is yours for the living and you can have it as fast as you get to doing what it takes to live this life.

On the spiritual path you are not the judge, you are the one wanting forgiveness of all, not the release of punishment they have incurred according to man, but that they know God, know Truth and in that knowing can turn from man, repent, and rise to knowing God aright and live that expression of harmony and abundance as long as they see the expression of God in every saint and sinner alike.

Just know all that comes to you from God is harmonious, of its nature of harmony for all. If it isn't, if there is a judgement, a you or i, personal, hubris, ego, it is you thinking and not God because it is rife with duality. That is the finger test of all that you are knowing: if it is of God it is always an harmonious answer, good for **all** without force or sword and you feel this response as peace, the relief of knowing all is and it is good, God's got you.

Check yourself for structure of prayer, it is an understatement to say you have to know of who you speak when you say the name I: I, God, Father not i, personality/ego Carol, Dillon or Scott. Always remember "*i* of my own self can do nothing, it is the **Father** within, He doeth the work."

Good/harmonious for all or good just for you? This is the easiest way to check yourself, make sure you are living Truth and not duality disguised as Truth. There is only one I and it is God the Father, God the Son and God the Spirit.

Anytime words akin to "God told me to do it", "it was God's will I do X", "God says you should", "the Bible says", "God made me do it", "I am God's warrior", "I do the work of God" etc, are heard from your lips or another's you are witnessing *duality, humanhood, consciousness of man, cause and effect* **not** God, not grace, not Truth or life eternal because they are statements of *i*, of man, of ego and power not ordained by God nor under grace in any manner or form.

Death, resurrection and ascension:

Spiritual death, resurrection and ascension are not physical experiences but experiences of consciousness. It is a conscious act of rising from the consciousness of man to the consciousness of God which is the experience of heaven on earth, peace be with you.

To rise in consciousness you have to die daily to the things of man to be resurrected/remade in the consciousness of God and then live your life as a servant, instrument, happy to do the Father's will.

It is the ascension of consciousness from the *corporeal* to the **incorporeal,** not by physical process but by an activity of consciousness. All takes place in consciousness.

I is God in manifest form, God expressing.

The I that you declare, I Kelly, I Brent, I Jim is the child of God when you know your Truth. Say I. **I** was never conceived, **I** have always been. **I** was never brought forth from a womb. **I** is God and **I** is the spirit of God in man, the expression of God individually appearing as the son, you and me.

God the Father

God the Son

God is the Father and God is the son. God manifests/expresses itself immaculately as you, as the I of you, the identity of you. Your true identity is God expressing itself, God revealing, unfolding and disclosing itself and this I has every property, quality and quantity of God.

There is no demonstration to make **except** the demonstration of the **Father within,** conscious awareness of God and that brings the allness of God to bear in your experience. This is the **first step** to living under grace.

Man thinks he can manifest *material* things, bring what they want into expression by thinking a certain way. Patently false. The only thing there is to manifest is **God** in awareness because God is all there is. When you bring God into awareness within you are simultaneously opening a way for the imprisoned splendor, the allness of God, grace, to flow from you to bless the world and to return to you as your outward supply, fruitage, bounty, harvest.

You do nothing but bring God into awareness and that is the demonstration or manifestation of God which brings the allness of God to bear in your life as grace, the added and needed things.

You cannot manifest *things,* you can only manifest **God** and God being all comes into expression for your peace, your enjoyment, for your experience but it begins within, always within and that is why man cannot manifest anything of a lasting nature because they are trying to manifest things though *mind* manipulation, affirmation and *belief* in a power apart from God. That which man experiences is only *temporary* in expression because it is of the temporal world/duality but the experiences of God are **eternal** in expression because God **is** eternal expression.

The 15th chapter of John summarizes the entire mystical life of man.

It contains the secret of man's harmonious, immortal and eternal life starting now, here on earth. If you abide in the Word, spiritual Truth and abide by the principles of Truth/God consciousness and let God abide in you, you will bear fruit richly for you are the branch and God is the tree or vine. If you do not keep God on your forehead, on your arm and over the entrance to your home, metaphorically, not as the Hebrews who took it literally, you will be as a branch cut from the tree and die. You will live a life of chance, of revolving episodes of good and bad and that is called statistics or odds.

The spiritual man is not a statistic bound by human thoughts and conditions rather the spiritual man is under God's grace. God laid out a code of life we can follow and it isn't a code reserved for those in holy places, it is for all, you, here and now to be available to you in your business life, personal life, whatever activity you participate in. God can prosper your business, your profession, your talent, the sciences, humanities, national and international affairs. You are protected, fed, maintained and sustained by your **awareness** of the presence of God within.

Any activity that makes you feel you are being made to compromise your integrity to receive pay will change now because God goes before you to make the crooked places straight. This may result in your getting a transfer out of the situation, the person causing friction gets moved or released, whatever is best for you, because what is best for God will come about. **By no effort of your own you will find a place of peace-God will change circumstances to bring harmony unto you when you are of its harmony.**

The mystical life is the life you live when you recognize that the invisible presence within you is the reality of being and that it forms the joys of your outer experience.

When you find the source of your joy, prosperity, happiness, wisdom and love within you and it develops fruitage in the without, the outer world, the visible tangible world you are living the **mystical** life which often results in your living the **monastic** life.

The monastic life is the life lived **within** yourself and is the definition of "in the world but not of the world."

When you find your Self, your I, keep it secret, sacred and silent. Tell no one because:

This relationship between you and God is secret.

This relationship between you and God is sacred.

This relationship between you and God is silent.

Tell no one, tell no one, tell no one. Keep this growing light concentrating and brightening within you. Let it be the secret within like the glow of new love pours forth. Let the only thing known of your inner life be what is sensed about you in your presence. This will be the measure of your change in consciousness from that of mere human to that of joint heir in the kingdom.

Can you say YES to everlasting life in the arms of grace maintained and sustained in every way as a branch **connected** to the vine which bears fruit richly? It is the nature of the branch to bear fruit as it is eternally supplied with Life which is God. This understanding of oneness with God is the connection between its tree/vine and your branch constituting oneness.

All that is of the tree goes to the branch not by choice but Law, by the Law of expression, the inherent Life of the tree must flow outward from source to whatever is connected to it. It knows nothing of, nor can do anything for, that which is not connected to it but the branch connected to the tree has the whole of the tree, has the Life of the tree, the only Life there is. The outer expression of the oneness of tree, God, and branch, you, is the visible abundance/fruitage you experience in the visible world as grace, God in action.

Understand however when the fruit is gone that doesn't mean the supply is gone. The harvest is the visible supply but the supply is eternal and remains forever in the tree, ever in the branch as long as the branch, you, choses to remain connected to the tree by having conscious awareness of the tree/God.

All expressions of God in form are miracles because the definition of miracle is **not by/without the hand of man in activity to bring forth the effect.** All that comes to you byway of your relationship with God are miracles because they come from within you for you from Source because you are **of** the Source of all that is. No human thinking or doing was involved in what you are experiencing now in fact the opposite is true: because of your not thinking or doing of self, little s, you are with Self, capital S, God, where grace is found.

Spiritual awareness, God consciousness comes into the realm of man with the study of metaphysical Truth. These Truths settle in and and at some point the Truth of being, of oneness, is experienced. **This mystical experience of God contact, union, is the experience that reveals man as spirit and not flesh and blood,** and is that which instantly transforms a philosophy student into a mystic, a finite man to infinite spirit with every good thing yours by birthright as child of God, joint heir to God's kingdom.

Everlasting life and infinite supply in the form of grace shall pour forth from you heralding God's glory to the world through silent expression, healing those receptive to spiritual healing/God contact/God awareness and in return are blessed to the degree you share the grace of God.

Sometimes the impression is money and spiritual things don't go together and that is utter nonsense. As long as you are engaged in a human activity under your present system of finances money is an important factor. People say Truth should be free and that is utter nonsense too. In fact the most expensive pursuit in the world is the pursuit of Truth. The Master recognized that when he said "sell all that you have if you want to find the pearl of great price. Give up all for My sake."

There is nothing cheap about Truth, there is nothing inexpensive about Truth, the price is so high very few people in all the world are willing to pay it. The price to be paid is **surrender.** Surrender of your human ego, desires and demands upon God. You must surrender control of your life and trying to control others lives. You have to give up all that you *believe* and for some this is a price too great to pay because they cannot trust what is on the other side of humanhood is better.

Man thinks that unless he gets for himself what another could give won't be as good because you always keep the good stuff for self and give the other stuff away. That is not the way it is with God. You get the cream, not the non fat milk, you get the fatted calf not the desiccated husk of wheat. But until you know, have faith through direct impartation that the best is not of this human world you will live off of husks and muddy water instead of feasting.

At the mystical level of consciousness thought must never be permitted to dwell on supply as if it were something outside of yourself, something to be attained, earned or deserved.

Supply is the realization of I in the midst of you that has come that you might have Life and that you might have it more abundantly. Eternal supply is knowing God aright and that is only achieved by having the mystical experience which is the awareness of a presence within not of you but with you and this is God, universal consciousness of creation finally able to help itself come back to the fold, back to harmony to once again be of all that is instead of separate and apart from infinite supply and expression.

Consciousness and prayer

When I found Joel S Goldsmith on my path I knew instantly I was home. All the *metaphysical* teachings of Earnest Holmes, Neville Goddard, Emma Hopkins, Robert Collier, Dr. Joseph Murphy, Genevieve Behrend and Emile Coue had caught my attention and I devoured their works but there was always something missing or were philosophies I just couldn't accept/get behind. I knew they all lacked the same thing as each was seemingly built upon another, each just a more highly tuned *human* consciousness coming forward *adding* a new patch to old jeans. Don't get me wrong, I learned from each successive iteration of religion/metaphysics but they all lacked something, something I was to know that would bring the feeling of YES!! That is what I was missing for understanding!

All of them had the same basis ie do good/get good, thoughts become things, you already possess what you want you just have to tell God to release it for you. They all felt ritualistic, mechanical, follow the rules, keep your mind blank, don't react, act like you already are/have in other words be good, do good, think good, don't judge, just keep on smiling, chin up, positive thoughts, light at the end of the tunnel.

All these things you had to keep in your mind so you didn't forget how to *get* your good. You had to be constantly trying to manifest through thought, action and deed. Work on the dream board, write it out 50 times a day for 5 days then burn it dancing on one foot in the drizzling rain under a quarter moon but only if you hear frogs croaking, otherwise it won't work. OMG!!!! Don't get me started on affirmations and denials! They make you look like a crazy person about to sneeze and fart at the same time because your brain is so confused your face cannot keep up.

Through metaphysical/mind work I had some shifts in my life but I needed to stop, I was like a madwoman constantly hunting, searching for that thing, that aha moment that changes your perspective immediately and completely because *i* was *mentally* exhausted. Though *i* knew there was something more *i* just didn't know how to find it. *i* had looked in all the places *i could think* to look for my answers so *i* felt a hiatus was due. Notice the little *i* denoting me, personality, human. But Joel came up as a book suggestion in my feed and of course I had to check him out because not once in my years of study had his name come up.

Joel revealed the answer to the single most critical question I had and I was stunned. It was so absolutely simple on the surface but it hit me as the deepest Truth I had ever known and the answer to the reason *i* could never find God is because God is not a *thing* to be found **it is a shift in consciousness that you feel within your own being that brings a feeling of peace where it was not before.**

You **feel** God **as** peace, love, benevolence, forgiveness where it wasn't before. When God is in your awareness it is **felt** as a presence no different that a person in your proximity but within you, **of** you. When you have the experience of God revealing itself within you know God **is** and is within you and each individual to ever walk, is walking or will walk this earth.

The missing link between man and God is consciousness, knowing by way of an actual experience/feeling God is and is within you.

When this hit me the entire world of God opened up within me. Truth was felt and recognized for what it was and I heard God say "hello my Child, **I** have missed you! Hug! Are you hungry? **I** have a table laid just for you! Come! Feast!"

It was in that moment I knew without a doubt I had found what I was searching for-the understanding of how to have a personal relationship with God-and that is only possible when God has been realized within your own being as the Truth of your being, child of God.

You have most likely already experienced God:

Years ago when I would get mad during an argument if I was asked *why* I was mad I couldn't articulate it; I just was. I learned the understanding would come to me later on, just slide into awareness with a BAZINGA! That is why!! It makes so much sense now! and then I could have a conversation with the other person as to why I was mad because I truly knew. I was experiencing God giving me that which I desired to understand to deal with the situation and heal it. I knew it came **to** me, I just thought it was of myself, not knowing it was of **Self.**

I know this is common for a lot of people, to rest, to wait for the reason so you can understand it from a different perspective, not what was going on but **why** it was going on. Human man always reacts to the "what," the appearance, feeling etc, instead of understanding and healing the **why** which is always at its base duality.

God has been with you throughout your life and if you look back over times when miracles happened, perfect happenstances, the peace from within that released you from prison/bondage/slavery you will realize God is not foreign to you and as you bring these incidences up in memory they bring back the peace and joy of the experience and it was **good always,** never led you in the wrong direction, never made you feel anything other than harmonious. I say this to show that the God you know of man, what you have been *told* is a fallacy, a myth, an unreality because you have absolutely experienced, albeit without understanding, the true God, the God within that is love, support, kindness, understanding, rest, peace, direction, vitality, release and relief.

Now do you see God as the harmony, good, peace unto your life? Can you imagine that feeling of accidentally getting grace multiplied and within **your control** by how much you desire to be in oneness with God? I desire God endlessly for the reasons mentioned above, to remove illusion from the world, from myself and from those of my consciousness so that they too may become receptive to that which makes you whole once again. Blessed be he who walks with Thee for thine is the kingdom of heaven, consciousness of My peace.

The reality of God in your experience:

You will see the examples of my relationship with God detail a much different expression of God than the God man denounces and fears. Hmm. What is the difference? God within is real, the God outside of man is not real therefore what you have experienced in any way shape or form-*God did this, caused this, it is God's will*-was not the Truth of God therefore what you experienced was not of God but *separation* from God living as *mortal* man. Why? Because you do not know God and the only way to know God is by way of actual experience of the presence of God within.

When you know the true God within that is **only ever kind and loving,** you want to be with God, the real God because that is how it was meant to be. You are the child of God not the puppet of man, the slave to other man, forgotten by God or beyond redemption.

You are the child of the most high so dang it start acting like it and stand up and make a choice for yourself, rise up in consciousness, learn Truth, what it is and where it is and what it does for you and then you will not only know the true God you will be living as you were meant to, with God, hand in hand never to part.

"Walk with me" he just said. His hand is out gently like you do for a scared dog for that is truly what man is, fearful of everything but show it a bit of love, kindness, trust and they blossom, open, are born anew. This is the way of the Father, from scared and guilt ridden to trusting sidekick of the most high. Your God is awesome!

I am certain there have been times in your life where you have felt the peace descend or the answer drop in or you got that second wind or found you weren't frustrated doing what you were doing but were in the zone, flow of what you were doing. Looking back on those moments now with the Truth that it was God giving what you received I want you to answer one question: was the quality and nature of what you received from within better than what the world gave as an answer? Was what you received coupled with a feeling of can do spirit? I got this? Oh my gosh I need a piece of paper to write down what just began flowing!

Is this the God man talks of? No. It is the complete opposite of man's idea of God. Ahh. There is the difference. *Man's* idea of God. You my friend have actually experienced God in a pin head amount by complete accident and even that almost imperceptible relaxing in the silence or just letting go of what was bothering you brought forth something amazing that left a lasting impression on your consciousness in spirit and form. That is the feeling of what God is when it is known in **your** awareness, **the experience of God is the experiencing of harmony, peace, joy.** That which came forth from within, what you received seemed to come complete with directions as God brings itself forth fully formed for you to bring it into expression out in the world by way of your conscious oneness with God.

The God man believes in breaks my heart because the Truth of God in awareness is so beautiful it cannot be rightfully expressed except through the actions of one who is of this knowing and living this knowing as their nature.

Open Sesame-the magic of opening up to God

When you say "God, I am done with this life, you can take me," God hears "I am ready to be made anew" and since you are spirit, just unaware of at the moment, you cannot die so instead you rise in conscious understanding of Truth which makes the world anew **in your experience.**

If you tell God you are done with this world you aren't going to die, God isn't going to take your life, make you dead physically but it is going to take away your *sense* of human reality and remove the *perception* of physical death.

When you say you are done with this world you had better be sure that you mean it because that is the magic that opens the door to this infinite experience.

All that you need to do:

Being in the consciousness of harmony is all that is necessary for the manifestation of harmony in your experience.

God is food for the soul

The pain of loss, separation, longing, hunger for what has been lost to you in the human world is felt at the very core, very soul of you. But what you feel isn't the loss of a person or thing but of a connection. Your soul is the seed of God and wants to go home where there is safety, support, love, joy, ie what you were looking for from human relationships. Your soul isn't crying out for what you lost it is crying for you to pay attention to it and find out where the true pain is coming from-the need to reconnect with Source, God.

The pain of loss isn't the pain of what has been lost it is the pain of **you** being lost. **You are lost** and wandering because you believe your happiness can be found out in the world and that is the illusion of all mankind. The happiness that already exists must be discovered within and when that happens the soul is happy because it is literally being fed, nourished with the Life that is its Life, suckled, and finally sated with Self and this translates into your expression being of this same nature and quality.

You no longer look outside of yourself for what is needed rather you sense within and know your abundance in all forms necessary already is and in that you give thanks to God for thy grace is my sufficiency unto every need.

Every human problem is an opportunity to find a spiritual solution which raises your conscious understanding that much more about God, the world and your place in and of it.

When the soul hurts it is crying out for you to ask it what it needs. When that pain squeezes your heart, takes your breath away and you think you could lay down and not get back up ask within, ask that which you know is in pain what it needs to stop hurting. Scream out loud or within "what can I do to help you? What can I do to stop your pain?" And from the silence, when you can think no more, are exhausted by life, the answer will come.

"Come home Child, I have missed you, you are my son in whom I am well pleased."

What you have been seeking from the world to ease the pain has actually been the cause of the pain. The world is the equivalent of an empty candy wrapper, a bite of tasteless brûlée, a beautiful car with no engine.

What is to be found within your own being is the crème de la crème, the best, the most satisfying, the most perfect expression of being. What your soul is trying to do is get you to get quiet, mentally bend down to this part of you, this child within, and ask it sincerely, honestly and passionately "what can I do to make us feel better because when you cry I cry and when you are lonely I am lonely but nothing I do or find or bring to us stops your crying. Please help us stop crying."

And the answer will come as a wave of something you have never felt, that which you thought would have come to you by now with all the relationships you have had, all the love you thought you had experienced. But no, this is different, this is beyond measure, it is a fullness, a wrapping, no, it is wholeness. You feel new, different, lighter, brighter. You soon find yourself focused on this feeling within and the need to know what it is, how to reproduce it to have it as your permanent "resting face." Welcome to the spiritual path my friend, welcome to the spiritual path where the sidewalk ends and God begins.

Why is it you only seem to find God when you are down? Like zombie blank in the eyes, white noise buzzing in the head can't think kind of down? Because your mind is finally empty of all the ways and means *you* yourself can fix, alter or change the situation. You are as Shel Silverstein says "where the sidewalk ends." There is nothing left to think, you have run out of road, dead end. Full stop. Stuck. Your mind is momentarily quiet which is all that is needed for God to be heard.

What you don't understand is God didn't come to you when you were down and out because you were down and out. **God has always been there waiting for a time to say hello** but your thinking mind has been too busy thinking and learning and achieving of your own thoughts and desires to hear the voice within.

God will wait until you get good and quiet. God doesn't compete with the human mind because **God only knows you when you chose to know it,** look within and wait for it to show itself to you, make itself known which brings the Truth of your being into your awareness-I am that I am.

Until you are done with the pain of the world and also the excesses of the world you cannot chose to be other than you are because you are happy being where you are even though it is painful. You push through, that is what it means to be human right? Push and shove and take and rise and fall and do it all over again.

But you aren't human, you are an expression of God, spirit in form therefore the ways of man are not the ways of God thus the nature of man is not the nature of God. Man is the result of spiritual man not knowing who he is and that causes man to feel pain. **To make the pain go away you must address the root of the pain** and the pain is the soul of you trying to get you to look within for the answer instead looking outside to that which feeds the pain. That which is within nullifies the pain through grace ie Truth of knowing Self, the God within.

The fruitage of spiritual living

By your fruitage/expression of supply will your conscious awareness of God be known.

Fruitage, bounty or abundance is the visible expression of your inner relationship with God.

One thing you will be actually chastised for by *human* man is the faith or belief you put in the invisible. Do not worry what man says, think on this:

The integrity, validity, Truth of a spiritual practice, regardless of name, is validated by the expression and abundance of the practitioners of the practice. Are they peaceful and kind or judgmental and moody? That which is in evidence cannot be faked but the tongue can and will deceive for its own purposes.

As a student myself that has had a front row seat to the transformations in consciousness available to anyone who seeks in earnest to know God I live every day experiencing miracles, some small and some that drop me to my knees and make me ugly cry. Every day I experience God in my midst as God **is** the Law unto everything out in the world which is harmony, peace, ease and joy in my experience.

I experience things that make me smile and inside I see God smile as we recognize its handiwork together, give fist bumps and sparkles for the joy that is tangible in my midst not of myself but because the allness of God is as free flowing as my breath connecting with those receptive, those in need, to heal the sick and feed the hungry, for benevolence to be shown and harmony to descend.

This is the power of God and your only job in this entire existence, your reason for being is to go back to God so you can continue on now knowing who you are to experience the allness and fullness that is your birthright.

There can be no peace among man if there is no peace in individual man and that can only happen when you have a relationship with God, Self.

You control the flow of grace/God in your experience

Once you know that God constitutes individual consciousness then how much God do you have? As much as you can accept and become aware of. You can have a little understanding of Truth or the whole of God. Understand you aren't getting parts of God's allness if you only study a little; you get the allness of God but it is sporadic, hits here and there of grace, a little less duality.

The more you study and live your Truth in expression the more you recognize God in your midst as grace, the added and needed things on a more and more consistent basis ie it becomes your atmosphere and it is then you can say with knowing "I live by grace."

Requisites for illumination:

Nothing can be accomplished without the attainment of spiritual consciousness so the question is how do you attain it?

The first thing you need to do is surrender yourself-your will, your desires, your ego, your pride, your likes and dislikes, your judgements and your fears. You have to surrender all that the world has heaped on you that has become your shell, your protective way of thinking so that you can come out on top because these things of the world are the barrier to the attainment of God's presence.

If you go to God wanting something you are going to God as a beggar and unknowingly accusing God of withholding from you itself which is already within you just waiting for your awareness to become the activity unto your life. This is the only reason the prayers of man have not been answered: God knows nothing of lack, illness, poverty, pain **because those concepts are not of God consciousness,** they are man's way of describing the world around them and nothing more.

My Peace

This world is not to be saved by might or power nor by any agreements men make among themselves but by the still small voice that only operates through your consciousness, through the consciousness of the individual who opens themselves to it and is silent enough to hear it.

The still small voice reveals Truth of man's world so when you leave your house go out with an inner assurance, an inner peace that you are carrying something greater within you than anything you will ever have to meet/do/face in this world and it is closer to you than breathing, that voice, that smile of God, that something that the Master called My peace.

My peace doesn't come *to* you my peace is something that you let flow out **from you** because you embody it, it is **of** you and has to be **released** from you. Wherever you go you have to carry **Truth**-"my peace goes before me, this presence goes before me, my peace is thy grace and thy grace is my sufficiency in all ways." You carry that and people feel that benediction which you are releasing and then they feel your peace as relief or release from something that was weighing on them.

Don't expect to *get* My peace, you can't. You of spiritual knowing must **give** My peace to the world by letting it flow from within to the world and in doing so receive that which has been cast upon the water-the grace of God you released for all mankind to benefit from-returned upon you 1000x. You walk up and down this world smiling with the realization God's grace is your sufficiency. Just think what that does to all those fears of bombs, car accidents, divorce, bankruptcy, loneliness and lack!

Thy grace is my sufficiency and your harmony is my salvation.

Now you will find that you are dispelling the fears of the men and women you meet without saying a single word for it is the presence within that is the Comforter. Everywhere you go you are dispelling fear **if you realize thy grace is your sufficiency, My peace I give to you, My peace, eternal peace, divine peace, immortal peace.**

You do not feel like others who present in the world and that is because you want nor need anything of the person you have encountered moreover you are open and giving of that which you are of, grace, and that my friends is like the best fair food you can imagine! Inhale, take a big bite and feel a little less stress in your life. Want to feel that feeling again? Get curious.

You of the spiritual path are carrying God, the allness, the wholeness, the nature and quality of God out into the world when God is your expression. God is not controlling you, making you act a certain way it is the Son looking **to** the Father how to be, how to express **as** Truth and the easiest way to express as the Father is to move your butt over and let God go first. Easy peasy.

You are the instrument **through** which God's grace reaches this world and without you it will not be known as it needs to be to bring man back into conscious union with the Father as it was in the time of the awakened/illuminated man Jesus who **knew** himself to be the Christ, the living **expression** of the God he **knew** to be within himself. Jesus was the Christ because he knew who he was-the son of God not the man of earth therefore he was illumined, knew more than what the world could provide-Truth of being.

The name of God given to Moses, I am, would have been lost but for God's presence on earth **as** Jesus the Christ which means Jesus **of** God knowing. After his crucifixion the disciples carried **the Truth of God** out into the world and for the next 300 years true Christianity reigned. But true to man's need for power the teachings reverted back to the practices of the *Old Testament of law and punishment* dolled up with the *name* **Christ**ianity but not the **nature** of Christ which is forgiveness, peace and eternal life.

Why is what you experience as *orthodox* Christianity not true Christianity? The designation Christianity means **of Christ knowing** but there is no God in the laws of man, there is no God in the awareness of man and there is no God outside of man. What is called Christianity today is missing the one thing that defines true Christianity-**Christ knowing**-knowing God by conscious awareness, knowing **I** am that **I** when **I** know **I** am not *i*, human man of shifting emotions guided by personal desires and false beliefs rather ageless, dateless, infinite as the stars and as perfect as the Father who created all before time was.

Without those few who knew the Christ by way of conscious awareness of the God within themselves there would be no Bible, no written record of the coming of **individual Christhood** and the meaning of the coming of Christ. There would be no organized religions based on a single Godhead and there certainly wouldn't be a possible way to understand our connection to all that is without them.

There is a responsibility that comes with knowing God and that is sharing God aright and in that way will receive the bread you cast upon the water pressed down and flowing over, the added things, the joyous things, the beautiful and practical things as God in manifest form. Do not malpractice yourself by taking credit for the work of God through you and **remember which I you speak of** when it passes your lips because that determines always whether there is the presence of grace or the presence of man in your midst thereby defining your experience.

Man can never find God with intellect, human senses, reasoning power or searching the writings of the ages.

Man can only find God when God makes its presence known within individual consciousness by way of an inner, intuitive experience that reveals to you in a moment of awareness the Presence within.

This can only happen when man **wants** something other than what the world has provided, both the good and bad experiences must hold no sway over you, you are done with that, you are ready to go beyond what you know, be willing to learn, willing to not be in charge rather be shown without your human input of finite ego a new life.

The spiritual life is completely separate from mortal/human life therefore you must stop bringing up your human conditioning with all its judgements and barriers to higher understanding and be empty of thought so the consciousness of God can fill you. You cannot add new wine to old skins meaning you have to empty the vessel of the old to make room for the new. Learning is only effective when it is desired to be learned meaning you are willing to do what it takes to achieve knowing God face to face.

It isn't an all out dumping or purging of your human understanding rather a gradual yielding of your personal ego to **let** God show you a better way to express that is harmonious, easy and does not bring negative karma/consequences to bear.

Remember, two cooks in the kitchen messes up the perfection of the experience therefore *you* need to step out of the kitchen, **release your *human* consciousness/understanding and be willing to be taught.** You have to become a child again, forget all you know and let new understanding become Truth unto your consciousness.

God does not exist in your experience unless God exists in your consciousness.

Until you have conscious awareness of God within your own being and have chosen conscious union with God you are man whose breath is in his nostrils, living in a world of duality, pain and all the other things inherent in man's experience of life.

The only way something becomes part of your consciousness is when it becomes **known** to you, becomes a part of you by your awareness/conscious knowing of it. Consciousness equals awareness of something thus making it known to you as a reality and not fantasy, belief or blind faith.

Something has to happen to bring new awareness into your consciousness and that awareness comes only from having an experience which brings awareness of the experience into your conscious knowing; you know it because you experienced it.

Let us say there is a family of raccoons living under your house. They have been there for years but you only just noticed them. Now you know they are there. They are part of your consciousness because you are aware of their existence now, you experienced them in some way. Now that you know the reality that there are raccoons living under your house you have a choice to do something but no matter what you do you're **conscious** of the raccoons now where before even though they were with you, under the house, you had no awareness of them **because they were not a part of your conscious realization** therefore they did not exist to you because you were not **aware** of their existence.

This is exactly like God. It has been with you always but until now, or for some reason that brought you to a place of despair, you became aware of its presence. Just because you were not aware of the God within does not mean it didn't exist in you. Your awareness of this presence is what brings this presence, God, into conscious activity in your life and this is brought about by you having an experience of God's presence within your own being, in the silence behind the human thinking mind, in the seat of consciousness, the kingdom, the garden of Eden, heaven on earth.

"I will never leave you nor forsake you" is Truth you now know because you didn't have to seek God, you merely had to become **aware** of where God already **is.**

Conscience vs. Consciousness:

Man understands his *conscience* to be that of an angel on his shoulder gabbing about while the devil sits on the other shoulder trying to talk louder than the angel. This *conscience* is what man calls the "moral compass" which is **nothing** in and of itself.

This conscience is **not** consciousness. Conscience is synonymous with duality. Why? Because *your* conscience, that which is trying to balance behavior/action with their possible consequences, is the definition of duality-do good or do bad, reap good or reap bad. *Human* conscience is merely the mental tight rope of life being walked between two opposing forces trying to procure the optimal results for your efforts of being good or saying chuck it all and being on the nightly news.

The all of human man, from being to thinking to doing, all the processes of the mind that go into being human man are of duality/unreality and only becomes reality when the consciousness of man is risen to that of Truth and when the consciousness of all form is realized, recognized, revealed as that of, not separate and apart from, God, allness, oneness, then the conscience, the thinking mind, will come willingly under the governance of the consciousness of Self and harmony is restored through oneness.

Spiritual man has no conscience, no thinking/devising/planning mind because there is nothing to decide, nothing to control, maintain or support so the thinking mind rightly oriented to God serves as a **deductive** mind and not a *creative* mind. What that means is from here on out you don't decide/chose how you are going to progress in this experience rather you rest, trust, listen and respond to God within. This is how you rise in spiritual understanding by which to experience harmony of being: peace, abundance, good fortune, joy, the added and needed things.

Conscience is of man's thinking mind-duality.

Consciousness is your connection to Truth, God. It is knowing you exist and what you exist as-child of God, joint heir to the kingdom, prodigal son returned home.

Conscious awareness

All conditions are healed by the awareness of the **healer** and that awareness is that **God is as all** and God's presence reveals the condition was never real/physical but a figment of imagination, illusion of the mind, what humans call reality. Once the reason for the perceived discord has been discovered to be *separation* from Truth-that you are not human but **spirit,** of God, you can begin to die daily to the unreality man holds as Truth-that there are two powers.

This is how the conscious awareness of God is born-once you are shown Truth about one wrong thinking/belief you understand that if one image you held as true is actually false, then all the perceptions of your world **must** be false if they are all based on the same premise of two powers.

Your consciousness is the access to infinity and with this you have the whole secret of Life.

Now there is nothing to do but practice and no place to go for you are Home when you are in the consciousness of Infinity.

I live and move and have my being in infinity. I dwell in that secret infinity so there is no place to go for all is provided within this infinity.

You have to **know** God to **share** God and you have to know what you are sharing to understand the import of the sharing. It is only at your level of God understanding that you can share God understanding.

You could not impart Truth to me because water does not flow uphill; you cannot teach what you do not have conscious understanding of and I can tell you right now there is not one single pastor, preacher, priest, rabbi or evangelical teaching Truth to mankind. It may not be because they are complicit in the great hiding of Truth from the world but because no Truth is to be found in current religious theology by which to begin to get more Truth. When you spout from error you teach error which perpetuates error.

If you live Truth then all you can ever do, be and teach is Truth. Truth is of the One, the only intelligence which is creative, harmonious, eternal and Self perpetuating. This central intelligence is the Life flowing in and through you guiding and directing for harmonious interaction because within the kingdom of one consciousness all is and it is harmonious merely by the nature of the Law of like begets like. God is the earth and the fullness there of. **All is God in form and that singularity is the reason for the harmony of all that is.**

That which is called the kingdom or heaven is a risen state of consciousness that will always be harmonious and that which is of man will always be duality. One cannot become the other but you can chose which one to express from-spirit of One, Truth or human of duality, error.

We are all states of consciousness not persons

Jesus was a state of consciousness called Christ consciousness, that of God, and was so thoroughly touched by the divine that he did not accept outward appearances as Truth which released the error from his consciousness which resulted in a healing of erroneous belief. A healing is revealed Truth, God in awareness where error was which results in a state of grace, harmony in your midst.

Remember it is the **the awareness of God within** that reveals God **is** and grace, the allness of God, is the return for your knowing Truth.

Grace is not a gift, it is Law, like for like. You receive at the level that you give of God to the world through living the nature of God which is harmony/harmonious expression. The more you live in oneness the more grace you are releasing and this bread on the water is the Law of like begets like returned upon the sender, karma. **If what you give is good what you get is good.** Only by being an instrument for good itself can this be your return.

Karma is for human man too as we all well know so you can see in the consciousness of God what goes out is good and what comes back is good, **singularity of expression.** In the world of man what you give is not always what you get, good or bad, duality of expression/chaos/chance and that is the inherent unreliability, chameleon like nature of man who vacillates because he doesn't know who he is to be other than who he is.

Consciousness begets consciousness

Your consciousness is infinite because your consciousness is that of the Father-infinite, omniscient, omnipresent and omnipotent. As you unfold you realize you are not going out into the world to bring/get what you want rather you have learned to tune within to know the Truth of inharmony, lack, limitation, sin, sickness and disease and that is that **they are of man, created by man's false thinking and that all it takes to live Truth is to have conscious contact, awareness, communication with the source of all, the God within.**

What you immerse yourself in, what you go to first, what you find comfort in is what you become. You do not declare or exclaim Truth rather you receive Truth unto yourself and this Truth given to you is given to all who are receptive through consciousness not the lips. What you desire for yourself you must also desire for all of your brothers otherwise you are being a selfish human and subject once more to the duality of man.

You are consciousness, you are awareness but that which you are conscious of and aware of is not of yourself but of that which is the Truth of you when you are in the consciousness of Truth. You possess nothing in and of yourself because there is no you separate and apart from allness, God. You are an individual expression **of** the allness you express.

You are not the allness, you are **of** the allness because of your awareness of your spiritual nature; this is the conscious knowing that allows all that you are of to come into expression in the outer world as the added things. There is no you and there is no me separate and apart from our identity as child of God therefore even though we are individual expressions expressing we are of the same source, your consciousness of expression is the same as mine, harmonious, therefore we are one in our expression which is God therefore our interactions are that of the nature of our consciousness which is God-harmonious and fruitful, peaceful and joyous, true brothers. It is also of the quantity and quality of God which is infinite and perfect.

Now do you see why there is never anything to ask God for? That there truly is no lack, illness, pain, error or fear that you need to ask God to rectify/change on your behalf? Do you see why when you do ask God for *things* you get no thing? Not because God is trying to punish you but because **God does not know of *things*** ie lack, illness, pain, error or fear so there is nothing for it to rectify or change.

It is also a sign of not knowing Truth of God if you still ask for *things* because not only in asking do you show you do not know Truth but to ask for what you think you lack means you are looking outside yourself for that which will be the change you want. **There is no God outside of yourself** and until this is understood and that God outside of you has been laid bare as the illusion it is you cannot grasp the understanding of the true God already set up within you just waiting for your awareness of its presence.

If you do not have the consciousness of the presence of God you lack the one element that does the healing work. God is always present with you for the Christ, risen son of God, is the reality of your being but until you get quiet within and enter the consciousness behind the thinking mind of man it can be of no benefit to you.

Understand there is not just one risen Christ; all will rise back into their Christhood to live in oneness with the Father. Jesus was an **example** of what it meant to be the Christ which was to free man from their belief in duality by living the expression of the spiritual man free from the *beliefs* of human man.

What takes place in your inner communion is what becomes grace to the world and your bread on the water. You communing with your source is what brings forth the spiritual food that feeds the world whether the world recognizes it 50 years from now doesn't negate the fact that what will become in a future now is dependent on what you do spiritually **now.**

Once you reach in consciousness for God you will have God

You have to have conscious recognition, realization of the God within to partake of God's world and all that is necessary for you to do is learn to get quiet within and listen for what is already within you. It may not happen the first couple of times but it will; get comfy, relax and smile, you are waiting for your best friend to come for a visit!

Bread crumbs

Pray for right teachings and soon a book or person or that which will suit you perfectly will appear in your awareness. What appears in your experience are what I call bread crumbs, the trail God lays out for you to follow to learn, become illumined, experience revealed Truth. It is what man calls coincidences; those things that you become aware of now that your focus is in and not out. They are God's way of opening your consciousness to Self step by step, showing you Truth which is needed to help you surrender your duality, see grace in your midst, feel the true nature of the Father every time you connect the dots, follow the bread crumbs and feel God respond within as your gift of oneness as peace, harmony, joy or a kiss on the forehead.

Every time you feel something brewing within, a lightness, a giddiness, ask Father: "what am I to pay attention to Father? I can feel a shift coming, something I am to know that is just going to rock my world." By acknowledging you are aware of God you bring God on the field and will get a response. Every day is like a treasure hunt with God. What am I going to stumble on? What is going to touch the very Christ of me and drop me to my knees with gratitude and love? What little nugget of wisdom is going to take me further from man and closer to God?

Your **expectant** atmosphere of being with the Father from waking until waking (you ask God to keep your consciousness open while you sleep blissfully) is what allows God to express in your atmosphere. When you are expectant of the Father you are living in the consciousness of the Father and receive what is of the consciousness of the Father-everything.

God consciousness does not overcome/take over/replace your mind because **mortal mind is not really a thing rather a construct of survival techniques** man employs for the expression called living. Once man realizes his true nature as son of God, joint heir to the kingdom, infinite and immortal in his oneness with God, the one Presence, the one Life, the mortal mind dissolves into the nothingness dreams become upon waking.

God doesn't take over your mind, God shows you the Truth of its existence within you and when you are ready Truth will dawn in understanding and you will have had the experience leading to actual awareness, signs following, knowing God is and I am. The only thing you are to do is remind yourself of spiritual Truth when faced with any duality/polarity/opposites because all are but illusion.

Thank you's, I love you's, you're awesome usually get a quick response from within; a silly face, a kiss on the forehead, a wink, a smile, some acknowledgment that you were heard. Remember this relationship is forged in the silence but it is the allness of your life, this is a relationship that is as constant and continuous as you put forth the effort to study and live God in expression and it is right with you as you are with it therefore God's presence can be brought into expression by giving gratitude to it, asking it to come onto the field or just saying "hello, I love you, thank you for this glorious day and I can't wait to see what you have in store for me! Whoot! Whoot! Let's get this train a movin'!"

How, by what name, you address God is your business. Mostly it is my BFF in my mind and I call it Father. It rarely addresses me but a few times it has been Daughter (big fat ugly cry on that one!)

I don't relate my experiences for any other reason than to impress upon you the JOY this relationship brings! You can literally receive any kind of help you need just by asking for that which God can give-peace, harmony, love etc. I am never alone, ever. Not that I have a constant back and forth, it is quiet up in there a lot but its presence is always available to be felt, rested in, trusted.

So much of God can seem contradictory but once you get into the rhythm of your relationship with God, because it is a relationship, you will at times stop and compare the "becoming" you to the "old" you, the way you used to feel when you were by yourself, separated from God, source. Has there been a shift in your level of comfort being by yourself more? Are you seeing signs follow as your life becomes more harmonious? Smoother? This is grace and this is only the beginning of what God will do in your life when you are in oneness.

Once you realize your consciousness is the door or access to infinity-infinite supply, love, joy, life and peace, you will no longer look to man whose breath is in his nostrils and no longer fear what mortal man can do to you because figuratively speaking you will close your eyes and get into the silence of listening and witness God's grace take over. In time it becomes spontaneous, it acts to provide for you before you know what you have need of but **go and tell no man what ye have seen.**

The Word of God

The **Word** of God means "the consciousness of God" or "Truth of God revealed." The way it is used biblically is very confusing if you do not have the mystical definition. Any word used to describe the Truth of God whether Word, Source, Supply, Consciousness, Meat, Wine, Water, Bread, Omniscience, Omnipresent, Father, Sword etc, that is **capitalized** denotes it being in reference to God, as food for the soul, as water to sake the thirst of longing, as the supply of all that is, as the grace that returns to you, that it is always present where it is known, is what reveals itself so you may know it aright.

If you don't understand a word or how it is used in spiritual context see if it is explained in the terminology section and then take it into prayer and ask for understanding so you may rest. Do not lean on your own thinking rather ask, ask, and ask silently within because this is the only way to live the life of God under grace, heaven on earth, peace instead of chaos.

Every time you are with God you are healing those who are receptive to healing.

Every moment you entertain God in your consciousness you are revealing Truth to the consciousness of those who desire to know Truth. Not by your own power or desire or will but by the God of you for the God of all to awaken.

This Truth came to Joel: **Conscious oneness with God is the healing principle** because the healing principle, that which frees man of their false beliefs to once again live Truth, is knowing God **is** by way of an actual experience which reveals the Truth of that which is unlike God as no thing real. Your oneness is the evidence of this Truth and makes you free from believing in anything other than Truth: God is. I am that I am therefore the allness of God is the allness available to you through expression, your expression of oneness with the Father releasing grace to heal in proportion to your time spent in oneness.

I want to reiterate what it means to be in constant prayer, oneness, to pray without ceasing because it sounds harder than it truly is:

1. To pray aright is to listen for the soft, small voice of Truth
2. To listen you must have no thoughts of the world of man.
3. To have no thoughts of the world of man means you are not in your head thinking, chewing, devising. You are not in the past or in the future but in the present moment relaxed, being and doing like those around you. **The difference between human man and spiritual man is on the inside, in the silence.**

Spiritual man is in the moment, now, with no thoughts going on because there is nothing to really think about because God is taking care of things. It can be a hard concept to understand when it is read; when you experience it you will know. Suddenly you realize you were silent up in there, maybe humming or not but you definitely weren't in your head like you used to be. Progress grasshopper, progress.

The nature of those you encounter is governed by the Law you are under as that is the nature you are expressing and like begets like therefore if you are of the nature of man you encounter duality. If you are of the nature of God you encounter grace (most of the time.) What you express is for the most part what is reflected back to you. I say most of the time but know your expression did register just maybe not until later. Being grace to the world means you are harmonious and that is what matters on this journey.

The presence of God is to bring all under its dominion at least temporarily when God is in their midst as you and through you. Therefore the path of your travels could be envisioned as a swath of new growth seen as lushness where barrenness was before. You are the bringer of the needed rain, you are the soother of the soul, you are the **instrument** of the only presence that can do this for its creations and as a creation of God you are tasked with bringing Life to the husk of man, enlivening and invigorating the soul to wake man from human unreality.

Man worshiping a God outside of himself is no different than worshiping the light from a lightbulb instead of the source of what makes the light. **The light is the emanation of the electricity, the effect, not the source of the electricity in expression.** If you were to limit yourself by looking to the bulb for light in and of itself sooner or later you will be disappointed because the bulb will burn out and you would be without light but as long as you know the source, the electricity, you will have light even if you have to produce a new bulb.

So it is with you. If you are looking to God for love you will always have it but if you are looking to persons they will come and go, may turn to the evil side of duality but if you are looking to God, whatever happens out there in the world will make no difference. This one will get washed away, that one will turn away, Judas will betray, Peter will deny, Thomas will doubt but it will make no difference as you expect nothing from man, not loyalty, fidelity, confidence or assistance. All you expect is of God.

If you expect your good from man you will soon meet with Judas, Doubting Thomas, Denying Peter. Even if you don't have that happen you will have all twelve of the disciples go to sleep on you but it isn't just other man that betrays you but you when you depend on man and the world.

When you look to person, place or thing for gratitude, supply, love, companionship, anything that happened to Jesus through his disciples can happen to you through those to whom you look. This is the lesson Jesus gave through the disciples: each served their purpose temporarily but not one of them endured but Jesus' Life principle endured **because even without the twelve disciples he still walked out of the tomb in his own body.** The same body that had been wounded.

Your body cannot change even by dying, it is spirit in form but you can change the appearance of your body by changing your concept of your body. You must come to the realization that it is already perfect through knowing why that is true: **God is as all therefore God is the source of all that is expressing.** God is the very activity of your body, capacity of your body so how can it be less active today than it was yesterday if God is the activity and capacity of it? If God is the activity of your supply, how can your supply be less one day than another? Supply is invisible, eternal and infinite. *Personal* awareness of fluctuations in *outward* fruitage or bounty that cause fear and anxiety is in the *belief* that *you* are responsible for your supply and that it can go up and down.

The fluctuation in the health and strength of the body comes only from the belief that you have health or a body of your own instead of realizing God is individual being, God is the source of being and of body and then realize that the only capacity you have is God capacity. This is not only a God capacity for expressing gratitude but also a God capacity for expressing health, vitality, youth, vigor, strength, wisdom, abundance and all the added and needed things.

The quality and ease of your life is directly proportionate to the amount of time you are resting and listening for God while living what is an outwardly normal and natural life ie home, family, fun, work etc. The more you are under the Law of good the more the Law of good operates in your experience therefore if you are encountering more duality than you think you should be at this point of your journey, check yourself, are you expressing as God or man? The proof is in the response you receive from those in your presence and the peace or chaos you feel within. **The quality of your experience is the quality of your expression.** Like begets like, can it be any simpler stated? When I am at rest God is, when I am thinking and doing God is not therefore grace is not my expression or my return.

Thank you Father for the Law of harmony I am under.

Your consciousness of Truth as spiritual man is already within you but as human man of duality it is as yet unknown to you therefore a rock lives more its nature than you are at the moment therefore whenever you can be in the presence of men or women who are dedicating their lives to a spiritual pursuit and are thus of a higher conscious understanding of Truth do so. It doesn't matter their religion as long as their life is a dedication to God, if they are in some manner **living the Christ way** then be with them, let them be your tribe.

There does come a time however you must stop relying on the healing of others and begin healing yourself ie you must learn to stand on your own infinite consciousness or you will lose your demonstration (of your oneness with God) ie there does come a time you do have to come into the recognition of God as your individual being and learn to go within and not to one of higher understanding to keep pulling you along.

Understand this **doesn't** mean don't commune with others of like minds, it doesn't mean stop reading and studying. No! It means to lean more and more on the impartations **from within your own being** as that which you are to know and not continue constantly with a healer or teacher to raise you up in consciousness.

If the teacher doesn't step away and let you exercise and strengthen your own connection with God it will never be the connection you want for only you can get yourself back home to the Father's house, only your footsteps, your living Truth in expression will get you to the garden of Eden but that never means you cannot rest along the path and meditate with peers as well as teachers and healers, **it is merely the degree of *reliance* you place upon another that determines the degree of your Christ consciousness.**

To pray without ceasing is to commune within yourself.

The God you are seeking can only be found through your own consciousness. Your consciousness is the access to your true health, wealth, happiness, peace, freedom as received from God, Law unto harmonious expression.

Man cannot give you your freedom, armies cannot give you peace. Only God can free you from the prison of fear the world of man has created for you to exist in. Those who take up the sword will die by the sword. The way man thinks will always end in death, his or another's, but always ultimately his.

But if you really seek peace for yourself, for others, neighbors, enemies, the world, seek peace within yourself because if you succeed in making access to God in your consciousness enough God will come through to free you and the world.

10 men with access to God will free this entire world of its fears and wars. It isn't necessary that a million find God, it is only necessary for one to find God, that one will establish the works.

You might ask why hasn't this been in the past to be what you are experiencing today and the answer is this:

Consciousness

This is the secret, this is the key, this is that which was unknown. The meaning of consciousness spiritually discerned means the awareness of a presence within yourself that is of you but not you. You are conscious of a presence of love, benevolence and peace tucked right within where you can enjoy each others company on this eternal journey called life.

Prayer is a spiritual activity and it is your communion with God. **Prayer in its highest form is God's impartation of itself to you.** The attainment of spiritual harmony is never accomplished by words or thoughts. Words and thoughts only help you lift yourself into that atmosphere of prayer/communion where they are **no longer necessary.** In this atmosphere you are in **silent** communion with God and God's grace imbues you.

To assimilate Truth there must be a preparedness and a readiness for it in consciousness. The Master illustrated this with the three states of consciousness:

1. Barren soil
2. Rocky soil
3. Fertile soil

There is no use in giving this to one who is still living by the laws of Moses, who thinks God is going to do something for them just by asking somewhere up there. This message can never be given to those who have not glimpsed of the fact that God is love but also omnipresence so that the responsibility for the demonstration of this oneness is upon the individual for the kingdom of God is already within you. You can see there is a lot of preparation before an individual can come to believe the kingdom of God is within them because the world is seeking for it up there in the heavens somewhere far far away.

Man who is happy on earth regardless of circumstances is barren soil meaning if the seed of God is awakened through a Truth felt in one of this consciousness it will not prosper, will not take root because the ways of man are so much more comfortable and familiar.

Man who is of rocky soil doesn't really want to know God but wants the things of God, has some soil covering the stony ground to give protection to a seed newly touched with Life but the depth of the soil, the depth of conviction to know and grow is only so thick meaning it is thin thus though the life of the plant began there isn't enough to sustain it and again it dies and you know no God.

Then there is fertile soil. That man who is done with this world, wants a different way, is ready to just stop if they only knew how. This is fertile soil, this is the consciousness that when it is touched it begins to grow immediately because the desire to know more and more is the Life that feeds the seed to grow strong, put down deep roots, take in as much nutrients as it can and pull Life from the ground to sustain itself, is of the Life that brings forth bounty of its kind.

You always meet others on the level of **their** consciousness, you give bread for bread, not pearls of great price for bread for that will not nourish consciousness rather turn it away. You can only help people from their level of consciousness which is why so many *born again Christians* can be overbearing because they are trying to share the God that they only understand *intellectually* meaning they have not learned that God is an experience which becomes their expression of harmony because God is the harmony they feel.

Whether you see it with your eyes, sense it with your body or envision it in your mind it is all the same-illusion-because what is seen and sensed comes not as it is but as it has been experienced before. A bomb in your experience has no more power than a bomb envisioned in your mind. **Nothing can kill the spiritual man therefore there is no power within man or outside of man that can harm you, change your nature, take you from the I you know yourself to be.**

Remember, spiritual man doesn't die, spiritual man is incorporeal spirit in form and that spirit continues on to the next experience with a knowing of Truth they didn't come into this life with. You "leave" this visible expression in form with a raised consciousness of who you are and that is where you start going forward from this visible form just as you started this iteration where your consciousness was when you "died" the time before.

Only human man experiences death. Spiritual man may not express in visible form anymore but that is not death to spiritual man that is merely a transition, a moving on in an eternal experience.

Your faith is in the still small voice within you and when it utters its voice the problems of earth just melt away. Learn to be still, learn to listen and let God bring Truth to bear.

It doesn't matter if you find God tomorrow or ten years from now; seriously what does it matter? You are infinite being after all!

But what you may want to consider is how much longer you are going to keep suffering the errors of man, how much longer are you going to feign ignorance of the Truth you feel just begging to see the light of day within you.

You could find God in ten years by ignoring the feelings within because you just can't get yourself over the hump that God is within and spirit is your nature and for ten more years wonder when the pain is going to stop. Or you can just say "you know what, what have I got to lose? Seriously, if nothing else I will be a better human than I am now and if I can go that distance, why not just a little hop, skip and a jump over to spiritual knowing?"

This journey is joyous, lighthearted (most of the time) and adventurous so let it be so! There is no heaviness, no church speak, no rituals, no judgements just you enjoying the company of your new bff, listening, asking, practicing and getting used to seeing the world as it truly is.

It is being overjoyed, beyond grateful for the harmony that got you to work on time when there was no conceivable reason that you could or would. It is the chain of events seen in hind sight that had no possible way of being orchestrated by man's hand, the miracle on the highway, the peace that washes over you in your time of need. This is God in your life, this is the harmony that can be your life not here and there but every moment.

I can easily, every day, see God's harmony operating my life from what is given me that day to do to what sparks my imagination to bring forth or to just rest. Week after week I can look back and see how what was given me to do one day was needed to have been done for the next step to be able to come to fruition at the exact moment it was needed which was the progress to the next encounter that brought this person with this skill onto my radar through a thing given me to do that was done as I was given to do.

The key is when you get the impulse, do. Don't procrastinate and do what you want to do because you just missed your exit buddy. That was God saying "take next exit one mile ahead." You blow past that moment of perfect harmony and you may have to stay on that there road for another six months. And you wonder why you aren't making progress.

When you get the impulse/impartation it is because it is to be done then forgotten. It is a step in a process you cannot see so if you don't do what is needed to be done harmony stalls. When and how and why? Who knows, I just know there is a lot of time you are free to be as you would naturally be in this experience and on those occasions you need to play an active role you do what is given you to do then you are off on your own again. My point is this life isn't a constant physical doing, going and producing. Not at all! Yes, you want to be in God consciousness to the degree you want to know God and live under grace but when it comes to the doing I want you to remember one thing:

You are no longer encumbered by the stress and hardship of humanhood, you live within, enjoying literally the little things of life because you see the God of them and it brings you immense joy. You are truly free of anything to think to do of your own accord, the "I should" thoughts, and into this space God fills with peaceful, purposeful activity that is always supported by grace, God in action, in whatever form is necessary whether that be funding, space, customers or understanding. God never asks anything of you beyond being aware of its presence and resting in it.

To be in the world but not of it means to live your daily life as you are accustomed to living it **but without concern and without believing that the values of life are external to you.** For instance not to believe that your safety and security is in or of anything in the external world. If you need a fortress or high tower, if the seas need to part or a cloud by day or a flame by night God shall be it. If you need a hiding place God shall be your hiding place and the Master also reveals **I am** the bread, the meat, the wine and the water.

So if you need meat God shall be your meat along with wine, water and bread. Do you need to be resurrected out of your sins? out of your diseases and lacks? then God must be the resurrection. When you find yourself in God or when you find your home in it, when you realize the divine presence within you and learn to commune with it, tabernacle with it, pray in it and through it everything in the outer world conforms to this inner pattern of harmonious expression.

In other words the secret desires of the heart, when they are spiritual, when they are loving, in the direction of equity, justice, equality and benevolence, when the issues of your own heart are in that direction, all things work together for good in the outer picture. All of the outer picture conforms to one of harmony and peace because it is revealed to you that "I am in the midst of you. I will never leave thee nor forsake thee. I will be with thee unto the end of the world. Rest in me. Rest in the Word, Truth."

In this consciousness of being the weight of the world falls from your shoulders, the lines leave your face for there is no longer fear. How shall you *fear* what mortal man can do when there is a divine presence within you? How shall you fear the external world of illusion when you know Truth? You don't and that is why you can rest.

To human man the language of the spiritual world is strange, mysterious and not at all straight forward but that is only because they do not yet understand it cannot be understood by the *human mind*.

Houdini was the greatest magician of his time and people marveled at his talent but Houdini didn't think this about himself. There was nothing mysterious about what he was doing. **He was applying principles he understood and only to those who were in magical darkness were his tricks difficult and mysterious.**

So it is to the illumined consciousness; there is no mystery about the word illumination or the term the Christ or the spirit of God that dwells in me. It is simple, it means only that there is something unseen you are aware of that is within you, is a rear guard and a way-shower, your comfort and your laughter.

We call the Bible the Word of God but it isn't; it is written Truth **of** the Word of God, the consciousness of God. The Word of God is not corporeal, physical, tangible and cannot be handled with the hands. **The Bible contains the revelations of those who have received the Word, the Truth, conscious of God and reveals the Word of God is available to you because it is within you.**

It is only when you stop thinking in terms of opposites ie health *and* sickness, wealth *and* poverty and begin to think in terms of God **as** all that you are and all that you need that you transcend/rise above not only bad humanhood but even good humanhood. You **transcend** the 10 Commandments and rise to the consciousness of the Christ that was illumined in Jesus that gives/reveals the only two commandments you ever need to embody which acknowledge that:

1. there is but one God, one presence, one expression, one Soul, one Life, one Source and one Law of all that is and **each and everyone of us is of that same one.**
2. Honor your fellow man as yourself-see the Christ in every person regardless of how they outwardly present for human judgment. You can honor your brothers and sisters by knowing the Truth of them and by that knowing provide the means for them to begin expressing the Christ you know them to be.

Knowing these two commandments *intellectually* will not work; these commands have to be **lived,** they have to be accepted into consciousness and practiced over and over every time error presents so that you **can** forgive your enemy because you know they are merely ignorant not evil.

You do not criticize, judge or condemn a person who has made a mistake; you are not condoning it but in proportion as he seeks to rise above humanhood because of the desire for God's divine love **it is your duty as one who knows Truth to reveal Truth within yourself to give that helping hand, grace, by perceiving the nature of God as the very soul of every person.**

Any good *human* being can piously overlook the faults of others and even personally forgive them their sins. Any good *human* can do that but it takes one of **spiritual** vision to be able to say **I cannot see anyone for the face of God is all that shines, the soul of God looks out through all eyes.**

In other words you see past appearances, labels, judgements of what is presenting as human man and see their Truth shining out desperate for awareness, acknowledgement that the person before you isn't human and messy and flawed but perfect but for a little dust that wipes right off.

Such a realization does not heal sick or sinning people, it makes them "die" more quickly to the *illusions* of man so that their spiritual selfhood can be revealed. The sooner mankind dies to his humanhood the sooner their Christ consciousness, God within will come forward and be revealed through expression.

It has come time to stop thinking in terms of being healthy or wealthy rather to think in terms of being whole, complete, full. The time has come to know the spirit of God indwelling so that you may claim your heritage as the child of God, join heir in Christ to all the heavenly riches.

Death, resurrection and ascension:

Not physically but symbolically and means when you go from man of earth to child of God back **with** God under grace. You have to **die** daily to the things of man to be **resurrected**/remade of the consciousness of God and then live your life as a servant, instrument, happy to do the Father's will.

It is the ascension from the corporeal to the incorporeal, not by physical process but by an activity of consciousness. **It all takes place in consciousness.**

Up until your questions are answered you must continue to ask questions to satisfy your mind and it will finally understand its role as it is-deductive not creative. One of the reasons people fail to find God is because the mind is afraid of what is to come. **The mind is the most powerful tool you have but the way you have been using it is the cause of all your pain and suffering.**

Oh, you thought you were governing your life? Ha! Nope. Your thinking mind governs your life, not the I of you, the *i* of you, ego, personality. The thinking mind keeps throwing lies at you, making you look over here and then over there and then it tells you how to respond so you come out on top. This is the reason it feels so hard to change-you think you are the thinking mind and that you are not thinking of the right ways to get yourself into a place of peace and harmony.

You cannot manipulate your mind to do what you want, your mind is conditioned to respond to what is outside of it to protect it and not subject to your will or desire for it. It is only when you begin to understand that it is the consciousness of the world, the unseen thoughts and feelings of all people on earth, **something outside of you that is the basis for your actions-duality.**

The thinking mind has become the all of a person. The thinking mind is what produces the expression out in the visible world therefore man thinks someone homeless is less intelligent or capable of thought necessary to participate in the world than one who has a home and a job.

This judging from appearances is the reason for all the pain in the world.

Just because you may be dirty or hungry on the outside does not change the Truth of the within- the Christ. All men are created equal, **all are of God.** The equality of man is our nature but if you don't know your nature you do not know you are equal to all other man no matter how either expresses because man judges solely from appearances/material standing.

Man believes his nature to be man, not spirit thus the sentiment of equality to man means born with all the rights of another citizen under the laws they live under. This understanding of equality quickly turns into heirarchy among men, a pecking order of higher and lower, deserving and undeserving, "blessed" and down trodden.

When you know your true nature you know the true meaning of **equality-all are of God and all have the potential to rise back to the kingdom.** All are equal in the kingdom because all are of the singular consciousness of creation just at the moment unknown.

Why do you plant a seed? For the purpose of fruitage, harvest, bounty but you do not plant a seed expecting to have fruitage the next day. In fact you do not just drop a seed on the ground and give it water. There is preparation before the seed goes into the prepared ground and then there is the time between seedtime and harvest. Learning to know God through studying and practicing are what lead to the harvest but only after the seed has been sufficiently nourished and protected (secret, silent and sacred) will it bring forth visible fruitage.

---

3 stages of consciousness awareness man progresses through:

1. *Material/medical*-matter for material healing
2. *Mental*-mind over matter/mind over body/others
3. **Spiritual**-God, allness, oneness

Mental and **spiritual** realms/consciousness are different and separate. *Mind* and **God** are different. *Mental* and **spiritual** healings cannot be combined because mental healing is nothing more than the opposite coming to bear temporarily through personal might, denials or affirmations because it is of the thinking mind of man/duality therefore unreal, temporary, *illusion* of change when no change has actually happened because man cannot change himself because human man is a *concept* of being and not the **Truth** of being.

Divine consciousness is the reality of your being therefore limitations, discords and sins are not *of* you rather superimposed pictures, illusions of error born of the atmosphere of duality.

Man is the product of what he accepts in his consciousness. Even those who are advanced along the spiritual path must begin anew everyday because you cannot live on yesterday's manna. No one stores up enough Truth yesterday to fulfill their needs today. Every day you must open your consciousness anew for God to fill you with inspiration, ease, support mentally, financially, physically and visibly. In opening yourself up to God each day anew you put yourself in a position of rest, peace, your will not mine Father.

God is infinite and how could any one of us grasp the tiniest part of infinity? There is always something richer, something truer that unfolds today, something that enriches your consciousness today and becomes greater fruitage tomorrow. This is the way of the spiritual man.

There are degrees of consciousness therefore you do not meet everyone on the level of spiritual awareness as that is your level and not the other person's. If they still live in duality you don't have to agree with them and you don't have to argue with them, you let them be at their level of understanding of the world around them and bring God onto the field silently and secretly to reveal peace within the situation. By being grace, peace and calm in expression you are the instrument by which God awakens others who are ready and accepting of this peace, this place of rest.

Spiritual living is merely realizing you want God's qualities and quantities instead of human qualities and quantities. It is a relinquishing of self in favor of Self. It is the realization that in turning from the ways of man you are not giving up anything of value rather you are getting rid of all the stuff that has kept you from living in prosperity.

It can be very distressing to come to the point where you reach out for God. It is called the dark night of the soul but you would be so lucky for it to be only one night. For most of us it is an ongoing process of getting lower and lower until you either hit the bottom or decide to stop before you go splat.

There have been many dark nights leading up to the experience of being done with life; some would call it mortally wounded, blinded or stricken dead, when you are helpless and hopeless and have no strength, no vision, no direction to turn. It is in that moment if you are willing and ready for different God will speak or make its presence known within you. "Son, I am in the midst of thee, closer than breathing, nearer than hands and feet. I am the bread, the meat, the wine and the water. I am the resurrection restoring unto you even the lost years of the locust. I am Life eternal."

Doesn't get much clearer than that but you do not *understand* the words intellectually through the thinking mind of man rather **experience** them because you are in direct communion with God making you one with all that the Father hath which is the source of all experience and that brings forth the bounty, God in expression, that is the allness unto your life.

―――

When a problem or error presents after you have accepted the fact that **all answers to all questions lies within you** you take a moment to say "ok Father, here is the problem presenting and the answer is within, ie **what have I in my house** that will bring harmony into expression?" And pretty soon you will find the answer comes because God is within you and **you are asking God for it.** Think spiritual medicine to the rescue every time you "catch" error, feel it in or on you in some way just like you feel the first signs of "illness" coming into your awareness. Feel it? What do you do when you feel a cold coming on? You grab for something to relieve the symptoms and stop further involvement in the illness.

Spiritual living is no different, you go within to the spiritual medicine cabinet for that which dispels error. One elixir for all manner of human disfunction-Truth. God is and God is what you have in your house and it is eternal, harmonious and infinite in nature.

―――

All discord and disease has its origin in the *belief* that you have a mind and a life separate and apart from the allness and perfection of God's being.

There is but one Truth you must remember: there is no Law or power acting upon/against/counter to you rather you are the Law unto your body, business, home and supply **when** you know Law, God. **You** have dominion over all that is in the sky, earth and under the water. **You** are

Law, have dominion unto all no matter name or nature when you know your true nature as child of God.

Understand dominion **doesn't** mean dominance. Dominion means knowing Truth thereby not resisting evil/illusion and not picking up the sword/reacting humanly. Knowing you have dominion merely means you are cognizant of your higher conscious knowing which frees you from the effects of duality. Dominion is knowing God **is** therefore all else is no thing and **not** doing by force what you think needs to be done by the human definition of *dominance*.

There is a universal ignorance which has gripped the mind of practically every individual on earth that makes them unfriendly to Truth, antagonistic to Truth because Truth received in consciousness wipes out the very things man has come to depend on-*personal* pomp, glory, fame, fortune, power, prowess, achievement. **Therefore the *human mind* is in rebellion at once to anything that would destroy what *it* wants.**

But you aren't trying to destroy your mind, you are learning to use it as it was **intended** in the beginning as a **deductive** center for God's impartations, that which is given you to do from God within, its work for its purpose for you as you.

The human mind doesn't like to hear "I of my own self can do nothing," "why callest thou me good? There is one good, the Father in heaven." The human mind is set on glorifying self, see me, my strength, beauty, prowess, my beliefs in action.

There is only one thing keeping harmony from your personal experience and that is the universal belief you are separated from God.

To rightly understand the nature of God begin to perceive that it does not go out into the world to destroy your enemies rather it is to be admitted into your consciousness to destroy the **enemies within yourself.**

What enemies? All phases of personal sense from the greatest evil of self preservation to the least evil which is believing you are good, or philanthropic or spiritual or moral, benevolent, kind or any other attribute you give to yourself. **Only the presence of God in you allows those qualities to be your qualities because of your oneness with them.** Man has no qualities of himself, things have no qualities in and of their form, nothing in the outer world has any power or qualities because all is of God and become yours through expression when you are of God by willing choice.

The function of God is to purify you and me. You are not to call upon God to do something to someone else, you are to realize that **God functioning in your consciousness dispels error in you first and then your friends and then your enemies.**

The only thing that separates you from your harmony is knowing God aright. The difficulty lies in the *word* "God." The moment you think the *word* God you separate yourself immediately from God and the moment you start to think of synonyms of God the further away from God you get. Why? Because all you are doing is projecting a *word* into thought, only projecting an *idea* or *concept* and then you begin to worship that *concept*.

When you *think* of the *word* God you immediately begin to worship the *word* thinking the *word* is God and it isn't, it is only a *word* trying to explain what is unknowable to man which always ends in limiting your scope/vision/understanding of God so when you try to think of God as life, love etc, you are only having a vision of a specifically natured super being aligned with what you *need* from it.

When you are *tempted* to fight, resist, deny a sin, a false appetite, a disease, lack or limitation in any form just stop yourself and remember, contemplate Truth, God's Truth imparted to you within you. **The battle is because you dropped back into duality** for the moment, separated yourself from God consciousness of harmony that keeps everything just humming along. You have picked up the sword of two expressions, of *personal choice* and the only way to get back into conscious union with the Father is to **put up the sword,** stop reacting humanly to fix the situation and bring the only solution there is to bear, God in awareness.

Acknowledgment/acceptance/use of good and evil paves the way for labels. Labels are judgments, choices, decisions made through emotions/feelings/desires. Labels are shadows and shadows change the shape and depth of darkness. What is good today maybe bad tomorrow based solely on your needs, wants and desires at that moment. A good vacation can turn bad, a child is deemed bad one moment and good the next. Shadows/labels hide Truth.

What is Truth? Truth is God, capital T. Truth reveals itself as harmony, peace be with you. All God made is good and if it wasn't good it wasn't made. Read that again. It doesn't say **wasn't made**

by God. It says it **wasn't** made. If it wasn't made it **doesn't exist** as object reality rather subjective, illusory, of the mind.

The Bible clearly states every Truth about God but man cannot understand the Bible as it was meant to be understood because man doesn't have an awareness of God within, God consciousness, I. The Bible is written by I for I not i. The Bible is about you and only you when you know your Truth, child of God.

"The things of God are folly to man" and that is why so few people actually understand the words in the Bible as they do not recount necessarily actual experiences in an outer world but mostly refer to the duality of man's mind and is **trying to get man to look within** to the Truth of being which is that we all embody the Christ consciousness, the seed of Origin which is the connection to infinite intelligence, infinite expression, infinite supply and eternal life.

The Bible clearly states every Truth about God but man does not read the Bible as it was meant to be read-without your emotions and sentiments. It isn't to be read to be understood rather to take it within your secret, silent sacred place to ask "what does this mean Father?" and then await your answer.

Human man thinks he knows the answer to problems that present but man only knows how to *react* to the situation in a way that is self-serving instead of **responding** to the still, small voice within. Man tries to solve problems on the level of the problem-human-but a problem can only be solved byway of a higher understanding and that is the spiritual understanding of is.

To know that you know nothing of God is to admit you wish to know how God ordered this world you are living in and experiencing so that you can get the **most out of your expression in this form.**

It was not a physical act of getting up from the banquet of the swine and a physical journey back to the Father's house. The banquet of the swine is nothing more than our daily lives lived separate and apart from God and the journey back to the Father's house is not one that is to be accomplished by physically going any place **but by an act of consciousness in which you give yourself back to God.** This act of consciousness can never take place until there is first the recognition that you have been wandering in a far country, in the land of materiality and mentality and that it is necessary to return to the Father's house, to the source of Life to live that life.

The journey back to the Father's house is accomplished within yourself as an activity of consciousness and that activity of consciousness is meditation, prayer, silent listening for God's governance which are the basic **principles** of spiritual living.

This is the Truth saints and sages have been trying to reveal in human consciousness and only one thing has prevented the whole world accepting and living this consciousness:

Whereas all of this is true it is of no avail to anyone except in proportion as they attain an inner realization of it. So all of this Truth is really foolishness to man and it is of no avail if it is not understood as it was meant to be understood.

It only becomes the Life of you when you have attained that first spark of inner illumination/consciousness that reveals to you this **is** Truth. The only reason you can go to a spiritual healer for help is because they have attained a greater realization of the Truth of your true identity than you have but you can go and do likewise when you have received a degree of this realization.

It is only when Christ has entered in that you have the capacity to know Truth, to receive Truth and to **respond** to Truth.

Man says "if there is a God why does man suffer? Where is God in all of this? Where is God in the earthquakes, floods, hurricanes and eruptions? Where is God in the violence of man, the inhumanity of man? Where is God in all the chaos of man?"

God is not in the whirlwind, the chaos of good and bad, that is a storm all to itself unknown to God. God is not in the errors of the world, God is not in the world of man.

How is this Truth if God is equally present? Omnipresent? Omnipresence is based on **individual awareness** of God within not out in the world everywhere present like atmosphere. If God were outside of man the atmosphere outside of man would be harmonious. Since man is not harmonious you have to assume God is not outside of you to be found so you must look where you have never thought to look.

These conflicts of scripture can only be reconciled when some of the veil drops away, ie you know some Truth by which to discern Truth from belief, and it will only drop away in proportion to you searching within yourself because it is your conscious connection to God that allows the Bible to be understood.

Prayer is not beseeching, begging, pleading or threatening God for what you want to have/happen in the world around you. Prayer begins in the mind with a specific treatment-the knowing/remembering of Truth before entering into the silence for God's presence to be felt or known within.

Prayer is communion with God, **silent, sacred and secret.** It is the impartation of Itself, the all of the universe, to you within your being when there is none of the world to interfere.

Treatment is the conscious remembering/reminding of the little self, i, you as human man, of the dominion of God as all over all by remembering Truth, one will suffice. Then you rest on that one remembrance, a short passage of scripture or Truth like "grace is my sufficiency in all ways," let it float away and await Truth felt as peace and harmony ie that which would constitute to you the all encompassing love of the Father flowing within you, bringing a smile, bringing tears, bringing relief and joy. Hi Father! Big hug! Bigger kiss! Muahhh! Remember you are returning home within yourself to God and it feels no different than the excitement, love and peace you feel upon being with those out in the world who bring forth those expressions in you.

If you have prayed aright, asked correctly for God's grace by letting your listening attitude hear the impartations of Truth unto your being from within, you will bear fruit richly. If however you have asked and not received it is because you ask amiss/incorrectly.

God is spirit and can only provide that which it is, spirit. Therefore if you pray for *material* things, for change in any outer/human circumstance or condition you are going to God to get *things* it knows nothing about and cannot give. Man and spirit are separate. God knows Self, the awakened Christ in man, but God is completely unaware of man who lives in the atmosphere of duality because duality is not of the consciousness of God because God is singular, harmonious, is.

Now do you see why human man is not known to God? **Because human man is not of the consciousness of harmony** rather of i, me, my, what i want and not what you want; two different wants therefore *duality* of consciousness. There is no thing other than God therefore if you think of yourself as i instead of I, of God, you are revealing yourself as separate from I because you are not identifying as the correct I, the I of God in which there can be no other i. Human man is i and God is I. Spiritual man knows I am that I am, I and I are the same therefore they are one in the same but I and i are two completely different expressions of identity-I is reality, i is illusion caused by not knowing your true **Identity**.

Do not think that by saying the words **I and my Father are one** that makes you child of God, that all that is necessary to live in the kingdom, in the garden of Eden is to give lip service to receive.

There must be an actual contact, awareness, relationship, oneness of being that takes place within you because this awareness of God within is the Truth that makes you free from the duality of man and is the only way to rise above, to live in the world but not **of** the world's errors.

Unless something has taken place **within** you that brings the assurance of God's presence into your awareness there can be no benefit to or change in your life because God does not function in the human world therefore cannot improve humanhood. God can only show you by way of imparted Truth that the *beliefs* of *human* man are the *errors* that keeps man from living his **true nature as the child of God, joint heir to the kingdom.**

Living true Christianity, Christ knowing, is separate from all other religious or metaphysical teachings **because it is not *religion* it is a relationship and it isn't of the thinking mind but of consciousness.** This is not a way of achieving the things of the world, the desires of what *you* want humanly. The first thing you have to do is stop desiring the things *you* have been desiring. This is the hardest price for many to pay, the price of surrendering your will and your desires and it is because you have no faith, no trust in what comes after you give up your human desires and your human actions of ego and strife.

Practicing the presence of God

The Word of God in your consciousness is transformative, transforming, brings awareness of Truth to your consciousness and returns the mind back to its original purpose of deduction from the erroneous belief in it being a creative center. As you let go of the things of man, of expressing duality, of opposites, as you empty yourself of world beliefs and ways you begin to fill your consciousness with the Word of God and this is **practicing having the experience of the presence of God felt within** which once again reveals Truth-God is and only the things of God are Truth and that Truth is harmony in your midst.

Knowing the Truth of God and resting in the feeling of Truth brings God to bear not only in your conscious knowing but facilitates the availability of grace where there was none because only one with conscious awareness of God is able to bring grace to bear for those seeking grace, that which is not of the world of man because man's experience of the world is chaos, duality.

To be protected by God is to know there is no reality to anything in man's world because all in man's world is seen and experienced as *material opposites,* always as duality and always through the senses. Duality is an *illusion* not a reality therefore all the error duality "creates" is illusion as well. The reality is there is only one expression and it is creative. To be creative it must be harmonious. To be harmonious it must be of single nature/origin. God **is** harmonious expression.

Being harmonious implies there is perfection in every part of your existence ie your health is, your wealth is, your enjoyment is, your life is and is is the allness and fullness of God expressing. So you see when we speak of God being good we don't mean the good of man which is merely the opposite side of not crappy, this is the allness and the fullness of God, perfection, so when we say the good of God we mean beyond man's understanding of man's good. This doesn't mean scads of money, fame, rock star lifestyle; it means though you may have only two dollars to your name you now realize what is in the hand is merely what is visible supply, not the extent of your supply. Your supply is of God thus it has to be the nature of God-eternal and harmonious.

I don't want you to get hung up on the words/names used to express this creative consciousness man calls God. God, like every other word known to man, is just a label, means nothing but to those who understand the back story of the designation. What we call God is the embodiment, allness, entirety of all that is termed Life, the Law unto Life-the immutable Law of creation and expression that governs, maintains and sustains all that it is the form of-all that is visible and invisible.

The quiet of consciousness cannot be felt if the mind is busy because what you desire is behind the noise so the noise, chaos, chatter and confusion must be put to rest. How? Bring up a Truth and let that be the segway from earthly thoughts to God thoughts. Yes you are thinking but only as a distractive method to get you off of man and into God. Then you let that Truth become your environment within and then you get quiet and God pops in and says "I love that you come to spend time with me." This is an example of a spiritual principle called practicing the presence of God where you bring God into awareness for purpose or for the pleasure of its company, it is knowing where peace is and spending time with peace. It is because of this time spent with God you rise in conscious knowing which is the purpose of living a spiritual life.

Practicing the presence is a continuous acknowledgement of "*i* of my own self am nothing without God. Without God *i* am a husk, an avatar not in play." *i* look alive but *i* will also look dead at some point if *i* don't find that which is my sustainment, my life, that which *i* need to plug into to be functioned the way **I** was made to be functioned-by the one consciousness of my creator.

As creation you are under the knowing of God just as a child is under the knowing, the consciousness of their parents while young. Children look to parents, "can I? Is this safe? I'm scared." The parent is there to answer, "yes you can, no that is not safe, why are you scared? **I am with you always.**"

You live **by** the consciousness of that which you are **of,** God; you have no consciousness of your own because you don't have the capability. **You are the receiver not the sender.** God broadcasts and you receive, you don't create, you do what is given you to do.

This is the error of man. God uses us to express **itself,** its harmony and abundance, peace and love to the world; you don't use God. This is the correct orientation for man to be spiritual man and until you understand who is really running the show you won't even be on the stand by list.

Every person who finds God within makes it more attainable for others to find God. You are a source, an outlet for grace to flow from to awaken others. Your purpose and your job in a nut shell are:

1. Find God, good/harmony by being done with "this world"
2. Learn God, good/harmony through dying daily, study and practice
3. Love God by having a deep, personal relationship
4. Share God/good/harmony through silent prayer, treatment
5. Reap God, good/harmony through signs following
6. Live eternal life with God, good/harmony as risen, illumined spiritual man

---

The kingdom of infinite wisdom and love is already established within you.

When you understand this you will not make the mistake of trying to make the finite human mind understand God for the things of God are foolishness to man even as the things of man are foolishness to God.

Therefore to try to grasp with the human mind what God is is foolishness, it cannot be accomplished, never has been accomplished in fact after Moses received the name of God he couldn't voice it. He was able to reveal it to his brother Aaron but they couldn't share it because they were not given the understanding of **how** God comes into individual awareness.

God has to reveal itself within an individual. No one individual can reveal God to another but one spiritually illumined individual can lift the consciousness of others to where they can **perceive** that which is already within them.

In other words the kingdom of God is established within you whether at this moment you know it or feel it or benefit by it and to become aware of it you need to be lifted up in consciousness to where you can apprehend, where you can discern that which is invisibly present. That is why in the ancient schools of wisdom Truth was always taught by degrees, taught over a period of years because it was the time necessary for conscious understanding to dawn so that they could move onto the next level of spiritual understanding.

What is interesting is all that needs to be known about God can be written on one sheet of paper but that *knowledge* has never benefited anyone because **it must be felt as Truth in consciousness** to be lifted above the words read to where the meaning comes to you from within, the aha moment of instant clarity of understanding where you can say "before I was blind but now I see, where as I was in darkness now I am in light, whereas I had no comprehension now I understand."

You cannot tell another about God, you can only be the expression of God that makes them want to seek what you have that sets you apart from man in expression.

You can only demonstrate the level of your own consciousness.

Christ consciousness is not acquired by knowledge, not even the knowledge of Truth. You can **know** all the Truth ever revealed through all the philosophies and mysticisms and still not have one single grain of Christ consciousness. You could quote the Bible, be generous, loving, kind, giving but Paul reminds us if you give away all you have to the poor it would be no indication of your relationship with the spirit. **It is not any degree of human wisdom or goodness that you may attain that brings forth the Christ.**

It might be far more simple for a deep died sinner to attain the Christ than for a very good person for the reasons you can understand: the sinner is so aware of the fact that "*i* of my own self can do nothing, *i* am unworthy, the least of these, undeserving." That person has so emptied themselves that they are ready to be filled with the **I** of God whereas one living what is felt to be a fairly good life is apt to get the idea "*i* am good, kind, loving, *i* am doing just fine on my own, what is God going to do for me *i* haven't already accomplished? Life is good, why do *i* need God?"

As long as there is a trace of the belief that you yourself are the good that brings good to you, that you are deserving or worthy, in that degree you are setting up a barrier to the awareness of the Christ because the Christ cannot be known when your vessel is already full of *yourself*, your beliefs, goodness, right of actions.

Man thinks in his mind to justify actions. Spiritual man has no actions of their own so there are never any actions to justify, just harmony. You are like the child clinging to the Father's leg and will not leave, this is where you want to be and nothing of man can ever entice you because you know the Truth of the Father you are clinging to.

It isn't what you know of God, it is your application of that knowing in your life that expresses **as your life**. To humanly know something is akin to faith, it has no basis of Truth until it is **known** as Truth by way of revelation. **You have to experience God to go from *knowledge* to knowing**; this is the only way for the old man of earth to die and the new man of Spirit to be expressed. When you express Truth something of the old man dies. That Truth came alive in you but can only be expressed from the new man, not from the old man because there is no Truth to the old man, he is not under the Law of God neither can be.

Why God?

I was cleaning the kitchen one day thinking about my mom. She can be trying, so can I and in this new paradigm of taking care of her and not being able to separate myself from her as before I have had to be even more aware of my oneness with God. I forget to be kind most likely because she is my mother and that after the fourth time of being nice I tend to get snappy. She gets hurt and I get angry. With myself. I had to let go of the fact she is my mother and let God go first, let grace be my expression and there has been almost no tension, she is happy and I am not angry with myself, quite the opposite actually.

Back to the question **why God?** Because God feels good. When I am with God, letting God go first, be my expression the bitchy side of me cannot emerge because it is not *of* me because I am *of* God, peaceful, kind, benevolent, as sister to sister, brethren. When God expresses through me harmony is my experience as is my mother's.

To live in God is to be unable to be mad at yourself, guilty or fearful in any capacity because when God goes first those things of duality cannot express or present therefore are not in awareness thus not experienced. **To want to feel peace, love, kindness, joy is to want to know God.** So much of our lives are spent in the past and in the future always expecting somehow different from now in effect merely through time but no effort. To live now, in the moment is effort in that it is a different action, serves a different purpose, fills a different need, but is the only way to change the now of now to a different now of future now. You must want what God has to receive of what God is-peace of knowing you are sinless and you smile and you walk on knowing your return for sinlessness is the allness of being. Not a shabby trade off if you ask me.

Spiritual illumination/consciousness is our bond and it is a bond of love, it is set apart from any other form of relationship that exists between man. This is not a human relationship, this is a relationship that has evolved because of your prayer work within yourself with the **goal always being conscious union with God.**

In the moment you make contact with the infinite invisible you have made contact with all supply-what you shall eat, what you shall wear. Through the contact with the infinite invisible you have made contact with the infinity of being, the allness of being and that appears to your senses as the added things, those things humanly necessary to an abundant experience.

The added things:

When you desire to know the true God you will know the true God and in that will be made whole, Self complete. Your only desire to know God is to feel the love of God and live the life of harmony.

This is your reason for going to God. This is your main reason-to know God, be known **of** God and live within its presence/allness/wholeness. **The added things are the forms of God that**

come into your life because of your oneness, the forms of the Father made manifest for your use, your enjoyment, your support, for practical reasons and for the unexpected joy of realizing God in your midst in form as it appears for your enjoyment, use and sharing with your brothers and sisters.

The added things are God in expression but not the main reason for desiring God. Your need for God goes beyond the visible for peace unto your being; things themselves do not bring peace but the Father is the Gift of peace, supply, wholeness and completeness.

In the consciousness of God you **choose** to do the will of the Father, defer to its intelligence, the height of consciousness of which you have only a grain of in comparison. It is the will of the Christ to do the will of the Father and that is healing the sick, raising the dead, forgiving the sinner and feeding the hungry.

The activity of the Christ of you, being in oneness, is the healing unto man, the bread, the wine, the water and the meat of life given of freely so all may partake of the experience called Life under grace by knowing God aright.

Where there is spiritual consciousness there is no bondage to person, place or thing and there are no limitations to what you can accomplish.

Christ awareness is what brings about resurrection and ascension.

The Christ is embodied in you. The Christ is the son of God, the **spirit** of God and it manifests/expresses as you when you become **aware** of its presence within.

The acknowledgment of this presence within brings forth a miracle. In man's experience all power is outside of them, the power of climate, weather, infection, the calendar, age, peace, war, sin, all out in the world acting *upon* them. But all of this stops the moment you acknowledge Christ dwelleth in you. This now gives all power unto you, the spirit **of** you. God gave spiritual man dominion over all that is through the son of God within you, the Christ or the transcendental consciousness.

Why has the world not know of this presence to bring it into expression for the good of all? The Hebrews never have acknowledged that the Messiah, the Christ, has come. The Christians acknowledge the Christ came for three years and left and are waiting for the second coming.

Both Hebrews and Christians are without a Christ. One waiting for the Christ and the other awaiting the return of Christ **which is the acknowledged absence of Christ in the experience of 99.95% of human man.**

God has presented itself to you within the temple (you) many times. God did not send you to earth without an indwelling Christ but man has abandoned the Christ in each but God has never forsaken you.

Since nothing can happen to you that is not of your own consciousness you have to open your consciousness to the Truth of the Christ within, that you are the visible expression of God, sinless, complete and eternal.

I was never meant to imply individuality, personal, self, *i,* me or my.

I is the universal Law of creative expression expressing as all that is-invisible spirit in visible form of which all is of including you.

Consciousness is the governing influence of harmony, indivisible ie singular and can never be unlike itself because God is too pure to behold inequity-that unlike itself, ie duality caused by separation from Truth, therefore what is called bad or evil has no existence/reality because it is unlike God and God is the only reality of all existence.

You lose your fear of the outside world when you realize God is real by way of an experience of the presence within because there is nothing to fear when you know you are eternal in nature.

You keep your mind stayed on God by recognizing God as the soul of all those you meet by reminding yourself God is the Truth of those you meet. This is not only keeping your mind stayed on God it is also loving your neighbor as yourself which brings grace to bear where no grace was.

There will be roses but there will be some thorns, it takes a while to get to the point where your previous karma has exhausted itself and you are reaping only the karmic good that you have been sharing, your bread on the water, as the grace that you release of God as a vessel or instrument of God's divine harmony to the world.

No one ever receives the grace of God or the visitation of the Christ just for the purpose of enabling them to retire to a life of boredom. Of those who have much much is demanded, of those who even receive just a grain of Truth demands are immediately made upon it.

So if you are asking how can you experience Christ more fully in your life be prepared for the answer-you will be busier than you have ever been **but it will be a different kind of work**-you will finally understand the purpose of this existence which is to return home in conscious knowing to live Truth, God in expression.

If you are ready for the Christ you must be ready for the Christ within you to be called upon by those looking for the spirit. When you become aware of God you are saying that you are **choosing** to serve as the Christ, as a **servant** of God. If you receive the illumination of Christ it is for the purpose of sharing that knowing with the world by way of the grace you allow to flow from you as God's instrument of healing to the world.

This is the only way that God gets into the conscious awareness of those looking for Truth. Truth can only come by way of one who knows Truth and reveals Truth not as your Truth but as that which you are to take into God and have God give back to you the Truth you are to know.

If God's response/impartation is a mirror of what you brought in then what you were given was Truth but it has been defined specifically for you for your understanding directly from the mouth of God. If however God's answer is a polar opposite to what you brought in then you're understanding should be that what you brought in was **not** Truth and that you have now been given Truth that dispels the error which had been introduced into your consciousness.

Truth reveals error and it is in this way you correct your perception of life by living by the Truth **received** and not the error *believed*.

We are all states of consciousness **not** persons. Jesus was a state of conscious awareness, conscious of the Christ within and expressed as this consciousness which is benevolence, charity, kindness and peace. He was so thoroughly touched by the Divine that **error/duality was not in his awareness which is the definition of living Truth,** walking a spiritual path.

To be able to look past appearances and say "what does hinder you? Pick up your bed and walk" is Truth in awareness and is what reveals the unreality of fear, pain, disease, lack and infirmity. Therefore being of the consciousness of grace is sufficient for all experiences because grace is the allness of God in your experience. **Thy grace is my sufficiency in all ways.**

When it is said "the dawning of the Christ in your consciousness brings peace" it means Truth has been revealed which allows you to rest, let the error go, not react to it and harmony is your resting place. You feel God, the singularity of expression of is and it is always and eternally the same spiritual perfection which can in no other way be experienced than as what it is-peace and harmony unto the very center of your being. This is why you must be of the **state of consciousness** that willingly accepts God as the Truth of your being to experience the Truth of your being which is harmony, peace, love, allness-because they are qualities of God and not of the consciousness of man with a flexible moral code.

Spiritual consciousness does not overcome or destroy matter or material conditions but **reveals Truth** that no such conditions exist which finite man's senses *react* to. Spiritual consciousness knows the letter of Truth and reveals the appearance as the illusion it is, a condition of the human mind that believes in two powers/expressions ie harmony and strife, good and bad, nice and nasty and employs expressions of duality in the execution of their daily living contributing to or trying to mitigate the chaos around them.

So far as it is known Jesus never left written word yet his teaching is the foundation of the morals and ethics for much of the world. Many other mystics or seers left only the words spoken to their immediate followers yet by spiritual power, grace, these messages have become the Living Water through countless ages.

The wisdom of the ages uttered by spiritually illumined men and women encircles the world and is not confined to time or place. The Truth that fills your consciousness goes out from you like rings created by a stone hitting the surface of water making ever-wider circles until it embraces all of humanity.

All that is necessary to your fulfillment is included in the infinite consciousness of God which is your consciousness when you are **aware of God's presence.** In an individual way God expresses itself as you and your abilities are really the abilities of God expressing outwardly as your abilities. Your activity/life energy is the degree of God consciousness active in you making the responsibility for you God's responsibility.

By gaining the consciousness of God's presence you have the whole secret of success in every expression of life.

It is **you** of higher consciousness knowing Truth, not the other person, who must release God to flow to go before you to make the crooked places straight, to make your life smooth and fruitful. Therefore the grace you release returns to you as harmony within your experience/being. You of the higher consciousness are responsible for releasing this internal splendor so others may taste of the honey of God instead of the ash of man and in this way and this way only your bread is returned upon the water pressed down and flowing over-abundance with 12 baskets left over to share.

There is only one consciousness, one spiritual awareness and those that are receptive and responsive to it are of it.

This consciousness is always fruitful revealing peace, joy, abundance, harmony, the needed and the added things.

You have control over the weather, not by going to God begging for safety from it rather by knowing the Truth of weather/natural events. What is Truth? God is all, that which is seen as weather, threatening or not is nothing more than God in expression in that particular form **but it is the same source as you and God can not harm itself.** It is not in its nature to harm part of itself so how could a hurricane take you from the consciousness you know yourself to be? You can never, no matter what form or what expression you take, not know who you are for you are eternally I am.

Does that mean you will never leave this visible expression? No, the experience of spiritual man is that of continuous evolution of consciousness of which your visible body is of therefore you will leave this expression but this is not death rather transfiguration, change.

You will find that you can be a great healer simply by smiling. Through the simple recognition of the Christ of every person and addressing this Christ brother to brother you reveal Truth and receive harmony. A smile of recognition is more powerful than all mental striving for outer healing and the spiritual healing will be sweeter and more lasting because it is a direct result of one child of God recognizing another child of God and seeing a brother in all ways.

God's protection of and for you comes from your knowing Truth-God is and God is within you. This is your shield against the sword of man; not to fight, not to resist but to know God goes before you to make the crooked places straight. It has no opposite, no opposition, that which is is eternally so. That which is eternal is harmonious of being thus the is-ing, the be-ing of God is perpetual good in your experience to the degree you are one with God. Think of it this way: your life, your experience is paved by your love and devotion of God, your connection, need and desire for its presence. This alone is what paves your path of good and this path is yours to dance upon and experience as long as you are in conscious union with God.

Do not seek wealth, health or power; seek the realization of the presence of the Christ in all man and all things will be added unto you. Behind the wisdom of the world there is one word that makes all wisdom come alive-consciousness.

Consciousness is the secret word and the secret behind the Word.

Where the consciousness of the presence of God is **not** recognized there is bondage, slavery, sin, false appetite, lack, limitation, disease, fear, pain and man's inhumanity to man. But where the consciousness of God is present there is liberty, freedom, wholeness, completeness, peace of being.

You have infinite capacity because God is the actual Self of you therefore through meditation, inner listening, prayer, you contact and draw on its infinity. Once you can draw on your source there is no handicap in your experience the Self of you cannot overcome but the point is there must be that desire otherwise it cannot be. You know as well as I do AA has helped many millions of people but there are many who have tried it and not benefited from it because the will to be other than they express at the moment wasn't there, that inner desire, drive, capacity to want to achieve it so it is that there are many students along the spiritual path that go no further than being healed or trying to get on a platform to display their ego.

There is no limit to your spiritual capacity, even the full christhood. Those who awaken to this spark will go on from there and give it all they have to attain it however what degree is stored within your consciousness is the degree that will be carried into the next incarnation.

You will never be without you because you were created as you and that is your permanent identity. You may be a man in one iteration/incarnation and a woman or something completely unknown at this moment, the next. **But you will always know you are I am.** You will always be I, always the I of your own identity. And the reason is when you were formed in the bossom of the Father in the beginning it was as in individual expression of that infinity.

The purpose of this life is to continue rising in conscious understanding to break free of who you think you are to live the expression of who you truly are-child of God.

Why is God allowing X to happen?

God isn't allowing it, God isn't even aware of it because there is no God where God is not realized in consciousness therefore until you make your contact with God you have no God on which to depend.

God doesn't permit or create the errors of your experience rather **your sense of separation from God is causing it.** Pray without ceasing, keep your mind stayed on God and you make this a continuous experience/dispensation of good. You don't have to take thought because God goes before you to do those things necessary for your experience and that's why you never have to tell God what you want or need.

You never have to tell God you need money or companionship, home or clothing, you never have to tell God about anything. God is the infinite intelligence of the universe, that which **is** the universe, seen and unseen, maintains and sustains it without any human advice or interaction. If God can do that for the universe can you trust your expression to that same presence and power?

Most people think they believe in/know God but by the time you come to a mystical or spiritual life you have gone beyond the *belief* in God. You have come to the **conviction** through awareness of its being in, as and through you. You radiate God like an aura when the mind is stayed on God and it is felt by those open and accepting of God's grace but the operative words are **receptive, open to, desirous of and surrender to.**

It isn't heaven *and* earth it is heaven **on** earth through conscious knowing of Truth.

There are those who could never agree that human ingenuity, physical force, mental pressure, and unlimited capital are **not** necessary. But you know that by the application of spiritual principles you can live a normal and harmonious life completely fulfilled.

You experience this fulfillment not through affirmations but by **realizing** your oneness with God constitutes your oneness with all that is and will express itself **as** home, friend, student, money, book or teacher, anything of which you have need because the Father knows your needs before the advent of their desire in you. It is in this way you receive without asking which is the Gift of God unto you, grace in your midst.

In the spiritual healing ministry many people will come seeking loaves and fishes ie healings without making any changes to their consciousness instead of seeking for God itself. This is not your concern. You are not to be concerned with appearances rather you just do you, you bring God into awareness to heal the sick, feed the hungry, comfort the poor. You just sing your song of harmony and those who are **receptive** will receive it.

All you are ever tasked to do is bring God on the field to dispel illusion from your awareness and move on. The world at large is not your concern, you bring God to bear **for yourself and those receptive.**

Don't put your faith in your practitioner, in idols, books or ritual, let it be in the Truth that God *is,* that is what your practitioner is realizing for you-God is the only Truth, Presence, Substance, Law and Expression of all that is and that includes you, pure spiritual perfection in form.

When you go within and seek for Truth, light, peace, harmony or understanding you are in conscious oneness with the source of Truth and what is needed will be received.

There is a kingdom of God. This is not just a passage in a Bible, there is literally, actually a kingdom of God and it is within you and you only have access to it as you come closer and closer to living by grace rather than by taking thought.

Living by grace does not stop the reasoning process in normal affairs, on the contrary it makes the reasoning process clearer. If you have a problem **and** you have been able to attain even a moment of God contact you'll get the answer to your problem and it will be one that no human could have worked out for you because it will be of harmony for all not better for one over others. Can you see why human man could never come up with the solution God gives that is perfect?

Some may get angry because others seem to be progressing faster than they are and call this a false teaching because it isn't working for them. It doesn't matter how much you want God in your life, God can only come into your awareness in the degree you are willing to stop being who you think you are and let God reveal who you truly are. You cannot fight God and want God at the same time but that is exactly what you are doing when you don't want to give up the proclivities of human expression. The only reason it may seem others are progressing more quickly on their spiritual path shown outwardly as abundance, peace, harmony and beautiful expression of talents or skills is because they are in it to win it. No going back. This is it, it has to be kind of attitude.

You have to trust and trust is gained through practice and study because only then are you able to prove to yourself the Truth of the still small voice within and it is this which brings you to the awareness of the presence of the Father within and this is what cements this path for most. **When you have met the true God how could you go back to the false God** except for the fact you are not yet done playing in the world of make believe? That is fine, admit you are not ready and move on.

To be jealous or angry of another's success is to be human through and through and proof there is still work to be done within you before you come to this practice of spiritual living.

If you truly want to be here do the work-study, practice, meditate, heal and nothingize 24/7. If this is the life you want it is the life you have to practice living which means **dying to who you thought you were to reveal who you truly are.**

What is prayer/meditation/silent inner listening?

To rightly understand the nature of prayer is the most important function of any individual on the face of the earth. When prayer is rightly understood it brings all of God's love, peace, harmony and abundance to bear for yourself first and foremost but also to all who desire the grace of God in their experience.

Prayer is your contact, your agreement and your relationship with God.

Prayer is the means by which the relationship of God the Father and God the son is established in demonstration-the Word made flesh, the consciousness of God manifest in visible form, the sufficiency of grace.

Prayer when understood is the means by which you overcome material sense, material living and bring yourself to that place where your life is supernaturally, spiritually governed, protected, guided and experienced. You get to a point where food goes from delicious to good. Not that you don't enjoy food but that the experience of God, when thy grace is truly your sufficiency, becomes the feeling of fullness, sating the unknown source of hunger with the consciousness of God instead of the things of man-food, sex, activities.

God doesn't take away your enjoyment of food, friends, companionship or work rather it reverses your focus. The outside world doesn't hold the same pull, sway, mesmerism over you because the within of you is now alive and active and these experiences of Self are beyond any food, activity or experience you could have in the material world.

The true definition of prayer is inner listening also called meditation or silent contemplation but all mean you are awaiting the presence within to announce itself which is the confirmation of the reality of its existence.

To pray **aright** is to pray only for the things of God-wisdom, love, patience, kindness, forgiveness, Truth of understanding etc. You cannot go to God for things to improve your human existence therefore you must go within devoid of the human parts of you that want, desire or need ie ego, pride, judgement.

Prayers of need are never answered. Why? Because there is never any lack in the kingdom. How could there be if you understand that you are **of** the only creative intelligence there has ever been and as such are completely supported, supplied, maintained and sustained by your creator, your source of being when you are in the flow of it, within it, experiencing it.

If you understand "all that I have is thine" how can you ask for things that you need? You already have all that is of God so how can you need or desire a thing if you know your true nature to be the child of God eternally supported? **You cannot and that is the error of your prayer** and this is the reason you will never see a righteous man begging bread-the righteous man knows his source of supply and the allness and fullness there of already established within him.

Prayer is how you make a way for the imprison splendor to escape, the divine love and healing consciousness of God or grace of God. Through meditation, inner listening a realization of the presence of God comes and peace washes over you, what you know to be confirmation of a healing having taken place has been released out in the world going about the Father's business and somewhere in the world there are those reaching out for Christ healing and receive it because of your oneness with God.

Now do you see why you do not demonstrate persons, places, things or conditions? You can only demonstrate the presence and activity of God and let God do all the performing, adding to, removing of the outer world because God reveals the Truth of anything unlike its own nature and expression and what can that be except the belief in a selfhood apart from God which creates an atmosphere of duality?

Man's consciousness must be above animalistic, above bad humanhood, above good humanhood, above intellect, knowledge and human purity or chastity to be ready to accept the next level of consciousness which is that of spiritual identity.

The people of Moses' time would not have understood more than the 10 commandments because that was even a stretch to their understanding/need because their level of conscious understanding was limited to the visible things, of pain and pleasure, reward and punishment, have or take.

Christ consciousness is the next step which frees you from the mindset of the 10 Commandments to the reality of being which has nothing to do with who or what you thought you were and nothing resembling the world experienced through human senses.

The Christ consciousness makes you free from the desire for that which does not belong to you, makes you free from erroneous traits of character, from limitation of any sort.

It is wonderful to realize that the man who is set free in Christ, who is free of all human entanglements, was at best only a short time before *a good human!* It is merely a transition from one sense or state of consciousness/realization/understanding to another. All the experiences under Moses and Christ will be those of you and me; you won't be crucified bodily but you will rise from the tomb when your conviction is of sufficient degree.

Communion/true prayer:

To get into the atmosphere of silent communion with God just sit and close your eyes. Let your body relax, move as necessary so that after a few minutes you are not aware of your body so take the time to get comfortable. Take your mind out of your body and relax in that space behind your closed eyes. Just find a place where you don't see/sense identifiable form but more observing your inner space, whatever vacuous quality that brings to your imagination.

Now bring a Truth to bear.

God is all, I am of God substance and form, grace is my sufficiency, I am that I am.

Ask and you shall receive. Ask for the things of God and those things will be given-peace, joy, harmony companionship and supply from within. Now just rest knowing God will answer you and in the answer you will have your peace. The still small voice that is within each and every one of us will be heard, felt or somehow known to you and peace is felt as you realize you're not alone, have never been alone and now know it is God's good pleasure to give you the kingdom of heaven on earth.

The moment you have God awareness through the Christ of your own being you have no more life to live, the responsibility is now on God's shoulders. From now on all you have to do is follow where God leads you into greener pastures, beside still waters, out of the valley of the shadow of death and on to eternity.

To correctly understand the nature of prayer is the most important responsibility of every individual on earth. To pray that the reign of God be established in the consciousness of all man, that all man be opened up to the still small voice within to bring each individualized expression of God back into the consciousness that was and will be again their true nature is to pray righteous prayer ie prayer that is answered with the awareness of God.

When prayer is rightly understood it brings all of God to bear in your life and in the lives of those of your consciousness accepting of God's presence. The conscious awareness of God within brings wisdom, abundance and peace into your home, community, the nation and the world.

Learning to pray aright, to go within and listen for Truth, guidance, understanding and support is the most important thing for you to spend your time on.

The whole world is proof of the failure of man to get anything through prayer/praying to a God outside of themselves and is proof **there is no God outside of yourself.**

Intuition rightly understood is God.

That which people call intuition is that which happens when the mind is quiet, there is nothing going on and intuitively, from within yourself, you get an impulse, an idea, a revelation, an "I get it!" moment. Intuition is that which comes to you from within but it isn't your mind thinking it, it is that you have inadvertently opened the door, the channel, the flow of God intelligence, grace, revelation.

Many people follow their intuition because they have learned over the years that it doesn't let them down. That is God. **That which comes to you from within not of your thinking mind is that of God bringing grace/harmony.** I believe they present to us as chances to grasp the source of miracles because that is what they are, things that happen without the aid of human hands. These impartations, inspirations will eventually lead one to desire to find out more about them, where they come from and ultimately what they mean and this is the definition of a spiritual path.

For myself my journey began when I discovered something that I called "pushing the universe." There were times I felt the inharmony within, pushed it down and tried to ignore it because I wanted what I wanted damn it!

One day I got that feeling within, an irregular heart beat and nervous tension in my body, slight buzzing in my head. I realized it came at the time I was to make a big decision. This had happened over the years but it was only then I somehow began to associate the feeling with something that would end badly, not an omen of bad tidings but just a "hey, you have done this before, thought this way, rationalized it and worked it all out knowing it was a tightrope walk at best" but the *i* want of me always seemed to get the best of me and then *i* would regret it because there would be a mess to clean up and in many cases the loss of investment, inventory or property because *i* had gone beyond my human limits in some way. Were you paying attention to the little *i*? Me, my, ego, pride talking?

So this time when *i* got that feeling *i* stopped and said to myself, "no, *i* am pushing the universe, going against something and **I** can feel it and for the fist time **I** am going to honor it." 2 weeks later grace was revealed though I didn't know it as grace. Because of not going against the feeling within me I met my husband who is my best friend, my true partner in all ways to this day. Boy, what I would have missed if I hadn't changed the consciousness behind my behavior; I wanted to do life differently than I had been and that simple thought blossomed into what you are reading today.

This is the path you step onto when you stop pushing the universe, stop trying to manipulate, orchestrate or in any way try to determine your future through personal action. Your future is determined solely by your understanding of self and in that understanding find Self, God, the allness of being.

The point is this-all have experienced God at one point or another and may have at first thought it was God but then changed the designation of source because no one talks about how God is with you helping you out so to keep from feeling like a freak, weirdo, nut, you put it down to a one-off, a fluke. But in doing that you have denied the reality of God and suffer the pain, the karma of living without God to live amongst man where you sort of fit in but continue to feel the ache of emptiness you are hoping to fill with the things of man and the world.

Know this: if it was from within, given freely and was exactly what you needed to bring **harmony** to self, situation or future (you could see how it could play out ie harmonious in all ways) God has touched you and will do so again if you do what you did-get quiet, rest and ask for Truth, God, harmony to be bear.

That is all you want from intuition isn't it? That which you do not as yet know? That which will bring peace within you? Peace through right solution? No peace can be found out in the world if it first is not within you to flow out to be the peace you experience. You bring your own peace, joy, harmony and supply with you wherever you go and it is of you through you out into expression.

When people say to trust your intuition it should be with this caveat now that you have an understanding of what it is you are being given: Truth from God from within will always bring **harmony** to all situations and to **all** involved if they are receptive to God in awareness. If what you do, how you *react* to the situation is for *personal* gain, *personal* satisfaction, *personal* anything it is of your *human* thinking mind thus of duality and you will experience the results of human living.

True prayer is never addressed outside of yourself nor does true prayer expect anything from outside your own presence. The kingdom of God is within you and all good must be looked for there.

Rightly speaking there is not God *and* you but God ever manifest **as** you and this is the oneness which assures you of infinite good.

God is as all and your relationship with God through communion/inner listening is the constant recognition of this Truth.

It is not possible to *get* anything through prayer and the principle behind that is this: God is the source of every form therefore **if you haven't God you haven't the form** but if you have God you have all that God is the form of. Therefore when you are consciously one with God you are consciously one with all that is and all is available to you because it is God in form and not material/matter/physical in nature *separate* and *apart* from God to be *gotten* through human means.

Pre-awakener:

Pre-awakeners are those things that take you out of human thought, make you stop and wonder "did that really just happen or was that my imagination?" These instances that take you out of the world of sense and inside to quiet contemplation are another tear in the curtain of the unreality of life as you have been living it. These pre-awakeners are the little embers of a fire just being kindled that eat away at your certainty of life as you know it. You become curious about what is inside of you and little by little you realize the world with all its enticements, desires and perceived rewards begins to look less and less appealing.

This shift is a tipping point on your journey because when you get to living less in the world and more within yourself, learning, exploring, enjoying the peace within you suddenly feel you are missing out, getting old, shouldn't feel happy about staying in. "I'm getting boring" you say, "I'm losing friends because they say I have changed!"

And you have; you are becoming more and more open, transparent to the complete shift from man to spirit. This isn't a test of God, it is the feeling of middle ground you had been searching for, it is the peace and harmony you have desired by pulling yourself out of the world with its noise, lights, force/fake happiness but in a way it feels like you are giving up/losing things.

But what are you gaining? What honestly did the world hold that brought you the peace and harmony this inner world provides? It may feel lonely or solitary right now, it should, you are cleaning house, your house/mind/consciousness but know this: God **is** all, God **is** you, you are **of** God, you are one with **all** spiritual thought and being and within that simple statement is revealed the kingdom of God smack dab in the center of you and now real living begins as spiritual man supported, maintained, supplied and protected by omnipotence, omniscience and omnipresence.

Omni-only, one, the all knowing consciousness and the constant eternal **presence** is your shield, your protection from the errors of man, it is your atmosphere, your "bubble" of God in, around and through you at all times going before you, staying behind, sharing this bubble of God so others may know what it feels like to live in the reality of invisible presence instead of the illusion of power with no Source or Law.

Preparation for meeting God within:

You may be sure that if anyone is lifted in a given moment from mortal sense to the divine there has been a period of preparation preceding it, probably many years, most likely many centuries, and then, just at that moment came the full flowering of realized Truth.

I want you to contemplate this one Truth: you have been in existence as long as God has been because you are, we all are, individual expressions of God therefore we must have begun our existence when God began its and since God has no beginning and no end neither do we.

I was working with a Sister who had the realization of her true nature during our time together and though as amazing as it was to witness her receiving Truth, what was the real jaw dropper was that she realized the Christ of her had been working for possibly hundreds of thousands of years to bring her to this moment of realization.

She finally understood the still small voice within her was the God of her, that she had returned to the Father's house, that she was the prodigal son of the Bible returning to the consciousness from which she came, the real her, spirit, of Source, not human but God expressing and as such heir to the kingdom and its abundance of supply and support.

You are whole, you are complete, you are home when you realize the Truth unto you. Until this understanding blooms in your conscousness you will continue to go around again and again in this form of being until at some point you reach the point of understanding that God can do nothing for you until you find the God within. This is the whole purpose of you being in this visible form-to once again find your Truth of oneness, of isness and return to the Father's house, divine consciousness so that you can move on to the next adventure after this visible one which may also be visible or not but regardless of what it is you will do it as spirit and not man separated from God.

Preparedness:

You are prepared for the knowing of Truth when you are prepared to accept Truth and this preparation is merely the desire to know the unknown, you are preparing your mind to be open, accepting and desirous of that which it seeks. You cannot go on a camping trip and have expectations of it being a wonderful time if you don't prepare. You don't go to a job interview without preparation. In all things you desire you prepare yourself by being open and receptive to what it is you are desiring. If you desire to know something you are open to all that it is and if it doesn't jive with something already in your thinking mind you have to let go of what you *thought* was Truth to let the actual Truth come on in and get cozy.

There are usually many years of preparation before you finally desire to know other than duality/chaos in the form of pain/weight of the errors you suffer, until you say enough is enough, there has to be a better way, a more harmonious way of living, of having and being than this! Ding! Ding! Human living-pain, suffering, lack and illness-have been the **preparation** you needed to finally get where you want to be-with God, home again.

This is also the reason why there will be those you will not be able to help, not be able to heal spiritually because they are not done with the world of good and bad, they are still having fun or have not gotten to the point where the suffering has become an impetus for change. There may be one of this mind in your household, the wild child, the addict, one the world of sense has taken over. These are **never** lost causes, you treat and heal silently, sacredly and secretly and as you do the results may not be evident as far as a change in behavior/consciousness but know without a doubt grace is absolutely working the way is does and the fruitage will appear in the now for every moment experienced is experienced in the now.

The final part of preparedness is **surrender.** You must be nothing, know you are nothing before you can **become** everything **through** oneness but it is this admission, this humility that is the **key** to everlasting Life, **knowing** you are nothing without the awareness of the Source of all good and wanting beyond anything else to once again be within that love, harmony, peace, abundance and joy.

That is all there is to **salvation, rebirth or transfiguration**-a change in consciousness from that of human consciousness capable of good and evil to that of God consciousness, singular, only, harmonious expression.

Heaven on earth is a state of **consciousness** experienced inwardly and expressed outwardly through the revealed Truth that God is **I** and you are of that **I** when you know yourself to be **I** child of God and not *i* human man that is born and dies.

It is an agreement wherein you listen and respond to what is given you to do and God does the rest. Easy peasy.

---

2 parts to spiritual living/prayer/inner listening:

Realization of oneness

Demonstration of that oneness

Prayer is an attitude and has nothing to do with words or thoughts.

It is the attitude of opening yourself to God or of placing yourself in the position to receive God. It is an attitude and it is also an altitude. It is the attainment of an attitude of expectancy, of oneness, of being; an attitude of being a transparency, instrument, means by which Grace/God can come to earth. The attitude cannot be voiced better than Samuel's: "Speak Lord, thy servant heareth."

These are not mere human words they are an **attitude of prayer** and it shows an attitude of listening, receptivity and humility. It is an acknowledgment that there is something above and beyond yet closer than breathing, nearer than hands and feet. Prayer, when it reaches its highest point is really an attitude of **let me be filled with you Father.**

It is an attitude of the expectancy of spiritual harmony **knowing** thy grace is my sufficiency in all things. No one knows what thy grace is yet when you can take the attitude of thy grace and not know the form it will take, this is not only an attitude but also a very high altitude of prayer. It is a fulfillment of Paul's statement that we be unclothed of mortality and be clothed upon with immortality. You cannot be clothed upon with immortality while you are living mortality so here is another attitude of prayer: "let me be unclothed and clothed."

To be able to close your eyes and open consciousness to thy presence or thy peace-this is the correct attitude of prayer. Then you become a beholder of Life. This is another attitude, that of being a beholder, awakening each morning and wondering what things God has in store for you. **Get into the rhythm of being a beholder** and you will find that the spirit fills each hour of the day with what is righteous for you.

Unless you can believe that there is an invisible presence called consciousness and an invisible activity of consciousness that is living your life, there is no way to become a beholder. Remember Paul: "I live yet not I, the Christ liveth in me." When you can feel or witness that there is an invisible something living your life expressing as the added and needed things in your experience which you could not have brought about, you are living a life of praying without ceasing.

Until you can perceive there is a presence within you you cannot pray aright but when you can close your eyes and know that it **is** then you will discover there will be impartations to follow and obey. Only in this way does **all prayer become an attitude of listening, of letting, of beholding** because from then on this presence, God in awareness, lives your life, it performs that which is given you to do, the same presence that makes the demand fulfills itself through you.

This is why the Master could say: "I can of my own self do nothing ... if I bear witness of myself, my witness is not true ... the Father within me, he doeth the works." In other words it is not the human sense of i, personality, ego rather it is the **consciousness of I am** that does the works through you.

Remember the human is the son of a bond woman but the moment you have no human desires, the moment you have the awakening which is the seeking of spirutal Truth, spiritual grace, spiritual peace then you are the child of the free woman no longer subject to material or mental laws but living by grace and **God's grace is your sufficiency in all ways.**

Praying without ceasing:

There must be a principle by which to live, one that is simple, basic and sound that orders all below it into perfect harmony:

Impersonalization of all good and evil means to not give reality, validity, emotion, reaction, ie power, to that which doesn't exist knowing that the only expression, the only Law, the only Life of you and me is of God, the grace of God, the good of God, completely separate and apart from the good man knows as the opposite of his bad.

God orders your world, it is the guiding, maintaining and sustaining principle, energy, Life and Law of your expression in this form. To know Truth is to purify yourself of the beliefs of man/duality and live under grace but this purification, this clearing of the old consciousness of its beliefs **must** be practiced **daily** in the form of "dying daily," dissolving errors by knowing Truth as they present to you or others. To remain pure you must keep yourself in the flow of grace which is the effect of being of God consciousness as your nature of being.

You will know pretty soon if you are being "double minded" because your healings will fail, you will see conditions as good and bad and react instead of knowing Truth and begin to encounter karma which had passed you by for a while. Karma isn't punishment from God for disobedience rather it is just an **error returning to you** to show you the error of *your* way of being, living, expressing.

To pray without ceasing merely means to listen and observe the world around you not thinking and reacting to the illusions of man that may be presenting.

Why is it ok to pray for wisdom/light? It is an acknowledgement that at this moment you don't have all that you are entitled to as child of God and in acknowledging that and turning to your own Christ for that light you are praying aright.

Pleading and begging are not praying but is taught as such under orthodoxy but is actually paeanistic and has nothing to do with God, grace, spirituality or Truth. True prayer, prayer that does what prayer is meant to do, have communion with God, is silent, secret and sacred, it is a listening attitude, a receptive attitude and a surrendering to that which is so much smarter than you to learn from, lean on, laugh with and cry out to for understanding to once again find your peace.

Prayer is a recognition of God's presence.

Why? Because if you are praying aright you are listening for God to commune with you, be with you, talk with you. When you pray aright you are **with** God; what more of a recognition could there be than already knowing the Self of you?

You profane prayer when you bring in personal desire, worry or fear. How can you be established in God and fear and doubt for the outcome at the same time?

Prayer isn't thinking thoughts it is waiting for Truth to come from the depths of your own being. No strain, no mental effort you merely let it flow forth from within your own being.

The really cool thing about prayer is that everything needful flows out from and comes back to you and has nothing to do with work done by your hands or thinking mind. This is grace, the activity of God in your midst in visible and invisible form. Grace is your bread on the water, that which is to be yours through your oneness with the Father.

Grace is the return for your living where grace is-God consciousness-and this return in visible and invisible form is best explained by the human word **confluence**-when everything comes together at a specific point of now. It is the resulting experience of living your nature as spirit.

Everything that happens in your experience is a confluence of events that gives opportunity to know something greater than yourself. Every problem, confluence of events, is an opportunity to know God and every expression of grace is a result, confluence of events, of the opportunities taken to stay in oneness with God and brings with it a deeper understanding of Truth and more God in awareness.

Your prayer becomes less of thinking thoughts or declaring Truth except as a prepatory step and more in the sense of awareness, of receptivity that enables you to sit back and say "alright Father, I am ready to receive of you" and then into you comes this divine impulse either in the form of some statement of Truth or just as the feeling of warmth, peace or release. Be for warned: you cry a lot on this path with sheer joy out of no where when God pops in to say hello and give you a hug.

When that contact comes you have had the actual experience of God and it is this experience of God in your awareness that lives your life harmoniously. Up to that time it is merely a statement in the mind and a statement in the mind is far from demonstration. **It is when the statement in the mind becomes a feeling in the heart that you can then know that you have hold of the hand of God and the hand of God has your hand.**

So above all things make this practice before leaving home in the morning, make it a point to establish that contact. In the beginning of your practicing this path it will take time for you to make God contact and feel it. This is not to say you haven't already made contact in some other way either by way of intuition or being in the flow or feeling like you are not you at times because of the ease of work.

When you are new to sitting in the silence it takes time to get yourself into the consciousness of God because the consciousness of man is hard to shut off. It will come, one day you will suddenly notice you went right into the silence with no fight from your mind. One day you will notice you are giving a treatment without realizing you are doing it. Just like everything worth knowing it takes time to know because it isn't just reading and repeating, **it is knowing it well enough to teach another because it is who you are, what you do and how you express your life which is God's life available to all who desire it.**

Prayer, inner listening, is for the realization, awareness, and relationship with the presence **already of you.**

To pray aright is to pray for the salvation of others, those in need of God's love and guidance. To pray for your friends and relatives already within your consciousness of God serves no purpose because **the purpose of prayer is to bring God to those in the deepest of sins, with the greatest need and the most receptivity to knowing that which is other than what this life of duality provides** and that is why it is important to pray for those who are ignorant of Truth so they too can rise.

There is only one way to live as a mystic-to live by the principles/rules set out for one **wanting** to be back **with** the Father.

What are the principles/rules of being a mystic, of one in conscious union with God?

Know God by way of an actual experience of meeting God within that blossoms into the most beautiful relationship through prayer/inner listening.

Know the Truth of all man as child of God and do not malpractice your brother by judging by appearances.

Know the Truth of error as illusion, maya, echo, no thing real/tangible therefore do not react/find no need to pick up the sword.

Forgive 70x7 because you cannot go to God for forgiveness if you hold others in bondage to unforgiveness.

Heal indiscriminately so all may know peace for only peace within man will stop the atrocities of man against themselves and the world.

It is not hard, it is merely a lot of words saying be kind, loving and generous knowing God is and is within you forever pouring itself forth for your peace and supply.

Prayer is a state of conscious receptivity.

The Word of God is nothing that you say rather that which God utters within you.

One form of meditation is called contemplative meditation because you silently bring up, contemplate, some idea concerning God, a Truth, one of the red letter passages from the New Testament, think upon it for just a few moments then become **receptive and let** the impartation/meditation come through from God.

Practicing the presence of God-the foundation of spiritual living

There is a spirit in man and this spirit ordains, heals, resurrects, lifts up, illumines but it must be an experience and to have the experience of God within you as your true consciousness you **must practice the presence of God in your life.**

How do you practice the presence of God? Meditation, prayer, going within the silence and listening for God to speak, to be felt, heard, sensed or in some way makes its presence known within your being.

The more you live in the Word, Truth of God by way of mystical literature and scripture, the more you live in the awareness of the Spirit and its function the more you experience God in your awareness as your expression.

Practicing the presence brings about an inner peace in a greater measure than you have ever known before because the peace of the Father is unlike anything called peace by man whose breath is in his nostrils. It brings the day nearer when these experiences come as daily occurrences and you can finally understand the meaning behind the worlds of the Master: "The Spirit of the Lord is upon me because he hath anointed me."

The actual experience of the Presence felt within you is confirmation of its existence, the Truth unto your being and when the experience happens within the miracles take place without seen by the natural man as supply, abundance, bounty or luck.

If you have been led to a spiritual way of life you will not have the ability to forget to meditate throughout the day nor will you be able to go hours without talking to God. If the spirit of God dwells in you you will be unable to go through hours of the day and night without conscious thought of God as you would be unable to go without food. As food is necessary to mortal man so is the conscious awareness of the presence of God vital to the spiritual man.

Spiritual food is essential to the son of God and that food is received through communion/ inner listening.

The reason for prayer is not to benefit one but to benefit the many. You are asking God to become active in the consciousness of **all** mankind, **all** those receptive of God's presence.

Remember you do not pray for God to improve circumstances in the human world rather pray the son of God be revealed to individual man, the son of God be raised up **in** individual man and that God's governance reign on earth-peace and harmony among man.

The mission of the Master wasn't merely to multiply loaves and fishes nor was it to transform physical bodies from sickness to health nor to raise them from the dead. **The mission of the Master was to take you into a new dimension of life in which you find the reality of your being which is spirit in nature.**

Prayer:

Man:

The dictionary definitions of prayer all conform to a concept of prayer based on the erroneous belief that there is a God somewhere waiting for man to ask for something and have it received if God is in a good mood, you are good enough or if he even cares. Unless of course your family is under a generational curse of some kind/generational belief, in which case you and your children will be held accountable for all those past sins you had nothing to do with therefore your prayers go into the reject bin.

Spirit:

Spiritual man knows whatever of good that comes to them is a direct result of their understanding of the nature of their own being. The understanding of spiritual life unfolds in proportion to your receptivity to Truth, **not praying up to God** but letting God **unfold and reveal itself within to you.**

This is the highest concept of prayer. It is achieved as you take a few minutes throughout the day/night to meditate, commune, **listen,** pop in for a smile or a hug. In quietness you become a state of receptivity which opens the way for you to feel or become aware of the very presence of God.

There are two stages to true prayer/meditation:

1. Go within and remember Truth to dispel the error presenting either to your senses or those of a patient.
2. Get silent, stop thinking, close your eyes and just relax in the weightless atmosphere of your being/consciousness. It is in this silence God imparts Truth about the illusion seen as reality and in the moment of this revealed Truth God is present. When God is present the healing has taken place for the presence of God is Truth revealed-God is and only

God is.

Having gone through your initial experience of maintaining the activity of Truth in your consciousness, remembering Truth, contemplative meditation, you come to the second stage of true prayer where through meditation-inner listening-you are able to receive Truth from within your own being.

In this second stage of prayer you stop thinking Truth within your mind and you open your inner ear to hear God's impartation. When you can open your inner ears and receive impartations from within you are receiving the Word of God and this is when you are living by grace.

This is when you are not taking thought for your life, what you shall eat or what you shall drink but are aware of an invisible presence within your consciousness that brings harmony into your experience without any effort of trying to be other than you are. God reveals who you are but only when God is the first contact made meaning always let your awareness of God's presence go before your human ego.

For 53 years I was unaware of this indwelling presence. I knew myself only as my personality, my human form and what I did as my profession. I didn't know there was anything other than what was visible until I realized that there were words, thoughts, feelings and pictures that would pop unbidden into my awareness, consciousness by no effort of my own. When I became aware of **receiving** things that were timely and perfect that left me feeling lighter, happier, able to let go of the ick I had been feeling I began a deep dive to uncover what it was I was experiencing which led to God and the ability to understand Truth.

My first understanding of God was that my soul (which I always felt resided in my heart space) was my connection to God *outside* of me. I didn't understand that my consciousness, the silence that was within when impartations came was actually the Christ consciousness and my direct connection to God and not just a "letter drop" I felt my soul to be, kind of like a dead end.

Then one day everything clicked into place. All I had read, all the wrong turns and the backward miles, all my errors in judgement and beginning to trust led me to the place where I was willing to die to find that "something" else. I actually did die as all of you who are called to the spiritual path will. I had begun the process of dying daily to the nothingness of error when understood from the spiritual standpoint and not man's.

I finally had the experience of all mystics throughout the ages. From within me God came forward and kissed me on the forehead and from that day til this my consciousness has been transformed into that which almost constantly has some image, vision, thought or feeling of God in, around and through me.

(God is Law but God is also a personal relationship and as such is he to me within rather than impersonal it. Personal choice as it will be for you.)

God runs in the background in a way, not intrusive rather comforting and entertaining with his sense of humor surprisingly playful. He is my best friend, my heart. Without his presence I am the dirt of the earth, dry and lost to time. But with him I am his, eternally fed by grace, living my life in a way that is pretty much unending harmony unless I take myself from his presence by reacting to the world/duality. What I, and you, experience are the expressions of God in visible form as all manner of supply necessary to live the life of the prodigal son returned to the kingdom.

How do you live eternally by grace? By walking the talk. If you are voicing within yourself Truth of God, that it **is** the sufficiency unto all its creations, you and me, and are truly living your nature as child with God at the helm **though a thousand may fall at your side, ten thousand at your right hand none will come near you**/your conscious awareness for where there is light there can be no darkness and in the light is where all should endeavor to live.

God wants all its forms, individual expressions of Self, all man, to get onto the path that will make your life easier because though it is your life in expression **it was never meant to be yours to take care of or provide for.** You were created to live and rejoice not live to make a life separate and apart from God. That still small voice wants you to come home so it can take care of you again in a manner befitting the Prince of Peace.

That still small voice you think of as intuition is the universal creative consciousness expressing or God, whatever you want to call that which is the One, the Only. God is as all; there is no thing real/tangible or objective called *matter* or *material* in or of this spiritually created universe.

The error of man's thinking is that he was born and will die therefore must do everything in his power between those two points in time to ensure self preservation in whatever form or means necessary, even killing and this is the reason for *human* birth and death-separation from Truth, God, **eternal** expression.

If you are to attain the highest concept of prayer you must stop praying in the ordinary sense of *words* and make your prayer a continuous realization of the presence and allness of God, 24/7/365 knowing God is guiding and directing your every thought, word and deed.

It may sound daunting like you are going to have to keep running over bible verses or saying godly things. No and absolutely not! To be in **conscious oneness** with God merely means to be in the **present moment** where the thinking mind is not thinking because it is not in the past and it is not out in the future fantasizing. When your mind is occupied with its own human thoughts you are of the consciousness of man. God is only found in the silence so you have to be in a state of consciousness that produces a silence of thought/thinking and that is the present moment, now.

You cannot focus on two things at the same time that is why when you are thinking in your head you get into accidents, forget to do other things, become emotional and you cannot hear that which is softer than your own cacophony. **To be in conscious oneness with God is merely resting in the silence, the peace, the harmony this state of consciousness brings to you** and this is the state of being you are supposed to have always entertained because in this state of now there is no human thinking going on and that is the way it was meant to be.

There is no humanhood, man separated from God, **that is the illusion** therefore that which is an illusion can have no consequences thus a state of harmony remains.

But what of all the things in your life that are needing attention? Ah, attention or meddling? That which needs your attention God will put in your consciousness to do as part of your day. There may seem to be a mountain of ick coming your way because you are cleaning up messes/human karma but you are not to do anything of your own "I should, I better, I can help things along if I do X" language because that is the little *i* trying to fix humanly the things you did humanly but are now living spiritually. The two cannot go together, either you navigate or God does but your navigation crashed the bus more than once already.

You have to learn to trust. Yes, huge word and hard to do but the sooner you learn to trust, to rest, to **respond** to what is given you to do and not do what is not presented to do, the sooner things really start to straighten themselves out. Every time you try to help a situation along that you have given to God you are showing you trust yourself more than God. Starting to see the logic you have been trying to live by?

To pray for your enemy doesn't mean you are asking God to prosper them in their wrong doing, let them off easy, but to release sin and discord from their consciousness for it to be felt by them as an experience of God that brings relief and release so they may put down the sword and pick up the shield, put on the robe of IS. You don't just release your enemies, you release the enemies of nations, those who have offended nations, races or religions when you bring God to bear, Truth of being.

Prayer in its highest sense is not available to human man because human man thinks prayer is talking, telling God what needs to be done. These prayers do not reach God. Prayer is only and ever a silent communion with God for the sole purpose of hearing its voice, not your own thoughts.

God is only where it is **known** so close your eyes, open your inner ears and get ready for your guest!

How do you pray aright?

Prayer is inner listening/awareness so therefore you are to be waiting, think game avatar before play, for the presence of God to be felt, heard or known in some fashion. The thing that human man wanting to know God must learn to do is find the place within that feels like the avatar looks, ie waiting, resting, being not thinking of what is going on out in the world.

Prayer isn't concentrating to hear or forcing your mind into silence rather it is being **expectant** of what God is/brings into awareness-harmony, Truth to rest in when the world agitates temporarily. You are just within yourself waiting for your best friend to join you.

But how do you get from the world of inner noise to the quiet of inner listening? You have to get behind the noise of the thinking mind to get into the quiet to find God within. Some people think they must force their mind to stop thinking, that they must still the mind and that is not the case, you never want to force the mind to still rather give it something else to think about instead of what is going on out in the world of man. The mind is a very useful instrument and the more alive and alert it is the better off you are.

You have no right to still the mind but the mind will still itself in a rightful manner if you make no effort to still it but keep the mind stayed on God. If you force the mind to stop it is an act of repression or suppression and even if you succeed it is going to break out sooner or later and be worse than it was before. You have no right to still the mind **but you have a right to steer the mind and keep it active in the right way.**

When you want to meditate don't try to still the mind. Take a bible passage, a red letter passage, a psalm, a short one, my peace I give unto thee ... Don't repeat it power parrot fashion but take it something like this:

My peace ... let it resonate ... give I unto thee ... my peace ... that is Christ peace ... christ peace I give unto thee ... oh, I didn't know what it meant ... mind gets quiet as the thoughts float away and you rest in the arms of peace you brought into your experience by bringing God forth as peace, my peace, God's peace within you, of you, as you, for you, for the world.

In the silence that unfolds as the last thought floats away is where God will meet you, come into your awareness in some manner that reveals God is.

Prayer in order to reach God must rise above both words and thoughts.

The words and thoughts that are used in metaphysical work have a legitimate function up to a certain point in that they may lift you into a higher atmosphere where you can drop them. Man is so trained to use words and thoughts he cannot easily master the art of silence so to help settle the chaotic mind you can begin your time with God in **contemplative meditation** where you bring to mind a few words or simple thoughts of God to get your mind out of man and in with God. You just sit with the words of Truth, let them just float away and you remain in this place of inner silence awaiting God, **you are holding space for the Father to enter in, make its presence known.**

The words themselves are not any part of the healing they merely prepare you for an act of prayer which is inner listening for God to come onto the field, into awareness revealing Truth. Prayer is a stillness and a silence, not an activity of the mind and if you wish to see answered prayer watch the nature of what takes place when your prayer reaches the atmosphere of no words and no thoughts, where all you are is receptive to that which you know will make its presence known.

"Not my will but thine be done."

God performs that which God has appointed/revealed for you to do. You cannot therefore seek God's help for *your* will but you can seek God's guidance to establish God's will **in you** so you may be an instrument of God's grace, allness, will, purpose and the recipient of the grace of this activity of consciousness.

True prayer: **hearing** God in the silence within because you are quiet of mind enough to be aware of the soft, small voice uttering "I love you Child."

Where do new ideas/inventions come from? From the invisible. They come into consciousness and then from consciousness they are expressed, brought into form in the outer world for the benefit of all man.

Do you see the benefit of meditation/prayer? Of knowing God aright? How could you compose without meditating, without sitting down and getting silent within yourself and letting it flow from the invisible? How could you invent if you didn't close your eyes and listen within?

This is the understanding of **therefore in all thy getting get consciousness and everything else will appear externally.**

True prayer is like sitting with your best friend. You don't have to talk rather just sit together in the peace with an occasional sigh or I love you.

When you sit with God it feels warm, inviting, home, comfortable, easy. Woosaaahhh. Being with God is the **prayer of communion** and it comes about after you have attained some measure of life by grace, a life in which God is fulfilling itself as your experience.

Now you are entering a level of consciousness in which spirit is your only health, your only supply.

The highest concept of prayer is the constant dwelling in the realization of God's presence:

"I dwell in the house of the Lord now and forever." Psalm 23:6

"He that dwelleth in the **secret place** of the most High shall abide under the shadow of the Almighty." Psalm 91:1

But what does it mean? To dwell in the secret place of the most high is to be within yourself in conscious union with God as your guiding influence, its ways not yours. **To live in the secret place is to be in oneness with God and not outside in the world creating and experiencing duality.**

To dwell, to be, to stay, to remain **with** God and not man is to let God be the only voice you listen to, respond to rather than the cacophony of the human mind expressed as human living.

There is no reaching out to God, no trying to get God to do something, there is merely the statement:

With him (man) there is an arm of flesh but with the Lord our God there is the the arm of grace, the allness of the Father always present, always available, always harmonious and eternal.

It may seem strange that you don't have to tell God your problem or that you don't have to ask for anything, not even make statements or affirmations. Just sit and let spirit enter in.

Do this throughout the day. I call it checking in, just a "hello Father, I love you, flow Father flow," just something that takes you within to the place that the world cannot disturb and then you bring peace forth as grace unto yourself and those around you.

You must develop a sense of receptivity so that you can become even more aware of the very presence of God in its holy temple which is your consciousness. In the secret place of the Most High, which is the Holy of Holies, which is your very own inner knowing/consciousness you receive guidance, wisdom, illumination and spiritual power. In quietness and confidence shall be your strength.

Inner communion=prayer

contemplative meditation=treatment

Contemplative meditation is the knowing of specific Truth before inner communion which is the healing/revealing. This process is the healing agent to all error of man-knowing Truth then waiting for Truth to present from the only source of Truth-God within, and in this way and this way only the mesmeric influence/hypnotism is broken because God has just revealed itself as peace felt. Just like a hypnotist snaps their fingers and brings you out of an inner illusion believed to be realty God revealed within is that snap that brings you back to your Truth, **God is!** and out from under the illusion or mesmerism of man.

You heal yourself, all the ills, conditions and circumstances, when you begin to realize the Truth of these things. God reveals Truth through inner communion and that Truth stands with you, arms crossed, looking at the same error as you. You look at Truth metaphorically standing beside you and it says "I'm here aren't I?" And then look back at the error and it dissolves like a sand sculpture touched by a single drop of water and all that is left is is, harmony, God in awareness.

Prayer does not improve humanhood and that is why prayers that try to do so are not answered. God can only give you the fruits of God-the allness of God, the harmony of God, spirit in form received, not the things of man worked for or taken. Prayer can only bring that of which you are praying to-God-therefore you pray only for what God **is.**

When you come to the place where you desire the companionship and resting place of God over the baubles of man you are praying aright ie walking the spiritual path leading to full enlightenment and ascension.

Communion:

Communion with God is true prayer. It is the unfoldment of individual consciousness to its presence and expression and it makes you every way whole. Communion with God is in reality listening for the still small voice. In this communion or prayer no words pass from you to God rather the conscious realization of the presence of God **is** realized **as** Truth and harmony is your expression. This is the Christ state of being and never leaves you where it finds you.

Pray for your enemy:

If I am I am and you are I am then all are I am, we are kin, we are family, we are one so when you curse your enemy and wish them dead you are wishing the same on yourself because you and your enemy are **you.**

You pray for your enemies not for anything of the world but for them to awaken to the God within. When that happens your enemy now knows their true nature and will greet you as the light of God he is.

Father, let all be forgiven without penalty and open the consciousness of those we call our enemies that they might know the Truth of oneness.

The prayer of forgiveness has nothing to do with wanting them to be freed of their obligations/penalties/legal judgements; that is of the world and will be done in the world as man sees fit as that is the way of man. You pray only that they may know God as you do, as you who once was ignorant of Truth.

Be careful not to judge another man's sins or have comment on appropriate punishment because this attitude is of man, duality, ego and will prove to be deadly. Deadly in that if you are of the consciousness of man you are accepting the belief of human man: man is born and dies and that is the end of that. That is the death you are subscripting yourself to knowingly, by choice.

I cannot stress enough that God is a willing choice for singular purpose-**to experience wholeness unto your existence.** You have to keep yourself where you want to be by living in conscious oneness, walking the walk and living the life of the expressed Christ. God will not keep you on track, that door is always open and lost sheep are not his concern, they wander back when they wander back when they want what the Shepherd has. You absolutely control your own destiny: human man of earth or risen spirit of God joint heir to the kingdom?

Prayer is not an activity of the human thinking mind.

Do not expect the allness of God to function in the world of man, in *the dream* that has mesmerized the children of God into thinking they are separate and apart from it.

God is the only way to break the mesmerism of the dream/illusion and awaken you to the fact you are not finite but infinite and that you are not human but spirit. Do not go to God to adjust anything in your or anyone else's human experience, the dream man dreams. The awareness of the presence of God wakes man from the dream to live wide awake in oneness with God.

To finally realize you have been living from the wrong consciousness, your personal ego/pride/wants and desires is the beginning of the awakening into your true identity.

You either live in the world or in God, in the consciousness of the world of man with its duality or in the consciousness of oneness/harmonious expression with God.

When you no longer seek God for help with a human matter rather seek it for the peace it embodies you are awakening from the dream into the reality of being of how this life is supposed to operate through you not upon you.

If when you meditate/pray/commune words, thoughts or feelings come into your mind don't fight them, don't tell them to go away, just let them come and **know they are not your thoughts** but the false beliefs of the world temporarily inhabiting your thinking mind. Since you know the reality of human thoughts you know they are not yours per se but just things that are floating in the atmosphere of man that slipped in through a crack but never worry! Respond to them as you would any other illusion-**this is of man and not of God therefore it is not Truth. You are returned to the nothingness you were before man lost the consciousness of God within, you are an echo of consciousness past.**

Prayer when understood is the means by which you overcome all material sense, material living and bring yourself to that place where your life is supernaturally governed, protected, guided and experienced.

I talk a lot about answers received from within. What are you to do with them? Pay attention to what is received, not just that it *was* received. If it is to forgive your debtors release them consciously and move on. What is received is both the answer and the action, the study point by which you become more illumined, are raised in conscious understanding as that Truth given becomes Truth to you.

In the beginning of this new way of being the answer received is taken at face value, go and sin no more, there is no lack in the kingdom, etc, and rest in the feeling the presence of God reveals within you. Then as you progress, understand more of God consciousness, you realize the answer is also something to remember as the errors of the world present ie **get up and walk, sin no more,**

release debtors. Keep doing what has been given you to do-know the Truth of error to dissolve the illusion.

This action is practicing the presence of God which is the healing consciousness. By keeping your mind stayed on God, on the Truth of God and not of the world at some point you will begin to get the deeper meanings of Truth and you are more able to discern spiritual writings because you are reading it with a spiritual eye ie God is interpreting the meaningless human words as the scriptural Truths they actually are.

Only one of God consciousness, a mystic, can understand what is written by another of God consciousness because to man the things of God are folly, don't make sense and **this is the complete error of man trying to live by the *words* in the Bible instead of the consciousness back of them that brought them into being.** The Bible wasn't meant to be read and parroted it was meant to be read and returned **to you** from God not interpreted by man with no Christ consciousness.

---

2 types of prayers:

1. Those of the basic principles of spiritual living for personal unfoldment, to know the things of God to live more in the consciousness of God, to experience more of God in expression. Remember secret, silent and sacred until your footing is firm and conscious awareness has been established and experienced.
2. For all mankind for their illumination. These prayers come after you have begun to rise in consciousness and understand completely "love thine enemy as your brother." In this state of consciousness you know all error is merely ignorance of Truth and **your only prayer is for their ignorance to be lifted so they may see the face of God as you have.** You want nothing more than the world to feel God as you do, the completeness, allness in every breath you now take.

You want everyone to live in God consciousness for the way it **feels,** what it provides and what it accomplishes when you are an instrument of God letting grace flow through and out from you to heal the sick, feed the hungry and clothe the poor.

It is when you know God thereby know yourself that you can begin to pray for the world because your prayers are of God consciousness and not that of man wishing for a God to overcome the enemy. You have to be able to know the true meaning of prayer, live in it and be it before you can desire, not feel obligated, but desire to share God.

God is a need, a longing, a thirsting and a searching that will end in ultimate union if that is your desire. You will succeed at the level of your devotion to God through study, meditation, communion and healing. To the degree you **know** God is the degree of God in your experience. **God is impersonal Law; this is merely a numbers game, the more you are in the more you get out.**

When you have God awareness within, have had the mystical experience, you are automatically returned to your spiritual Truth but that does not mean you are **under grace** yet. That comes through the **relationship** you create with God through prayer, inner listening and dying daily to the errors of man.

To be risen you must **raise** your consciousness and Truth building upon Truth is the only way to come into full enlightenment. This doesn't mean you don't get to enjoy the things of God until you have full enlightenment, no! The minute you begin to practice, die daily because you want nothing more of human life, you are increasing God awareness and dropping the duality of man. As you progress in living in the consciousness of God you receive more and more grace, the allness of God in expression in the form of harmonious living and the added things manifest of God for your use.

Prayer is a mystical revelation, elevation of consciousness by contemplation of principles that transcend human thinking and as such are incomprehensible to philosophers and scientists because it is of the invisible and the philosophies of man deal strictly with what is visible, tangible and measurable.

Intellect hinders spiritual growth because intellect/knowledge is of the mind of man and intellect says there is no thing real that cannot be sensed by the body thus it is impossible to have an intellectual conversation about a spiritual/invisible subject. Know this however: the spiritual consciousness will be the risen consciousness of every man at some point of their existence when knowledge alone no longer satisfies the hunger for Truth within.

Remember that true prayer is a listening attitude within the silence of your consciousness. Affirmations and denials are useless because they are of the mind thus of duality and are not a spiritual activity and do not take you above the thinking mind of man into the kingdom because you're still thinking like a human and no human can ever get into heaven.

When it comes to thinking about God and the things of God just to say them will do nothing for words have no power however if you take those words inside and let them sit quietly at some point God will explain to you that which was not understood or bring to mind that which brings the peace man knows nothing about.

If you are just mindlessly repeating things to yourself hoping that they come true that is nothing more than a form of self hypnosis, mental work not spiritual Truth. But occasionally repeating them to yourself to remember as you go into silent listening, to use it as the step before awaiting God's presence, then that is exactly what will put you in the spiritual atmosphere of God's presence.

Some people do not need to use Truth after a while, they can simply go within and sit quietly because no words are necessary. To say a Truth even without going any further is to bring that Truth into consciousness and once again relax into the peace **that you *know* what those words mean.** That is the whole difference between someone who **knows** God and someone who has a *blind faith* in God.

Man lives believing there is a negative influence playing against a positive influence ie. God against the devil etc. The belief in two powers has been the atmosphere of humanity from inception therefore it is the atmosphere of humanity. Just because it is the atmosphere of humanity does not mean it is the correct one or that the true atmosphere of God, oneness, grace, is lost. It is not.

It is merely hidden under a million years of mortal man thinking itself separated from God and thinking that it has to fend for its own survival. In this human mind set of dog eat dog, kill or be killed everything is a threat and the i of you believes it deserves to live over the i of another and that is the justification of man to take, maim, defame or kill for its own survival.

Man thinks himself separated from God because he has forgotten that he is an eternal spiritual being. Until the desire within the soul of man is awakened and supersedes the desires for even the good stuff of human living (vacations, new cars, diamonds) you go on living the best you can and if that means living by the 10 Commandments under the law of man and being a good human without an actual experience of God then that is what you do.

But you never stop opening yourself to God because I had been talking to God for years and didn't realize it, didn't understand the potentiality of the voice within. In a way you kind of think that you're crazy especially because there's, well, no one you can talk to about the true God of is.

I thought that that voice was everything other than God because to be honest I didn't think I was special enough to have a relationship with God and as I sit here I cry saying that because I remember how much it hurt wanting it so badly and then years later realizing I had already achieved a measure of it but didn't know it.

I guess what this means is don't get discouraged if you think God isn't listening/responding because when you finally do have that mystical moment of contact and it begins to speak it will be revealed to you all the times in your life it **was there with you** and that you did in some way, shape or form try to understand the presence that you felt. But you may have as I did feel unworthy of God. I mean holy cow right?!

You are **not** God, you are **of** God. God is the Creator; you are the creation that can never surpass the Creator but as such can never be separate and apart from the Creator. God is ethereal, spirit, incorporeal, invisible and you are the same but in form to experience a world of spiritual forms.

"I will listen for thy voice" is not just a hymn it is a spiritual state of being. In a few moments of peace and quiet something will come to you from within, a feeling, words, message, some light and you will know that God is on the field, harmony is restored and off again you go about your business with God in awareness making the crooked places straight leaving harmony in your wake like the sweetest perfume.

Righteous prayer is the only thing that soothes the soul through peace and understanding however the praying of human man and the praying of spiritual man are two completely different activities resulting in different outcomes.

Human man begs, pleads and threatens for what they want, sometimes adding time, date and location to help God out. Man is always wanting God to *do something* for them then denounce God as bull pucky when they do not *get* what *they* wanted.

Spiritual man knows God therefore knows that to ask for anything of the world is useless because God can only give of itself, **consciousness** and cannot give *material* things as man asks for. Spiritual man receives the added things directly from God not by asking but by being one with it because God is supply unto itself through the Law of like begets like.

You cannot go to God with a request that you be healed physically, mentally or financially. You cannot go to God to pray for your employment or your success, that has been the fruitless prayer of man for the last 1700 years. Only when you seek God for the benefit of God, the receiving of what God **is** will your prayer be fruitful.

When you pray, pray that God's grace be active in the consciousness of all of mankind. You do not pray for improved humanhood rather you pray the son of God be revealed in individual man, the son of God be raised up within each individual man and pray that God's governance reign on earth.

Why pray for God's governance on earth? Because man cannot find peace; peace for man is merely the time between wars where he is preparing for war not enjoying the peace time. To pray for a specific person to become the leader is fruitless, but to listen for God to reveal to you from within that person which has an awareness of God or who is ripe to understand God then that is the person you want in government regardless of your personal choice.

The practicality of this is obvious if you are truthful with yourself and admit your mind is limited whereas God's is infinite, knowing all from a higher perspective than what you can see at street level to give you a revelation not of man but of spirit, Truth.

The duality of expressions man lives by is man's sense of their power and the power of/in those around them. Duality gives man the right to react to any situation in any way *they* deem necessary to express who they think they need to be in the moment to guard against another's expression of perceived good or bad, strong or weak, smart or not, influential or not, wealthy or not, happy or not, and respond accordingly. This is the definition of duality-doing what serves you and you alone.

Those doing altruistic deeds, following a calling they say is given by God are of duality. Any good deeds done to further *your* sense of importance, good, benevolence, begging money and doing things for others that they are unable to do for themselves etc, brings you no closer to God than if you were to do nothing for mankind.

Do gooders are those who will suffer the most because they believe through *their* acts of kindness, benevolence etc, *they* become kind, benevolent. They think what *they* do in the human world defines them and will bring them the bounty they feel will come from God because of all the good work *they* are doing for their fellow man.

God knows nothing of your life as human. Remember that. You have no power, you think and behave as if you do but that is what you have been taught to believe-to believe in the illusion instead of living Truth. You cannot rise in the human world and get the attention of God. **You must die to all of the fallacy of the world and seek Truth within.** You must understand God is not among man where God is not known so **if you are not knowing God you are not *of* the allness, wholeness and completeness of God.**

When you go in for Truth you want to become so immersed in the peace of Truth, the love and support of God, its constancy and consistency, dependability and reliability that you forget the claim you went within to release. This atmosphere of being supported, loved, protected and safe is the feeling of being immersed in the allness of God and **is** that which dispels the illusion of something other than God.

Prayer doesn't make human life easier/better it elevates you above the duality of human living to oneness where duality cannot dwell.

True prayer is contemplation not of you or me or your bank account rather contemplation of God, the things of God, peace, love, harmony, supply, grace. It is an abiding in the secret place of the most high, it is living, moving and having your being in God consciousness, infinity.

If you have prayed aright, asked correctly for God's grace by letting your listening attitude hear the impartations of Truth unto your being you will bear fruit richly. If however you have asked and not received it is because you ask amiss/incorrectly.

God is spirit and can only provide that which it **is,** spirit. Therefore if you pray for *material* things, for change in any circumstance or condition of the world you are going to God to *get* things it knows nothing about and cannot give. Human man and spiritual man are two completely different beings. God knows itself, the awakened Christ in man, but God is completely unaware of man who lives in the atmosphere of duality because there is no duality in the kingdom of heaven only in the mind of man who thinks himself separate and apart from God.

Take that which you don't understand into contemplative meditation until light dawns, the click of God on the field, presence felt happens and then it has been experienced as Truth because God came forth and put the seal on it with its presence and it is the difference between reading Truth and experiencing it that determines the degree of Truth within you.

Prayer is an attitude built on an understanding of Truth-secret, silent and sacred.

Meditation/prayer/inner listening is sitting in your bliss. I await your company Father!

Praying for peace is ineffective because peace is already where God is realized and if God is realized in the one praying there is no peace to ask for because the awareness of the presence of God is **peace unto you.** Paul said and it was true then and it is true now-**you are not children of God except the spirit of God dwells/is recognized/known in you.**

When you have gone from man who speaks of God in quotations to man who speaks of God with assurity of its reality within you it becomes **my friend, my strength, my guide, my peace.** In this observation you yourself can feel the shift, that Truth has been realized and the God of air quotes is now known to you by way of actual experience and peace is your dwelling place because you know the Source of peace-God within.

When you go into prayer you do not try to change a bad condition into a good one rather you have to be high enough of knowing so you can go down the middle and say "what I am looking for is a spiritual idea or plan Father not one of my own limited, human thinking" then sit back and witness God in action.

The fruitfulness, validation, result of righteous prayer is known by the good in your experience. If you are praying but not seeing the fruitage, the peace, the abundance, the harmony go within and ask God to show you where you are erring in your prayer. Most often it is a bit of humanhood in that you may still be talking instead of listening. You must be obedient to God's consciousness, what you are told is what you are to do to stay in oneness with God and show forth the fruitage/abundance/result/effect of that relationship and your devotion to it.

Fruitage is God as manifest form. Your fruitage, abundance, peace and harmony reflect the degree of God activity you bring to bear in your experience by right prayer and reliance on God in all ways for all things.

Take time to let what you read sink in. Don't *try* to understand it. If you don't get it just ask within for assistance, "please help me understand these words in a way that makes sense to me." Don't get frustrated, frustration is a human thing and God doesn't recognize it because you have separated yourself from it if you are experiencing anything but harmony. Realize this often during the day. God will explain these things and let you know you can let X go. Let go and let God.

Very Important!

You cannot talk about this to anyone not of conscious knowing or you lose your demonstration. What does "to lose your demonstration" mean? It means that by your throwing pearls before swine you are trying to use your humanness to introduce God to someone instead of letting the Christ of you awaken the Christ within another by way of your expression of harmony, the Christ of you be-ing.

To make sure you stay on track you must have conversations daily with Self, you know just shooting the breeze about your day to true communion/silent listening for deeper knowing. As your relationship grows, as you learn who you are you begin to trust God, depend on God, rely on God. You feel safe, supported, comforted, you trust implicitly in this final version of you, ie God, origin, and in this way you learn to hear and do what is given you to do by keeping your inner ear and inner awareness open and alert to its direction or laughter or smiling face. Fist bumps are also on the menu as well as explosive laughter and a wicked sense of humor if that is your flavor.

Who did Jesus say he was? The son of God sent to free mankind through knowing Truth. Free from what? The illusion of power of things and persons, slave to the illusions of the world man has created to protect self over all others. The Truth that all men have God within that maintains and sustains them in every way is absolute Truth but only if you go within and ask this presence to make itself known to tell you for itself.

Knowing God is having the letter of Truth always on your forehead, your arm and over the door to your home, metaphorically. You live and move and have your being in this Truth when you have had the experience that cements Truth, the awareness of the presence of God when God itself came forth within your own being and said "I have waited long to welcome my child home."

Sometimes Truth realized is instantaneous, the aha moment or the words remembered, the keys found or the perfect response. Other times the words that state Truth stay words for a long time meaning you can read or hear something for years and know it has a specific spiritual Truth behind it that will set you that much freer from the world of man but you are unable to go past the academics of the words, the metaphysical Truth, their face value. Don't worry that you don't always feel God on the field as long as you went within earnestly for God, to rest in God, to find comfort, understanding within to let go of the without as nothingness.

The more you go to God the more God is with you even when you are not going within to be with God. You are a cup full of humanhood emptying out little by little as spiritual Truth begins to take root. The more you die to duality the more God/Truth fills in the vacuum.

This time can be thought of as God bringing to you the experiences that will, if you are living in the Word and listening for its voice, crystallize as Truth within your being. No one can make you believe anything until your consciousness confirms it to you as Truth and once it has been received it is yours eternally.

Truth only comes by way of silent receptivity within you; though Truth is revealed in writings they are the Truth of another given to the world to be taken into the silence to receive your own revelation of that Truth as it pertains specifically to your level of conscious understanding.

You can pray for anything you want as long as it is *not of the human world*. Never pray for anything that is of man because you cannot demonstrate effects, things, you can only demonstrate the **cause** that produces them and that cause is God therefore all you can pray for are the things of God to receive the things of God and then all the added things will be added unto you because **God is as all.**

You are looking for Truth that only comes in the click, the contact with God as it reveals Truth about the rumor or condition. God places the seal on it, a feeling of it being done. You have accomplished nothing for yourself or the world until you have had God's seal placed on it in meditation or by an inner assurance of **it is done,** Truth revealed, inner knowing, peace descends, a release.

It is not the words you say, think or write but what is felt, known or revealed as Truth, the consciousness you have attained during your meditation/prayer/inner listening. Reading, listening and learning merely lead up to the point of realized Truth, priming the pump so to speak. The click, the awareness of contact is the important thing, not your thoughts or knowledge but the inner release, God on the field.

If you end up on the floor bawling like a baby just remember I warned you, the feeling of God is like an embrace, an "I've got you never going to let you go hug" and in that feeling of safety, love, security and true inner peace you give it all up, let it come up, the good, the bad and the ugly, cry it out and let God hold you while you do it. It will drain you to your core but leave you light, free, unencumbered to an obvious degree but now you have to keep the ball rolling. You want that feeling again? You have to do what allows it to flow-study, practice, meditate and heal error as it presents to bring grace to bear where there was no God in awareness.

Seek and it shall be given

Ask and you shall receive

For all things of heaven are within you but you have to know God to receive and to receive is to be ever faithful knowing God **is** your sufficiency in all ways.

The highest concept or idea of prayer is the recognition of God as omnipresence, omnipotence and omniscience; the recognition of God as ever present, ever available and the recognition of God as Law unto your being but with no attempt to make it so; all you are required to do is defer your will to God's governance and listen for the small soft voice for guidance, support, understanding and companionship.

Now that I have found God the emptiness I would feel without it would be unbearable, would literally suck the life right out of me because once you taste the honey of Life all else tastes hollow and leaves you wanting for there is no thing like it among man whose breath is in his nostrils knowing only duality.

What is sin, error and duality?

This section is going to deal with sin, error and duality which are the *beliefs* of man that keep him from knowing God aright. Here you will come to understand why there is no evil in the world, no Satan, no bad, and no good for that matter.

Always remember that which does not make sense is not to be discussed out loud with human man but taken within the silence to let God bring understanding because you can only get Truth from Truth and human man has no Truth to give.

What has fooled the world about error is that error always expresses *as* something therefore people **think error *is* something,** has reality, is objective, visible, tangible in the visible world. Man believes *things* are responsible for the negative in this world when in reality it is merely illusions of mind created from personal history/conditioning by having been born into an atmosphere *of* duality, of error, evil, devilish experiences and consequences.

How could you experience anything other than the atmosphere you exist in, that of the world's belief in duality **unless you remove yourself** from the world/consciousness of man to see the reality that is not available in the knowing of man? **That is the purpose of this practice of spiritual living,** to give you the vantage point of Truth from which to experience a life of harmony, joy and abundance free from the errors of man that cause man to fight and die and do it all over again.

There are only three things you need to know to live the spiritual life:

1. The nature/Truth of God-all that **is** visible and invisible
2. The nature/Truth of Prayer-inner listening
3. The nature/Truth of error-illusion, no thing real

That which has prevented many great spiritual leaders from achieving Christ consciousness is the fact that they know all about I and the Father are one and all about the Spirit of God **but they are**

still knowing two powers and still thinking of God in terms of *over* error, *using* God or praying *to* God making God their wishing well or servant unto *their* cause or claim.

Until a student has completely ruled out of consciousness that they are going to *get* God to do something for them, be *their* messenger or servant they cannot have the healing consciousness therefore **the study and practice of spiritual principles is necessary for spiritual development which leads to spiritual illumination or Christ consciousness.**

What is called commandments in the Old Testament are merely laws of man by man, no God involved merely a sliding scale of morality with corresponding punishments.

The commandments of the New Testament are Truths of God by which to abide in/live by/express as one who wishes to experience life lived by that choice-God instead of man, Truth instead of error, reality instead of illusion.

The good of man is not the grace of God rather just the opposite swing of the pendulum of life. The only good in the world is merely better than the opposite of bad and that good and bad are merely perceptions of what level of discomfort, disharmony and chaos is personally acceptable to you therefore **there is no universal standard** by which to truly gauge/qualify good and bad, happy and sad, sick and well, lack and wealth thus making it *subjective* according to personal history.

A world without a belief in a power apart from God to act on you leaves only that which was in the beginning-God/harmony. God is the only Truth but to know Truth you have to understand that **how you perceive the world** around you is **not** the reality of the world around you. **You have added labels/qualifiers/personal beliefs of evil/bad/error/sadness/lack/illness/disease to the perfection of God** because of your perceived separation from God, source, thus you feel vulnerable and label to protect, label to order, label to identify that which presents to you.

Man has even changed the atmosphere of the universe according to their limited understanding. Who said the person who looks like they lack actually lacks? Who is to say the person who appears to be sick is really sick? Who is to say the person who appears sad is truly sad?

Do you see by putting labels on things you know nothing about purely because of what is presenting you are adding your flavor, your spin, your personal interpretation to what **is**? What you see on the outside is not the Truth of what is actually there. You are looking at the poorly wrapped gift assuming what is within is of the same quality therefore you reject it mentally out of hand.

You judge what is not seen by what is seen because you have no idea there is anything other than what is visible to be known.

You have to see **God's** Truth in your awareness instead of your perception of what is. God knows Truth because God **is** Truth. How do you see with God awareness? By becoming aware of the Father within and learning through study and practice the principles of Truth to express as Truth, oneness with God which is what allows you to live under grace.

Illusion:

All of what man experiences is a perspective of what **is** and a perspective is nothing but a personal thought therefore what man experiences is a result of a perspective *believed* to be reality. It is like fighting a ghost and losing. This has taken me a long time to get Truth on. We on the spiritual path talk all the time about what error is-duality-the illusion/perspective/judgement created in the mind believed to be real-being the entire reason for man's living *as* man instead of child of God.

But there is another illusion more subtle that is the root of all perceived error. The Truth is that all that is visible and invisible is God expressing that human man has erroneously named and categorized as being matter, *this or that,* different materials, chemical makeups in different forms denoting individual/scientifically categorized expressions ie grass, metal, sky, animal. **This** is the illusion that perpetuates the *belief* in separation from God. There is **no** this or that, there is **only** God as all form and until you begin to see that Truth and release the material nature of man you are not taking the many opportunities to share grace.

You feel embraced by God in the sense that you understand when you are in oneness with God you are in oneness with all things because you are of the nature of all that is because you are of the consciousness of all that is. The house, the dog, the cat, the food, the land, the clothes you wear, the gadgets you use, the perfume, the foot powder, the q-tip are all God expressing in form.

You begin to get a completely difference sense of being when you understand there is only one creative expression of all creation visible and invisible therefore **its nature of infinite harmonious expression is our bond,** what makes us all of God no matter form because there is **no thing** besides God. Until you understand this **distinction** between God substance and man's naming things as they appear to be ie material/matter in form, you will be living duality because if you don't realize all is of God you are going to give power to that which cannot have power and again live duality.

Illusion:

When human man hear the phrase "life is but an illusion" they immediately think what they are living, life itself, this world, the physicality of it is an illusion, that existence is all in the mind and that this is the Matrix, a projection, unreality. And in essence it is.

The **unreality,** the illusion is that things, people and conditions have power over you and in this human experience you are always fighting these conditions. This is the *illusion* because there are no conditions to fight or desire because there aren't any when you know Truth, when you live from the consciousness of Truth and not the consciousness of illusion/error/duality. **The illusion is that you are man, that you live and die and have to get what you want.**

The **reality** behind the illusion is that you are immortal spirit, incorporeal expression of God in form and need not struggle or fight for what **is** already yours. When you know how to release to the world the allness of God through meditation and prayer you are supplied to the degree of your dependence on God and not man for the things of life.

Wake up from the illusion you are human and it will be like when Ne-Yo discovered his true reality-mind blowing but satisfying, settling, a new conscious understanding of the Truth of being, that final piece falling into place to make it all make sense. Now that you know your true identity, true existence can be experienced from here on out, no more fake living, no more confusion rather knowing Truth has made you free to live as you were created to live as harmonious expression among man but no longer of the consciousness of man which is chaos.

Coueism:

Spiritual living by principles of Truth is to bring light to your humanhood to **outgrow** humanhood; but just denying you are human and stating you are already this or that or have the mind of God is a form of Coueism-**claiming something for yourself you haven't demonstrated.**

Coueism along with **all** other mind treatments/healing modalities are nothing more than forms of self hypnosis trying to break the universal hypnosis of man. It is nothing more than trying to improve that which doesn't exist by way of optimistic autosuggestion and not any manner of spirituality, knowing Truth or experiencing Truth.

Man is trying to hold onto the human sense of life while at the same time praying for grace/intercession. You are trying to get rid of the evils of man while holding onto the good things of man. It won't work. You cannot improve *humanhood* with **God.**

The veil that separates you from your visible demonstration of the reality of God, the presence and all that is of God working for good in your life, is the clinging to of human good, fame, fortune, the desire to get rid of human evil in others or get that which will improve/increase yourself.

Your goal has to be seeking the spiritual kingdom and spiritual grace. If you cling to the human world you have to use the weapons of the world, both physical and mental, but in the moment that your goal changes and you seek the kingdom of God you can put up your physical sword and mental sword and rest in the presence of God.

God isn't a power in the way man thinks of power. God is power because there is no thing and no one above it so essentially top of the food chain. There is no *thing* in the world of man that can hurt God or its creations, you, me and everything visible ie the universe, as long as and only if you know the Truth that **God/harmony is the only power/presence** and live that Truth.

The only sin of man is the belief in separation from God which has resulted in spiritual man of singular expression knowing **is** now living as human man expressing *duality*.

Everything runs down hill from this sin because it has become the atmosphere of man. It is normal and natural for human man to judge and label, ascribe power to things and people and to express as they deem necessary in all situations to satisfy their desired outcome. It is normal to fight, lie and defame, everyone does it it just depends on the degree to which you use subversive tactics that makes you a good person, sort of a bad person or a really bad person in the eyes of man.

What man doesn't understand is no sin, no act of omission or commission is worse than another because the **original sin is the only sin that perpetuates the belief in sin, not the reality of sin** therefore no sin of man is *his* sin however the **consequences** of the sin are theirs to bear and it is **the sin punishing the sin,** the cost to *you* of the error committed, the pain you experience because of living this duality that is your every chance to stop and say "no, I won't live this way any longer. Show me another way to live" and in this way begin the process of knowing God aright, the God of is, harmony, peace, eternal and dependable, rock, temple and high tower.

Man believes God a thing to be picked up and used in times of need, when *their* personal powers of good and bad are not enough to protect them, to bring them something they lack in the moment to make it all work out in their favor. Man only calls on God in times of need and for the rest of the time man calls on himself to be all that is necessary to get what he wants by being what the situation calls for depending on the outcome *personally* desired. Human man believes in his own power to create the life he envisions living and through human power-mental and physical, by hook or by crook, will get it and if not then pray to God to do *their* personal bidding.

When God doesn't seem to be doing what human man wants God to do for them they shove God onto the shelf and take over the doing of whatever it was they felt God wasn't taking care of or doing too slowly. Man has no concept of the ability of God because they don't know God thus only believe in their own power and when that power fails to bring about the desired results *then* they call on God hoping to pull the proverbial rabbit out of the hat, the Hail Mary.

Duality, man, is when you believe you have a *choice* of how to behave/react in and of yourself in any given situation. Oneness of being, God consciousness, is expressing as the nature of harmony you **are** regardless of the situation presenting not because the situation demands it but because it is the only way you know to express as the nature you are-child of God, harmonious and benevolent.

Duality is the atmosphere of the world, chaos, therefore of man but what man doesn't realize is duality is choice, a choice to do as *you* want regardless of what is right or let **God** bring harmony to all. Human man has no understanding of peace thus cannot strive to embody it. Just the other day I heard someone say "you have to have the capacity to do bad to survive in this world, that it is the hallmark of a strong *man* to be capable of violence **but the key was to keep it controlled."** How can there be peace when there is always the capacity to do violence? How can you give of love and peace when there is an undercurrent of "what if" always in readiness? You cannot therefore there can be no God expressing.

Man thinks his strength is in his ability to stay alive but **your strength comes from knowing you cannot die** and in that knowing can begin to live your fullest potential as your true nature of Spirit because when you know Truth, where supply **is,** where peace **is** and where joy **is** nothing of man can rock your boat and that is exactly the attitude born of knowing God aright. God is the boat, the ocean, the sky, your North Star and the wind gently moving you forward completely under its governance and care.

Show me evil.

Look around and show me evil or bad like you would show me a chair, a car, your smile. If evil is a thing, a reality, that which has the powers you ascribe to it, it has to have form, be of substance **not associated with another form but is unto itself.** What does the form called evil or bad look like? What substance is it of? A chair is God in form, a tree is God in form, your smile is the expression of God, the entire universe is God substance in form so if God is all, omnipotent, omniscient and omnipresent, **how could there be an actual form of that which is in addition to all that is?**

For that matter where is the embodiment of what man calls good? What does that look like in its form? Let's put the forms of good next to bad/evil like you would put a kitten next to a gun, and discern their differences since one is perceived as good in form and the other as bad in form. Oh, snap. You can't. Why? **Because good and bad are perceptions, judgements or biases.** Good and bad are labels man uses to describe the world around them, *qualifiers* of things, not the Truth of things therefore are **not** things in and of themselves. This is the reality of good and bad man lives and dies for-an *illusion* of Truth based on your perception of Truth which is nothing more than *personal belief.*

When you can show me, in your hand or out in the world that which is evil or good in and of itself and not attached or associated in any way, shape or form to something else as a conditioning, label or judgement I will concede my Truth of being. Go on, I'm waiting, I have an eternity.

Living duality is the tightrope of death. You are trying to keep the world in a nice tidy box so nothing spills out and nothing untoward gets in. You believe by your having an even temper, being less outwardly reactive you can control your surroundings and you can to a point and it feels like you are sailing along on the ocean with just a few big waves to dodge. The problem with options, choices, duality is you are not the only one in the mix making them therefore what someone else wants will butt up against what you want and if they really want it you won't be able to keep your peace because it is an act, not a change in conscious understanding of why you truly have no need to react.

When you remove options from your consciousness you are left with **is**. All **is** and **is** is God and God **is** harmonious expression. So when you take away the good and bad you are left with **is.** Just **is,** I am, you are, that is all that needs to be known because that is all there **is** to know. Everything **is** and **is** is God and what is needed will be given in proportion to your devotion to knowing and living this life of **is** without opposites, without personal will, without duality.

When you are of the beliefs of man you are the expression of man capable of being both good and bad because that is the consciousness you are of; you believe it is normal and natural for man to express in any manner of behavior, any emotion or willful act they desire whether good or bad because that is what man is, a fickle beast, a chameleon for all occasion to get/have/do or be what *they* want. All man know this about each other and do it just the same as breathing. Human life is synonymous with duality, it is what man is because he expresses it-duality, two minds of good and bad and never of God unless God is known in consciousness to be under grace.

When you are under grace, God, you do not express anything of your little self, i, duality, for you are an **instrument** of God deferring *your* will, *your* perspective/labels/judgements of good and bad and are **being** the expression of the consciousness you are **of** by choice-God consciousness.

Grace is the allness of God in action and is that which is peace/inner knowing to those receptive of it.

Grace is the normal and natural dispensation/expression of conscious oneness with God.

Grace can only be expressed by those of God consciousness.

Why only through those who are of the consciousness of God? **Because grace is a dispensation of God,** spiritual creation manifest in form. You have to be of the consciousness of grace to give of grace because you can only express what you embody within. No God, no grace.

Spiritual man, the grass, the fish and the foul, the atmosphere, the cattle on the hills and the wheat in the fields **are** God in form, are of the same source but of individual expression.

The harmonious, infinite, eternal expression of God is the constant renewal of the world around you.

Human man is not of the consciousness of God therefore is not expressing the infinite eternal nature of God which is harmonious ie good.

God needs an awareness of its being for it to express through that awareness out into the world. What this means is it isn't *you* who is being loving, kind, helpful, understanding etc, it is that you are in conscious union with God therefore **you are an avenue through which the nature of God may pour forth in expression as you** through you to aid those receptive of spirit, to be touched by spirit radiating from you as you.

You only express grace when you are under the Law of grace because grace is of God and grace is the gift of God, the allness, the wholeness, the completeness unto your being that comes into expression received in proportion to your degree of oneness.

In this way you are an avenue of expression of God, allowing God to be of the words that come from your mouth, not the human you of duality. When you step to the side and let God go first, be your expression to the world it is you who is seen as the one expressing harmony, good, peace to man thus when you are under grace you express **as** grace, God in action, **because that is your consciousness of being.**

When you are under grace all your needs are met, you are peaceful, carefree, happy and what happens when you are peaceful, carefree and happy? It expresses out into the world as you being of these qualities. So, how could you, being in this consciousness of bliss, of joy also be angry, hateful, sad or egotistical?

When you are in love, get a new car, are wearing your favorite outfit, how do you go all Tasmanian Devil on someone? You can't because your consciousness is of the joy you feel, the love you feel, you are in the happy place the world can't touch, can't diminish, can't take you off your cloud of joy.

The opposite is also true. One who is felt as hostile, mean, not right, antagonistic, false is expressing exactly the consciousness they are-human duality/personal desire. What man doesn't understand is that you cannot hide who you are because as Emerson said "who you are shrieks so loudly I can't hear what you're saying" ie **your** consciousness **is** your expression in the world.

Thoughts never stay within, they become the outward expression, a mirror of your beliefs, pains and fears by which people perceive your presence-good, bad, welcoming or unwelcoming.

Therefore one who is of human consciousness of duality is expressing their consciousness which is their lack of conscious awareness of God. Without conscious awareness of God you cannot express God qualities so what you feel off of man is their human thoughts of who they are in the world as the costume, appearance they wear in the world. They have nothing to give other than their finite selves and since all is of God and humans have none of God in their consciousness, they can express only what they have-duality.

When you come into contact with one who is of higher conscious understanding they feel graceful, have a presence that is not that of man but of something higher. Most think of this feeling as one of higher standing, better morals, better upbringing, more opportunity, privileged.

Nothing could be further from the Truth.

The most enslaving unreality that plagues man to continue being man instead of becoming child of the most high is the *belief* that you can become that expression by buying, learning, getting or doing the things of the world.

Spiritual oneness **is** what self assured, success, peace and **knowing thyself** looks like to man therefore spiritual oneness is what you wish to have if that is the expression that you are drawn to become.

That person is the expression of God in your midst, spiritual man. The unassuming, easy to talk to, feel like I know you, thank you for that smile that lifted my burdens. It matters not what it was, it was how it **felt** that made everything lift and a smile found its way out. You don't know what it was, but something was different about the interaction and you were left feeling the world didn't suck as much as you thought it did.

Sit quietly, settle on a simple statement or question of God: "I want to know Truth God. Help me to understand you and this experience." Then listen. Just relax and await your guest; your listening expectancy is music to God's ears because your silence, emptiness of man's world/thoughts allows God consciousness to fill all space.

You will get something, something that lifts you a bit, lightens you a bit, releases you a bit, runs tingles through your body, gives you a little more than you had of something you needed. This is the spiritual man's way of life-listening. Always listening. Do it again and again and again until you are constantly open to that voice of wisdom and comfort, love and laughter as your being; **you are a partner to this experience, not the doer of this experience.** Your life will be that of an instrument of God bringing this wondrous experience to others who seek release from this world of man to find spiritual harmony among man to help them continue rising in conscious understanding until the atmosphere of the world is more spiritual in expression than duality.

Duality is anything other than is.

Man thinks from the standpoint of this *or* that, right *or* wrong, kill *or* be killed, take *or* be taken. If in your mind there is a choice to be made determined by *you* you are expressing duality. This *or* that, this *and* that, you *or* them. However, if in the same situation you see **is,** not a choice of how to accept it, ie by label or judgement, you are expressing oneness, singularity of expression, grace.

Singularity of expression: expressing the consciousness of God, Source.

- God expressing itself as all that is **is** singularity

- You expressing as God **is** singularity

- The true atmosphere of the universe **is,** being, harmonious, eternal expression of Self, singularity

Therefore **knowing** God aright is the **reason** for **your** singularity of expression because knowing God reveals the Truth of your singularity of expression **as** your true nature of being.

Duality of expression:

-The atmosphere of the world, the way the world works with its good and bad, highs and lows, haves and have nots is duality predicated on the belief of being separate and apart from God, wholeness, completeness, allness.

-Man expressing *himself* is duality not by choice but because it is the literal atmosphere you live in, it is the atmosphere you were born into, believe in and live by as your operating system by which to prosper self above all others.

-human man's operating system is always personal i, me, mine not yours.

Therefore what is seen in the world that can be judged good or bad is of the human mind of duality, of the atmosphere of the world because spiritual man in oneness sees the world through the eyes of God, is, all is and the nature of is **is** harmony in expression.

Original Sin:

The only sin of man is ignorance of Truth. All error stems from this one sin, the **original** sin that there is God *and*. That is why it is said you are not responsible for your sins because it is the atmosphere of man, the belief of man since man set foot on solid ground.

You are however **responsible** for the consequences of the sins you commit in this world of man and karmic law because though ignorant of Truth you are not ignorant of moral values and the laws of your human existence.

When you are aware of the Father within you are no longer ignorant of spiritual Truth which brings you out from under your ignorance of spiritual Truth but does not erase the consequences of current actions; **its purpose is to keep you from incurring negative consequences going forward.**

You have to close this chapter of life consisting of dual living, dual expression, being capable of being whoever the heck you want for your own purposes, slam it shut and say you are done living this kind of horror nonsense! You want action, adventure, love, laughter, peace and joy in your life and **knowing Truth** and relying on God in all ways is how to bring those expressions of harmony into your experience.

Now you are learning to live in the world but not **of** the world's consciousness of duality. You have risen in conscious understanding and now understand that there never was nor could ever be any power against God because there is no thing but God expressing as eternal harmony.

The chaos man experiences is merely his feeble attempt at trying to find meaning in a world devoid of its source of meaning-God, life, allness, wholeness, completeness, oneness, the living of is.

You start out as a student aware of discords and inequalities and practice making the mental adjustment by what has been called treatment, healing or knowing Truth but eventually will be like the mathematician who does not have to constantly think of how to do calculations rather knows mathematical law is constant thus always arriving at the correct answer **as long the principles of the law are met.** This practice of nothingizing error becomes innate, natural, it becomes the normal and natural activity of spirit in form living a visible experience-you.

After you have seen enough inharmonies on the street, in your business, news etc, the correction is made automatically. All error/chaos stems from different points of view, one wanting what the other has, anger, fear, frustration all of which are *humanity* in action. Since humanity is an illusion in and of itself, *whatever you are witnessing as a result of human thought and action is always an illusion and by knowing this Truth you bring God on the field, grace to bear.*

Eventually you reach a place where you are not consciously declaring Truth and yet the moment an error strikes your consciousness the adjustment is made. Now when you are called upon for help you have very little conscious treatment to do and very little remembering of Truth. Your state of consciousness is automatic, is spiritual therefore your connection to God keeps God in your atmosphere thus negating the need to bring God on the field because he is with you pretty much 24/7.

It is at this point you are no longer knowing Truth but have risen to that place in consciousness where **you have become Truth,** one with God knowing only one presence of good, grace, God. It is from this place of awareness that your new life begins, the life of living heaven on earth.

The only punishment you ever receive is that of your own misdeeds, omissions or commissions. Thoughts and deeds perpetuated as a human without God come back to you good *or* bad. The error punishes the error by the laws and emotions of *human* man and has **nothing** to do with God.

You change your response to life when you know the Truth of life and stop living the illusion of life. Why? Because Truth reveals there is nothing to react to because there is no Presence, no Power, no Law, no Substance and no objectivity *to illusion* thus it does not nor can exist as a reality therefore there is no thing to react to, fight against, fight for or change. Why? Because there is no thing you do not already possess, the allness of God already **is** within you and **knowing this is what changes your response to the world around you.**

You now know the Truth of all error is duality-man expressing *as* good and bad because they believe there are good and bad people and forces they must be prepared for, react to. That knowing affords you the opportunity to further remove the hypnotism of man's world by healing the error and bringing grace to bear just by knowing "this world" meaning the illusion of man or "maya", Sanskrit for illusion, and let the error go as the nothingness it showed itself to be. This is why it is said "do not resist evil." It doesn't mean not to resist in the sense of giving in, bowed down, belly up getting taken advantage of. No! You do not resist evil because if you **know** the Truth of evil you know there is no thing to fight because **all evil is individual perception,** therefore no thing, nothing, just illusion believed to be reality.

This is the beauty of knowing Truth, there is nothing for you to carry, nothing for you to do except heal error by knowing Truth which brings grace to bear for you and those receptive. This is the freedom of being of God-there is nothing for you to do, God is the governing influence, the mover and shaker behind the scenes with dominion over all that is because all is of it and all you are to do is respond to it, God within, not man. In this way you fulfill your purpose as child of God helping others find their way home to live the promised life of peace be with you while you receive your bread on the water pressed down and flowing over until you transition onto your next adventure.

The *illusion* is that this world is a *material* world. The **Truth/reality** of this world is that it is **spiritual consciousness in form.**

This world is spiritual not material. This is the illusion man has accepted as the universal understanding of all that is because man does not have the ability to see beyond the visible so it names the visible as if it were something separate and apart from the invisible but **God is all that is** and this is the true fabric of this world, **spiritual** not *material,* **one substance of all that is** not *random forms of matter* that miraculously work together.

The thing about sin/error/illusion is that when it presents it is now, immediate, in your face and you feel you have to do something about it/react. What you do is go within to God and wait for God to break the *illusion* of error by coming into awareness. The awareness of God is felt as peace and harmony which is spiritual healing because oneness has been restored.

The difference between human man and spiritual man is in the **perception** of the world around them: spiritual man **knows** what **is** through God awareness and human man experiences *what seems to be* through individual perception.

When error presents to one of spiritual consciousness you are given the choice to accept the error as reality and react as a human would or know error is an illusion accepted as reality by one who doesn't know Truth, God.

If you accept the illusion of error as reality and react you have slipped from God consciousness back to human consciousness of duality and are affected by the duality you accept ie fear, the threat of lack, illness, pain.

If you do not accept the illusion of error as reality you remain in the consciousness of God, in harmony, emotionally unaffected by/non reactive to the error because you know the Truth of error thus do not experience the effects of the *belief* that error has power to somehow affect your life negatively or positively thereby freeing yourself of the consequences of accepting the illusion as reality and reacting.

There will still be the crashed car or loss of job or pain of some kind but spiritual man does not see it as either good or bad but rest in **is, knows there is a reason for it and it will be revealed as harmony in some form.** Think of it as a reshuffling of your deck bringing more spiritual perfection into your experience. All that you experience as spiritual man on the path will end up harmonious if **you** continue to **let** God tell you what is happening by inner listening/prayer/communion and not react to what seems to be happening.

Harmony is within you to the degree you live in it for it is a **dwelling** place, your consciousness of God within, taking care of it all and in that knowing rest. This rest is harmony but harmony is only within you when you are with God. As a new student on the spiritual path you slip in and out of human consciousness of duality into spiritual consciousness by way of the spiritual Truths you are learning. I can honestly say there are times through out my day when I get that startled feeling inside, a feeling of something beginning to run down hill before I stop myself, mentally and physically and remind myself of Truth. "What are you doing? You know how this works. Stop reacting and just roll with it. Address what needs to be addressed, ask the questions that need to be asked and in the end harmony **is.**"

What I have noticed is that when something goes sideways if I don't react and just do as I am given to do it all works out to my benefit. For example I suddenly realized I need something done for a project I didn't know I needed done but couldn't continue on without doing so was not prepared and the person for another aspect of the project was suddenly unavailable and I felt very vulnerable to be honest. But, and this is the hard part to do, if I understand that when my world **feels** like it is falling out from under my feet **it is because it is revealing what is supposed to be.**

I lost my plumber for a project and asked him if he knew another plumber and a person for the part of the project I didn't know I needed to do and both of the people he referred me to worked out better for me in the end than the original person would have! Harmony! But without the first plumber falling through and giving me references I would never have gotten the people I was supposed to have on the job. I did nothing but take a deep breath and say within "I know there will be harmony in the end of this seeming chaos, I know from experience not to meddle, not to get all worked up and not to think into the future. I will handle what is given to handle, I will let you as I address situations in the words and tone necessary to the process going forward. I trust in your orchestration Father and I know, because **I know where I live in consciousness 95% of the time, that this isn't human karma coming back for an error** so it isn't for me to worry about but I'm still learning not to freak when personal error presents."

Thank you Father for being dependable, reliable and consistent in your expression because Truth/God **is** Law-dependable, reliable, consistent and eternal unto **itself.**

It doesn't matter what your sins are they represent generations and generations of **man's sense of separation from God.** Your sins, poverties and lacks are going to continue, not because it is God's will but because "you, worst of all, who say they love God but do not love your fellow man therefore you are a liar for to love God is to love every form of God and that is the sinner to the saint."

God is made evident, visible, tangible as individual you and me and **there is no such thing as loving God if we do not love each other,** forgive each other and release them and *self* from judgement or condemnation.

Everything that presents to you as anything other than good/harmonious/God is a judgement on your part; no matter what anything presents as, looks like, feels like or sounds like it is not yours to judge because the only Truth anyone can know about anything in this world is that it **is,** it happened but you cannot know how it will **affect** those involved therefore your views are *subjective,* unnecessary and have no bearing on the outcome thus are merely a *distraction* from Truth-if God is, and you know God is because you just had a pow wow with it twenty minutes ago, then there cannot be anything unlike itself therefore spiritual man expresses harmony no matter the expression of the world around them.

Harmony is only found where forgiveness is found therefore to have harmony one must forgive the ignorance of man and not condemn by judgement any man and the Bible states this clearly: "neither do I condemn thee but go and sin no more lest a worse fate befall you." **This isn't judgement, this is seeing right past appearances, healing the error and bringing grace/harmony to bear where there was none.** What the person does after this is of no concern to you. Every man choses their path and yours is to heal the errors of man **not** walk the path for another man. You do what is given you to do, bring God to bear at every silent opportunity while living the glorious life that unfolds from bringing God to bear for the benefit of your brothers.

You get to a "what do I care" attitude, what I am seeing is merely the *human* expression of the consciousness of lack, limitation, death and disease *believed* to be powers that can affect you in some way. However if you know there is only one power/expression of good/harmony then all other so-called powers must be no thing but labels/judgements ie unrealities therefore you don't get your knickers in a twist, don't feed error with *reaction* rather you release error as the illusion it is without fighting it **because you now know what is experienced by the senses is false** and the Truth of the matter comes from within and you rest for there is no thing to react to if you know Truth.

Duality: Chaos in expression

Human man lives by their *individual* will which creates inharmony because **all** man live by their *individual* will which may or may not be the will of others they encounter thus always the possibility of chaos/conflict in every circumstance or encounter.

Oneness: Harmony in expression

Spiritual man lives by God's choices, God's will which is harmony in expression because when all are of the same consciousness, the same will, the same expression there is harmony, there is nothing to cause inharmony because **there is only one from which all express from.** It isn't the harmony of *your* being, it is the harmony of God bringing harmony to all.

When you let God be your expression you are expressing God and you are known as the living Christ. You are **being** your nature, you are expressing Truth, you do not do for yourself as human man does trying to take or get from the world rather you rest with God and become the expression of abundance, joy, harmony and peace to the world and that returns to you. You cannot give what you do not have within and you cannot receive what you do not give of/share and until you know God aright you have nothing to give except duality.

While the world fights a power called evil, medical practices try to overcome or cure disease and theology struggles to overcome sin, you are learning Truth about human appearances called sin, disease and error and now understand the unreality of these expressions. They have no power, no

Life to support them, no Source and no Law therefore they exist *only as beliefs accepted as Truth,* illusions accepted as conditions which is nothing more than the misinterpretation of what really **is.**

100% of the error you encounter in your life is because you "played someone else's game" meaning you *accepted* something of the world of duality. You took it personal when someone sped past you on the road, you took it personal when another was rude, you let snide comments get under your skin, you allowed temptation to sway you, you judged, commented, felt fear, anger, annoyance, slighted and allowed your *ego,* your *i,* your little *self* to be your expression. You experience error when *you* **chose to do something without God in awareness.** No God in awareness=no grace in your experience=errors in your experience.

Every time you allow the world to affect your harmony you have allowed the *false* atmosphere of man to *control* you, take you away from the harmony that **is** your resting place to suffer the chaos of man once again. Let go of the world and just ride this eternal ride with God right beside you so he can point out all the potholes to avoid so your journey is without incident.

With every expression of sin and disease that appears before your eyes/picked up by your senses you learn to look at it and say "never again can I fear you, never again can I hate you, never again can I love you, there is no power in that which is sensed."

This doesn't mean these outer things are not useful, water is useful, shelter is useful, cars are useful, money is useful, food is useful, electricity is useful; many things are useful, many things are beautiful, harmonious and joyful **but none of them have any power for good or evil except such power as your thinking makes it so.**

When you stop and see what **is**-a dog, two cars crashed into each other, an eviction notice or the loss of a job-and see that it holds no power either good or evil, then you will find that divine harmony establishes itself in your experience. This principle **reveals** that you are suffering from those things you hate, fear, desire or overly love and when you no longer hate, fear or love them but treat them as a part of this universe and each thing serving its purpose you will find in one way or another those things that should not be a part of your experience will be withdrawn from you, those things necessary to your unfoldment will be provided for you then you have to watch yourself after they have been provided you don't think that they are good; **they aren't good they are useful, beautiful, enjoyable etc,** the only good they are is **inherent** in their source, God.

What you have to understand is that when you are **not** reacting to error you are not alone in this thought, you are with God when you become aware of error to heal it. To say within "error, maya, illusion, arm of flesh" is not saying it and hoping for the best, you are **knowing** it is error **because you are with God** which is your proof of what you are saying. If God is there is nothing else.

You are not left twisting in the wind when you find God and leave the ways and means of man which were your support though it was support only in your imagination. The **difference** is that the things of man are visible and measurable so you have a visual interpretation of what is going on for you, around you. With God, invisible, incorporeal within you your focus must change from the without/visible to the within/invisible where true allness resides because this is your support. If you *pretend* there is no error but *fear* you are wrong you are still living duality and will not see the benefit of living in God consciousness and feel it has failed you. No. You have failed yourself because you are not walking the talk and will suffer the sin of your duality, your choices.

In the human world thoughts are things, *thoughts* are believed to be as *material* as *things* are therefore *thoughts* cannot be **God.** Why? Because thoughts are only of the mind and are not tangible/objective as form. To be a thing out in the world where it can be touched, tasted, smelled, seen or heard it must have form and the only source of all forms is **God** because this is a **spiritual** universe not a *material* universe.

Truth vs belief

The understanding of a belief held as Truth and Truth revealed about a belief can be a bit confusing. A belief is released as the no thing that it is when you have a revelation, something clicks that brings an understanding beyond what you previously understood.

Belief is nothing more than a personal perception taken as Truth until such time a higher understanding of that belief is known. When this happens you are not a believer of that belief anymore because you now have a better understanding, higher knowing than the knowing you were at that formed the belief.

When it is said "error dissolves" it doesn't magically poof away rather upon second glance realize the *error* of *your* first take of the situation, "my mistake Father, all is harmonious because you are here."

Duality is the *perception* there is something besides is, God being, expressing.

There is no *thing* other than God in expression therefore there is no *thing* in the world that is other than **is** except the *belief* there is *other than* what **is**-good, harmony, allness and peace. God **is** and cannot be divided, is as it is which **is** eternal harmonious expression of all that **is.**

Evil doesn't exist as entity or identity. **Evil exists as a belief in two powers called carnal/mortal/human mind** therefore if you wish to lessen evil in the world you must begin to recognize even if a natural *disaster* threatens it is only the emanation of carnal mind, the *belief* that weather has power to change your nature, kill you, and as you do that watch as the storm evaporates, changes direction etc, because when you **know** all is of God you have dominion over the storms because you know their Truth-they are not good and they are not bad, they are God therefore knowing the Truth of them removes the perceived power of them and you rest. Why? God cannot kill itself therefore nothing of nature can kill spiritual man because nature and spiritual man are one. You can leave this experience which is seen as human death but with the knowing you are eternal comes the knowing that you are free from any and all fear of man, the greatest of these being human death. When you know your Truth you lose your fear of anything of the world of man and rest in God.

God is all and all is good therefore God cannot do anything against one part of itself because it would be against its nature of perpetual harmony predicated on like begetting like. God can no more harm a man, strike a man down or "call a man home" because that which is creative and harmonious cannot suddenly change its nature to be other than it is but human man can and does as a way of expression.

What is judged good or evil is not of the world but of the human mind, flows out from the human mind into expression but when you understand "*human* mind" merely means the *belief in two powers* you understand that all evil flows out **not** from *you* but from the *belief in two powers* that is the **atmosphere** of man, the invisible soup of hundreds of thousands of years of man's fear and pain caused by believing they are separated from God. This is called the human condition.

Simply remind yourself of the nature of evil, that it is not of or belonging to *something* or *someone* thus is unreal/illusion so by **impersonalize it, separating it from person, place or thing, you take away its perceived reality** and in that knowing of Truth you are free of the *influence* of the error because you healed it, revealed the Truth of the error as no thing real.

The minute you sense error on your part against yourself or another immediately ask for forgiveness-"that was wrong of me Father"-then make the appropriate adjustments for though you have asked and were forgiven, the error must be rectified in the world of man of cause and effect. You created an error and you must correct it, pay the corresponding *human* judgement otherwise the forgiveness you ask for is merely lip service trying to cover your butt.

Forgiveness is predicated on you knowing that though you erred if you change your ways because you see the error of your ways you will no longer suffer the human consequences of those ways because you have grown beyond the consciousness that created those errors. This is a numbers game in essence. The more Truth you experience as grace in your life the more you rest and trust in Truth. The more you trust the more grace you receive, the added things, signs following.

It is your **devotion** to God and **not** yourself that brings the allness of God to bear in your life and not just the paltry scraps man thinks to be treasures.

People aren't evil even if you refer to them as a Hitler or Genghis Khan but they will be evil if you see them as evil. If you believe there are sinful people you open yourself up to experiencing sin, the belief in lack opens you up to lack, the belief in disease opens you to disease and the belief that those who are born ultimately die.

The only sin is ignorance of Truth.

The very desire for something good, even something as good as to be of service, is a barrier to spiritual development because you have no right to want anything, even to want good.

There is only one righteous desire: to want to know God. Then if God places you in some form of service you perform the works given you to do. Don't worry, you will love it because God is You 2.0 remember? You are God's expression of Self and you get to reap the bounty of omnipotence, omniscience and omnipresence because where you are God is.

These works you do with joy as you permit yourself to be a transparency, vessel, instrument through which the harmony of God may flow.

When error appears in front of man, man reacts and gets to work mentally, physically or emotionally doing something. Spiritual man when confronted with error knows there is nothing humanly to do thus seems undisturbed by them. To human man this can look like hardness, uncaring, not my problem kind of attitude but man cannot nor will ever understand what spiritual man does that is so powerful that God is loosed to be and do what God **is**-good, grace, benevolence, kindness, charity, love, comfort, peace.

Man is akin to a chicken with its head cut off still thinking it is alive going through the motions but with no purpose, no sense of direction, with a blind eye to Truth all the while looking outside himself to the world to reattach his head.

There is no condemnation when you are under a belief of error, whether it is of sin or sickness. There is no error personal to you. **All error is a universal belief which you accept therefore manifest.** It is this acceptance of universal beliefs which cause you to come under the effect, duality, which gives the illusion you are sick or sinful.

Think of the significance of the First Commandment, "there is only one presence which is power" therefore to fear or hate or judge is to give up your God bestowed dominion because you have fallen back into human thinking of duality.

There is no such thing as overcoming evil, nor God healing your diseases or fixing your bank account nor reforming sinners. Overcome false theology here and now by accepting the First Commandment.

The Bibles of the world tell of two powers, of good and evil but that is because scripture has been accepted from the standpoint of literal translation instead of read in the light of spiritual inspiration/understanding. Scripture cannot be interpreted *intellectually,* merely as an historical document because it is **revealed Truth, metaphysical Truth** of inspired sages, seers and mystics. In this light there is but one Presence, one Power and I am that I am.

The advantage of one who seeks a different experience than that of human man is one who realizes what he searches for cannot be among man, the world, the visible therefore it must be where man is not and that is the invisible, the within of self, consciousness. Consciousness is where Self is found, that which is not of finite man but infinite spiritual perfection, the I of you.

Most religious seekers seek in the metaphysical, in the written *words* of man for **God,** in the suppositions, philosophies and theorem of man which are only the extent of the highest man's *thinking of* **God** because man doesn't have the capacity to **know** God.

Those on a true spiritual path now understand what is sought is spiritual in nature and cannot be found in a materially perceived world. Therefore it comes down to knowing what it is you seek and then knowing where it can be found.

The advantage you have right now is you are being shown **what** Truth is and **where** Truth is found.

Why do you come to a place in your life where you begin to seek? Because you have been touched by grace, the allness and wholeness of the Father because you in some way asked, genuinely want different and in that desire for what is not of man, this earthly experience, have opened the way for different to manifest in your reality.

What does the search for Truth mean? It means you are seeking that which at the moment is unknown but know it will bring peace and relief to the weary human you are. **What you are seeking is a personal relationship with God** to be made whole, to feel peace, to rest in the arms you knew were there to hold you. This is the reason you are here and the reason you will stay because this is home, this is security, this is peace man of earth will never experience because it is of God and you must be of the consciousness of God to receive of all that God is.

Spiritual consciousness, God awareness, is the awareness of your being as individual God being. It recognizes the entire universe as consciousness formed/appearing, universal Law of creative expression, God governed by divine principles of itself.

Spiritual consciousness does not overcome or destroy matter or material conditions rather knows that **no such conditions exist** even though human/finite sense presents them for your acceptance or rejection. It allows you to see behind the appearance of good or bad to **is,** the harmony and peace of God as all that **is.** No qualification, no judgement, just **is** for **is** is the Truth of that which *appears as* good or bad.

How do you get from good/bad to is? You stop judging, having a personal opinion of X because it was created by God so it is, all is, unqualified, unjudged, pure, harmonious is. Man determines the degree of good or bad solely on personal experiences that have left him with biases, judgements, likes, dislikes and fears.

By classifying something as good or bad instead of is you have created the illusion of power outside of yourself and given permission for this illusion to alter your emotional state, good or bad, like or hate, fear or joy, desire or reject and in this way set up the duality/dichotomy of thought that is the downfall of human man.

The duality of man's mind, the belief that there are inherent qualities of good or bad, that bad can become good and good can also turn bad is the reason man suffers and dies. Why? Because there is no good and bad, only **is.** Man has created the atmosphere of good and bad to compensate for the lack of inner connection with God that is the rudder, the wind and the sail of your life and without this you flounder and sinking more than you float.

God wants you to float. Stop kicking and sinking, treading water and getting no where. Let God help, let God do for you what it used to do before man decided their needs and desires superseded all others and began acting on that belief with no understanding that all were brothers. If only man would remember this there would be peace on earth for **one with God is a majority.** When you understand the mystical meaning of that you will never be alone another second of your life for this understanding is what makes you free from the effects of the belief in duality thus knowing the absolute reality of God, harmonious expression of all that is.

All illness, discord, mistakes, lack and fear are created by the mind of man then experienced in the world around them. Man wants to be released/healed of their ailment/circumstances therefore pray to a God outside of them for the relief sought-get rid of this, make it better, make it go away, change it into what you want because what you have isn't that.

Do you see that all a human knows to ask for is the *opposite* of what they have/do/are experiencing and when received in a measure must be continually protected/monitored/worried about because it could all go away in a blink? What if you were able to ask for something else? That which is lasting, fulfilling, Truth to stand on? What if you were to ask for God?

Why would I want God you ask?

God is steady, reliable, consistent **Law.** Law **is** eternally. Gravity, mathematics, music, astronomy, physics. All laws are immutable, unchangeable, eternal is. When you come back into the consciousness of God, of the Law of universal creative expression, you become one with the Law that governs the universe which means you are no longer alone rather supported, maintained and supplied by this eternally expressing **Law** and this is why and how you are harmonious-you are free, you are safe and you are home.

Every form of error that would touch you must go through your mind, your thinking mind, cognitive mind, the ego/personality of man with its judgements and biases. If however you do not accept the error in your mind ie you see it for the illusion/ignorance it is, it cannot affect you, change your state of being.

You cannot say you **know** God and *believe* in/live by using two powers. Your dominion, your protection over **experiencing** error lies in **your ability to let slide, not react** to whatever erroneous thought, condition or appearance presents out in the world or within yourself by **knowing** nothing can take you from the harmony of God unless *you* allow it.

Nothing of the world can disturb you as long as **you** see the things of *man* for what they are-misplaced attention on *self* and the *world* and not with **God** in harmony for peace among man.

Most of this study has been about releasing error in the outer world but there is error concerning the body that needs to be addressed. The body will try to keep its power, its need to get your attention and focus once more on what is truly an illusion-your physical body that thinks *it* can have pain, disease, inharmony, that *it* can be in and of itself as *it* was **before** you knew Truth. I and others have found that which has been spiritually healed tries to get your attention as if it were *real* and in need of *your* attention once again. Let us say through prayer and treatment harmony has been revealed in the form of a few of your physical ailments having gotten better/changed but every now and again *it* acts up, the stomach gets bubbly, the joint or nerve pain seems to return, the headache, the hands and feet hurt.

You are on the spiritual path, you are the living expression **of** God therefore you **know** your existence to be spiritual from consciousness to visible expression of form not flesh and blood therefore the "body" cannot of itself be other than the expression of your consciousness of God, **is,** not *it* separate and apart from God therefore what you are feeling are *echoes.*

Echo by definition is the remnant of something *thought* to be real therefore it as well cannot be real.

Echoes are those things that seem to come back into your awareness, of *something past* that were healed and revealed as no thing, illusion, and this is merely an *echo* of that *illusion* trying to get you to *do* something, *react,* treat it as flesh and blood instead of spiritual perfection.

Important! Always use your judgement of right medical care, no one is in your shoes so if you are concerned about a returning pain have it checked. Do what you chose to do whether it is to rest in a revelation or go to the doctor. Your life is always yours as are your choices **just spiritually heal yourself first** then do as **you** feel necessary to bring relief of your symptoms and peace to your mind.

Healers do not need to know the errors patients bring to their attention **because all error stems from the belief in being separated from God** so if you bring God into awareness you have broken the mesmerism, the belief, that God is outside of you to *get* favor with or from and the healing is done and those receptive to the soft still voice within will receive grace, peace, whatever is needed because you knew the Truth of error within yourself to bring it into the awareness of others.

Sin:

Why do people behave the way they do taking, lying, harming and killing? Because they don't know who they are. You are not a sinner no matter what you have done, it is only the name given to the act being committed. Unfortunately man in his love of labels **combined** the sin with the person creating an unreal or erroneous appearance calling the sin the person and the person the sin-thief, killer, abuser, defamer etc.

Sin is never personal, it is not a thing, a person or a place. It is no thing more than an action viewed through the lens of judgement, of good and bad. If it is deemed bad by one it is a sin but if it is deemed good by another then it is a blessing. How can one form express as two expressions at the same time? It cannot and if you can see that then you will soon see why good and evil do not exist except in the mind of the one who accepts that there are good and evil powers at play in their life.

There is no good and there is no evil there is only **is**. Spiritual living is **is,** the activity of Truth in your consciousness **is** the fabric/basis/reality of true existence not what is brought into awareness by the senses of the body and altered by the mind.

Sin has always been associated with the person performing the sinful act but if you read that again you can clearly see it says sinful act. The **action** is sinful, **not** the person, ever.

"Though your sins may be scarlet ye are white as snow."

This clearly states that no matter your sin the Truth of you will always remain perfect for the **Truth** of God is **untouched** by the *beliefs* of man. Your soul is of God, the mind used for deduction is of God, your consciousness is of God and you are the visible expression of God.

All is of God but for one thing-human man who is not under grace nor ever can be because they don't know they are truly sinless and perfect in the eyes of God.

There is no good and no evil, just spiritual wholeness, completeness and perfection where I am.

You will always be faced with discordant appearances but you will be in a state of consciousness that does not respond to them, does not accept them as real, doesn't fight or battle them. The battle is not yours, it is God's. "Stand ye still, see the salvation of the Lord, they have only the arm of flesh while you have the Lord God Almighty." You never need to battle, never need to fight, never need to sue or be at war with another.

This world of man is of getting, achieving, accomplishing, striving and struggling. It is a world of two powers. To some extent you have already left that world if you have come to realize that life need not be lived by power, by might or struggle, but that life can be lived by grace and that you are on the path to experiencing that grace in greater measure. You must choose your path. Do you want God to do *your* will and supply you with what you *think* you need or do you wish to enter the spiritual realm of life in which you surrender yourself/will to God and live your Truth, child of God, heir to the kingdom?

Not my will but thy will be done in me and you. **Thy grace is** your sufficiency in all ways. Not what you tell God you want or need. You surrender your desires and accept the grace of the Father, the all knowing within you. Feed me in accordance with Thy grace and Thy wishes. **You ask for nothing, seek nothing but the peace being with the Father brings.** Abide within yourself in an expectant knowing of God's grace, harmony, peace, abundance and companionship. Your mind doesn't have to work because you are turning within only for the purpose of being in communion with God and for the benediction of God's grace upon you and the world.

Choose you this day whether you are going to be in this world and think of yourself as human going to God for your daily needs or whether you are going to accept yourself as child of God who is heir to all the heavenly riches. Choose right now and if you choose the child of God **never pray to God for anything except its spirit be upon you and his grace be realized within you.**

You do not ask that God *do* something for you but that **you awaken to its presence** and its works for you, through you, as you.

You are under human law while you are taking advantage of an eye for an eye and a tooth for a tooth/duality. As long as you are *resisting* evil, as long as you are *using* the weapons of the world the very knife you throw at someone will come right back to pierce you in the chest-karma, cause and effect. You experience duality when you indulge the human way of life and there is no way of expecting grace while you are doing it. You can pray for grace for a million years and it isn't going to come to you. You are only going to have grace when you give up the weapons of the world and come to the understanding of Job, **He hangeth the earth on nothing** and if you just stand there in that nothingness the spirit rushes in to pick you up and carry you through.

It is in this way Truth is born, it is in this way all unfoldment comes from within and is the fulfillment of scripture-I am that I am.

There is no reality to *mental* powers, those of healing or those of evil to cause ills. That which is perceived as *power* is merely personal perception based on the *belief* that another can have power over their mind/life through *thought*.

It is your perception and degree of *fear* associated with it that makes something "strong or weak" against your being. I'm strong of body, I don't get sick. My body is weak, I get everything. Duality from personal perception, illusion not Law.

Man has the capacity to sin again, this is why you have to be **alert,** this is why you can never **stop** praying/listening and communing because there is a trap awaiting those of this belief. Why? Because prayer, inner listening, communion is your **only** connection to God and without it you have only man and duality. The only way to stay in the kingdom is by staying in the consciousness that constitutes the kingdom.

You have to be in it to win it/receive it!

What is grace and demonstration?

There will come a time when you enter a period of life called living by grace. Man shall not live by *bread* alone but by every word that proceedeth out of the mouth of God through inner communion revealing thy grace is your sufficiency in all ways. *Bread* is what is called the substance of man's experience that cannot satisfy because man is not whole without God, Source, without **spiritual** Bread, Meat, Wine and Water; the things of spirit, of God, of Truth.

When this becomes your experience it never again becomes necessary to take thought for your life because God takes thought for your Life, it reveals to you what you shall do each day, it opens avenues or channels of good in your experience and you begin to live the life of the child of God.

In this experience you receive all that is needed and wanted through grace, not by the sweat of the brow, not by earning or deserving it but by virtue of inheritance from God.

You are here to do the will of the Father so all may know the Father aright and return to their rightful place as joint heir to the kingdom of God.

I (the Christ of individual man/individualized expression of God) am come to do the will of my Father, God, and my Father's will is this:

I have come to heal the sick, raise the dead, feed the hungry and clothe the poor, open the eyes of the blind and preach the gospel. **Therefore the ministry of the Christ is to assure that God's kingdom be established on earth as it is in heaven,** that there shall be no death, no disease, no sin and above all things, if any of you are living in fear that God is punishing you for some sin lose that fear for it is not true, God has never punished anyone for any sin, there is no provision in God for punishment of any nature-God is too pure to behold inequity.

You are **not** here to do *your* will, make something of yourself, become something notable as society would have you believe. You are here to do the will of that which you are of, God, universal creative expression. This is the mistake of mankind from the beginning because *you* know nothing but think *you* are to do something with this self. However if you are knowing God aright through inner listening you are learning *you* are not to do anything of yourself, of your own mind of desire but to let the I, the **God** of you do it all **through** you **as** you.

When you know God aright you have no desire of the human world because all you could ever want is wrapped up within you just waiting to be recognized so it can become to you what you didn't know it could be-real Living, real Life, living Truth, living from the consciousness of Truth, God, Source of all that is visible and invisible.

To receive the grace of God you must retire from the world of sense, learn to silence the material sense of needing to *do* to survive and instead turn within. God **must** become a living reality to you, a divine presence felt just as you sense another person in a room but within yourself. It must become friend, confidant, teacher, comforter, rock, center.

The God of you **is,** is within and is sensed or felt as any other presence in the outer world would be because it **is** the spirit of every man of earth when you know God aright.

The greater your realization that you are living by grace and that this grace is established within you, the greater the contribution you can make to the world. This is your reason for being here. Remember: what you and I can receive from our studies is only that we may have more to contribute to the world by healing and bringing grace to bear. Let your prayers and treatments be the realization of this Truth:

The kingdom of God is already established within you just awaiting your awareness of it to begin harmonizing your life by **its** expression of peace and harmony unto your being which you express to the world because you just feel so dang good! This is sharing God's grace, God's allness which is healing to those who seek.

As you progress on this path, have been practicing the presence and nothingizing error, the burdens of life become lighter ie sickness not as often or acute, financial stress or even lack gradually gives way to sufficiency. Concern for one's self disappears as every need is met without taking thought or planning or worry or fear on your part.

The peoples or powers which before were feared now fade from view either disappearing from your experience or are released from your consciousness and become powerless. Your desires for baubles and things and experiences become less demanding, fears evaporate, you become assured, confident within yourself and this metamorphosis of consciousness becomes evident not only to yourself but to those who you meet and deal with every day.

This inner presence has also become your inner power. God's presence becomes your power and this power is not physical/force rather it is knowing Truth that **God is the only presence, only reality and it is the knowing of this one Truth that keeps you from the error of expressing and experiencing duality.** God awareness begins as an occasional experience and as you **encourage** it by being open to it it becomes a constant awareness of its presence. The forces outside of you, the illusory forces that create desires and fears, pain and anger begin to diminish as you become more conscious of Truth that produces and governs the outer life harmoniously and fruitfully from within.

There is no longer fear of the evils of the world nor is there intense pleasure in the happier things of the world. It is possible to have the pleasure of the world and enjoy them or not have them and not miss them because there is a constant harmony humming away within that needs no outer cause. In God consciousness there is an inner light that is felt that is an emanation of God. God is **felt** as a divine presence or calming influence within. It is **felt** by those who come in contact with the man who has found his inner Self and is reflected in his health and success outwardly in the world. It radiates from him forming an atmosphere around him which is the illumination, the perfume of God and the presence that goes before and stays after.

When you find your inner life you have found your eternal peace, joy, harmony and security. Even in the midst of a failing world you will stand unmoved and untouched because you are in the presence of God, know the Truth of oneness and are freed from living an earthly life to begin living a spiritual life. When you are no longer limited by the five senses and have attained even a grain of spiritual understanding or Christ consciousness you will find yourself unlimited in the terms of here or there or now or here after. There's a going in and coming out without any sense of time or space, an unfolding without degree and a realization without an object.

Expression, activity, manifestation or demonstration all mean the same thing: God on the field, the presence of God realized, God in expression, grace.

The manifestation of God or demonstration of God is the harmony, peace and all the added things of God visible and invisible in your experience.

To live by grace is to see every person as their Truth, child of God, regardless of what the senses reveal.

To live by grace is to forgive 70×7 but go and sin no more lest a greater sin befall you.

Grace:

There are those of whom the term graceful is used to describe. This doesn't mean any visible attribute but rather their spirit, the life that imbues them, the light, the peace, the harmony felt in this one's presence, the feeling that you are left with after they have gone, what they have left with you lingers and entices revealing a desire to be likewise instead of the fumbling human you seem so often to be.

It is the God within that is alive and present that you feel and nothing else, nothing of the person themselves rather what is in and through them as them in your experience. This is the experience of God in your midst and this is what your expression will become the more you become one who is of these qualities through study and application of Truth.

Grace is the gift of God, it is God in action. The activity of God, the activity of spirit is grace. Grace is the allness of God in activity in your experience. Grace is that which appears as the added things, the expression, the nature, the quantity and quality of God in your life and is the giving of God to itself.

There is only one gift of God, not gifts plural and this gift is grace, the allness of God unto your experience.

Grace is the absence of all power because grace is the allness of God which transcends duality. God is not a power that overcomes another power, it is the presence that reveals the non power of anything other than itself and in that acknowledgement the presence of God reveals no power is necessary to remove error or evil because no power is needed to reveal and release that which isn't real ie illusion of the thinking mind.

You do not fight error or wrongness rather you see it for the personal/human nature it is and not Law thus revealing it **isn't** a thing, is no thing, nothing and dissolves.

When it is said error dissolves it doesn't magically poof away. It wasn't anything but an illusion of your mind, a knee jerk reaction or echo of an old habit ie judgement or personal perspective, to begin with and when God is in awareness you merely realize what at first registered *as* error just **is.**

The cycle of grace:

Illumined consciousness touches receptive consciousness then becomes illumined which touches receptive consciousness and on and on it goes.

Materialists divide and hoard and believe all supply is limited while spiritual man shares knowing full well the infinite and unlimited nature of God. The materialistic man has to count numbers, amounts and degrees. The mystic **knows** the infinite, omnipresent nature of God. The mystic is not fooled by appearances, not concerned with numbers, amounts or degrees except in the practical every day living of exchange. Mystics do not measure in materialistic/finite standards because the infinite nature of God cannot be divided.

The grace of God, the infinite nature of God is a spiritual **activity** which appears practically for use in visible form.

What is the nature of grace?

-More than you need, left over to share

-Moses-the manna/grace falls fresh each day

As risen man you enjoy the things of the world but you no longer need to possess the things of the world because you know tomorrow will bring something else for your use/enjoyment and that is why there is no need to hoard that which comes freely and constantly. Hoarding only throws you back into duality; **what is given freely to you must be released as freely from you with no strings, no pangs of possible lack.** You trust God because you have reason to trust, signs have been following therefore why, how even would God stop being God?

This can be a sticking point for you, it was for me. It is probably the hardest thing to learn to do, trust. Why? Because there has not been one single thing in your experience that has been reliable, without question, without fail. Supply can be the hardest thing to have faith about because supply to man is a live or die situation. If you don't have money, if you haven't busted your butt to bring in the money you feel it, the fear, the anxiety, the possibilities of what will happen if you don't have money. I mean just look around! Yes, and you are looking around at *human* man suffering the sins of their beliefs. What do you believe? Have you seen signs following?

This was in a way my last mental stand but as you will find with any mental hurdle, habit change, growing in consciousness, once you relax into the ways of your new life you are **being,** not *trying* to be. In all of this work, dying daily, letting go of belief/error there is an exchange of perception, understanding from that of man to that of God. At first there is you the human grasping for anything it can get its hands on because your humanly created God is disappearing by the minute and you feel unsteady, afraid but as you rest, let go of you, i, human, your consciousness of Truth grows and you rest, first after forgetting to trust/know Truth, then automatically because Truth has become your consciousness of being, your operating system.

You have to make a way for the imprisoned splendor to escape, the divine expression of God or grace of God. You do that through meditation, through realization of the presence of God within and then when God comes into awareness peace washes over you. This feeling is the confirmation of a healing having taken place and grace has been released in consciousness going about the Father's business and somewhere in the world there are those receptive to grace and receive it.

Now do you see why you do not demonstrate persons, places, things or conditions? You can only demonstrate the presence and activity of God and let God do all the performing, adding to, removing of the outer world because God in awareness reveals the illusory nature of anything unlike its own nature and character.

God's grace, the allness of God, flows through you in proportion to how much you have died to the ways of man and by your conscious awareness of God within. You have to die to one to rise in another. You cannot put new wine in old skins therefore that which is an erroneous belief must be illuminated with Truth directly from the God within to make way for more Truth to fill you, illuminate you, buoy every step because you are supported by the within.

My husband and I were on a mini vacation for a family wedding and had decided to take my vehicle. While there we lost the alternator and for the next four days prayed heartily when we had to go anywhere. We had to leave the vehicle 150 miles from home and my husband had to go back and get it the next weekend.

Within 5 days of getting my car fixed my father came down with a medical emergency that had us running all over town at all hours of the day and night for 8 days while at the same time moving my mom into my house and my dad into my mom's. Long story. Suffice to say if I hadn't known there was a reason for the alternator going out when it did I would not have had a good vacation. But I did know it would all be ok but had no idea of the harmony that would transpire.

If God had not put the idea in my husband's head to take my vehicle, if it hadn't had trouble at that time the trouble would have come when my father was in need of being transported to a hospital with a life threatening condition. You cannot understand how thankful I was knowing the reason for the breakdown was to ensure I could safely get my father the care he needed and not end up on the side of the road at 3 in the morning helpless.

This is why you cannot judge what is seemingly going wrong in your life when you are on the path. There is harmony coming but sometimes there are things that need to be prepared/removed/changed for that harmony to appear, **for when the confluences of your life lived in oneness manifest as the added and needed things.** You have to go with the flow, see where it leads, let it come so it can go, let God be the harmonizing influence to your life.

It is hard at first not to react, it is a knee jerk reaction to want to do something, figure it out, to get angry and lament "why me?" But you are going back to humanhood to try to explain what is happening spiritually. You must be empty of humanhood and so fully immersed in God that you can wave your hand at error, your's or another's knowing it is merely a stepping stone to harmony when you are rightly walking the spiritual path.

How do you measure your spiritual progress? By the degree that your concern is not for gain, something added or removed from your life but rather that your understanding is grounded in the realization of omnipresence. As your conviction or confidence grows in the unfolding of good then are you coming into living by grace.

In this consciousness you realize "Son thou art ever with Me and all that I have is thine." You can measure your acceptance of the spiritual teaching by the degree of concern that you are **losing** about personal welfare because you have no personal welfare to provide for, God is taking care of that.

Sometimes hardships come into your experience as a result of living by grace **but,** and I can attest to this by personal experience, just as Joseph was sold into slavery and suffered the choices of his brothers, there was a reason for the experience and all Joseph could do was trust, have faith that the Father's will be done through and for him and that it would be for the purpose of harmony, his and those of his consciousness.

The very moment you begin this absolute reliance on God, the will of God and the love of God you may find yourself being moved in very strange ways and some of them you may not like not knowing what the ultimate destiny is to be.

Having gone through one particular painful discord, being in the throws of excruciating pain it wasn't until six months later I was able to look back and see the **why** of what I went through and am able to see the love and grace of the Father that was being manifest in my experience now.

Yes, there were times I was concerned that the pain would be my new normal but about 4 weeks into the pain I got an impartation from God and it took me to my knees. Within came the words **everything heals** and it was in that moment I knew that it was God behind what was going on with me, though I should have known that from the start. Nothing in your life is an accident if you are under grace but there are things that sometimes need to be changed, died to that you aren't even aware that need to be died to.

As far along the spiritual path as you get there are always going to be things that pop up that need to be addressed as error presenting but also the realization that as long as you are **living honestly by grace** and not dipping your toe back into humanhood, whatever the disturbances might be, stop, take a breath and ask yourself, "what is the purpose of this Father? What am I not seeing that needs to be released from my consciousness? Oh, that's ok, you don't have to inform me, I just needed to come inside and know that you are the cause and the effect of everything in my life and that is always good."

The shadow of the valley of death may be where your footprints are right now making you feel like you are in a hell that won't ever end but regardless of the error that presents God is right with you governing your life, walking the path with you to bring you out the other side a bit shinier but you have to let it play out God's way to get God's grace, remember that. You must be where grace is to receive grace and grace is not of human man.

In the beginning of your journey there are going to be things that may make you feel that the God you just found and began to depend on has abandoned you into the wilderness of pain, suffering or anguish you thought would never darken your life again. That is not the Truth! What is Truth is that when you and I **die daily** to the things of the world we are dying to the things we **recognize** as duality.

If you know by demonstration that you are living under grace then what you are suffering is not because of thoughts or actions that dropped you back into humanhood with its good and bad duality but rather **it is God getting in there and rooting out the deeper stuff** you don't recognize as humanhood for you to witness and release now knowing Truth through oneness.

Coming through the experience having had the inner conversations with God along the way brought me that much more into wholeness. As known spirit you are already whole, complete and that is why when you pray for parts you get nothing because God cannot add to that which is already whole and complete, **it is you who must realize that when error presents in you or to you there is nothing to change except the consciousness from which *you* are expressing.**

To pray without ceasing merely means to be in the moment of now, always now, not in the past and not in the future but now. Now is the only time the human mind isn't chewing on something of man, of earth, of duality and God is not in the thinking mind of man. To be in the **now** is to be present, aware of what is going on within yourself, what is being given or shown and that can only happen when you are in the present moment, now.

There is no time in the kingdom of God because God is eternal, no past, no future just now and that is why you must also be in the now to know God because that is the only place God can be found-**now**-not in the future and not in the past. What does it mean to be present/now? If you are going to have a conversation of great importance you would be listening, waiting for information not thinking of what the conversation is going to be, not getting angry, nervous, fearful or even curious because thinking takes you out of the now, out of listening and into thinking.

This presentation of yourself in a waiting, receptive attitude ready to listen to what the other person has to say is being in the present moment, now. There is only this moment and it is filled with all you need to know and will express to you as that which is to be known because God whispers it in your ear for your benefit.

The **only** demonstration you can make, is available for you to make, is the demonstration of God by letting God shine through you to the world. Your conscious contact with God is a blessing to you and a blessing to everyone you come in contact with and everyone who comes after.

There's only one selfhood and it is where I am; the Father and I are one.

All discords, limitations and inharmonies of this world are based on *belief* and not **Truth** therefore everything that is inharmonious, limited or chaotic is merely what you think it is through the senses therefore not real, merely illusion, nothingness, mirage, shadow.

You treat all claims of error the same because there is only one error that causes all claims-the belief you are separated from God. This is the secret to overcoming this world for that which is in the world creating the illusion of discord is because of a single universal *belief*. What is universal belief? All believe it thus it isn't even realized to be a belief and not Truth.

All man are born into an atmosphere they were never meant to experience but because the *experienced* atmosphere of the world is duality how could one chose to live other than by the expressions of the world?

You do not pray for the demonstration of things rather you pray for the demonstration of your oneness with God by going within and asking it to come onto the field, **asking God to make its presence felt to confirm its existence.** This confirmation of its reality of being as one with you is the demonstration that brings all the added things into your experience.

Man limits his prayers to one thing or another or a couple things but they are part and parcel, limited in scope. Spiritual man asks for allness, wholeness, oneness, completeness and in this receive the allness of the Creator, a complete transformation of conscious understanding and thus by asking for God, to know God, to rest in God you receive all that could ever be received, the fullness of the Father.

It is sinful to limit, to put any mental limitation, direction or instruction on prayer. You have no idea how God works, how grace will manifest or how many other people must do their part in your expression of grace. God is the governing influence of the universe so how do you or I presume to think we can order from God like Amazon and have it delivered the next day?

Man when he prays can only see what is right in front of himself, what he *needs* at that moment to survive or enjoy because the mind of man is all about things and emotions, feelings and possessing.

The spiritual man rests. When you finally understand that it is not physical work that brings you supply in God's kingdom but inner knowing of Truth that reveals grace as bread on the water returning to you do you live Truth that God is the Source of all your supply.

You are so content with what is going on **within you** that the world seems to just fall into place; there are still hiccups but the smoothing out of your life is noticeable if you start paying attention to the happenings in your life.

No one wants your treasure if you don't value it as a treasure. In spiritual work insofar as possible give help to all those who ask through silent prayer but do not give of the gems of your spiritual wisdom as spoken/revealed Truth until they are prepared to receive it. The Master so instructed us to give milk to the babes and meat to those who are prepared for it and you must be wise in speaking Truth.

As you open yourself to God as a servant and a son you can be sure that God will fill your consciousness to the top. Those who come in contact with you will also be blessed by the consciousness, the awareness you have of God within **however** not everyone will catch the import of what you have given to seek to know more. Most people who look for God are looking for sustainment in the *human* world ie better house, better health, better relationships etc. These people seek only for loaves and fishes and **not** how to bring forth loaves and fishes for themselves.

Many are not seeking God for comfort and love rather they seek to be avenged of wrongs done to them or for another to be punished for their sins but to leave them unscathed. If you pray only for yourself you have put up the wall that keeps God from working in your life and this wall is called selfishness. Everything in God's kingdom is for all and not just for yourself however **what you receive in return for what you give freely is yours,** your grace returned to you pressed down and flowing over-abundance beyond measure.

Seek the realization of God's grace in the now as a sufficiency unto this moment of now. You will find that having attained it now, known by the presence of God on the field, it will never leave you nor forsake you because now is the eternity in which your good appears.

When you go any place with complete silence of *human* thought, wish, will or desire where you are is filled with the presence of God. There is no need ever for words or thoughts. There must be a complete silencing of the *human* will so the allness of God can penetrate the atmosphere of man and fill all space.

Let the God of you, I, and not the human i always be the first contact with the world in all ways and this is accomplished by your conscious awareness of God within. Before you grace goes and after you grace stays to bless those who remain there to conduct their business in an atmosphere of grace brought into their awareness by your knowing God aright.

Grace is God in outward expression therefore you are an expression of grace in your oneness with the Father. The miracle of the Father is revealed to you in your living a spiritual life inwardly as peace beyond man's understanding, harmony, joy and outwardly as abundance, fruitage, luck or blessings but all are merely the allness of God flowing through you, working in your life because your life is its life when you come back into the kingdom and give up, release, shake off the erroneous form of natural man/carnal man/human to reveal your true nature as spirit.

As long as you live and move and have your being within the spiritual temple of your consciousness realizing only the presence of spiritual grace you are living in and through God and God is really living as you; you and the Father are one because there is no you, there is only God expressing as what is known to the world as you.

Spiritual power means introducing the Spirit of God, Truth, into the situation, not to prove right or wrong but to bring **harmony** to bear for the good of all so all may benefit from you knowing God.

When you come under grace no human laws operate. In the spiritual realm which is a state of consciousness living by God's divine love and support, there are not two powers battling one over the other or one overcoming the other or one removing the other, there is but one. There's no opposition, no contention, no confusion in the realm of spirit. There is only a state of harmony which is itself the Law of illumination to every phase of materiality. When you come into the state of grace you no longer have good health or bad health nor do you have abundance or meager supply rather you live in a state of harmony in which there is neither good nor evil, just being, divine being, spiritual expression, one expression of which all is of.

The revelation of life lived by grace instead of under the laws of man consist of the revelation that conscious awareness of God within each individual is the Law of resurrection, healing and protection to the body, business and home. You begin to see how consciousness expresses as harmony and bounty when there is an awareness and deferment to God within.

The Bible says "if ye abide in Me and My Word abide in you, ye shall ask what ye will and it shall be done unto you."

This doesn't mean you are asking in the sense of *give me a more beautiful home or a new dress* rather you are asking for the continuance of infinite grace, asking for the continuous realization of the omnipresence within.

Every time you receive an impartation, a feeling, a flush, a smile, relief, peace unto your being you have confirmation of God's promise-I will never leave you nor forsake you.

If all man treated all man as kin, the loving kind, how would one cheat another? Maim or kill another? How could one man take advantage of another or crush another man's soul? In the kingdom all is given so there is nothing one man would ever need from another man thereby allowing them to move and have their being in harmony.

The reason man cannot be harmonious with other man is because in man's mind someone always wants something from them so it is up to them to take first which perpetuates the never ending cycle of chaos felt and witnessed daily as the fighting and dying for the *human dream* of success.

So many people say they are doing God's will. Unfortunately because they don't understand the Bible by way of spiritual illumination they take it literally and feed the hungry and lift up the poor in the *literal* sense through physical labor and mental grinding while asking for money to support *their* worthy cause.

If what you are wanting to do or are doing as your *calling* is costing you money, taking away from instead of adding to your peace and joy, if you have to advertise for help and ask for donations what you are doing is not supported by the God you say you are doing work for. How do I know this?

When God calls you to do something it provides the means through grace. It is not your job to do anything when you get an impartation, it is not your place to *react* in a way that demonstrates fear of lack of money or understanding, your job is to rest in confidence that if that is what God wants to happen in your world it will provide the means for God is the supplier, maintainer and sustainer of itself.

God is the supply and means unto all impartations. It may not be tomorrow or next month but when it comes into visible form or higher understanding you immediately know and can trace back the events that led to the current happening. It is like lightening flashing through you as your deductive mind connects the dots and once again you are flooded with love for God for its ways, perfect in every aspect from timing to quality to individualization. The grace of God is better than you could organize, plan or procure for yourself because it is always perfect in its expression.

Your inner light will shine only in proportion to your withdrawal from the outer world, not by your leaving the world or its pleasures and joys *but* by your leaving your **dependence** upon them by dropping your faith in person, place or thing and by taking away the power you give to person, place or thing.

Grace, the allness of the activity of God, translates itself into your experience as tangible form which may well be houses, money, clothing, vacation, friendship or property but it is **God** in manifest form not *matter* or *material* separate and apart from God.

This is the distinction that must be clear. When you go to God you are going to God for what it is first and foremost-home, peaceful, safe, a place of learning and resting and second merely as a matter of course, the Law of like begets like, the return for the time you spend with the Father. By dying daily you receive God in form and expression/feeling.

What you receive is God because all is of the same Source individually named according to what it is/does according to human standards of qualification. **All is God** and you cannot call God *matter* or *material* because it is not. Matter and material are merely labels, identifiers man uses to undersand the world and the properties of the world through study and testing but none of it is other than God, that is what must become clear in your understanding.

There is no thing called matter or material in substance or form when you understand **God is as all** so to man a tree is a tree completely separate and apart from anything else in make up/expression. But spiritual man knows a tree is God individualized **as** the form man has *labeled* "tree."

You cannot possibly bear witness to the Christ identity of your parents, husband, wife, coworker, children without its eventually softening and mellowing them. You can be certain that the I of every member of your family is begging you to see them as they truly are, the I of them, and not as they appear to be while under the influence/hypnotism of this world.

You will come to that place in consciousness where you live by grace, where you have attained a measure of God knowing and can more often than not find yourself in the same relative place of inner harmony regardless of any changes that take place personally, politically or economically ie you are more immune to the ups and downs of the *human* experience because you are no longer living what constitutes the human experience-duality.

Man will still fail you, defraud you, try to use you but in these times see through the eyes of God to the Truth of all man-they behave this way only because they know not who they are. In these situations you give of God's grace to bring an awareness of rightness into their expression and remember you are not dependent on man, the paper money of man or the laws of man for return of what was lost. They will suffer the return of their error while you receive the abundance of God over and above what was lost to duality.

Not by might but by grace are all things made right.

There are always going to be celebrations, excursions, vacations, adventures, activities and they are all for your enjoyment but in God's world you don't get attached to them, want to hold onto them past their expiration date (mine, you can't have it). You enjoy what is brought into your life and you willingly let it move onto its next home because you know that as long as you let it flow from you freely it will flow **to** you freely. You are the log jam in the river when you start thinking like man again-me, my, mine instead of I, Self.

The key to the kingdom is to keep the flow going knowing it is unending and what you release will come back to you in another form for the current need or desire of God expressing as you. You have to remember God is today as it has always been and will be tomorrow. It is only your humanhood rising up within making you panic when you think lack, have a fear or get angry that separates you from the grace of God, the good, the harmony of being.

The moment you realize that you do not get your satisfaction or your supply from the external world you are under grace. You can bring yourself under grace this minute by relinquishing the desire for anything and anybody in the world by the realization **I live by grace, by the grace of God** and in that second you have left the laws of man, mortal living and come under grace.

Just relinquish your desires and you are under grace. Relinquish the belief you need something in the realization that God knows your needs before you do and you are under grace. You do not reach out mentally or physically for anything.

Only do not go back and sin again, do not go back tomorrow for fear of lack or fear of man or fear of disease. Keep yourself living in the realization "thank you Father, I have no needs but you" and soon this will be the Truth unto your experience.

Once you are touched by mystical teachings you are drawn closer and closer to the ultimate realization of the name and nature of God as your true identity. When you realize the name and nature of God you are free of the dual nature of man and brought under one expression of good, God, is, and furthermore in proportion are a free flowing instrument of grace to the world. Those who are touched by grace are those ready for grace and their true identity will be revealed if they take the opportunity to know more.

There is no grace in the world as good, rather the only good in the world is the opposite of bad. Grace is the allness and perfection of harmony and it is only found where there is an awareness of God's presence because grace is the activity of a spiritual universe expressing itself in substance and form of all that is.

Grace reveals the laws of man/human as the nothingness they are.

There is no power of the thinking mind. The mind allows man to process information; it was never meant to be a power, a thinking and devising center rather a vehicle for expression-holding a paintbrush, pen or hammer, ears to hear the world around you, a mouth to bring forth knowing or perfect pitch. The mind and the body are one not two. They work together in concert for the purpose of carrying out that which is given you to do each day byway of impartation from within.

The only consciousness that has any power is the consciousness of God which is your conscious awareness of being when there is no thinking going on. The body performs the functions of consciousness by way of the mind sorting and calculating information that allows for smooth performance/execution of the job given you to do. **The mind is a tool** but man allows himself to be the tool and the mind to be the power back of the tool. You are no tool my friend and it is high time you knew that but to live that Truth you must understand the role of the mind and put it in its proper orientation to the will of God and not the will of personal i, me, ego.

Your mind only runs away with you when you are thinking which is being a human afraid and alone. The racing mind is a sign of not being in God consciousness where the mind can be quiet so if you want to quiet your thinking mind let God be heard, get quiet, make tea, set out cookies and get comfy for your visitor who fills all space with "peace be with you child, I am here. Are those scones?"

The Master Christ Jesus washed the feet of his disciples, touched the lepers and served in any and every way to show that it was not he himself that had power but that it was the grace of God operating **through** him, not a grace in him alone but a grace that would operate in **all** who were willing to leave their nets and empty themselves of self to be refilled with Self and live the allness of God in expression.

"To leave your nets" means to stop living the duality of man, stop depending on man and the world for what you need to instead live in oneness with God experiencing life as it was meant to be.

If called upon to share with others you can do so without the feeling that you are taking something of your own and giving it away thereby leaving yourself with less because all that you have is of God. If called upon to do extra work you can do it without feeling that you are using your strength because the allness of the Father is your support in all ways.

You will find that at the end of a day spent in God consciousness you are not tired. You are not weary of mind or body **because you were not the one working.** Yes, you are the visible expression of the work done but the **Life** used to support your actions was of God. When you are with God you are supported in all ways and that means from the thoughts that come into your conscious knowing to make the process smoother and more productive and also the energy that moves you through the day.

Your perspective of time begins change, it does not have the same feeling in your life ie you will do something strenuous or involved and then three hours later not feel like it was just done that day but rather is just in the past, done because you don't feel drained as if you performed that task. It is an odd feeling especially for those who are clock watchers for their cues of life. You will work through dinner, you won't be hungry and you will be enjoying your time because it is more productive than ever before.

You also seem to have more time, life is smoother, your head is less chaotic, more at ease and you are not full of tension and anxiety rather more chill, relaxed, jovial, you are happy, truly happy because you feel fulfilled, whole, complete and that becomes your expression and your attitude and it changes every aspect of your experience.

Grace is the wind beneath your feet that never seems to end and carries you through and beyond all that is given you to do.

Healing and Treatment

Why you are here:
You are here to do the will of the Father.

The Master said: I am come to do the will of the Father.

What is the will of the Father? **Heal** the sick, raise the dead, reform the sinner and feed the hungry. This is accomplished by you knowing Truth and revealing it within yourself which is what brings Truth to bear in your experience and those accepting of it.

In the human picture there is disease, sin, fear, war, jealousy, envy, hate, malice, germs, contagion, accidents etc, therefore the Master came to give us a principle which first of all would clear away the sins and diseases of which we are now victims and then this principle would see that we had no return of them.

The principle the Master gave us is this:

There is but one power and **that power unto you is your awareness of the presence of God within** which reveals all sin, fear and disease are not powers in the atmosphere of God/consciousness of God, they cannot exist therefore you can say "what did hinder you that you are sitting there crippled? That disease has no power if you know Truth so rise, pick up your bed and walk." And in that highly developed spiritual consciousness in which the Master knew no power but the presence of God those who understood rose, walked, saw and ate.

So in the Master's consciousness he saw the powerlessness of anything that the human mind could conceive. He saw that temporal power, the power of a Pilate, or the power of germs, climate, fear, jealousy etc, were not power but *perception* of power.

But remember he had a highly developed spiritual faculty, a high degree of God understanding, knowing, awareness, connection and instantaneously saw the nothingness of any presentation of power other than that of God because he had been witness to the healing grace of God time and time again therefore knowing there is no Truth in the *expression* of blindness, hunger, lack death.

He could stave off the errors and evils of the world, stop them from continuing because he knew the Truth of them: no thing real. Then if the person suffering the error got the conscious understanding of why they were not as they thought they were they were no longer under the effects of the belief because when the cause is seen to be illusion so must the result.

The visible condition expresses only as a reality until you know why you cannot have any condition of the body-you are not flesh and blood separated from the allness of a spiritual God, you are of God not individual pieces and parts that can fail. You are whole, complete and eternal.

This is exactly what takes place in spiritual healing work and when you are somewhere as near as high in spiritual consciousness as the Master your healings become automatic, ie innate because **it is who you are.**

Your relationship with God:

When someone has all of the attributes you think you want in friend or partner you do not look at other people as potential partners because where you are has all you will every want or need. In this scenario the world of single persons holds no sway over you because what you have at that moment makes you blind to what might otherwise be *temptation*. You are so happy where you are because it satisfies your every need (exaggeration for point) you are sinless, you are committed willingly, happily and now know no other way of living except with this person.

You have expectation of this relationship going on forever and know it will be full of adventure, learning, probably some crying but mostly you will be enjoying all this life has to offer with your new forever friend to experience it with. This is your happy place where you express to the world without words the joy you feel because of the secret relationship that has you all a-glow.

Now change the other person to God within. This is the exact relationship you are to have with God that will express as the needed and added things.

Do you see now that having a relationship with God is no different in aspect than having a relationship with anyone else? The defining difference between human relationships and the personal relationship of knowing God aright is the difference between in and out. Instead of going to man for answers or supply, comfort and peace you go within to your best friend who knows where all the good stuff is stashed and how to bring it into your awareness.

What spiritual healing is

Spiritual healing is the cornerstone of spiritual living. You cannot live a spiritual life if you do not recognize that which you are trying to release from your consciousness as error/duality, that which is the false life, the illusion. To grow in conscious understanding you have to let go of false beliefs to be filled up with Truth and to let go of false beliefs they must be recognized **as** false beliefs, the illusion they are.

Spiritual healing is simply recognizing error for the non reality it is born of the thinking mind, internal vision, illusion, maya, nothingness, arm of flesh, or "this world" as Jesus referred to the cause and effect of the belief in two powers man employs as their operating system of activity/action/living and expressing.

Spiritual healing **is** your individual salvation and the salvation of those of the world receptive to God's presence, God's allness, wholeness.

Spiritual healing is of two parts:

1. First is **treatment.** Thinking words of Truth to take your focus out of the world and inside with God. This step becomes less necessary as it is training yourself how to get into the silence which after a while is automatic but sometimes you need words to help you get there.
2. The next step is **prayer/meditation/inner listening.** Prayer known in its rightness is **inner listening** which is also the true definition of prayer. By letting Truth remembered gently float away you are left in the peace of those words and you rest and wait for the presence of God felt within.

The presence of God felt is the **demonstration** of Truth: God is and is within you which is the **healing** of human man's *belief* in *separation* from God. This activity done in the silence of your own being is what **heals** man of his *belief* in separation from God by way of your knowing the Truth of God to make it available to all who seek Truth.

There will be times someone asks for assistance with something the world has said is *impossible* to heal, is *fatal,* no cure and you many feel overwhelmed and insecure about your ability to handle such a *hard* case. **There is no one expression harder to heal than another** because all are caused by the same error, what is called the original sin: the *belief* in being separate and apart from God, allness of being.

A healing reveals the Truth of God within the healer which looses this Truth into the atmosphere for all who desire what is not of this world to receive of what is not of this world by virtue of the higher consciousness of the healer.

You are not healing individual *ailments, errors or circumstances,* those are *labels* of man. You are **revealing** the *cause* of all ailments, errors and circumstances is the *belief* in being separated from **God.**

A healing is a demonstration of God's presence:

The all of all that is **is** God therefore all the things people give power to-disease, poverty, fear, the calendar, time, age-cannot exist, are unreal therefore have no power and cannot do to you what power you gave it whether good or bad. Even good power must be realized to be a non power for if there is good power in the world, because it is under the hypnotism of duality, there must be bad power too. What is good can become bad and what is bad can become good in the human experience.

When you are of the consciousness of God you know God **is** as all and is **is** perfect harmony so whatever of the world that is not of this harmony is not real. Is is what something is. *Duality* **is** *judgement* that relabels God's perfection of **is** according to personal history. The *judgment* is not nor can ever be **objective** therefore it must be *subjective* and as such nothing more than illusion of the mind expressed which is the outward expression of your nature as human man not spiritual man.

The cause of every discord is separation from the consciousness of God which is the supplier, maintainer and sustainer of its form-you.

What does separation from God mean? It means **you are separated from the Truth that you need to know to live the life God intended for his individualized expressions-you and me.** You are separated from the consciousness that **is** the consciousness of the universe.

Human man is of their own singular consciousness, each man thinking and doing according to their own limited understanding of life because they do not realize there is the intelligence of the creator of the universe within just itching to help you get your life on track so that it may have another avenue of expression through another prodigal son returned home-a much better experience of this visible existence.

Basic premise of spiritual healing:

1. God is individual being thus all are individual expressions of God, perfect, harmonious and eternal and as such do not have a body of flesh that is born and dies but **is** eternal consciousness in form constantly renewing itself.
2. When you know your Truth you know all that man suffers is because he reacted to illusion instead of bringing Truth to bear which flows out into universal consciousness where those receptive can receive of it and can then begin to express it as their Truth thereby bringing more grace into their experience because more Truth is being expressed for the good of all man.

The secret of spiritual healing:

You break the hypnotism by recognizing evil conditions are merely hypnotism appearing and **the recognition is the healing/revealing of Truth.** You don't do anything after you recognize the error for what it is-hypnotism, duality, two powers, this world, maya, illusion, unreality, figment of the mind.

Example-you look out at a horizon, you recognize it as a horizon. Can you get rid of the horizon? No, that will never leave because it isn't there at all, it is a misconception of what is being seen but even though the appearance stays there you aren't fooled into thinking the horizon is anything more than an illusion, like a mirage or train tracks that seem to merge in the distance. All *illusions* **look real** as something but there is nothing to them, no substance, no form, no law to support them, they are merely figments of your mind, your eyes playing tricks on you.

Now before Columbus horizon had a completely different meaning. To those looking at it from a distance it seemed to be the edge, the end and that perception, belief kept man from venturing toward it for fear of falling off the edge of the world. But what happened when Columbus proved the horizon was a visual trick, illusion and of itself was no thing? **The Truth was revealed** to the world and for those who already had an idea that the horizon wasn't the end had their thoughts validated through actual proof of identification.

Those who had a consciousness of life that looked to the stars, the heavens for answers instead of the ground beneath their feet were more consciously ready for the next level of conscious unfolding of the world around them. Those who were more simple in their thinking, who could not see beyond the appearances of what they thought they saw refused to believe that the world didn't end at the horizon and would not be swayed no matter what proof was given because they themselves didn't have the **conscious** ability to think that there could be anything other than what **their senses told them** was reality.

This is where man is today, still seeing error, injustice, lack, disease and calling it reality.

As long as you believe in horizons, mirages or merging train tracks you will be fooled by them but what happens when you realize it is just an illusion? Nothing. It just falls away from your mind, it is no longer a condition, just an illusion and you are not bothered by an illusion, it isn't going to stop your progress or make you feel like you have to figure something out to make it go away.

Any outer experience ie what you see, hear, taste, touch or smell, that presents as other than **harmonious** is *not real but a personal judgement* of your *human* mind.

Whatever is *inharmonious* in your awareness is nothing more than a *personal* judgement which has caused *you* to experience a moment of *duality* caused by separation from God in consciousness.

How you achieve Oneness with God ie spiritual healing of self:

1. First you must know what God is and where God is-all that is and you are of all that is therefore God is already **of** you.
2. Know the true meaning of the word prayer-inner listening/meditation **not** talking
3. What consciousness is-your connection to God, all that is
4. Where consciousness is-behind the thinking mind in the quiet of your being where inner listening takes place
5. How to correctly meditate/pray to have the mystical experience-to listen within and await the presence that has always been with you
6. Have the mystical experience and understand what it signifies-you meet the Father face to face within your own being and this consciousness of harmony as your expression is what ordains you to heal the sick, raise the dead and feed the hungry. Emanuel-God with us, oneness, heaven on earth
7. Know the nature of error-suggestion to be accepted or denied, illusion, maya, duality, the arm of flesh, man's existence as opposed to the arm of God, spiritual Truth of

      harmonious eternal expression.
8. Impersonalization and nothingizing error to bring God into awareness which reveals error as no thing real because if God is all, how can there be anything else?

These are the building blocks that awaken you to the conscious knowing of the presence within which free you from man's illusion that there is something other than God expressing you must ask God to battle against. This is spiritually healing oneself of erroneous beliefs and bringing God to bear where there was no God in awareness.

The entire practice of spiritual living is to bring you back to this awareness of Truth so you can once again live your Truth, your true nature as child of God, joint heir to the kingdom, to live in heaven on earth bringing God to bear for more and more God to be known in individual consciousness. One with God is a majority and knowing this is your ordination to heal silently, sacredly and secretly the errors of the world as they present in your awareness.

Understand! This isn't a practice to go out into the world and be a do-gooder, corner proselytizer, soap box pulpit nonsense. Spiritual Truth is the way by which you remove sin, disease, lack, limitation and death **from your experience** individually and ultimately the world **by revealing the ignorance that separates man from Truth.**

Error only comes into your awareness as error when you are being *human* ie judging, disparaging, comparing, otherwise all would be harmonious because that is how you feel **inside.**

The key to spiritual healing:

God is not omnipresent in your experience **until** God is realized in your consciousness. Therefore God only becomes a demonstrable experience to the degree the principles of living in God consciousness are known, practiced and lived.

This is the purpose of treatment-to bring you to the state of consciousness in which you can realize/become aware of God within to release the world outside.

Example:

I was having trouble with a friend, the relationship felt like it was on the rocks and I needed clarity on the situation because it was stuck in my head and affecting my mood. I closed my eyes and started up a conversation.

"Father why is this going on? What do I need to know to be released from this anger, pain and confusion I am feeling?"

And from within came "what does it matter? What does it matter if the relationship ends? What does it matter if it gets resolved? Either way you will be harmonious so let it go. You good?"

I smiled and said, "yes, Father, right as rain," and in that moment I was released and harmony came because I didn't resist what was happening, I didn't try to get the other person to see what they had done and apologize I just gave it to God to give back what he wanted for me-harmony.

Always remember the struggle is not yours, give it to God and you will be on your way in no time lighter and brighter for the chat.

This is the all and all of a spiritual healing, **peace in awareness** which can only be God in awareness for all is of God coursing through you as the Life of you. You receive of God what God **is** and to spiritual man it feels like peace, joy, relief, companionship, wholeness, satisfaction, contentment, woosah.

You must know God to receive the allness of God and you can only know God by way of an actual experience of God within. You cannot fake it because the **entirety** of spiritual living **is** the demonstration of you oneness with God in expression. No God awareness=no demonstration of God/grace in your experience.

Knowing God aright is the healing principle

"In thy presence is the fullness of life," "thy grace is my sufficiency" are not just pretty sentiments they are absolute Truth by which you live your life when you know God. **Conscious awareness of the presence of God within your own being constitutes a spiritual healing and is the key to living a spiritual life.**

The purpose of spiritual living:

1. To know your true name and nature as the child of God
2. To attain the Christ consciousness which is the consciousness that revealed Jesus **as** the

Christ-the illumined one
3. To know the nature of error, nothingize error and attain illumination through imparted Truth and to understand the **practicality** of living a spiritual life instead of a human finite existence.

God vs man: unconditioned vs conditioned consciousness

1. God is one cause of harmony manifesting one effect of spiritual perfection which is harmonious, infinite, eternal incorporeal spirit omniscient, omnipresent and omnipotent **where it is known.** God **is** and only God **is** the source of all that is visible and invisible constituting all that is of the universe. All is God and God is all there is. God is called the **unconditioned** consciousness.
2. Man is *duality* of expression of self, personality, ego, i. Man is the expression of opposites, *personal* judgements as to good and bad, right and wrong of the *appearances* in this world. Man lives and dies thinking he is separate and apart from God. This is called the *conditioned* consciousness.

Why is this distinction important? Because it is a matter of life and death. When you know your Truth, when you know you are child of God and express out from this consciousness you are living Truth. When you know your nature as eternal and infinite what *power,* what *expression* of force could man have over you? Isn't the *belief* of death the reason man is human man and not spiritual man? To pick up the sword and protect oneself from the *illusion* of death is the hallmark, the distinction that separates human from spiritual man.

You receive the fruit, the effect, the added things of your consciousness which is the cause and effect of all that you experience. Spiritual man will receive the fruit of the Father, harmony, abundance, peace. Human man will receive the fruit of man, of the good expressions and the bad expressions, of the good happenings and the bad happenings.

Mental vs. Spiritual healings:

Mental healings seem to bring "healing" in the renunciation of the symptoms but since mental healing is merely a heightened awareness of *the human mind* and has nothing to do with God/spirit, mind healing/any healing that is of the mind of man that has no awareness of God will **never** heal/reveal Truth rather merely allows the patient to feel *temporarily* better until their next illness/problem comes around.

Mind healing, any *metaphysical* healing that doesn't have God consciousness as its base is always subject to the two powers inherent in the human experience. If you have *intellectual* knowing of **Truth** with a healthy side of leap of faith, sincerely practice healing yourself and others you can bring about a *temporary* change in yourself/patient but you are *mentally* knowing **Truth** because you have not had the experience of God within to take your healing out of the realm of *intellect/ man's finite knowing* into the **mystical** realm of God.

All modalities of healing are on the mental/human plain **unless** there **is** an awareness of the presence of God within the practitioner doing the healing work. Only this is **spiritual** healing of which its purpose isn't to *change* your human condition into good rather open a way by which you can feel the presence of God which is the all encompassing harmony of your life, not piece meal but all of it, all of you, your expression and your experience.

But here is the kicker. If you don't have curiosity as to how you were healed silently, sacredly and secretly you are being human and will return to this practitioner, other practitioners and other healing modalities to temporarily make it seem that your illness/error has abated but only until the next time something of the world makes itself known in your experience.

But if you get curious-how the heck and why? I want to know this to share this because it is awesome!!! Then you will find that healing brought out something deeper in your conscious knowing that will be permanent. Why? **Because you are seeking the source of the healing and not the healing itself.** You want the understanding behind the loaves and fishes, not just the loaves and fishes. You want to know why, how and mother may I have more?! This is the desire all of us will embrace at some point.

This is the start of your spiritual experience, everything has to start with a seed. That seed is Truth and is found in the New Testament, the red letter words of Christ Jesus not speaking his *personal* words but the **Word of the Father** within. The Christ is the allness of God tucked right inside of you like a secret pearl of great price that once you know is there will cause you to leave your nets, your homes, and your family (metaphorically), leave the world and go within to God because you now realize this within-ness is Truth and not the world that is seen and experienced through the senses.

Conscious oneness with God is the healing principle.

Conscious oneness reveals Truth-God is and only God is

Conscious oneness with God is your true nature

You heal merely by knowing the nature of error

You are a healing agent every moment you are with God

Knowing the source of Truth brings Truth to bear, God on the field.

Communion, oneness heals

Knowing the Truth of error heals

Nothingizing error heals

Healing means bringing God to bear, grace in your midst

Healing is grace in your midst

Grace is the allness of God in action ie among man as what is needed to bring harmony, God to bear.

Being one with God is the healing principle. Why? Because when you bring Truth to your consciousness you bring Truth to bear among man where it wasn't before. You reveal Truth within yourself and this is the ripple, the aura, atmosphere, expression that goes out from you to those in need not of your volition but of God's as and through you.

It may seem like I am saying the same thing over and over but it helps me to break it down Barney style. The "if this then that" until I get to that one sentence that brings the entire message into focus, codified and simple to understand. But you might grasp the meaning from any of the statements because we all interpret words and the way they are used differently according to where we are from and our history but know that the mystical meaning of words, the way words are used in spiritual healing, **never change and in this are unified across all nations and all languages so as to be universally understood.**

God is singular in expression meaning it will **always** be a message of peace, harmony and forgiveness.

God within is the Truth of your being and this can only be understood byway of an actual experience of God within your own being. This reveals the Truth that "I am that I am, the Father and

I are one, I am the prodigal son returning home, I am the individualized expression of the one source of all that exists visible and invisible." This revealed in consciousness **heals** you, **returns** you to your true state of consciousness as spirit and not man.

Healing understood mystically is that which restores man to his true nature, *true expression of being as that of harmony, spirit in oneness with God.* A healing reveals man's error of thinking and Truth reveals the consciousness of self as Self, child of God. You have always been a prince but have borne the weight of a pauper only to one day stumble on that which reveals your true nature, that of a prince, one of standing and bearing because of his heritage.

Does this pauper now knowing himself to be a prince continue to live the way he had been? Wouldn't he return to his kingdom, to his Father whom he has never known but feels drawn to beyond reason? Would he expect anything other than welcoming arms from one who created him? Would you run or walk to the union of Father and son?

This is mankind with calloused hands and hardened hearts unaware of the stamp of prince across his forehead. If you but look within you will find the sign pointing to the Truth you unknowingly bear witness to-the Father within, God, wholeness and allness unto your infinite expression.

What God is:

God is not a conqueror, a super human being to be used by man which is why the Hebrews and Jews didn't believe Jesus to be the Messiah; they felt the Messiah would be a *giant, a power over other nations* **for them.**

God is the **gentle** Revealer of Truth, "I am come that you may have Life and have it more abundantly" and all you need to do is seek where Truth is found-within the silence of your own being.

God doesn't change the world to suit *you* when you pray rather God helps you to see that you, not the world, is the cause of error appearing in your midst as reality. The world is fine, it is your perception, consciousness of the Truth of what this world is, of who you are that needs adjustment and that is called healing or revealing Truth.

The purpose of treatment:

To develop spiritual consciousness, the awareness of God within, to have oneness of being so that you can live under grace, the allness of God, as it was intended.

The treatment part of a healing is remembering specific Truth to help you focus yourself. Written Truth become mystical Truth when they are revealed within you from God then released to the world. Metaphysical Truth, also known as **the letter of Truth,** are necessary to this mystical experience because you take written Truth into the silence asking God to give understanding to you for **your** peace.

Truth is not understood by man; man *reads* Truth and can only understand their face value while spiritual man knows Truth to be deep, rich and **experiential.** You must have an experience of God to know God and you can only ask God for understanding when you know where and what God is.

Silence:

Silence is the greatest protection from the duality of man. Silence is the healing activity of individual consciousness and **is the creative principle of all existence.**

In this silence you become receptive to the inner voice, the voice of the inner Self, and as Truth expresses itself to your listening inner ear you become aware of the healing influence-there is only one presence-with signs following.

Your receptivity to the Kingdom of God, God consciousness, God awareness, God knowing constitute what is called **a healing atmosphere**-you are healed/released from the altered reality that is man's experience of God's world. It is in this atmosphere of God you are reminded of your name and nature and **that is all there is to healing, bringing Truth to bear.**

This knowing of one presence releases you from the duality of man, frees you once again to embrace your true nature as the child of God and live the life you were created to live. It is only in the understanding of the Truth of **one** presence that your are made free from the erroneous way human man thinks and can rise to a higher plain of consciousness/existence where duality has no effect, no power and no presence/objectivity because you in your exalted state of oneness can clearly see there is only harmony behind every seeming error when you know the Truth of error.

Spiritual treatments don't overcome evil, **they show the nothingness of the belief in what man calls evil** as merely that of a universal belief in more than one expression which in and of itself is an error. Thus if the cause is not real there is no result/effect.

Purpose of treatment:

If God is omnipresent, omnipotent, omniscient, all and it is good, how can there be that which is destructive or evil?

There **can't** and that is the purpose of treatment-to **remind** yourself where power is and where it belongs-the power is in and of God, not of man, mind or matter. All of Life is God; God is the **source** of all that is in individualized form man calls matter classified according to man's interpretation of data therefore every element on the periodic chart is unique but their cause, their origin, their source is God. Whatever that source may be it is the **only** source from which everything else is individualized and it is no different than you and me as individualized expressions of God. All of Life contains all of Life, God, and expresses as needed for each individual expression to express.

Everything is an individualized expression of one Source and that is what is called the directive, creative intelligence that is Law unto the whole of existence, the nature of God expressing, the rhythm, order and harmony of a closed system where everything is provided, maintained and sustained by Self-the creative intelligence of harmonious existence. God is the singular source of creation resulting in harmonious manifestation of Self.

Then why are most not experiencing harmony if all is God and God is harmony? Because man is **unaware** of this harmony because man thinks his nature/name is human with his own mind regardless of the will of others and in that duality of wills lies the chaos of man forever battling what isn't real instead of resting in what is. Man cannot see beyond his nose to find the source of the sweet smell of a strawberry on a hot day or to find out why the flowers follow the sun. Man is not interested in the why or the how **only** what it can do for him.

Spiritual man on the other hand does take time to smell the roses because in their consciousness is the knowing that this is the perfume of the Father and it is good. Thank you Father! Spiritual man sees not the world around himself but sees the creator of all that **is** around him and revels in all that is manifest.

You don't have to believe in God per se but in that which is the intelligence of the universe we inhabit, that from which you come, that which made all that is. I still don't know how to explain the word intelligence as it applies to the creative ability of an unsee force to bring forth itself in form. Whatever it is it is and has proven to be Law, unchangeable, infinite, of only one nature-good/harmony/order. Call it what you will, it is this order that man is not in the flow of.

It is in this order that harmony reigns. Why? Because in this order there is one consciousness of good and spiritual man is of this consciousness listening to this consciousness which is your guide-what is given that day to do, hear a nugget of inspiration, receive a Truth bomb, a smile, a hug. God, Law unto creation, whatever you want to call the harmony of life/nature untouched by man **is** the reality of this world.

What is healing and treatment?

When you present yourself to a spiritual healer they do not examine your mind or your body. They don't need to know your name or even what brought you there. Why? Spiritual healers, mystics, have arrived at a state of developed or evolved consciousness that enables them to look through the *appearance,* the claim or problem, and know Truth. In the light of spiritual Truth error is revealed as no thing. God in awareness nullifies all that is not like God in nature-harmonious.

To the mystic you are not seen as a human being made up of good, of bad, of mind and of matter. You are not seen/known in that light at all. The evolved spiritual consciousness is not looking *at* your body or *entering* your mind; they are communing with God **within themselves.**

A healer knows your Truth even though you do not. **I know who thou art, the child of God.** In other words wherever there is an evolved spiritual awareness there is the discernment of your true being, true nature and it is for this reason when healing is at the spiritual level it is **without effort** because healing is the result of Truth known in consciousness-God is and if God is there can be nothing else. This is the consciousness of spiritual man and there is never effort in remembering Truth.

God being infinite spirit is omnipresent where you are therefore you cannot have two powers in the presence of God because God **is** omnipresent, present all the time. You don't have to battle error/evil/bad when you know: **if God is there is nothing else for God is omnipotent, om-**

nipresent and omniscient where it is known. All and only. Therefore there is not and can never be an *other* being, presence, law, power, cause or effect separate and apart from the allness that already **is.**

As a mystic you live in God awareness not merely when someone asks for help but 24/7/365 and in the same way you cannot turn off and on the Truth "God is the only power." **You live in that consciousness continually** so no matter how many times expressions of external power are presented to you they do not rattle you, change you, affect you. Why? Because you no longer live by the physical senses that perceive false powers as reality but express as the consciousness that knows only harmony, good, is.

You must understand for spiritual healing to have an effect the desire of the one asking for help has to be turned **to** God and **away** from man. To get a healing from a spiritual healer you must desire not wellness but **wholeness** and by that you must desire God, to be made **whole** in God, of its image and likeness-harmonious expression of being-not just an easier human experience with more good than bad.

This is not to say you won't get healings that **seem** to be better humanhood but, **and this is the turning point, the fork in the road:** if you want more than to live ailment to ailment, healing to healing trying to piece yourself into perfection **you will have to raise your own consciousness and have the mystical experience.**

You turn to a spiritual life to rise above the effects of the world upon your body, mind and finances and through study and practice of the principles of Truth you receive the understanding of Truth that allows you to rise to and beyond the conscious understanding of the healer you once went to.

Now you are a healer of man same as the practitioner. You have been **ordained,** not by paper or man but by God itself because by knowing God aright you are ordained to share God with those who seek God.

Your ordination to disciple to the world is in the experience of meeting God face to face within. Your ordination is complete when you know your true nature as child of the most high and live the principles of spiritual Truth in expression.

It is the degree of conscious oneness you express that determines the nature and degree of the healing because it is directly proportional to your degree of living God consciousness **but** understand it is not the sole responsibility of the practitioner for one who does not want to be healed **spiritually** will not be healed spiritually and will continue to suffer duality. The one seeking relief must be the one opening the way for the relief to be brought into awareness and that is only by letting go of everything you think you know to learn what is Truth by which to truly live and not just exist.

Spiritual healer and spiritual healing:

If you go to a healer that healer cannot bring to you anything of this world, nothing for your finances, nothing about your neighbor, nothing about how to correct any mortal situation you may find yourself or another in.

Though you may go to a healer for the things of the world that is not what you will get. When you go to a healer it is not for the physical healing or material relief rather to bring forth God in the awareness of the **healer** thereby bringing God into the world by way of the healer with a higher conscious understanding of God acting as a vessel for divine grace to touch the consciousness of the one asking for help.

This grace, activity of God, is what awakens the sleeper in all of us. And the sleeper is not the Christ of you, it is *you* the human you who is asleep to your true nature of being. Therefore bringing God into your conscious awareness is the only thing that brings God into the world to bless others, awaken them to the within where the meat, wine, water and bread of God (Truth of supply and support) becomes the meat, wine, water and bread of the visible world that supplies your every need from the source of you.

What healing work is:

God the Father, God the Son, I, is the creative principle of the good of your experience, is your source of strength, **I can do all things through Christ who strengthens me,** and by this realization does the Christ become active in your life.

All healing work is an experience within your own being/soul. Anyone who tries to do healing work just because they have read all the words in a book or know all the statements of Truth or denial to make will fail though in the beginning they may have a small measure of success because they may have a bit higher human consciousness to lift a lower human consciousness up but human mind manipulation can only go as far as the human mind which is the reason for the conditions of man right now.

Healing work is not the product of thought, thinking or making it so through right thinking, determination, mental manipulation, affirmations or denials rather true spiritual healing work is the product of a divine inspiration or illumination that flows from the center of your being out from you, not something *of* you personally but of that which is the **living expression** of you. If this weren't true the Master wouldn't have said "I can of my own self do nothing." He should have been able to do a lot of things because of all he knew **but even with all he knew he couldn't do anything, it was the Father within that doeth the work.** Jesus was the **instrument** of God revealing the promise of God-eternal life, eternal supply, harmony and peace.

Holding space

To hold space is a phrase thrown around a lot as of late and I know people mean well with it and it does do good, there is nothing wrong with it at all however your ability to heal would increase dramatically if you **understood** the act of divine Love you are performing and the miraculous effects it has on the individual as well as the world when it is done with right knowing of what it is, what it is doing and what its purpose is.

What you call holding space for that which will bring peace/healing/relief to enter is spiritual consciousness without the consciousness of it being a spiritual act. **You are doing what a mystic, a true spiritual healer does-goes into the silence and holds space,** remains in the silence and waits, makes a place for the spirit you know to come to do that which only **it** can do-bring a change to the situation for the better ie harmony for all.

On the mind level it does work but is still of duality/chance/can become what it was again however if that which you hold space for is a spirit manifest within that you are aware of, have contact with, you are entering the "spiritual realm of mysticism" and could easily follow the spiritual path laid out here with very little difficulty because it is merely an **acknowledgment** of what it is you call spirit and to remove duality from your experience if it isn't already. These two changes set your feet squarely on a true spiritual path with a road map to follow for maximum success.

The principle of healing

When Jesus "fed" the people with Words of Truth or actual food he was shocked that they would come back the next day to be "fed" so he called their attention to the fact that where they saw loaves and fishes, the visible, they hadn't seen the **miracle,** the **principle** that **provided** the loaves and fishes.

What Jesus was trying to show the world wasn't that God would *give* you material good, edible loaves and fishes but **spiritual** food to sustain the Self of you. Jesus came to give mankind a **principle,** a way by which to **receive** of **spiritual** food for an harmonious, abundant eternal life and this **principle** is:

Conscious oneness with God through awareness of God within is life eternal.

If you receive a healing it is not because God decided now was the time to do the healing, you receive a healing because you opened yourself up to that which was not in evidence out in the world and received what is not of the world-Truth-which maintains and sustains you in your spiritual identity **when your spiritual identity is known to you.**

Healing is not improved humanhood:

Healing is the revelation there is no humanhood only the *illusion of bondage to beliefs and conditions* that form your perception of the world which is an internal picture and not reality. Visions, illusions are internal, not external/real/objective and are only false renderings of circumstances *according to your beliefs and conditioning.*

What is a spiritual healer?

Spiritual man has not degenerated into a mortal and mortal man is never going to regenerate into spiritual being. What has transpired is that the teacher/practitioner has attained the spiritual capacity to look you in the eye and see the spiritual son of God and not believe the evidence of the senses, not believe the appearance whether it testifies to sin, disease, lack or limitation. This is the spiritual healer. Not the one who prays to God that you be healed, they have been doing that in orthodoxy for thousands of years. **The spiritual healer is one who can look you right in the eye and say "I know who thou art! The holy one of Israel."** Therefore when sin, disease, false appetite, lack etc, appear in your experience you can knowingly say "this is maya, this is illusion," "this is the world of man, of sense perception trying to fool me into doing something/reacting."

This is predicated on a further revelation **prayer and meditation are not to be used for increasing man's humanhood or improving it.** This is not the Christ way, it is the way of religionists and failure. You can only gain the world as joint heir to the kingdom of God when you find God and finding God must be the only desire not the loaves and fishes/material things of the world.

How to begin healing/treating yourself:

There are no wrong healings, there is no right or wrong way to perform a healing; it comes down to the consciousness of those involved be it healer and patient or you for yourself. Because you are in a human state of consciousness you have to start with words and thoughts, the metaphysical/human mind works first. This first part of prayer is called **treatment,** where you bring to mind a Truth on which to dwell, to rest in.

The words and thoughts of the treatment process merely get your mind "out of the world" and switches you to God's world or consciousness. By bringing words of **Truth** to mind the *world* view is released/floats away and Truth is revealed in consciousness. How? In what way?

God is felt, sensed or heard within and is the confirmation revealing the Truth of the unseen and this is why no where in the world, in the *minds* of man, in the *beliefs* of man can the peace and harmony of **God** be found.

There is no expression/grace of God in evidence where there is no conscious realization of God within individual man to express as grace.

If you have no consciousness of something it doesn't exist to you, you are unaware of it therefore you cannot express it. God is not where there is no conscious realization of its presence. God cannot be found, known if you do not look for it where it is, **within you.** If you are consciously aware of it within you then you have God in your midst, awareness, constant companionship, supply, support and eternal life and Truth that keeps you from falling back into duality.

A healing is a revealing:

A healing doesn't change your physical condition per se. You aren't healed of a disease, lack or limitation, fear, sin or false appetites, cancer, deafness through physical or material means, you are **freed** of the *belief* in two powers which expresses in your life as those erroneous conditions.

You as a healer do not magically reverse/heal their physical/material problems you **reveal** the cause of their problems as the *belief* they are flesh and blood that is born and dies rather than the **child of God,** spirit in form.

A healing reveals that when you are of the consciousness of God, harmony, you cannot be of the consciousness of man therefore are **not** affected by the *beliefs, illusions or expressions of human man*.

A healing is a temporary relief/reprieve and another illusion of man will become evident unless you take over the healing of self instead of going to a healer when the time comes. Healers are like books, good for a time, necessary for understanding but at some point you have to put the book down and start writing your own story, ie you are responsible for your life. There is purpose in learning through healers and teachers but if you become dependent on them for their conscious knowing you are not knowing anything yourself except the phone number to call for help.

Help thy self. You use a raft to traverse a river but do not carry it beyond the other shore for you are now on solid ground and no longer in need of that which is behind you as much or not at all. This side of the river is yours, your practice, your communion, your resting and healing of self and others. The tools you used in the beginning helped you learn the steps you were to take but the steps are now yours to take with the Father not a healer or teacher. Not to say don't ask for help when it is needed but learn to depend on the Father within, **do not lean on thine own understanding nor on any other than God.** Take all in to God to get Truth from God and in that way it has authority, dominion over the errors that present *as* reality.

It isn't the words that do the healing it is the Truth **of** the words, the knowing what the words **do for you,** not what the words *sound* like to human ears that interpret good and bad judged by personal experience.

Silent ministry:

All true spiritual teachings/mystical teachings, healings and experiences are **silent.** The sharing of God is silent, sacred and secret. This work is **not** to be public, shared with the masses because the mass mind of man will try to crucify you, publicly humiliate you, try to tear God from you because they don't have the consciousness necessary to **know** God and this is why **secret, silent and sacred expression of spiritual living is of the highest order.**

Then how are others brought onto the path if you are not to proselyte from the pulpit? By **their** conscious need for that which they cannot find among man. You will be found, you will be called upon and there is nothing you need do. But you say, "this book reveals that which you say shouldn't be given to *man.*"

You reading this are **not** of the mass mind of man, your Christ has been awakened and have been **following** the bread crumbs God has been dropping because it feels your readiness for different.

Those who seek what I and other mystics have, oneness with the Father through an awareness of a presence within our own being, will seek it until they find it through no act of that which is being sought. God is the consciousness of all that is of its consciousness and if you seek God you are opening your consciousness knowingly or unknowingly to that which you seek and will receive in the measure of your desire to know.

The **caution** for beginners is that until you know God you cannot express God to another in words that make sense because at the moment it doesn't make a whole lot of sense to you even though you feel within that it **is** Truth. To be able to articulate Truth aloud can only happen when you go past the stage of learning and are implementing without thought the things you have learned. You have to be the expression **of** Truth before your foundation is rock and not a mix of rock and sand, a slippery slope that can leave you more broken than you were.

Silent, secret and sacred. These are the **conditions** the seed of God needs to put down roots and grow strong and be well into maturity before it can be revealed to the world because only at this stage of spiritual understanding have you born the visible fruits of your invisible work in the visible world as absolute proof of which you speak.

All work starts in the invisible, within the secret, silent, sacred place where God is and will only produce fruit when the principles are followed.

Let God be your resting place:

It can be difficult at times to live the spiritual life because man, no matter how far along the path, still has some desires-to do, to be, to bless, and that is a barrier to spiritual development.

The dissolving of the barrier begins when you let go of desires, wants, wishes or telling God how to do its job and go within to it because you want to learn from it, be comforted by it, rest in it only for the reason of needing to be with it, God, the Comforter.

Go to God asking only that its harmony of expression be established in you and realize your oneness with it thereby becoming consciously one with the creative principle of your being. That is it. Now you should be devoid of needs, wants and desires because you finally **feel** God **as** fulfillment, comfort, wholeness within your own being. By being consciously aware of God you are one with God and not separate as human man believes.

When you and God start working together you will be amazed at how much God does through you as you; it is what you could have only wished to have accomplished after a lot of hard work, money and time. Sometimes the path is completely different than you could have ever imagined and you can chose not to follow at any time, God does not hold any of its images captive in doubt or ransom.

Sometimes those changes in direction are however exactly what is needed to bring more of God into the world, reveal **your** innate talents, your healing abilities, your beautiful smile that makes others smile back.

The difference between spiritual healing and medical healing:

One thing you need to understand: the word healing does not mean to spiritual man what healing means to human man therefore **because it is not a physical healing** you do not necessarily become free of the symptoms immediately, or more quickly than you would humanly expect **but** what does happen is that the cause, the illusion thought to be power for bad is shown to be no thing when God comes on the field/God in awareness.

Spiritual healings can and do often have immediate results that defy human understanding but that is not the purpose of the healing; it may have been the desired effect but it wasn't the true purpose you sought a **spiritual** healer instead of a *medical* doctor-you didn't want your body or circumstances healed, **you wanted your life healed,** to find peace, harmony and health, abundance, joy and rest. You want to stop repeating the same patterns whether mental, physical, moral or financial. This is what you seek, to find wholeness wrapped in peace with a big dollop of harmony on top.

When it comes to ailments a lot of spiritual students question the rightness of medicine. That question can only be answered by you and the answer will depend on how far along the spiritual path you are-the degree of your oneness with God determines when and what you chose to use of this world. **It is always your choice,** never dictated by God, spiritual teacher or man.

Even if you receive peace from within and the healing is done, if you are squirting, leaking, broken or uncomfortable beyond your limit you may want to seek medical attention. You have to understand medicine benefits those who use it for what it is **but don't worship or give power of good or bad in or of the medicine or profession.** Medical advancements were brought into universal consciousness from God through one for the good of all man so use it, just spiritually heal yourself first to continue breaking the universal mesmerism of a power opposing God which produces the errors you experience as human man because that is the consciousness you are expressing from.

It is akin to the story about the man stranded on the roof of his house during a flood. A boat comes by to rescue him and the man says "no, God is going to rescue me." A second boat comes by as the water is getting higher and faster and again his response is the same. And a third boat. Finally the water sweeps the man off of his roof and he drowns. Standing before God the man is distraught. "I have loved you all my life, I have prayed to you every day of my life and I prayed for you to save me and yet you let me die." God looks at the man and shakes his head sadly, "wasn't three boats enough?"

What this means is that God being all shows up as some form of good/needed/visible or invisible thing and to not look a gift horse in the mouth! Whatever brings peace, relief, joy, abundance, is of kindness, benevolence, charity, unselfishness is of God no matter the form-person or object, what it is or how it presents. The aspirin you take for a headache is God substance. It has no power beyond the chemicals it contains that act on the *physical* body for its purpose, it is not good and it isn't bad, it just is for the purpose it is for-body pain unless it is abused by man.

God doesn't tell you what you can and cannot do, God merely tells you "I've got this," and you can do as you feel from there because you got the healing, God on the field, in your awareness. Take an aspirin, go to the chiropractor, do what you need to relieve the error expressing as pain just know what is expressing as pain/error in your experience is an opportunity to understand

why it came into expression and how to change your expression going forward to not suffer the same error/pain again.

Remember every error you encounter is an opportunity to raise your consciousness; why else would they come into expression except to show you the duality of your expression so you can heal yourself to become more the expression of harmony?

Expressing life at your level of understanding is all that is asked of you with the caveat that your level of understanding is constantly being increased as you live more and more in God consciousness.

I have mentioned a medical issue that started shortly after I really got on the spiritual path. It was a pinched nerve in my neck that made it impossible for me to do anything but sit or lay down for almost 8 weeks. I went within for a healing the moment I felt it pinch and felt the click. I proceeded to do steroids, acupuncture, chiropractic, heat, ice etc for the pain. Oh the pain! It was beyond anything I had ever experienced before and was really wondering if this was going to be my quality of life going forward and honestly that was a dismal prospect but I knew God was harmony and there would be a reason I just couldn't see at the moment.

About 4 weeks in God spoke, "everything heals" and in that instant I broke down crying with relief. Understand though I knew God was harmony being new to the path it was honestly the first time I was really taking God out for a spin on pain within me not error outside of me, of someone else, I could nothingize and release ie it was very personal to me. Don't get me wrong, I had been knowing God for awhile but this was the biggest thing so far in my experience to trust, to **know** it would get better and that there would be harmony revealed. I did trust and it did heal, not physically but spiritually as my mri and my doctors don't understand how I could be completely pain free.

In the beginning of being pain free I found myself worrying about re-injuring my neck and going through that pain again but then I realized when something is spiritual healed, if I stay where spiritual healing comes from I will remain healed because it wasn't a physical ailment per se, it presented that way, **but it was a way for God to get me to do what it needed me to do-sit and type this work-and to raise my conscious understanding so I could reveal Truth to you.**

This is what you have to remember, understand and rest in completely. What comes into your life once you are truly on the spiritual path that *seems* to be error isn't of your making with returning karma but the moving and shaking behind the scenes that gets you further along the path. It can be jarring and you might freak and slip out of oneness because *you* have to do something about this pain/problem. By all means do what you need to do medically but know it isn't duality upon you but spiritual healing that is more like pulling a bandaid off really fast to get the healing started.

The material world of man you have so carefully constructed is going to get a make-over and for some it is going to be a complete demolition and rebuild but look forward to it! In the past living as human man you had no assurance of the outcome of what seemed to be error but now you do and if you rest in that knowing that **there is a purpose** you can get through it better, easier because you know God is directing the remodel as it is his house you live in and not yours.

Receptivity/degree of received healing:

Spiritual healers are **not** doctors or psychologists or coaches, we **do not** know anything about anatomy, physiology, biology, broken bones or germs. The only reason we can bring forth a healing is that the only ones who come to us are the **sons** of God. The healing is **dependent** on the recognition of that ie the consciousness of the **patient** determines the amount of healing they receive and also whether there is a permanence to the healing or not.

Those who go to healers to heal themselves of the ills of the world but want to continue endeavoring in the world will continue to suffer ills of the world. However if one comes to a healer with the same kind of human ailment/problem but is done with this piece meal fixing of self, wants more than what the world offers this is the **consciousness** that is open to different, open to that which is unknown. This is **receptivity** and is fueled by need, thirst, a hunger that is not sated in the human world.

This is all that is necessary to awaken to the Father within and when the connection has been made you know God to be real and that spirit isn't lo here nor lo there, it is omnipresent where God is **known.**

The importance of NOW:

The present moment, now, is the only time the mind is quiet to hear the soft still voice of God.

This is the key and the sticking point if you aren't careful.

To be in God consciousness you have to be present, in the moment, **now;** you cannot be thinking about stuff, the *past* or the *future*. The only way to be **with** God is to be **with** God in consciousness not off in your own little world of thought. How can you have a conversation with or be waiting for God to come into awareness if your mind is elsewhere?

As long as you stay in the present moment, now, and not back in the past or out in the future, every moment is now and you are with God and not man of earth and **this is the key to spiritual healing-God in awareness, the healing consciousness** lived as your consciousness, your actions returned to you as grace, bread on the water pressed down and flowing over.

Only when you live in the now, in the present moment, on a **fairly consistent basis** are you under a **measurable degree of grace** ie a more consistent experience of peace while being protected from duality because you are with God being an instrument of God so there is no duality in consciousness to react to therefore none in your experience.

Spiritual integrity:

In the human world of judgement you may be forgiven your ignorance or put on probation but on the spiritual path there is no probation, you pay. You pay every time you fail to perceive duality and nothingize it by experiencing chaos instead of harmony. You stand or fall by the degree of your **spiritual** integrity.

What is your spiritual integrity? Your realization of one Self, one Consciousness, one Soul, one Spirit, one Life, one Law, one Presence, one Being in God through the Christ of every man from before time, the **consciousness that was the expression of Jesus** that **revealed** him **as** the Christ.

You have to rightly know God as the only presence and have oneness with God on the inside and common man or woman on the outside. Outwardly you keep your language, the language of the man on the street but inwardly you have to live your life as a saint. Why? Because you know you are being measured by your expression which is what is going on inside of your *thinking mind*. You are not punished *by* God but punished by the thought returning upon the thinker, you. Your deeds return to you regardless of their content, what you sow is what you reap, consequences, karma-good and bad of man or grace of God.

You and only you are responsible for your errors as you are no longer ingnorant of karmic law/cosmic law and now aware of spiritual Law where your thoughts and actions return squarely on your shoulders.

You never channel God, you never try to channel God. You are an instrument, God uses *you*, you do not help God in any way but by being open to its presence. To try to do anything would be falling back into duality because you know of your own self you can do nothing ... unless you forget that and think you are suddenly powerful.

Grace is the gift of the healing consciousness:

Grace meets all needs because it is the allness of God so whatever is needed to bring relief, harmony, release will be given to those asking for those things. **Grace is temporary in nature and only becomes a permanent dispensation as your oneness with God becomes a constant dispensation unto your life.**

All grace should come with a big warning sign: "temporary relief only if you do not seek to know how your relief was gotten," ie what it takes to be able to do that for yourself, bring peace to bear.

Psychologists would call it self soothing, making it a mental game of hide the fear and produce the smile, but it is bringing Truth to bear, God on the scene, to dispel error which is the peace, or soothing to your being. Truth is the tonic to the jangled mind that just wants to find a place of rest. You have to learn to rest in Truth no matter how foreign it feels because this is the Truth that when known makes you free from the errors of man to find freedom in God. The sooner you learn to rest in the Truth given you of God the sooner your life will bear the fruit of your oneness.

The secret of spiritual living is knowing the reality of what is called good and evil which enables you not to judge as good and evil but to see **unconditioned** Truth, all is, just is. That doesn't mean there won't be times you need to correct an error of a student but it would be a correction of the human sense they are permitting to handle them and probably need some outer form of correction so they may receive a healing and rise in Truth.

This only applies to students and patients because it is not your job to correct the world, only at times to help a student or patient see their duality so they can correct the error they are

making. It is not wrong to bring to the attention of one under your tutelage the error of their thinking which is leading them away from God and back to duality with the idea they can mix and match the qualities of God and man to fit them perfectly; it cannot be done.

To help one progress sometimes the sword must come through the teacher/healer when the student cannot see it or do it themselves because they are missing a point of understanding or have not had a revelation on it. Your bringing attention to some things at some times can be that which makes them go within to ask God to give them Truth of what they were told.

It is never to criticize but to remove obstacles so they can continue on their path of illumined conscious understanding.

A spiritual healer nullifies error with Law and does it through grace.

A spiritual healer/revealer is not one who develops ways of *using* Truth over error or using treatments to overcome disease. A spiritual healer **is that state of consciousness** which knows God alone **is** the reality of all that is and anything else is an illusion, unreality born of the universal mesmerism/hypnotism/belief in two powers of good and evil.

Unless you are expressing Truth as your livingness you are of the *mental realm* of man. You may be thinking of **spiritual** things but you are *thinking* of spiritual things *mentally* and no **healing** can take place. There are sometimes *mental* healing though the result is not a **spiritual** healing rather a *suggestion,* a temporary uplift/fruitage of self hypnosis *thinking* "I am well, I am rich, I am perfect, or God will take care of me."

When you accept a *suggestion/duality* as Truth and respond to it you have had a *mental healing, a psychological or psychosomatic or hypnotic healing* but it is in **no way spiritual** because you have merely *reacted* to a suggestion of your or another's *thinking* mind and will find yourself back where you began.

It isn't the treatment, the going within and asking God to show you Truth that does the healing it is **your consciousness of being child of God** that does the healing because in that knowing you bring the only presence there is to bear in the situation-the presence of peace which is the allness of being-God in your awareness.

The absence of supply is with those who do not have conscious awareness of God, who do not abide in the Word and do not let the Word abide in them. Lack is of those who do not dwell in the secret place of the most high and have cut themselves off from the only supply there is. The Word of God is the bread, the meat, the wine and the water unto your life and is simply the conscious realization of God's presence within your consciousness. You are aware of a presence within that is not you but is the source of you. You have just met God face to face.

This is the key to all of the kingdom! All of the supply, all of the love, all of the experiences to come as the individualized expression of God rests on your awareness of **who you are** and are in constant, conscious contact with that presence because it is your teacher, your guide, the smarter you you trust to take care of you because you depend on it and not man whose breath is in his nostrils living precariously balanced between good and evil.

Matthew 3:3 A voice of one calling in the desert, prepare the way for the Lord, make straight paths for him.

When you are lost, nothing left and you call out to God, Father, that is what opens the door you didn't know was closed for God to enter your life and make its presence known. When God is your navigator, your guide, the road of life is easy, peaceful, abundant and fun. God goes before you to make the crooked places straight.

It isn't what you say with words that heals:

It is the state of consciousness, of realized Truth from God through you to the world. It is your state of consciousness, your conscious communion, communication with God that allows its allness to become evident as healings ie raise consciousness within the patient/student asking for the dissolution of an illusion which they call a problem.

Healings are never physical, they are spiritual. A healing happens when the healer gets a click or confirmation, contact with the Father within which makes itself known in words, thoughts or feelings. It is the revelation of Truth that has always been, "I and the Father are one, all that I have is thine."

Do not try to heal someone humanly either mentally or physically, you are not a doctor of any kind nor claim to be. The healing spiritual healers do is not a healing in the human sense of the word rather it is a revelation in conscious knowing of their true nature of being by way of the healer's higher consciousness of God.

Conscious oneness with God is the activity that heals/reveals Truth and this is the reason absent treatments/healings are valid. You do not need to be in the proximity of a patient as long as your consciousness and the consciousness of the one asking for help are correctly oriented to God and not man.

When you as the healer get the awareness of God all those in conscious union with God receive the awareness of God in whatever form/experience is necessary to bring peace, harmony, understanding or benevolence into expression for their good.

Whenever you are faced with a problem regardless of its nature go within your own consciousness for understanding. Instead of running around seeking answers from this or that person, instead of looking for a solution outside of yourself merely turn within. In the quiet and calm of your own being let the answer to your problem unfold.

Do not be discouraged if the answer you seek doesn't come the first couple times you go within, just keep yourself open to God's impartation of Truth in whatever form it comes. As you learn to depend on God, as you learn to depend on this infinite source of all that is for the working out of your problems and experiences you will become more and more adept at quickly discerning God's brand of harmony.

Too long man has sought health, peace and prosperity outside of themselves. Now it is time to go within and learn that there is never a failure or disappointment in the whole realm of your consciousness, nor will you ever find delay or betrayal when you find the calm of your own soul and the presence of an indwelling being.

You are I am:

You cannot take credit, even secretly, for that which you do on the spiritual path. On the spiritual path you are one with God, there is no you-personality, will, desire-separate and apart from God, you are one, I am is your name, the name shared between you and God and every other person on earth. Whether someone is on the spiritual path or not they are I am. They are the sons of God; **the only difference between the man of earth and the man on the spiritual path is the conscious awareness of the Presence within** which is the God of creation sitting in the bosom of its creation-you-waiting for that moment of recognition where from then on God is active in your life with the only intent that of bringing you back home, to remember who you are, why you are here and to experience your Truth of being as eternal and infinite.

Socrates said "man, know thyself." **Know thyself as child of God** not man of earth, spirit not flesh, immortal and eternal not mortal and finite.

The solution to any outer problem is automatically taken care of in the realization of inner peace/God on the field. The peace within produces harmony and joy without. The peace be still within appears as the daily manna without. The realization of this divine presence, this feeling of divine Love through you is the temple of God in which you live and move and have your being even when you are out in the world of mortal man.

The world of God within is your abiding place, the place from which you discern all that is of the outer world, not as you see it but as God reveals it to be and in this way error is healed and grace flows to those in need.

The role of a healer:

The role of a healer is to realize for themselves, **not** the one suffering the error, that there is no Truth to the claims of man no matter the claim because all stem from the same belief-separation from God thus in need, lack or inharmony.

By bringing Truth to bear/God on the field the claim of duality is revealed as no thing real which is the Truth that brings grace to bear for those receptive.

To behold an appearance, whether good or bad, happy or sad is to know it is malpractice/false/illusion and that is that. No acceptance, no rebuttal, no concern, no argument, just a mental error/malpractice presenting which if you do not accept dissolves.

Discord that touch your consciousness aren't real conditions or people they are just universal malpractice, nothing more than a projection of the carnal mind living the belief in two powers. All there is to evil is the belief in two powers, mental impositions that hit your senses and if you react, battle, fight, refute or try to ignore them you lose because **in resisting you establish evil in your consciousness as a "thing", a "reality" when it is nothing but a mental imposition to begin with.**

Spiritual treatments don't overcome evil, **they show the nothingness of the belief in evil** as merely that of a universal belief in two powers which in and of itself is an error. Thus if the cause is not real neither can the result.

Important:

Healers are not God to their patients, healers release their patients **to** God so they may know Truth and begin their journey home to the Father.

Anyone who has done healing work has been the instrument through which others have attained their freedom/Truth of being not because of your desire to heal a headache or a tumor but by freeing the mind of the one asking from false pictures, illusions, wrong thinking. Where the spirit of the Lord **is** harmony **is.** Where there is receptivity God is on the scene. It only takes one person with an awareness of God, the leavening, or the catalyst, to awaken others to receptivity.

There is no power in knowing Truth, **the power lies in your application of this Truth** as it pertains to your life. Truth reveals there is no power to overcome because there is no opposing force just a belief, error of mind, illusion, universal hypnotism of an unreality taken as Truth.

This is the definition of resist not evil because evil is no thing but an illusion of personal mind, has no Law, no Source, no objectivity. How do you fight, battle or protect yourself from an illusion in another person's mind? You don't because there is no need to, illusions have no power to do you harm when you know they are illusions.

If all you need is given by God what is there to fear or fight against, pick up the sword against? Protect? Save? Hold onto? Take? Covet? This is why when you know God you can rest because there is only one thing for you to do in this life now and that is listen for God and to do as given to have **eternal** harmonious expression and return.

Dying daily

The path of spiritual awakening is not a straight line, it is an upward spiral of continually revisiting beliefs you *thought* were Truth to find higher levels of understanding on which to rest which is what allows you to easily release the *belief* in light of revealed **Truth.**

It has been revealed that which will lift you up out of mortality/human living and *perceived* death is the Spirit of Christ within each **when it is known in awareness** and this is your connection to Truth/God and the **knowing of Truth** by way of a relationship with this inner Self is what reveals abundance unto your livingness. This Spirit is available to all but there is a price to be paid for it to be active in your life and that is **surrender.** You surrender who you think you are and what you know as finite human and allow yourself to be shown Truth, that the life man experiences isn't Truth by way of a spiritual principle called **dying daily.**

Spirituality/Truth/God knowing cannot be added to a vessel already full of materiality/human belief. You cannot add God Truth to your *personal* sense of self and get better humanhood. You cannot attain the kingdom of heaven if you are not choosing to live in the consciousness of Truth that **is** the kingdom. Your vessel must be empty of self, human beliefs and actions, before it can be filled with Self, the knowing and living **of** Truth.

The spiritual principle of **dying daily** to the erroneous beliefs of man is what allows you to empty yourself of what is not Truth to be filled up with Truth which is the only way to experience through expression your true nature as Spirit, child of God, eternal, immortal and infinite.

There is a story about a man whose horse ran off. The villagers said "oh, how sad," and the man said "maybe."

The next day his horse came back with six more horses. The villagers said, "how wonderful" and the man said "maybe."

The next day the man's son took one of the horses out riding, got bucked and broke his ankle. The villagers said, "how sad," and the man said "maybe."

The next day the village was raided for men of fighting age. The man's son was not considered because of his broken ankle. The villagers said "how wonderful" and the man said "maybe."

You as man cannot know the over arching picture of the why and wherefore of life and because man is myopic, short sighted, he *reacts* to immediate circumstances and from there the end is already written-either good or bad can be the result of your reaction; duality is a crap shoot/double edged sword. However if you are in oneness with God you wouldn't *react,* you would **observe** without judgement.

You are the instrument that allows God's allness/wholeness to be what is received by those who seek God in their experience. Just know that if human man has no belief in God, God will not be known until that man begins to desire what is not of this world. Then God will be found because God is desired and not more and better *material* good/human experiences.

Any who seek God aright, for only the desire of being in the presence of God, will find God and all the world will be theirs for they will be joint heirs to the kingdom of all that is good and harmonious for eternity. I know it sounds like fancy, almost impossible that you could know God, be one with God, have a relationship with God within but you can, it is real and if you want it it will be yours and there is nothing on earth that can stop it for what God has put together no man can put asunder/break. No man can keep you from God, **only you can keep you from God.**

To die daily means to deny yourself the ability and the choice to judge.

It means to witness without involvement of emotion or reaction. To go inside and ask God to reveal **its** reality of what may be presenting to you instead of reacting as a human to a situation and becoming an instrument of man's chaos instead of an instrument of God for harmony.

Protective work:

It is important never to lose sight of the **non** power of *effect* in man's world. Germs are effects, disease, weather, climate, false appetites, all of these exist as *effects,* that which is experienced as the **result** of believing you are separated from God but because they are effects of the *human* world of duality they have no power in and of themselves to do/be good or to do/be evil. The effects experienced by man are merely the effects of their *thinking mind* coming back to them as what they *already* believe something to be, do or cause.

Protective work begins with knowing, living and expressing Truth that **nothing** has power/expression/presence but God and that there is **no** power in effects **except** the power man gives them. Therefore dominion over the errors and evils of this world is experienced in proportion as you recognize God, spirit, to be the only presence, the only Law and the only nature of expression-harmonious.

When we talk about the nature of expression of spiritual man as being of a single nature of expression, harmony, it sounds as if spiritual man cannot express duality. This is true of the highly risen spiritual man, think Jesus the Christ but it isn't a complete dispensation of harmony right out of the gate, it is the letting go of belief/duality and filling up with the singular expression of harmony that brings you to the place of singular expression.

You aren't going to have an immediate 100% change, flip of a switch from chaos to eternally harmony but **that when you are with God in consciousness you are harmonious** because you are **of** the consciousness of harmony and not of the consciousness of man which is duality/chaos.

You as a human man newly revealed as spiritual man are not going to experience complete harmony because you are not going to be where harmony is **on a constant/consistent basis until you have been a while on the spiritual path.** You are still full of human behaviors and beliefs but as you die daily to the things of man you become more harmonious because harmony is what you are entertaining in your consciousness.

You are living more and more in God consciousness, spending time with God having a true relationship with God through inner listening and best friend chit chat thus are of the consciousness of harmony more and more in expression because God feels good within you and that is what you express as, ie you feel good to others and that is how they respond to you which is the definition of grace in your midst.

When it is said "harmony is the only expression where you are" means **your expression when you are with God is harmonious because it is where you are in consciousness.** Grace, the allness of God in activity goes before you to make the crooked places straight and it does make your experience much more enjoyable and peaceful than if God hadn't been known to you but understand this doesn't mean everyone is responsive to grace, of a lightened mood, of something relieved or lifted therefore though there will be harmony where you are because **you are of the consciousness of harmony** that harmony must be your **expression** to be the personal messenger of **peace be with you** to get the harder nuts to crack a smile and feel something not of man, something that brings peace to a weary soul.

Dying daily is putting off mortality and putting on immortality. There will be loneliness on this path but only for a bit until you begin to realize you are never alone.

Every sin, lack, disease or discord you encounter in your life is another opportunity to "die daily" to the universal mesmerisms that present in your life as the result of the belief in two powers. This is an opportunity to bring God to bear and watch the error die to your conscious awareness as the nothingness it is.

These moments that allow you to bring Truth to a situation are truly blessings from God in the sense that once you meet a problem, any problem big or small, with Truth through spiritual understanding you won't have that problem again unless you forget your Truth and react to illusion as reality.

Knowing Truth shall make you free from the bondage of human thought, from human error to more and more God realization, unfoldment and enlightenment. You will never have to backtrack/do over that demonstration of God as long as you stay in God consciousness which is now, not in the past and not in the future.

To rise in spiritual consciousness you must put into practice spiritual principles and to practice is to participate in the activity of dying daily to error so you become less aware of it in your experience which means more harmony. To become harmonious **you must experience individual moments of harmony that become a constant dispensation, ie normal and natural, not that which you are trying to be but are.**

If you don't practice you cannot attain the Truth you seek to be. Each practicing of the principles dissolves a little bit more of the human thinking mind, are dying daily to the erroneous beliefs of man while filling up with spiritual Truth that is your rock, your high tower, your assurance of dependability and reliability unto the care and supply of your eternal experience.

To practice a principle is to be the principle in expression.

As long as there is an i, me or mine that is in anyway trying to achieve anything, accomplish or get, be glorified, there is a selfhood apart from God that is trying to maintain itself. This is duality and it is this you are dying to, the i separate from I to become **I** am. But to do this you must let go of the human ways by which you interact and interpret the world around you. It isn't a denying of anything, it is knowing the Truth of error as illusion separate and apart from any visible form and in that knowing error cannot exist as a reality to be feared or reacted to.

This is dying daily to old beliefs because you have been shown Truth which allows you to release the old and rest in the new. This is the **most important step** in spiritual growth because if you do not die to beliefs you are trying to add God to human living and it cannot be done as thousands of years of praying to a God outside of man attests to.

It is possible to die daily and it is merely the realization that as you must not desire ill health you must not desire good health, as you must not desire lack you must not desire abundance, as you must not desire an evil nature so you must not desire a good nature. God is not of the opposites but **is,** harmonious and perfect.

When you are harmonious of body, relationships, and finances you don't think about them because there is nothing to be thinking *about* them, they just **are** and all just **is** and it **is** good/harmonious. Have you ever noticed that? When your body is "feeling really good" you forget to think about your body, ie what was wrong with it because nothing **is** wrong with it at the moment, it **is being** and this is experienced as harmony.

When there is money in the bank you don't think about buying that something something you have had your eye on because you are not concerned about the money, it **is** there, finances **are** harmonious. When your relationships are going well they just hum along without contention, without confusion, easy, peaceful, it just **is** and you rest in that which **is** harmony.

You wouldn't make chaos in an harmonious relationship; it is harmonious; why would that even cross your mind? That is not even part of your consciousness at the moment because all **is** humming along just fine with what you and the other person are putting into it, both parties are happy and life **is** smooth. This is the understanding of harmony, when life **is** it isn't off the charts fireworks and sparklers and can't get up in the morning down in the dumps rollercoaster.

Spiritual life is not of the highs and lows, good parts and bad parts of man's experience rather is peace, ease, smoothness unto all the different aspects of your life working in concert to create an harmonious **atmosphere** to exist in supported, supplied and maintained by the quantity and quality of God which is the definition of divine Love.

The Great Reset: Winnowing the chaff of man from the fruit of God.

Prayer is a spiritual **activity.** You must participate. Nothing can be done *for* you, only **through** you which implies activity on your part and that activity is dying daily so God consciousness can fill the vacuum left by letting go of long held beliefs. It can be painful/confusing at times but only temporarily, just don't allow yourself to fall back into old ways to ease the pain because it is familiar and this is new territory with new consequences you don't know but know this: all of the consequences are the same as source-good, God.

I and my patients have compared our coming into awareness and the time shortly thereafter as the internal changes of Spirit manifest or as harmony and order once again become your nature instead of the natural/material man of earth who is "out of order."

Here are a few of the things noticed after the awareness of God has happened:

1. Your body starts to change, you stop analyzing it and instead begin to understand its purpose in this life and begin to love it. You are happier, you seem to be able to converse without letting emotion interfere, you don't care about 99% of anything you used to. Your food intake will begin to drop because most people use food, like any other "thing" to fill that which feels empty. As you fill up on God you don't need as much from the world to satisfy the hunger because God is the only **food** that can do that. Your ability to have small talk, to actually want to have any conversation at all drops dramatically for you find nothing you are able to converse about other than dogs, weather and vacation spots. It isn't that you are above man rather you just don't have as much in common because you are dying daily to the beliefs of man while all man knows to do is talk about their false beliefs. You become aware of the errors of humanity left and right and do your best to heal them as they come and find all the conversation, friendship, companionship, love and joy within with God.
2. The Law of God begins to reset your life and in your experience something big seems to hit the fan just when you feel you are doing good, staying in God consciousness and it takes your feet out from under you/allows you a chance to question all of this spiritual stuff because you wonder what you did to bring it on, you were walking the walk!

I encountered a major medical problem, another a huge family drama etc. which make your head spin because dang it! I was doing what I was supposed to do! It was only at the end of it I could look back and see the Truth of God's will, God's way, the flow of the Law of consciousness, all that is, harmony and order, one with the flow instead of against it. It is **re-ordering you,** bringing up in your experience those things of you that are not **of** harmony to release them, die daily to through going within and resting with the Father for the Truth of what is being experience.

It is akin to the feeling when a project starts to go sideways but somewhere along the downhill slide you are turned in another direction where the right person, the right solution, the right something is waiting for you. It is human nature to suck in your breath, pucker the lower cheeks and pray to make it out the other side and you still may get that feeling when you have been on the path a bit but now you can check yourself, take a breath and smile because though it feels like the floor is crumbling beneath your feet a rock/harmony appears, God in your midst to supporting you all the way through to the ta-da of grace in your midst.

This to me was a difficult thing to lean into because I am a wee bit of a control freak, like my duckies ordered, polished and combed. Living from God consciousness takes away the need for me to be a control freak but just like anything else we do on this path of surrender it is one step at a time, realizing a little bit sooner each time the freak out feeling comes into the chest, "ok, I have felt this before and it always ends good though it feels out of my control but *i* am no longer in control so *i* need to let it play out," self talk to get myself back into conscious oneness with source I temporarily forgot was my safety net in life.

You do what presents to be done, ask the questions that need to be asked and let God be your thoughts on how to proceed, who to talk to, what to say etc. I have learned to move to the side, metaphorically, and push the big guy forward and let his words be my words and in this way keep my harmony.

These things you may or may not encounter are not tests by, from or of God to test your faith. It isn't a test, God doesn't test and there is no faith in spiritual knowing, rather it is a quick, hard and uncomfortable reset from which moving forward will be that much easier. This is a gross analogy but it makes the point. If you are having stomach issues and you know that if you throw up, your body is wanting to, you will feel better, you just have to do it, get through it. You let yourself be guided by that inner knowing to be rid of whatever is bothering it and instantly you begin to feel better, the ick has been released and you are you again.

Or you can keep forcing it down, feeling the nausea for as long as you resist that which you are given to do-throw up. You have to get through it, let it all go, stop fearing whatever it is you are fearing and trust what is being asked of you is for the best; without it, not doing what is given you to do, you continue to suffer needlessly. No matter what you are going through there is a reason, a purpose that will become evident as you move along this spiritual path and it will be good, great, better than you could have ever thought could be.

During my experience I was basically couch/bed bound but I could make myself get up and do stuff through the pain but I was definitely unable to be and do what I wanted so I did what I could-write. It was only later that I could see what had been given me to do was the visible starting point of my spiritual journey and you are reading the fruit of the Father, the fruit of oneness as my books are his Word, his consciousness in and through me out into the world to you.

Did I know this at the time? No. But I did know because I had experienced God and knew it to be good/harmonious, that this would be too if I stayed my course with God at the helm. During this time I meditated, prayed and know beyond a doubt that I had a spiritual healing, I felt it and I felt an immediate lifting of some of the pain but the physical pain had to linger so *i* was forced to linger and do what was given me to do.

But when you get through these adjustments by dying daily and dropping human expressions the other side will make all that you have gone though just a distant memory but remember: the path you took got you here so never, never think of your past as a waste of time; **it is the necessary preparation you need to desire God, that which is not found in the world of man.**

I didn't know it at the time but the reason for my "medical" situation was to put me into an environment in which I had no choice but to begin writing because my normal life was not available to me. The visible condition created the time necessary for me to get done what God had put before me to do.

There are many other things I can connect, and will continue to be able to connect to this singular event/reset as each comes to a recognizable conclusion as having started with that event. If I hadn't been still and trusted, if I hadn't been told from within "all things heal" to know without a doubt that this too shall pass I would not be seeing the fruitage of my devotion to the Father now created in that now of reset.

The point is you have no idea, I have no idea, what is still to come in this unfoldment but this I can absolutely promise you: whatever you go through, no matter how confusing or painful just trust. We don't use mantras or statements like sugar free candy but when I'm in pain it overwhelms me and I need something to help me get out of me and into God I do say sometimes over and over as my reminder: **your will Father, I know there is purpose in this I will see later, I trust you.**

After you have been living the spiritual life for a while you more easily recognize error before you *react* to it, accept it, take it on as your expression because it hits up against the new consciousness you are expressing from and it rings a bell. **This is not real, of me, this is duality, of the world.** This is a healing! You automatically did what you have been working toward-knowing error. It touched you, you recognized it for what it was, a suggestion of something *outside* of you and that recognition is the healing which allows you to release a belief in the light of Truth.

This is 100% of what living the spiritual life is. It is knowing the Truth of God, the Truth of you, the Truth of error and **living those principles in expression.**

Spiritual man's quality of experience is based on the degree of grace in their life which is directly proportional to the degree of deference of personal will for God's will for you as you.

Dying daily is the giving up of the sense of personal possession because when you live and move and have your being in God's kingdom there are no personal possessions, all is **of** God therefore what you possess is **of** God and not *yours* and that is why it is so easy to share, give of what you have-love, joy, peace, benevolence, abundance-because more will be given.

The overcoming/dying daily/healing of error or revealing of Truth is never the overcoming of something out there in the world it is always a dying of *personal* self to a *belief* that has been accepted in your consciousness as **Truth.**

The overcoming is done within your own consciousness **because you are the one who knows what error is** and why it must be addressed-to bring grace to yourself and those receptive to God.

All you are ever asked to do is remember secret, silent and sacred is the way of spiritual living in the kingdom of heaven on earth. If you speak *your* words before God comes on the field you are trying to be a part of the healing process, trying to *humanly* fix a situation but you can do nothing, it is the Father within that doeth the work, you are an instrument playing the music of the conductor; you are not the conductor.

Man thinks he needs to react to every error/slight in their experience to mitigate the damage to their life. But man is reacting to *illusions* which would have no effect on their life **if** they knew the Truth of what they were reacting to.

It can be hard not to react at first because it is habit but if you remember that what is going on *out* in the world of man is a kaleidoscope of personalities hitting, bouncing and *changing* with each interaction into something that it wasn't you can walk in the midst of man being untouched by the personalities/expressed consciousness of man all the while bringing grace to bear, God in the midst of man where God was not known before.

Protective work:

Your protective work is your reminder of the non power of the beliefs of man and is done first thing in the morning to reestablish you in oneness with God. You start your day in the realization that:

Power does not act upon you it flows out from you and it is the expression of God, good, and now you are so established in God that as negative appearances touch you throughout the day you are prepared for them, recognize them for what they are-illusion.

After having been on this path for a while it is no longer a routine of going into the silence and waiting for God to come on the field to tell you the healing is done, rather you establish your oneness first thing in the morning so God is on the field unless you react to error and let it have time in your thinking mind, ruminating etc. Therefore it is a simple recognition/awareness of the Truth of error as it presents and grace flows, the healing is done and you have placed spiritual bread on the water to return to you pressed down and flowing over.

A spiritualized consciousness is a consciousness in correct orientation to God and not *man*.

Once an individual knows the name and nature of God he is a free man and you cannot bind a free man in superstition, ignorance or any form of slavery when they know the true name and nature of God. On the other hand you cannot give the name and nature of God except to those who are prepared for it for they will misunderstand it, misinterpret it to mean they themselves are God and not that they are a willing **instrument** of God to work through and as their life.

This is a big distinction and big slide backwards if you think *yourself* to be the power and not the **vessel** through which the power flows and blesses. The allness of God cannot be used for personal gain or desire. What you desire must be what you desire for the world to experience as well as yourself, that is the only way one day all will be harmonious-if all want the same for others as they want for themselves. That is Love, that is harmony, that is abundance without end.

What does it mean to be prepared? You must be ready to go to God **willingly** because you have realized that it **is** Truth. The time you spent living humanly before you came to God is that which **prepares** you to leave the world of confusion, error and suffering behind. Done. Hands washed. Hasta la vista baby! You have to be done with the ways of the world; that is the **preparation** needed to go to God because you cannot have both so the choice must be made definitely. Remember this is not a dipping pool this is the deep end. You will swim, dance and walk on the water once you completely submerge yourself in it. This is where the magic happens, deep within the cool calm and peace of the within where God is.

Recognition of that which is within is what brings the within alive to live your without.

There is only one power but it is not a power of protection from evil in the sense of force or overpowering another but the power of knowing what is real and what isn't real. This **knowing Truth** is the rock on which you stand that is dependable, reliable and true because knowing Truth allows you to chose how you want to live **knowing why you want to live it.** If you want to live with God it is because you love knowing God, love being with God, depend on the certainty God/Law provides in your life when you are living with and not against it.

Or you can chose to take your chances back on the checker board, craps table or roulette wheel and keep doing it your way. All of life is a choice and being on the fence/ambivalent, having a whatever may come attitude **is** a choice of laziness, mental miasma or mental apathy-just don't give a hoot as long as the right parts of your life are supplied-the outer ie don't mess with my mindless actions and gluttonous appetites for all kinds of adult candy, don't take away my ten second stimuli, idols, rituals and false beliefs.

Bible passages and mystical writings are not the power of God. The power of God is the **understanding** of the words God gives back to you, not the words you take in. The degree of God in your consciousness is the power of God at your back. Your consciousness of God is dependent on you knowing Truth so during the day you let Truth come into your consciousness to feed you. It may be with a passage of scripture, a metaphysical Truth or mystical poetry, it may be the lyrics of a song, words on a billboard, it could merely be the feeling of God walking with you.

The more you entertain God in awareness the more you experience harmony which is your **protection** from duality, error, misstep, recrimination, back peddling, making amends, pain.

God is the bubble wrap that protects you from the errors of man around you.

The spiritual message is not an activity of the mind or body so it cannot become imbued in your consciousness unless the mind is quiet, peaceful, silent. Empty your mind and let everything extraneous drop away and **rest expectantly** for God in your awareness.

- you have to **clean house** for your guest, God. Remove the clutter, open the curtains and relax on the couch expectant of the visitor sure to arrive.

- you have to set up an internal environment; expectant but relaxed silence in which God can announce itself and function as your individual expression.

It is your responsibility to maintain the listening attitude. "I, if I be lifted up, will lift up this entire world back to the Father's house, into God consciousness."

The reason to die daily is to empty yourself of human beliefs so as God imparts itself within you there is room meaning you are not going to stand there and argue with God that what it is saying or showing isn't the Truth as *you* understand it. You have to come to God empty, willing to learn at any cost and the only cost, the only thing you must give up **is your belief in an expression apart from the expression of God** which is knowing Truth that **has** the potential to keep you from making mistakes **if you lean on it in all ways.**

You have to die daily to erroneous appearances by dropping *your* perception/judgement of them. Man is wired to compare and contrast self to others in an attempt to elevate self to a higher status of self importance. This is the problem with man in a nutshell.

In reality there is no individual self, no individual mind therefore all man tries to accomplish by his own thinking mind is futile because the mind man uses is not a creative mind but a deductive mind being used incorrectly thereby giving incorrect results.

There are many opportunities daily to stop and remind yourself of the presence of God within you. At any given moment you should be giving thanks to God for the food on your plate, the spring in your step, the smile on your face, the roof over your head, the car under your dominion, the peace and harmony unto your body. Never miss an opportunity to say thank you silently (or softly to yourself) for that which comes into your experience that is God.

All that brings peace is of God. The good you are experiencing, if it didn't come by way of your oneness with God, is temporary in that if you don't keep holding on, protecting, fighting for or building a wall around it someone else will come along and take it.

Only the things of God are permanent good because they are constantly renewing from within yourself and not dependent on outer circumstances. If you receive things by no power, thought or action of your own it is of God and is yours as long as you have need of it. When you are done with it, regardless of name or form, you pass it along as God's grace to another.

When you die daily to the things of the world you are crucifying/letting go of your personal beliefs, faith or dependence on a presence or power outside of your own being. As you rise above your outer dependencies you are ascending into the state of consciousness in which, regardless of the storm/error that presents, you can close your eyes and say **My peace is with me.**

Do you see that from the moment you release your beliefs of the world of man, see error for the no thing that it truly is you **have come into the realization that a state of peace within is life eternal and harmonious and from that moment you have made the ascension from this world into the kingdom?**

This is what is meant when it is said "I have overcome the world." You have overcome the *belief* there is something you *need* from the world of *man*, of *duality*, of *material* form. You have found

Christ within to be your salvation, your supplier, your healer and redeemer. You have found the source of eternal life within your own being where it can never leave nor forsake you.

Witness how this reverses the trend of your life. Whereas mortal man receiveth not the things of God because he is too busy seeking the baubles of *this world,* the spiritual man is not only **receiving** but he is **sharing.**

Spiritual treasures cannot be hoarded. For he who has much more will be given, for he who has little, that too will be taken from him. Spiritual treasures-grace-must always be expressed and allowed to flow from within to the without so you secretly and sacredly carry grace into your home and into your business and then you take the next step and let grace flow to your enemy.

The reason to forgive your enemy? Ignorance. They are ignorant of their true nature **as you were** living in a world God never intended for its creations to experience.

Father forgive them; for they know not what they do (behave the way they do).

If you ask Me I will give you living waters (Truth of oneness), I will give you meat and you will never hunger. I am come that you might have Life and that you might have it more abundantly.

It becomes easier to say "Father please forgive them, they know not what they do" now that you understand man creates chaos only because of his ignorance of this inner peace just as you and I were ignorant of it before we had the mystical experience.

Always remember you were them before you knew Truth. You are not above anyone **you are merely less ignorant so humbly thy self** and remember "I can of my own self do nothing, it is the Father within He doeth the works." Make sure all glory goes to God and that human arrogance, hubris or ego do not color the picture.

Prayer for the "enemy":

Understand there are no enemies in this world, there are only those ignorant of their Truth of being. You as spiritual man forgive 70x7, forgive ignorance of action because you were ignorant at one time too.

What man calls an enemy is merely someone who is opposite them in a particular view. You have *perceived* enemies because your human-ness wants something another doesn't want therefore these two expressions are the definition of duality ie individual, ego driven minds wanting, which is the chaos of man. When you are of God under grace there is only one expression of all that is therefore no duality, no chaos, no confusion and no fear.

The only reason for enemies is fear. If you know God you no longer are capable of fear for the most part thus rest and greet all as they are, brothers, kin, of the same Father. Human man treats every encounter as them against the world where spiritual man treats every encounter as God expressing in their midst and that is accomplished by being **of** the consciousness of God which is your expression of peace.

Therefore when you come up against a national enemy, a business enemy, a personal enemy know they are not your enemy rather you before you were enlightened, fed, brought to a resting place by knowing Truth. It then becomes your place to bring peace through inner communion/prayer:

Father, let all be forgiven without penalty and open the consciousness of those we call our enemies that they might know the Truth of oneness and find salvation this moment wherever they may be, in sin or in sickness, immorality or fear.

Understand when you pray for you enemy you are not praying for them to go unpunished. Firstly that is not your concern and second their sins were committed in the world of human law and will run their course of human correction. **What you are praying for is them to know God.**

Your prayer of forgiveness is to bring them out of ignorance so they may continue to search for Truth because you don't want to see your enemy, your brothers, killed you want them to rise and have eternal life just as you do. This is how the errors of man begin to lose their hold on the world. The more Truth and grace among men the less duality being expressed. Because of your love of God there will be more loving God. It becomes exponential in its potential to bring all man back to God.

This is the love of the Father and the love you must have **for all are of God as you are.** This is how you continue to rise because if you hold someone in bondage through fear, anger, hatred, greed *you* will once again be in bondage to human man/duality and will not know grace until you willingly chose to live the principles that return you to the kingdom.

What is supply?

Supply is grace and grace is the allness of God that flows back to you proportionate with your expression of God.

Supply is omnipresent within you and must flow out from you. You carry it with you just as you carry your integrity, your loyalty, your fidelity. You cannot leave it behind because supply is God and your supply, visible and invisible, is commensurate with your giving of God by being an expression of God ie harmony.

The more you live in the consciousness of God, seek its presence, have conversations with it, keep your mind within instead of getting caught up in the wounds of the world the more grace flows out from you healing those receptive to the presence of peace, God, and back to you as the added and needed things.

God is impartial Law, Self perpetuating infinite supply unto you if you are of the consciousness of that which is perpetual supply. You have to be in it to win it. Not one toe, two feet or everything but your nose. 100% baby, all the time, whooping it up on the middle path, enjoying the peacefulness of the path, the certainty of it, the Truth of it as you go along your merry way much happier, lighter, freer and calmer than before.

It is all supply to all of itself all of the time, that is the meaning of joint heir to the kingdom. All of the kingdom not degrees of the kingdom. Yes the degree of commitment to following the spiritual path is the degree of your supply, returning grace but the **allness** of all that **is** is yours in the degree of your oneness. The degree of your oneness does not determine the degree of God you get. You get all of God all of the time you are in conscious oneness. The more you are in oneness the more you are of the consciousness thus more grace returned upon you for being in oneness and releasing grace as a result to bring peace to those receptive to God's presence.

The amount of supply in any and all form you experience outwardly as peace, prosperity, harmony and benevolence, love of your fellow man, is directly proportional to your relationship with God. No awareness of God=no relationship with God=no spiritual supply=death.

Human man lives by what the Bible calls "bread alone," by the sweat of your own brow and the life blood of your body which today is averaged at about 82 years. You are living your life completely *independent* of God's supply. Sure you do the occasional prayer or church thing but it is all just for show, being there so others can see you while judging those around you. You may say *of course I believe in God! What kind of a heathen do you think I am?* but when asked **where and what** God **is** have no answer to give because it was just a parroting of what all the cool kids were saying; lip service.

You may pray every night, not have sex, go to church three times a week, not live your life outside of a few others trying to win their way into heaven by virtue and pride; both *human concepts,* so God knows zip nada about what you are *trying* so hard not to do, all that is evident is you are not in the kingdom and God has no idea you are wayward.

There isn't God *and* supply, whatever supply means to you. **God *is* supply,** God is **all,** one Presence, one Law, one Life, isness, oneness, allness, wholeness and Self completeness. God is, singular, not good *or* bad but **is,** without judgment, without condemnation, without labels, unconditioned, pure, harmonious and eternal.

A *material* sense of **spiritual** creation has led to a *material* sense of **supply** and because of that prayers are uttered to God asking for clothing, food, housing, supply, health etc, when one of the principle of spiritual living is **God is the source of all supply**-the earth is the fullness of God's glory-whether it appears as vegetable, animal or mineral, all **is** God consciousness not *matter* separate and apart from the one source that **is** the all of creation.

Man is trying to *get* from the world what God would **supply** freely if man would just stop looking outside for that which **will** fill the emptiness within.

Spiritual Capital:

When you arrive at the realization God is the source of everything necessary in your life you arrive at the realization you have spiritual capital.

Spiritual capital is the supply unto your life through knowing God aright, the only source/cause of all that is. In the human world supply is what is acquired through your own effort, your own hand, your own sacrifices. Spiritual capital is your **spiritual bank account that is yours through no work of your own hand/effort.**

Think of God this way. Niagara Falls is massive and seemingly unending in its supply of water. To look at the falls from the front you have no idea where the water comes from only that there is an unending supply of it being experienced by those witnessing it.

The source of the water is behind the falls from the Great Lakes which are supplied by streams and rivers feeding into them. From the front of the falls it looks unending but if you were to get a different view, get a more **illumined** view of the whole system you would see there is a source unseen constantly feeding water to the expression which is the falls.

You are the falls. You are supernaturally fed, supported and maintained by an invisible source. God is constantly filling and flowing through you and back to you but the source is not visible to the eye that has not begun to see past appearances.

When you arrive at this revelation you have spiritual capital and this is absolutely infinite, eternal and omnipresent. But as far as the world of man is concerned this makes no sense. It rests with you and all the other mystics of the world to express to human man that living by grace is not only practical but the most profitable way of living there is.

I was just making some breakfast talking with God thanking him for all that I have, how blessed I am, beyond measure. To be immersed in God, live in a world I know to be that of the presence within me, that I am of creation and not separate from God. To know all that is of my world, my animals, my family, my home, everything is God, perfectly harmonious. When I touch the counter, feel water on my hand, smell food cooking I know I am partaking of the allness of which I am. I express the harmony of my relationship with God as money in the bank, ease of relationship, a confidence never before enjoyed and peace unto my life for the most part.

I know that when I am with God grace is flowing to the consciousness of all those receptive to the still small voice regardless of space and time but, **and this is the revelation given,** realized it wasn't for that reason I have a relationship with God but my relationship, that which makes me feel alive, living Truth is the most important thing **because of how it makes me feel**-harmonious and peaceful. The fact that healing is the **result** of this relationship is secondary to my relationship and **that is why healing is effortless.**

Healing is effortless because it isn't a thing you do, it is a result of **who you are being,** what nature you are expressing as, and when you are with God simply because it is your absolute happiest place to be you are healing, bringing God to bear where there was no God before. Your oneness of being is the avenue of illumination, revelation, Truth to those seeking what you are giving of.

You and only those on a true spiritual/mystical path can bring peace to the world but it isn't through trying to do so it is by having a personal relationship with God which is the wholeness of Life you have been seeking from man and the world.

This is the understanding of **"conscious union with God constitutes the healing principle."** Communion with God **is** the healing agent to all of mankind and it is done through you but without thought or effort on your part. Healing is the unavoidable conclusion to the allness and wholeness received within from Source expressing as it must as your expression, your nature of perfect peace, harmony and good will to all.

When you let this presence within become what it is supposed to be to you-your guide, your rock, your resting place and your only source of understanding/Truth-you will realize how absolutely reliable and dependable Truth is because Truth is Law, immutable, unchangeable, constant and eternal in nature.

When you begin to see the world as God in form your reverence for what is changes, you caress the world with your inner eye and it is good and you can't help but smile because you are surrounded by God, harmony.

All the money in the world cannot be used as food for it is merely symbolic of supply. Money is the only supply/measure of wealth to mortal man but to spiritual man supply is of God. **Spiritual man's supply is his conscious awareness of God as all,** providing all that is necessary because God knows you better than you know yourself and knows before you that which you desire.

God is you when you are one with it and what it desires for you is to live in the kingdom of heaven on earth, to experience harmony and laughter, abundance and benevolence, the good things of this world without attachment to anything knowing there is always more to come.

God wants you to live not merely exist! An existence of monotony is torture to the soul and presents as depression, anxiety, fear, sadness, anger, confusion, apathy, disease, addiction, deepening darkness, abuse in all forms given or received, no self worth, feelings of failure, disappointment, dissatisfaction, don't care whether you live or die attitude and suicide.

The atmosphere man so desperately holds onto because of its seeming reality **is** the source of all that ails man and keeps him struggling and dying, swallowed up bit by bit from birth to death until there is only a shell of form devoid of the awareness of the one thing that would give it infinite existence-the awareness of the presence of God within all individualized as you and me.

It is the Father's good pleasure to give you the kingdom. Good pleasure. What part of that is keeping you in the world that provides most everything *except* pleasure?

When you know that knowing/deferring/loving God is the key to all supply you will ever need you realize there is nothing to *get* for all is within just waiting to become manifest in visible form in proportion to how much you allow God to govern your life-a little or a lot-and this is reflected in the amount of fruitage, supply, blessings felt/experienced in your life.

You may think money is supply but money is not supply, God's grace is supply. Don't go to God for supply rather go to God for God. All the money in the world cannot be used as food, neither gold nor diamonds can be eaten. Money is not supply except in the human three-dimensional world and even then it is here today and gone tomorrow, has value one day and is worthless the next.

In the kingdom you are not dealing with money as supply you are dealing with consciousness **of** supply, your consciousness of the fact that you embody everything necessary for a fulfilled experience as the living expression of God and leaning on God in all ways.

Man clings to yesterdays manna, to that which they possess not seeing the unfolding bounty that is the reality of Life.

Spiritual man freely gives, shares because he knows God is today as it will be tomorrow so if God is supply today God is supply eternally therefore spiritual man does not hoard, refuse or keep that which came from God whether grace or substance in form. There is always more supply when you know supply is infinite, eternal and of the quality and quantity of its source, God, universal creation which perpetuates eternally because of its purity, singularity of expression, is, and is no other ie there is no duality of man in spiritual man because that is the defining factor between human and spiritual man, their nature of expression. It is this that it is meant by "by your name you shall be known," the name of God, I am, or the human name of Man, Bob, Tyrell, Simon or Gale.

The abundance or fruitage of knowing God aright depends on 3 things:

1. Know God is your selfhood, the Truth of you and the Truth of everyone you meet.
2. Your supply has nothing to do with *man* and everything to do with your **relationship** to God through inner listening/prayer.
3. That it is the Father's good pleasure to give you the kingdom and then relax, truly let go and let God.

When you feel the assurance of God within and express **as** that assurance, the knowing, the faith born of experience then you are living the spiritual life of eternal supply.

The spirit of God, once it is allowed to come into your consciousness, operates out here and draws to you all that is yours-teachers, conditions, books, circumstances, messages, doesn't matter. Whatever you need will be brought to you because nothing is impossible to God because God is every possibility.

You never demonstrate material supply, your supply is the spiritual fruit of your conscious union/awareness/oneness with God. Your level of conscious understanding of God is the degree of supply you receive. God is impartial Law, does not give or withhold for God is eternal expression eternally expressing not supressing.

You alone control the flow of grace, good into your life by the amount of God you express to the world through your living in conscious oneness with God.

Neither do you ask for supply because if you know God you know it is infinite supply and if you are aware of God's presence in oneness with you then you know **you are the supply unto yourself** so by *asking* for supply in any form is to pray amiss and not be answered.

Prayer is communion, listening, resting in the silence and to do these things you must be out of the thinking mind and within consciousness. You have to **want** to be in oneness with God but you also must be of the consciousness through which that can be accomplished and become a reality to you, your soil must be fertile, wanting to **know** God not shut it out with what you *believe* about God. The fertile soil is the receptive consciousness, that which is expectant, eager to hear, eager to know, eager to live reality not illusion of sense.

Your received supply is directly proportionate to your union, awareness, oneness with God. You knowing **who** you are is the opening of the floodgate to eternal good, supply, harmony, peace etc, experienced. You can only experience that which you are consciously aware of. If you have no **awareness** of God you cannot experience God as your life lived under grace as your sufficiency.

Never connect/associate your supply with anything visible. Your source of supply is invisible yet tangible in form, unseen yet it is the only reality. **Your supply has no relationship to human man.** Your supply has to do with your consciously realized relationship with God which becomes the return of your supply.

It is not your function to know how, where or by what means your supply will come, it is only your function to live in God awareness and be expectant of that presence to do what it does: always and eternally is-ing/being.

Money is an instrument/form of human supply; it is a form of expression of supply, but it is **not** supply. Every time you have any thought of needing money, clothing, food, housing, companionship you should remember: **money is not supply** it is a form of supply but supply itself is infinite and omnipresent because **God is supply.** God is infinite, God is omnipresent (where there is awareness of its presence) and wherever you are God is, **therefore you have infinite supply just by knowing who you are and expressing that nature of being** meaning you present as the expression of your consciousness which is wholeness and allness, peace and harmony, kindness and joy.

Never judge from appearances or you will be limiting your capacity to receive. If you look at your wallet you are judging by appearances. Remember the story about Niagara Falls? You see only the result of some invisible source. The falls are the expression of a larger source behind it but from where you stand you cannot see what it is, only that it is therefore the source of the falls is not visible however that does not negate its existence as the proof of its existence is pouring forth right in front of your eyes.

All that you are, all that you have is the fruitage of your own state of consciousness and what you have not achieved is your lack of conscious awareness of God and nothing more, not a deficit in you, not because of where you were born or your financial status but merely because **you do not yet know what you need to know**-God in awareness by way of an actual experience of God is called the mystical experience that reveals God is and God is within you.

The realization/awareness of God within is all supply unto your being.

Treasure is not supply, treasure is the visible manifestation of supply and supply is God. As long as God is your consciousness your supply is infinite.

Money is not supply, money is a form of exchange in your experience but it isn't supply and to get money humanly often is to find it doesn't give the satisfaction it seemed to promise ie the temporary nature of joy/happiness of getting what you want is a perfect example of the fleeting nature of man's experience of good and why he tries so hard to hold onto the little he has.

The Branch connected to the Tree of Life

You might be wondering if there is anything you might do or not do that would stop the flow of good/grace/God. Yes. You can forget that there is this invisible bond between you and your creator, forget the Father is the husbandman and that all of God's good **is** always flowing forth.

I am the Tree/vine, ye are the branch; He that abideth in Me and I in him, the same bringeth forth much fruit; for without Me ye can do nothing.

Unless you recognize your conscious oneness with the Tree of Life you will be purged, you will remain as a branch separated from the Tree using up its own energy in the form of human years and then you will whither and die.

You are purged from the Tree of Life not by God but by *you* choosing not to abide in Me and let My Word abide in you.

This is the secret and the only way to become the prodigal son returned home.

You have to have your consciousness/the place from which you respond to the world, in God and not out in the world of man. You must defer to God for your direction, comfort, solace and purpose of being. The thoughts of God, the words of the Master are Truth of God and what you need to know to once again return to the Father's house here on earth.

Every branch in me that beareth not fruit He takes it away might lead you to think that God indeed does punish you but that is not true.

What is true is that if you **do not abide in Truth,** do not maintain **your** conscious oneness with God you are separated from God by your choice.

It will be you separating yourself from God's grace thus being purged, destroyed, burned up and withered away-no longer of God's awareness/kingdom/heaven, eternal and immortal.

To abide in the Truth of oneness is to live and move and have your being in the consciousness of the Father.

This doesn't mean you are connected to other people by the mind rather you are connected to the invisible as are others on the spiritual path. All are connected to the invisible and it is in this way that all men are one, **connected** to Source which is our connection to each other **through** source, not *individual mind*.

Your connection to the invisible, the Christ mind within, makes every place on which you stand holy ground. Every time you think thoughts of hopelessness and despair it is as if you acknowledge you are a branch cut off from the tree, that you are separated from God forgetting you are and have all that you could ever be or want. Your peace, your rest, your trust and your Truth are only found when you are one with Source, the branch **connected** to the vine/Tree of Life, God, sustainment of all that is aware/in conscious union with it.

Nowhere in the Master's message are there any words of condemnation; in fact the Master said **"neither do I condemn thee but go and sin no more lest a worse sin/fate befall you."**

If you return to the old *material* state of consciousness where you once again start taking thought for your life, how to make money, how to heal your body, how to have a better life, how to protect yourself etc, and do not abide in the Word of God, in conscious oneness with Source, you will be purged again and again ie live and die and live and die, without realizing the **purpose of life is to rise above death into immortality by way of knowing Truth.**

Every time you **forget** you are a branch **connected** with the invisible Tree of Life, the husbandman, the Father within, you are committing the **original** sin which began **spiritual** man living as *human* man-**thinking you are separate and apart from God** forgetting you already possess all that you are asking God for humanly. By *reacting* to duality you are forsaking, albeit momentarily, your relationship with God, the consciousness of harmony.

Just remember every time you leave God consciousness you are willingly putting yourself back into the duality of man and all the consequences thereof. You are again a branch cut off from the Tree, your Source. You will experience lack and limitation in all manner of supply **unless** "ye abide in Me and My Word abide in you, ye shall ask what ye will and it shall be done unto you." John 15:7

Human man juxtaposed to Spiritual man

I was trying to think of a more understandable definition of the difference between living God in expression and living man in expression and God popped in with "knock off."

Man's reality is a cheap knock off of God's reality. The life of man can look good but it is rarely as good as it seems to be from an outside perspective.

The life of man is a house of mirrors reflecting back distorted images you take as real but it is just an illusion, a distortion, not you, not real, not a true representation of you. Man only sees the form, the surface, that which presents and not the source behind what is presenting. Just as with a knock off luxury item. It looks good, feels good, impresses and inflates but the stitching starts to fray, the material starts to peel, the hardware breaks down. You polish it up, wipe it down, paint over the flaws and carry on with your knock off parading as designer.

You are designer baby! Not a knock off so stop living as a copy of someone else's perfection because unless you realize your own perfection you will always be a copy, a fake, unreality but know **you are nothing less than an individualized expression of God, creator of all.**

Man is only looking for something real, honest, trustworthy and dependable to cling to, that which makes sense of this thing called living. Knowing God through awareness provides that which you seek.

The human world depends on powers, always seeking one power to overcome and destroy another power. This is what constitutes the human experience; their very security is always based on external power but just when they get the power it isn't power anymore because someone else has more power.

Is there no solution to this? Will there always be more and powerful? Must we have these powers to protect ourselves? Or will man eventually destroy themselves looking for greater and more destructive means of power over others by which to rise themselves?

The dependence on a power, personal or outside of them, is the human side of life and when you realize **the secret of life is in no power** then you have achieved spiritual freedom through knowing Truth.

When you have nothing left to depend upon but an absolute silence into which the spirit of God can come do you have security.

God is the only security that will last. You will never secure peace on earth as long as it is achieved through the ways of man ie treaties, wars, promises and truces. Security will come only when you ultimately realize human weapons are of no power, our armies are of no power and that there is a stale mate and something else must take its place and then will come peace on earth and with it good will toward all man.

It isn't what goes into the mouth that defiles you it is what comes out of your mouth-you either express as man of duality or man of spirit. God doesn't care if you smoke or what you smoke, drink, eat rich foods, snack on crickets. The more of God consciousness you imbibe the less those things of the world attract you, demand your attention and soon they may not even be a part of you. The point is this: God asks you to give up **nothing** of your human ways **except** the belief in duality. All the rest comes in due time.

Do not think you must be pure before you present to God, God is the purity you already are, God just helps you uncover it and live it to its fullest. Does that mean you will never partake of the things of the world? Of course not! A drink, a smoke, decadent foods may be part of how you enjoy life but **only if you are not desirous, dependent or experiencing karma as a result.**

God doesn't **make** you give stuff up, God releases you from them as you grow in conscious knowing and that is why spiritual evolution is so effortless-it requires no thing of you but to follow where God leads skipping to a song only you can hear.

That which has been the **missing** piece to understanding God, living a spiritual life and receiving the abundance set forth for God's children is:

1. **Conscious** awareness of the presence within as that of God and in this knowing of God as Self $1+1=1$, wholeness, completeness, oneness, union with source, your true nature and origin.
2. It is by this **conscious** understanding of oneness that you live in the kingdom here on earth, living among mortal man calling no attention to oneself but silently, secretly and sacredly correcting error and releasing God's healing grace to the world.
3. It is in this inner contact all reality of being is received and the Truth of error is revealed

as the universal *belief* in separation from God which results in the experience of duality ie good and evil, good luck and bad luck, or just good and bad. All error stems from man's *belief* in being separated from God.

4. **Only as you become consciously aware of the presence of God is the presence of God functioning within you.**
5. It is only your acceptance of God, your conscious realization of God and an actual **experience** of God that allows God to function in your life, be your life, do your life with you just doing what you are needed to do and the rest of the time enjoy your family, your work and your relationship with God.

You are the temple of God.

This must be so if the kingdom of God is within you then you are the temple in which God functions but this temple was not made by hands meaning it is not material or matter but spirit in form, God manifest.

Now here is the mystery. People look at themselves in the mirror and they see what seems to be a corporeal body and immediately identify this with themselves whereas this body is **not** you, this body is **yours,** you are incorporeal spirit and you are **not in** this body. You have never been in this body and you have never looked out from within this body. Surgeons have looked from head to foot and haven't found you and they never will. You are **not in** this body and this body is **not you,** this body is **yours.** Is there less of who you know yourself to be when you cut your nails? Your hair? Have a foot or other body part removed? Are you less you because there is less of your visible body? Of course not because you are not in your body, your body is yours therefore not intrinsic to you being you. Your body is an expression of **your** consciousness in form.

Where am **I?** Not of the body you think yourself to be of. **I am** not here, **I am** risen, **I am** not in any tomb, any corporeality, **I am** not in any tomb of body or matter, **I am** the living temple of God visibly expressing.

All that you could ever need to know about God can be read in less than an hour. Reading about what God is is one thing. **Becoming one with** God is what takes the time and effort on your part to put in.

Man goes to church to be filled up, to be kept on track, to have something to think about during the week that might make them a better person or to feel cleansed of sins. **You cannot begin to learn how to be a true Christian until you start wanting to be a true Christian.** If you go to church once a week or on holidays you are paying lip service, want something for nothing ie only willing to expend a few hours a month or year. You can continue on that path until the dogs come home and never know what spiritual life is all about. You can devote hours a day to reading the Bible and memorizing verses to bring up at parties and discussions but until you take the time to stop, get quiet and listen for God within that is all you will be doing-waiting.

The actual meaning of the word **learn** doesn't mean to pump in, it means to allow what is within to flow out to bring Truth to individual consciousness, that is what you are learning, what comes from within you that is new and not a rehashing of man's words from human mouth to human ears. I am not saying don't go to church, it serves a purpose **just don't put your faith in what is being taught.** Take yourself there with God awareness and see if the people, the sermon, the preacher don't start to change their ways.

Churches and religious gatherings are not to go to learn from **but to release Truth to** not by words but through conscious oneness with all that are there, seeing others as the Christ and see if the atmosphere doesn't begin to change to more reflect the peace you are bringing when you bring God into their midst.

All you are ever called to sacrifice are your "ways of the world" ie duality, no other sacrifice is ever asked.

It is your right as spiritual man to draw upon God for supply, support and protection. But to receive you must be in oneness and in turn that oneness becomes the allness unto your life experience, the experience of a life lived by grace.

Silent, secret and sacred-no one is to know you are studying about God, no one needs to know and no one should know. This is your love affair, your journey, your enjoyment and your personal experience. Man will tear at you for these beliefs because man cannot believe until he is ready to. To the world you say you are "working on yourself," only you and those of your household/consciousness ie teachers and other students, are those you speak to about spiritual matters for only spiritual man will be able to understand your questions.

Understanding omnipresence:

How to understand omnipresence when so few feel God's presence or understand the implications of it.

Envision the sun shining on a scene in your mind, some place where there are at least a couple of people walking around. Now feel as a cloud comes between you and the sun. The cloud is cutting you off from the sun that is all around you but at the moment, though sun shine is **omnipresent where you are** there is a cloud, a barrier, *something* keeping the sun from reaching you.

God is omnipresent but unless you know God, are aware of God, know where God is and who you are in relationship to God you are cut off from God. There is a cloud, a barrier, between you and God and God knows nothing of the barrier. Does the sun know a cloud just shielded its rays from hitting the ground? No! The sun does what the sun does because it can do no different.

God is the same. God is not a thing, a person or anything you can name or identify, label or conjure up. God is a name designating that which created this world that is unexplainable and unknowable to man.

The barrier between you and God is your name, what you identify yourself as, your nature of being. 99.998% of people will identify as human, flesh and blood Roger, Doug or Pat. If you have a name God knows nothing about you because you are man, disconnected, unaware of God, you are under a cloud while at the same time another stands under the full glory and warmth of the sun, soaking it in, basking in it, reveling in it.

Man's barrier is his identity-i, me, mine, Erik, the man with an ego/personality separate and apart from every other person on earth. Human man is an island alone and adrift always protecting its own at all cost.

You come out from under duality, that which is "blocking" the sun, by breaking down the illusion of darkness by dying daily to error by knowing Truth until soon the cloud is gone and you are running free in the warmth, free in the arms of God, free knowing **I am the child of God.**

When you know who you are you know your name and by your name shall ye be known.

The clouds are only there because you are holding them there through ignorance of the sun on the other side. Let them disburse, let them become the nothingness they truly are, blow them to the four corners and watch the earth melt, error dissolve.

This world is not to be saved by might or power nor by any agreements men make among themselves but by My spirit, by the still small voice that only operates through the consciousness of the individual who opens themselves to it and is silent enough to hear it.

The still small voice reveals Truth of man's world so when you leave your house go out with an inner assurance, an inner peace that you are carrying something greater within you than anything you will ever have to meet/do/face in this world and it is closer to you than breathing and is called **My peace.**

My peace doesn't come to you my peace is something you let flow out **from you** because you embody it, it is of you and has to be **released** from you. Wherever you go you have to carry **Truth**-"my peace goes before me, this presence goes before me, thy peace is my grace, thy grace is my sufficiency." You carry that and then the people out in the world feel that benediction which you are releasing and then they feel your peace as relief or release from something that was weighing on them.

Don't expect to *get* My peace, you can't do it. You of spiritual knowing must **give** My peace to the world by letting it flow from within to the world and in doing so **receive** that which has been cast upon the water-the grace of God you released for all mankind to benefit from-returned upon you 1000x. You walk up and down this world smiling with the realization God's grace is your sufficiency. Just think what that does to all those fears of bombs, car accidents, divorce, bankruptcy, loneliness and lack!

Thy grace is my sufficiency, your harmony is my expression.

Now you will find that you are dispelling the fears of those you meet without saying a single word for it is the presence within that is the Comforter. Everywhere you go you are dispelling fear **if you realize thy grace is your sufficiency, My peace I give to you, My peace, eternal peace, divine peace.**

You do not feel like others who present in the world and that is because you want nor need anything of the person you have encountered moreover you are open and giving of that which you are of, grace, and that my friends is like the best fair food you can imagine! Inhale, take a big bite and feel a little less stress in your life. Want to feel that feeling again? Get curious.

You of the spiritual path are carrying God, the allness, the wholeness, the nature and quality of God out into the world when God is your expression. God is not controlling you, making you act a certain way it is the Son looking **to** the Father how to be, how to express as Truth and the easiest way to express as the Father is to move your butt over and let God go first. Easy peasy. You are the instrument through which God's grace reaches this world and without you it will not be known as it needs to be to bring man back into conscious union with the Father as it was in the time of the awakened/illumined man Jesus the Christ.

The name of God given to Moses would have been lost but for Christ's presence on earth as Jesus the Christ to reveal Truth to the world. When Jesus left this expression the disciples carried the name of God out into the world and True Christianity, awareness of the Father within through conscious union, was the Christian religion for 300 years before it was abolished because it gave too much freedom to individual man. What was brought forth in its place is what exists today-the Old Testament dolled up with the *name* Christ but not the **nature** of Christ, called Christianity which it is not because it is based on mosaic law not grace.

Why is what you are experiencing as orthodox Christianity not true Christianity? The designation Christianity means **of Christ knowing** but there is no God in the laws of man, there is no God in the awareness of man and there is no God outside of man. What is called Christianity today is missing the one thing that defines true Christianity-**Christ knowing,** knowing God by conscious awareness, knowing the name of God and the name of you.

Without those few who knew the Christ by way of conscious awareness of the God within themselves there would be no Bible, no written record of the coming of **individual Christhood** or the meaning of the coming of Christ. There would be no organized religions based on a single Godhead and there certainly wouldn't be a possible way to understand our connection to all that is without them.

There is a responsibility that comes with knowing God and that is sharing God aright and in that way will receive the bread you cast upon the water pressed down and flowing over, the added things, the joyous things, the beautiful and practical things as God in manifest form. Do not malpractice yourself by taking credit for the work of God through you and **remember which I you speak of** when it passes your lips because that determines always whether there is the presence of grace or the presence of man in your midst thereby defining your experience.

Unless you have a God experience/mystical experience all the things of God are but *philosophy* to man who does not know the Truth of God but give thoughts and ideas of what God is through their finite understanding of life.

Beliefs are not Truth.

Truth is Law and Law is unchangeable and eternal. Beliefs are subjective and individual thus rendering them unreal/illusion.

God has no pleasure in your dying, turn ye and live.

God never has had any pleasure in your dying and God has **never** been responsible for a death in the history of the world and the only reason death has ever taken place is the ignorance of spirutal Law. The **ignorance** of the fact that there is only one power/presence of harmonious expression thus no power/presence in/of infection, contagion or heredity **except** the power you *give it* through erroneous belief in opposites.

Don't make the mistake of blaming your patient/family member because they are under some belief of ignorance or sin or disease. Always remember that whatever you believe you or another is suffering from isn't Truth but **a universal belief, the atmosphere, a false understanding of how this life works according to man, history, all of recorded history** which mankind has accepted and yielded to.

Never blame anyone for their actions and never try to make them better than they are, *you* can't because you are trying to do something yourself instead of being the instrument of God.

Never tell someone to be more loving, kind, generous or forgiving because they cannot be other than they are until **they know Truth** by realizing that those qualities are of God and not of human man to express.

Do not make the mistake of worshiping someone else's consciousness; worship only the Truth that comes **to you** from within your own consciousness for that is the only way Truth is known.

Truth is given only to those who seek it and those who seek Truth never fail to find it.

Your daily life **is** your spiritual life. There is no distinction made because when you know Truth you know the sabbath is every day, every second of every day when lived in christ consciousness **for the sabbath means a time of quiet contemplation of God** which for *man* is a mere act, rote, ritual of refreshing/washing conscious clean of errors once a week on what is termed a holy day.

Every day is holy and every day you are in conscious union with God is the sabbath. It is merely a resting from the concerns of the outside world to rest in that which **is** your strength and peace but man uses it as a washing machine to shine himself up so he can go get dirty again but after a while there is a stench that just one holy day a week can't wash off.

Our nature as spirit dictates we live as spirit which is conscious, constant union with God. In this way and no other are you child of God, joint heir to the kingdom. There is no separation from this union unless you inadvertently fall for the illusion of error/duality otherwise God time is all the time, where you want to be because of the ease and **practicality** of **letting** God govern, direct and fulfill your life through your visible body in an experiential world of spirit of which to partake.

But to partake of the allness that is God you must be of the **consciousness** of God expressing the **nature** of God. Give God get God. It is really that simple once it rings true in consciousness, then there is no stopping this train! Unless of course you try to navigate!

Remember God is **always** the navigator, that is the only way this works. You do as it is revealed to do because when you navigate you crash/are of duality which is what you are working away from. You let God go first, first thought, first contact, first words and in this way and this way only will you find harmony expressing in your experience.

You only express what **you** allow to be expressed, you always have free will as to how you express yourself to the world, the nature you believe yourself to be and in that choice **take complete responsibility** for the consequences/karma returned to you pressed down and flowing over whether of man or God.

Do not say after one month this isn't working. It isn't that **it** isn't working it is that *you* aren't working it, you aren't studying and practicing and giving up duality. You want to, you say you do, you try but give up saying *it* isn't working.

To the degree you allow God to have governance over your life is the degree of expression of God **as** your life. If you are not expressing the nature of God more and more and human traits less and less you are not walking the talk you are merely mouthing the words, *do as I say not do as I do*, which is duality on its face.

God is always known by its nature which is harmony. If you are not getting more and more harmonious you are lying to yourself about the work you are actually doing to know God. Knowing God is up to you and you alone, no one can do it for you so if you aren't seeing results **you** aren't doing the work. Plain and simple. God is and when you know this for yourself and stop screwing around with duality it is then that you reap the benefits of knowing God aright.

The power of God:

The power of God is not the kind of power man ascribes the word power to. The "power of God" is the **presence** of God within you expressing its nature as you. Therefore the power of God is your **awareness** of God's presence within and the nature of that presence in expression-harmonious.

The **power** of God is in the knowing and deferring to the **presence** of God and it is this knowing and deferring that allows human man to become aware of their true nature as that of harmony which frees you from the chaos of man, from the dual expressions/nature of man, frees you from the illusion of human living that is of pain and suffering, lack and limitation, illness and death.

The **power** of God is in the knowing of what and where the **presence** of God is and knowing this presence is **of** you. You are not flesh and blood, you are an expression of God and the knowing of this Truth is the eternality of your existence.

You are protected from the ways of human living by **knowing Truth**-who you are-and in this knowing have no fear, no desires and no needs of your own for you are whole, complete, supplied and maintained by that which you are of but only when you know Truth to **live** Truth in expression. Man lives by erroneous beliefs and suffers the duality of those beliefs but spiritual man lives by Truth, God, and reaps the allness of God-spiritual perfection.

You do not give of God to *get* the things of the world, *material* good, you give of God to **feel** God, grace, allness and wholeness because that is your return for sharing God with another. This is the blessing of giving and scriptural Truth:

To receive you must release, give; if you hoard no more is given because to receive you must give of the allness you embody so others may feel the wonder of knowing God aright.

You already are of God and it begins to function through you when there is an awareness of it and this awareness reveals Truth to you and this is why you can more easily surrender your will, your ego, let go and let God. It is true you already have it, it is true you already are it but it is not true that you are yet demonstrating it because the experience itself must come to you, meeting the Father face to face, the mystical experiencing.

This is when God, grace can come into demonstration and not just be words you read but measurable activity of good/harmony in your life where there was not any before.

The world is an illusion:

The illusion isn't what is seen, ie tree, car, rabbit, air, man; it is how man has **classified** all that exists visibly *as* material substance/matter according to *man's* system of theory and discovery based on all things being *separate and apart* from each other therefore a tree is unlike steel which is unlike flesh in their composition, base make up, chemical analysis, expression.

Human man experiences everything around him as matter/material separate and apart from God but it isn't and **that** is the illusion. All that **is** is God, God in form, all form, all creation, all that is visible and invisible is of the same source expressing **as** what is necessary for this world, this universe and its inhabitants to exist. All that was created in the beginning, invisible, spirit creation, becomes visible/manifests as that which is needed according to the consciousness of man as being spiritual man. As the consciousness of a few rises byway of God awareness the consciousness of all mankind is raised because what is given of God to one is given to all who are receptive.

The illusion: mountains, sky, earth, cars and people, houses, ie *matter/material* in form separate from all other form.

The reality: all is of God, **spirit** in form.

Once you know Truth you can never look at anything the same because **now you know the Truth of every single expression is God in form.** All is God and this is why all is harmonious. This is why all that is of the world works in concert, all that is **is** for all that is and why your body functions the way it does with your nose away from your feet and your butt away from your nose.

If all were not of one expression there would be no harmony between man, animals, minerals and plants meaning what would man eat if what created man did not also create that which sustains them? What if that which created the plants didn't put the sun and moon in the sky, rain to feed and soil to nourish? What if the rocks ate people and plants produced rocks? Do you see why there can be no other explanation than a singular source of all expression?

All that is didn't come into expression out of random dust particles; all that is is **intelligence in and by design.** The water you drink, the dirt that nourishes the plants that feed the animals that feed you are available to you because **you are the reason for them.** All that is this universe was created, brought into expression by God for God's greatest expression, you when you know your Truth.

When you can understand that each ice age, each cataclysmic event this world has experienced over man's measure of 4 billion years has been with purpose, is of the Divine Idea so you could utilize what was created then **now.** Everything that has ever happened, changed in and of this universe was by design, with purpose, each phase of existence building upon the one before it, what man calls evolution and is the reason there are natural resources for industry to produce what maintains and sustains us today.

If there hadn't been the animal and plant life of each epoch, if there hadn't been clouds of poisonous gases, earthquakes, eruptions and floods that changed, covered, removed and deposited, you would not have valleys of fertile soil, fresh water from hidden sources, deposits of life saving salt and all manner of flora and fauna your body can utilize. If there were no singular consciousness of creation there would be no natural resources like water, metal, gas, coal, oil, salt, minerals, crystals, plants, fish in the sea and birds in the air to sustain and maintain you **now.**

The minute you sense error on your part against yourself or another immediately ask for forgiveness-that was wrong Father-then make the appropriate adjustments for though you have asked and were forgiven the error must be rectified in the world of man of cause and effect. You created an error and you must correct it, pay the corresponding judgement otherwise the forgiveness you asked for was merely lip service trying to cover your butt.

Forgiveness is predicated on you knowing that though you erred if you change your ways because you see the error of your ways you will no longer suffer the human consequences of those ways because you have grown beyond the consciousness that created those errors. **This is a numbers game** in essence. The more you know Truth the more you can rest and trust in God's Truth. The more you trust the more grace you receive, the added things, things following, peace in your experience. It is your willing devotion to God **not** yourself that brings the allness of God to bear in your life and not just the paltry scraps man thinks to be treasures.

Human man does not express love, God expresses itself through you as that which is felt as love coming from you. But what of those who give off everything but love in their atmosphere? They do not know harmony, God, rather they experience duality completely under the hypnotism of good and bad being *of* things and people and cannot express anything unlike their nature of duality.

One of duality may express what they feel is kindness, helpfulness, consideration but it is always tinged with human want so when they come into proximity of another of duality there is an underlying current of chaos because either or both could change their nature from good to bad and blow the whole situation up into something it never was except for duality and the human reaction which creates chaos and not harmony.

Human man, self, has nothing to give but duality and duality is no thing but personal perspective therefore human man can give nothing that is real, of Self, God, to another. The only way to ensure harmony in your experience is **to be** the harmony that is your expression and to be harmony you must be **of** harmony and to be of harmony you must **know** where harmony resides-with God and only God therefore to give of anything that is of Truth to another you must be of the Truth you desire to express.

God goes before you and makes the crooked places straight. The Law of harmony you express from becomes the Law of harmony of your experience/expression therefore where you go harmony goes before you as the state of consciousness that will greet you.

Truth is not revealed with the mouth but in the silence.

If God **is** error **isn't**.

Self surrender is the price of God.

Gratitude is the currency of God.

Eternal life, wholeness, purpose, joy and abundance are the gift of God.

No one is exempt from the relationship of oneness-you are **of** the Father, spirit is your nature so even if at this moment you feel no God within, know it is inevitable (yaaaa!) because you are **of** it, cannot escape it and will come to the point where you will give up all you *believe* to **know** that which is Truth.

God is only and ever awaiting your recognition of its being within you and your awareness brings its governance of peace and harmony unto your experience.

God doesn't give life, God is Life so to have Life you must have God in awareness.

Separation from the consciousness of God is not knowing harmony as the atmosphere and currency of your life and is the definition of duality.

You are already the child of God in your essence but so was the prodigal son when he was eating with the swine. He was still the son of the king, heir to everything but it didn't seem to do him much good. Neither does your heirship in Christ do you much good until by contact with this presence within your own being you re-establish that oneness then the infinite good of God flows through. But regardless of how high you ever go, even to the consciousness of Jesus the Christ, you will still be at the point where you will have to pray for light, wisdom and understanding. **You never stop knowing God, it is what you will do for all eternity** learning and growing and being more and more like the source of you until you ascend having completely released the duality of man from your consciousness and are living wholly God consciousness. This is the entire purpose of this life. To return to the Father and live the Life of the Father and not the life of illusion as human man.

Your state of consciousness is your demonstration of God thus far. If you are here you came here by an activity of your own consciousness and if you hadn't been prepared for it you would have been led somewhere else. Do not second guess choices that keep you moving forward, that is fear and you know fear is only what you make of it-reality or illusion.

There is no such a thing as mental powers, those of healing or those of evil to cause ills. All this proves is there is a stronger suggestion overpowering a weak one. What makes a thought or suggestion stronger? The consciousness of the one perceived to be the receiver/how much that person believes another can have power over their minds/lives through thought.

It is your perception and degree of fear associated with it that makes something "strong or weak" against your being. I'm strong of body, I don't get sick. My body is so weak I get everything. Duality from personal perception, illusion and not Law.

There are moments as your oneness deepens when you lose the feeling of yourself. This is when you glimpse what it is like to be higher in consciousness just for a second. In the moments of its coming it is unfair to say that there is a you, you have been so completely dissolved there is only the realization God is there and not you, you are behind the hand picking up the cup but not the one controlling the hand picking up the cup. This isn't an out of body experience it is an out of personal self feeling as if seeing through another's eyes. It is and you are. You are experiencing just for a moment what is to come and it can be scary but know all is harmony for all is God which means all that you experience on this path is **purposeful** with the ultimate goal of living by grace, harmonious, joyous and free so absolutely nothing on this path can hurt you, damage you or do anything to you you don't want it to. **The only thing this path can do is make it easier for you to go from human to spirit.**

Most of the time when you are in oneness you are aware of you and a presence, you are *being*, listening to God and talking with God as you go about your day in what humans would call a work/play flow, effortless expression regardless of what task is being done. You are under the Law of God because you have deferred personal will/ego in favor of following where God leads. When God leads the road is straight. When man leads there is no road, just a lot of footprints going nowhere.

Your world is the product of the measure of the I that you are showing forth. If you were wholly unconditioned by the atmosphere of man then your world would be entirely abundant and harmonious. But you have only been able to manifest a certain degree or measure of that infinite divine consciousness therefore your world is exactly the measure of divine consciousness that you are realizing ie you know what you know and that is where you are now until you understand another Truth and release another error of man's thinking mind and rise in consciousness again. Whatever still remains of error in your life represents the degree of your consciousness still living the duality of man.

The integrity of the practice is known by its fruitage and those who are on a spiritual path, when practicing and living Truth, are the best of the best healers because they are almost constantly **in conscious oneness with God which is the healing principle itself, that which does the healing.** Therefore the healing percentage of a true spiritual healer will be much higher than one working in the metaphysical/mind realm.

The ability to heal is the fruitage and by your fruitage you will be known. If you become a healer with a high degree of healings it is because you are so in oneness with God you know without thinking the nature of error and the universality of error and know it to be one thing and one thing only-the belief of being separated from God. **All error branches from this one belief into the myriad of forms it has taken in the human world as discord, disease and death.**

Though it is called a healing it isn't a healing as man understands. A better word might be **revealing.** You bring harmony to a person by bringing God into **your** awareness which brings the allness of God into **your** experience which does what is needed by its omniscience, all knowing. You have revealed Truth **to yourself** to dispel the error presenting and this Truth has been felt by those asking for God.

God is a presence not a word. God **is** an experience and God **is** knowable by actual experience. God is not what you read or believe without having had an actual experience of God. To know

God is to sit in the silence of your own being, set the table, open the door, pour the coffee and await your visitor!

The more you give silently of the Truth you **know** the more it will multiply itself upon you but if you try to give anything before it has become revealed Truth to you it diminishes what you are sharing and you will have **less of it.**

Until then do not teach anyone because **you have nothing to reveal.** Why? Spiritual consciousness comes out of an attained consciousness and not out of *intellectual knowledge.* Anyone can read and get a glimpse of the meaning but until that which is read is **returned/revealed as Truth,** practiced and lived it has no value to yourself or another because it is merely words until it has been **experienced.**

God is the harmony unto your being when there is only one guiding intelligence of harmonious expression and a corresponding receptivity to do what is needed to be done of a visible nature/by your hand to do.

God=harmony=harmonious expression=grace in your midst

When you are **of** creative intelligence instead of man's finite knowledge and understanding you are within the allness of all that is, one with it by the nature of your being. You are of the same source as the couch you sit upon, the ground you walk on and the air you breathe. All is of the source of original creation in different forms but all are of the **only** source there is-creative intelligence expressing as all that is visible and invisible.

Man is the only inharmonious expression because man is the only one of God's creations that has the capacity to use the mind incorrectly as a thinking mind instead of a deductive tool to aid God activities. Man of his own thinking and doing does both good and evil. **A mind of duality cannot be in oneness with God** and not being in oneness is what keeps you out of the allness of God.

You cannot intellectualize God, you can only know God by way of an actual experience of God within bringing awareness of where God is which reveals the nature of your being as spirit, child of God.

You are a progressively unfolding state of consciousness and you have always been unfolding to the point that you are right now where you can accept the Christ consciousness, are ready for oneness and **willing** to let God live your life from here on out.

The key is not in you doing, it is letting God do for you.

It is not having to forgive the unforgivable, give the forgiveness in and of yourself, it is not doing to bring money or supply to yourself, it is letting God be the avenue by which all that is for you can come into expression as and for you. You do not forgive someone unforgivable in your eyes, you give it to God and forgiveness flows from you as the very consciousness you are to the situation at hand. You merely give God a way to bring the harmony you yourself cannot bring about. What you are not capable of doing is and has always been meant for God to do **through** you to bring harmony which is your natural state of being. Let God do all the work, you just open yourself up to what becomes of that flow in your experience.

The Self of you does the forgiving that you, human, ego, i, cannot provide. What you can and do provide is a way for the qualities of God to flow out and express in your experience.

What is of God cannot be given by man but neither can it be taken by man. No man no matter how they try can take your peace *unless you allow it* by coming out of the consciousness of peace into the consciousness of duality and picking up the sword. Therefore the peace of God is yours no matter what is going on outside of you because **peace is yours as long as you are with God.**

The words in marriage vows, "that which God has joined no man can tear asunder" has nothing to do with the vows of marriage or the laws of man it has only to do with communion, you and God, that what was joined in the beginning no man can change or make an untruth.

Spiritual literature has nothing to do with human or mortal man ever, it always references you and your relationship with the I of you, God within. This is another example of orthodox religion using spiritual Truth in a human way to elicit a response of control through fear and condemnation.

God didn't create *human* man and human man is not created in the image and likeness of God. ***Human man*** **is spiritual man separated in conscious knowing from Source thinking it is alone and must fend for itself.** Before the belief in good and evil all **man** knew the principle of life was within their own being, the Christ consciousness, the seat of the Father in which to entertain thoughts of the Father.

You are a child of God who has tried to live life by their own finite mind and physical power, surviving by brute force, manipulation or going with the flow hoping to get along by going along. You were born into an atmosphere of duality which conditions you to see and measure opposites: love and fear, desire and unworthiness, lack or riches, health or disease, happy or sad, alone or together. All of man's life is based on one or the other possibility of that which in and of itself has no opposite but in fact just **is.**

A car is. It may be a good car or a broken down car but it is a car. Peanuts are enjoyable for some, deadly for others. Your hair is fine, thin, curly, gray or healthy but it is still at its base hair. Just hair. Things are not this or that they just are. It **is.**

The label you give person, place or thing is your qualifying/labeling or judging according to and depending on *your* conditioning, habits, upbringing, faith, belief, family history. This is why there can never be **peace** on earth brought about by *man*. Peace can only come to earth when enough men have found their true nature and are the beacons that lead the rest into the light of spiritual illumination which results in spiritual living which will be **peace** on earth because **God's** presence will be experienced more than the *duality* of man of times past.

God is only present where there is an awareness of the Christ within and are being an **instrument** through which God's grace flows out to bless, be a benediction to those receptive to the spirit of God.

Your desire and receptivity of that which you do not know becomes the resulting consciousness which you will express **as** when you are **of it.**

Years ago when I would get mad during an argument if I was asked why I was mad I couldn't articulate it; I just was. I learned the understanding would come to me later on, just slide into awareness with a BAZINGA! That is why!! It makes so much sense now! and then I could have a conversation with the other person as to why I was upset because I truly knew.

Most people believe they are angry/reacting to what is immediate to them but a lot of the time it is something buried that has been triggered. Hindsight is 20/20! I was experiencing God giving me that which I desired to understand to deal with the situation and heal it. I knew it came **to** me, I just thought it was of myself, not knowing it was of **Self.**

I know this is common for a lot of people, to rest, to wait for the reason so you can understand it from a different perspective, not what was going on but **why** it was going on. Human man always reacts to the "what," the appearance, feeling etc, instead of understanding and healing the **why** which is always at its base duality.

God has been with you throughout your life and if you look back over times when miracles happened, perfect happenstances, the peace from within that released you from prison/bondage/slavery/unforgivingness you will realize God is not foreign to you and as you bring these incidences up in memory they bring back the same emotions and they were good always, never led you in the wrong direction, never made you feel anything other than harmonious. I say this to show that the God you know of man, what you have been *told* is a fallacy, a myth, an unreality because you have absolutely experienced, albeit without understanding, the true God, the God within that is love, support, kindness, understanding, rest, peace, direction, vitality, release and relief.

Now do you see God as the harmony, good, peace unto your life? Can you imagine that feeling of accidentally getting grace multiplied and within **your control** by how much you desire to be in oneness with God? I desire God endlessly for the reasons mentioned above, to remove illusion from the world, from myself and from those of my consciousness so that they too may become receptive to that which makes you whole once again.

Blessed be who walks with Thee for thine is the kingdom of heaven, consciousness of My peace.

The only reason man is holding onto the world is because they don't know what God feels like or what you feel like when God is living your life. When you find that which tickles you, brings you peace and makes you smile you hold onto it, stay where it is, attach yourself to it, soak it up, roll around in it happy as can be and are careful not to lose it because it becomes your anchor, your safe place where everything makes sense, is easy, light and joyous with your best friend always in residence for comfort and companionship.

The only reason man hasn't found God aright is because they haven't been taught the true nature of God as divine love, allness. You have been made to believe the only way to experience allness/wholeness is to *get* them by winning, taking, manipulating, lying, hard work, long study and years of modifying your personality through emulation of those you admire/worship in *hopes* of living the life *you* think you desire-the job, the spouse, the house, the monumental feat accomplished but unless it comes from God it will be hard won and temporary because you are trying to be something you are **not**-*human*.

Prayer for all:

I want you to love the person you are allowing God to transform you back into, I want you to find your laugh again, breath deep and feel freedom fill you from head to toe. I want you to have a gentle smile on your lips that tugs at the corners when your inside conversation with God slips out into expression. I want you to consciously understand **who you are** and **why you exist** and let the feeling of God warm you, support you, guide you and provide for you in all ways.

We live in a click society. Click the button and get a prize for just a bit of money. God is a journey of unfoldment with no click button. God cannot be gotten materially, intellectually, monetarily or physically.

Truth cannot be gotten the way man gets things, through the mind of desire, work and determination. God is **revealed** when there is no desire for anything of the world because the world has nothing left to offer, nothing that fills the emptiness within.

Welcome to the land of living water, God awareness.

Man is out of order because man is not of the consciousness that is the order/harmony of all creation-thus the saying "man is separated from God," from God's consciousness which is the allness, the everything you ever need in this visible experience. When you know there is nothing of the world, of man that you desire, peace instead of chaos reigns.

When you feel lack you have forgotten you are already fulfilled

When you fear you have forgotten your Truth

When you feel alone you have forgotten you have a best friend

When you are sick, in pain, dying you have forgotten your true nature

When you are anything but fulfilled you have forgotten your Truth and all you need to do is go within and see Truth smiling back at you.

When you know your Truth harmony, peace, joy and abundance are what you experience and it is good.

We are all joint heirs with God therefore we all draw upon the same infinite source for our infinite supply. You need not labor, strive or struggle for that which is already divinely yours. All that anyone possesses at any time is the level of their own state of consciousness therefore belongs only to the possessor. That which you have is the result of the fruitage of your state of consciousness and has nothing to do with you doing in the world to get the things of the world.

You can have as much of God in awareness as you desire by removing the boundaries of human duality from your awareness. Nothing you can get from another or through your own power will ever really be yours rather it will always be a construct, an illusion of the human mind subject to the laws of man, duality.

When things are gotten by human action instead of received through grace, your connection with Source, it has the potential to be good or bad wherein that which you receive through no effort of your own is eternally yours and is harmonious because it is an outpouring of your state of consciousness (God consciousness) in visible expression.

All that the Father has is yours. The realization of this Truth would enable all men to live harmoniously, joyously, successfully without fear of one another, without greed, envy or lust. You would be in the land of milk and honey where all is provided for you by way of your relationship with God.

The awareness of God as the source of all that is necessary for life under grace will forever solve the problem of supply and therefore establish and raise God's reign of peace on earth because man would no longer need to *get* rather man would be active and alive **doing and being** the expression of God as God presents itself to the world as you.

If it isn't the Father revealing it you can say rise all you like and nothing is going to happen because there is no power, no effect, in the *saying* of words if there is no conscious understanding of the Truth behind the words. "I of my own self can do nothing" is one of the most profoundly true statements ever uttered. So as long as you of your own self can do **nothing** there must be a period, even a split second where you know nothing, are nothing, desire nothing but become a vacuum so that the Word of God, the consciousness of God, the bread of life can spring forth within you.

Moses was slow of speech but the Lord promised to put the words in his mouth and did. When you find yourself in any situation you don't need to think clever thoughts or work out in advance the outcome you desire, rather you **let God go first** meaning before you think, before you open your mouth to speak from your human identity of frail ego, stand back of yourself and let God go first. Let its words be your words, let its countenance, its nature of harmony, its divine love of all that is be your expression in the world.

Step aside and let God go first in all ways. You need the humble faith that says "I can of myself do nothing so I will let God come forth and show me harmony in my midst."

There is no God on earth except through the consciousness of those who have an awareness of God and make way for God to function through them. The natural man receiveth not the things of God, the natural man knoweth not the things of God. The natural man is not under the law of God.

God can enter your experience only **through** you, your consciousness. You already have the kingdom of God within you but must open out a way for the imprisoned splendor to escape as Browning puts it; you must become aware of it to benefit by it.

There is no way to get God to come *to* you, it already **is** within you. You must open out a way for the presence of God which has been with you from before the earth was to manifest in your experience, become the activity of your life.

You will not find God in a book but you can read a book to remind yourself to go back to the kingdom of God within yourself. Metaphysical Truth/written Truth/the Letter of Truth is intrinsic to spiritual living and leads to mysticism which is living Truth, expressing as the presence of God within **feels.** This is what is called the mystical experience and is that which separates spiritual man from human man-the knowing of God within by way of an actual experience of the presence of God within.

This experience is the key to spiritual living and is the only way to live in the kingdom, in the garden of Eden, to be in the world but not of the world for you are no longer of the consciousness of man rather of God living among man to share God's grace to bring peace to man through your expression of harmony.

If you wonder why it takes a long time to attain the mystical consciousness remember that it takes as long as is necessary to develop the conscousness that can look at error and know Truth, see God at work/always being without attempting to make something happen that you think needs to happen to move things along through human means/actions.

But what if something, a tree, looks like it is dying? Remember that this is the place in which this principle is even more necessary than when you are looking at a healthy tree where you can readily agree that God is functioning. Now through spiritual discernment alone you have to agree that there is no evil, no death, no destructive power therefore there is no need for God to change anything, improve anything or heal anything. **So whether or not that tree is dying is up to who is beholding it.**

The one who can behold that tree and smile because of the spiritual discernment of seeing God at work will watch that tree be raised up into life. The beholder of God in awareness bears witness to God in action.

When the Master says "Ye shall know the Truth and the Truth shall make you free" remember that the Truth that you are to know is that **I in the midst of thee am mighty.** That My peace is your salvation, that quietness and confidence is the prayer, that you do not attain your good by might or by power but by gentle Spirit.

You let God's grace flow through you and you tell no one of this happening, remember go and tell no *man*. Tell no one what things you have discovered, do not throw pearls/wisdom before swine/those not ready to leave the world of man/not of the consciousness of spiritual discernment.

These things that are whispered to you in silence, the Truth of God's allness unto your life, all supply, all support, all maintenance, shall be shouted from the housetops as demonstration not by you telling the world of God's grace but by **demonstrating** it by the supply/bounty you express as the result/effect of living under grace.

You are the visible expression dedicated to the service of God, ordained of God. The Christ has ordained the minister and the temple.

Only the awareness of God will lead to Truth, not human knowledge which is finite.

Salvation:

When you sow to the spirit God is the harvest, the fruitage, grace received in visible form and invisible expression. It is your choice to sow either to the spirit and reap life ever lasting or to the flesh and reap corruption-sin through duality of powers at play in your experience. You cannot sow to both.

By sowing to the spirit you wipe out **further** karma, the penalty/consequences of wrong doing byway of wrong thinking. Understand you are instantly forgiven when you ask God for forgiveness **but that doesn't mean you are free of the karma associated with the transgression.** But, when you have been walking the walk for a while there is no negative karma/duality returning upon you because you aren't creating any. All of your former wrong thinking and doing is wiped out in a moment of repentance not through years of suffering, trying, paying a penalty, self flagellation and guilt rather this moment you are set free however the Master said "neither do I condemn thee **but go and sin no more lest a worse fate befall you.**"

Thy sins be forgiven you, not after death, not after years of torture but in the moment of repentance. **When you repent you are saying you are washing your hands of your old ways knowing** they have not satisfied the hunger deep within though you have tried every avenue available to man to find that inner satisfaction.

Man cannot find the satisfaction they crave on earth living as human man because satisfaction is a product of knowing God aright, it is the way you feel because you know God and know where God is and this knowing is what makes you feel satisfied, harmonious and peaceful and becomes your expression to the world. This knowing is your **salvation,** your freedom from all the ills of human man living in the atmosphere of dual powers.

―――――

Remember God knows nothing of your life as a human, not about your sins, accomplishments, money, investments, housing, pain or joy. God only knows God and it can only know you as the individual expression of itself when you seek to know it. It is only in the seeking of Truth that you find Truth and it isn't something you can actually find, it is something you realize, become aware of deep within yourself. It is a recognition of another within that is the Truth that had been sought, the quenching water to your search for understanding of being, of Life.

The more you commune with God the more of the river, the avenue of supply, is available to you until soon there is no river of supply but the allness of supply. Think dribble to flood.

Always remember you can stop sinning/being human at any moment-before the thought is finished, or after it has been erroneously formed, at the first sign of discord realize your error and correct it. The sooner you recognize your own errors the sooner you can correct yourself and return to the consciousness of God and keep yourself under grace.

Do you see now it is you, has always been you who has separated yourself from God through thought and action? Before knowing God these experiences affected you but as a Truth student when you fall back on your outdated human ways the sting of error is much more keenly felt. Why? Before you didn't know God's peace and love so there was nothing to compare the returning karma to meaning karma/chaos in some form was all you had ever known.

Fast forward to knowing God and living by some measure of grace. This is nice you admit. Smooth, peaceful, balanced and easy, so much easier! Now act like a human, do something of duality-see unreality, sin, disease, lack, do something of omission or commission and let yourself feel the feeling of being separated from God in consciousness. When you are at this stage of God understanding you will feel much more discomfort than before for the same transgressions because you now **know the feeling of God** and you lose it when you fall back into duality. The pain of error felt by the spiritual student is more acute than one who doesn't know God. It is like being separated from your best friend for a while, it feels empty, unsettling, cold and you will do what is necessary to have them back in your life.

Spiritual work is wholly spontaneous. It is not based on memorization, ceremony, ritual or rules, it is a livingness and within that livingness you are being. There are no formulas or rote repetition or use a treatment from the day or week before because this work doesn't lie in the realm of the mind. That which you devise, work out through the thinking mind is of man therefore is not of spritual knowing that **Truth resolves every error without you doing anything** as long as you are living the principles of Truth.

Keep the realization of your relationship with God secret and sacred. This relationship, maintained in silence and secrecy, appears outwardly as harmonious human relationships and experiences.

It can be hard! I had an experience that was a true miracle and wanted so much to tell my husband about it but I knew I couldn't because it wouldn't have made sense to him how it came about because it was my demonstration. A few times I almost did tell him but I knew the moment it left my lips it wouldn't be the same to **me** anymore. Why? Because I shared a secret moment between me and God. Could I tell my teacher if I had one in flesh? Absolutely! Because they would have a complete understanding of what the experience revealed-God as the only reality of expression. So it stays locked up inside of me where it brings joy and gratitude, more devotion because each Truth revealed and experienced builds upon the one before and these Truths are what flow from me to the world bringing back more miracles for me to witness.

You do not use spiritual power, you allow spiritual power, omnipotence, to flow through you. You do nothing but be open to God with the understanding what God **is** is free to move from one of higher consciousness out into the world as a free flowing release of God's allness, peace to those ready and receptive of it for the purpose of healing or awakening to the God within.

The healer does not try to direct, control, channel or use God for a patient's purpose. Your role as a spiritually enlightened being is to further the contact of God with the unawakened individual identities of God ie human man.

Every person who has not had some form of spiritual awakening of Truth that **I am the consciousness that was in Christ Jesus** is asleep. Human man whose breath is in his nostrils is experiencing an unreal perspective of reality where they stumble around aimlessly even if they think they have a direction all mapped out for their lives.

Having a relationship with God **is** your goal in life and in that relationship realize you are not flesh and blood but **of** the image and likeness of God-consciousness expressing. I believe once you know a few things probably never said to you in this way you will see truly how easy, relaxed, enjoyable and fun a righteous relationship with God is.

Spiritual illumination reveals the harmony of being and dispells the evidence/experiences of material sense. It does not change anything in the universe for this is a spiritual universe but it changes your **understanding** of the universe. Always there have appeared men bearing the divine message of the presence of God or the Divine-Buddha of India, Lao Tzu of China, Jesus of Nazareth. These and many others have brought Truth to man and man has confused the **message** being given with the *messenger* in visible form *giving* the **message.** Man has put *faith* in the *messenger* and not in the **Truth** being given **by** the messenger.

By putting faith in Jesus the *man* instead of knowing God aright through the indwelling Christ man has failed to comprehend it was **the consciousness of God as and through Jesus that made him different, made him the Christ, illumined of God.** By trying to seek good through Jesus the *man,* man has failed to find the omnipotent, omnipresent and omniscient Christ of their **own** consciousness and this is the fate of 99.95% of man today who looks outside of himself for God.

In this new consciousness you are less angered by the acts of others, less impatient, less disturbed by their apparent failings. Why? Because the peace and quiet of your own soul/consciousness/being is the Law of harmony and success unto **your** world of daily experiences, goes before you to bring grace to those on your path in need so it is grace that greets you wherever you go and less humanhood.

God is not a power that is going to do something, God is the presence that **is** whatever is needed to bring harmony unto you. Watch this carefully because until now the whole world has been losing its demonstration. Man thinks of God as a power over evil and that is setting up evil as a power and that defeats you right from the start.

Evil is not a power and that is why the Master could say "resist not evil." In other words his entire demonstration was **not** proving that God heals sin but in saying "what does hinder you?" sin had no power and Jesus was not going to make a reality out of sin by condemning anyone for it. He didn't *believe* God healed disease, he said "what did hinder you? Pick up your bed and walk." He never thought of God as a power that was going to do something, he **knew** God as a presence and by being **of** the consciousness of this presence there was *no thing* to do anything to and no body to do anything for. **God is the answer to every problem.**

God is the answer to every problem and that is why you don't have to know the name or claim, all you have to know is the name of God, I. When you get God it will see that the patient is taken care of, you don't have to know the basis of the claim, all you have to know **it is an absence of God that is bothering the patient** and if you can bring to them the consciousness of God's presence then it makes no difference what their problem was because they have no problem now because all that is deemed a problem by man is merely an illusion, ignorance of Truth **God is as all,** and God is all good in which nothing can enter that defiles it or makes it a lie ie duality.

All error no matter name or appearance/claim is an illusion created by the atmosphere of man believing in two powers which is only and always a separation from God in conscious knowing.

The presence of God within you greets the divine presence of another and it is the greatest joy in the world for another to be recognized in their Truth and not judged by their messy humanhood.

To see all as they truly are without judgement is to see the Christ in all, not the human judged by appearances. No matter what appears to be, know God is back of all just unrecognized as Self, source, the life that sustains for an eternity, not 3 score and ten of human life.

Dolly Parton is a real world example of living by grace; not lip service pretending to be godly but true God consciousness, spiritual living. She has so much supply she gives it away and never seems to lack. You know from interviews God is her rock, her home, her life and it shows as the consciousness she expresses from. She not only gives glory to God, she **lives** her glory **in** God as child of God giving of her love of God to the world through her expression of love, kindness, benevolence, and joy.

Then there are others who are famous, rich and through circumstances lose their wealth, fame or life. Why? Because they are living from the consciousness of man-get, take, favor, live a life consistent with what man *thinks* would be awesome, idiilic in today's society but rarely is what it seems to be on the surface.

Practice and study are the key to staying in God consciousness, in the now, in the present moment where you are in oneness. It is not doing anything, not something to learn or keep rolling around in your head. Being in God consciousness merely means being with God, chillin' up in there. You know how you are when you are just humming away, the mind is empty and happily quiet as work just flows from your finger tips. That feeling within is the consciousness of God being lived and expressed as your peace while doing what is needed to be done.

There have been secret fraternities throughout the ages, the original being Masonry and within this organization the secret of spiritual identity was known and taught to every Mason and the reason Masonry became a world power for good. Later it was accepted more or less as a ritual and ceremony rather than a spiritual principle (changed to accommodate the mind of man and not the spiritually discerned) but all secret fraternities were founded on this basis of knowing your true identity as spiritual in nature and living the expression of that nature.

When the Christ dawns in individual consciousness the sense of personal self diminishes. The Christ becomes your real being. You have no desire, no will, no power/ego of your own; the Christ overshadows your personal selfhood and you happily allow it!

To take no thought is to refrain from conscious thinking and to let divine ideas fill your consciousness. Since you are individual spiritual consciousness you can always trust that consciousness to fulfill itself and its mission. You are the instrument facilitating the divine activity of Life expressing and fulfilling itself through you.

More and more you must become a spectator or witness to life, to let it just be without your input, your mental or physical reaction. Too many times we humanly interject ourselves into situations and that involvement just messes up the mix. Stand back and bring God onto the field, into awareness. Let it **reveal to you** the Truth of what you are seeing, let its Word flow gently into your being to calm your mind or to give you that which you are to do.

One of the major things man has to relearn is to stop reacting, stop taking everything personal and stop thinking that you lack in any way, shape or form. You the human are never of any use to a situation however the presence of God among the godless is the salvation unto the situation and God can only be present if you bring God onto the field to do its work.

Your work is done, you brought God onto the field. From here on out anything that you are to do is because of the impartation from God as to what **it** wants you to do, **not** what you humanly want to do or think the situation needs of you. **No situation needs you;** you got yourself into the situation by acknowledging/reacting to it now get yourself out of it by healing it.

You must learn to be a beholder of Life and its harmonies. Each morning you should awaken eagerly to watch the new day unfold, be excited and expectant that the day will bring God into view where you never witnessed it before. Why? Because as your spiritual awareness radar becomes more attuned, more automatic, you don't need to ask God to come onto the field (though it is always nice to feel; the awareness within brings lightness and joy) rather your oneness of being has become your normal and natural expression.

Several times each day bring to mind the fact that you are literally witnessing God all around you now that you know what God constitutes. You are witnessing the revelation of Life eternal, the unfolding of consciousness and its infinite expression, the activity of Spirit and its amazing formations.

In every situation of your daily experience learn to stand back of yourself (i step to the side metaphorically in my mind) and see God at work, witness the play of Love upon your affairs and watch God reveal itself in all those around you.

Truth cannot be known by the human thinking mind because Truth cannot be intellectually discerned. Truth is a **spiritual** quality and it must be spiritually discerned. It must enter your awareness through spiritual sense, spiritual consciousness. This spiritual sense is attained in two ways:

1. By the reading of spiritual or inspirational literature which includes practice and study.
2. By contact with those whose consciousness is of the same consciousness of God.

Spiritual consciousness is contagious ie it is impossible to be in the presence of those who are making even the slightest degree of effort towards this awareness without receiving some if it from them.

The greatest awareness is found in the word **receptivity.** "Speak Lord; thy servant heareth." "Be still and know." "I will listen for Thy voice." Always it is **be still, listen and be receptive to revealed Truth,** more and more light, more and more understanding. There is an infinite reservoir of spiritual good and by opening the inner listening ear you open your consciousness to an inflow of the Word, the consciousness of divine Spirit.

When you have had the experience of God within you are advancing to a state where your interest is in God and the things of God, where you must pray without ceasing and this life must be a dedication, not a dabbling. This is an all or nothing ride if you are going to take it because if you think you can jump in and out, on and off the spiritual band wagon you're going to suffer the sins of the world more and more acutely every time you let your mind wander back to the duality of man to *get* something or do something that involves picking up the sword whether mental or physical.

Ye are the light of the world and there is not an individual on earth who is not here as part of a divine plan. Everyone has their own particular mission, everyone here is to serve some particular part of God's purpose.

As a *mortal/human man* you do not fulfill that mission as no human has ever nor can ever fulfill a **spiritual** mission but by **letting go** of your humanhood, the *i,* ego, personality, divinity and the divine plan are **revealed.**

The Spirit of God is ever-present to lift you up out of every infirmity but it **has to have consciousness and form to express through.** Jesus was illumined of God, knew God through awareness and it was this union of being that made way for those miraculous and instantaneous healings in Galilee. There had to be disciples to carry on the healing/revealing of Truth because **God always acts through individual consciousness** just as it acted through Moses, Elijah, Peter, Paul etc, as it has acted through mystics, healers and teachers of the recent past.

God operates through the instrumentality of individual consciousness when *individual* ego/personality is purged of desire for self-glorification, self-profit or for whatever it is that the temporal/

material world represents to you. Only when you let go of the world can God express **as** the fullness **of** your world.

There are no large or small amounts of God, there is only the infinity of God. Think of grass, all the grass in the world; if you could burn it up all in one day it would be growing again because there is only infinity. You may have a certain amount of dollars to your name today but that doesn't constitute supply because if you spent it, gave it away or destroyed it, it would begin to multiply the very next second because infinity is flowing so spend it, give it, whatever you like because you cannot stop the flow of infinity as long as:

You recognize God is infinite consciousness expressing itself in your life.

God is always now. God cannot quit expressing itself on a certain date anymore than it can start expressing itself after you have given a treatment. The patient isn't really any better after a treatment than before, it is only now they are exhibiting more of their divine selfhood. You don't make them better than they were before you merely bring out in your treatment a **greater measure** of **their** divinity for **them** to recognize/feel/become aware of and get curious about what it was that touched them.

You always meet others on the level of **their** consciousness. You give bread for bread, not pearls of great price for bread for that will not nourish consciousness rather turn it away. You can only help people from their level of consciousness which is why you do not give of words that hit up against a wall of resistance rather express how knowing God within makes you feel, this is what you want the world to know of God.

There is no God in *words,* there is only God in **expression.**

The path of spiritual awakening is not a straight line, it is a spiral. You continually revisit beliefs you thought were Truth and find higher levels of understanding on which to rest upon to easily release the erroneous belief in light of Truth now known.

You can approach any subject of this world spiritually without a preconceived opinion of right or wrong by seeing reality-God, is, not duality. When you open your consciousness to a spiritual solution it comes forth in a human way that you could never have thought of or planned. All over this world there are prayer groups praying for world peace and 99% fail. Why? Because they are going to a spiritual God to find a human solution based on their idea of right and wrong-subjective/erroneous/duality.

How do you get where you are to be? By constantly keeping your consciousness open and listening for the Word of Truth as it is the light unto your path. Keep desiring God, keep the knowing open to what **is,** not what is desired by you, i, self. It is this love of God, the desire to know and have constant communication with it that brings back to you abundance in the form you understand abundance to mean as well as all the added things.

All that is necessary to know Truth is to ask in earnest. The knob on the door is always and only on your side so it is always and only up to you whether that door gets opened or remains shut, whether you start on the path to spiritual living or remain human living the life of duality.

He performeth that which is appointed me to do

God's presence, knowing, understanding and wisdom through you as you is the Life of you because whatever is revealed to you through conscious realization now belongs to you, Truth received not by studying and memorizing but by awareness of what **is,** what is revealed to you moment by moment as life unfolds from the river of infinite knowing flowing through you by virtue of your oneness.

"He perfecteth that which concerns me"-God does a far superior job compared to you no matter your level of skill because skill is dependent on personal knowledge. God created all there is to know. God's infinite knowing trumps your finite knowledge so let the big guy show you some new moves. Just know sometimes the move shown can be the loss of a job or something equally as surprising but **know it is all good,** it is to put you where you are supposed to be, where your talents and personal expression are to further your experience of God as you.

So many people say they are doing God's will. Unfortunately because they don't understand the Bible from a spiritual consciousness they take it literally and feed the hungry and lift up the poor in the literal sense through physical labor and mental grinding while begging for money to support *their* worthy cause.

If what you are wanting to do or are doing as your *calling* is costing you money, taking away from instead of adding to your peace and joy, if you have to advertise for help and ask for donations what you are doing is **not supported by the God** you say you are doing work for. How do I know this?

In all impartations God supplies the means. It may not be tomorrow or next month but when it comes into visible form or higher understanding you immediately know and can trace back the events that led to the current happening. It is like lightening flashing through you as your deductive mind connects the dots and once again you are flooded with love for God for its ways, perfect in every aspect from timing to quality to individualization. The gift of God is better than you could get for yourself because it is perfect in its application of its plan for its life as your life which is over-arching and complete not finite and myopic like man.

If you experience the presence of God it will be proof to you of its existence but more so it gives you a **principle** whereby you can help your neighbor, friend, family and enemy without their permission, acknowledgement or recognition. You do not need the permission of man to bring grace to man, it is the will of God to awaken all man to their Truth and Truth reveals the true nature of man as spirit and this is the grace of God in action.

Silent, secret and sacred is our bond between God and all of that which is God. You change nothing rather you are the way by which change can happen.

When you pray for peace you must be willing to give peace for only what is released can be received.

You don't have to do anything to attain God's peace except be open, desirous of it. This is the life of inner silence, the life of listening, the life of true prayer.

It is a secret way of life lived within your consciousness but not a life in which you keep secrets. It is the secret, God, you happily share with those ready and receptive of knowing God.

You have nothing of your own, all is of God but you are of God so all that is of God is yours and will be given therefore you have no need of having/getting/hoarding because you receive by grace, manna daily, in proportion to the degree God is your expression.

You have to practice the principles of Truth for them to become evident/experiencial in your life because this is a cumulative system-the more you study and put into practice what you are being taught the further along the spiritual path you are going.

When I started my journey it was at a time when I *needed* or was in lack and supply did eventually come, but there were months and months during which I had to remind myself each day **your grace is my sufficiency** and mean it. Each day your consciousness is being transformed from *I want, I need I take* to **I have, and I know why I have.**

You must cast bread on the water to get it back because you can't get someone else's bread.

You of yourself do not give or receive rather it is an ebb out and a flow back of abundance without the hand of man being involved. Remember this is a supernatural universe not a material universe thus all is spirit/consciousness in form not matter or material in form separate and apart from God. **When you change the fabric/consciousness of the experience you change the nature of the experience.**

I am not body I Am consciousness, Spirit, Life, Truth. The seed drops to the ground and the Life of the seed becomes the Life of the tree again. Stop identifying yourself as the trunk of the tree or the body and identify your **Self.** Realize you are **I** consciousness and that **I** goes on and on and on and becomes the next form of which **I** may appear as you individualized.

Your outer demonstration can be no greater than your inner acceptance of and living the life of the Christ in oneness with the Father.

The easy way to remember the difference between I God and i self is this:

You are either the **I** am of God or the **i** of individual man.

Peace on earth starts in your household first. These are the embers that spark the flame of desire to know peace not only for yourself but for the world, all man.

Spiritual intelligence can only bring spiritual things not the material things of man's world of duality.

Remember if you are to claim God as your consciousness then you must claim your consciousness to be a benediction or blessing unto all who are drawn to you. This is Law and if violated, meaning you are not a benediction to man, not living the nature of God, you will suffer the sin, the error of duality. You cannot ride two horses in the same race and until you can ride a horse sitting backwards you are of no service to anyone, especially yourself.

God is only where it is known in consciousness by way of an actual experience of God. Where God is realized/known freedom takes place, the freedom to know how to live under grace instead of under the mortal laws of morality.

Where God is not realized the bondage of man to the illusion of two powers continues and man lives a false life.

God isn't dormant in you, **your** awareness is dormant and needs to be awakened.

Awake thou that sleepeth-you. You must awaken to that which is within.

The impulse of God when there is work to be done feels like a desire instead of an undertaking because it is not you who is undertaking it meaning all the things of your body you used to put time, effort and money into ie to get strong and healthy, mean nothing when you do the work of the Father because when you are in oneness what is given you to do through your visible form is supernaturally supported by the Life that is living your form. The energy, intelligence, physical strength, ingenuity, dexterity etc, **are of you** so not only is what given to do never difficult it also provides new avenues of learning and awareness.

It may seem strange that you don't have to tell God your problem or that you don't have to ask for anything, not even make statements or affirmations. Just sit and let spirit enter in.

Do this throughout the day. I call it "checking in", just a "hello Father", "I love you", "flow Father flow", just something that takes you within to the place that the world cannot disturb and let peace be your expression to those around you.

You must develop a sense of receptivity so that you can become even more aware of the very presence of God in its holy temple which is your consciousness, in the secret place of the Most High, which is the Holy of Holies where you receive guidance, wisdom, illumination and rest. In quietness and confidence shall be your strength.

When you meditate if unbidden words, thoughts or feelings come into your mind don't fight them, don't tell them to go away, just let them come and know they are not your thoughts but the thoughts of the world temporarily touching your consciousness. Since you know the reality of human thoughts you know they are not yours per se but just things that are floating in the atmosphere of man that slipped in through a crack but never worry! Respond to them as you would any other illusion-this is of man and not of God therefore it is not Truth.

The duality of expressions man lives by is man's sense of *their* strength or weakness and the strength/weaknesss in/of those around them. Duality gives man the opportunity to *react* to any situation in any way they deem necessary to express who they think they need to be in the moment to guard against another's expression of perceived good or bad, strong or weak, smart or not, influential or not, wealthy or not, happy or not, and *react* accordingly. This is the definition of duality-doing what serves you and you alone.

Pray for right teachings and soon a book or person or that which will suit you perfectly will appear in your awareness. What appears in your experience are what I call bread crumbs, the trail God lays out for you to follow to learn, become illumined, experience revealed Truth. It is what man calls coincidences; those things that you become aware of now that your focus is in and not out. They are God's way of opening your consciousness to Self step by step, showing you Truth which is needed to help you surrender your duality, see grace in your midst, feel the true nature of the Father every time you connect the dots, follow the bread crumbs and feel God respond within as peace, harmony, joy or a kiss on the forehead.

Every time you feel something brewing within, a lightness, a giddiness, ask Father: "what am I to pay attention to Father? I can feel a shift coming, something I am to know that is just going to rock my world." By acknowledging you are aware of God you bring God on the field and will get a response. Every day is like a treasure hunt with God. What am I going to stumble on? What is going to touch the very Christ of me and drop me to my knees with gratitude and love? What little nugget of wisdom is going to take me further from man and closer to God?

Your **expectant** atmosphere of being with the Father from waking until waking (you ask God to keep your consciousness open when you sleep to further its work) is what allows God to express in your atmosphere. When you are expectant of the Father you are living in the consciousness of the Father and receive what is of the consciousness of the Father-everything.

You are the way by which the imprisoned splendor can touch those receptive so as often as possible during the day give God as love, comfort, peace and joy to release God into the atmosphere of man, the consciousness of man for those receptive to receive of God.

Revel in the feeling of God's presence in every kiss of wind, every hint of fragrance, the sun on your face or rain on your head. You smile, you can't help but smile because you are one of the very, very, very few who know **why** they are smiling.

To pray for things you desire to make your life happier, wealthier, healthier or for dominance over another in any form is to pray amiss, miss the mark, fail because God doesn't know human man or what he suffers. Why? because if someone is suffering they are human and cannot be known of God. But to pray for, seek, desire more that is of God ie light, wisdom, understanding, love, guidance, Truth of being-these things lie within the awareness of God to receive for they are the things of God and not of man.

The Truth of life comes from God not from man. God is spirit and must be know spiritually through the activity of God in your consciousness for the things of God are but foolishness to man. Man cannot understand God because man lives as finite flesh and not infinite spirit. **This is the switch that must be flipped,** Truth known in your consciousness to rise you from man whose breath is in his nostrils to the son of the most high, joint heir to the kingdom of heaven to experience here on earth in this form.

Being in oneness with God makes life effortless **not** inactive. It makes you busy but not the busy of man. The world of God is supernaturally supported, you are just the leg work for your part but all that comes before your point of activity was done by God, by its perfection of seed time and harvest so all that is necessary for your expression is in place.

The seeker and the sought are One.

You change your response to life when you know the Truth of life and stop living the illusion of life. Why? Because Truth reveals there is nothing to react to because there is no Source, no Law, no power and no objectivity to *illusion* ie does not nor can ever exist as a reality therefore there is **no thing** to react to, fight against, fight for or change. Why? Because there is no thing you do not already possess, the allness of God already **is** within you and knowing this **is** what changes your response to the world around you.

You now know the Truth of all error is duality, the belief in God *and* the belief in a power against God and in that knowing just think or softly say "this world" meaning the illusion of man or "maya", Sanskrit for illusion, or silently say "this isn't right is it Father" because you know illusion when you see it, and in this way let the error go as the no thing it has shown itself to be. This is why it is said "do not resist evil." It doesn't mean not to resist in the sense of giving in, bowing down getting taken advantage of.

You do not resist evil because if you know the Truth of evil there is no thing to fight because all evil is *individual perception* not Law therefore no thing, nothing, illusion thought to be Truth.

This is the beauty of knowing Truth, there is nothing for you to carry, nothing for you to do except heal error by knowing Truth which brings grace to bear for you and those receptive. This is the **freedom** of being of God-there is nothing for you to do, God is the governing influence, the mover and shaker behind the scenes with dominion over all that is because all is of it and all you are to do is respond to it, God within, not man. In this way you help others find their way home to live the promised life of peace be with you until you transition onto your next adventure.

To live the spiritual life means to feel the presence within, the connection, the safety and security, the dependability and reliability, the unchanging nature that is the rock on which you stand. Being in the consciousness of God is normal and natural, runs in the background like a favorite song but when you need it, feel fear, get angry, you ask God to come on the field to be the comforter, bring itself into your presence and feel the calm descend, the pulse slow, the anger dissipate and the apology forming to both parties involved, yes you included.

Forgive yourself for erring. We all do it. All you can do is catch it, heal it and do what is required of you to bring peace to the situation ie amends, apologies, judicial correction. And you grow from there. "I'm not going to do without listening for you first God, and then yes, I'm going to listen even if it is not the answer *i* would like to receive. Your way or the highway is my motto now Father."

Spiritual man has the capacity to sin again and for this reason must live in the now, the present moment so you can hear the voice that is your guide, your Truth, your place of inner peace that is unknown to human man who only knows peace by accident.

What does knowing Truth have to do with natural disasters? Ah, human man calls them natural *disasters* while spiritual man knows all to be God expressing, not *good*, not *bad,* not a *disaster,* not a *horrific* event but rain, wind and temperature **being** what rain, wind and temperature do at certain times. It is not good, it is not bad, it is, and it is of God therefore to see the Truth of weather is to remove the power from it thus knowing it for what it is.

This isn't to say stand out in the middle of a storm with a pitch fork in your hand, head up, mouth open like a turkey screaming to the four corners of the world "do with me as you please." That is not knowing God and I hope your life insurance is paid up. The **knowing** that storms and things of *nature* are of God removes the perceived threat/fear/consequence to your being/expression/life experienced as lack, loss, pain, suffering and death. A weather event is of God and you are of God so how can that which you are of take you out of infinite existence? It cannot.

You may lose this visible form of expression but that is not **you,** that is no thing more than a form by which you experience outwardly what is your Truth inwardly. You are **not** in your body, your body is an extension of your consciousness in form but **your body is not you,** the I of you. You are eternal in nature and incorporeal in form therefore nothing can change you, nothing can hurt you and nothing can take you from infinite expression when you know that to be your Truth.

If you are threatened by weather you can escape it and you won't need God's help; all you need to know is this: this threatening storm isn't a thing at all it is an activity of the human mind thinking there is something other than God facing them. All is God therefore the storm is nothing but an image in thought that has no power and in that realization the illusion that there is anything other than God in your midst it will dissolve.

What you are witnessing is still there, God as weather, but it is no longer separate and apart from you, has no power other than of its source, God, therefore there can be only harmony in your midst. Can you leave this expression because of the storm? Ie humanly die? To man yes you may have died but spiritual man can't die so that is merely another illusion of man who doesn't know God.

Suicide doesn't end your life, it merely prolongs the suffering of the human experience in that when you die as a human you come back again at the level of consciousness you left the world the last time.

Suicide does nothing that you think it will but if you realize there is no death, that you will have to come back and do this all again in the hopes that at some point you become aware of your Truth why not take the steps now? Right now you can die to the life you were living which is in essence the reason people commit suicide; a death of humanhood, of duality, of living "this life." No matter whether it is this life or the tenth from now **the purpose is always the same**-to get you to a point where you begin to question why you are here and instead of getting stuck within your own thinking finite mind allow that which is of higher understanding to give you that which you are seeking humanly.

Life will never change to suit you, you must change to experience Life as it was meant to be lived and only then will you understand why suicide changes nothing of your existence except adding to the lifetimes you suffer needlessly separated from what you seek-peace and understanding of which both belong to God.

I was talking to God saying the blessings are just too numerous to count and his reply was I am living the life of blessings, this is the flow of grace visibly manifest, God in my midst. Thank you Father, my heart is full.

God is the Law behind all that is known to be **constant/eternal** universal expression. Therefore if God is Law and Law is constant/eternal/unchangeable that is unequivocally stating God is constant, impartial, impersonal, like begets like in the degree of expression/identity/knowing therefore God cannot be a man, personal, give or withhold, play favorites or make you jump through hoops to get what is already yours by birthright.

Man *created* a God like that for control of other man and it's called our *Lord* of the Old Testament and you now understand there is nothing spiritual about man or man's laws. Spirituality comes only when you **leave** the ways of man, child of ignorance and willingly choose to express harmony as the child of the most high. There is no God in the laws of man because there is duality in the laws of man, not grace.

The qualities a thing, person, place or condition express to you are what **you bestow upon them by your reaction to them.**

Therefore if you express as human man you embellish what **is** with adjectives and verbs, descriptive language based on *personal* history. Nothing ever just **is** to man, it always has to be qualified/judged and filed according to the *thinking* mind. The nature you express as is evident in your description of the world around you. If you see bad people, chaos, lack, limitation and pain you are human because those descriptions are the qualities you give the situation, you embellish according to your history and personal nature, ego.

Spiritual man knows Truth, there is no this *or* that, this *and* that, there is only **is**:

A dog running away from the owner

A man taking that which doesn't belong to them

A weather condition

A court decision

A fight

An accident, arguement

Those are seen through the eyes of a spiritual man. Human man would qualify the dog as bad, the man a thief, a deadly weather condition or an unjust court decision, a losing fight, a horrible accident or a heated arguement. Do you see the difference? Do you see how when something is seen in its Truth there is nothing more to discuss about it? It is and there is nothing to change about it. But qualifying something leaves it open to interpretation, bias and another point of view.

There are no two points of view in the kingdom, there is only one consciousness and it is God being God, is-ing. Is cannot be divided and that is what a point of view does, it opens it up for individual interpretation based on individual history and not Truth therefore anything man comes up with as a descriptor is not real, false, unreality, illusion, duality.

―――――――――

There is no grace in the world as good, rather the only good in the world is merely better than the opposite of bad and that good and bad are merely perceptions of what level of discomfort, disharmony and chaos is personally acceptable to you which means what you call borderline bad I may call fantastic and what you call great I may find acceptable therefore there is no universal standard by which to truly gauge/qualify good and bad, happy and sad, sick and well, lack and wealth thus making it *subjective* according to personal history and this is the reason there is no Truth to the *belief* in good and bad because there is no Source, no Law and no objectivity to that which is *subjective*.

This spiritual Truth trips people up and it did me as well because how can you be living an unreal life if you feel real? How can there not be bad, evil or that which is definitely not the good, the ripe juiciness of life? Because *human* man has added a component to the Truth of God that completely changes every experience of every person in the world-the belief in a power apart from God.

A world without a belief in a power apart from God to act on you leaves only that which **has been from the beginning**-God/harmony. God is the only Truth but to know Truth you have to understand that how *you* perceive the world around you is **not** the reality of the world around you. You have added labels/qualifiers/personal beliefs of evil, bad, error, sadness, lack, illness or disease to your experience.

Man perceives the universe according to their limited understanding and by putting labels on things you know nothing about purely because of what is presenting you are adding your flavor, your spin, your personal interpretation to God's Truth. What you see on the outside is not the Truth of what is actually there. You are looking at the poorly wrapped gift assuming what is within is of the same quality therefore you reject it mentally out of hand. **You judge what is not seen by what is seen because you have no idea there is anything other than what is visible to be known.**

You have to see **God's** Truth in your awareness instead of your perception of what is. God knows Truth because God **is** Truth. How do you see with God awareness? By becoming aware of the Father within who has been waiting patiently for you to answer the knock, open yourself up to that which is new, fresh and alive and finally live the fullness of life you were created to experience.

Don't believe ever that the function of God is to increase your material good. Too many metaphysicians have spent years trying to make a spiritual God increase their human sense of good instead of being willing to abandon the human sense of good for the spiritual perfection of is, unqualified life.

Once you understand the nature of harmony mere human good will become of very little import in your experience. You will still have human good, laughter, fun, friends, adventure, but the experiences won't be for experience sake rather knowing the source of what you are experiencing is the allness of God manifest as that which you are experiencing.

God doesn't think, God is consciousness, is, being. Man is forced to think because man is trying to figure out who and what he is in the world. God **is** the world, God is what you are searching for and it is within the silence of your own being and that is why you haven't found it up until now. When you find God you won't think either, not in the way you did before because you will have allowed yourself to come under the governance of **is.**

Man thinks God to be outside of himself thus all that God is supposed to be to man **is outside of man to get or obtain.** How does man try to get from God? By asking, demanding, begging, ordering or subverting because, well, God is too slow and I know what I want so with God's blessing I will plow through this world to get what I want.

The truth of God however is the complete opposite and this is the **difference** between human man and spiritual man. God is within, is your being, is everything of this visible and invisible world for all is God. Therefore you do not try to *get* God to give what you lack you **rest** knowing the supply of your entire existence is within you.

This life is a closed system of Law-that which is and always will be is Law as Law by definition is unchangeable and that is what makes it dependable, reliable and constant. You are of this Law when you know there is a Law to be of and chose to live by it. That which governs the universe, the stars, planets, atmosphere, the seasons, the weather, the grass, births, seed time and harvest, your nose in the right spot and your feet made for the purpose they serve is Law, God, Law of harmonious expression that Self perpetuates eternally.

There is nothing other than the Law of harmony by which to live and express from. When you defer to the wisdom that comes from within you are never in conflict with yourself because you are of a singular consciousness-God-not you *and* God. Not duality *and* grace because it cannot be done. It is one or the other and your choice determines the quality, quantity, nature and expression of your experience.

When you understand this statement you know Truth:

You will never see a righteous/spiritual man begging bread.

All demonstration of supply is God in form:

What have you in the house? What do you have of God you can give to another? A smile? A helping hand? Silent prayer for God's presence? Greeting all as brothers?

This is the secret to infinite supply because when the Master told the old woman "begin to pour" she "released," poured from the container holding just a little bit, gave of what she **had** and it continued to flow and flow and flow, never running dry. Christ Jesus used that same principle in the multiplication of loaves of fishes. There was a multitude and they were enhungered. And the disciples said "we haven't enough" but the Master said "what have you?" They answered "a few loaves and fishes."

"Begin to break." That was and is the answer. The disciples, spiritual man, had to do something to get the flow of grace going and what better way than doing the work of the Father by feeding the hungry? They had to know that what was needed would be, they just had to begin to share of what was God's to begin with. Jesus said "begin to feed" and to feed is to share and so as they took what they had and shared it they found it multiplied and **that is the secret of eternal spiritual supply.**

From the moment you accept the fact that you have within yourself this infinite storehouse of supply then you can take of what you tangibly or consciously have and pour, or break or share it and watch how the flow continues. This great Law of multiplying loaves and fishes doesn't just apply to visible supply but **understanding.**

If you take what what you know to be **Truth** and begin to apply it, live it, pour it and share it (silently, sacredly and secretly) it multiplies itself as more grace and more Truth in consciousness.

The ability to receive impartation, called intuition, 6th sense, or "a way about these things," is knowingly or unknowingly being open to universal consciousness through inner listening.

This was one of the things that Edison did and talked about openly. When he needed an answer he would put his hand to his ear and gaze skyward. He was listening for the answer he knew would come as it had so many times before. Did he know he was actually communing with the Father or the Universal consciousness? Or did he just know that if he asked a question within and let it float away it came back towing a big bag of answers?

Communing with Self, listening within are **tools** employed by artists, writers, composers, dancers, musicians, architects, scientists, landscapers, astronomers, all who create, to bring that which is new into expression. Man cannot bring into expression anything new only God can and it comes by way of **being open to God.**

The entire message of Jesus the Christ was to reveal to man that the kingdom of God is not in holy mountains or holy temples, not in holy books or holy people, that the kingdom of God is not lo here nor lo there but is within **you** just awaiting your recognition of its presence.

You are no longer *of* the atmosphere of duality once you have sufficiently grasp the principles of spiritual living so that you are no longer *seeking* health, wealth or happiness as the world gives it rather are **open** to the miracle of grace that is only found through your connection with that which **is** grace, God, **but only when you return to the Father within.**

Remember no *man* will ever get into heaven, Eden or into the conscious awareness of God because man is not God's creation therefore man cannot partake of all that **is** God's expression/kingdom. Human man is an erroneous expression of spiritual man who has amnesia (separated from source, direction, governance) and is living separate from God as man in a world of dual powers/expressions of good and evil.

God must be sought individually because only then is the consciousness of the one seeking ready to accept that which is sought. This is why it is said "the things of God are foolishness to man" because man is not ready, receptive of God at that particular time. But he will be.

As spiritual man, as healer, teacher or student, you are **never responsible for another.** Each person walks their own path and the return of that path is revealed by the fruitage, the abundance, the peace in and of their experience. Each person choses the depth and degree of their relationship with God and it is secret, sacred and silent.

This is what is meant by letting the world burn up. You can only save yourself and those who desire to be saved by knowing Truth. You cannot force, coerce or demand one come to your understanding because then you are living duality. **Spiritual living is freedom.** No one holds you in bondage to them or their ministry and no one is ever turned away. Who can put God in a box and charge admission for that which is literally where you are when you know where it is? Closer than breathing, nearer than hands and feet.

The way God feels **is** the blessing. The meaning of "God be with you" is the same as "peace be with you" because God is the peace within you and you desire them to feel the love of God, the allness of God, to have the joyous life of knowing God.

We talk about peace all the time but what does it mean? If all of the different facets of your life are humming along, no medical issues, no relationship issues, no work or self inflicted issues you are chill, peaceful, all is good and you **feel** it. Life is less jagged, less on edge, less end of the month worry, less heartburn or tummy issues. I'm serious. Your body registers your emotions right in your gut and if you begin to track your good and bad tummy days you will notice when you are peaceful **all** of you is peaceful.

So many expressions of duality of my form have left my experience meaning the aches, pains and illnesses I used to experience have lessened considerably or are gone and I feel ageless, I feel radiant. Don't get me wrong I still feel little niggles here and there, a pinch, a poke an ache but I tell them to "shoo, you cannot be here. You are an echo of what I used to *believe*" and turn my attention to something else.

Remember your body is not yours it is of God, consciousness in form therefore your body is spirit, too pure to behold inequity/duality/illness/disease.

I still wear glasses and I'm sure there will be "medical" issues that need some form of human intervention (after spiritually healing it of course) because I probably won't be without duality in this lifetime but seriously does it really matter if one or two things hang around if most of the duality of my expression has been healed?

Remember no thing that has a *name* can be real, cannot be in or of you, cannot hurt you or kill you because anything that has a *name* is of *man's thinking mind* of duality which has been proven to be unreal.

God is not present when you are *thinking* through a problem. God only comes when *you* know "*i* of my own self can do no thing, it is the Father within who does the work." When you get to the point of surrender with your inner ears wide open God will come into expression as the perfect answer, solution.

It is only when you ask for God's help that God has the opportunity to fulfill itself as grace, harmony and abundance unto your experience.

It makes no difference whether our governance is Republican or Democrat, exchanging one set of men for another will not solve the problems of this world. The only thing that will solve the problems of this world is the awakened indwelling Christ within those who run for office regardless of party designation.

Do not use your human thinking when making choices for governments and bodies of government. Rather go within and ask God to show you the correct choice. By going to God and asking for **its** choice you rise above the selfish thoughts of humanhood as to which individual will better fit your individual life and go into the realm of which candidate would benefit man in his individual **growth.**

To know Truth is to go within to **listen** and not to use your *senses* to make a human *judgment*. Life with God means you go to God for its omniscience, **you lean not on your own understanding but on God for all things** and there can be no error in your experience.

The things of God aren't things that bring temporary/temporal happiness or intrigue but experiences that deepen your understanding and love for your Father and fellow man as you live in the world but not of it. You are free because there is nothing the world has that you want; what you want you have found within, all the fullness of life pouring forth the glory of God's love for its expressions.

We are all children of God but until you have awareness of God within you are mortal man asleep to reality living as that which you truly are not. This may sound harsh, but until God within has been met and accepted as Truth God doesn't know you. Why? Because God didn't create human man and if God didn't make it it wasn't made/isn't real.

Human man is the expression of a spiritual consciousness that no longer knows its source of supply and feels fear in the face of little or no supply or domination by another. Man is nothing more than the sum of his fears. Not his loves but his fears. If man were a product of his love he would be risen spirit.

What is fear? Irrationality based on misinformation-*i* am alone-is the fear of all man and this fear predetermines man's life to be that of struggle, pain, useless emotions and (perceived) wasted time. Why? Because fear is the base of duality and man is nothing but duality embodied that is born and dies **until** man stops fearing and starts listening, resting and being.

What can hate directed at you do to God, the all of you? What can jealousy, malice, envy or even love do to you when God is your consciousness? Nothing, nada. It bounces off of you for your shield, your robe of God is the atmosphere of your expression, the Law unto your being, goes before and remains after you bringing grace to those receptive to the consciousness of God.

Worldwide warfare against individuality, individual identity is against your relationship with God. All of that which sets men in herds or unites them for a common good, all of this is a denial of the spirit of the individuality and the freedom of man.

Families, groups, government troops, sects, gangs and tribes all serve to create *loyalty* between members of the group rather than the group serving each other not with loyalty (because at the base of loyalty is fear) but **divine love**-God-thus bringing God to bear as the consciousness of those gathered.

Biblical promises, Truth do not apply to human man. No spiritual promise applies to a human man or all human man would be saved. Spiritual promises apply to you when you are in spiritual oneness, when you are no longer living the life of duality.

If so be the spirit of God dwell in you are ye child of God.

Only when you make your contact with God are you returned to your nature of spirit because you know the Father to be within as the source of what was received. Without this contact, awareness, you are merely a man who was born and will die.

In order to achieve this consciousness you have to make the return journey of the prodigal son, you have to get up from the banquet with the swine, this world and its duality, and return to the withinness of the Father and the world falls away. You have to abandon all previous concepts of life, all of your beliefs, fears, truths, likes and dislikes, what constitutes good and what constitutes evil to live free in God.

Turn and live with God for God has no pleasure in your dying which you will surely do unless you go back to your nature of spirit. Understand that the promises in scripture do not apply to the human you and me, scripture applies only to those who have gone home to God in consciousness, who are no longer living as man but rather the individual identity of the one God expressing as you.

As you practice the spiritual principle of sowing to the spirit you will begin to find more and more of your attention on My kingdom and Thy grace rather than form and effect. You will begin now to think in terms of spiritual grace, spiritual harmony, spiritual relationships and not better human relationships, not better human health, not just dollars and things.

You will find yourself no longer thinking in terms of a better material body or looking for material good rather you will be absent from the body (not constantly picking at yourself, your skin, your shape, the you the world sees that you feel is never good enough or always comparing and falls short) and present with the Father and as you do this you will find that the body, forms and effects appear harmonious.

Books on Truth and teachers are very helpful along this path but they themselves are not the answer, they are not God however they contain Truth that allows you to find the Truth you have been seeking.

The language of Truth is very clear to one who has the capacity to understand, has the raised consciousness of which Truth is written. The Master stood before Pilate and Pilate said "what is Truth?" And the Master doesn't answer, turns around and walks away. Why? Wasn't that an opportunity to *convert* Pilate? *Tell* him all about the kingdom of God? No! **The Master knew there was no use presenting Truth to a state of consciousness not prepared to receive it because it would not enter.**

But he did not hesitate to say to the disciples "I am the Truth" because he was speaking to those of an understanding higher than that of the natural man who doesn't know the Truth of **I**.

God has never created a disaster, a sin, disease or anything of any evil nature. Therefore with a knowing heart you can open your consciousness to the experience of God's grace, that thy will be done, and then rest in the Word, the awareness of God's presence within doing the work.

Rest and behold what things take form by virtue of God's grace. Only when you surrender *your* will and your desires will you bear witness to God's presence and see what great things God does through the consciousness of those who open consciousness to it.

Revelation/Truth is shocking because the nature of revelation always destroys your pet beliefs, theories, things you have come to accept as if they were gospel/Truth. Revelation is a shock because of what it **does** to you when you realize how wrong you have been, how wrong your ancestors, parents, friends, religions and society at large have been but then you rest with a peaceful heart because you know Truth and can now live the Life of Truth.

No Truth is ever to be taken as your Truth whether from teacher, book or service. Truth is only received by way of enlightenment, an aha moment, intuition/conscious knowing however what is given as Truth by me for example, is Truth **revealed** to me to **share** with those receptive to Truth. It only becomes Truth unto you when God comes forth with it interpreted for your level of conscious understanding by which to grow in understanding.

The mystical words of Truth that make up this book and all mystical writings are Truth that we individually have received from God to bring peace unto our own being and to those in the world receptive to My peace, those aware of an inner going on not of the body but behind the scenes so to speak.

Truth revealed is only and always trying to get you to wonder where that impulse came from, where that perfect answer came from, where that perfect peace came from. That which man calls a problem is merely God trying to get you to stop what you are doing and look for a better way of doing it-its way not yours.

If two, three or four things happen/line up in your life, human man will most likely disregard it as happenstance, mere coincidence, aligning of the stars, good luck and take it for a temporary happening. But if man got **curious** as to **why** things happen the way they do they would soon learn why and how they happened and how to make them happen more frequently in their experience. It is accomplished by walking a true spiritually based path of enlightenment.

Just remember, Truth is given through the written or spoken word but it only becomes **your** Truth when God speaks Truth back to you and then you know Truth because Truth just spoke, doesn't matter in what way it was expressed or received, the fact that Truth just validated Truth is all the Truth you need to rest upon.

All principles of Truth are Law unto God. Not following the principles of Truth doesn't bring the wrath of God to you, you bring the repercussions/consequences of not following the principles to bear upon you-karma, cause and effect, the duality of man in your experience.

You are never punished for your sins *by* God you experience the return, the *consequences* of your actions under the Law of like begets like, as ye sow so shall ye reap.

The kingdom of God is within

I in the midst of you am the only power. Is there any other power but I? Any other God than I? Only I in the midst of you is mighty.

You can receive this very quickly if you can make up your mind in advance that you aren't going to ask it for anything you would ask the world to give-cars, money, resolution to any human problem, health, material goods, new business, new marriage.

It is God's good pleasure to give you the spiritual kingdom and spirit is the only thing in a spiritual kingdom.

God's grace isn't that of a material nature yet when it appears it comes in a tangible visible form man labels *material* good. The barrier to receiving grace is trying to online order some preconceived idea of what form your supply should take ie what you think you want/need instead of asking for that which will continue to rise you in conscious understanding which then expresses **as** your visible supply.

Truth, when it hits your consciousness, is perceptibly felt, is the Spirit within that quickens/makes itself known inside of you that reveals the reality of your true being and it is wonderful!

In this now of your acceptance of spiritual sowing you immediately start the process of reaping/harvest. The crop you reap begins when you plant the seed. The seed sown is grace, the allness of God in action and in due time sprouts appear and then will be the harvest or fruitage.

Sowing to the spirit and not to the flesh can only happen when you turn from the flesh, the world of man. Scriptural language calls it repentance for God takes no pleasure in your dying. Turn ye and live is God's motto, turn from sowing to the flesh, putting your faith in matter, the externals of life, the baubles, the forms. Everything exists in the invisible and externalizes in the visible as the fruitage of the Truth you express and this creates a life harmonious, joyous, abundant and everlasting.

Man has been raised by man but when man sees the spiritual man he knows he is missing something, could be like him but doesn't know how. How do you become like this other man? You must leave your pack, the way you were raised, the all of who you are because you are not a man therefore will never find fulfillment as a man because you are so much more than that! You were never meant to suffer, be hungry, cold or die, you were meant to live and have your being in this reality you have now glimpsed.

All you need is understanding to open the floodgates of God's infinity into your experience, release all that is of God for the sustaining, maintaining and supplying of your eternal life.

Mystical Terminology

#1 reason for the need of mystical interpretation of terminology

Mystical language is not readily understood by those who have not studied Truth or have not had the mystical experience and this is the reason for mystical interpretation of scripture. This isn't an introduction of new meanings it is returning to the **original meaning** of the words used by those in **union** with God. It is a language not understood by the *intellectual* human thinking mind but by the **soul** faculties, the **Christ** of you.

This is why so many people have no understanding of the Truth they are reading; they are trying to *interpret* spiritual **Truth** by the modern/non spiritual meaning of the words used. You must know the mystical meaning of the words read to have oneness with God.

---

2 Another reason for the need of clarification of words

It is not just mystical interpretation but dialectic differences, the way words are used amongst groups, sects, states and countries at large. A pop is a soda is a fizzy water. A slipper is a sandal or a flip flop. The way a word is used by an individual sets up a rightness and a wrongness to another's use/understanding of the word. This is the reason for so much confusion.

I'm sure you have been witness to an argument where from an outside perspective do not understand what they are arguing about because they are saying the same thing just in different ways but the base of what they are trying to express to each other is the same as the other is trying to express to them.

The meaning of the words of man do not mean what they mean universally (boot/trunk, fag/cigarette) but once you begin to hear, speak and receive through God, there is no confusion because there is no dichotomy from which the words come, they come from a single source, single voice, single meaning with a single interpretation-as it is given from God as Truth.

This is why it is of the utmost importance to not *hear* the words of man for their understanding but to stand back and let God bring the meaning to you from within then there is never any confusion to cause inharmony because it is not a man and a man in a conversation but a raised consciousness open to God to bring understanding of Truth from the source of Truth by way of the one of higher consciousness knowing of God.

4th dimensional living is spiritual living

There are two parts to spiritual living.

Metaphysical Truth-the written words of Truth which when taken into the silence will be given back to you and will reveal Truth which allows you to rest, release error as no thing and once again be in the consciousness of peace.

Mysticism-the living of your relationship with God expressing the Truth you know which is harmony unto your experience.

4th dimensional thinker:

Man turns to God *for* something-money, houses, companionship, freedom from sin, immorality, lack, ill health but God can give you none of these because God has no concept of these *negative* qualities/circumstances. Therefore God doesn't know these problems exist, not because it is ignoring them but because **they do not exist in its consciousness of harmony.**

What you have in your consciousness, what you believe to be true of you and your life is the life you are living. If you think like human man separated from God then you are and are living in the *3rd* dimension which is man giving power to anything out side of them-God, weather, disease, death, other people, lack, their own body.

A **4th** dimensional thinker has risen above, grown past, knows what is experienced by human man is in error because it is viewed through an invisible atmosphere of the belief in two powers of good and evil. A 4th dimensional thinker knows there is no other power than the knowing of Truth-God, harmonious expression.

Therefore any teaching that **doesn't** go beyond the mind of man, does not go up beyond human knowledge and understanding is **not** a spiritual teaching and you are not on the spiritual path for you have not touched Spirit. The spiritual life absolutely requires spiritual contact, inner realization of and deferment to the God within for without this you do not leave the atmosphere of man's erroneous thinking to find source and fount of all that is Truth.

12, 70, 200

Not the number of anything but rather representational of those of the world in oneness with God; the consciousness of those which make up the number. The 12 refers the consciousness of those living as true servants of God in oneness, healing and sharing the grace of God as their livingness. The 70 refers to the consciousness of those on a spiritual path and the 200 represents those who do not know God aright.

These reference the **consciousness** of the 12, 70, 200 **not** the number *limited* to that group ie it is a numerical representation of how few actually stay the course to full enlightenment, live the life of the Christ completely. It is not a human measure of numerical expression but a revealed Truth of the consciousness of man trying to rise in conscious understanding of what is not of the world.

You are of the 12, the 70 or the 200 depending on your conscious knowing and living the Truth **I and the Father are one.**

A house divided against itself

This has nothing to do with personal relationships, human relationships. A house divided is a term denoting a **divided consciousness,** that of good and bad; it means you are trying to ride two horses in the same race, you are trying to relying on spirit *and* on yourself/man/matter at the same time. You are trying to add spiritual teaching to human living to improve human living but you can't. You are either with God or not and if not you are living duality.

A spiritual healing reverses the entire material/mental picture

A spiritual healing reveals that you do not live by bread alone **but by every Word out of the mouth of God,** the spirit within you coming forth as you to the world. Spiritual living completely stops you struggling for *effect* and allows you to rest and in this resting (being with God instead of trying to be "you" individual ego) bring forth fulfillment.

You do not demonstrate *your* daily bread, you demonstrate God **as** your daily bread, fresh manna from source because **God** is the infinite storehouse of your supply not the world, not man, not job or inheritance. God is the fulfillment unto existence.

Abundance

A sufficiency with 12 baskets left over to share.

Active surrender

The act of being in a constant state of surrender/deferment to God's will **for** you. It is a willing choice, one made of knowing life with the Father is where you want to be and by surrendering your will to the will of the Father you are giving all choice of **expression** back to God where it belongs which is the only place from which comes singularity of expression-good.

Active surrender takes the responsibility of living off of your shoulders and allows you to rest, do and be as God desires for you as its expression of perfection.

Almighty

There cannot be an Almighty and other powers and this Almighty is everywhere present where it is known in consciousness. Right where you are on the highway, in adultery, in disease, or on the cross God is there in the midst of you.

God already is omnipresent, the all-presence, omnipotent, and omniscient therefore do not go to God for anything. Go within yourself and awaken, awaken to the realization that God already **is.** All that the Father has is awaiting your awareness and acceptance.

Anti-christ

What is anti? According to man it mean "against, in opposition to, false, not real" but anti means unlike. The *anti of Christ* **is** the carnal/mortal/human/material *mind* of man. *Human* man **is** the *anti, unlike* of **God** and which, if it is believed to be a power, will destroy you because if you believe you are human you will die like humans do.

There is no evil to be protected from, removed from you, there is no evil to overcome to get good. Evil is impersonal, comes from an impersonal source and that source is merely the **universal be-**

lief in good and bad/evil. That is all there is to the mortal mind, the mind of man, the anti christ, that which is unlike God in expression/nature.

There is no mortal mind as a thing, an entity, there is no devil or Satan as an entity, a being, a reality, is not objective, tangible. All are nothing more than *individual* perception based on appearances. All are *conjecture* of your mind playing out a vision/scenario of what you *think* is happening/transpiring.

The universal belief in two powers is the impersonal source of all that is good and bad and evil in the world. This belief is ingrained in your psyche from before you were born, it is your conditioning, your programming, your family histories around and through the environment in which you were born. In this way instead of seeing the world **as it is** you *interpret* the world according to *your* likes and dislikes, good and bad which becomes your ingrained responses to life. But this is not truly *your* response but those of others, their fears, loves, hates, desires and biases *taken on by you* without your given consent/consciousness of choice to accept or release.

This translates into fears generationally placed in the atmosphere of the child before conception and onward being the food/conscious reality of the child until the child decides to think with their own mind which many parents rebel against because it usually goes against *their* way of seeing the world thus wrong on every level. This is a major reason for dissent among family members and why so many seeking God stop seeking because it is seen as weird, wrong, not our way, fairy tale, never worked for me, can't hack the real world so you live in an invisible world etc. All fears and judgements based on duality.

Everything you have learned was conditional, based on punishment and reward, be this way or else, do this or else, this or that. Duality is your reaction to the world in ways that you feel will protect yourself from harm, lack, illness, loneliness but it does the opposite. Duality can only beget duality thus your thoughts predicate the result and in the human world the result is always duality so you are rolling the dice every time *you* make a decision because you are, well, making a decision which is duality at its base.

The entire error of man is in the *belief* there are personal choices to make. In the human way of living yes, you make choices based on *your* desires and the desired outcome.

In the kingdom spiritual man does not make choices for himself rather rests in the Word of God/consciousness of God/oneness in which you resist not evil (because it is an illusion thus no reality, nothing to fight, just know Truth and it dissolves) and by not fighting/resisting an illusion you do not pick up the sword, fall back into duality. As spiritual man you rest in the words God speaks to you because they are always without fail of peace, harmony and love **of you as the perfection you already are.**

I desire nothing but God within because that feeling alone is what lifts my feet off the ground making the effort in my life almost nonexistent. The feeling of God within is so comforting, so safe, so empowering to go boldly forward as his expression that you do and in that doing of sharing, releasing and giving of the spirit you are blessed, your cup will overflow with signs following of your love of God.

Anti-Christ

You are not your sins, you are released from your sins and fears when you know these are not *of you* but are of an impersonal anti-Christ, the belief in two powers. The anti-Christ is nothing more than a belief there is something other than God in expression.

The definition of *anti* is not against but *unlike*. The anti Christ is anything *unlike* God in expression which is human man therefore all who express as human instead of spirit are in Truth the anti christ, *unlike* Christ because they are living humanly not spiritually.

Think of sins as spots of mud on your being. They are **on** you, not of you therefore they can be wiped away. Though your sins be scarlet, the dirt, you are white as snow-true spiritual nature-that is too pure to behold inequity ie more than one power or an opposing *expression* to Self, harmony.

If you hold everyone in this light that you yourself just bathed in there are no sinners, no irredeemable souls for nothing tarnishes the soul and you must see that though appearances may bring *judgement* from *man,* one of spiritual illumination sees past illusions/judgements to the Christ within and this is how you begin to forgive yourself, your neighbor, your enemy and bring God onto the field to awaken those who are lost in this world.

The *anti* of God is the *belief* in more than God in expression as all that is.

Ask questions of God, get answers of Truth from God

As long as you are on the spiritual path the greatest blessing that can come to you is your ability to question. Not to take things blindly, not on blind faith but continue to question as a Truth student, not as a doubter rather a receiver of Truth that allows you to grow more and more into the image of God's consciousness which you express as.

-How do *i* awaken to God?

-How can *i* make way for God to become active in my life?

-How can *i* be of help to myself in bringing God into awareness that I may know this indwelling spirit?

-Is there anything *i* can to do have a greater experience of God constantly and consciously?

-Can *i* get to the point where as Paul said "I live yet not *i*, the **Christ** liveth my life."

-Can *i* get to the point where **I** truly understand why **I** have no need of taking though for my life, what **I** shall eat, what **I** shall drink, what will sustain me eternally?

These questions don't indicate doubt rather indicate you are a **thinker** not just a blind believer, a sheep. You are a thinker, you **want** the experience of the Christ, you **want** to live and move and have your being in God. You **want** to know that this indwelling Christ **is** living your life.

If you ask the question that means you are ready for the answer not from the standpoint of merely having an easier life but because you really want to enter into the Christ life.

The spiritual life isn't easy **at first,** it is straight and narrow but honestly, being at the level of conscious understanding that I am at I will truthfully say that if the struggles in your life have gotten to the point where you are reaching out for the unknown the benefits of the spiritual path manifest quickly in that you are able to experience the fruitage of your conscious connection with God first as internal peace, a better sense of knowing who you are and by which consciousness you express from and then outwardly as abundance. But more than that after you realize God is real trust is established and you defer all governance of your life to it to let it establish its harmony within and without.

Think of God as not only the smartest person but also your best friend that whispers within you Truth unto every situation when before as natural man you would have reacted in a way that would entangle you either through action or just the conflicting thoughts because of the way you have become accustomed to reacting.

There is no place for reaction/judgement/human emotion in God's kingdom. Why? Because what is there to react to, do something about when everything **is?** Is stops all further thought, reaction, comment. IS is IS. This might sound like you have to stop being happy or joyous and be meeehhh. Blah. Milk toast.

The complete opposite! By not reacting and just being you do not restrict your flow of grace, you do not put up a wall of humanhood between you and God. The duality of the world, the fact that man believes in another expression that must be protected against splits your mind into what is good and what is bad and this duality of focus blocks out God and you experience duality instead of is, peace be with you for you are home in Me and I am home in you never to part as long as you desire to be where I am.

Atheist-anyone who fears anything

If you have *fear* in your consciousness you don't **know** God which is the definition of atheism. Those who say they believe in God yet *fear* contagion, disease, bombs, dogs, spiders, growing old, death etc, do not know God either for if they did they would live their lives expressing the reality of God as harmony, peace and good will toward man and not fear.

You cannot have both God and fear. One is of God, Truth and the other is of man, illusion. Man can never enter the kingdom of heaven because they don't have the conscious awareness of God as source, oneness, allness.

Attachment

The difference between spiritual man and human man is attachment, ie not being enslaved/a slave to *things*. When you live in the kingdom you know where your supply comes from and in this knowing enjoy but do not do anything to hold onto whatever it is. It was **provided** by God and that makes it eternally yours so why try to hold onto something that exists in your experience for as long as you want it? When you are done with it it moves on, you give it away, you share the bounty that is of God, not of your hard work.

This is why it is easy for one on a spiritual path to be free with things meaning if they are with you enjoy them if they aren't that is fine too because you have no *need* of them or their experience at the moment but if you ever want to experience or have it again it will be provided through your infinite supply because of your oneness with infinite supply.

Aura: sensed and seen

What man has seen and named as the human aura/energy/vibration is merely the feeling of grace/peace/God *or* humanhood being expressed/felt. This is man's finite understanding therefore when someone is said to have a very pleasant aura/energy/vibration it is actually grace/peace/God they are sensing but humanly labeled it as being *of* the person themselves, ie their personal energy, personal vibration, *personal,* of themselves.

This brings us to what man calls energy vampires. You know those people who when you are around them leave you feeling emotionally drained, have had the vitality sucked right out of you. It isn't that they are taking from you it is that you are empty of God and feel the *absence* of God in what *they* are giving. Two empty vessels. You cannot give of what you do not have and *human* man has nothing of **God** to give therefore you feel no God qualities in your interaction, how could you if neither of you are giving of God? You cannot give of what you are not aware of already possessing.

If your good, kindness, compassion and love were of God instead of you *trying* to be those expressions in and of yourself you would not even notice an energy vampire because you don't care what others bring to the table, what you bring trumps anything and everything of man, your dish is the hit of the party.

If you feel drained after being around someone it is because *you* are not of the consciousness of God but of the consciousness of man. Why? because spiritual man wants nothing, needs nothing, expresses nothing of themselves personally and gives nothing personally. Spiritual man is God expressing and this expression of perfect harmony is the nature, the cause and effect that will release human man from the slavery of their own mind of lack.

Therefore if you start feeling run down, tired, exhausted, confused, out of sorts you are out of God, out of the flow, out of the consciousness, out of the harmony of God. Go within and get back into oneness and through practice, study and living the principles of spiritual living you will find you are like the Everready bunny that just keep going and going and going because you are going on God's energy, God's allness, nature, quantity and quality of Life.

It is not uncommon to be able to get by on one, two and even three hours less sleep because you as spiritual man do not use of your finite human energy and physicality to perform daily tasks rather God's allness of being flowing through you doing/supporting all that is given you to do.

Baptism

The risen spirit is ordained to impart Truth to those who seek it. "If I be lifted up I shall draw all men unto me."

Baptism: the visitation of the spirit, ordination of the spirit, the mystical experience of meeting the Father face to face which makes God a known reality to you.

This is why there is no ritualistic/human ordination in spiritual living-all are ordained to share the Truth of God when God's presence has been felt within and oneness has begun.

Bible

Man reads the Bible from the perspective of a God above/outside of man and because of this man thinks *things* outside of them have power to control them and *they* must be strong in and of themselves to resist these forces.

But when the Bible is read from the correct understanding that God is creative harmonious expression through you out into the world, that God is **within** you, that you are **of** God, your entire understanding of life changes. You are no longer separate and apart from allness, you are **of** allness. You cannot lack, be sick, have pain or desire anything of the world if you are already whole. What can be added to wholeness? Nothing. There in lies the understanding of **no** desire.

Man of God has no need of desire when what is expressly for you comes unbidden because the Father knows of your needs before you do. Man of God is already whole, so whole and so full of Life bursting within them that it flows out to touch others who are receptive to this touch.

Just like some people do not like to be physically touched, some do not like to be touched by the feeling of grace, the feeling of love, the feeling of acceptance and Truth. God is an experience; you **feel** God and in this way and only this way you know God. Some people are not ready to know God and may leave this world before they do know God but never fear at some point in their experience they will know God and become the light unto the darkness just as you are now but understand this:

This is the reason some people will never accept your peace, will not be associated with you and this is exactly the reason for the words "though a thousand may fall at your left and ten thousand on your right nigh will come near your door step." The presence of God is an uneasy feeling to those strongly rooted to the earth, to material goods and material thinking. To them you hold no interest because your nature is not theirs therefore you are not of the birds of a flock that stick together ie live duality.

Obviously until we rise completely there will be some humanhood in our experience but rejoice! You are like a stink bug to a bird, something to be avoided, ignored, not even registered because you are out of their consciousness, their world and the fact that you do not fear to man removes their power. Can you leave this expression/humanly die? Absolutely, but you aren't dead and in the act of resisting not evil, though "dead" are risen further in the only way that matters in this expression, conscious knowing of the Truth of God.

Carnal mind

Paul recognized the potential for evil in man as the *carnal mind,* the collective consciousness of the human race that believes itself separate and apart from God. The carnal mind, the atmosphere of duality, created this atmosphere where man needs, wants and fears therefore man is always faced with *temptation* ie choices.

Temptation is never a person or thing tempting you it is your *human mind* tempting you to believe God is separate and apart from you and that you still *need* something you don't have. To rest in the arms of God is the most satisfying thing you can do for many reasons but the main one is there is **no desire for anything** thus no temptation because you know as spirit there is nothing being withheld from you and God knows your needs before you have the desire so again there is no temptation to *do* anything to *get* something because there is nothing to *get,* only God in awareness to **receive** of God through grace, the allness of God in action.

Do you see how when you know the source of all that you need you have no desires? No one can tempt you into doing anything against your nature of harmony so whether error presents in the form of personal desire, sickness or lack learn to recognize it as a temptation, something to accept or not, something that is *tempting* you to believe in a selfhood or a power *apart* from the allness of God.

Central Intelligence

God is the central intelligence of the universe, God **is** the universe. God is the only actor and we, spirit in form in conscious union with God, are individual expressions of this central intelligence.

You do not possess the intelligence of the creator of the universe but you have **access** to it. What is this intelligence? In human terms there is no comparison. The word intelligence to man is so finite and minuscule to use it to try to define that which is the all of all that is would be impossible.

Let us just say this about the creative intelligence of the universe: this we call creative intelligence is the Truth of you and me. It is of itself we are formed. We are literally of the dust and the air, the grass and the hills, all is of the same creative intelligence expressing visibly and invisibly.

Human man is the only expression that can be assisted to grow beyond the confines and limitations of man's thinking mind. It is only this knowing **beyond what is currently known that propels humanity into the next generation with more conscious understanding of the world around them** than the previous. This is evolution and it is God expressing through those who knowingly or unknowingly contact the spirit within and bring forth new invention, understanding, bettering the world for man to continue to awake to Truth which frees man to begin the journey back to the central intelligence which you are of and stop living this life of duality, this life separated from the Father, the comforter.

Life never began and will never end, it is cyclical. You did not know your spiritual heritage until now. For thousands of years you have been on your way to this exact moment. Everything that has ever been of the consciousness that you are, every thought, error, pain, pleasure, choice, leap of faith, every literal breath has been to get you to this moment. Why? Because the moment you meet God and understand the upside down nature of man's world and see the practicality and literal common sense of God's world you are beginning the much shorter leg of this visible journey because you are now the prodigal son returned home. You know your Truth and you are willing to learn how to live this path, practice the presence of God to bring the allness of God to bear in your life and in the world for all man for no man is your enemy when you know the nature of all called man.

Why do we exist? God just said for its pleasure. Expression is its pleasure because it is its nature. It does what it does and because it is Law there is no limit to what you receive because as ye sow so shall ye reap. Tit for tat, degree for degree. The entire purpose of getting to this point of conscious understanding is to gain the conscious understanding of **how to go home,** to know and live heaven on earth, sharing God's grace and have a damn good life until you transition out of this form.

The central intelligence monicker makes me think of a cell. A cell **is,** exists to serve only its purpose through chemical, physical and physiological responses that express as the cell being, the innate **intelligence** necessary for it to express, serve its purpose of being.

The reason for disease among human man is the actual God of you is not what is living the form because you are unaware of your nature as spirit. Therefore the *cells* are living themselves by their innate *physical/material* nature therefore when a few go rouge, get drunk and multiply they start popping out funky cells and then you have cells creating erroneous copies of *themselves.* In human man each cell has its own intelligence and though they work in concert they are free to be as individual cells.

When man knows his connection to God and is in oneness with this consciousness this immediately brings you into eternity because you are **of** the consciousness of that which is eternal therefore you are as well. Now that you are back in your rightful place, child of God, you are **spirit** in form and perfection is your constitution. In this light your body is not made up of a billion *individual* cells rather God is the expression of your body which is harmonious which to man would be health.

A child born into the world of duality is being brought into an atmosphere of chance, unrealities and illusions thus will suffer the consequences of the duality inherent in the world. This is why "bad things happen to good people." First, there are no truly good humans because they are of both good and evil thinking and doing and second, this world is a crap shoot held together by a shoestring strung between two red hot pokers. No one said this life was going to be easy and they weren't kidding!

A child born into this world from parents on the spiritual path will be born as spiritual child already of the knowing of Truth, it will have its Christ consciousness already open and ready for more Truth in the atmosphere of its home. This child will seem to thrive, be beyond understanding in personality and ability and will be the light unto the next generation which is the only way to perpetuate the knowing of God by bringing as much grace as possible to bear in the world **but** for the next generation to be more spiritually governed **those of this generation must have their awakening to Truth.**

Children

Children need to be directed not punished. There can be discipline in direction but it is not punishment of force, anger or irritation. It is the discipline of Truth, knowing Truth and living Truth. Children are animals and must be directed or they become the lower consciousness of the next generation instead of the higher. We are not to teach children like they are taught in school where things are shoved in and learned by rote rather by example, understanding and quiet time. Children today are kept so busy trying to *make* children that succeed in life by having numerous skills and talents along with knowledge and standing but this only perpetuates the belief in duality, that you of yourself must do something. You cannot make a child into your image and likeness rather are to allow **their** true image and likeness to emerge as that of child of God.

None of that outer chaos matters to a child and it should definitely not matter to you. What is important is bringing up the next generation in an understanding that is different than the world around them and to do that you must employ different ways of getting through to the soul of the child, the consciousness and not just punishing according to outward expression.

Parents do not know, or lose sight of, the Truth that their children are not *their* children but are God's expression even when they are the screaming foul monkey demons of horror movies. But if parents know how to correct along spiritual lines there should be no reason for the rebellion in them that makes them problem children later.

Man looks at children as extensions of themselves and that is the problem with parenting. **Your children are of God,** are of the consciousness they were when they left their last iteration. **Your children are complete strangers to you because their consciousness was already formed before inception.** The child is the visible expression of the consciousness of its atmosphere. When a parent raises children through God realization most of what you are doing as a parent happens in the silence of your being which becomes the atmosphere of your home which becomes the atmosphere from which the child expresses as a more calm, observant child that takes in the world instead of demanding from the world.

Your children, though not your children, are a reflection of the atmosphere outside of them until it is revealed true reality is the atmosphere within the silence, invisible, sacred and secret. Then and only then does the innate consciousness of the child begin to change to that which is Truth, that which it has been seeking thousands and thousands of years for. This is you, the child who was but is no more, the old man of earth has died and you are now the new man of spiritual understanding.

Discipline is not punishment and the child can feel this. Punishment is for who you *believe* they are by their actions whereas discipline is behavior correction through knowing the Truth that you are not your actions or sins but pure and discipline is to reveal the purity without demoralizing, malpracticing or damaging the child's sense of self which you are revealing as God. God could no more punish you than it could stop being itself. Therefore you in the consciousness of God cannot punish because it is not of your nature. You heal, you correct and you pray and that brings more and more grace to bear in your children. Even the hardest nut to crack will open at the softest whisper of that which feels to be missing.

The conduct of all those around you is dependent on your consciousness because your consciousness brings the Law of your consciousness to bear. Therefore the consciousness of a human teacher becomes the consciousness of the child **if** the child has not already started to be filled with a consciousness higher than that of the teachers out in the world.

If children are not rightly directed at home through the spiritual consciousness of the parents the child will be educated by the masses, by those of duality and will need to wander this earth as you did before finding Truth. The children of each successive generation are begging, pleading, screaming at the top of their lungs to be given something different than what has gone before so they don't have to suffer and their children's children no longer have to suffer.

The only way this world can change is with you knowing and living your Truth to impart it to your children so that as they continue to transition into different phases of this eternal experience they are doing it as raised consciousness instead of human consciousness of duality.

Christ and Messiah

Mean the same thing: enlightened one, illumined of Truth, teacher, messenger of God, **servant** of God. You **serve** God by helping those who desire to know God aright by being the expression of God which is an avenue of grace to all who seek.

Church doctrine

Church doctrine are *laws of morality* made up by *man* therefore cannot be the Truth of **God.** If it doesn't come from within you it isn't Truth/dogma of God and has absolutely nothing to do with spirituality, Truth or having a relationship with God.

The life of the spiritual man is governed by the awareness of the Father within, what comes from the Father and no thing of the world of man.

Communion

Communion is the act of turning in to listen for God and is the definition of prayer. It is the unfoldment of individual consciousness to God's presence and it makes you every way whole.

Communion/meditation/true prayer

To get into the atmosphere of communion with God just sit and close your eyes. Let your body relax, move as necessary so that you are not aware of your body so take the time to get comfortable. Take your mind out of your body and relax in that space behind closed eyes. Just find a place where you don't see/sense identifiable form but more observe your inner space, whatever vacuous quality that brings to your imagination.

Take all into God-questions, problems, concerns, confusion, joyous experiences, healing of self and others-and from within will come exactly what is needed for your peace. You don't always have to bring God into awareness to be with God you will get to the point where God pops in with a smile, a Truth bomb, a response to a healing given as done.

Conditioned/unconditioned consciousness

Conditioned consciousness: the thinking mind of *man* with its judgements, likes, dislikes, belief in two powers. Also called the human mind, mortal mind, carnal mind.

Unconditioned consciousness: the consciousness of **God.** The consciousness that was Jesus in expression free of all human traits and qualities of duality, of judgement or bias. The unconditioned consciousness knows and lives **is,** God in awareness.

Conditions

Conditions are merely the *accepted error* in action that you experience as *effects* of your *thinking* mind.

Conscience of human man

Human man lives by *their* choices, desires, wants, needs, likes and dislikes ie by their point of view and because each person's point of view is different chaos is the only possible result.

Consciousness of Spirit-also the point of view from which you express life but it has nothing to do with you *personally*. Spiritual man is akin to bees in a hive working and being as you were meant to be-through the consciousness of the intelligence that created you. You were never meant to *think* to do; you were created to **respond** to an inner impulse, force, life, consciousness of your creator thus living as and by your creator's consciousness/point of view which is good, has no opposite.

Conscience vs. Consciousness

Man understands his *conscience* to be that of an angel on his shoulder gabbing about while the devil sits on the other shoulder trying to talk louder than the angel. This *conscience* is what man calls the "moral compass" which is **nothing** in and of itself.

Conscience is not **consciousness.** Conscience is synonymous with duality. Why? Because *your* conscience, that which is trying to balance behavior/action with their possible consequences, is the definition of duality-do good or do bad, reap good or reap bad. *Human* conscience is merely the mental tight rope of life being walked between two opposing forces trying to procure the optimal results for your efforts of being good or saying chuck it all and being on the nightly news.

The all of human man, from being to thinking to doing, all the processes of the mind that go into being human man are of duality/unreality and only becomes reality when the consciousness of man is risen to that of Truth and when the consciousness of all form is realized/recognized/revealed as that of, not separate and apart from God, allness, oneness, then the *conscience,* the *thinking* mind, will come willingly under the governance of the **consciousness** of **Self** and harmony is restored through oneness.

Spiritual man has no *conscience,* no thinking/devising/planning mind because there is nothing to decide, nothing to control, maintain or support so all of man's thinking mind is now at the **service** of consciousness, **deductive** not *creative*. You don't decide/chose how you are going to progress in this experience from here on out, you rest, trust, listen and respond and in that way only do you rise in spiritual understanding which expresses as abundance, good fortune, joy, that which brings peace.

Conscience is an act of man's thinking mind-duality.

Consciousness is existence, knowing you exist and what you exist as-unqualified, spiritual perfection.

Conscious awareness

You do not suffer the conditions of sin but suffer the *effect* of a *belief* of being separated from God; what you experience is the result of **ignorance.** You are ignorant of the Truth that the *labels and judgements* of good and bad/evil are not real/objective but mere thoughts and images in your *mind* you *react* to. Human man reacts to that which does **not** exist in the visible world.

Once the reason for the perceived discord has been discovered to be *separation* from Truth/God in conscious knowing you realize you are not *human* but **spirit,** of God. Now you can begin to die daily to the unreality that there are two powers or expressions in a world of singularity because you have met that singular expression face to face.

This is how conscious awareness of God is born-once you are shown Truth about one wrong thinking/belief you understand that if one image you held as true is actually false, then all the perceptions of your world **must** be false if they are all based on the same premise of two powers.

Conscious capacity

Your conscious capacity is that which you do/use to express yourself. Human man of duality has the conscious capacity to do good and to do evil because man believes in good and evil as being expressions of man and thing.

Spiritual man in oneness has only the conscious capacity of God to express from which is the consciousness of harmony. This is why spiritual man does not need to pick up the sword to protect himself against outside forces because spiritual man doesn't express duality to invite duality in return.

If there seems to be some form of agitation around you you silently bring grace to bear and move on, no thing more needs to be done because you have done the most benevolent, loving act one can do-bring God to bear among man for peace among man.

Contemplative meditation

When you contemplate the Truth of God in the inner silence and then await its presence as confirmation of Truth in your awareness which dispels illusion/duality as a reality.

Continuous dispensation of grace

The goal of spiritual living is to have a continuous dispensation of grace which is the activity of God in your life. It is as simply as being in the present moment, now, to hear God's voice which keeps you in the expression of God and not man. The more you are with God just chillin' the more grace is in your experience because you are with the source of grace.

Conversion/rebirth/Ascension

Born again of the Spirit.

Correct letter of Truth

Prayer is what you live by, not a prayer of words or thoughts but silent communion with the Father within. **Silent** listening is the true definition of prayer and is the **only** connecting link with God. Prayer can start off with words of Truth thought within, to rest upon to take the mind out of duality and into the atmosphere into which Truth comes. The thoughts quiet and you settle into the feeling Truth of God brings forth-peace, release, lighter load-and rest until you feel done or until God comes on the field.

It isn't necessary for God to come on the field, have actual words or visions just the feeling of peace that washes over you or whatever it is within you that tells you God is and God is within.

Cosmic law

Cause and effect, karma, man's laws. Cosmic law is only about man, the beliefs of man, the livingness of man under *mosaic* law of *Lord* God.

The entire teaching of the Master, the New Testament, was to teach you/show you what *cosmic law* was and then how to **surmount/rise above** the *duality* of cosmic law to be under **grace** through **oneness.**

Coueism

Spiritual living by principles of Truth is to bring illumination to your humanhood to **outgrow** humanhood. Just denying you are *human* and stating you are already this or that or have the mind of God is a form of *Coueism*-**claiming something for yourself you haven't demonstrated.**

Coueism along with all other *mind* treatments/healing modalities is nothing more than forms of self hypnosis trying to break the universal hypnosis of man ie duality as a result of a *sense* of separation from God. It is nothing more than trying to improve that which doesn't exist by way of optimistic autosuggestion and not any manner of spirituality, knowing Truth or experiencing Truth therefore will not result in a higher degree of conscious knowing than before you started your study.

Creation

According to the Bible God created the universe in six days and rested on the seventh. Read without the consciousness that is illumined, of God awareness, this seems ridiculous and it is.

This again is a perfect example of *reading* the Bible instead of letting it be given back to you from God as it was meant to be understood. God didn't create the universe, all that is, in six *human* days, **the six represents the different stages of consciousness man goes through** on their way to spiritual enlightenment which when you reach, achieve oneness, have had the mystical experience of meeting the Father face to face, you have reached the **seventh** day on which you **rest** because you are **home.** What is being reference is your transformation, coming into your Truth of being. The numbers are **representational** of the stages of conscious knowing you go through as you journey from man of earth back to child of God.

The words in the Bible cannot be understood by the human thinking mind therefore you must present them to God for the understanding behind what the words mean to the human thinking mind.

Curiosity

Curiosity is a necessary attribute of the spiritual man. Curiosity didn't kill the cat, it took its nine lives and gave it one of eternal expression. Be curious.

Darkness

Darkness is the **absence** of light. Darkness has no properties, no substance, no form thus doesn't exist in and of itself.

Sin, disease, lack and death, like darkness do not exist because *words* have no substance, no form, no reality/existence. What God didn't create doesn't exist except as a shadow, figment, thought of the mind, illusion which is the definition of subjective, unreal.

Only that which is objective is real/experiential and because God is as all, God is the only reality/Truth to experience.

Death, resurrection and ascension

Not personally but symbolically; when you go from man of earth to child of God then back **with** God. You have to die daily to the things of man and be resurrected/remade in the consciousness of God and then live your life as a servant, instrument, happy to do the Father's will.

It is the ascension from the corporeal to the incorporeal, not by physical process but by an activity of consciousness. All takes place in consciousness.

Deductive awareness vs. the thinking/creative mind

Spiritual man has a **deductive** mind of awareness which is the Truth of being.

Human man has a *thinking/creative* mind which is a false expression of being caused by the *belief* in separation from creation, God, Source.

Spiritual man does not use the mind to *think;* the mind is an avenue of awareness by which to do the works of the Father. The **deductive** mind is an **instrument** through which God works through you as you.

To say you have no thinking mind doesn't make you stupid, it makes you aware of your true nature and **the only way you can live your nature is to defer to God as the governing influence and supply of your life.** Awake or asleep God is the Truth of sinner and saint alike. All knees will bend and all will rise to the kingdom of heaven but it is always and only **your** decision/choice as to when your knee will bend and your journey home begins.

Deductive mind

Your mind isn't for thinking but awareness and knowing Truth. To be used the way it was intended the mind is more of an antennae for **receiving** impartations, impulses from God and not a broadcasting station for the little *i,* the personality, *i* Kelly, Brandon, Mikeala, to tout itself. When the mind is used for the purpose of knowing Truth, that Truth then becomes the Law of harmony unto your experience, it sets you free from every sense of limitation-physical, mental, moral or financial. The Truth that you entertain in your consciousness takes over your life eliminating discords and in-harmonies and brings about peace, harmony and freedom.

Warning.

The power of God is not a power you can use for personal gain, personal power or even personal good. What you desire for yourself-peace, comfort, release and relief-must also be for your *enemy* as well as for your **friends.** You cannot desire anything for yourself you do not desire for all man to have/experience because all are your brother and you want **all** man to feel peace to be able to express peace.

The Christ within rises all boats, not just yours. In fact, if you try to *use* the omnipotence of God you will definitely see the results crystalize in your life as human disharmony: wanting something only for yourself is selfish and God is abundance, giving, not hiding and hoarding.

Matthew 13:12 "for whosoever hath, to him shall be given, and he shall have more abundance. But whosoever hath not, from him shall be taken even that he hath."

What this means is he who has much of God awareness is constantly opening up a way for the imprisoned splendor to escape to bring itself to earth and what goes around comes around that is the Law of like begets like, you are blessed with the abundance you shared of God's grace. If however you have no awareness of God you are living and existing on the little life energy the cells of the body provide until they don't and you will continue to experience the ups and downs of believing in two powers. What little life you have inherent in what you think to be a *material* body wanes and is lost, not being sustained by God and you die as man believes, leave this expression but you only come back again and again with the hope you will continue to rise in consciousness to that above man but you won't until you chose to take the opportunity given to know **how** that is accomplished.

Dementia

If you learn to communicate with one not of healthy material mind through spiritual awareness you are communicating with the Self of them and the appearance or lack there of of personality doesn't matter because what is important to the person is the way they feel when you are around because you see them, not their declining state of life.

If you can see the Truth of a person to their dying breath you have given one peace beyond measure because maybe for the first time in their life they are being seen as child of God and right then and there their body is released, the aged is no more and youth is returned. In this glow of God all will benefit regardless and sometimes specifically because of lack or decline of mental thinking and reasoning ability. When you lose your senses all you are left with is God.

Demonstration

Human man believes he can demonstrate, bring into being through some form of power *they* possess that which they desire to have, be or do. It is usually used in context with manifesting, bringing into being through thought, ceremony, spell, affirmation or denial. It is of *their* power, *their* ability to *create* matter ie money, houses, cars, people, jobs, clothes, opportunities etc, through ritualistic *thought*.

The demonstration of **spiritual** man is always and only one thing demonstrated-harmony in awareness/God. How do you demonstrate harmony? By being the expression **of** harmony. When duality is brought to your attention by your own experience, that of a client or family member you **heal the error by an actual awareness of the presence of God within yourself.** The awareness of the only presence there is within you reveals the unreality of what is expressing outside of you.

Harmony is your choice and your reward. Do I always keep it together when confronted with duality? **No** and neither will you. It takes many times of forgetting God is running this show before you automatically defer and let God have at it. It takes repetition, dying daily to learn why you have no need of reacting but you will get there. You have to remember this is a way of living not a one and done kind of thing so enjoy the ride, watch the seasons change and do a happy dance every day just for fun.

Demonstration

A demonstration is hearing the voice of God within as proof of the existence of God as creator of all and it is by this which you live your real existence. A demonstration is the attainment of the **meat** the world knows not of, the demonstration is the attainment of **peace be with you** because God is within and you are in conscious union with God in the inner silence of your being. This demonstration is available to all who come to God of earnest seeking and righteous desire.

Dependence of man vs. spiritual man

Man of earth is dependent on earth and man for all that they need and want for survival and expression. Man goes to work to make money, man goes to school to learn, man pays another for services and product. Man fears constantly about loss of money, job, car, home and man constantly searches for purpose by looking to the world to supply the answer, the need you can fill through your own knowing, energy and finances.

Spiritual man has found the harmony of living through knowing Truth. In this state of knowing you do not look to man for money, happiness, supply or abundance, you don't go and do and try to be because as spiritual man you know who you are and where your supply comes from and it has nothing to do with man or the material things of man.

Spiritual man is dependent only on God for all that is needed and no longer depends on self, i, me, my, finite knowledge, limited strength, cunning, thinking, devising mind to get from man what is needed because you know all you need comes from within you to the without as grace in your experience.

Divine Love

What is divine love if not forgiveness? Isn't forgiving another and knowing you are forgiven the greatest feeling in the world? The greatest release and relief to your being? Does it not give one a second breath, a second look, a second chance? Is that not what God is? 70x7 you will be forgiven. Why? Because no matter what you do as a human nothing can keep you from God if you desire God over man.

The only thing that will keep you from God is the bondage you place on yourself and others and this bondage/inprisonment is enslavement to a pain, an injustice, a hurt, a transgression, lack, fear, disease, omission or commission. You must forgive as you would be forgiven for only in forgiveness is there total and complete freedom of being and that is what God is when it is known in awareness.

Divine Love

Human affection/love is not Divine Love because 100% of all forms of *human* love are selfish. What is divine Love? Love that wants nothing of you, is given freely without thought of return, it is a place to rest, it is healing grace, it is peace be with you.

Divine Love

Harmony/harmonious expression

Divine order/harmony

The first Law of creation is that of perfect harmony which can only come from a singular expression expressing. Harmony is Law and is the measure of your God consciousness which is expressed to the world as you, your supply, joy, peace, abundance, your expression of health, wealth and happiness.

Do unto Caesar

There are things the world requires of its citizens and those things are called the things of Caesar, of man, of earth, but are necessary as a part of our responsibility to our **brothers,** not our government. Spiritual man is still responsible as are all others for the things of man-taxes, schooling, armed services.

To not take up the sword doesn't mean being a conscientious objector. To not take up the sword means **to not use mental or physical means to solve a problem** but to let spiritual power that you are fully aware of as being the only power pour forth to go before you to awaken receptive souls, to bring peace into expression so harmony is the atmosphere of all those around you.

Dogma vs. doctrine

All dogma are doctrine but not all doctrine are dogma.

Dogma:

Truth revealed by God through a mystic, one in conscious union with God. That which is revealed within is Truth, God, harmony unto your being and expression.

Doctrines:

Human interpretations of Dogma, the Word, Truth of God.

Every *religion* has its *own* rules, teachings of *morality/conduct* and blind faith proclaimed as Truth by *man* interpreting the *written* word with **no** God contact or awareness of God.

Doctrine are nothing more than one person's *beliefs* followed as rules/law for conformity to what *they* want their world to look thus make others live according to *their* rules laid out as **God's** rules.

Nothing gets you to God but Truth in awareness and Truth is revealed within, **dogma.** Human man receiving an interpretation of Truth from the *mouth* of man is *doctrine,* false teachings of law and duality not God and grace. Even the words of a mystic, though Truth, are not to be taken at face value but taken within for God to speak Truth to you-dogma.

Dominion

The Truth that must become your Truth is that of **is,** consciousness expressing. God **being** consciousness **is** in the midst of you, that which **is** to be your savior, your presence, expression and your dominion over everything in, above and below the earth.

When it is said spiritual man has dominion over the things of the earth it means because of his understanding of his true nature he fears no thing of earth or man. A man who knows his Truth fears no man or beast, bomb or tsunami, not even death and it is by this Truth peace descends and becomes your expression no matter outward appearances.

Dominion

Dominion comes through recognizing the spiritual nature and identity of every individual. This transforms your world and gives you dominion over sickness, sin and ultimately death. In the recognition of your spiritual identity you are now tabernacling with that which was never born and cannot die.

Dominion

People think the word dominion means power *over* something but dominion is your realization that there is **no power, ie no expression** apart from the harmony of God to *need* a power over. One expression of harmony predicated on one presence that **is** harmony. It allows you to know as you go through life nothing can kill you, you are infinite being living confidently under grace, God's harmony, love and supply and with this Truth of being you have dominion, (one power/expression of Self) over the world (2 false powers/expressions of self).

This inner knowing of God as all **is** the protective power, dominion; not a domination of force but **a dominion of knowing Truth.** Only those who know God is nearer than breathing, closer than hands and feet have dominion over the *things* of the world but this is not *domination* over other man in the sense of being superior in any way. Dominion is **knowing** who you are not *domination* over others as a physical force. The two words result in completely different experiences.

Dominion allows you to rest in God knowing all error is illusion and knowing this Truth of one power is in and of itself dominion over man's way of thinking and behaving thus freeing you from its effects because if you don't abide by duality in your consciousness it is **not** of your expression therefore are "out of the loop" so to speak and away from 90% of the error human man experiences. Why? Because **all** error you used to encounter was created by you *thinking* you were separated from your source of Life.

Dominion or domination?

Dominion of God over all that is for peace and prosperity or domination of self by self or another for continued enslavement to beliefs?

Door

Entrance, gateway, threshold, barrier, that which is seen as that which must be opened, crossed, gone beyond to progress.

Duality

Man has the ability to use his mind for good or evil to suit individual purpose and each man has his own mind. The world shows forth the effects of the mind that can do good and evil and this is the **definition** of duality, more than one mind thinking and desiring and doing-your human thinking mind and the myriad of other thinking minds all trying to live separate from God experiencing the chaos of this separation.

Dwell

I will dwell in the house of the Lord-I will dwell/live/have my being in God Consciousness. I keep my consciousness connected to God; my mind is silent of human stuff and is just there like the bouncy dot at the end of a cursor, open, receptive not for something to come from outside but for something to drop within, a revelation, a hi there, a nugget of illumination, a Truth felt.

Where you dwell is where your thoughts are. Dwelling in God means resting in the silence. You have to understand it is not the silence of emptiness, it doesn't echo and make you feel light headed or woo-woo, spaced out. When I say empty I mean inactive, just chillin', all's good, God's got it so you are not alone it is just quiet up in there because you are harmonious, nothing to chew on, worry about, care about because when you dwell in the consciousness of God you are of the harmony of God; that is the entire purpose of this life, to experience harmony which is the atmosphere of God in your awareness.

Dying daily

You cannot put new wine into old skins.

Your consciousness cannot be a transparency through which God works while it is double minded. Which Master shall ye serve today? God or Mammon?

The saying goes "God is a jealous God" but I would like to rephrase that in a less Old Testament way to reflect grace and not law. God is God and the nature of God is good, peaceful, harmonious, allness expressing and you must be as well. God doesn't throw you out, denounce you, get all irritable or grumpy that you live duality and not oneness with it. It merely means if you are with God you get God, if you are with man you get man.

It isn't a jealousy thing at all it is a *this or that* not both. God knows nothing about you until you open yourself up to it within consciousness and even then God knows nothing of your transgressions because transgressions are of two powers and God knows nothing except Self therefore God only knows the pure, untouched perfection of you, ie no baggage thus no judgement or condemnation from the Big Guy.

Think of your thinking mind as a glass full of dirty water, the dirt being duality causing turbidity, turbulence, cloudiness, uncertainty. As you begin to understand spiritual living, die daily to the errors/illusions/maya the water in the glass begins to clear, is less murky, less turbulent, less uncertainty. The more you study, imbibe/live Truth, release error the clearer and clearer the water gets; you are emptying out the duality of man that clouded your mind to allow the pure Water of everlasting life promised by God fill you to overflowing.

Dying daily: peeling the onion or ten thousand petal lotus

Dying daily is the peeling away the layers of human conditioning to reveal Truth unto your being, your true nature as child of God under all the dirt of humanity laid on top of you, **not** in or of you, but on top. You are white as snow no matter how scarlet your sins **but to be able to live a life above sin you must remove the condition that creates sin** in this world and in your life. What is this condition that wreaks havoc on the minds of man? The belief that there is any power other than God/harmonious expression.

Man believes there is both good and evil and within this duality can never find balance, peace, rest for man is all about judging and placing everything neatly into their own box of understanding. Can you see now why there is no Truth to what man sees or experiences? Because two people in the exact same situation will never behave/see/understand the situation the same because they are not just seeing, they are *recreating* it according to their experiences/history. Therefore that which is experienced by the senses is never the reality of the situation or object because man unknowingly throws their baggage on the assessment.

It is the spiritually minded man who can see beyond appearances, beyond the confines and prejudices of their own experiences/history and see what is truly before them because they see it through **is,** as God intended it to be experienced. It is a flower, it is a storm, it is a meat packaging plant, it is a passing from this expression. These things **are** and if you see them as they **are** they bring up no change in emotion, no correlation or correspondence to previous experiences by which to judge and you remain peaceful.

Elohim

Biblical name of God meaning

Many of One

One of many

Error

An error is merely an illusion with no objectivity, no form, no Life and no Law thus no reality.

Error

You do not fight error.

You do not use Truth to overcome error.

You do not use God to overcome error.

You recognize error is no thing because it is a judgement based on *personal* beliefs and not **Truth.** Therefore you are not dealing with *powers* that need to be overcome rather you are dealing with your *thinking* mind trying to tell you what it thinks is there and that is the problem.

The *thinking* mind cannot tell you any **Truth** therefore all *error* is because you *believe* what the *thinking* mind tells you instead of what **God** tells you.

Eternal vigilance

Eternal vigilance is the price of spiritual living. Stay present, not in the past or future but in the now which is **praying without ceasing,** die daily and always remember where your dependency lies-with God, not man.

Evil

Evil **isn't** a thing, isn't objective (tangible or visible) therefore does not exist. Evil is a *personal* interpretation/assessment of what **is** thus is **only experienced by the thinker.**

Faith

Faith is **knowing** God is the same yesterday, today and will be tomorrow because God **is** and can be no other.

Faith is **knowing** all already is just waiting for the right time, seed time and harvest, for it to come into your awareness.

Faith **reveals** there is nothing you need, nothing you lack, nothing you cannot experience when you live and move and have your being in God consciousness.

Faith in God is the **result** of the mystical experience with signs following.

Faith

Faith is an activity of consciousness just as much so as integrity. Faith is always present in you even though like integrity, it may be dormant. The recognition and acknowledgement of the omnipresence of God as an activity of individual consciousness starts the flow of it into visible and tangible effect and begins to change blind faith into knowing through awareness.

Human life is but a dream and you must wake up from it to live the real life of living under the grace of God as your source of all life and not man. What you can get or obtain humanly through mental or physical force can be received without human effort if you can learn how to rest in the promise of God-that it is responsible for you but can only take on that role of governance and provision when you allow it to because you now know God to be your consciousness of being.

When thought dwells on person, place or thing you are functioning in the dream, the unreality of man, chaos caused by duality. When thought dwells upon God you are in the kingdom under the protection of Truth which bears witness to your eternality.

Faith

Blind faith is believing without experiencing **but** faith in the form of desire rightly directed will result in an actual experience of God changing blind faith/hope to knowing which is the hallmark of a mystic.

Faith healing

Faith healing is the belief a person is a direct conduit of healing from God outside of them to come into expression and perform a miracle *because of them.* Faith healings are healings in the sense of man ie the renunciation of symptoms but this is only temporary, psychosomatic, self hypnosis **unless** the person healed digs into the how, the cause, God, and stops focusing on the what, the effect, the change in appearance/condition.

One who does faith healing can easily become a spiritual healer by knowing where God is, who you are in relationship to God and what duality is. You already have deep faith there is a God that does heal you just have to tweak a few things and you will no longer have faith *in* God, you will have **met** God face to face.

Fake person

You know how sometimes you can just feel the fake coming off of a person even though they say and do all the right things man of earth says but their expression doesn't match their actions and that is duality. A fake person, one acting to elicit a response, has no God freely flowing **from** them because there is no God within awakened to Truth.

This person is completely rooted in the material world, in duality and yes, the person is fake, not because they are behaving "fake" but because they **don't know who they really are** and are trying to make themselves into something through their own limited understanding of who they can be by imitating what is out in the world.

Man expresses their nature through behaviors associated with states/stages of consciousness and they change as you outgrow old habits and thoughts. Therefore as you walk the spiritual path your expression will change because you are changing within and this is the understanding of "by your name you will be know, child of God or man of earth."

Fall from Grace

It is at this moment you can change your life and the lives of others not by physical or material means but by silent contemplation of Truth heard from within and releasing that Truth as your expression to bless and awaken those ready to experience living with God as it was in the 1st chapter of Genesis.

Human man is not experiencing the harmony of the 1st chapter of Genesis, living in the kingdom. Man lives the 2nd chapter of Genesis where man has eaten of the fruit of good and evil, *of the knowledge of man*. The first fruits/experience of human duality.

Why did *knowledge* cause spiritual man to be cast out of the garden of eden? Out of the consciousness of peace? **Because knowledge is of human man and man can do good or bad with this knowledge** thereby experience both good and bad which is *duality*.

Knowledge is of man's thinking mind not Truth given from God. Knowledge comes from *outside* of man, is *learned* rather than being **revealed** within. Knowledge has nothing to do with God and cannot be lived in conjunction with God for knowledge is of man's finite cumulative understanding of the world around him **and this knowledge can be used for good or evil.** Knowledge is subject to duality because its source is duality-man.

But knowledge is good right?

Knowledge is what man has *surmised* about the universe not knowing the **Truth** of the universe. Knowledge is that which man puts into his mind to make sense of this world but Truth functioning **as** consciousness negates the need for thinking, learning, stuffing in of information because there is nothing man needs to know that God cannot **give** him by going into the silence and listening for the soft, small voice to impart all that is necessary to know:

I will never leave you nor forsake you and the reason I am presenting to you is for your benefit so you may have life and have it more abundantly.

In the beginning God was all the knowing spiritual man needed, it was God that provided all for his children. So what was it of the tree of Knowledge that caused so much pain? *Knowledge* is of man, **Truth** is of God. Man and God are separate therefore if you live by knowledge, man's thinking mind of reasoning/conscience, of the belief in good and evil you are not of the consciousness of God thus are not of the nature of God-harmonious and eternal.

Man is not known to God because man is an aberration of spiritual man because it lives by its own thinking and not by God's be-ing. Being out of the kingdom merely means being out of the consciousness of all that is which is already created ready for expression in your experience. If you are not **of** the consciousness of supply you are not able to receive supply.

That is all that the fall from grace means: **you are no longer of the consciousness of God by which to receive the things of God.** You have to be in it to win it! Remember that!

False appetite

The seeking for that which you feel you are missing, that there is some *human* connection or material expression that will fill the emptiness but it isn't anything human you crave but that which is not known to human man.

Fate

Such a tricky word for a human to unpack. Man says in dejection, resignation "my fate was written in the stars before I was" to explain their current circumstances of error. Fate is always looked upon with sadness, regret as if fate was a culmination of your upbringing, socio-economic status, schooling, parents, country of origin and skin color with no input from you making an iota of difference. To man fate is set, unchangeable, you are only following the path already laid out for you by "God" and another better one laid out for another.

That is the incorrect definition of fate. **Your fate is to return home to the Father,** to rise in consciousness from savage man who takes to man who follows the rules to man of spiritual enlightenment. That is your fate and it is the fate of all who believe themselves to be human-to return to living in heaven on earth so you may become the enlightened consciousness of which you didn't know you were, to live eternally in the consciousness of your creator, God, universal creative consciousness of harmonious expression. Your **fate** is to experience life with, in and of the harmony of God, not suffer and die.

Father

"Therefore call no man on earth your Father" is revealing that the creative principle of one is the same for all. **Therefore we must be equal, of one source** and this source is God, the Christ within, oneness. All have Christ consciousness but until it is known and active in your experience you will not show forth the individual talents given by God because you are not of **God** but of *man* until you have the **mystical** experience by which to know your Truth and your **only** Father.

Fear

Man's operating system is fear and that fear operates the thinking mind creating consequences and circumstances that you don't want to experience. Fear of being alone, fear of being left behind, fear of not being loved or loving someone. Fear of fame, fear of not getting fame.

Spiritual man has **no** fear rather our operating system, that which we are tuned into and respond to is God within. Spiritual man **responds** to God but man of earth *reacts* to man.

Fear

Every discord in life is because you are ignorant of Truth-God alone is the only presence expressing as all that is. Anything you feel that has power in your life is based in fear and **fear is the result of separation from the consciousness of God.**

Fear controls **all** *human* choices.

Fear

All fear arises from the belief your life can be terminated at any moment through lack, disease, accident or otherwise. Fear is the only motivating factor behind the life and activity of man; it is the driving force, maybe not understood as such but fear controls a human's behavior from taking the last bit of cereal in the box to stealing another's property because it is better than yours.

Fear, deeply seated and finely camouflaged, is expressed as personal and professional over achiever, prowess, constant doing, comparing, changing, conforming, praise seeking, condemnation, untoward behavior toward others that only benefits you. Lying, cheating, manipulating, physical and mental violence used to give you domination/control over your life because you know there is only you in your life to do it all and only one lifetime to do it in and he who dies with the most toys wins.

Fear and healing

You cannot be healed of fear, it is impossible because where there is fear there is the belief of danger and if there is a belief of danger there must be fear, they are co-joined, inseparable but fear is dissolved in the realization of God. You don't get healed of fear, you get God, you get a realization, attain an awareness then you find there is no thing to fear and that is the only thing that makes fear go-**the realization there is nothing to fear.** That is the Truth of every spiritual healer. **No spiritual healer can be successful if he fears the condition he is called upon to heal.**

No one can be a spiritual healer while they are in fear for in them there is not yet God. *Human* man cannot be a **spiritual** healer and all the Truth written is not the healing agent either, it is knowing the Truth of God by actual experience of God within and then you know **Truth**, God is and God is with you to help you rise.

When God is Truth to you error melts, is no longer a part of your experience because knowing Truth has made you free to live as you were intended to live-through, as and by your nature-incorporeal **spirit** in visible form and not a body of *flesh and blood* of its own making, own care and finite supply of inherent life.

Flesh

The Word became Flesh: God consciousness, invisible/unknowable manifest in the visible/knowable as form of all that is individualized. Think **available for use by mankind, manifest creation, knowable.**

Freedom

Freedom is not won or gained, it is **realize.** God known within as your Truth of being frees you from the *duality/chaos* of man.

You can never be persecuted for your religion if your religion is but the outward expression of your inner **relationship with God living Truth.** Words and actions are persecutable, grace through silence is not. You cannot be persecuted for being a person who sees no evil and expresses no evil.

Freedom

Freedom cannot be given to you by another. Freedom is only experienced when you **know** Truth. You can't *get* free *from* anything-husbands, wives, lack, ill health, etc. Even if you do succeed humanly in separating yourself from your perceived bad situation it will only be a temporary good, never permanent and real because you do not ever get free *from*. If you ever get free *from* something it is only to become *attached* to another thing.

The only freedom that results in complete freedom is a freedom **in** Christ, spirit, spiritual consciousness and that is why to leave one religious *organization* to join another religious *organization* is to find freedom from one only to get bound/enslaved to another.

That isn't freedom; you cannot *find* freedom by leaving one country for another; you can improve your lot in life, your ability to express humanly how and what you want to express; there is no denying the millions of immigrants that have improved their lot, living conditions, freedom of personal expression, physical, mental and moral wellbeing, found wealth but by virtue of that visible, physical change have **not** found peace, happiness, safety, security, full expression of Self because those things are not to be found in flags or countries or unifying songs, mantras, ways, laws or beliefs, they are found only in the realization of **no power.**

"I shall not fear what man can do to me, I shall not fear what circumstances or conditions can do to me, I shall not fear what infection or contagion, weather or climate can do to me" and in that loss of fear which is the result of raised/illumined consciousness, knowing Truth, you find harmony that only comes when you are free of man's ways of duality.

Freedom in God

Whenever you are going through a period of illness, unhappiness, frustration, lack of peace or lack of prosperity remember that **this has nothing to do with your outer world.** You will be tempted to believe that the external world is causing the difficulty but this is not so. If you can discern that this represents a battle going on **within yourself** you will quickly achieve victory just through the ability to discern that no person, condition or situation is doing anything *to* you. This is a battle within you in which your **higher Self is seeking ascendency** over the *mortal/material/carnal* sense into which you were born.

Every moment of every day man fights man for things man cannot give because what man is looking for is the ascendency of their higher Self for freedom, to not live as animals but to live a life of harmony with supply, good will and joy but man has no idea that is what they are seeking because the material world says there is only material things to seek to fill the void within.

What man seeks is **freedom** and freedom can only be attained individually. Freedom is not collective, it is individual for no man can free you, only you can free you.

Man does not realize it is freedom they seek and it is only found through God, the higher Self of being. **Man unknowingly seeks a spiritual principle** and yet man knows nothing of spiritual principle/Truth therefore man associates the feeling of emptiness as lack of *outer* things/satisfaction and thus perpetuates the horrors of man trying to *create* a life for themselves separate and apart from their Truth of being which does and will fill all the emptiness within.

No matter the names man gives to express his present conditions of lack they all stem from one thing: living separate from God, source. It is merely coming to the Truth within yourself that you **are of God** and this Truth will make you free from the weight of the world for God is the state of consciousness where there is no weight to bear for God has lifted it from your shoulders in the revealing of your true name and nature.

Fruitage

Fruitage/abundance/visible supply/harmony **is** God **as** manifest form. Your fruitage reflects the degree of God activity you bring to bear in your experience by right prayer and reliance on God in all ways for all things.

All men are created equal as all have the spirit of God within. It is not God's responsibility to do anything but be there when you are ready to experience God therefore this life of grace is completely yours to chose or reject, how far you go, how quickly you rise in understanding, how much you practice the presence and go into regular communion to the point of not having to go into communion because you are always together.

You determine the degree of your demonstration by the degree of your **desire** for God. The purpose of your wanting God must be righteous-for the knowing of God and Truth-for there to be a conversation and union between you and God. You can lie to yourself all you want, you can even make excuses to God but God is not there anymore, you have shut it out the second you thought something for yourself ie a want, desire, judgement, excuse or condemnation. You are on your own Mister. Toodles!

So how do you get back into God's harmony? Know Truth of your error, forgive yourself and those you hold in bondage and open yourself up to the consciousness of God within. But because you erred there will be consequences meted out because of the duality you reacted to as reality. You are not being punished by God for your sins, remember God knows **nothing** of your existence when you are not of **its** existence/consciousness, you are receiving the return of your actions, the law of karma, cause and effect upon you.

Frustration: separation from God

When you feel yourself losing it, getting frustrated, start to feel anxious or fearful it is because of one thing: you have closed the door on God, you have left its consciousness so once again you are functioning as a mere human and in that limited capacity you do get anxious, fearful etc.

This came to me one day as I was getting frustrated and began to make mistakes. I stopped and thought: why am *i* in this mood? And God said "because you are out of my flow." I was frustrated and in that mindset was human. I took a breath and smiled. "Ok Father, you are right, *i* was doing when it should have been you, the **I** of me doing all things through me for me as me."

You will feel yourself relax, deflate, a little chuckle helps open your consciousness to God, "thank you Father for always reminding me of where home is!"

Garden of Eden

The garden of Eden is a poetic expression of/for the nature of God-good, perfect-and is nothing more nor less than a **state of consciousness.** This state of consciousness is the awareness of the Christ, the Soul of God within each form called man. When this state of awareness through actual experience of the God within has been achieved you release all you have ever believed to be true about yourself and others and learn a new way of expressing-as individual expression of the one true God instead of human ego/personality.

God

God is the universal Law of creative expression expressing eternally; it is the consciousness of being, the governing influence of harmony/order perpetual and eternal in nature. God is **not** a he, a thing, a being. God **is.** Unqualified. Pinnacle, only, indivisible, all and only harmonious creative expression. Anything not of these qualities was not created in the beginning by God therefore does not exist in the kingdom/consciousness/creation.

What was created that is not of God's kingdom? Human man whose thinking mind is of duality, a mind that can be used for good and bad and believes God to be separate and apart from him.

God

God is the highest concept of being.

God

Even though God is impersonal Law when you are in a relationship with this inner presence you personalize this presence as a being, a he/she/it because when you have a relationship, any relationship, it is personal.

God is the Life, being and consciousness **of** you because you are **of** God. You are the individualized expression of God with the ability to know beyond the thinking mind of man.

God

God doesn't punish. Ever. God **cannot** punish you for your actions; the actions, sins, acts of omission or commission come back to you. The *consequences* of *your* actions come back to bite you in the pocketbook, body or mind because **God** has **nothing** to do with your *human* living or consequences there of.

God

God is the infinity of your individual being. Demonstrate this, prove it, begin in whatever way is open to you at this moment to let God's grace flow **from** you. Do not pray that God's grace come *to* you rather **open** out a way to let God's grace flow **from** you. This presence within you goes before you to make the crooked places straight ie harmony waiting for you as the Law unto you because it is the Law of your expression.

Your realization, awareness God is as all is what releases the allness of God, grace, into the world for others and returns to you as your supply, bread on the water, spiritual karma which is the perpetuation of good.

God

There is an invisible Law that **is** all that is and all that will come into visible expression. Think of oil in the ground. How is it that this viscus fluid which served no purpose to early man has become a staple of modern man? Because the consciousness of man has evolved, grown, gone beyond its former confines of understanding into that vast beyond of unknown through conscious oneness with the creator of that oil and its purpose to mankind along their evolutionary path.

Only as the consciousness of man opens to the consciousness of all that **is** can man dip into the great storehouse of knowing and allow that which was heretofore unknown to man come into expression. All has always been coming into expression as part of the Divine Plan it just needs you to get quiet, go within and let God give you that which was previously unknown to benefit the world in some way.

God

God is not a religious anything, **God is not religion.** God **is** being, **is** the unseen singular presence of creation. God is nothing you can define beyond saying it is the intelligent, directive harmony of all that is and you are an individual identity of this intelligent, directive harmony **when** you have an awareness of it by way of an actual experience. This experience is what is termed "meeting the Father face to face." This is the mystical experience, the experience that reveals your reality of being not as man of flesh and blood rather incorporeal perfection in form, child of the most high.

God is a presence

God is creative expression; **the** creative, maintaining and sustaining presence that **is** the universe. God is not a power over anything or anyone, God is as all. All is God in image and likeness, substance and form and maintains and sustains all that is of it.

God is as all that is, visible and invisible

There is no matter/material substance or form

To mortal man the natural makeup (base chemical makeup) of man, animal, mineral or plant is not spirit in form, God, rather a limited concept of life called *matter/material*. This is why any attempt to heal, change or correct the *physical/material* universe is evident you have not develop sufficient spiritual consciousness to understand that **there is no changing of the human scene through mental knowing/knowledge** rather a growing into a conscious reality above human duality where you live with a conscious connection to the one expression of creation which is the Truth of you.

Christ consciousness recognizes all life to be of God in expression therefore what *appears* as material to the human senses is not reality but merely the illusion or **false sense of what it is of** ie it isn't wood, it is God expressing **as** that which man calls wood. This is also a duality not always recognized. Man thinks of God *and*. Always God *and* you, God *and* the world when the reality is God **is** as all that is. Spiritual consciousness discerns all is of God and not matter/material in nature.

There is no *matter* or *material* in all of the universe because the creator of all that is termed physical, that which is visible to the five senses, is **spiritual consciousness manifest in form.** Therefore you cannot think from that level of sense perception but must remember to disregard appearances, turn from the picture before your eyes and become aware of the eternal Truth-**spirit** is the substance of all that is visible and it comes from the invisible.

All that is of the world as form/expression is of the same source no matter the outward form/expression. It may look like gold, steel, a living dog, a lustrous diamond or a dead tree but the Truth is all is God expressing in the form expressed/seen and all is enlivened, lived by Source regardless of how lifeless something seems to your senses.

There is no separating God from form because God is the source of all form.

God is Husbandman

Jesus compared God to the husbandman, the one who tends the "garden." Jesus said "I am the true vine and my Father is the husbandman. Every branch in me that beareth not fruit (the false beliefs/error of man) he takes away and every branch that beareth fruit he purgeth it that it may bring forth more fruit" ie the fruit, expression of God must be given, released for more to come into expression. "The vine does not eat of its own grapes/fruit."

It was through this revelation that the Master was able to feed and heal the multitudes and through this same realization any individual, teacher or healer can be the avenue through which God/good/grace flows from and back to as bread on the water, supply, peace, abundance. The good you release of God returns pressed down and flowing over revealing the eternal bounty of living under grace is a never ending cycle of perpetual good.

God is not a power

The secret is that in the moment you achieve the realization of God's **presence** you are aware there is no need of God being a power because Truth reveals there is nothing unlike itself that it must be a power over and you rest.

God is not religion

God is not a religious belief, God is not religion, God is spirit, the unseen, singular presence of creation harmonious and good. God is no thing you can define for yourself because you would be trying to define that which man doesn't know because *man* has not been face to face with the Father within. Therefore anything you think you know about God as a man is solely conjecture based on your *ignorance* of Truth.

Spiritual man has the companionship of the Father 24/7 and knows nothing man says about God is true because you cannot **know** God until you have an **experience** of God and when that happens, when you find the Father within, you are no longer *man,* cannot unfeel what you have felt and now know yourself to be **spirit.**

You can reject it, a lot of people do and they are absolutely miserable because the human side of them, their upbringing, their parents' demoralizing chatter, schooling, religious learnings etc, will not let the God of them be heard. This dichotomy of mind is that which literally makes people insane. They are trying to negate their Truth and in that loss of hope hate life, hate themselves, hate the fact that they cannot go to God and cry like the child they are and get the comfort that is their birth right.

Insanity is doing the same thing over and over expecting different results. Let the possibilities of your life become realities. I'm not just talking about God I'm talking about living. Let yourself live but to live you must change and to change you must be open, release old concepts (die daily) and see the world in a different way (one expression not two) and soon you will be living a completely different life but you have to **allow** yourself to do so. Forgive yourself, forgive the world, forgive 70x7 and just keep **open,** keep **silent,** keep sacred the experiences you have in this new consciousness of good and let the inner living begin.

It is a natural progression of man of slavery to become man of spirit. No different than the evolutionary chart of man as that from ape-ish to man and all the iterations in between. I'm not refuting it I am using it as the example of the same path of progression from **one state of consciousness out pictured as realized form, function, advancement to another** until the desired state of consciousness is reached-that of which you are, spirit in nature, etherial in form, prodigal son returned home.

God is supply/grace/God in action

Stop thinking about having, being and doing and center on God. God is your dwelling place. That is all you need, not a physical/material dwelling place but God. When you have God you not only have the dwelling place but all that is necessary to keep it up. In the same way God doesn't provide shelter from harm, safety or security and praying to God for those things is a complete waste of time.

God itself **is** your Hightower, God itself **is** your fortress therefore pray for the realization/awareness of God, for the realization of omnipresence and you will find that even though you walk around without any form of physical protection your **spiritual presence** guarantees that none of these evils will come nigh thy dwelling place. How can it? The place on which you stand is holy ground because in God is eternal harmony where chaos cannot invade.

God rains on the just and the unjust

The grace of God rains/touches on the saint and the sinner alike. The grace of God can touch any in need at any time it is asked for but grace is not a permanent dispensation, good in your life, **until** you know God aright.

Why? Because grace is a dispensation of God and for grace to become you permanent dispensation ie ongoing expression you have to be where grace is-God.

God is available to any who cry out in earnest for God's allness in some form. It matters not whether it is the prayer of a long time Truth student or one who just found rock bottom and is crying out for something other than what they are experiencing. All who seek receive **but it is up to the receiver to know what to do with the Truth received,** the peace felt, the knowing imparted, how to make it a livingness and not just a spot o' luck.

Those who seek to understand where the change, the peace, the harmony, the good came from will find it while there are those who receive a healing and will look at it as good luck, better human circumstances etc, but will soon find themselves right back in the position they were in-duality-therefore all of life as man is chance, back and forth, good to bad and back again. Man is a never ending cycle of trying to *get* from life that which God **gives** freely.

God realized

God realized is infinite, omnipresent supply.

God: material vs. spirit in form

God is the very substance, essence, Life and Law of all creation.

Man calls what is seen *material* creation but there is no material creation in all the universe for all that **is** is spiritual creation. God didn't *make matter* because God is all that is. All that **is** that man calls *matter* is **spirit** about which man *entertains a material concept*/view out of *ignorance* of **Truth.**

Man has a material sense of creation just as man has a material sense of man but there is no material man, there is no mortal man, there is no man that was ever born or has ever died; you have **always been the child of God.**

God's power

God's power is not power as man understands the word power to mean; knowing God within as the harmonious expression of your life is the expression of God **as** you which is your protection from the chaos and inharmony of human man. Knowing Truth is what keeps you in the kingdom so you can stop making easily avoidable mistakes on the spiritual path. Knowing all you every will need resides within you just awaiting expression through your spiritual awakening is what keeps you on the path because God is dependable. Yes, dependable. God is Law, Law is unchangeable so if the law of gravity holds today it will be holding a billion years from now. God is not like man, cannot change its mind because it hasn't a mind, it **is the universal Law of creative expression that only knows itself.**

The "power" of God is in **living** the Truth of God, that's it. Live in God and you will experience what words inadequately describe.

God's protection/God power

When people speak of power it is always of force, physical, mental or mechanical but the protection of God, the power of God is the **knowing** that if you live in conscious oneness you are protected from 95.9% of all the ills that befall mortal man thus experiencing heaven on earth.

God's will

Will is your expression. What you want is what you express outwardly and what you want creates conflict among man because all man want what *they* want.

God's will isn't like your human will of want and need, God's will merely means God expressing instead of human you expressing. God's will is nothing more than the Law it **is** in expression. God's will is not a personal will of choice determined by selfish desires of need or greed, like or dislike. God's will is what it **is,** harmonious expression which is harmony unto all situations.

Good and evil

Good and evil are *concepts* not **object** reality. Concepts are *individual* not **universal** therefore are not Law, have no Source therefore no Life to sustain them because they are merely *figments* of the *human* mind that cannot be found out in the world as **object** reality.

Good and Evil

Do not associate/identify evil with yourself but remember also not to associate/identify good with yourself. All good is of God and you are the instrument/transparency through which the quality and quantity of the Father appear. Nothing is outside the possible as long as you are not claiming any qualities or virtues as your own but acknowledge you are the **instrument** of God, not God.

I can of my own self do nothing, it is all the work of the Father **through** me.

Grace

The healing, revealing, sustaining influence, expression, effect, result of oneness with God.

Grace

The grace of God is the spirit of God in action which brings visible and tangible good into your experience.

Grace

Grace is the allness of God in evidence. Grace is the visible and the invisible, the needed things and the added things. Grace is harmonious expression, benevolence, love, kindness that flow through and out from you to touch those receptive, desirous of the grace of God whether that is something known to them or not.

Grace is not a favor God does for one over another. God's grace is the activity of God in visible and invisible expression that supports, supplies, maintains and sustains your eternal experience. Grace is the allness of God that pours through you and back to you as bread on the water-your blessings, your supply, your joy, harmony, your needed things and the added things in the degree of your oneness.

Grace in your experience

There are no coincidences on the spiritual path. All you experience is the hand of God, grace going before you. I talk to God a lot, out loud (alone) and silently. "Thank you Father" falls from my lips at every green light, perfect parking spot, good find, easy of transactions, kind people. Happy accidents? No, it is all God.

That near miss on the highway wasn't near at all. Grace kept it from happening not because of your driving skills or the other person's driving skills but by being in God consciousness you bring grace to bear in your experience therefore God **is** the expression of the drivers around you-harmony. God **is** the cause and effect/result of your experience and it is harmonious, good, great!

In all ways let God go first. Let God have first thought, first gesture, first word, first expression. You step aside, watch, listen and learn. Harmony is your expression when you let Harmony go first. What you are doing, saying and expressing is either the expression of the human you of duality or the God/harmonizing influence of you. Think of it this way, God's first impression is bound to be much better than yours could be humanly and the outcome when God goes first is much better for you in the end than if the human/ego/personality of you had gone first.

Always follow God's lead by letting God go first and you will experience harmony.

Graceful

There are those of whom the term graceful is used to describe. This doesn't mean any visible attribute but rather the Life that imbues them, the ease, peace, and harmony of their expression that stays with you after they have gone. What they have left with you lingers and reveals an ache to be likewise instead of the fumbling human you seem so often to be.

It is God you feel and this is the experience of grace, good, benevolence-God-in your midst and will be your experience when God is known to you by way of meeting God face to face within your own being thereby being able to say with understanding "I am not separated from God!" and this Truth in awareness is the only thing that allows you to release the false *beliefs* of man as the *illusions* they are.

Gratitude

Gratitude is the currency of Love. Gratitude for God in your life is what keeps bringing grace into your life. Gratitude is the awareness of God as all and giving thanks for all that is of God, the food you eat, the clothes you wear, the house you reside in, the vehicle you drive, the peace in your midst, the health of your countenance, the joy in your laughter and the ease of your finances.

All is God because God is all there is and when you come to that realization you cannot help but grin like a dang fool when you look around and see the Father pouring forth its perfection at every turn. This is what you are grateful for and it will become a constant dispensation of grace in your midst when gratitude for grace is your expression.

Gratitude-your purpose

When you receive a spiritual healing you don't receive a physical healing as man would want to fix, change or alter their lives, you receive a **demonstration** of God's omnipotence, omnipresence and omniscience in your experience and that is what to be grateful for.

The **key** to Life is "if so be the spirit of God dwell in you." That is it. If God **is** your consciousness you are home, right where you are meant to be and just rest, listen and enjoy the ride while God navigates your experience.

Greatest possession

What is the greatest possession you could desire? Truth.

Truth is more desirable than the whole earth.

Ye shall **live** Truth in **expression** and this **frees** you from the *duality* of man to live eternal **oneness** with God.

Once you **know** your Truth **as** child of God you possess the only thing worth having in this experience which is the allness of Life.

Harmony

When you live in the atmosphere/consciousness of harmony you are harmonious. When you live in the atmosphere/consciousness of duality/chaos you are of duality and chaos.

You are always where you are in consciousness and that place of expression is what the world experiences of you and it is either of harmony or chaos, God or man. It truly is that simple once you have the principle of Truth by which to discern the entire world around you and finally feel that you know Life, can have Life and can share this Life that is joyous, easy, abundant and free from all the baggage man carries as their expression.

Spiritual man travels light carrying only God while human man carries an 80 lb ruck sack trying to sprint up hill wondering why they never seem to get where they desire to be.

He hangeth the earth on nothing

What does this mean? In the spiritual realm no one thing is dependent upon another in other words when you are doing spiritual healing it isn't even dependent on **you** knowing Truth, it is merely dependent on an **absolute silence and stillness** where you hold space for the Father to fill with **its** presence and **it** doeth the works of bring **itself** to bear, bringing harmony to the situation. **Conscious oneness is the healing principle of God, that which reveals Truth in the midst of error.** The healing is the harmony brought to bear in the situation ie relief, release received.

Everything is alright Child, I have you for you are mine, always and forever my perfect expression.

Healing

Intercession, mediation, opening a way to bring God awareness/Truth of being to another not by self but by/through conscious oneness **with** Self, God. You with the higher consciousness of God are the **instrument** by which man who seeks what is not of this world can find what is not of this world-God within.

This seeking is the Christ of you, the spirit of God within all man craving to return to what makes it in every way whole so you may be the light of God to bring others into the light from their life of darkness caused by being ignorant of Truth.

You heal ignorance by revealing Truth-God is and is within you.

Healing

A healing is the recognition of the Spirit within which is the real Self, not the self thought of as the human. When this Truth is realized all perceived powers of man-disease, lack, pain, even death-dissolve into their true nature of nothingness because there is only one presence, God, harmonious expression so how can there be other than harmonious expression?

This is the illusion a healing dispels. When the Truth of being is realized you embody a world separate and apart from the *sense* world. You are a world unto yourself existing in the human world but not **of** it for your world **is** the kingdom, consciousness, your conscious oneness with God where there is all you will ever need without anything from the outer world of illusion. Your inner world of spirit is the only reality not the outer world which is merely a projection of *human* thought with its many expressions for man to fear.

Give no thought to appearances.

During one of my trying times when error was presenting in a very personal way I asked God to give me that which would allow me to let go of the illusion without trying, faking it because I just wanted the ick to go away. I received "what does it matter?"

Really what does it matter? What does it matter what happens in life if you know with God, even if in the moment all is upside down, painful and confusing you will come out the other side more harmonious than you were before. If that was the end of our friendship there is harmony because it wasn't where I was supposed to be. If the friendship is better because of the grace brought to bear then there is harmony as well. God is a win/win.

However there may come a time that feels like you are losing ground just when you are really getting the swing of spiritual living. This honestly is to be **expected** and everyone needs to be aware, not afraid but aware that when the tremors of restructuring start to be felt rest, know, ah, this. This is good, it is uncomfortable and **must** be trusted and not fought against and all will be good just stay the course, let God lead, let God go first in all ways and in that way you are always safe from picking up the sword and incurring human karma.

Healing

Healing isn't healing in the sense of man's healing. Spiritual healing is spiritually healing man of the *belief* in duality/two expressions. It is a healing **influence** that dispels error by revealing Truth- God is and is within you.

When you have the realization/awareness of God within by way of an actual experience of God then healing takes place because Truth has been revealed. The healing of the error shows definitively the reality of one power, within, perfect, harmonious good is-ing eternally, perpetually. This is God and this is what a healing reveals within oneself.

Healing, spiritual

In spiritual context a healing is when Truth has been revealed within your own being that ultimately brings you to the realization of your true nature as spirit, individualized expression of the one expression, God, universal intelligence. The realization of your true nature reveals you are one with the Father therefore no longer human in nature, that was a costume or belief but was not the *reality* of you. The reality of you has been found to be the consciousness within that speaks to you, guides you and is the source of all the needed and added things.

All humanhood falls away as Spirit returns home to the Father, I and my Father are one not two. Now life as it was meant to be lived begins and you are under grace forever more as long as your consciousness is stayed on Thee, pray without ceasing, love thy neighbor as yourself, pray for your enemy that the Truth of God be revealed to them and like the Master forgive 70x7.

The only way to be free of this world of chaos and death is by knowing God aright.

Hell

Hell is not a physical place it is a state of consciousness you express thus incur. If you are going through hellish experiences it is because you are expressing as human man, of duality and feel the error of this expression as that which returns to you.

Hell is your choice not God's.

Hidden manna

Hidden manna is grace, the infinite good within you; it is the allness of God pouring forth for your experience and expression. It is like the lakes behind Niagara Falls, the source of that which is visible, **the falls in action,** but from the vantage point of the falls the source is not seen ie unseen, out of conscious knowing but is the source of the expression seen as the falls.

Human conscience

Human conscience: personal judgment that assists in distinguishing right from wrong according to individual self.

Spiritual man does not judge or make choices of how to behave rather expresses from the consciousness of God, the expression of harmony where you do not *think* from a place of i, personal, rather **listen** to I, universal/God.

Spiritual man has no need of a conscience because spiritual man does not decide, spiritual man **abides** in Truth and Truth does it all for you through you as you. You already chose God over duality therefore there is never another choice to make, you rest having already chosen harmony and to have that harmony as a reality you must **express** what you desire to experience and that can only be done when you are in oneness with the source of the harmony you wish to experience.

human faith

Human faith is nothing more than superstition or belief. It is only when one has an actual experience of God that you realize "faith" means nothing more than belief used as a shield, soap box or sword but is of no actual good to you until it is based in Truth/actual experience and then it becomes realized Truth, faith through awareness, knowing by experience, Truth unto you.

Human man

Human man is not the child of God

Human man is not spiritual being

Human man cannot experience heaven

Human man is born into certain death

Human man is a *concept of expression* given of man about man to define the form the individualized consciousness of God expresses as. All is spirit in expression therefore human man is spiritual man unaware of his true nature.

Human man vs spiritual man

When you read that man of spirit is not subject to the laws of man it can be very confusing. What it means is that the laws of man are yesterday's news, that is the Old Testament of laws and punishment whereas the laws of God are higher in consciousness than just brute force and punishment. God's Law of peace, love and forgiveness is the Law governing one who has risen in consciousness above the need for physical/material laws of man because they have grown beyond the consciousness of i, ego, small self and realize there is a big Self, One Self.

How does spiritual man transcend human laws? By being of a higher understanding/conscious knowing than man who doesn't know God. As child of God you are no longer living in the mindset of man of duality therefore you are free to see that if you stop fighting man, stop fighting yourself for a place in this world and defer to the One who can show you your **true place** in the world you no longer struggle, life becomes easier, smoother, less pendulum swing from good to bad and reside in is. When life **is** there is no struggle, no needs, no wants and no desires. It **is.** Say "is" to yourself. See if you can take "is" any further in discussion in your mind.

Now take good and bad. Think of something that you love, or something that you hate or fear. Once that is in your head you can ruminate, chew and reorder it and along the way your emotions are churning and bubbling and you are either getting happy, sad or angry.

This is the difference between man of earth and man of Spirit. Man can always find something to keep his mind cranking out useless emotions and fears that keep him from getting anywhere. The spiritual man however is always in a state of isness, ease, just is. Nothing else to say. The issue is dissolved and no longer a part of you. Instead of reacting spiritual man sits without judgement and lets God bring to consciousness the reality of what is being presented and in that revealing of Truth spiritual man rests because Father has said "it isn't what it seems, this isn't Truth, move on, what does it matter?" Ok, thanks Father! Love you!

Human mind

The human mind is the processing center of man, the decision maker, the interpreter, judge and jury of life because the mind *seems* to have abilities to discern what is good or bad for you and wants to decide for others as well. It has become a *reasoning* mind, a mind that weighs and balances consequences then makes a *choice* as to how to proceed for maximum self benefit/survival.

This is the error of man. The mind is not for *thinking* rather is an avenue of **awareness,** a **deductive** mind that **processes** what is **given** to do that is then done by God through you as you. God is the knowing that allows you to perform what is given to do. You don't *think* of what you are going to do beyond what is normal and natural for you to do ie work, home, family. That which is to prosper you will come from within to your conscious knowing and God will lay out your spiritual journey from itinerary to lodging, enjoyment to quiet contemplation while you are just along for the ride experiencing the life laid out for you when you let God be the boss and you the intern with great benefits.

All of this life when it is lived righteously is that of teacher and student, Father and child. You do as your teacher instructs using its conscious understanding of what is to be done and the way is imparted to you. All that you will need to know will be given through impartation.

Human mind

The human mind is not God, is not creative and has no power. With my mind I can know you are in a room with me but with my mind I can't place you here in this room, I cannot *create* your existence in this room, all I can do with my mind is to be **aware** of your presence because my senses tell me so.

You cannot know Truth with the mind for the mind is not made to know Truth, the mind rightly known is an instrument of consciousness because the senses register the outer world. Your mind *reacts* when you are of duality but when you are one with God the mind becomes a **faculty, a tool** for deduction, it is through the mind you become **aware** of that which is the Truth of the world around you.

Spiritual man does not create but spiritual man is in the flow of all creation, of all that is already created but you have to be **of** the consciousness **of** the flow and the flow is God in your conscious knowing.

This is literally the only secret to Life-**know God by actual experience and it is by this knowing signs follow-all the needed and added things.**

Human parenthood/children

Human parenthood is only the *visible* manifestation of **divine parenthood.**

The Truth of every human birth is the divine expression of God **but** because the child is born into an atmosphere of duality/no God awareness in their parents, their expression will be of duality which is the reason for all *human* suffering before and after birth.

However children born from an atmosphere of God knowing will be the expression of that knowing, of perfection ie without the expression of error therefore seen as healthy before and after birth. Once you begin to perceive you are not merely the visible expression of the union of two finite humans it is then that you break the law of heredity, you break its good aspects and its bad aspects and you understand yourself and all others to be expressions of creation, of Truth and not a limited concept of false beliefs in expression called *human* man.

Humility

Going to God knowing you know nothing but desire more than anything to know everything.

Hypnotized by appearances

The error of man lies in the duality of good and bad powers at play against you in the world. You *react* to the appearance of good, you react to the appearance of bad, you *react*. You have given what is out in the world power over you by accepting it as Truth when it is not. By accepting and reacting to what is out in the world you have given man/the world **the ability to change your mood, your expression.**

How does *reacting* to a stimulus/effect/vision/illusion give it power *over* you? Think for a moment of something that you saw in the last week that brought forth a pretty strong emotional *reaction* from you, good or bad. Now I want you to think of all of the ensuing conversations that came from that heightened *emotional* state. How long did you ruminate on that subject? How many people did you talk to about it? What actions did you take either for or against the situation? Do you see that all the time spent on that which can have no effect on your life was of no benefit to the situation in fact detrimental because it kept you down, ruminating, fearing, hoping, etc?

If this isn't the power to control you I don't know what is. And it is you *letting* the power of *appearances,* illusions in your mind, control your thinking, your actions and your consciousness of being. Every fear you have, every joy you have controls you, has power *over* you in some way that will not allow you to just be without judgement or involvement.

It is this human need to be a part of everyone else's lives that creates the chaos in the world-someone always trying to control another or the world around them by using mental, physical or material force/power instead of bringing harmony to bear by bringing God into awareness to heal those who seek thereby lessening the chaos of the world one man at a time.

I am I am: what it means

Every person must come to the place of "I am I am." This is the definition of the word **mystic,** one in conscious union with God, realized oneness with God and the actual experience of God-conscious awareness of its presence within you, felt, communed with, rested upon and prayed to for the things of God-its wisdom, peace, patience, benevolence, supply, understanding.

Mysticism is the practical application of this union to bring about a life lived with God as God's expression to the world. Every mystic that walks the spiritual path knows and reveals through silent meditation, prayer and treatment that **I am that I am** in expression and deed. **I am** the visible expression of God as harmony and healing to the world.

Idolatry

Idolatry is a *belief* that *items* can be imbued with the **spirit** of God ie edifices, statues, idols and then *worshipped* as if they *were* **God.**

To *worship* something is to believe *it* has power in and of its form to do something to or for you. Man worships other man, wooden object, golden calf, self etc, all of which have no power because **there is no power in the world but that of God.** Every time you pick up your prayer beads, light a candle, touch holy water, *take* communion, perform ritual or right or pray to a God *outside* of you you are worshipping *man* and not **God.**

There is no way to *worship* God. In fact if you *worship* God you do not know God aright because you cannot worship that which is **within** only that which is *outside* of you and by now you know there is nothing outside of you that has any power of good or bad thus cannot do anything to you unless *you give it the power of thought* believing it can come into expression as you *envision* it.

Ignorance of the Law of God

Ignorance of the Law of God is disobedience, though disobedience is willful and ignorance is not knowing but once something is known it cannot be ignorance anymore and becomes a willing/willful choice.

You are only ignorant of something once, after that you are enlightened and **responsible** for your choices ie returning karma. You can try to be ignorant of God after you know God but that is willful and as human man once again in expression will reap duality.

Ignorance-the silent killer

Ignorance is the most deadly weapon/killer there is among man, more deadly than all the weapons of mass destruction, all the wars down through the ages and all the disease that has ravaged the human form.

Ignorance is the cause of all that has brought death and destruction to man so if man were no longer ignorant of their Truth there would be no wars, no weapons and no death because what breeds instability, chaos and fear would be no more.

When you are no longer ignorant of something it is because something more fundamentally true has been revealed within yourself and with that revelation grow in conscious understanding and move on to do it again and again. This is called illumination and it is the only cure to ignorance.

Illumination

Spiritual discernment that sees through the appearances of duality by knowing omnipresence, omnipotence and omniscience where I am.

Illusion

Figment of the thinking mind, not real, subjective not objective, what man calls reality.

Immaculate Conception

Immaculate conception is that which comes into expression of itself eternally ie without the hand of man. This is also the definition of a miracle. Both reference the nature and expression of God, all that is perpetuating itself eternally.

Impersonalization

Separating the sin/power/appearance from the form *named as* the error itself ie murderer, thief, adulterer, liar, manipulator. The word is not your Truth, that is the word man has given to the error in judgement you have made.

No thing that you have done, good or bad defines you. Those were actions expressed because you didn't know how to not express them ie you didn't know how to be peaceful let alone remain peaceful because you as human man have no idea what peace feels like, why it benefits you therefore do not search beyond good and bad as descriptors of yourself and your experiences.

Once you begin to feel the Truth of the words "child of God, spirit in form not flesh and blood, full and complete not in lack or want" you can more easily see how man is living, how you used to live by qualifying, judging compared to now where you understand all you did as a human was because the world around you was doing the same thing. Not right obviously but what else is there to do but experience what is around you, the atmosphere of the people around you? You can't, neither can anyone else and this is why the sins you have committed were not your fault, they were the result of living in an atmosphere of others doing the same thing.

What you are responsible for is the return of the error, the consequences. What man has no concept, no way of understanding is that every error/bad circumstance was for you to stop and examine why it came back at you the way it did. In every instance without fail you, if you are completely naked and honest with your Self, in someway either started the ball of antagonism rolling or kept it rolling because you *felt* hurt, slighted, shamed, afraid, threatened, bullied, challenged etc and reacted, did something.

What we tend to forget is that at any time, at the first blush of erroneous thought/action, after you have lied yourself down to the three foot mark of a six foot hole, even as the first shovel of dirt stings your eyes-you can ask God to come into expression to stop the ever increasing karma *you* are incurring.

You can stop returning karma just by taking responsibility for your actions because it is your guilt over your actions, doing instead of stopping, walking away, taking a beat, that eats away at you and keeps you angry at yourself which is why you react-you are already on edge.

To release the burden and yourself you have to admit you have been human just like all of us have and realize you have a choice going forward to not feel this way again and that is by learning what peace is, where it is and what it does for you.

Maybe for the first time in your life you realize you **do** have control of the quality of your life because you now know how to change your expression, stop your human self and bring peace to bear, God into awareness. Peace releases your from the belief you are merely *human* who is flawed and messy and reveals **I am the child of God learning to be what that means.**

The world is showing you at every turn its duality, chaos and confusion, that there is something wrong with this livingness, we all feel it but have done it all the same but what you may not understand is each man creates the atmosphere of hate, anger, fear and lack that is their world/experience.

One of the greatest **benefits** to being in oneness with God is that God makes all the decisions while you reap all the peace of **not** *making choices/decisions.* Why? Because if you are not making choices based on finite information it cannot come back to bite you in the butt meaning no negative karma, nothing to fix. End of story. What God wants to be done may be very hard for *your* ego or heart to take but know without a doubt if you follow the will of the Father peace will be the path you walk because you are not doing your will that takes you away from your source of peace.

Importance of secrecy

Why is secrecy so important? Think of man and their judgements and beliefs. Anyone who is not of the mass mind is ridiculed, cast down and cast out from society and **until** you have imbibed enough Truth as to who you are and why you are **you cannot share with others.** Why? Because man will tear at you until you think you were wrong to believe in God the way you do, the only way, the truthful way. Man will bring you back down to earth because man destroys that which it doesn't understand and in this case that will be you. Keep this inside until you can stand on it in the middle of the valley of death, in the middle of chaos, in the center of the storm and know you will be safe even if this body is lifeless because you are not the body, you are eternal spirit in form.

At the point you are strong, when you know Truth and are past the confusion of this new way of living, then and only then can you share because your expression of Truth speaks louder than any word you could speak and it is the expression that keeps the wolves from attacking for they feel your Truth and walk away.

You are protected by your knowing Truth and man knows no Truth but will try their hardest to take yours from you if you are not at the point where the weapons of man cannot hurt you.

Impulse

To have an impulse as a *human* is to *react* to that *outside* of you.

To have an impulse as **risen** son is to **respond** to that from **within** which is to be known and done.

The feeling of God is an impulse that comes unbidden from within and will without fail bring peace along with a solution. That sudden feeling to do grocery shopping later than earlier and find you would have had to go to the store twice because of an unannounced guest. That feeling that made you turn where you didn't think you should only to find out it was right. The feeling to call someone to find out if they need some help. Spiritual man lives by these impulses, they are the flow of God in your awareness and the more you do as bidden the more you receive for your listening attitude.

God isn't a reward system for doing good over bad. God **is** the gift when you live is, spiritual **awareness.**

Inspired revelator

One who reveals Truth

Mystic/Jesus/Gautama, **you** when the Christ has entered in/come into your awareness.

Integrity

Human man's expression of self to do right in the face of evil or to resist evil. Life for one of integrity is a constant struggle between good and evil because they have more to lose than one who has little by way of little integrity. Understand integrity is a *personal* assessment of *their* morality therefore is of man and not of God.

Intuition

Intuition rightly understood is God. That which people call intuition is that which happens when the mind is quiet, there is nothing going on and intuitively, from **within** yourself, you get an impulse, an idea, a revelation, an ah ha moment.

Intuition is that which comes to you from within but it **isn't** your mind *thinking* rather it is **that you have inadvertently opened the door, the channel, the flow of God intelligence, grace, Truth.** It is God giving itself to you to bring good/harmony to you.

Many people follow their intuition because they have learned over the years that it doesn't let them down. This is God. That which comes to you from within not of your thinking mind is God revealing grace/harmony. I believe they present to us as chances to grasp the source of **miracles** because that is what they are, that which happens without the aid of human hands. These impartations, revelations will eventually lead one to find out more about them, where they come from and ultimately what they mean and that is the definition of a spiritual path.

For myself my journey began when I discovered something I named "pushing the universe." There had been many times I felt inharmony within, pushed it down and tried to ignore it because I wanted what I wanted damn it!

One day I got that feeling within, that irregular heart beat and nervous tension in my body. I realized it came at the time I was to make a big decision. This had happened over the years but it was only then I somehow began to associate the feeling with something that would end badly, not an omen of bad tidings but just a "hey, you have done this before, thought this way, rationalized it and worked it all out knowing it was a tightrope walk at best" but the *i want* of me always seemed to get the best of me and then *i* would regret it because there would be a mess to clean up and in many cases the loss of investment, inventory or property because *i* had gone beyond my *human* limits in some way.

So this time when *i* got that feeling *i* stopped and said to myself, "no, *i* am pushing the universe, *i* can feel it and for the first time *i* am going to honor it." 2 weeks later grace was revealed though *i* didn't know it as grace.

What **I** would have missed if **I** hadn't changed the consciousness behind my behavior! **I** wanted to do life differently than *i* had been and that simple thought blossomed into what you are reading today.

This is the path you step onto when you stop pushing the universe, stop trying to manipulate, orchestrate or in any way try to determine your future through your actions. Your future is determined solely by your understanding of self and in that understanding find Self, God, the allness of being.

The point is this-all have experienced God at one point or another and may have at first thought it was God but then changed the designation of source because no one talks about how God is within you helping you out so to keep from feeling like a freak, weirdo, nut you put it down to a one-off, a fluke. But in doing that you have denied the reality of God and suffer the pain, the karma of living without God to live amongst man where you don't fit in and continue to feel the ache of emptiness you are hoping to fill with the things of man and the world.

Know this: if it was from within, given freely and was **exactly** what you needed to bring **harmony** to self, situation or future (you could see how it could play out ie harmonious in all ways) God has touched you and will do so again if you do what you did-get quiet, rest and ask for Truth to bear. That is all you want from intuition isn't it? That which you do not as yet know? That which will bring peace within you? No peace can be found out in the world if it first is not within you to flow out.

When people say to trust your intuition it should be with this caveat now that you have an understanding of what it is you are being given: **Truth** from God from within will always bring **harmony** to all situations and **all** involved. If what you receive is for *personal* gain, *personal* satisfaction, *personal* anything it is of your mind, duality and you will suffer the sin.

Intuition

Listening to Joel the meaning of the word became clear. He was talking about Edison and how he worked mathematical problems. He said there was a place where the reason/thinking mind ends and intuition takes over. This is exactly what contemplative meditation is. You take a bit of what you know that you want more understanding on and let it roll around until it ebbs into stillness and then you wait for intuition to take over.

That is the human view of intuition and it is the **spiritual** definition of contemplative meditation which is a spiritual prayer, inner listening for the Father within to bring that which is desired to be understood or known.

In-tu-it-ion-**In to it.** You go in to it, within, to hear Truth, get the answers or that which washes away pain. Man is unknowingly employing **spiritual** techniques to receive spiritual answers but think *they* are the one intuiting them, bringing them forth, and that is the **error.**

You of yourself can do nothing it is the Father within who doeth the work. You do not bring forth from God what you want, God reveals what it is you need to understand at that moment to grow in conscious understanding. Sometimes it is a tasty bite and sometimes it is the whole enchilada, guac and all!

Intuition is turning **in to It,** God, and can be used to refer to the way God operates in consciousness for they are the same in that respect. They are both a going within to have that which is not known revealed but the comparison ends there because man believes it is their *personal* ability to tap into something called intuition that makes them better seers, healers, astrologers, tarot readers, angel communicators ie mental/metaphysical healers.

Mind healers and metaphysical healers believe *they* have special abilities that allow them to tap into the unseen setting themselves apart by their intuitive *powers.* There are very powerful healers, seers, astrologers, and readers but to spiritual man who knows Truth they are merely manipulating appearances with a higher than average chance of being right because they are unknowingly tapping into spiritual Truth which gives them a higher potentiality of being right among men but unable to partake of spiritual Truth consistently through knowing God aright.

What is done through the mind is not intuition it is merely manipulation of that which is already a manipulation ie duality. Man can only temporarily reorder/restructure their lives because re-anything is merely changing the outward appearance with no change in nature/consciousness. What was sickness today is wellness tomorrow but sickness of another sort two weeks from now. How is that a healing? How can your future be revealed by that which is outside of yourself? It has no connection to you or to Truth to be anything other than an illusion, intrusion for you to experience through thought or fear.

The point is when you need anything you just pop **in to it** and rest a bit. Refreshments in twenty with a side of Truth for your afternoon delight!

Is

We use the word **is** constantly yet have no idea of what it means.

According to Merriam-Webster **is** is Middle English, from Old English, akin to Old High German *ist* is (from sin to be) Latin est (from esse to be) Greek esti (from einai to be) or in combined form, Later Latin, from Greek, isos **equal.**

Definition of is:

Present tense, third person singular of BE

Dialectal present tense first person and third person singular of BE

Dialectal present tense plural of BE.

What is BE?

Present participle-being

Present tense first person singular-am

Present tense second person singular-are

Present tense third person singular-is

Definition of Be:

To have an **objective** existence, have reality or actuality; live; I think, therefore I am

To have, maintain, or occupy a place, situation or position

To remain unmolested, undisturbed, or uninterrupted, used only in infinitive form **let him be.**

Is must be harmonious because is **is** Self perpetuating, eternal, infinite. Is **is** the functioning of all that **is** and have named it God. I am because God **is** Self perpetuation of eternal harmony in outward expression.

Is

When you live as spirit there is no good and there is no bad, there is only **is**. What is **is**? **Is** is that feeling of perfect flow in your life. There **is** easy, harmony, happiness, big sigh, life **is** grand with a smile that lights the sky. **Is** is harmonious expression; only that which **is** exists infinitely. The is of God, the harmony that **is** the consciousness of God is of a nature indescribable. How do you rate peace? The feeling of freedom? the knowing of God within? You would rate it according to how you would feel if you **lost** it. If God suddenly stopped talking to me I know he isn't gone for it is infinite but the emptiness of my own being, just thinking about it makes my breath catch on a sob.

Is

That which **is** is Self expressing Self. A dog isn't bad, it **is** a dog that has not been trained. Money isn't good or bad, it **is** a mode of exchange. Weather isn't good or bad, it **is** weather. Is only becomes something other than is **when you put your spin on it according to your history.** You may think rain, thunder and lightning are amazing while another hides in fear because of their past history ie irrational fear, of those elements but they are **no thing** other than rain, thunder and lightning expressing **as** what they are.

All **is** when what **is** is not qualified or judged, not seen through the conditioning of your history. Is **is.** Period. All that **is** is God expressing without judgment, without history, without anything of the *mind* of man coming in to alter what **is.**

Isness/is-ing-the power of God

The power of God is not power in the sense of force but in the sense of being present in awareness as all that you could ever want or need. All that **is** must be good/harmonious otherwise it would contain duality which prevents harmony therefore that which is **is** because it is of **singular** source, no duality and that is the only thing that begets infinite existence-harmony.

Law unto yourself

You become a Law unto yourself by your oneness with God therefore the laws of man, the beliefs of man, the powers of man have no power over you because by being of the consciousness of the only Law there is-good, harmonious eternal expression, God-you are not bound by or affected by the laws and beliefs of *man* because you embody, are **of** the only true Law there is-harmony.

Therefore when you are in oneness you are **of** the only Law there is, you are knowing the **only** Truth-God is-and this is the governance of your life, that which you live by and it is within you not external to you therefore you are Law unto yourself.

God is Law unto your being therefore becomes the Law unto your expression. This is Law, Truth not belief, not faith, not fancy. Law. You are only consciousness expressing and from where you express-God or man-is the governance of the expression unto your experience.

Life

Functional activity/expression of conscious creation man calls God.

Love

The greatest power/presence on earth or in heaven or in hell is the power/presence of Love but Love is not an emotion, a word or a statement. Love is an **action,** a doing, a being. Love can never be expressed in words in fact the very words "I love you" can be covering up its opposite. The spoken word of love has no more relationship to Love than the spoken *word* God has any relationship to the **experience** of God.

No one is going to ever know God by saying God and no one is going to Love by saying love. Love is God in activity, not just one but a **series of actions** and those actions must be God in expression which means care, thoughtfulness, forgiveness, consideration, cooperation, benevolence.

Love was expressed by Paul in the same way, "the greatest of these is Love," not the *word* love but **being** Love, the expression of God flowing out from you to return as peace and harmony.

Love

Love is praying that the kingdom of God be established in the hearts and souls of **all** man, that the gentle governance of God be the governing influence of mankind and that all man willingly surrender to the wisdom and ways of God. Pray the will of God be established **in** you and that the will of God be done **for** you, let God's love flow **through** you that you may be wise, loving and benevolent toward all of your brothers and sisters.

Man

Man is the illusion resulting from the belief in both harmony and chaos, good and bad, that there is duality in and of all possible outcomes.

To live God's harmony you must give up that which constitutes duality and that is only the personal judgement/bias placed upon that which is seen, touched, tasted, smelled and heard. If you stopped qualifying everything according to *your* likes and dislikes there would be absolutely no chaos in the world around you and as more become one with God the more harmony there will be out in the world and soon the whole world will be harmonious.

Spiritual living is an individual path but by individual attainment and sharing God through your expression you begin the enlightenment of the masses one person at a time.

Manifesting

Man has always been told told he could manifest that which he would like to have in his life by thinking and believing they already have it. This may be true in the human world but it is not of any spiritual nature, has nothing to do with God or anything related to spirituality.

Man may be able to *manipulate* his current circumstances by dream boards, secret writings, spells, chanting, following the stars, giving sacrifices of things or of self but just as surely as they come into your experience they will leave because they are not born of the spirit, of the grace of God, supported and maintained by God infinitely.

Manifesting spiritual supply

There is no such thing in the world as demonstrating material supply. It is an absolute impossibility because there is no *matter* to get because this is not a *material* world. The only thing that can be manifested is **God** in awareness which is your supply unto every need.

Human man thinks he can manifest things of the world through mind power/perceived power but inherent in what is "manifested in man's world" is the duality of man's consciousness and as such has no permanence because man is trying to obtain and retain an illusion which is nothingness. Man tries to get and keep figments of his imagination in tangible form by manipulating circumstances for purpose but it is just a temporary change because you have no way of controlling the will, thus the actions, of the one you manipulated thus the beginning of the Hatfield's and McCoy's, chaos because of duality.

Do you see how nothing *gotten* in the human world has any permanence because you are *taking* not being **given** and what is taken can be taken again. What is given is eternally yours until you decide to give of it to share the gift that was given to you.

Master/Teacher

Servant of the Father

Jesus was Master, teacher of Truth, servant of the Father doing the Father's will to bring peace and harmony to those receptive to living differently than man of duality, chaos, pain and death.

Materialistic concept of life

The belief that all that is is separate and apart from God in substance and form.

Man classifies all that is as matter, material according to the periodic table which is a man made classification of that which was at one time unknown.

The Truth is all is of God, creative consciousness expressing. Since God is the expression of all that is there is no separate *materials* that make up different forms rather there is one **consciousness** expressing as all the forms needed. Spiritual man knows there is nothing called matter or material in this world, only God expressing as the needed and added things. All is God in form.

Mental power

Mental power is what human man thinks is *their* ability, their strength, their cunning, their intelligence over another.

Mesmeric influence

Every phase of discord that comes into your experience is a mesmeric influence from which you do not know how to protect yourself. In other words when you are in the midst of an epidemic of any disease you are not necessarily suffering *from* the disease but from the mesmeric *belief* in *disease* as a **reality.**

The world of man is predicated on this mesmeric influence of a belief in a power other than God/good which is duality. This mesmeric influence has been in existence since before time was and has been lived as reality because those who knew it was mesmerism, a false reality, are long gone.

It has only been with the mystical understanding of Biblical Truth that error has been revealed to be no thing and the reason to not resist evil and not to pick up the sword.

Mesmeric influence

It has never been revealed to you that every discord coming to you is a mesmeric influence that you can accept by reacting humanly or dismissing it as ignorance, no thing thus being unaffected by it.

An example would be you being in the world during a pandemic. You are not necessarily suffering from the actual organism in your body but the *fear* of it getting on or in your body. Remember like begets like, what you fear is what comes upon you. Probably just as many people died from the mesmeric influence, the fear, of the disease as from the effects of the organism itself on the body.

No matter how deadly viruses and other microbes seem to be in the *human* experience they have no Law behind them, ie if polio can be eradicated by a vaccine there is no Truth, no Law of God in or of the effects of polio. Therefore all disease, all the things the medical community works to correct the *effects* of are nothing more than the *belief* in the *ability* to get sick, the *belief* you are not the child of God **unable** to get sick because **you are consciousness in form** not *physical* flesh and blood.

Metaphysic

Greek-meta ta physika, "after the things of nature" referring to an idea, doctrine, or posited reality outside of human sense perception. In modern philosophical terminology metaphysics refers to the study of what cannot be reached through **objective** studies of material reality ie the study of what is not visible.

Metaphysical Truth is the revealed Truth of mystics, that which has been received through communion, consciousness. This revealed Truth is the Truth of God received by mystics to bring the knowing of God to man. When you go into contemplative mediation you take a metaphysical Truth into consciousness to get your mind out of the world of man and in oneness with God. You rest with Truth to bring Truth into awareness, God on the field which is the definition of a mystic, one who has direct union/communion with the Father.

Metaphysical healings

Metaphysical healings are a combination of mental and spiritual/unseen healing modalities but are of man, mind, duality therefore have no powers except to those who believe in two powers ie that something can be other than it was merely by *thinking* it into expression.

Spiritual man can see the error of these healing modalities because they do not heal byway of Truth realized rather by *belief* in their *power* to do so and since man has **no** power in and of himself the nothingness of the belief is revealed as nothing more than a *temporary* exchange of good for bad.

Metaphysical vs mystical definitions-keep 'em straight!

To help remember the difference between metaphysical/metaphysics and mystical/mystic I used the first two letters as a reminder of :

Metaphysical-the "me" of men-personal-human-duality

Mystical/mystic-"my" relationship with God-spirit-oneness

Metaphysics

A branch of philosophy defined as the study/theorization of things that are theorized, hypothesized but unable to be proven scientifically ie that which is not seen but is felt to exist. But even if man were able to study the unseen it would only be explained through the intellect, the thinking mind therefore would **not** be the Truth of the unseen rather what is *thought* about the unseen.

The things of God are nonsense to man and always will be as man cannot understand that which is spiritual, of a completely different state of conscious understanding, invisible to the senses.

Metaphysical Truth is the Truth of the invisible, God, received by those in oneness with God and given to man to contemplate in the silence to raise their conscious understanding. Metaphysical Truth are not supposition, not theory or thinking but Truth from the source of Truth.

Metaphysics

A major branch of philosophy concerning the existence and the nature of things that exist; metaphysics concerns the nature of, and the relations among the things that exist.

Metaphysical idea: that reality exists **independently** of one's (thinking) *mind* and yet **can be known** is called realism.

https://simple.m.Wikipedia.org

Derived from the Greek meta ta physika (after the things of nature) referring to an idea, doctrine or posited reality outside of human sense perception.

In modern philosophical terminology metaphysics refers to the *study* of what cannot be reached through **objective** studies of *material* reality.

Https://www.pbs.org...metaph-body

Metaphysics: The study of existence and the nature of reality

Began as at treatise by Aristotle dealing with first principles, the relation of universals to particulars, and the teleological doctrine of causation.

Teleological doctrine is the philosophical doctrine that final causes, design and purpose exist in nature.

A philosophical doctrine is a particular theory, principle, position, system, code of *beliefs* or body of teaching. These are the famous "-isms" of philosophy and for our study it is mysticism/spiritualism/realism, the **knowing** of God by an **experience** of God which **dispels** every *philosophical* supposition ever entertained by *mortal* man.

Middle Path

Another name for the spiritual path, being, is. The middle, zero change, not good and not bad but God's allness, living under grace eternally supported, supplied and maintained by Source.

Mind of man

There is no creative mind. The mind is deductive and aware but it is not creative. Your thinking mind cannot encompass spiritual presence or spiritual power, your mind can only grasp that which is of the world of sense ie tasted, touched, heard, seen or smelled and this is why it has been said *thoughts* are *things*. *Thoughts* are as *material* as *things* therefore thoughts and things cannot be **God.**

Mind of man

Human man erroneously believes they have power to create but succeeds only in creating *illusions* based on *personal* experiences which immediately forms an *opinion* based on biases which is an expression of your *belief* and not God's **Truth.**

The mind of spiritual man is an avenue of awareness for conscious expression but has no creative abilities. The mind of spiritual man reveals that which is, Truth. All of spiritual work is based on the fact that the creations of mind are not Truth/reality rather are illusions, counterfeit, *seem* real but have no reality, no substance beyond the visioning mind they are being envisioned in, cannot be touched or sensed in any way in the visible world.

Miracle

That which is done/is experienced without human footsteps/hand of man.

Monastic life

In the world among man but not of the consciousness of the world. Exactly what spiritual living is.

Morality

Man's attempt at living the laws of man to the best of their ability, feeling what is right to do trumps what they want to do for personal reason. A moral *man* is an upstanding citizen when viewed by other men but moral man is still *mortal* man because when push comes to shove he will still pick up the sword.

Motive

Your motivation, the why, determines the outcome of all situations because your motive is either selfish or unselfish, of man or God. Even if you don't really know what you are doing/trying to become as long as your motive is for **peace, joy, love and understanding** you will receive what you need but if your motivation is for *more and better material things* you are praying amiss and will not receive what you desire rather what the world desires for you.

Mystical consciousness

One thing about mystical writings that makes them impossible for mortal man (the things of God are folly to man) to understand is that they were written by those who had **attained** the awareness of the Christ of their own being and were expressing the consciousness of God therefore wrote **from** the consciousness of God.

Like begets like therefore someone of the Christ consciousness can understand the Bible and other mystical writings because they know what the words mean not by their human definitions but by their expression within you.

Once you make contact with the Christ the higher conscious understanding of the impartations that you receive as intuition become crystal clear and is the Truth that allows you to see past the illusory expressions of the world to witness Truth-God is.

Mystical nature of the words of spirit

The problem man has with the Bible and all other spiritual/mystical writings is that they do not know that the meaning of words used by man of flesh and the same words used in spiritual writings sometimes have completely different meanings and it is only to the degree that you understand the spiritual meaning of the words that you will understand the deep meaning of spiritual literature.

Meat, bread, wine and water are all substances of the human world, things of substance for the body however in spiritual writings these are also food but of the **Spirit** in reference to the feeding of the soul, of the consciousness by way of imbibing, communing and communicating with God. God doesn't *bring* you meat, bread, wine and water God **is** that which feeds, enlightens, raises, fulfills and sustains you.

Mystical prayer

The mystical prayer is listening expectantly to hear the voice of God to hear Truth, receive the conscious awareness of God's grace so that you may be instructed or illumined.

Mysticism

All mystical teachings are exactly alike in that the basis of all of them is **conscious union with God,** realized oneness with God-the actual experience.

There could not be a mystical teaching unless there was a mystic to have had the experience of conscious union with God.

The appearance of Jesus, the visible man was nothing, could do nothing. But there was this inner selfhood which had been **realized,** attained, and consciously lived. This was his mystical selfhood which brought him the healing gift.

Name and nature of God

I am (name of God, Self)

I am (your designation of Self when you know Truth)

incorporeal, eternal spirit (nature of God)

Therefore I am I am when I know the Truth of my being.

No competition

What you demonstrate is yours eternally until you decide to give it or share it. It is of your consciousness and can only be given to you because it is the return/demonstration of your conscious oneness with God. Anything that represents an activity of your oneness is yours. This is the freedom of God consciousness, you are of infinite supply so give freely, share, enjoy and let go because tomorrow brings more spiritual Truth, manna, supply unto all your needs.

Non resistance/resist not evil

All discord, regardless of name or nature, has no power or presence that needs to be overcome; it is an arm of flesh, the nothingness of man's mind of duality. You must recognize then you have no need of fighting or righting the error by way of your thinking mind but stand back in consciousness, the place within where there is no thought rather just being (think avatar waiting to be engaged by you) and watch as God reveals Truth and that Truth resonates within you, flows out from you as the grace of healing to all who are receptive.

Non resistance, non attachment when confronted with error is to be unaffected emotionally, to relax and know all error is illusion. Being in the consciousness of God is to be truly relaxed, going with the flow at every turn because you are in the boat of God on the river of God doing things with God completely supported and supplied by God on your journey.

Normal and natural

What do these mean? They are different for human man and spiritual man.

Normal and natural for human man is to be within their rights, legal and moral, to kill for self defense or imminent harm or for any reason the court of law and the court of man deem acceptable.

Normal and natural for spiritual man is harmonious, peaceful, quiet and without power therefore rests in the harmonious expression they are of. Whatever happens to spiritual man is good because of who he is and it is never just good for them personally but also for the good of all who desire that which is being offered-harmonious expression of being.

Depending on how you present, man of earth or man of God knowing, determines what is "normal and natural" thereby shouting to the world the source of your consciousness.

Now

Manna comes fresh every day, God's grace, the treasure of this moment, the continuing now. The meaning of the word now to man holds a different meaning than the spiritual now.

The spiritual now is an eternity since it is always now. You never get past now nor does now ever fade into the past. There is only this moment, continuing but what man calls the future is just the extrapolated view of now. The validating factor of oneness with God is the never ending quality of its existence expressed as an unending line with no start and no end-a circle. You were never born and you will never die for your creation was from the beginning before the world was and eternally is.

Now

To live oneness in the atmosphere of God you must live in the present moment. The past doesn't exist and the future is merely a now moment a little beyond this moment but all time is **now.**

There is no ticking off of time in the kingdom of heaven, in God's awareness for there is only now. Whatever life you are living now is the only now you have any control over. Time is a human construct and has nothing to do with God. God is now. So if the only time is now what you are conscious of now-consciously being, living, expressing-is what you will be conscious of being, living, expressing when tomorrow is now.

Therefore if you want a different tomorrow than you are living today you must change your now to change your tomorrow. Everything is now so if you begin to walk the spiritual path now then two weeks from now you will embody more of God consciousness/awareness which will present itself to you as a higher awareness now.

The understanding that needs to become Truth is that you cannot hope for a better tomorrow because there is only now. So if you want a better tomorrow you have to chose to be better now.

All the "I'll be nicer next time" or "I'll do the right thing next time" or "I'll be more loving/kind/considerate tomorrow" creates exactly what tomorrow will hold-all the lack of yesterday because you cannot change the future, you can only change the now. The now becomes the now later so who you are now is who you are tomorrow unless your today is other than it was yesterday.

Yes this sounds like the old joke "whose on first" but this is a large key to spiritual living so if you don't get it, heck try writing it, just come back to it every now and again and one time it will be revealed and you will follow the understanding easily because you are at the higher consciousness you needed to understand it, you just weren't ready for it until you were. This is all of spiritual life. If it doesn't stick don't worry about it just circle back, give it a little try on again and go about your business. It will come, it has to come because **your ascension back to the full consciousness of God is Law and fulfillment of scripture.**

Now: God's measure of time

The now of consciousness does not become the future as if something miraculous is going to change between now and then because there is no *then,* there is only you as you are in this moment extrapolated out further. Therefore if the thoughts, beliefs and judgements you are of right now are the same two years from now nothing in your experience has changed for you to experience different than you have been.

How do you become different now to take that new consciousness out into the further nows? The future now is nothing more than this now expressing therefore if you are not satisfied with this now you won't be satisfied with the future now. Why? Because it is always now. You can change in the now to be a different you in the now but **you** have to **do** something now to experience different than now in a future now.

Nothing happens between now and now unless **you do it consciously.** Thinking and wishing are lip service and lip service is what you will reap but if you die daily, change your now by spending more time each day with God soon your nows are always harmonious because you changed in the now to become this expression in the coming now.

You will know by the fruitage of your experience, the grace you experience in spirit and form, if your now is changing. If life is becoming harmonious, easy, just flows then you are seeing the Truth of God manifesting in your life. God is real and you experience the reality of this inner Truth as you become more and more like God in expression.

If however you still seem to struggle, have disagreements and feel unsettled or agitated you may be asking to know **Truth** but are still living *duality*. You may be giving lip service to Truth to make yourself look good but you cannot lie to God and you cannot lie to yourself when faced with Truth: if you are not aware of grace coming into your experience you are not praying aright. You are still *telling* God what to do or *talking* instead of listening. You may still be judging, it matters not. You fix it by going in to **hear, practice the presence and giving your choices over to God.**

If you want God to live your life you have to stop trying to navigate so God navigates, directs, makes the crooked places straight and you just drive/do what is needed to be done as given you to do.

What you are looking for in your experience of now is harmony. Harmony is a place of mental stillness, not by might but because there is nothing to think about, plan, worry or care about. Harmony is the hum of you being, it is the feeling of lightness, weightlessness, free to take a deep breath because you are unburdened by the things of the world. Harmony is the middle ground, not the grey between dark and light, good and bad but harmony, a completely different level of being unknown to most humans.

The harmony you experience now is what will be of your future nows if you continue to do what you are doing now. God is Law, like begets like therefore if you are of the consciousness of God you are of the Law of God which is dependable, reliable and eternal. You cannot say that about man in any degree.

Omnipresence

God is here and now where you are when you are of the consciousness of God-good/harmony. You never need worry about being away from a holy center or church or being separated from your Bible/readings because it makes no difference where you are **because God is the consciousness you live/express from and God is within, of you.**

You can never be separated from God unless you separate yourself in belief by not abiding in the conscious realization of the presence of God where I am.

Do you see now why if you know Truth Truth will make you free from the duality of man? That God has never been separated from you in your trials when you thought you were separated from God by sin rather you shut yourself off from God by your own belief in separation from God but God cannot separate itself from you because it is literally you but you are unaware of this as a reality.

Sin does not separate anyone from God it merely separates them from the willingness to open their consciousness to God and to God's presence. Poverty is not a sign one is separated from God it is only a sign that they have separated themselves in *belief* from God thereby cheating themselves of the benefits of God's presence.

Omnipresence

When it is said God is omnipresent it means God is forever pouring itself out into visible form/manifestation, being, forever flowing, forever appearing **where it is known.** There is nothing for you to do other than have the awareness of God within, be an instrument of God's grace to the world and listen for that still small voice of the Father to chime within you as that which is given you to do.

Omniscience

Omniscience, all knowing, doesn't mean knowing like man knows by thinking; omniscience is the automatic, normal and natural expression of a closed system of singular source eternally bringing forth itself in form as constant renewal of Self, this universe, you, all that is. God doesn't think, God **is.**

Your body in man's view is as close to a closed system as you can get biologically because all living things needs things from the outside to survive but the system called body, if it were self sustaining, would be akin to the point I am trying to make to God, the universe, being a closed system.

Your body functions in and of itself so it seems, the systems that make up the body work together without thought, independent of your thinking. The body is being, the body is **living** itself. When we talk about God **being** this is what is meant. What it is perpetuates what it is through Self creation and expression.

On the wheel: going around and going nowhere

Human life is fruitless, it is the constant motion of standing still/going no where, living and doing all day every day only to wake the next in the same general place. Even a big event that sways your pendulum of good and bad will even out until you are once again standing still in constant motion; the going around and around each day going no where.

"Being on the wheel," where man goes around and around but is standing still is because he is **not growing in consciousness.** To change the standing still to progressing/movement there must be a change in consciousness and God in awareness is the change.

One

The beauty of one is it **is.** There is no chaos, no division, no difference. There is no conflict in one because there is nothing in one other than itself therefore it will always be itself. That which **is** eternally **is.** One cannot be changed in and of itself because what is one but eternal sameness?

Chaos or conflict comes when two or more exist in the same space and then the perpetuation of two or more is constantly changing because of it being more than one. One is stable, unchanging, dependable and reliable, under the Law of like begets like. Two or more is unpredictable, shifting sand for even if it is spectacular right now, it wasn't a moment ago and won't be a moment from now. Think basic collision theory which is perpetual chaos.

One is one. Two or more is unpredictable/unknown because of the way they collide and combine in a random fashion based on chance, proximity, similarity or difference.

You always know what you have or get when you have one of something but when there is more you cannot control how they interact because you are not dealing with singularity but duality which creates chance, options, possibilities.

Oneness

You do not establish oneness with God, you **are** one with God but to bring this Truth into expression you must dispel the belief in separation by becoming aware of God within.

The only reason you are not experiencing oneness is because you have been taught to pray to a God outside of you that does not exist.

Opinion

That which you are never to give for opinion is just another word for judgement, selfishness, coercion; they are self serving words that are of your *human* desire to be noticed, seen. The way you serve God is through the service of healing, of revealing Truth within silently, sacredly and secretly **not** giving your opinion outwardly.

Spiritual man has no opinion of another person rather listens for Truth that comes directly from Truth, God within and this Truth may be shared if the person receiving it is of the consciousness to understand it otherwise you merely say you cannot give an opinion on that which you do not know the Truth of and *words* are never **Truth.**

Ordination

Man's ordination of clergy and other holy people is not the ordination of God but of man. Man determines when other man have reached a sufficient understanding of man's interpretation of God to spread the fallacy to others. The ordination of man is in and of itself no thing real because you cannot be ordained by God of that which you have no understanding of and that understanding only comes from an actual experience of the Father within.

The rising in consciousness from man to spirit is what ordains you, gives you **permission** to be a servant of God knowing Truth and releasing it to free all of humanity from its universal hypnotism in the belief there are two powers in this world that must be mitigated, avoided or controlled in a way that makes you feel you are in control of your life.

Ordination

True ordination is when man has realized the Truth of himself and has become one with it. This actual experience of God within is the ordination, the right that allows you to speak Truth to the world silently, secretly and sacredly. You are ordained, given the green light to share Truth of God because you are one with God.

Man ordained by man is merely given a certificate, a recognition for knowing what all man could know if they wanted to. That is not true ordination because it is of man about man.

Original

That which is and can be no other. Original is. It is the only **because** it is the original. Anything other than what **is** is not of the original because that which **is** is not divisible, changeable or dependent on anything else and is infinite in nature.

That which **is** cannot be altered nor can it every stop being.

That which **is** is eternal because that which came into being out of itself is only and always itself: harmonious, pure, and singular in source.

This is the exact definition of God, universal creative consciousness expressing as you when you know your Truth.

Anything that isn't Original isn't real, isn't of the expression, Life and Law of the Original. This is what is meant when it is read "if it wasn't made by God it wasn't made." That which isn't **of** the nature/expression of God isn't real because all there **is** is God.

Original sin: man's belief in separation from God.

The belief God is outside of man as something to attain favor with for more and better material, earthly living.

This belief is the only thing separating you from the allness of God you were created to experience. Once you understand your heritage, your Truth, your nature you are no longer human; you have returned to the Father's house and are once again **of** the consciousness of God no longer separate in expression.

Perceived death

When death touches you or another you can smile and know:

I can lay down my life, I can raise it up again. I can walk in or I can walk out. If you destroy this temple in three days I will raise it up again.

Only when this rings true can you repeat with the Master: "I have overcome the world. Whether I live on this plain or on another, I am eternal."

Personal expression of emotions vs. God expressing as allness through you

All that was created in the beginning was good and if it wasn't good it wasn't created. Only God created and it can only create itself, good/harmony. God is the only expression of all creation.

You are of God therefore God/good/grace flows through you. It is God flowing through you, the **embodiment** of all that is harmonious/spiritual. Your feelings, your emotions of love and peace, joy and companionship are **not** yours, they are of God and if you have conscious awareness of God then you have all that is of God flowing in and though you as you.

This is the hang up a lot of people have-they think they *personally* are able to give or withhold love. You cannot. You either radiate what is **of** your consciousness or you don't. You can only show forth God, good, in proportion to your openness, understanding, awareness and devotion to God which in turn is seen outwardly as increased consciousness of imparted Truth and visible supply.

A child may think when they get older that their parent withheld love from them. This is incorrect. The parent cannot withhold love *however* their lack of God consciousness, ignorance of Truth looks to the world as if the parent had no love to give. Why? Because God is the only source of harmony there is to express. When you are in a relationship with the God within, desire its presence, this relationship of oneness is the alchemy that allows all that is of God to flow through you out to the world perceived as love being given **of** the one God is flowing through.

Therefore the flow of God **through and out** from a person is the only way they are able to express anything good/harmonious to the world. Otherwise it is personal ego expressing in a way to elicit a personally directed response for their selfish purposes.

God is unable to be selfish. All God **is** is for its creations. Human man in his finite existence struggles for survival because he thinks he can die and must protect at all cost that which he has struggled to acquire. Those who have returned to the spiritual path have nothing of their own to keep for all is of grace, God, infinite supply, joint heirs remember?

When you are living in the consciousness of God all needs are met through grace at your level of awareness-your understanding at this time of God/Truth is how much of God's being is being expressed in your life either emotionally, financially, morally or physically. Therefore the only thing human man has to give are the things of earth, not God.

To come into oneness reveals the nothingness of man's thinking and places you right in the middle of yourself with God. With God there is only good therefore the expression of one who is on the spiritual path is not their personal expression but God **expressing** as love, peace, kindness, to the world.

Sure there are random acts of kindness, random expressions of joy, peace and love in your life but it is not you *personally* that has created this atmosphere. It is God's grace touching you from one who is walking on the spiritual path in an atmosphere of God because God rains on the just and the unjust.

Point of context and spiritual understanding

Mark 11:24

Therefore I say unto you what things soever you desire when you pray believe you receive them and ye shall have them.

Therefore when you ask God for the things of God whatever they may be know they are yours because you are basically asking to have what is already within revealed, brought forth for further illumination. God can only give of itself, of what it **is** and God is not in the world where it is unrealized. If someone is still *asking* for the *things* of man they have not the first Truth that is the foundation of prayer: **I and the Father are one. In this knowing lives the secret to all life-all is God and all supply comes through your relationship with God.**

God cannot destroy itself nor favor one of its expressions over another, neither can weather, the moon, the sun, stars or tide battle each other nor does God use floods and storms to wipe out civilizations and kill people. God cannot destroy itself because it is all of all that is. God is the source of all that **is,** unqualified, in this visible, tangible experience. All is God!

Point of view

Another name for **duality** is point of view because there is never one point of view because the very name testifies to the multiplicity it represents.

Poor: biblical meaning

Biblically poor means poor of **spirit,** lacking God knowing because why would you counsel those who were rich (in spirit)?

The down trodden man means mystically the lack of spiritual awareness and the life thereof as being empty, lacking and painful as the lack of spiritual knowing expresses as the life you experience. Why? **Consciousness.** Who you know yourself to be within expresses to the world as you in visible expression. The outside is always the exact expression of the consciousness of being within.

Power

There is no power outside of you and no powers ascribed to you because the only power in and of the universe is creative intelligence that is omnipotent, omniscient and omnipresent. When you know this as Truth you can rest. When you have this revelation of no power against you your body lets out a big sigh and you feel all the fight, tension and fear drop from you. Like at the end of exercise or hard play, in the end you rest, let all of what was the activity fall away as the game or experience is over.

Spiritual man rests while human man reacts. Spiritual man knows there is nothing to react to because he knows God is real and is the essence flowing in and through him, not theirs to use but theirs to release to bless others and in that bless themselves, bread on the water, pressed down and flowing over.

When this clicks it will make the world completely different because you won't be experiencing it as a man eating jungle but a paradise that continues to reveal its wonders and beauty the more you die to the duality of man. It is you knowing the Truth of God, of Life that allows you as spiritual man to witness the same error as mortal man but **remain peaceful** knowing the error is merely a *belief* in power that does not exist.

Physically weak man picks up a weapon. Mentally weak man controls men. Spiritual man rests in Truth and walks through the fires of this world putting them out as they pass. This is the "power" of God, bringing peace to man by which man may find their peace.

Power of God

The "power" of God is its presence in your awareness. God is an atmosphere impermeable to the things of man ie duality. God's power is in its **nature** of one, wholeness, allness and completeness. What man calls God is a **closed system** of perfect harmony and peace humming away, bringing forth only the perfection that **is** wholeness, completeness, oneness to that which is **of** it.

Man is always leaking, exhausting, releasing energy/power and must go in search of it by taking it from another or refueling. Man has no power to create so he can only draw from the world what he needs to exist. God on the other hand is all that is necessary for existence because God **is** existence. Man is trying to express who they think they are by manipulating circumstances, negating negatives and increasing positives and that is why some parts of life are good and others not so much. Man always has to chose-money or time, money or sanity, status or inner peace, power or victim. In God there are no separate areas of life. In oneness with God harmony is the only operating system, is the infinite governing influence of creation.

Power of God

The power of God/God power is merely knowing Truth that **protects** you from committing errors of duality thereby not incurring error by picking up the sword/reacting. The presence of peace reminds you there is no fight to be had in all the world and in that knowing rest, remain harmonious which is the expression of God.

Power of God

The power of God is not a power as man understands power to be-force, of one over another, one killing or subduing, bringing under control person, condition or situation.

The power of God is in you **knowing** there is only one expression possible of God-harmony-and if you are in oneness with God that is your expression (for the most part, we aren't perfect for a loonnnngg time) and returns to you as bread on the water, grace returned for grace released. Remember, God is **Law** not a super being therefore is **impersonal** and your return of grace is also impersonal as a measure, degree to which you shared grace. You get back what you give. Technically you get more so if you keep that in mind it does help to keep you in the safety zone of God consciousness.

Yes there are times things aren't completely harmonious but that is a human perception because you may be holding onto a judgement causing you to feel this way ie you had a determination/desire/expectation in mind for yourself.

Harmony is a state of being and it is a choice. I can let people get to me if I have not had a moment with Father to get into his sunny vibe first thing in the morning but because I don't want to experience inharmony **I make sure I am the harmony wherever I go so I am never out of harmony unless I drop it.**

You only have what you possess and bring with you as you so if you expect kindness it must come **with** you and flow from you to another so that is their return because the kindness from you is God going before you. What you experience is God going before you to make the response that of itself because what is given is what is returned so if you give grace it will be returned in a way that is harmonious to the situation, keeps harmony as the only expression thus experience.

Does this always satisfy those new to the spiritual path, those used to winning or getting? Not always because the personal sense of *i* is still very strong and fights against both parties involved getting harmony which doesn't always mean getting what you wanted for yourself. Ahh, there it is. You didn't *get*. You tried to *use* God to get what you wanted and just found out you can't have your way *and* God's harmony. It is one or the other because the two cannot ever exist in the same atmosphere/consciousness. Why? Because one is of God and one is of man; one is real and one is illusion.

Power of God

The power of God is inherent in its singular expression that has no duality. **The awareness of God within is the absence of duality** and the absence of duality is harmony. Harmony is the nature of God and the Truth of you which is the **healing** to all the errors and consequences of *man*.

Power of God: protection

God is, singular, no duality and the power spoken of God is not power as man knows power as a force to be used rather it is the power inherent in knowing Truth that protects you from making a mistake. That is the power of God, it is a protective presence that makes you free from the effects of duality in your experience.

God is both cause and effect, good and good thus living in the consciousness of God, knowing the reality of the opposite of good as nothingness you will eternally, infinitely experience the results of the consciousness in which you abide-God of both cause and effect being good or the mind of man with duality of cause and effect bringing strife, struggle and confusion.

When you know something is good, feels good, does good and is perpetual infinite good why would you subject yourself once again to the instability, confusion, and pain of trying to live in a world with both good and bad as possible result? I know why and it is the human condition you are trying to overcome and that condition is **fear:** defer your will, your life, your existence back to God, take your chances on an unseen force of good or keep your will and keep living the life you can see and experience which offers up a plethora of options other than good for you to partake of but it is known, familiar, safe to the ignorant.

God-cause and effect both good

Man-cause and effect can be both good and/or bad

You can see one is better but until you know through experience God **is** better you will continue to experience the life you have been living of chance, duality, good and bad.

Practicality of spiritual living

Spiritual living is practical living. What you desire for yourself you must also desire for all man. In this way you are never asking selfishly, for only yourself, but by praying for it to be of the consciousness of all man receptive to God's healing grace you are freely giving bread on the water, grace, and it will return to you pressed down, shaken together and flowing over. What you do for your brethren will be done unto you and to receive you must give **not** of yourself, your possessions or your time, but of the God you embody.

Pray for your enemy

If I am and you are I am then all are I am, we are kin, we are family, we are one so when you curse your enemy and wish them dead you are wishing the same on yourself because you and your enemy are one. You pray for your enemies not for anything of the world but for them to **awaken** to the God within. When that happens your enemy now knows his true nature and will greet you as the light of God he is.

Father, let all be forgiven without penalty and open the consciousness of those we call our enemies that they might know the Truth of oneness.

Understand to pray for your enemy is not for them to escape the karma they inflicted upon themselves and others through ignorance but for them to have a moment within that stops them and reveals a different path, something new. **You pray only for the salvation of man, that they may know God as you do and rise from the ashes of man as you have.** The prayer for your enemy is always forgiveness, forgiveness of ignorance and by bringing Truth to bear you are doing your part as child of God to put a chink in that armor of ignorance so it may someday completely fall to the ground revealing Truth, free of the duality of man to stand naked and unafraid before the world silently knowing I am that I am and though you were blind now see and in this way become a light unto the world bringing the Love of God to bear among man where there was none.

Pray for your enemy-why you should

An enemy can be personal or impersonal it merely is that which is of ignorance and not Truth and since the life of spiritual man is without force/sword what we have at our disposal to get rid of "enemies" is opening out a way by which the hearts of man can be touched by God.

What is the purpose of praying for your enemy? To bring them to the knowing of God, the feeling of God that allows their lives to be transformed from that of chaos to that of peace. If someone is driving you nuts, persecuting you, your family, is on your mind for some reason or other and you want it to stop what better way for it to stop than for the one in darkness being human in expression to be given a revelation of their Truth that starts them on the path you walk?

If you want something in your life to change you must pray for the change you want for all which is to awaken to their Truth to stop being who they were to become who they are. To pray for your enemy is to make everyone your brother, your kin, you, God in expression which is harmony in your midst.

Pray without ceasing

To pray without ceasing is merely to be in the now, in the present moment because God is only in the now not in the past or in the future. When you are in God consciousness by being in the present moment you are in oneness with the Father and that is the definition of prayer, silent inner communion. It is where you share grace without effort silently, secretly and sacredly with your fellow man and it is where you release the errors of man as the ignorance they are.

"Father they know not what they do" is what you bring into the silence and then God gives you Truth.

And the Father's response comes from within "because they know not **who** they are." And then peace descends and you realize what you are seeing and experiencing isn't real but an illusion. This is healing, the dropping away of long held beliefs and convictions about life, dying daily and praying without ceasing.

To die daily is to see through the veil of unreality, see past the image, the illusion, the pretense and judgement and to know what it **is** at its base and it is always God expressing.

Prayer

Prayer does not improve humanhood and that is why prayers that try to do so are not answered. God can only give you the fruits of God-the allness of God, the harmony of God, spirit in form received, not the things of man worked for or taken. Prayer can only bring that of which you are praying to-God-therefore you must pray for what you can receive **of** God. When you come to the place where you desire the companionship and resting place of God over the baubles and bright lights of man you are praying for the things of God, to have more of what God is in your life and thus continue to walk the spiritual path leading to full enlightenment and ascension.

Prayer

Prayer is an action, a doing, a being, a listening, a living and expressing the consciousness you share with God.

There is no prayer/praying being done where there is no resultant change of consciousness. There may be some kind of an attempt at prayer, a mix of begging and listening which cancels out the listening part, there may be some false concept of prayer but true prayer, living out from God consciousness, **must** results in a change of your conscious expression. If you don't feel different, don't see and experience the world differently you are praying amiss because if you were praying aright you would be expressing the consciousness of God, the nature of God which is good.

This absolutely has to bring change to your life because your consciousness is that which you experience within therefore consciousness is always expressed as your being, it can be no other way.

If you do not feel to be a different person, one with more understanding of the world around you by way of more understanding of the world within you need to go back to foundational Truth and see where you are erring. It is just a side jaunt, no biggy, just get your compass out and find your way back to your path.

Prayer

Prayer is the absence of human desire in the recognition/presence of **is.** When desire is spiritual, of God, about God it is prayer. What desires are spiritual? When the desire is not only for you and those you love but for **all** of man. Spiritual prayer is **unselfish** prayer, the prayer for all to be, have and do within the consciousness of God so all can live in harmony.

Asking, even demanding illumination, light or understanding is all right because you are asking for that which God can give you and commensurate with your expression of illumination is your return of grace, God in action, the visible and the invisible supply unto your life of harmonious oneness.

Prayer

How you awaken to the realization of the presence of the Christ within.

You have come into this world believing you are human. You have grown up in this understanding/belief. You have been taught to turn to human sources and persons to support your existence. You have been trained to look out to Moab, to the external world for help, success, activity. You have **not** been told to depend on the spiritual presence of supply.

The first step is the conscious realization of your oneness with God, the realization of your true identity. Then comes the understanding of the nature of error as illusion, mirage, suggestion, world hypnotism, no thing real.

Prayer is silent communion where you await the Word of God. The Word of God is the consciousness of God and the Word of God made flesh means the visible manifestations of God's grace in your experience. Therefore to be receptive to the Word, consciousness of God means to learn to be still and listen for the voice within.

Prayer

Truth revealed from God by way of conscious union dispels the darkness, the conditionings of the mind, duality in and of the human perspective of being, your un-reality. Your true reality comes only when you acknowledge and communicate with the presence within. This act of turning in, turning away from the outside world is to find peace the world knows not of. It is in this peace you experience the Truth of Life-in the world but not of the consciousness of the world.

Prayer

An attitude and an altitude of consciousness. When you are so high in consciousness that your attitude is purely a "speak Lord, I am listening" you are in an attitude of prayer and the voice of God which is always speaking is now heard.

Prayer

Inner attunement whereby you become receptive to what God has to say to you or an inner attunement whereby God's spiritual blessings are revealed to you.

Prayer is inner listening to hear Truth **from** God, being receptive of God's allness and not you telling or demanding from God.

Prayer

Inner contemplation of what God is, not what you want on earth/in your life. Prayer is silent meditation, communion within you to know God aright so you can be in the flow of all that is because it is your birthright, your true nature of expression.

Prayer: silent listening

Prayer is your contact, agreement with God, prayer is the means whereby the relationship of God the Father and God the Son is established as demonstration, the Word made flesh. Prayer when it is understood is the means whereby you **overcome** all material sense and material living and bring yourself to where your life is spiritually governed, protected, guided and experienced.

Praying without ceasing

To pray without ceasing is to keep one's consciousness open to God always knowing who you are, the risen Christ, the individual expression of God. Rest in Me all the days of your life.

To pray without ceasing sounds hard, like you are going to be constantly thinking or saying or trying to be until you become. That is not the case at all! You merely rest in the Truth you know: you are the child of God and in that knowing bring God into awareness which releasing God to flow out to the world and in that measure is returned to you as that which you expressed of God to the world.

To pray without ceasing is to rest in the Truth you know and let that Truth be your expression.

Pre-awakener

Pre-awakeners are those things that take you out of human thought, make you stop and wonder "did that really just happen or was that my imagination?" These instances that take you out of the world of sense and inside to quiet contemplation are another tear in the curtain of the unreality of life as you have been living it. These pre-awakeners are the little embers of a fire just being kindled that eat away at your certainty of life as you know it. You become curious about what is inside of you and little by little you realize the world with all its enticements, desires and perceived rewards begins to look less and less appealing.

Preparation

The time before you desired to know God. Preparation is the trial and error of life, the falling down but always getting up and keeping on in the same direction-to know God. This burning desire, absolute necessity to understand Truth **is** what prepares you to accept the reality that God **is** your individual consciousness when it presents in your awareness.

Preparedness

You are prepared for the knowing of Truth when you are prepared to **accept** Truth and this preparation is merely the desire to know the unknown, you are preparing your mind to be open, accepting and desirous of that which it seeks. You cannot go on a camping trip and have expectations of it being a wonderful time if you don't prepare. You don't go to a job interview without preparation. In all things you desire you prepare yourself by being open and receptive to what it is you are desiring. If you desire to know something, you are open to all that it is and if it doesn't jive with something already in your thinking mind you have to let go of what you thought was Truth to let the actual Truth come on in and get cozy.

There are usually many years of preparation before you finally desire to know other than duality/chaos in the form of pain/weight of the errors you suffer, until you say enough is enough, there has to be a better way, a more harmonious way of living, of having and being than this! Ding! Ding! Human living-pain, suffering, lack and illness-have been the **preparation** you needed to finally get where you want to be-with God, home again, not of this world of chaos.

This is also the reason why there will be those you will not be able to help, not be able to heal spiritually because they are not done with the world of good and bad, they are still having fun or have not gotten to the point where the suffering has become an impetus for change. There may be one of this mind in your household, the wild child, the addict, one the world of sense has taken over. These are **never** lost causes, you treat and heal silently, sacredly and secretly and though the results may not be evident as far as a change in behavior/consciousness now know without a doubt grace is absolutely working the way is does and the fruitage will appear in the now for every moment experienced is experienced in the now.

The final part of preparedness is **surrender.** You must be nothing, know you are nothing before you can **become** everything through oneness but it is this admission, this humility that is the **key** to everlasting Life, **knowing** you are nothing without the awareness of the Source of all good and wanting beyond anything else to once again be within that love, harmony, peace, abundance and joy.

This is all there is to **salvation, rebirth or transfiguration**-a change in consciousness from that of human consciousness expressing two powers of good and evil to that of God consciousness, singular, only, harmonious expression.

Heaven on earth is a state of **consciousness** lived inwardly and expressed outwardly through the revealed Truth that I am that I am.

In a way it is an agreement, you listen and respond to what is given you to do and God does the rest. Easy peasy.

Principle

There is only one power and that power is **knowing** God is both cause and effect thereby the only expression of God is good, harmonious. This knowing is what keeps you from falling back into the error of human duality and this knowing is dependent upon the **principles** of Truth you know **and** express that keep you in the flow of God.

Expressing the principles of Truth is the only way to **live** Truth. Principles are the actions/expressions of the Law of God, Truth, and must be your expression to allow the fruits of spiritual living to be the fruits of your experience. Therefore when you are living in God consciousness you are the expression of God consciousness because you are **being** the principles, being God in expression.

Principle

According to Merriam-Webster principle can only be a noun, referring to a "fundamental truth", "a code or law."

Principle/s are what make up the why and how of a Law, why it works eternally, infinitely. The principles of mathematics, music, physics, chemistry, light etc, were discovered to be universal Truth because no matter the circumstances the dynamics, the expression of each Law remains the same.

Nothing man can do can alter a Law, Truth, because the results are **independent** of man because they are wholly Truth, God, is, infinite Self perpetuation, a closed system completely Self sufficient in maintenance, support and supply.

Protection

God is your water when you are thirsty, your food when you are hungry, shelter in the rain, supply when it is needed. **God is the source of all you need which is your protection from any form of lack in thought or expression.**

When you say "Father" and smile you are saying I know you to be real and though there is no food before me now, no transportation now, when it is needed it will be. If you know your place, child, you understand there is no place God isn't with you. God is your rock and your high tower, your peace and your joy, your abundance and your charity, your benevolence and your laughter.

You never *work* to demonstrate supply when you are with God, you only **desire** to demonstrate **your oneness, your union, your nature as child of God** by letting God shine through you.

Protection

The protection of God is the living of your life within the oneness, the singularity of only good thereby protecting yourself from the duality of man which leaves your life to chance, like a pendulum swinging back and forth between good and bad. Oneness with God stops the pendulum swing and rises you above the need to express as good or bad. Your protection, God's protection of and for you is this atmosphere of peace, consciousness of harmony, balance, neither good nor bad but perfect, God's perfect where you live and have your being within.

Protection-the principle of awareness

The source of man's troubles is duality and getting up and going about your business without first saying "good morning Father! What's on the agenda for today?" leaves you open to the duality/chance/statistical nature of man's world. Why? Because you didn't bring God into your awareness first thing in the morning to cement its presence going before you to make the crooked places straight. You **protect** your day from the duality of man by making certain Truth is known, front and center.

As long as you know who you are, what you are to do and who is in charge your day will go without hiccup. God is Law unto this day, God is the governance, harmony, swiftness and perfection of your day and because God is omnipotent, omniscient and omnipresent there is no evil or destructive mental or material powers to act on you in the presence of God. "In thy presence is fulfillment of harmony, peace and thy presence is here where I am because thou art omnipresence."

The Law of God is the Law of all visible and invisible *expression:* harmonious by way of omnipotence, omnipresence and omniscience. One power of protection-knowing Truth, one presence-Self, one knowing-is.

Knowing God through an actual awareness of God within your own being **is** your protection from falling for the illusion of duality man calls reality.

Protective Power

God is not "protection or power" in the sense of man. God's protection for/of us doesn't go and subdue those we encounter on our path rather brings harmony to them in whatever way is needed so those we encounter have been touched by God, given some relief, brought peace to mind, brought money for a lunch they wouldn't have had and are not *hangry* when they are in your midst.

Know this Truth: God goes before you to make the crooked places straight.

What do you feel? Peace? relief? Thank you Father! This **is** harmony in your midst. God's isness, being consciousness, your consciousness, is expressed from you to go before you to bring harmony to the consciousness of those people and situations you are to encounter. **Your** trust in the harmony of the Father is what sets the harmony in motion. You are not *hoping* to have a good encounter, you are not worried that it won't go your way. You are **resting** in the knowing that when God is your consciousness there is harmony in your experience.

Protective work

It is important never to lose sight of the **non** power of *effect* in man's world. Germs are effects, disease, weather, climate, time, false appetites, lack, limitation, fear etc, all of these exist as *effect,* that which is experienced as consequences but because they are effects of the *human* world of duality they are *perceived* to have power in and of themselves to do good or to do evil. But they don't. The effects experienced by man are merely the effects of *their* thinking mind coming back to them as what they already *believe* something to be, do or cause.

Protective work begins with knowing, living and expressing Truth that **nothing** has power but God and that there is **no** power in effects **except** the power man gives them. Therefore dominion over the errors and evils of this world is experienced in proportion as you recognize God, spirit, to be the only presence, the only Law, and the only nature to express as-harmonious.

Protective work is the **realization** that only God is power by presence known and that which appears to you as power/might/force is merely a universal *belief* in things possessing power in and of themselves whether of infection, contagion, hereditary, astrology or a belief of any other power against you.

Protective work

Your protective work begins first thing in the morning with the realization there **is** a presence of harmony within your own being. It doesn't act *upon* you from *outside* of you it works **through** you and acts upon the world. You are the transparency through which grace, the allness of God, can act upon the world.

You are in complete control of the flow of grace in and through your life by your oneness with God, how much you defer your will to God, how much you commune, trust and rest in God. By your nature you will be known-spirit or human man.

As man of earth, mortal man you are subject to the innate duality of the world/people around you thus are always trying to mitigate the damage to your day by being pre-emptive, guard up, ready with words of power in your favor. Man is always trying to keep the ship upright in the storm of human duality. When you are with God you do nothing but sit in the boat, move the sail as instructed from within and do not freak out when big waves start to form for God is the waves and God is the boat and God is you so how could one part of God hurt another part of God? It cannot. You cannot die. You can leave this expression but that isn't death so even if you humanly "die" in the storm you are not dead for you are eternal as the waves, as the wind and as the universe for all is God and God is eternal.

Fear dissipates when you realize even the last analysis of human man is a lie.

Protective work

Your protective work is your protection from the *belief* in two powers and is done first thing in the morning to reestablish you in oneness with God. You start your day in the realization that:

Power does not act upon you it flows out from you and is the expression of God, good, and now you are so established in God that as negative appearances touch you throughout the day you recognize them for what they are-illusion/hypnotism-and let them go, pay no attention to them.

Once you have been on this path for a while it is no longer a routine of going into the silence and waiting for God to come on the field to tell you the healing is done because you established your oneness first thing in the morning so God is on the field unless you react to error and let it start having time in your thinking mind, ruminating etc. Therefore it is a simple recognition/awareness of the Truth of error as it presents that lets grace flow, the healing is done and you have placed spiritual bread on the water to return to you pressed down and flowing over.

A spiritualized consciousness is a consciousness in correct orientation to God and not man.

Once an individual knows the name and nature of God he is a free man, he can never be bound to superstition, slavery, never be made the tool of a church organization as the Hebrew were at the time of Jesus the Christ, an organization that took the life and soul out of its followers for its temples and temple priests in tithing, sacrifices and all day worships.

You cannot bind a person in superstition or ignorance or any form of slavery when they know the true name and nature of God. On the other hand you cannot give the name and nature of God except to those who are prepared for it for they will misunderstand it, misinterpret it to mean they themselves are God and not that they are willing **instruments** of God to work **through** and **as** their life.

This is a big distinction and big slide backwards if you think *yourself* to be the power and not the **vessel** through which the power flows and blesses. **The allness of God cannot be used for personal gain or desire.** What you desire must be what you desire for the world to experience as well as yourself, that is the only way one day all will be harmonious-if all want the same for others as for Self. That is Love, that is harmony, that is abundance without end.

Purification

The constant process of removing beliefs of duality also known as dying daily.

Purification of spirit

Everything in the consciousness of God is harmonious so no matter what you are going though even if it seems to not be harmonious, of God/good rather painful, confusing, seemingly wrong direction etc, as long as you are **of** the consciousness of God there is a reason, a purpose for the hell, discomfort or pain you are in and it is your **absolute** trust in God that brings the resolution/revelation of God into focus, why you had to experience what you did to grow in God consciousness to receive the revelation, the big reveal, the purpose, the why.

When Joseph confronted his brothers after what they had done to him and the subsequent years he had spent as a slave, he didn't blame them for throwing him in a pit. "Now therefore be not grieved, nor angry with yourselves, that ye sold me hither for God did send me before you to preserve life. So know it was not you that sent me hither, but God. And he hath made me a father to Pharaoh, and lord of all his house and a ruler throughout the land of Egypt." (Gen 45:5-8)

If you understand this passage you understand that your spiritual consciousness carries you through the purification process, even though it may seem that you go down in the pits and prison of sin and disease. God goes before you carrying you through those trying and purifying experiences until at last you are where you were meant to be-the spiritual man with dominion over all that is.

Always remember if you are truly in oneness and duality comes knocking and it feels personal **it is not;** it is something being shaken loose, some duality is coming to the surface to be recognized and released by knowing Truth. These big movers don't happen often because they are what I term big resets; they suck but without them, without the trust needed to get through them and come out more spiritually shined and polished on the other side you do not progress as quickly on this path because it is all about **trusting** the Law that is God, the Law that keeps the stars in the sky, the water in the oceans, the planes in the air and the plants and animals living.

Quick Keepers

Those Truths that you memorize or write down that are helpful to you when you get separated or don't know how to heal something, not more than three that are overarching non specific Truth that release you through their simplicity of realization and put you back into peaceful union like:

Thou art ever with Me

Thy grace is my sufficiency in all ways

Father please tell me the Truth of this error

Simple reminders of who you are and who is in charge. Your will not mine Father. **Not my job Father,** usually when it comes to body maintenance, health like issues ie sore back, "not my body Father, this is yours so it is in your care always."

Take an aspirin and a hot bath, heal it by knowing Truth and there is nothing said against relieving pain through physical/medical healing modalities as long as your **first** thought is spiritual healing and resting in the presence of God. Then address your discomfort how you see fit.

Receptivity

Receptive to God/presence of God in expression merely means responds to the presence, the feeling or expression of peace and harmony, kindness and ease in their midst. The reason for this distinction is because we all know those that no matter what they are sour, nothing changes or lightens their expression. It isn't that grace isn't present it is that the person has no desire for change and no change will be expressed in the moment. This is the meaning of **you cannot heal everyone** because not everyone wants what you are, they are not yet done with the world but know the soul of that seemingly unresponsive person did feel what was given and someday it will all fall into place because of the seed you planted by your knowing God aright.

Receptivity/degree of received healing

Spiritual healers are **not** doctors or psychologists or coaches, we **do not** know anything about anatomy, physiology, psychology, biology, broken bones or germs. The only reason we can bring forth a healing is that the only ones who come to us are the **sons** of God. The healing is determined by the conscious receptivity of the one asking for the healing ie man wanting a quick fix or spiritual man looking for Truth. The consciousness of the **patient** determines the amount of healing they receive and also whether there is a permanence to the healing or not.

Those who go to healers to heal the ills of the world but want to continue endeavoring in the world will continue to suffer ills of the world. However if one comes to a healer with the same kind of worldly ill but wants more than what the world offers this is the **consciousness** that is open to different, open to that which is unknown. This is **receptivity** and is fueled by need, thirst, a hunger that is not sated in the human world.

Receptivity/Ready/Ripe

Those who are ready for what has been missing and want it beyond anything the world can give. They want all that they can bring to bear in their lives when they know what it is and where it can be found.

Religion

Religion=relationship

God is not religion, your relationship with God **is your religion,** your expression through right knowing of the Truth you know yourself to be.

"Religion" is the living of principles that make up a way of being; religion is your expression as *self* or **Self** to the world.

Resurrection

You are resurrected out of your humanhood when you know your Truth. You are raised out of the physical senses of the body into the realization of your nature as spirit, child of God, joint heir to the kingdom where real living can begin.

Revealed Truth

Revealed Truth is the Word of God, the consciousness of God revealed through the consciousness of one who has God awareness-a mystic.

Righteous

One who knows Truth and lives the principles of Truth in expression.

Robe of Mysticism

When God becomes your life, when infinity embraces you this is sometimes called the Robe, the Robe of Mysticism. It means you are cloaked in it, covered in it, safe within it, embraced within it, of it.

Sabbath

Old law said the sabbath was on Sunday, the sabbath being a day to worship God but everyday is the sabbath for those who live in Christ consciousness therefore there is not one holy day set apart for the worship of God rather every day is sabbath in which your mind is stayed on God and your life is that of harmony.

The greatest quality/activity that ever comes into the experience of a spiritual student is freedom. You are free from:

-theological/church/organized religion beliefs and domination

-the laws of man

-the duality of the human experience

-death

Sabbath-being with God

Man wasn't made for the sabbath, the sabbath was made for man to utilize in accordance with his life at the moment. There is no one day more sacred to devote to God than another, all days are holy as God is all. 7 days a week for sabbath, 24 hours a day, every second is sabbath when you and God are one.

Secrecy

The most vital part of any spiritual practice is **secrecy.** You must practice the ability to keep secret about the works going on within you, to live God through practice without ever speaking about it to those not of the same consciousness.

Never under any circumstances speak of God, tell another about God until such time as you have completed the demonstration (of oneness within) and are fully living in the consciousness that enables you to automatically realize right here where I am in the midst of me is God and because of this relationship I have access to all that is of the Father because I am joint heir to the kingdom of God along with all the other prodigal sons returned home.

Self preservation

The first law of mortal man/human man

Signs following

After you have the awareness of God the signs, the proof of this relationship, follow first as the feeling of God alive and flowing in you as love, peace, joy and then out in the visible world. These are the good things that start coming into your life. I was at Walmart one day and within the span of 30 minutes I encountered 4 very obvious "God in my midst" occurrences and when I got to my car I cried because the love of God, what came into my experience was so overwhelming beautiful and amazing because **I knew why** I was experiencing good, ease, companionship, kindness-I was experiencing the life lived by grace where God goes before you to make the crooked places straight and the difference is obvious. It is the difference between a day that sucks from the beginning and gets worse or waking up to sunshine and birds-the feeling of God in your midst.

Silent ministry

All true spiritual teachings/mystical teachings, healings and experiences are **silent.** The ministry, the sharing of God is silent, sacred and secret. This work is not to be public, shared with the masses like an evangelical merely trying to get ten converts out of a thousand. Man will try to crucify you for your beliefs but at the same time would welcome the relief you reveal if they knew what and where God is. **Therefore the secrecy of spiritual living is of the highest order.**

Then how are others brought onto the path if you are not to proselyte from the pulpit? By **their** conscious need for that which they cannot find among man. You will be found, you will be called upon and there is nothing you need do through human means/thinking. You rest, God works.

The **caution** for beginners is that until you know God you cannot express God to another in words that make sense because at the moment it doesn't make a whole lot of sense to you even though you feel within that it **is** Truth. To be able to articulate Truth aloud can only happen when you go past the stage of learning and are now implementing without thought the things you have learned. You have to go beyond student, beyond teacher to **living** Truth as your expression before your foundation is rock and not a mix of rock and sand, a slippery slope that can leave you more broken than you were.

Silent, secret and sacred. These are the **conditions** the seed of God needs to grow within, to put down roots, grow strong and be well into maturity before it can be revealed to the world because only at this stage of spiritual understanding have you experienced the visible fruits of your invisible work in the visible world as absolute proof of which you speak.

All work starts in the invisible, within the secret, silent, sacred place where God is and will only produce fruit when the principles are followed.

Silent, secret and sacred

No one is to know you are studying about God, no one needs to know and no one should know. This is your love affair, your journey, your enjoyment and your personal experience. Man will tear at you for these beliefs because man cannot believe until he is ready to. To the world you say you are "working on yourself," only you and those of your household/consciousness are those you speak to about spiritual matters for only spiritual man will be able to understand your questions.

Soul

The soul is the seed of God that feels pain and longing for what the world cannot provide. It is the Self, the Truth of you seeking conscious union with Self, God, Truth to be complete again. Because man entertaining a sense of separation from God it is like keeping a part of you away from that which satisfies the whole. The soul bears witness to the hunger for Truth within and tries day in and day out for you to recognize the hunger could be sated, fed infinitely if you would find the Bread, the Meat, the Wine and the Water that brings everlasting satiation to that which you are-spirit.

But man lives in a world of illusion trying to make the universe work in their favor instead of letting the path revealed within you before time was guide your feet and unfold your livingness in God as you are meant to experience.

Source of all form

The source of all form is invisible. When you place a seed in the ground there is a Life force that acts upon it and that Life force is invisible, invisibly acting upon the seed and soil and later appears as blossoms, flower and fruit. The visible is the **result or effect** of an invisible power or presence man calls nature but by whatever name you call it it is God, an invisible, infinite expression which is Law so when you plant roses you get roses, when you breed chickens you get chickens, what you receive is what you gave.

There is Law operating, the Law of like begets like and is invisible, its action is invisible but the **result** of the action becomes visible and then becomes tangible as flowers, fruit, tree. There is within all this invisible Law in operation. You witness this in consciousness as your experiences come to you without human means.

Sowing to

To sow to is to give attention to, desirous of. When you sow to the flesh ie desire the things of the world you will experience the things of the world both good and bad.

When you sow to the Spirit you are giving your attention to God, you are keeping your mind in the present moment with your inner ears open always ready to hear the still small voice. It is having conversation with God, thanking God throughout the day, it is keeping your mind in the consciousness of peace, living in the garden, happy, relaxed, free and in this consciousness are releasing grace into the atmosphere of man to awaken those who are ready to awaken to the Christ within.

What you reap is the abundance commensurate with your consciousness of God. As your conscious understanding deepens, as the new habits like dying daily and letting God go first become your normal response your spiritual abundance will begin to increase noticeably to the point where you can clearly see God working/expressing in your life.

Sowing to the flesh

When you make attaining that of the world of man, material good, the end and aim of your existence, give power to form, power to material sense, relying on yourself to make something of this life.

You are only sowing to God to the degree you are transferring power from the outer realm to the inner, to the degree you live by the Word.

Spiritual Capital

When you arrive at the realization that God is the source of everything necessary in your life you arrive at the realization you have spiritual capital.

Spiritual capital is the result of your conscious oneness with God, the only real source of all that is. In the human world supply is what you have acquired through your own effort. Spiritual capital is your **spiritual bank account which is infinite.**

Think of God this way. Niagara Falls is massive and seemingly unending in its supply of water. To look at the falls from the front you have no idea where the water comes from only that there is an unending supply of it being experienced.

The source of the water is behind the falls from the Great Lakes which is supplied by streams and rivers feeding into them. From the front of the falls it looks unending but to get a different view, get a more **illumined** view of the whole system you would view it from above, from a higher perspective of understanding to see there is a source unseen constantly feeding water to the expression that is the falls.

You are the falls. You are supernaturally fed, supported and maintained by an invisible but knowable source, God, that is constantly filling and flowing through and to you but the source is not visible or available to the eye that has not begun to see past appearances.

You have nothing of your own, all is of the Father and that is the Truth you are revealing to the world; that if you rest, trust and listen you will be greatly blessed of yourself and those of your consciousness.

When you arrive at this revelation you have spiritual capital and it is absolutely infinite, eternal and omnipresent. But as far as the world of man is concerned this makes no sense. It rests with you and all the other mystical teachers of the world to express to the human man that living by grace is not only profitable but the most **practical** way of living there is.

Spiritual healing

Spiritual healing is completely misunderstood by man. Spiritual healing isn't healing in the sense of man who sees healing as the opposite of what is that is wanted to be rid of.

Spiritual healing is inner prayer for allness, completeness, wholeness and for a transformation of **consciousness** to take place. If your consciousness can change, see duality for what it is then you are on your way to harmony and all the good there is in this existence because you now **know** therefore your consciousness is not what it was rather it is enlightened, now knows Truth instead of false information.

This transformation of consciousness from man of duality to the singularity of spiritual man is the healing of your entire existence, experience, life. Not just your body or circumstances but all that comes, signs follow. Spiritual healing is a **transformative** experience that **reveals** that which you have never known but know instantly is Truth and will make you free **if** you continue to live in it and practice it until it becomes your normal and natural way of being, becomes your nature, your expression and what you experience, bread on the water returning pressed down and flowing over.

Spiritual healing

The realization of oneness with God. All that takes place in treatment/healing/revealing is the **mystic's** realization by way of a higher conscious knowing of God within themself that **all there is is of God** and what is being experienced is unreal, of man, illusion. Truth breaks the mesmerism and healing is revealed.

Spiritual illumination

Spiritual illumination is the bond between us. It is a bond of divine Love that is separate and apart from any other form of relationship that exists between humans. Spiritual illumination is what brings harmony to every situation because you desire no thing from man thereby instantly freeing those around you from your perceived human wants and desires.

Your living in God is what frees mankind, maybe only temporarily, but that makes no matter, when you are in their midst, there is harmony and this harmony becomes their happiness or lightness of being which is what greets the next person in their atmosphere lifting someone else in the process. Exponential baby! Exponential! And all you have to do is be, be with God and the whole world of error, duality, pain and suffering melt/dissolve/gives way for Truth to shine through and bring the gift of God, grace, in your midst.

Spiritual integrity

Go and sin no more.

Spiritual integrity

On the human scale of judgement you may be forgiven for your ignorance or put on probation but on the spiritual scale there is no probation, you pay. You pay for every deviation from your own ability to perceive error and nothingize it. You stand or fall by the degree of **your** spiritual integrity.

What is your spiritual integrity? Your realization of one Self, one Consciousness, one Soul, one Spirit, one Life, one Law, one Presence, one Being in God through Christ, the consciousness that was awake in Jesus that made him the Christ.

Spiritual life

Spiritual life is lived after one has conscious union with the source of being-God-as did Buddha, Lao Tzu, Bhagavad Gita and Jesus. The spiritual life can be lived as a seeker, a student merely by following the rules laid down by the mystics but the **activity** of God, the allness of God, harmonious expression of existence, only begins when conscious **union** has been made and is maintained through practice and study, ie living the union.

Spiritual living

Spiritual living consists of knowing and living the principles of Truth which are prayer ie meditation/silent inner communion/practicing the presence, dying daily and bringing God on the field to reveal Truth within you that yes, God is therefore error is no thing real.

Spiritual living

God is light. Where the presence of light is realized there is no darkness. If there is physical, mental, or financial darkness be assured the presence of God dispels it. You need not fear to go to God in sin, as a matter of fact the deeper the sin the greater the need for God. Acknowledge the sin and then open your consciousness to the realization of God's grace and be assured the sin will disappear.

You have to remember that though sins are not *of* you, you are still going to suffer the effect of the error committed. But you thought there was no karma in God's kingdom! There isn't (bad karma) but your error was committed in the consciousness of human man. The errors you commit in the world are returned upon you **until** you have the consciousness of God **always** within you guiding you as naturally as you used to guide yourself. It is in this relationship that you sin less and reap less error returned upon you.

Living in the atmosphere of God frees you from the duality/error/pain/confusion of human living.

Spiritual living

The willingness to give up the struggle for survival and let God express its own life as yours, its intelligence, supply in and through you.

Spiritual man

Spiritual man is human man now knowing their Truth that they are not separate and apart from God but of God and can now live the life of the prodigal son in oneness with the Father.

Spiritual power

The realization of your name and nature: I am the individual expression of the one God within me that is the creator of all that is seen and unseen.

Spiritual power

Spiritual power means introducing the Spirit of God, Truth, into a situation silently, secretly and sacredly not to prove right or wrong but to bring harmony to bear so all may benefit from you knowing God.

Spiritual power

The power of God/Spiritual power is merely knowing that which keeps you from error-God is, I am and there is no other thereby keeping you from falling back into the trap of reacting to duality.

Spiritual Protective work

Is necessary but the nature of protective work is protecting **oneself** from the universal belief in two powers. Protecting oneself from the *belief* in the absence of God, or the belief that God is a God to only the good.

God is not God to the good or the bad it is God only to those who desire to know it.

Spiritual receptivity

Spiritual receptivity is when you are no longer vested in the ways and means of man but are open to "signs from the universe" that there is more to know. This **willingness** is the receptivity you need to have to know God. Why? Who do you know goes where they are not wanted? I'm not saying God has feelings, it doesn't, not that kind, but unless you are yourself receptive you are not ready and until you are ready you have no interest in that which you do not know therefore you are not receptive.

Spiritual sword

Everything not necessary to the life of the son of God is cut away with the spiritual sword which is merely revealed Truth that releases, removes human error in awareness. The spiritual sword is Truth within helping you to die daily to the errors of man.

Starting your day

Before you leave your house or start your day take a moment to bring God onto the field, into your consciousness, say "good morning my Father! I love you! What adventures have you planned for us today?" Then feel its radiance warm you, the smile felt within your consciousness, the "I love you" that floats in as if on a gentle breeze. Let God be your livingness for that is what you are working toward or living in but understand it is a **relationship,** one that needs you to participate and not be merely an observer or lip servicer; you don't become awesome with no change in consciousness and that means putting in the work-meditation, practicing the presence, healing error and forgiving 70x7.

Suicide

Man thinks the greatest sin against God is suicide. No one sin is greater or lesser than another because suicide is nothing more than duality in expression ie man thinking man can die or be killed or take one's own life. If you only had that power! You cannot do anything to yourself. You are infinite being, not flesh and blood and suicide is no greater error than any other error of human duality because it is an illusion, that you think you can kill yourself is the illusion.

I'm absolutely not saying suicide is not a horrible reality for too many people. I am saying when you reach spiritual understanding you will see the Truth of the error as merely a belief that they could die and not a reality. Not a discounting of another's pain associated with the act but a revelation of Truth to bring peace, harmony, healing to the human act which has brought pain.

Suicide does not keep you out of the kingdom of heaven. **Not knowing God aright** keeps you out of the kingdom which is the consciousness of all man of the world.

If one commits suicide it does **nothing** to their soul. Why? Because God doesn't know you until you come back to the house of the Father which can only be done in consciousness therefore God knows nothing about human death because there is no death to spiritual man. Human man does not exist in the consciousness of God, the knowing of God until man is **of** the consciousness of God and then he is no longer man but risen spirit.

Suicide may take that person out of the visible world but their soul, their Christ, that which is the God of them remains eternally as I. "Though your sins may be scarlet you are white as snow." Nothing you can do in human form changes the way God sees you. Why? Because God is not of the world of human man and has no idea of what you are going through or doing in this human expression.

So if someone has committed suicide or is thinking of it know that though that may end a visible life, it doesn't change the fact that they, you, all are eternal spirit and cannot die.

When the spirit is no longer in association with a body of spiritual form it is still completely whole because it is of God, I. The body is merely an out picturing of the consciousness within for the purpose of this human experience. The I of you is the consciousness of your being, how you express to the world and it is always and forever perfectly pure for it is of God not man and nothing man does can change the Truth of God.

One who takes their life in the desire to be out of this world for whatever reason will come back again and again until the time their consciousness becomes aware of that which is not in the world but is within them. When consciousness seeks to know/be raised above what is in the world of man that is when one realizes they cannot die for they are immortal spirit and whether you find God in this lifetime or the fiftieth from now it doesn't matter beyond the years **you** spent trying to deny the feeling of Truth within.

Once you know God, how this life really works you will come to an understanding you cannot exit this life and come out better on the other side, you must go through this life endeavoring to understand it by way of conscious connection to Source which is the reality of you-not flesh and blood but eternal spirit, perfect under the dirt of the world/sin/error that has covered/disguised your true nature.

Leaving this world doesn't change your life, it merely prolongs the suffering because until you find God you will go around and around not understanding that **the purpose of this life** is to rise, be known once again by the Father and in that light live the eternal existence as the child of God.

For all of you who have suffered this experience I hope this understanding brings comfort. No one dies. We are all of God thus the consciousness of God is innate within us and when that consciousness is realized you live eternally, infinitely, complete and whole from that expression of harmony.

Supply

Do not confuse fruitage or harvest with supply. Supply is **God** and is always the source of the fruitage. The branch is connected to the tree and **through** this connection has all the supply of the tree flowing to and from it as visible fruitage/harvest. Given the right conditions the fruit will become a tree in and of itself but still with its supply within to once again bear fruit. But should the branch fall from the tree, the fruit withers and dies before its time because it doesn't have **Supply,** is not connected to Source of what it needs to complete its cycle.

God is the tree and you are the branch connected to the tree receiving all that is **living** the tree. Oneness of being is what allows the Life of God to flow through you bringing forth fruitage or visible bounty. Because you are **of** the tree you partake of all that **is** the tree.

Human man is a branch cut off from the tree unaware of the supply available to him thus uses only the life inherent in the *material* body by which to try to bring forth supply. We all know once a branch is cut from the tree the life it had quickly ends and the process of dying takes place. Human man dies because he is a branch not connected to the tree, is separated from God, eternal supply.

Surrender

Surrender is your complete acceptance of God as your being, source, true nature.

Sword

Those who live by the sword die by the sword-human force of any kind.

One of the principles of spiritual living is to **put up thy sword.** This means to stop using force in any and every situation ie mental, physical or mechanical power. To not retaliate, not react, not take the action personally because if you have been working the principles you should know that there is **no** evil only illusion therefore there is nothing to react to unless you yourself have gone back to believing in the power you used to give to an illusion.

Sword of the Spirit

The Master said "I have come not to bring peace but a sword."

The sword of Truth is the Word of God, quick and sharp, Truth to wake you up to Truth, to set you apart, **above** the errors of man you once held as Truth to see them to be nothing more than illusions of the human mind. It is for this reason the Master brought a **sword-Truth-**to help you cut away the kudzu that has taken over your mind, all minds of man, to reveal the true landscape God created in the beginning so you can once again flourish in this earthly experience.

The sword the Master brought-Truth of God-is to help you break your reliance, faith on material means, on your having to get or take to receive. The sword is the breaking away from the hope and reliance on *external* expressions ie whatever man has depended upon-armies, navies, money in the bank or their human mind.

No matter where you have put your dependence this sword of Truth must come to your consciousness and sever from you all such hopes, faiths and confidences until you individually and then collectively begin to realize that man shall not live by bread alone, by form, by force, power, by anything in the realm of effect.

Your dependence for supply, happiness, companionship, health etc, must be on God. You must completely rely on the promise of God to sustain, maintain and supply his creations of which you are. Right now you are dependent on yourself for all that you need in your life. In the human world it is all on your shoulders to make something of yourself, to figure out your purpose or not all the while trying to keep your head above water and maybe make it to the end of your life with the dignity of having lived a not so bad life.

System

A system is a group of interacting and interrelated parts of a whole that act according to the singular governance **of** the unified whole. A system is influenced by **itself,** is bound by **its** Law ie by **its** principles of expression.

Merriam-Webster-system

A group of interacting bodies under the influence of related forces/a body considered as a functional unit.

Every expression of God is **of** this system, of creation, the Divine Plan, God consciousness or conscious creation expressing. You are **of** the system which is whole and complete unto itself when you are under the influence of the whole, God.

Temptation

Nothing more than a choice created by a want/desire you have that is strong enough to pull you from the consciousness of God back to the consciousness of man. Temptation is not of the devil or caused by anything other than **your** desire for that which at the moment you do not have.

Temptation: a cause of duality

Temptation doesn't come from without, from man or the world, it comes from your inability to see another direction/option/course of events. Man blames that which is outside of themselves, devil, Satan, evil, as the reason/cause for their actions to not have to take responsibility for their actions. Not my fault, x made me do it, I didn't have a choice.

When you reach spiritual maturity you realize how idiotic excuses are. No thing and no one has any power to tempt you except insofar as they are facets of whatever your *personal* weakness may be. You have no dominion in your life until you come to the realization that **you embrace within your consciousness all that you are to externalize as your experience of living** therefore there is no thing to get, nothing to be other than the expression of harmony which brings all good things into your experience.

The added things

When you desire to know God you will know God and in that way will be made whole, Self complete. Your only desire to know God is to feel the love of God and live the life of harmony.

This is your reason for going to God. This is your main reason-to know God, be known **of** God and live within its presence/allness/wholeness. **The added things are the things that come into your life because of your oneness,** the forms of the Father made manifest for your use, your enjoyment, your support, for practical reasons and for unexpected joy.

The added things are **God** in expression but not the main reason for desiring God. Your need for God goes beyond the visible to bring peace to your being, things themselves do not bring peace but the Father brings both peace and supply, the whole enchilada!

The difference between man of flesh and man of spirit

The main difference between man of flesh and man of spirit is man of flesh thinks only of force by which to live his life through bodily strength, mental acuity and weapons of all nature and need. Spiritual man does not think of ways to use force to get their way, as the means by which to live their life rather allows his mind to be an avenue of awareness to carry out what is given that day in **consciousness** to do. God is the navigator, you are the driver. You do the work of the Father and in turn your work load is lightened considerably because you are not trying to do it all by yourself rather you are just along for God's ride of your life!

The difference between victory and glory

Glory-all rise

Victory-one winner and the rest lose

The Fall

The "fall" had nothing to do with a quince or a snake. It had to do with Eve *choosing* to receive *knowledge* from an *outside* source rather than **within** from **God.**

Living by *knowledge*-consciousness of man; expressing from man's finite understanding of what they *think.*

Living by **knowing**-consciousness of God; expressing as the allness of all that **is.**

You cannot live by knowledge of man and grace of God at the same time. To live by knowledge is to live by your own mind, your own thinking and doing. In this consciousness of living by *knowledge* you are separated from your source of all **knowing,** God.

The gift of God

The **gift,** not gifts plural, of God is the grace of God, the allness of God in action in and through your life when you know God aright.

Ephesians 2:8-9

"For by grace are you saved through faith; and that not of yourselves: it is the **gift** of God: Not of works, lest any man should boast."

The healing Christ

The state of consciousness that first of all knows God constitutes individual being and also knows that because of this no man is evil and no man is good. Every bit of good found in the world is merely the lesser side of duality however God's grace does fall on the just and the unjust so there is grace in the world that will bring about healing, relief. Grace comes by way of a **miracle,** without your hands/work.

The perceived good of human man comes through their efforts by resisting evil, fighting evil/error as if it were a thing to be feared or fought. There is no grace in the world of man unless spiritual man has awareness of and oneness with God to bring God to bear on earth among men whose breath is in his nostrils **that desire the things of God**-peace, joy, love, companionship, benevolence etc, and it is this desire for God alone that brings the gift of God, grace, to bear as the added and needed things.

The I of you

The I of you is the only thing not objective or subjective to you. Truth is God and God is I. Not the i of human man who lives and dies but the I of God.

The just and the unjust

I couldn't understand the statement "the rain falls on the just and the unjust" but this is another way of saying that when Truth comes into the awareness of one in union with the Father it becomes part of the atmosphere where it can come into the awareness of any calling out. It doesn't matter to God if you are sitting in church asking for his presence, his peace or if you are hiding from the police with a gun in your hand. If you ask in earnest God will come into awareness BUT understand God is harmony, is to bring harmony to you and that probably means to stop doing what you are doing otherwise you wouldn't be calling out for a Hail Mary.

As human man you are the unjust, un righteous, think God is outside of you.

As spiritual man you are the just, the right knowing, know God aright-within.

You become the just when you walk the path the revelation you received put you on but you have to take the first step.

The letter of Truth

The **letter of Truth** means the same thing as metaphysical Truth, revealed Truth, the written Truth revealed by mystics ie the red letter words in the Bible and **your** Truths revealed within for the good of all when you receive impartation, Truth, from the source of Truth God within.

That which comes from a mystic has been anointed by God through actual awareness to share Truth. The letter of Truth isn't mere words, they are the way, the **teaching** that brings you to an actual experience of the awareness of God, into its kingdom/consciousness of harmonious expression, into the flow of grace made manifest in the visible world as that which you need and desire **not** by your own hands but completely free of human involvement which is the definition of a miracle.

The Letter of Truth

The Letter of Truth are the written Truths given by mystics down through the ages and are the principles, the rules so to speak, of Truth, God, spiritual living. Within the Letter of Truth you find out what God is, who you are, what Truth is, what Truth does and how to let Truth work in you to experience God in awareness.

If you abide by the principles of physics, chemistry, electricity etc, you are versed in the correct doing/application of that particular law thus can know how it will respond because it is **Law.**

The principles of God are **the rules of the Law of God in action** ie what you need to do to **allow** God to work in your experience to **receive** of the constant, dependable, reliable, self perpetuating, unchanging result guaranteed because of the innate harmony of being, one source of consciousness that is of one expression-IS, not good or bad or otherwise but is, just is. This is Truth of all that is visible and invisible, all is, not qualified, judged, labeled or sorted into compartments within but seen for what its true nature is and that is as far as the **deductive mind** gets to go. All of life **is,** unqualified, un judged, without bias because all **is** and it is **God expressing.**

The mind of man is not creative but deductive

There is a consciousness within man but man doesn't know it exists; what man thinks is consciousness is merely human conscience, the thinking mind, where you mull over, repeat, replay, change, idolize, scrutinize, fantasize and minimize your life. Man thinks this mind has the ability to create/bring into outer expression what is being visioned but the activity of the mind that is within you is not creative rather deductive.

The mind of you cannot make anything out in the visible world that can be touched or sensed in any way. It can only create images within your mind that you lay onto reality that is out in the world to make you think what you are envisioning in your mind is real, but it is merely illusion. Your mind was created by God to be a deductive center, to be that which allows you to bring into visible expression what you receive through conscious oneness that is given you to do.

God never gives you an impartation then says "here, go for it," while it sits back and watches you crash and burn. No! God imparts the steps for success as you need them to progress. It is you open to the omniscience, the all knowing of God and letting that which is to be known through you be known. A new expression, a new material, a new application, a new invention. They are new because they came by way of your **conscious** union with God and were brought into form by way of the deductive mind receiving impartations giving you the know how, the impetus for the next step in its creation. You are bringing forth that which is of God so of course God is going to be the thinker and the doer in and of you as you with your deductive mind being the instrument through which invisible substance becomes visible form.

There is only one consciousness and that is God consciousness and that is your consciousness and my consciousness **if so be you are not entertaining the belief in two powers.** When there is no belief in good and evil your consciousness is that consciousness that was in Christ Jesus. When you accept and live the belief in two powers you are no longer of the consciousness of harmony for you are entertaining that which brings chaos-an *other* in opposition to the one expression of good/God.

Therefore every experience of your life is an outer expression of your current state of consciousness. Nothing happens to you from without, everything happens as an activity of your own state of knowing. As a human being before entering any of the metaphysical or spiritual approaches to life you are accepting, not knowingly but by virtue of being born into the atmosphere of the human mind devoid of spiritual understanding or need, you are accepting as absolute that there is both good and evil and judge by those standards not knowing they are beliefs and not reality.

The nature of My Peace

The nature of my peace is God. Peace descends; it is not found or gotten. It is an assurance **I am with you, I will never leave thee,** and you can almost sing your way through life with this refrain dancing on your silent lips.

The power of God

The power of God is not the kind of power man ascribes the word power to. The "power of God" is the **awareness of the presence of God within** you expressing its nature as you. Therefore the power of God, that which God can do for you, is only by way of your awareness of God's presence within and the nature of that presence as your expression.

The power of God is in the knowing and deferring to God and it is this knowing and deferring that allows human man to experience harmony of being which then allows life to be lived under grace.

The power of God

The power of God is the Truth of God in your awareness and as your expression to the world.

The power of God

The power of God in your life is you **knowing** it is dependable, reliable and infinite, was yesterday and will be tomorrow good, great, much better than you can do on your own. The only thing that can ever change your present circumstances of union/oneness with God, harmony, is you. If you fall back into duality, if you express your own will, if you chose to swim on your own you must be fully aware of the warning signs posted on the beach. "No swimming, strong undertow, enter at your own risk," and the risk is duality, no longer at one with God under grace.

The sins of the Father or generational curse

As you now know there is nothing that can keep you from God. No thing and nothing if you want God, desire to know God and to live God. No condition, circumstance, person or sin can keep you from God. Therefore the *sins of the father* are the same illusions you bear as the guilt, pain or lack you have associated as your label.

"Thou your sins may be scarlet, ye are as white as snow." Horse's mouth and all you might want to believe it and not the preacher that has no idea of the love of God while they spew fear of God.

Never trust anyone but God for God is the only Truth. There is nothing of you other than God, no thing and nothing. We all sin, we all do things we wish we hadn't and we all suffer the sin. We all cause others pain and we cause ourselves pain but only because that is the nature of the *human* world and up until now you didn't know there was another way, another option to living this experience.

The sword of the spirit

Truth is the "sword" that cuts you free from the illusions of duality. Truth reveals the unreality of man's world of duality.

The sword of the spirit must come to you to sever your belief in some far off God, all your theological beliefs about the nature of God-a God that punishes or a God that rewards, gives or withholds. All of this must be released by you through knowing Truth.

You must live not by your human wisdom, physical strength, education, bank account or reliance on others; you must learn to live by every word that proceedeth out of the mouth of God and until that has been accomplished that sword will continue to cut and cut and cut until all that you harbor that is not of God has been cut away, died to and you find yourself with more conscious understanding than you had before the sword did its work revealing Truth. Understand the sword is a **metaphor** not an actual weapon. There are no weapons in the kingdom; it is called a sword to denote the dying to the old ways, they are being released not killed, let go not over powered, revealed not destroyed.

The sword **reveals** the nothingness of error which is Truth for you to accept or deny ie keep living duality.

God is Truth and to live Truth you must live by the **consciousness** of that Truth-all is and all is of God and there is no other except in the mind of man *separated* from Truth.

The sword of the spirit

The sword of the spirit is the **dying daily** that reveals the true I of you as you release the i, ego, me, mine of you. To do this you must relax your mental powers of judgement/bias and let God flow into the emptiness you have created by **observing** instead of participating. Let God's thoughts be your thoughts and your North Star, your constant companion, the guide unto your life.

God cannot steer you wrong, you may think it wrong beause you are still trying to control the direction of your life but when you let go, throw up your hands and completely defer, give this living to God, go in whatever direction God faces you when you come out on the other side you will see the reason-either it was a situation you needed to die to the unreality of which can be harsh but necessary-the sword of the spirit-or it was a situation that seemed to have no real purpose to you but is intrinsic to the overview of God, the path already made straight as long as you follow the bread crumbs laid out by Father for you to follow.

Let life be a game, enjoy the ride, roll down the window, put on your favorite music and just let go, no destination, no time frame and your thinking mind is quiet, happy to go along for the ride because nothing is being asked of you, you can just be, maybe for the first time in your life you are free.

The will of God

The will of God isn't like your personal will of choice. The will of God merely means that which God is, allness, harmony, love, joy, abundance. The will of God is God being God, is-ing.

The will of God is the way/being/doing of God and the will of man is the way/being/doing of man.

Will is your nature expressing as spiritual man or human man and it is by your **will** you are known. It is the same as **by your name you will be known,** being i Kelly the personality or I child of God known to the world as Kelly.

The Word made flesh

When there is the dawning of understanding within, when words become more than words, when you stop and say aha! now I get it! the words have been made **flesh,** they have taken form in consciousness, they are real to you by your conscious understanding of the imparted Truth.

The Word of God

The Word of God means "the consciousness of God." To live by the Word is to live in God consciousness, to be in conscious oneness letting God be your expression.

The Word of God: the consciousness of God

The Word of God is invisible but the **effects** of keeping your consciousness linked up, open to, in constant communication with God by being in the now, the present moment and not in the past or the future, is what produces supply, bounty and fruitage in the visible world, God manifest in form.

The words "I have overcome the world"

To overcome something can be done in many ways but the word can be confusing. To overcome something sounds like a physical feat, to go over, above, beyond the peak. The spiritual understanding of those words means you **know** differently now than you *believed* before, you have **risen** above the consciousness you *were*. To say you have overcome the world is to know the Truth of the world-duality-and chose to live by grace-singularity. To overcome is to surmount, rise, go beyond by/through understanding **not** force or power.

The world is an illusion

The illusion is in how man has **classified** what they see.

Human man experiences everything around him as matter/material separate and apart from God but it isn't and **that** is the illusion. All that is **is** God, God expressing as form, all form, all creation, all that is visible and invisible. All that is is of the same source expressing as what is necessary for this world, this universe and its inhabitants to exist. All that was created in the beginning, incorporeal creation, becomes visible/manifests as that which is needed according to the conscious expression of man.

The illusion: mountains, sky, earth, cars and people, houses, ie matter/material classified by expression/humanly perceived nature.

The reality: all is of God visible and invisible.

Once you know this Truth you can never look at anything the same because **now you know the connection between every single expression is God.** All is of God in form and that is why all is harmonious when **unqualified** by man's thinking mind.

Thou shall have no other Gods

God is the only presence, expression, Truth and when you read "thou shall have no other Gods" it means you will not give power to anything of man for all power is of God. To have no other Gods is to have no other power and no other power means personal power or the power of the senses or powers of the world held by man to be real.

Thought

Thoughts are only of the Thinker, I, God, and are called impartations. Spiritual man does not have thoughts of their own thinking because thoughts are of the Thinker, God. Thoughts are pure, of God, Truth, divine impartation not of the mind but received in consciousness, it is the communication of God to you his child to keep you moving along the path of spiritual knowing so you can live the fullness that is within the allness it is.

Man uses the word think and thought interchangeably but for tense **but they are completely different in their mystical Truth,** one is of man of duality and the other is of spiritual man of singularity.

Time

Man's entire existence revolves around time. When to get up, when to go to bed, when to get a job, when to become an adult, when to have children. From cradle to grave life is measured in daily to do's to become something by the time you die.

Time is a man made concept that allows visible man to allocate and perform as part of a society, to participate with others in common activities. But time is a killer. As the clock winds down so do the days of your perceived finite life. You tick them off one at a time yet celebrate another passing of 365 measures of time with a party but all the time *fearing* time. Not enough time to do, find, be, have, explore, love. So every minute can become a death knoll.

It is not man's natural nature to be a thief, dishonest, that is always brought on by expediency, something of the moment for which they have no other way of fulfilling. Time. If man knew his true nature in which all supply already is, even though he hungered at the moment he would know God was with him, Emanuel, so would be his supply in all form and it would come to him at the right time. Spiritual man doesn't need to steal, cheat or lie because all of those actions are brought on by the belief in time. If you rest in now you are in the only "time" God functions therefore you are functioning in harmony with God.

If you think of time as that which has a beginning and an end you are dwelling in past and future which God knows not of therefore you are not **of** conscious oneness with God and fear the passing of time thus do things you would not do if you had unlimited time, resources and wisdom. A child steals food from the serving table before dinner not understanding there will be a plate waiting for them. A child takes another's toy not knowing their aunty brought back many presents from her latest travels. Man cannot wait but spiritual man knows he has all the time in the world and then some.

To be touched by God

Means that suddenly you are aware of a presence, a voice, a feeling within that is not of yourself. You are aware of God, you have been touched, awakened, now know Truth, **God is and God is within bringing peace and harmony to all who enter.**

To hold space

What is called **holding space** for the spirit to enter is spiritual consciousness without the consciousness of it being a spiritual act. **You are doing what a mystic, a true spiritual healer does- goes into the silence and holds space,** remains in the silence and waits, makes a place for the spirit you know to come to do that which only **it** can do-bring a change to the situation for the better ie harmony.

To judge righteous judgement

To see with the eyes of the Father to reveal all is and all is God no matter the outward presentation.

To still the mind

To still the mind is to not use the mind. Think of your eyes. You see **through** your eyes but you are not really **using** your eyes they just are doing what the eyes do. You do not see **by** the eyes, you see **through** the eyes. It is the same with the mind. The moment you start **using** the mind you are trying to use it as a creative force thereby **misusing** its function. Remember, you think **through** the mind, not **with** the mind because it is a deductive center not a creative center.

So the step from metaphysics to mysticism is accomplished in proportion to the degree to which you become a **beholder,** a witness, one who sees without any thought about what they are seeing and it is only in this way God can show you Truth through its eyes which are your eyes when you are of its consciousness and what will be known will be some form of good/harmony/peace.

Transcendental consciousness

Consciousness that transcends that of man of earth facilitated by your awakening to the Christ of your being to begin your journey back to God, oneness of being.

Treatment

A treatment is the recognition of Truth in yourself that touches the Christ of the one that asked for help-their Christ receives Truth from God by way of your raised consciousness **temporarily** raising the patient's consciousness to receive the consciousness/Truth of God, know or felt or not.

It has nothing to do with person to person mind control it has to do with openness to spirit of the one asking for help. If you the practitioner get the click, the world got the click, **all those looking for grace received it** in the measure of their need because you brought it into expression to share with the world which is loving your neighbor and your enemy as the brothers and sisters they truly are.

Treatment, purpose of

Man believes himself separate from God.

The purpose of treatment is to reveal Truth to man-God is and God is within you.

Treatment/healing

The realization of God's presence which is Truth that reveals error as no thing.

Treatment/treating yourself

Declaring that which is Truth that is not evident to the five senses. All treatments and healings are done on **yourself** because it is you who knows Truth to release/break the illusion thus bringing grace to bear in the world to be felt by all who are receptive.

True prayer

Hearing God in the silence.

True Prayer

That which you desire is within, not without. No amount of searching, begging, pleading or supplanting will bring to you that which you pray for because there is no God outside to hear you. The kingdom of God is within you therefore prayer, to be effective, must be directed **within** to where God is.

Truth

What is true of you and me must be true of everyone. To be true, Truth must be universal therefore since Life is God and my Life is God and your Life is God, it must be the Life of all.

Understanding the emotions around death

You have no physical relationships therefore your relationships are those of consciousness. This is the comfort, the reality, that allows you to get past physical death of a loved one. You didn't love the body, you loved the personality, the expression, the mind, the heart and I speak of these metaphorically. You loved the person they were, not the body they inhabited. **Therefore in sight or out of sight the consciousness of that person is still the consciousness of that person** and since God is the consciousness of all, that person is and will always exist as long as they exist in yours or another's consciousness because all are of God, eternal and infinite.

Unfoldment of Self

When you make inner contact with God and understand more the nature of God all that you need for abundant living will find its way into your experience because God **is** the substance of **all** supply and abundance unto your expression.

Universe

A self contained, self maintained closed system governed by a singular consciousness of harmonious expression, perpetual, eternal, infinite and invisible.

The harmonious expression of a closed system governed by a consciousness of perpetual, eternal, infinite good is experienced as harmonious living, being and expression among and by all its forms because they are One.

Victor vs glory

Victory in man's world always produces a winner and a loser. In glory, there is only Truth received of the Father, it is He that does the work for you through you therefore your glory is in the omnipotence, omniscience and omnipresence of God because in that consciousness you are **always receiving,** never a winner or a loser.

What about those who are being hard to love?

That was you and I once. We have all been five-year-olds living by our senses, taking, lying, stealing because we didn't know better. We all go through stages of growth, increased awareness, consciousness, and your mistakes show you it is time to grow and change your conscious understanding of who you are, what life really is and your place in it.

What is the conscious realization of God within?

It means to have an actual experience of a presence not of yourself within your own being. You are now able to hear the voice of God and this is the connection by which you begin to learn Truth and rise in conscious understanding to partake of oneness with God, come back into the kingdom, the consciousness of **is.**

What it means to live heaven on earth

The kingdom of heaven is the feeling of completeness, the allness and fullness of Life in expression. Grace is the allness of life returned upon you that allows you to live in the atmosphere of peace among man because you want no thing from man, desire no thing from man because all is provided by the Father through oneness.

This is heaven on earth, it is a state of conscious knowing that I am I am and with this Truth walk the earth sharing God, loving God and living God in awareness to rise others to their own point of awakening to Truth.

When it comes to the discussion of evolution vs creation:

Evolution is nothing more than adaptive increase that allows a species to continue its expression as the conscious expression around it dictates.

Understand this process is not separate and apart from God, it is God expressing as the evolved form that is the hallmark of Life-constant renewal of Self byway of adaptation, evolving states and stages of expression-God in form. This is what allows for what seems to be biological activities separate and apart from God but once you understand God is the source of all form, and as you recount your evolution from human man with no understanding of the Father within to where you are now in conscious union with God you can see how evolution is merely the creative consciousness of all that is moving this universe forward so that man can evolve to a higher conscious knowing by which to continue their evolutionary path back to Truth and live in conscious oneness with God.

Why you are human man and not spiritual man: no internal relationship to guide your life

Your Father has not been present to sit with you and have conversations, a back and forth dialog of "how can I help you son?" when you ask to learn what is expected of you and what the result for you is when you are of God governance.

God is always dependable and reliable and I know not one of us can say we have ever encountered likewise in man. Your Father can be your guide this minute to the unfolding Truth of this life if you want, it is always and only up to you how illumined you become, what you express as your progress in fruitage, outward abundance and healing ability but there are rules, boundaries.

Good old boundaries. Just knowing what you can and cannot do to get into and remain in the kingdom with God. No rituals, rights, gutting or pouring of icky stuff. No starving, carving or crying. Just stay within the lines and all is good. Yes, it is truly that simple, hard at times to do because of your personal will wanting to win but absolutely simple in application.

Through study and application of Truth, the letter of Truth, meditation, practicing the presence, healing, treatments and forgiving 70x7 you are living God, the nature of God, good, harmony, and your peace, your joy, your ease of being attests to the degree of God governance of your life.

These are the **principles, rules** you live by that become your Truth in expression when God is the governing consciousness or influence of your life. That's it. If God is in awareness you are God governed; simple, no muss, no fuss, just hand over the reigns and take a well deserved breath with the weight of the world lifted and back where it belongs-on God's shoulders not yours.

Word usage denoting human and spiritual man

Words for human man:

Natural man

Carnal man

Mortal man

Human man

Man of earth

Words for the spiritual man:

Child of God

Spiritual man

Messiah

Mystic

Guru

Servant of God

Yield

To get God on the field there has to be a **yielding,** a **transformation** of consciousness, a softening within yourself and the patient, a releasing of personal ego in order to make way for spiritual awareness.

Don't miss out!

Visit the website below and you can sign up to receive emails whenever Kelly Logan publishes a new book. There's no charge and no obligation.

https://books2read.com/r/B-A-KMOW-NBSWI

BOOKS2READ

Connecting independent readers to independent writers.

Also by Kelly Logan

365 Days of Truth Volume 1
365 Days of Truth Volume 2
365 Days of Truth Volume 3
Sense to Soul How To Have A Personal Relationship With God Through Mystical Interpretation of Scripture
The Cause and Effect Survival Guide
The Cause And Effect Survival Guide
Intuition: The Best Friend You Didn't Know You Had

Watch for more at www.betterbyintent.com.

About the Author

Kelly A. Logan is an author and contemplative teacher whose work explores the inner experience of God, consciousness, and truth beyond doctrine and tradition. Her writing focuses on direct spiritual awareness, mystical interpretation of scripture, and the quiet transformation that comes from inner listening rather than external authority. She writes for those seeking a personal, lived relationship with God—rooted in clarity, freedom, and direct knowing.

Read more at www.betterbyintent.com.

www.ingramcontent.com/pod-product-compliance
Lightning Source LLC
Chambersburg PA
CBHW080922300426
44115CB00018B/2911